# Poiesis

Poiesis (n.) (poy-ee-sis): 1: Making, manufacturing; a manufactured object. 2: Poetry; a poem.

# Poiesis
## MANUFACTURING IN CLASSICAL ATHENS

Peter Acton

OXFORD
UNIVERSITY PRESS

## OXFORD
UNIVERSITY PRESS

Oxford University Press is a department of the University of
Oxford. It furthers the University's objective of excellence in research,
scholarship, and education by publishing worldwide.

Oxford   New York
Auckland  Cape Town  Dar es Salaam  Hong Kong  Karachi
Kuala Lumpur  Madrid  Melbourne  Mexico City  Nairobi
New Delhi  Shanghai  Taipei  Toronto

With offices in
Argentina  Austria  Brazil  Chile  Czech Republic  France  Greece
Guatemala  Hungary  Italy  Japan  Poland  Portugal  Singapore
South Korea  Switzerland  Thailand  Turkey  Ukraine  Vietnam

Oxford is a registered trademark of Oxford University Press
in the UK and certain other countries.

Published in the United States of America by
Oxford University Press
198 Madison Avenue, New York, NY 10016

© Oxford University Press 2014

All rights reserved. No part of this publication may be reproduced, stored in
a retrieval system, or transmitted, in any form or by any means, without the prior
permission in writing of Oxford University Press, or as expressly permitted by law,
by license, or under terms agreed with the appropriate reproduction rights organization.
Inquiries concerning reproduction outside the scope of the above should be sent to the
Rights Department, Oxford University Press, at the address above.

You must not circulate this work in any other form
and you must impose this same condition on any acquirer.

Library of Congress Cataloging-in-Publication Data
Acton, Peter Hampden.
Poiesis : manufacturing in classical Athens/Peter Acton.
pages cm
hardcover ISBN: 978-0-19-933593-0 — paperback ISBN: 978-0-19-049434-6
1. Athens (Greece)—Economic conditions.  2. Manufacturing industries—
Greece—Athens—History.  3. Economic history—To 300.  I. Title.
HC37.A38 2014
338.4'76709385—dc23
2013043049

For Sarah, Gemma, Annabel, and Camilla

Nothing is easier than to admit in words the truth of the universal struggle for life, or more difficult—at least I have found it so—than constantly to bear this conclusion in mind
–Charles Darwin: The Origin of Species

# CONTENTS

List of Figures, Illustrations, and Tables   xi
Preface   xv
Acknowledgments   xvii

1. **Introduction**   1
    1.1.   Athens, the Manufacturing City   1
    1.2.   Original Sources   8
        *1.2.1. Ancient Literature*   8
        *1.2.2. Archaeology and Epigraphy*   13
    1.3.   Methodology   16
        *1.3.1. Embeddedness and Empirical Analysis*   16
        *1.3.2. Theories of Firm Size*   22
        *1.3.3 The Theory of Competitive Advantage*   33
        *1.3.4. Competitive Advantage and Industry Structure*   41
        *1.3.5. Applying the Competitive Advantage Framework*   44

2. **Industry Formation**   47
    2.1.   Early Manufacturing   48
    2.2.   Homer and the Households of the Rich   51
    2.3.   Hesiod and the Peasant Economy   61
    2.4.   Empirical Evidence   65
        *2.4.1. Metalworking*   67
        *2.4.2. Leatherwork*   68
        *2.4.3. Cosmetics and Perfumes*   68
        *2.4.4. Textiles*   69
    2.5.   Supply and Demand in a Competitive Market   70

3. **The Pottery Industry**   73
    3.1.   The Evidence   73
        *3.1.1. Original Texts*   73
        *3.1.2. Pots*   75
        *3.1.3. Potteries and Kilns*   78
        *3.1.4. Stamps and Graffiti*   80
        *3.1.5. Vase Paintings*   82
    3.2.   Industry and Workshop Size   83
    3.3.   Labor Force   87
        *3.3.1. The Process of Making Pots*   87

   3.3.2. *Staffing Needs*  92
   3.3.3. *Justifying a Full-Time Team*  97
 3.4. Bases for Differentiation  101
   3.4.1. *Fine Ware*  102
   3.4.2. *Coarse Ware*  105
   3.4.3. *Niche Products*  105
   3.4.4. *A Second Kiln?*  106
 3.5. Subsequent Changes in Competitive Dynamics and Industry Structure  108
 3.6. Summary  114

4. **Mining, Metals, and Armor**  116
 4.1. Mining  116
 4.2. Ore Processing  120
 4.3. General Metalworking  124
 4.4. Jewelry and Ornaments  128
 4.5. Coinage  131
 4.6. Bronze Armor  134
 4.7. Shield Manufacture  138
 4.8. Knives  144
 4.9. Summary  145

5. **Textiles, Clothing, and Footwear**  147
 5.1. Textiles and Clothing  147
   5.1.1. *Spinning and Weaving*  151
   5.1.2. *Scouring and Finishing*  159
 5.2. Footwear  162
   5.2.1. *Tanning*  162
   5.2.2. *Shoemaking*  165
 5.3. Summary  170

6. **Woodworking**  172
 6.1. Furniture  174
 6.2. General and Specialized Woodworking Segments  183
 6.3. Boatbuilding  185
   6.3.1. *The Trireme: Development and Configuration*  185
   6.3.2. *Responsibility for Building Triremes*  189
   6.3.3. *Manufacturing: the Hull*  191
   6.3.4. *Manufacturing: Components*  193
   6.3.5. *Shipbuilding and Supplying Industries*  197
 6.4. Summary  200

7. **Construction Industries**  202
 7.1. Public Buildings  202
 7.2. Monumental Statues  215

7.3. Private Housing and Infrastructure   225
  7.4. Summary   228

8. **Food, Drink, and Personal Care**   230
   8.1. Agricultural Products   230
       *8.1.1. The Athenian Diet*   230
       *8.1.2. Processing*   233
       *8.1.3. Food Service*   238
   8.2. Cosmetics, Perfumes, and Medicines   239
   8.3. Summary   246

9. **Athens's Manufacturers**   248
   9.1. Citizen Investors   250
   9.2. Citizen Craftsmen   270
   9.3. Women   274
   9.4. Foreign Residents   278
   9.5. Slaves   281

   **Coda**   289

   **Athenian Currency**   297

   **Appendix: Quantifying Manufacturing Participation**   299
   A.1. Supply Analysis   300
   A.2. Demand Analysis   311
       *A.2.1. Example One: Clothing (Chapter 5)*   312
       *A.2.2. Example Two: Shoes (Chapter 5)*   313
       *A.2.3. Example Three: Basic Furniture (Chapter 6)*   313
       *A.2.4. Example Four: Ceramics (Chapter 3)*   316

   Secondary Sources   319
   Photo Credits   355
   Index Locorum   357
   General Index   371

# LIST OF FIGURES, ILLUSTRATIONS, AND TABLES

**Figures**

1.1 Competitive Economics  34
1.2 Cost Advantage Example: Commodity Mining  35
1.3 Impact of Management  37
1.4 Capacity to Gain a Structural Advantage  38
1.5 Impact of New Entry  39
1.6 Competitive Advantage and Industry Structure (1)  42
1.7 Competitive Advantage and Industry Structure (2)  43
1.8 Competitive Advantage and Industry Structure (3)  44
2.1 Specialization and Unit Costs  54
2.2 Specialist and Generalist Unit Costs  55
2.3 Value of Mobility  56
2.4 Impact of Cost Reduction on Supply  58
2.5 Increased Demand for Quality  59
2.6 Demand-Supply Interaction  60
2.7 Advantage of Fixed Workshops  61
2.8 The Make or Buy Decision  71
2.9 Competitive Supply  71
3.1 Impact of Entry and Exit on Industry Prices  101
3.2 Pottery Costs and Volume  107
3.3 New Pottery Costs and Volume  114
9.1 Investment Returns (1)  250
9.2 Investment Returns (2)  258

**Illustrations**

2.1 Blacksmith—Homeric or early C20?  57
3.1 Fine Ware  76
3.2 Protocorinthian cup  77
3.3 Storage *Amphorae*  78
3.4 Pottery Workshop on the Leagros Hydria  83
3.5 The Caputi Hydria Showing Four People Painting  85

xii { List of Figures, Illustrations, and Tables

    4.1    The Finest of All Coins   132
    4.2    Berlin Foundry Cup: Molds for a Statue or Armor?   137
    4.3    Hoplite Shields in Action   140
    5.1    Menswear (Modeled by Demosthenes)   149
    5.2    Ladies' Wear (Modeled by Athena)   150
    5.3    Ancient Sandal with Decorative Cut   165
    6.1    Couch and Small Table   177
    6.2    Trireme with Full Deck (Model)   188
    7.1    The Erechtheum (Artist's Reconstruction)   206
    7.2    Luxury Private House: An Illustrated Reconstruction   227
    8.1    Ancient Olive Press   236

## Tables

    1.1    Impact of Division of Labor   30
    2.1    Farm Size and Allocation of Labor—Vologda district   63
    2.2    Annual Income per Consumer—Vologda district   64
    3.1    Kiln Capacity (Floor Area)   93
    3.2    Forming Labor Required to Fill a Kiln   94
    3.3    Stacked Kiln Capacity   95
    3.4    Pottery Industry Structure   115
    4.1    Metalwork Specialization   127
    4.2    Metals Industry Structure   145
    5.1    Textile Clothing and Footwear Industries   170
    6.1    Furniture Manufacturing   180
    6.2    Principal Components of a Trireme by Trade   197
    6.3    Man-Days per Trireme at Hull   199
    6.4    Woodworking Industries Structure   201
    7.1    Sources of Contract Workers   214
    7.2    Construction Industries Supply Structure   228
    8.1    Agricultural Processing   231
    8.2    Other Industries Structure   246
    9.1    Industry Structure Overview   249
    9.2    Roles in Manufacturing   249
    9.3    Knife Factory—Revised (*minae*)   265
    9.4    Furniture Factory—Revised (*minae*)   265
    9.5    Women's Roles in Manufacturing   278
    9.6    Role of Metics and Freed Slaves in Manufacturing   281
    A1    Representative Population Figures   303
    A2    Manufacturing Participation by Adult Males (c. 350 BCE)   306
    A3    Manufacturing Participation by Adult Females (c. 350 BCE)   310
    A4    Manufacturing Participation by All Adults (c. 350 BCE)   311

| | | |
|---|---|---|
| A5 | Manufacturing Participation by Social Group and Workshop Type | 311 |
| A6 | Sandal Consumption C4 Athens (for Illustration Only) | 314 |
| A7 | Basic Household Furniture C4 Athens (for Illustration Only) | 315 |
| A8 | Basic Furniture Items per Household C4 Athens (for Illustration Only) | 315 |
| A9 | Basic Furniture Labour C4 Athens (for Illustration Only) | 315 |
| A10 | Stacked Kiln Capacity (from Table 3.3) | 317 |
| A11 | Manufacturing Employment by Social Group and Industry Type | 317 |

# PREFACE

In the course of research for my thesis, and then for this book, when friends asked me what I was working on and I replied, rather unimaginatively, "Manufacturing in classical Athens," a common response was an incredulous "What did they make then?" with an occasional joking reference to "pots." By the time I have mentioned clothes, shoes, armor, houses, furniture, temples, boats, cosmetics, and jewelry, and clearly have more to come, they realize it was not a very good question, but they are not the only ones that might have known better. Despite its evident importance to the city's living standards—and to the survival of a large proportion of inhabitants—this is the first book for almost a hundred years to focus on manufacturing in Athens between 500 and 300 BCE. When I decided to apply what I had learned about manufacturing industries in my commercial career to what I remembered about Athens from my undergraduate degree, the openness of the field was both a shock and a challenge.

I have tried to create an account of manufacturing in classical Athens that covers all major segments and makes sense in terms of what we know about how business works. It traverses the historical evolution of manufacture for sale, tries to capture from all sources the most important things known or conjectured about manufacturing activities of the period, and then, using a framework derived from The Boston Consulting Group's research into business competition, describes how each of these industries most probably worked and the implications of different industry structures for expansion, income levels and lifestyle. It examines how different types of business and roles suited different status groups and the factors that led to subsequent industry consolidation.

The task begun here is far from complete. No doubt some important facts, or even classes of manufacture, have been omitted, despite the best efforts of many kind experts to direct me. There is scope for another book of at least the same length that does no more than refine the analyses with additional and better information. I hope that new discoveries will prompt new insights and that the framework applied here will prove robust enough to incorporate or adapt to future archaeological findings or different interpretations of texts.

I have taken a calculated risk in trying to make sense of limited and confusing sources. Many admired historians deduce as much as possible from facts that can be established with reasonable certainty and are cautious about going further. Here, I have taken such facts as I have been able to find and built on them using a simple microeconomic framework and the most plausible assumptions. The orators and Aristophanes give us plenty to work with.

If we listen to them we cannot but recognize the importance of manufacturing and the high level of engagement among Athenians of all status groups. If we add the frameworks that we know work effectively in explaining commercial activity in all the situations in which they have been tried, we can begin to make sense of the confused picture we have of how different types of workshops were run and by whom. The framework itself provides important insights—all both probable and falsifiable. It indicates that the ability of some operations to expand was based upon brand preference, which then tells us something about what Athenians valued. It suggests that there might have been quite large operations that made certain products, even though these businesses are not among those for which we have such evidence. Many of the ideas put forward about how particular industries worked can and should be challenged as lacking firm support, but they fit with contemporary insight into how commerce operates and add depth to our understanding of how Athenians lived their lives and in what ways the classical age was similar to ours and in what ways it differed. I believe this approach can not only be applied fruitfully to many other societies and periods, but also has important implications for the relevance of the discipline of history in today's world.

This book is not explicitly aimed at contradicting Finley's Embeddedness Paradigm (discussed in Chapter 1 and the Coda). An extreme version of that paradigm (probably not Finley's) refuses to analyze any ancient society using terms or concepts that were not explicitly captured in the writings of the ancients. Some scholars look for the symbolism of transactions instead, perhaps because their idealized view of Athens cannot bear very much reality. This defeatist attitude not only limits our ability to understand the people of Athens by ignoring what mattered to them very much, but more fundamentally it starts to deny the relevance of history to modern life. Unless we can recognize the affinities as well as the differences in our studies of other societies, it is hard to explain why anyone should pay or be paid for studying them. It is the enlightened scholar's task to use whatever facilities she has at her disposal to make sense of history and develop the lessons it can teach, which include in this instance the history of industries, case studies of industry conduct, the financial choices and survival strategies of individuals, and the balance Athenians strove to maintain between honor and cupidity, and among society, family, lovers, and business. Only by exploring these common realities can we start to understand the society they shaped and benefit from that knowledge. It is time to reject the pernicious L. P. Hartley fallacy and assert with confidence that the past is not another country and many of the things they do there aren't very different at all.

The original cloth edition of this book contained a number of regrettable errors in the backgrounding material on various products and in the Bibliography, which Professor Emerita Susan Rotroff generously pointed out and I have corrected here. The publisher has also taken the opportunity to correct a large number of copy errors that I and others identified. I hope that the removal of these distractions will make it easier for the reader to focus on the substance of the work.

# ACKNOWLEDGMENTS

Having remained connected with the classics throughout my business career and chosen to return to them later, my greatest debt must be to the teachers who inspired me at school and as an undergraduate. I was privileged to be taught by Michael Feeney, Dom. Denis Agius, Kevin Newman, Michael Winterbotham, David Mitchell, Martin Frederiksen, Robin Lane Fox, John Davies, and George Forrest.

For enabling me to carry out the requirements of a University of Melbourne doctorate, I must thank my supervisor, Chris Mackie; my academic referees, Vice Chancellor Glyn Davis and the Governor of Victoria (then Deputy Chancellor), His Excellency Alex Chernov; and the faculty members who helped me, K. O. Chong-Gossard, Louise Hitchcock, and Andrew Turner.

From the start of my researches, I received vital help and encouragement from Ed Harris, Paul Cartledge, Anthony Snodgrass, and Al Moreno. My thesis examiners, Ed Cohen and Ian Morris, provided very positive and constructive feedback, and it has been a pleasure to stay in touch with them. The three anonymous readers engaged by Oxford University Press made an invaluable contribution to the finished work. Sarah Pirovitz helped with the selection and sourcing of the illustrations.

I received important input on production technologies from my sister, Mary Acton, (Milton Abbas, Dorset, England, porcelain restorer); Kevin Beasley (Melbourne, Victoria, pattern maker); Rodney Broad (Meridian Sculpture Founders Pty Ltd., Melbourne, foundry manager); Ian Gregory (Anstey, Dorset, potter); John Hearn (RMIT University, Melbourne, Professor of Mathematics and Geospatial Sciences); Chris Kane (Dandenong, Victoria, clay wholesaler); Jennifer Mann (Woodend, Victoria, sculptor); and Craig Sitch (Manning Imperial, Redan, Victoria, manufacturer of ancient artifacts). Ian McPhee and Gillian Shepherd helped me find my way around the splendid Trendall Centre at La Trobe University.

At the wise insistence of my editor, Stefan Vranka, I received feedback on drafts from subject experts: Alan Johnson (pottery), Jack Kroll (mining and metals), Barbara Tsakirgis (textiles), Roger Ulrich (woodwork), Margaret Mills (construction and sculpture), Eleni Hasaki (pottery and sculpture) and Robert Curtis (food and drink). Geoff Kron put me right on some aspects of economic development. All responded promptly and courteously and provided invaluable suggestions and corrections. They are not to be held responsible for the defects that remain, let alone assumed to agree with my approach and conclusions!

The microeconomic concepts that this book relies on derive from the pioneering work in the theory of competitive advantage led by Bruce Henderson and his colleagues in the early years of The Boston Consulting Group; some of the ideas were further developed by my mentors, friends, and partners in Australia, especially George Pappas, Colin Carter, Ralph Evans, Maurie Koop, Thomas Girgensohn, Rick Boven, and David Brownell.

Finally, I must acknowledge my debt to the great Moses Finley. I disagree with his premises, his logic, and his conclusions, but he has set an important challenge to those who are truly interested in understanding ancient society, and it is one that I hope others will take up.

1 }

# Introduction

## 1.1 Athens, the Manufacturing City

Modern Greece has been described, perhaps a little unfairly, as "the richest country in the world that doesn't make anything."[1] Classical Athens could not have been more different.[2] Athenian Man was as likely as not to have made many of the products used in his own home and probably depended for a good part of his sustenance on manufacturing for sale. However rich he was, his wives and daughters would make their own clothes, working alongside some of their slaves and perhaps supervising others in the household's workshop. Every time he went outside, he would be surrounded by evidence of production: the smells and the smoke of smithies and pottery furnaces, the clack of looms, the hammering of carpenters and sculptors, carts rattling through the streets full of stone or wood or bales of fine cloth or jars of imported oils, all told of the physical, environmental, and social impact of manufacturing.

The opportunities offered by manufacturing also played a vital part in Athenian economic and political life. The social mobility, employment opportunities, and relatively even distribution of wealth that accompanied the rise of commerce helped Athens to avoid the revolutions that the Peloponnese suffered regularly between Cinadon's revolt in Sparta in 399 BCE and that of Diaios and Critolaus in Roman times.[3] Agriculture was the real capitalism, contributing to social inequality, and trade and industry the great levelers.[4] Drawing on widely accepted evidence and making conservative assumptions, it seems likely that over half of all the city's residents during the classical

---

[1] Lanchester (2012) 18.
[2] The classical period of Athens is generally considered to begin soon after the defeat of the second Persian invasion of Greece under Xerxes and end with Athens and the rest of Greece coming under the control of Macedon—approximately the fifth and fourth centuries BCE. The scope of "manufacturing" as used here is broad and includes mining and construction. It does not include primary agriculture, reselling, or service activities, though the role of finance is a recurring theme.
[3] Hodkinson (1983) 239–81.
[4] Francotte (1900–1901) II. 340–65.

period would have spent at least some of their time manufacturing products for sale or for home consumption.[5] Of course almost all slaves were involved, either helping with household production or working in a gang for one owner, but a reasonable estimate is that around a quarter of the free population of all status levels, men and women, worked at making things full-time.

A surprising number of historians have somehow managed to ignore this. Consult any reference book on classical Athens and look under "industry" or "manufacturing." At best you are likely to find a reference saying, "see under Crafts." Under crafts you will find, again at best, references to a few instances where a citizen craftsman has come to the attention of Plato, or Demosthenes has acted for an aggrieved workshop owner. Look at the most distinguished histories of those times—books that bring scholarly perception and insight to the politics, the diplomatic and military strategies, the status structure, the art, the literature, and the architecture—and see what they have to say about manufacturing. It is often ignored altogether. A highly regarded book published as recently as the 1990s and purporting to present a "portrait" of Athens in her glory days describes a city almost wholly innocent of commercial pursuits.[6] Nowhere in its more than 500 pages does it attempt to address how Athenians made a living. The 32-page index has no entries for craft, industry, manufacturing, metalwork, pottery, retailing, selling, vending, or workshop. Artisans working near the Agora receive a desultory two paragraphs amid pages describing the religious festivals and events that took place there. The fact that far more people probably visited the Agora daily to do business than would ever appear at regular festivals is completely overlooked. It is a portrait of a fascinating and charming city, but it is not Athens. To try to describe Athens without mentioning the prime activity and source of income of such a large number of its residents is perverse. Not only does it mean our ideas of the city are far removed from the reality of the lives, hopes, and fears of the people concerned, it also prevents us from understanding one of the most important dynamics in any society: how production was structured and what economic opportunities it offered to different segments of the population. Only a handful of historians, drawn on frequently in this book, have allowed manufacturing to play a part in their stories of classical Athens. To find an attempt at a comprehensive account of manufacturing as a topic in its own right, it is necessary to go back about 100 years.[7]

This book is an attempt to fill the gap. It summarizes the literary and archaeological evidence and the recent work of subject experts on each of the major sectors of manufacturing in which the residents of Athens engaged. By applying a conceptual framework derived from contemporary business

---

[5] See Appendix.
[6] Meier (1993).
[7] Francotte (1900–1901); Glotz (1926—original French edition: 1920).

strategy, it identifies how each segment most probably operated: which lent themselves to the employment of large gangs of slaves, which remained the province of small craftsmen, and which provided the best returns to capital and labor. It is a common mistake to see manufacturing as having undergone a steady progression from self-sufficiency based on home crafts to mechanized mass production; in reality individual craftsmen, small workshops, cooperative production arrangements, and large factories have coexisted over millennia in various societies, not least in classical Athens.[8] The average number of employees per operating business in Australia in 2000–2001 was 10.4, and, at the last count, over a quarter of businesses in contemporary Greece had fewer than 10 employees.[9] We know of many in classical Athens that were considerably larger. Differences in business combinations and interactions at different times and places help explain how particular societies work and how various groups within them manage to keep body and soul together. They determine, among other things, the relative power of capital and labor, the nature of employment arrangements, the relationship between ownership and management, the demand for different types of labor, and the availability of opportunities for income, wealth creation, and social mobility. Some conclusions drawn here will be contentious; some may be contradicted by findings or interpretations that the author is not presently aware of; some scholars will struggle to approach such a "modernizing" analysis with an open mind.[10] Those who are able to do so should find the approach helps to make sense of a confusingly varied set of activities and offers a robust framework for incorporating new information and developing alternative hypotheses.

The standard of living in Athens in classical times was high—and not just in relation to the period, but by comparison with almost any other society until recently.[11] Economic growth in Greece between 800 and 300 BCE was between 0.6 percent and 0.9 percent a year, twice as fast as in England and Holland before the Industrial Revolution.[12] Health, as measured by bone density, increased rapidly, despite urbanization, which tends to have the opposite effect.[13] Houses, though not luxurious, were large and comfortable by the

---

[8] All terms are used in their common meaning. "Factory" is applied here to a manufacturing workshop employing at least as many people as the average site that statisticians class as a factory today (typically about 10). Similarly, the group of manufacturing operations serving particular markets is referred to as an "industry" if it consists chiefly of such enterprises and a "craft" if not—a very important distinction, as this book makes clear, that would be obscured by referring to all manufacturing as "craft."
[9] Australian Bureau of Statistics, Business Operations and Performance, 2000–2001; Eurostat (2012).
[10] My reasons for being undeterred by the strictures of Finley and his followers are given in Section 1.3 of this chapter.
[11] Scheidel (2010).
[12] Ober (2010) 9–16.
[13] Ober (2102).

standards of the time, some with 240–320 m² of roofed space, larger than the median single detached house in the United States in 1997.[14] Average house size had increased by a factor of five or six since 800 BCE, and of course the new space accommodated proportionately more furniture and possessions.[15] Athens had the advantage of being in relatively fertile country and free from famines except those caused by siege, so whereas Rome had to increase taxes on rural producers as urbanization grew, Athens did not.[16] Massive imports of grain allowed her farmers to concentrate on cash crops and win important export markets. Wealth was more evenly distributed than in many societies.[17] The reforms of Draco and Solon had primarily addressed land ownership, which was and would remain for some time the major source of subsistence for the majority of the population, but they also created an environment where citizens were expected to be responsible for their own living (with regular handouts from the state) which went some way to reducing differences in wealth.[18] By classical times the basic daily wage was around six times subsistence requirements and half of Athens's population lived a life that would have been described as "decent or middling" in Holland and better than the typical Briton in the eighteenth century.[19]

Between subsistence and post-industrial societies, differences in living standards relate essentially to the consumption of manufactured goods. Humans have always been willing to trade resources for personal comforts like grooming, sex, or entertainment, but once these have become available at affordable prices in the quantities people want them, marginal expenditure tends to be on manufactured products up to the point, late in modern history, where advanced societies are sufficiently satisfied with material possessions to seek additional services with their extra resources instead.[20] Athens was rich in raw materials including marble, limestone, clay, and silver, and trading partners provided other luxury items such as fine cloth, spices, dyestuffs, and precious metals, often for further processing in Athens.[21] Classical times saw a major increase in output, especially in mining, metalwork, stone, timber, and housing, leading to labor shortages, the encouragement of working immigrants, and vastly increased imports of slaves.[22] Quality often rose along

---

[14] American Housing Report for the United States. US Department of Housing and Urban Development/US Department of Commerce, published 2000. Houses near the center of Athens were typically much smaller than this (see Chapter 7.3).

[15] Morris (2010) 30–50.

[16] Hopkins (1995/6).

[17] Kron (2005); Ober (2010) 12–17.

[18] Recent research (e.g., Harris (2002b)) suggests that Solon's reforms were not so exclusively focused on land ownership as had once been thought.

[19] Clark (2002) 830–48; Kron (2005).

[20] Becker (1965) 493–517; McKendrick (1982) 10; de Vries (2008) 78, 86–107.

[21] Hughes (2010) 62; van Alfen (forthcoming).

[22] Davies (2007b) 352.

with quantity. Conspicuous consumption became increasingly common in the fourth century.[23] Some couches and tables were highly ornate and inlaid with gold or silver, men and women wore jewelry of outstanding craftsmanship, and decorative ceramics or silverware for festivals might take several man-years of work.[24]

Rapid growth and high living standards were underpinned by a remarkable volume of trade.[25] The lack of Phoenician artifacts from the Archaic Age discovered at Athens shows it was not a very significant trading economy at that time, but the ever-increasing need to import grain as its population grew turned Athens into one of the most trade-exposed states of all time. By the fourth century Athens seems to have needed to import between 50,000 and 100,000 tons of grain a year (in addition to an apparently large quantity of luxury items), and securing this trade was an important factor in the development of her naval capability and many offshore colonies or cleruchies.[26] Athens's harbor taxes (Andoc. 1.133) indicate a trade value of 43.5 *drachmae* per capita in the fourth century, a level matching Renaissance Venice and two or three times higher than Great Britain at the height of her empire.[27] It has been estimated that by the end of the classical period, the average trading ship was over 120 tons, with some as large as 300, and Thucydides (7.25.6) has been interpreted as pointing to a class of ships of 400 tons.[28] It was only in the 19th century that the average size of ships constructed in the British Empire exceeded 120 tons.[29]

To encourage trade, Athens embraced expatriate communities. She fostered relationships with the Phoenicians by decrees that gave them various privileges and honors, including gold crowns, land ownership rights, honored guest status, and freedom from certain taxes (IG. II/III² 8388). Similar group privileges were accorded to the Kittians (IG. II² 337) and Sidonians (IG. II² 141). A case has been made that honorific occasions for individual traders became more frequent, the language more extravagant, and the honors more significant as Athens's diplomatic and military influence declined and she

---

[23] Morris (2005) 91–126.

[24] Tucker (1907) 64–66; Richter (1966); Andrianou (2006). The mix of non-agricultural activity seems to have been similar to that in much later societies, such as North India under the sultanate in the 13th to 15th centuries (Habib (1982)). Neither then nor under the Mughal emperors of the next three centuries did Indians spend much on housing, though they spent heavily on luxury goods (Raychaudhuri (1982)).

[25] Finley (1965b) 11–35.

[26] Millett (2000) 40; Moreno (2007) 312–13; 141.

[27] Andoc 1.133 shows the 2 percent harbor taxes (*pentekoste*) came to at least 36 talents, implying taxable imports and exports of 10,800,000 *drachmae*. The population at the time is estimated at 250,000 (Hansen (1986) 65–69). For comparison with Venice and Britain (using wheat equivalents), see Kron (forthcoming) 5–7 out of 49.

[28] Vélissaropoulos (1980) 63; Wallinga (1964) 28.

[29] Mitchell and Deane (1962) 220.

sought new ways to secure critical imports, but it is clear that Athens's interest in trade went far beyond grain ((Xen) *Ath. pol.* 1.11–12; Xen. *Vect.* 2.1–6; Isoc. 8.20–21; Dem. 20.30–40).[30] The Sidonians who "had amassed great wealth from shipping" (Diod. Sic. 16.41.4) were honored, but Sidon was not a source of grain.

The extent to which Athens relied on manufactured exports to pay for its imports is a matter of much conjecture, and several scholars have attempted to estimate the composition of Athens's balance of payments, based on the domestic shortfall of grain.[31] We know the city had a number of sources of foreign exchange, including the silver mines at Laurium, allies' tributes, and harbor taxes, but the original sources offer little help in quantification. Xenophon (*Anab.* 7.1.27) gives the state's total annual income at the start of the Peloponnesian War as 1,000 talents, of which Thucydides (2.13) attributes 600 to the empire. Harbor taxes a few years later were not considered worth much more than 40 (Andoc. i.133). We have no reliable numbers for annual silver receipts, though we know they were substantial.[32] It is tempting to infer that there was a large and growing deficit to be made up by manufactured exports, and Plutarch seems to suggest this (*Sol.* 22.1), but there is no strong primary evidence supporting an export trade in manufactures other than fine ceramic ware (much of it probably secondhand) and olive oil. For our purposes this matters little. The Appendix shows that even conservative estimates of domestic demand suggest a large and active manufacturing sector. Exports of some products might have been quite voluminous without affecting the activities and strategies of many competitors in the domestic market.

While some finished goods were imported, Athens had a long tradition of craftsmanship using local raw materials or unprocessed or part-processed imports. The Athenian assembly was far from the preserve of farmers and the idle rich. A sausage-seller in Aristophanes announces that in submitting himself to the Assembly, he is about to put himself in the hands of "lamp-merchants, turners, leather-dressers and cobblers" (*Eq.* 738–40), and Xenophon's Socrates lists crafts first in his description of the Assembly's members (*Mem.* 3.7.6). Many of these people would have been small farmers during the winter and served in the military in summer, but in town they were identified by their craft occupation. Others would have been year-round manufacturers, tending not to be away from Athens much and thus possibly over-represented in public activity in the city.

---

[30] Engen (2010) disagrees, but see Acton (2012).

[31] E.g., Garnsey (1988; 89–106); Moreno (2007) 3–32; Oliver (2007) 9–38; Engen (2010; 81–83).

[32] Analysis of coin variation suggests 3,600 talents of silver went into Athenian tetradrachms between about 500 and 480 BCE—and at normal tax rates the funds for the fleet to counter the Persians imply revenues of 2,400 talents—but production was variable and the state's percentage take unknown (Picard (2001)).

Crafts had been important in the city from early times and central to its economic development. Pseudo-Aristotle and Plutarch tell how Theseus divided the people into agricultural laborers and artisans (*Ath. pol.* 19.3; Plut. *Th.* 25.2–3) and found the artisans more numerous than the nobles and the "useful" (agricultural laborers). This is almost certainly anachronistic, but it does provide an important insight into how Athenians saw themselves. Plutarch may have been more accurate when he credits Solon with having made the crafts more socially accepted by enacting that sons need only support their fathers if they have learned a trade from them (*Sol.* 22.1), but this is otherwise unsubstantiated. Where Sparta was the archetype of the oligarchic, regimented, military-based state, Athens was a place of opportunity. By maintaining the tributes she received from the Delian League after the wars with Persia and investing them in glorious buildings, the city created a huge demand for craftsmen, far beyond the capacity of the local population to supply and attracting artisans from all over Greece. Of similar importance was the path to freedom that industry offered the more capable and loyal slaves. These factors in turn allowed Athens to develop her manufacturing businesses faster than other Greek states—even faster than Corinth, despite its naval power (Thuc. 1.13).

Craftsmen were well regarded: from the seventh century they ceased to be anonymous and started to claim credit for fine works. Images of craftsmen in bronze and on vase paintings became more common and they were rewarded and lionized by their fellow-citizens from at least the time of Solon.[33] Crafts often reflected strong family traditions: sculptor families included Myron and his son Lycios, and Antenor whose father, brother, and possibly two nephews were also sculptors. The great Praxiteles and Cephisodotus were probably brothers, and their sons, including Praxiteles II, and other descendants became sculptors too. Decorative artisans were generally adept at more than one craft—Pheidias the sculptor might have started as a painter and he was expert in bronze casting and architecture as well—but being competitive in some utilitarian crafts such as shoemaking or fine weaving increasingly required specialization.[34] Reselling specialized too: in archaic times, craftsmen or family members would sell directly to end-users, but by the classical period, the retail trade had emerged as a separate business and major employer.[35]

Aristotle (*Eth. Nic.* 2.1) observes that crafts are teachable; otherwise craftsmen would be born and not made. Plato frequently refers to the process of learning a craft—generally pottery (e.g., *Grg.* 514c; *La.* 187b; *Prt.* 324c). In their catalogues of distinguished artists, Pliny and Pausanias often name the artist who taught them.[36] Craft apprenticeships were of two types: for those

---

[33] Farrington (1944) 80–1. Images appear to have become less common from around the middle of the fifth century BCE (Treister (1996) 92–94).

[34] Burford (1972) 85–89.

[35] Bolkestein (1958) 45.

[36] Hasaki (2012a) 174.

such as music or rhetoric that the apprentice could not perform commercially until he was fully trained, the teacher was paid. For learning from a master craftsman in such trades the cost was high; the aspiring poor could only get in as assistants and would have found it very hard to get onto the advancement ladder. For other trades, like weaving, pottery, and simple metal-bashing, training was often within the family workshop.[37] Even where it was not, the apprentice would quickly make a financial contribution and so the teaching was free and the master would pay the trainee's upkeep.[38] There were no "national standards"; apprentices and their teachers were judged in the marketplace. Most workshops were too small for much task specialization; everyone needed to be able to pitch in anywhere, so apprentices would observe and learn every stage in the process, even if they were only to work in a very specialized part of it. Not all apprenticeships were happy experiences. Many lead curse tablets appear to be by apprentices cursing their masters, and a Boeotian *skyphos* shows a young man hanging horizontally from the ceiling—perhaps a punishment imposed on an apprentice by a dissatisfied master.[39]

Beyond the traditional craftsman, working alone or with a slave and family member or two, we know of a number of sizable enterprises, employing gangs of slaves. Typically these gangs would be managed by a slave foreman who would enjoy the profits after paying a pre-agreed sum per slave to the owner (*apophora*).[40] Some owners transited to such an arrangement after establishing the business themselves; Demosthenes's father seems to have managed at least one workshop himself, and Aristophanes implies that Cleon's father was active as a tanner at some stage (e.g., *Pax* 270; *Eq.* 44), though he might have inherited a working operation complete with foreman, as his son did.[41] Some owners like Nicias (Xen. *Vect.* 4.14) made a business out of leasing slaves for others to employ. A central theme of this book is how some product segments lent themselves to the creation of large firms and others did not.

## 1.2 Original Sources

### 1.2.1 ANCIENT LITERATURE

In examining what we can glean about manufacturing from ancient literature, it is important not to expect too much. It is difficult to think of any European creative writers before the mid-19th century who wrote explicitly about manufacturing or commerce, even when they were living

---

[37] Hasaki (2012a) 286.
[38] Burford (1972) 89.
[39] Hasaki (2012b) 255.
[40] The workings of the *apophora* system are analyzed in Chapter 9.1.
[41] Davies (1971) 319.

through the most disruptive economic developments: Dante only mentions merchant banking to assign punishment to some of those involved, Shakespeare seems largely oblivious to the opening up of the New World or advances in the local textile industry, and Goethe completely ignores the extraordinary development of the Ruhr Valley. Only a handful of the famously realistic novelists of 19th and early 20th century England and France ever turned their attention to industry—and then only as a cause of social unrest and family dissension rather than to describe the dramatic changes that were taking place in technology and competition. Industry still has few creative writers—and far fewer poets or philosophers—who take it as their theme. All that survives from classical times is a small and somewhat random sample of successful works of literature, and if we were to try to evaluate the role of manufacturing in modern society from a similar sample, we would come to some very minimalist and inaccurate conclusions about it.

The information we do have is far from consistent. The epic poets and tragedians display great respect for crafts and acknowledge the importance of technology in improving living standards. The philosophers and comic writers show us various sole operators and a few public figures known for the money they made or inherited from manufacturing, but make clear in their different ways that the commercial impulse is unattractive and that engagement in manufacturing for profit is nothing for a citizen to be proud of. The orators speak of large manufacturing enterprises and sophisticated business transactions involving lease payments, debt, securitization, and risk management, very often conducted by citizens. It is sometimes hard to believe they are all describing the same class of activities at approximately the same period.

The early poets provide some insight into the history of craft specialization and itinerant practitioners. Chapter 2 draws on Homer and Hesiod for evidence of early manufacturing arrangements and mobile craftsmen. They and the lyric poets show manufacturing was a part of everyday experience, most households made most of their needs for themselves, outstanding craftsmanship was prized, specialization was starting to emerge in some forms, and the rich, while largely self-sufficient, were customers for certain goods made by itinerant specialists.

For the tragedians, manufacturing was central to improved living standards. Aeschylus's Prometheus, like Hesiod's, can claim credit for the whole basis of civilized life—speech, numbers, letters, divination, navigation, and farming—because he "hunted out the secret spring of fire...which when revealed became the teacher of each craft to men, a great resource," and so "rescued men from shattering destruction" (*PV.* 109–12; 236). Before this they "lived like swarming ants in holes in the ground" (*PV.* 448–50). A Sophocles chorus attributes the magnificence of man to the fact that "his application of technology is beyond imagining" (*Ant.* 365–66).[42] Athenaeus later echoes this idea of progress driven by commerce and technology: "Nobody would describe the life of Heroes at the time of the Trojan War as pleasant. That description is rightly reserved for our way of life. For in Homeric times life was ill-provided and unequipped with inventions because of the absence of commerce and the immaturity of techniques" (*Deipn.* 12.511d).

Myths and legends retold by ancient writers often included descriptions of how various crafts had been introduced to mankind by gods or demigods, who became its tutelary deities and whose image stood in workshops to be invoked by practitioners. Pallas Athena presided over potteries and Hephaestus over smithies. Generally the gods had not invented the craft themselves, but learned it from a specialized being and then helped impart it to men. Hephaestus learned metallurgy from, variously, sea nymphs (Hom. *Il.* 18.395–405), the Daktyloi (Plin. *HN.* 7.197), the Chalybes (Aesch. *PV.* 715), Love (Pl. *Symp.* 197b), and the Cyclopes (Verg. *Aen.* 8.424–25); the latter "gave Zeus his thunderbolt; they were the first skilled manual workers, who taught Hephaestus and Athena all the techniques of fine workmanship such as is wrought beneath the sky" (Hes. *Theog.* 139–41). The more scientifically minded Romans looked to natural explanations for man's learning: Lucretius thought lightning lay behind the discovery of fire (*De Rerum Nat.* 1.895–901; 5.1091–95), as did Vitruvius (*De Arch.* 2.1), and that smelting had been discovered from observing an accidental fire melting ores (5.1241–49). Pliny was fascinated by technology and names inventors for dozens of items of armor, weaponry, and military techniques, including the discovery of flint (Pyrodes), the two-horsed chariot (the Phrygians), and stone-quarrying (Cadmus, or possibly the Naxians) (*HN.* 7.57). He offers three different versions of the origins of mining and smelting (*HN.* 7.191–98).

While we might expect a more earthy depiction of manufacturing in comedy and history, both prove something of a disappointment. Aristophanes brings a wide range of anonymous and representative characters onto the stage—farmers, soldiers, old men, domestic slaves, tutors, nurses, hoteliers, priests, and poets—but the closest we come to meeting manufacturers is the chorus of rural producers and craftsmen in *The Peace*, where the spear maker has a virtually non-speaking part. In *The Knights* the Market-Judge-cum-Seller-of-Strange-Things is lampooned as a typical commercial character but is not a manufacturer. Industrial connections of politicians are often referred to in order to make fun of the humble way in which they made or inherited a living, but we are not told, for example, whether all tanners became rich or just the forebears of Cleon and Anytus, or—if they were exceptions—what they were

---

[42] This enthusiasm is immediately qualified by a warning that man can use this capability for good or evil, and comes shortly after Creon's tirade against money as the root of all political evil (*Ant.* 313–14)!

doing right. Cleon's "Herculean valour in braving the stenches of his trade" (*Pax*. 752–53) tells us nothing about tanning operations that is not obvious to the most casual passer-by. Menander casts a similar array of characters, but with a higher proportion of slaves, the occasional addition of prostitutes, and some new service occupations such as cook, waiter, and doctor (*Aspis*). The *Epitrepontes*, which has arbitration as its subject matter, does not refer to a commercial dispute, even though a good proportion of the surviving works of the orators does. We can sometimes infer the structure of production from reselling activity in Aristophanes, but we learn little or nothing directly.

Historians of the classical period regularly address the economic motives and effects of war—the founding of trading colonies, the supply of ships and weaponry, movements of people, and the provision of public funds—but these are essentially macroeconomic matters. They describe triremes at a level of detail that is valuable for deriving production requirements (see Chapter 6) and sometimes specify large quantities of armor to be provided to Athens's youth, but generally ignore the production or sales processes of the goods in question. They also tend to display an ambivalence about the role of commerce in society that tallies with some of the writings of philosophers. Thucydides held that the acquisition of surplus wealth is acceptable—even laudable—if it is applied to living a good life, but "the desire to amass unlimited wealth...contradicts the notion of 'the good life'."[43] Herodotus (2.166–67) notes the Egyptians despise trade and value warfare, and speculates as to whether Greek states learned this attitude from them; Xenophon explains that "while in other states...all men make as much money as they can," the *homoioi* in Sparta were forbidden to engage in any economic activity (*Lac.* 7). Plutarch tells how King Agesilaus summoned a gathering of the Spartans and their allies and asked the artisans to stand up. All the Spartans remained seated (*Ages*. 264–65). Other cities including Thebes, Thespia, and Epidaurus had quite similar attitudes. The historians make clear that Athens was a less rigid society and one that tolerated, perhaps encouraged, the social mobility to which manufacturing products for sale can contribute.[44]

The philosophers regularly emphasize the moral hazard of unrestrained pursuit of material gain and advocate a life of leisurely contemplation as the ideal one for a citizen. Some scholars hold that this elitist attitude was so pervasive as to constitute a serious obstacle to economic or industrial development.[45] It is, of course, perfectly possible that Athens could have had a highly efficient manufacturing sector owned and operated entirely by foreign settlers, freed men, and slaves, but in fact there is plenty of evidence that citizens

---

[43] Kallett-Marx (1993) 17.

[44] The economic egalitarianism of Sparta, with which Athens is often contrasted, has probably been overstated (Hodkinson (2000)).

[45] Hasebroek (1931) and Finley (1973) are the best-known examples—see Section 1.3.1 below.

owned, financed, and worked in a wide range of manufacturing businesses.[46] Both Plato and Aristotle accepted the need for commerce and saw the profit motive as an important, if dangerously seductive, inspiration to endeavor. Plato gave craftsmen a place in his *Republic* (371e), even though industry was a much less valuable use of time than philosophical enquiry (496d–e). There is little sign of admiration though. Workers do not embody skills so much as appetites that need to be controlled (547b). Technology is of interest only to the extent it copies ideals (524d–31d). Plutarch observes that one can admire a work of art without wanting to be like its maker and that "if a work delights us because of its gracefulness, it does not necessarily follow that we should hold the man who makes it in high regard" (*Per.* 2.1). Similar sentiments are expressed by Aristotle and by Xenophon (e.g., *Oec.* 4.2–3). On the other hand, two of Xenophon's works, the *Oeconomicus* on the management of private affairs and the *Vectigalia* on public finance, show considerable economic sophistication, including a sound understanding of how supply and demand determine prices (*Vect.* 4.6) and the impact of compounding returns (*Vect.* 4.4).

We are left with the orators. Law was big business in Athens; one historian estimates there were 40,000 lawsuits a year, though this seems overstated.[47] Contract speechwriters offered their services in the Agora. The general interest in forensic oratory can be deduced from the large number of copies of Aristotle's *Rhetoric* that have been found. A surprising proportion of the 159 speeches that survive are about commerce—perhaps because money bought the best advocates, but also because several of these orators had commercial interests themselves. Lysias (12.18–19) and Demosthenes (27) both owned factories. Andocides was an early investor in what we now call public private partnerships, acquiring the right to collect harbor taxes for one year (Andoc. 1.133). Isocrates' father made flutes ((Plut.) *Isoc.* 1) which might have been quite a big business, as flutes provided much of the musical entertainment at both public and private functions. His son inherited a large sum but quickly lost it and turned to speech writing to restore his fortunes. These orators were not likely to adopt the philosophers' position that business was all a bit grubby and not a pursuit worthy of a citizen; nor, of course, were their clients.[48]

Given the amount of factual detail in the orators and the lack of it in other literature, they are a vital source—often our only source—for matters like the size of workshops and slave-gangs and the price and earnings of slaves. The proportion of business transactions that actually ended up in court is

---

[46] See Kron (1996) xi and, especially, Chapter 9 of this volume.

[47] Hughes (2010) 2; 43.

[48] Demosthenes held that earned wealth was respectable when the proceeds were spent on public service (liturgies), but he was not above using the commonplace of snobbery to score points off opponents (38.25–27) and makes a great deal of the fact that Aeschines had to work for a living while he, Demosthenes, did not (18.257–65).

likely to have been low—it is difficult to imagine that a business jurisdiction could survive if it was consistently high—but the surviving speeches nevertheless describe a vibrant and competitive manufacturing sector. Of course advocates often had reason to exaggerate, and some of their assertions must be treated with caution. It has been suggested that public rhetoric tended to construct "alternative realities" in order to preserve democratic equilibrium, and that we should never assume that we can get behind this rhetorical construction to understand how the economy really worked.[49] On the other hand, the legal process involved evidence and witnesses, and it is reasonable to assume that any assertions aimed at convincing a large body of judges must have been at least plausible and consistent with known events and practices, even if some of the details were exaggerated.[50]

To summarize, the only facts about manufacturing activity that can be usefully deduced from ancient Greek literature relate to the origins of manufacturing for sale (Homer and Hesiod), reselling arrangements (Aristophanes), and the size and profit profile of some of the enterprises that became involved in litigation. Later writers add little. Strabo and Pausanias show an informed interest in sculpture and construction, but essentially as tourists rather than engineers; the technical writings of Vitruvius, Galen, and others have little to do with the objects made by and for classical Athenians or the enterprises that made them. It was not until the late 19th century that historians started paying attention to ancient economic activity as a subject in its own right, and vigorous debates on how commercial it all was have raged ever since, prompted at least in part by the inconsistent picture in the primary sources.

## 1.2.2 ARCHAEOLOGY AND EPIGRAPHY

Moses Finley observed that it was self-evident that "the potential contribution of archaeology to history is, in a rough way, inversely proportional to the quantity and quality of the available written sources," and it is certainly true that archaeology is an important source of information on production.[51] The pervasiveness of manufacturing in Athens is reflected in archaeological finds and the evolution of the industrial city can be traced through shifts in the location of production. Although few if any areas were ever exclusively industrial, different areas at different times played the role of major production centers.[52] Traces of production facilities in and around the Agora, principally collected by the British and American Schools at Athens, are well documented by Monaco and give an idea of production locations and the

---

[49] Ober (1989) 153–54; Morris (1999) xxxi.
[50] Cohen (1992a) 26; Harris (1995) 15; Millett (2000) 31.
[51] Finley (1986) 93.
[52] Osborne (1987) 81.

layout of some workshops or *ergasteria*.[53] To deduce the manufacturing processes that took place inside their ruined walls presents more of a challenge. We can gain a good understanding of the part industry played in the urban topography but have less to go on in relation to what happened indoors. Even where we can work out the configuration of rooms, walls, and furnaces, they do not tell us anything about production processes.[54]

Potteries can be readily located through the excavation of ancient wells in which shards have tended to survive better than the detritus of other industries. There is also some evidence of furnaces that are unlikely to have been used for pottery, such as those on the Acropolis, which is a long way from the sources of water and clay that are essential to ceramic production, so these furnaces may have been used for working metal or other materials.[55] Most workshops were located on a thoroughfare and in the shade of a wall, and groupings seem to reflect a similar logic to the industrial clusters of recent times like Detroit for automobiles and Northern California for digital technology.[56] Practical reasons included easy access to raw materials (possibly sharing supply), exchanging new ideas, and neighbors who might borrow or lease each other's slaves when they were not required. The encouragement of such clusters is the basis of many contemporary national and regional industry policies, and today there are hundreds of cluster initiatives all over the world.[57] It appears Athens achieved them instinctively. Beyond these dedicated places of business, perhaps between 20,000 and 30,000 houses were involved in manufacturing goods for their own consumption or for sale, with workshops in or alongside the living quarters, as was typical in other cities of the time such as Abdera and New Halos.[58]

Epigraphic evidence can be revealing. Tombstones, honors for craftsmen and traders, and lists of people making religious dedications sometimes include job titles: we see a surprising number of descriptors for female agricultural workers as well as the expected preponderance of jobs in textiles for unattached working women.[59] Tablets cursing, say, bronze workers, written

---

[53] Monaco (2000) 19–46; for locations see also Sparkes and Talcott (1970).

[54] Monaco's sites AXII and DIII are fine examples.

[55] Tschira (1972) 158–231. Curiously, one of the best preserved of these sites is also one of the earliest, dating probably from the eighth century and thought to be active until the third quarter of the seventh. Just south of Tholos, site AXII includes a furnace of 1.3 meters in diameter in which the walls and floor are covered with one or more layers of polished clay; there is doubt as to whether this was used for pottery, as pottery furnaces were typically rebuilt after each use.

[56] Krugman (1991) 35–68; this clustering is partly explained by Hotelling's Law (1929), which attributes the observed tendency of ice-cream vendors to gather at one end of the beach to a desire to let customers know where to come and to compete for them when they do.

[57] Michael Porter, Letter to *The Economist*, November 17, 2007.

[58] Laziridis (1952) 272; Reinders (1988) 37–79; for estimates of household participation, see Chapter 9 and Appendix.

[59] Brock (1994) 343.

on lead sheets and rolled up and thrown into pits in order to reach the gods of the underworld, suggest there would have been many such tradesmen in an area. Public records, including decrees, building budgets, and accounts, give public employment head counts and rates of pay. Records of mining leases have much to tell us about investment patterns and the types of people who invested at Laurium.[60]

It has long been observed that Greek art of the archaic and classical periods never neglects representation of the crafts, but that representation takes many different forms.[61] We see lone craftsmen, some intent on what is obviously a complex activity, some doing something much simpler; people working in pairs, often perhaps a citizen of modest means with his slave; and, more rarely, quite large workshops with half-a-dozen people or more working on separate tasks.

Most valuable of all are finds of original objects themselves. Material evidence of occupations includes wood (foresters, sawyers, carpenters, furniture makers, boat builders); stone (quarrymen, stonemasons, sculptors, mosaicists, haulers); metals (miners, blacksmiths, armorers, silversmiths, goldsmiths, coiners); clay (potters, tilers); hides (tanners, cobblers); and more rarely reeds (rope- and basket-makers); herbs (healers, perfumers); and wool (fullers, dyers, and weavers).[62] All tell us something about the resources required to make various objects. Buildings attest to the quantity of work and the range of skills required (Chapter 7). Wells and cisterns filled with molds provide examples of test pieces and simple coroplasts from as early as 1400 BCE. The earliest pottery kiln found contained a number of pieces with holes in them, which must have been used to test firing temperatures (the hole was for fishing them out of the kiln). The manufactured vessels for the transport and storage of wine, oil, and grain are of a volume and consistency that suggests they cannot have been made for retail sale by part-time citizen craftsmen (Chapter 3). Finds of hundreds of loom weights and spindle whorls in specific places show that textile production was not always confined to the individual household's own needs but could take place on a large scale (Chapter 5). An early bronze-casting pit used to make a statue of Apollo for a small temple on the west side of the Agora in around 500 BCE contained charcoal, slag, lumps of metal, tools, and fragments of molds that were clearly shaped for the statue using the lost-wax method (Chapter 7.2).[63] The size of boatsheds in the Peiraeus, combined with descriptions of triremes by poets and historians, enabled a working replica to be built in the 1980s.[64] For some

---

[60] Shipton (2001).
[61] Rostovtzeff (1941) 1200; Beazley (1944) 6 presents one of the best-known examples.
[62] Davies (2007b) 346–48.
[63] Camp (1986) 164–65.
[64] Morrison and Coates (1986); see also Chapter 6.3.

finds, reverse engineering and chemical analysis can tell us more still—for example that the bronze used in major public statues was often recycled from other applications.[65]

The analyses of manufacturing sectors that follow draw extensively on archaeological evidence, combined with the expertise of modern craftsmen, to estimate the quantity and type of labor required to make different items. These data on supply are combined with what we can learn about demand—generally from literature or from considering what factors lay behind the buying decision—through a conceptual framework that relates competitive supply and demand conditions to industry structure and profitability. The result is a series of hypotheses about how each sector functioned that are consistent with the known data and are open to falsification by new finds or by experts with richer information. Importantly, the hypotheses add up to an integrated and comprehensible picture of how Athens made the huge range of manufactured items it consumed and what that meant for residents in all social groups.

## 1.3 Methodology

### 1.3.1 EMBEDDEDNESS AND EMPIRICAL ANALYSIS

Twenty-five years after Finley's *The Ancient Economy* was published, Morris observed that "any informed discussion of these [Athenian economic] phenomena has to start with Finley's model."[66] Forty years on, it is perhaps less necessary to describe in detail the arguments of Finley and his followers as to why Athenian exchange activity cannot be conceived in modern terms, nor the accumulated evidence that challenges this hypothesis on historical and sociological grounds.[67] Nevertheless, as the chapters that follow rely heavily on current microeconomic explanations of how business works, it is incumbent on us to address Finley's warning: "The economic language

---

[65] Camp (1986) 76.
[66] Morris (1999).
[67] *Finley and his followers*: see especially Finley (1959/60; 1965a; 1970 12; 1973; 1985d); Millett (1990; 1991); Meikle (1995a, b); *Historical objections*: Nature of trade: French (1964), Nixon and Price (1990) 166, 270; Morley (1996); Hordern and Purcell (2000); Reger (2002); Differences between ancient societies: Mattingly and Salmon (2001a) 14; Drinkwater (1978; 1981; 1982); Meaning of self-sufficiency: Isager and Hansen (1975); Hordern (2000); Harris (2002a), Bitros and Karayannis (2006); Emergence of a new mindset: Descat (1995); Faraguna (1992; 1994); Tandy (1997), Morris (1994; 2004); Interdependence of city and country: Osborne (1987; 1988; 1991; 1992); Millett (2000) 28; Cities as manufacturing centers: Jones (1964) 465; Bresson (2007) ch. 7; Management of grain supply: Andreau (1995); Stroud (1998); Moreno (2007); Engen (2010); Market-based price-setting: Loomis (1998); Bresson (2000); Feyel (2006) 422–27; scholion to Ar. *Eccl.* 814; Dem 34 39; 56 8, 10; Budgets: Faraguna (1992); Management of currencies: Stroud (1974); Management of interest rates: Inscription 2940 in Bourguet (1929) vol. III, Fascicule 5; IG. I³ 369; Respect for entrepreneurs: Bitros and Karayannis (2004; 2006);

and concepts we are all familiar with, even the laymen among us, the 'principles' whether they are Alfred Marshall's or Paul Samuelson's, the models we employ, tend to draw us into false accounts."[68]

Finley did not do justice to the ancients. He quotes with approval Hume's "I do not remember a passage in any ancient author, where the growth of a city is ascribed to the establishment of a manufacture."[69] This philosopher, "whose reading in ancient authors was wide and careful," must have missed Thucydides's opening statement (1.2.2) that it was the lack of commerce that stopped earlier generations from building cities—few ancient cities founded on trade can have owed their origin to exports of grain or timber, the only major traded items that were not more than partially processed. Chapter 9 shows that Demosthenes was being perfectly rational in discussing his inherited factories, despite Finley's scathing comments.[70] Aristotle may not have written anything called *Economics* himself, but he analyzes the physical and financial stages in trade very clearly (*Pol.* 1258b) and has a good grasp of how monopoly profits work (*Pol.* 1259a).[71] Both Aristophanes (*Pax.* 1198–1202; *Eq.* 644–45) and Xenophon (*Vect.* 4.6) understood how supply and demand affect prices, and the latter describes the science of economics in almost exactly the same way as Alfred Marshall (*Oec.* 6.4).[72] And even if the ancients were ignorant of basic economic concepts, it is a very large step to conclude that they could not act in an economically understandable way. We do not assess Tiger Woods's golfing skills by his ability to describe the ergonomic principles of his swing. Physical bodies obeyed the law of gravity long before Newton articulated it; why should we assume businesses did not obey the laws of competitive economics long before Marshall? J. M. Keynes had no time for Finley's sort of reasoning: "[The paucity of ancient writings on economics] means only that analysis had not disentangled the various elements in rational action, not that common sense neglected them."[73] Many historically important developments occurred

---

Commercial contracts: Cohen (2006) versus Pringsheim (1950) and Todd (1993); also Fuller (1939); Fried (1981); Harris (1988; 2001). *Sociological objections:* The unreality of arguments based on "Economic Man": Smith (1976) I. 116, 188; Knight (1921) 78; Sen (1977); North (1981) 5; Frank (1985); Hargreaves Heap (1989); Andreau (2002) 128–29; Weintraub (2002) 17, 23; Saller (2002) 252; Morris (2004) 22; Lieven (2005) 71; Ferguson (2008) 321; Lanchester (2010) 116; McFadden (2013); Complexity of individual motivation: Maslow (1943); Simon (1957); Becker (1957; 1968; 1976; 1991); Herzberg (1959) versus Mayo (1949); Hirschleifer (1976; 1983; 2001); Hirschleifer and Riley (1994); Coleman (1986a, b; 1990); Levitt and Dubner (2005; 2009); Personal motivation in modern business transactions: Stinchcombe (1959); Dalton (1959); Macauley (1963); White (1981); Sahlins (1981); Granovetter (1985) and Granovetter and Swedberg (2001 Intro.); De Long (2007); Limitations of human rationality: Kahnemann et al. (1982).

[68] Finley (1973) 23; cf. Polanyi (1957) 65–67; Pearson (1957).
[69] Hume (1822) 415; Finley (1973) 21.
[70] Finley (1985a) 24.
[71] Riezler (1907).
[72] Marshall (1959) 1; see also Aubert (2001) 96–97.
[73] Keynes (1921) 307; cf. Faraguna (1994) 552; 585.

with no verbal theory and, when they acquired one, "the theory was generally nonsense but the practice sound."[74] Quite often, managers of successful businesses are themselves unable to describe (and may not even understand) what underlies their success. In the 1980s, an Australian trucking company, which had a highly profitable business in armored cars in Australia, acquired one in the United States. This proved unsuccessful over several years, and the company, believing that making profits was a result of skilled management, kept changing the manager. This had no effect, for the simple reason that the company's profitability in Australia was a result of very high local market shares, keeping costs per stop low by having many stops on each route and less unprofitable driving time between stops. In the United States, local market shares and route densities were low. The managers had got their original business model right without understanding it. Could not the Athenians have done the same? Irrespective of whether Athenians could articulate—or perhaps even conceptualize—economic theory, Athenian manufacturing might still have operated in practice according to the same set of fundamental economic principles that we are familiar with today, and subsequent chapters show that it generally did so.

Finley nowhere explains why economics is the only sphere of human activity that cannot function properly unless it has achieved some (undefined) level of "functional segregation."[75] Religion, sports, warfare, and the arts were all more embedded in the main current of Athenian social life and values than they are in today's society, and were at least as deeply embedded as was economic activity.[76] Yet we do not question whether the ancients can really be said to have competed at sport or whether battles can be explained in terms of military strategy or whether the modern aesthetic can relate to classical sculpture and drama. Is there some reason why economic activity is seen to have undergone a conceptual shift resulting in a complete discontinuity of practice while other activities have not?[77]

This is not to deny that some of the differences Finley emphasized had important impacts on how business was conducted. Slavery itself makes for a very different economy, giving labor a capital cost and the owner an ongoing maintenance obligation. The fact that only adult male citizens had full commercial rights is another important difference, but how much this affected business dealings is not so clear. A practical people, the Athenians found various ways of getting around legal restrictions when they had to.[78]

---

[74] Haldane (1968) 60.

[75] An early case was made by Schmoller (1900–1904) and this notion seems to be taken for granted by many modern scholars, e.g., Snodgrass (1980) 124; Meikle (1995a, 1995b); Cartledge (1998) 15–17; von Reden (2002) 64. It is not clear why.

[76] Millett (1993) 180–81 is equally critical of "modernizing" treatment of ancient wars, but this is essentially on economic grounds.

[77] Rihll (2002) 8; 18 notes a similar debate about whether the Greeks actually *did* science, sensibly concluding that the only way to find out is to look at what they did.

[78] Cf. Black and Black (2011).

Non-citizens were prominent in many commercial activities and were protected from injustice as long as they paid their tax.[79] Tax-paying metics had explicit legal rights and even aliens without metic status could appear before the *dikai emporikai*, and, before that tribunal was established in 350 BCE, there were probably similar arrangements in place.[80] The inability to own assets or make even modest contracts in their own name did not mean Athenian women were inactive in commerce. They did a lot of buying and selling and, if necessary, husbands, relatives, or other male citizens could represent their interests (Dem. 41).[81] In fact they were probably responsible for the financial management of most Athenian households. It was the *oikos* (household) rather than the individual that controlled property, undertook liturgies, was accountable for tax, and managed income generation, including the production of goods for sale, and it was women who ran the *oikos*. The chief purpose of wills was to ensure the survival of an *oikos* lacking a male heir by adopting a new master, often through finding suitable spouses for the widow and daughters. Women had the right to object if a will alienated the *oikos*'s assets (Aeschin. 2.29). One way for the wealthiest entrepreneurs to ensure their business interests survived their own death was for their widow to marry the slave in charge of it (Dem. 36.14). Slaves enjoyed similar *de facto* freedom and played a leading role in many commercial activities, reflecting the Athenian citizen's distaste for direct personal involvement.[82] They often ran workshops on behalf of their owners, owned and operated trading vessels (e.g., Phormion—Dem. 41.31; Lampis—Dem. 34.5–10), acted as principal in banking contracts (Lampis—Dem. 34.23, 31), and made maritime loans (Zenothemis—Dem. 32). They could enter contracts and even litigate in their own name: Demosthenes represented the slaves Phormion (36), Lampis (34), and Amphilos (56). Some slaves undertook liturgies (Dem. 24.6–23; 33.4; Isoc. 17.9). The laws recognized their responsibility for business debts, and slaves living independently (*choris oikountes*) could do very well financially ((Xen.) *Ath. pol.* 1.11) and were allowed to own household goods.[83]

Finley's observations on limited rights tell us nothing about whether the transactions that took place in classical Athens can usefully be described in economic terms. It is quite conceivable that Athens had an efficiently functioning and profit-based economy, even if the structure of society meant many of the actors played different roles in it than they would today. Whether or not particular activities were economically rational, and whether economic

---

[79] Engen (2007).
[80] Gauthier (1972).
[81] Harris (2006b) 343.
[82] Cohen (2002 and forthcoming).
[83] Cohen (2000) 130–54; Pritchett (1953) 31–46.

analysis can sensibly be applied to them, can only be ascertained from examining what actually happened in commercial dealings rather than by inference from status or gender stereotypes. And if we really seek to understand what the ancients did in ways that we can relate to, we should be willing to try every heuristic, including the use of our own language and concepts.[84]

Finley and some of his followers also note that classical economics assumes that the objective of agents is profit maximization, whereas the topography and climate of Greece meant that the principal objective for most agents was risk-avoidance.[85] Since Finley's time, archaeological surveys and pollen counts have shown that the old view of Greek agriculture as inefficient and risk-averse cannot be correct; an agricultural system of that kind simply could not have generated enough food to support the population densities of the Greek world.[86] Between 500 and 200 BCE there was a shift toward intensively worked blocks of contiguous land, making heavy use of manure and often producing for the market, achieving dry-grain yields that would not be matched until at least the 19th century.[87] In any event, classical investment models accommodate risk-preference quite easily. Risk and reward are the critical components in investment decision-making and the chosen balance differs between individuals and for the same individual at different times. They can also reflect different time horizons; investment trades off current resources for future ones—the essence of agricultural risk minimization. It is possible, for instance, that the ancient Athenian investment paradigm put a higher price on risk than ours would in similar circumstances, but this does not change the nature of the equation, though it would change its solution.[88] It is also possible to analyze behavior assuming other objectives on the part of agents than profit-maximization.[89] The only way to discover what Athenians' objectives really were is to test their decisions against a risk-return model, as we do in Chapter 9.

An early reviewer of *The Ancient Economy* gently remarked: "One may respectfully suggest that the old, laborious methods, of collecting evidence and interrogating it with an open mind, will remain with us for a longish time yet."[90] The critical question is whether, when one Athenian resident of whatever status had commercial dealings with another, the limited rights of

---

[84] Harris (2013) 22; Braudel (1969) 83–90.

[85] Bresson (2007) ch. 2; Hordern and Purcell (2000) 178–82; Cartledge (2002) 160. This was probably not true of the rich, who may have made their money from storing goods at times of famine in the first place (Halstead (1987)). The beneficiation of silver ore shows quite clearly that Athenian investors could understand and respond to the profit motive (Christesen (2003) 41).

[86] Kiel (1987); Hansen (2006; 2008).

[87] Hodkinson (1988); Cherry et al. (1991); Jameson et al. (1994); Snodgrass (1994); Bintliff et al. (2010).

[88] Akerlof et al. (2010).

[89] Becker (1957; 1968; 1976; 1991); Hirschleifer (1976; 1983; 2001); Hirschleifer and Riley (1994); Levitt (2005; 2009).

[90] Frederiksen (1975) 171.

women and non-citizens, constraints imposed by social ideas of what was acceptable, an ancestral habit of worrying about risk before profit, or the limitations of his economic vocabulary made the outcome of the transaction different from what it would have been if conducted in a modern market economy, or whether the same economic laws prevailed despite the different context? By testing a variety of transactions and economic decisions from classical Athens against modern paradigms, we can assess how far the evidence supports inferences drawn from contemporary industry theory or whether it can only be explained in terms of a different, non-economic framework. We can also identify when Athenians appear to have made different choices from those a rational actor might today, and base conclusions about Athenian values on such facts rather than on inferences from selective readings of the limited surviving texts.

Finley's paradigm has dominated recent economic historiography of the ancient world to the point where many scholars have steered clear of economic matters altogether and very few have attempted to apply modern analytics. Only recently "on commence... à admettre que les Grecs avaient une économie et que, comme système, cette dernière merite d'être étudiée pour elle-même."[91] The *Cambridge Economic History of the Greco-Roman World* (2007) is informed by a more institutional approach and does not hold everything up to the harsh and unreal light of neoclassical economics, but even there a depressing number of contributions start with an explanation of the limitations to industrial development in rather Finleyan terms. To the extent that manufacturing features, it is in its macroeconomic context—large production facilities, state intervention and exports—rather than in terms of industry dynamics and competition between business establishments. Even among the few historians prepared to engage with economic subjects, none have tried to use the data available to make sense of the financial viability and conduct of participants in manufacturing industries. No one has tried to pick up where Francotte (1900–1901) and Glotz (1926) left off their detailed treatises on Athenian manufacturing, though a number of scholars have made major contributions in specific areas, such as the mining industry (Rihll 2001; 2002; Rihll and Tucker 2002), the life and work of craftsmen (Burford 1972), banking (Cohen 1992a), the laws governing commerce (Harris *passim*), and the economies of cities (Bresson 2000; 2007). Davies (1998; 2001a; 2007a,b) has laid out some of the challenges and choices in modeling economic flows in the ancient world. Others, like Andreau, Cartledge, Morris, and Osborne, have approached particular historical questions with an open-mindedness about economic perspectives that often leads to insight, and the work of all these contemporary scholars is drawn on here. Unfortunately for our

---

[91] Bresson (2007) 3.

purposes, it remains "striking how much of the economic historiography of the Mediterranean has concerned itself not with production but with exchange."[92]

## 1.3.2 THEORIES OF FIRM SIZE

Common explanations of Athens's supposed failure to build a large industrial base include a lack of interest among the right people, difficulty accessing credit, poor accounting techniques, an unsupportive regulatory environment, and the limitations of a slave workforce. A more sophisticated account suggests that firm size depends on division of labor, which depends in turn on the application of machinery. Each of these arguments has its own flaws, which we comment on here, and none addresses the question of the wide divergence in firm size that was a marked feature of Athens's manufacturing.

The lack-of-interest argument is, of course, a variation on the Embeddedness Paradigm, although it predated Finley.[93] Glotz believed that "the head of an undertaking was not driven by the need to collect as much capital and labour as possible because he was not driven by the necessity of getting the biggest possible returns out of expensive machines, in order to diminish his general costs and to obtain a progressive increase in profits."[94] Humphreys speaks of "small-scale, disconnected business ventures, assessed by the security of their returns rather than their potentiality for expansion" and attributes this largely to the social preferences of Athenians who were happier being rentiers rather than serious industrialists.[95] Hopper observes that factories were acquired by chance as a result of other financial dealings, and that there is no evidence of investments made to extend an enterprise, nor of any particular expertise or enthusiasm for efficiency on the part of owners.[96]

None of these views takes account of how the *apophora* system worked: owners were certainly happy being rentiers, because that is what they had chosen to be. Under the *apophora* system, owners received a regular fixed payment from the workshop or gang supervisor, generally a slave or a freedman, who ran the business on a day-to-day basis and took the risk and profit on the business himself. It was the supervisor who would have benefited from improved efficiency or expansion.[97] Provided the business made enough profit, returns to owners were unaffected by year-to-year fluctuations in the bottom line, as is the case with preference shareholders today. Given this clear demarcation between ownership and profit sharing in larger enterprises, even if many

---

[92] Hordern and Purcell (2000) 30.
[93] Finley (1973) 144–45; cf. Hasebroek (1928; 1931).
[94] Glotz (1926) 142.
[95] Humphreys (1970) 21.
[96] Hopper (1979) ch. 7.
[97] This system is explained in more detail in Chapter 9.

of the elite really were disinterested in commerce, it is far from certain that this would have limited the development of businesses. Snobbish attitudes to industry have been common in societies ranging from North America at the time of the revolution through India under the Raj to South Africa during the Boer Wars and are well exemplified in the national cultures of Western Europe until at least the mid-20th century.[98] There is no evidence that economic development in any of these places or times was especially constrained as a result. Elitist attitudes are social matters and do not usually affect economic activity.[99] Wealthy Athenians may have sniffed at those working in a craft or trade, because it indicated they could not afford to employ enough slaves to earn money on their behalf. Owning industrial slaves, on the other hand, seems to have been perfectly acceptable.[100]

The following pages give many examples of citizens, including some of the most respected orators, politicians, and generals of the time, who owned successful manufacturing businesses. Athenians not only found industry an acceptable way of making money, but they could also be honored for doing so, provided their profits were reasonable, decently acquired, and spent in a socially valuable way.[101] The noblest uses of wealth, frequently referred to by the orators in tones of great respect, were public services, especially the provision of trierarchies and military equipment. It was also noble to lend money to friends in need, often but not necessarily interest free.[102] It is likely that these expectations of social expenditure by wealthy citizens explain the substantial *aphanes* (hidden) economy and the difficulty historians have had in quantifying the wealth of even the best-known plutocrats of the time.[103] It is also likely to have made them more anxious for commercial success.[104] In short, there seems no sound basis for believing that, alone among life forms, ancient Greeks lacked a selfish gene.[105]

A refinement of this line of argument suggests that technological advance determines firm size (not strictly true, as shown later in this section) and this was impeded by social structures. The well-educated who might have had the technical knowledge were uninterested, and in any event, science had become preoccupied with abstract speculation rather than tangible experiment.[106] As Galbraith pointed out, "inventions that are not made, like babies that are

---

[98] United States: Jefferson, quoted in Rosenberg (2007) 6; South Africa: Hancock (1958) 332, quoted in Finley (1965a) 44; British Raj: Allen (1994) 230; 118; cf. Ruskin (1866) Lecture 1; Russell (1960) ch. 1.
[99] Pleket (1990) 121–22.
[100] De Ste. Croix (1981) 124.
[101] Bitros and Karayannis (2004) 10; (2006).
[102] Finley (1973) 152.
[103] Bitros and Karayannis (2004) 3–5.
[104] Osborne (1991) 120–48; cf. Xen. *Oec.* 2.5–6.
[105] Dawkins (1976); cf. Smith (1999) 1.119.
[106] Finley (1965a) 32; Farrington (1944) 141, 49, 88.

not born, are rarely missed," and the advantages of technical improvements may not have occurred to the Athenians.[107] In fact, several practical books on crafts, technology, invention, and discovery were written by leading thinkers, including friends and pupils of Plato and Aristotle.[108] Theophrastus wrote two volumes "On Metals" (now lost) as well as his treatise "On Stones," and his successor as head of the Lyceum, Straton of Lampsacus, wrote one on mine machinery. In each case, technical development had taken place in the absence of any body of knowledge that could be defined as theoretical and the theory that developed was an intelligent digest of utilitarian knowledge.[109] The hypothesis is also contradicted by most modern interpretations of the Industrial Revolution, which highlight the fact that innovation tends to come from entrepreneurial endeavor rather than scientific insight—the power of steam had been known for a long time and was first harnessed in Britain's coalfields, not in the rooms of the Royal Society.[110] Even before the Industrial Revolution, Daniel Defoe had noted that in England it was "better to improve than to invent, better to advance upon the Designs and Plans which other people have laid down than to form Schemes and Designs of their own."[111]

No more convincing is the suggestion that the people running workshops were constrained by capital from investing in business development.[112] No innovations were likely to require more capital than a successful foreman could finance out of his own retained earnings; if they did, and the slave or freed foreman was not able to borrow from the typical sources open to citizens, he could have persuaded the owner to invest a little more in equipment in exchange for a higher *apophora* (sharing the benefits of productivity gains), just as he would if he wanted to increase the complement of slaves. It is implausible to attribute the failure to apply, say, steam, water, or animal power to heavy material handling processes like turning a shield on a lathe or tanning to the fact that only the elite would have thought of it. It is even more implausible to suggest that there was no benefit in saving labor because slaves were free or because there was no economically functioning market for labor.[113] Eliminating the need for a slave saves both a capital sum and an annual labor cost equivalent to at least the subsistence wage.

The more general argument from limited capital availability is no stronger.[114] For a lack of loan capital to have acted as a constraint on development, two conditions must have applied: the sums required to start or expand a

---

[107] Galbraith (1962) 9 iii.
[108] Rihll and Tucker (2002) 287–89.
[109] Rihll and Tucker (2002) 290–91; 275.
[110] Schmookler (1966); Harris (1992); Kealey (1996); Pomeranz (2000); Landes (1969); Mokyr (2002; 2009); Clark (2007); de Vries (2008); Allen (2009).
[111] Defoe (1728) 299.
[112] Finley (1965a) 37.
[113] Glotz (1926) 142; Meikle (1995a).
[114] Finley (1952); Millett (1990, 1991); contradicted by Harris (1988) and Cohen (1992a; 1992b).

business must have been quite large and they could only be financed through credit. Neither condition prevailed. The amount of capital needed to start up or expand a typical manufacturing concern was modest. Tools were relatively cheap, raw materials were costed separately, and most fixed production items were put together from freely available raw materials by the slave workforce and therefore covered in their costs.[115] For example, a pottery kiln would have been made from waste clay and assembled by slaves, taking a few hours, and would not have compromised a daily firing routine. Whenever we hear of a value being put on a business, it is ascribed either implicitly or explicitly to the labor force. Most industrial slaves seem to have cost in the order of 300 to 400 *drachmae* each, depending on period and skill levels, a little more than it would cost to feed a slave in a year, so the funds needed to acquire industrial slaves were roughly within the budget of anybody who could afford to keep them. Technology limitations meant there were no economies of scale or major investment steps in most industries and therefore no disadvantage to slow and incremental expansion; a modest investment in a slave or two would be enough to start product manufacture and, if successful, this would generate funds to buy more slaves. Even larger businesses were valued at sums that would have been within the reach of several hundred citizens—a 20-slave furniture business was mortgaged for 4,000 *drachmae* (Dem. 27.9) and a small foundry cost 1,700.[116] Epicrates's perfume business went for 4,000 *drachmae* and was apparently worth much less (Hyp. 3.8). Harris identifies 13 *horoi* or boundary stones placed near workshops that were pledged as security.[117] The security value of eight of these workshops is recorded; two were for 6,000 *drachmae*, one for 1,750 and the rest for less than 1,000. The true value would have been higher than the security value, perhaps 50–60 percent more, but the sums are still not large. The largest industrial valuation we hear of is of Pantainetus's ore processing operations at just over three talents (Dem. 37.31), so the capital needs of even the largest workshops were probably not much more than the minimum amount needed to perform liturgies.[118]

To the extent capital was needed in industry, it seems to have been readily available. There are numerous examples of manufacturing businesses being bought, sold, claimed, mortgaged, and lent against: Aristarchus could borrow funds to acquire the raw materials for making clothes (Xen. *Mem.* 2.7.11–12) and Athenogenes to buy stock for his perfumery (Hyp. 3.6.9–10). Pantainetus's ore processing facilities and its slaves were offered as security

---

[115] See Chapter 9.1 on workshop cost structures and payment responsibilities; for slave costs, see Jones (1956) 194; Foxhall and Forbes (1982); 41–90; Ober (1989) 131; Kyrtatas (2002) 142.
[116] Glotz (1926) 268.
[117] Harris (1988) 362–64.
[118] Harris (2002a) 81.

for a loan (Dem. 37.4), as were the furniture-makers of Demosthenes's father (Dem. 27.9). Mantias and his son funded their mining interests with debt (Dem. 40.52). For his perfume business, Aeschines initially borrowed overseas at 3.5 percent a month, then locally, and eventually from friends at 1.5 percent per month (Lys. fr.38), the progression of sources and interest rates seeming to reflect a reduction in perceived risk. If the market failed, there were several alternatives to borrowing. To start a business, slaves could be leased, and Xenophon (*Vect.* 4.14–15) suggests that it was possible to pay the costs of leasing slaves out of the margin generated by their productive efforts. This meant no capital barriers to entry, or, in today's terminology, a workshop could be 100 percent geared to a lessor. Once a firm became established, any capital costs of growth, such as acquiring more slaves or working capital, could be funded organically from the business's earnings, as is common today.

The argument from accounting is intriguing. De Ste. Croix suggested that without double-entry bookkeeping the ancients could not untangle the prime determinants of profitability and were unable to collect income taxes or run businesses efficiently.[119] In fact, the medieval examples of more advanced accounting that de Ste. Croix cites demonstrate the pragmatic approach that characterizes most accounting practices, and no particular form of accounting was required in order to make such calculations.[120] Even the Medici did not systematically use the double-entry method, though it was known in Genoa as early as the 1340s, but seem to have confined themselves to three sets of accounts: the *libro secreto*, a general ledger; a *libro di intrata e uscita* (cash flow); and a *libro dei debitore e creditore*, or balance sheet.[121] Certainly financial calculations would have been easier after Fibonacci introduced Hindu-Arabic numerals and decimal calculations (as well as the world's first Net Present Value formula) in 1202, but that cannot be taken to demonstrate that no serious calculations were possible or attempted before then. Even the latest accounting techniques seldom cost activities precisely or provide a robust guide to decisions about the future.[122] Investment decisions generally depend on marginal calculations, while formal accounts only provide averages and many allocations of costs to activities are approximate at best and often arbitrary.[123] It is unreasonable to conclude from the fact Athenians could not achieve even the limited level of certainty that we can that they had no interest in making sound business decisions; better to ask with Hordern and Purcell, "how likely is it that an end to the impressionistic numeracy

---

[119] De Ste. Croix (1956); cf. Burford (1972) 58; Saller (2002) 55 on Finley (1973).
[120] Macve (1985) 248.
[121] Ferguson (2008) 45.
[122] Keynes (1936) 162–63; cf. Knight (1921)—the principle of "Knightian uncertainty."
[123] Macve (1985) 248.

of the past substantially changed the behaviour of those who aspired to the accumulation of wealth and status?"[124]

An inadequately supportive regulatory or legal environment is sometimes posited as a barrier to development, although Athens's commercial endeavors, both craft and trade, were supported by a robust legal framework that included common law, formal law, and codes of conduct to enforce contracts, all of which helped reduce transaction costs and increase economic activity.[125] Business associations of all types were governed by laws that covered the protection of property rights (underpinning access to borrowings), the enforceability of contracts, fraud, hire transactions, sales conveyance, warranties on product quality and slave health, deposits, loan default, and enforcement of real security.[126] Gaius attributes to Solon a decree legitimizing a wide range of forms of association as long as they were not in conflict with other laws.[127] The Athenians developed *koinoniae* or partnership agreements to define profit-sharing arrangements, and there are many examples in mining and in maritime lending, though these entities were not recognized as legal persons, so actions were against individuals.[128] Creditors could reduce the risk on maritime loans by lending to two people, one of whom remained accessible in Athens and was obligated for the whole loan amount, while the other made the voyage. The system for marking mortgaged property was sophisticated and well understood.[129] Athenians understood the value of this legal and regulatory infrastructure: "If you think that written contracts and agreements between partners should be binding and if you will not take the side of those who break them, those involved in lending will more readily make their assets available. As a result the port will thrive and you will benefit.... For who will be willing to risk his own money when he sees that contracts are not enforced?" (Dem. 56.48–50). Most importantly, the justice system was there for those who felt their interests had been unfairly compromised in economic transactions and, in contrast to the redistributive economies of the Near East, the justice meted out seems fair and consistent with appropriate expectations of economic behavior. In court, judges examined not a man's status but the nature of the case.[130] All in all, Athens was a better place to do business than many later civilizations.[131] It might be true that some mechanisms that facilitate enterprise, such as limited liability, had not

---

[124] Hordern and Purcell (2000) 293.
[125] Bresson (2007) ch. 1.
[126] Harris (2006a).
[127] Wilamowitz-Moellendorff (1965) 278; Vélissaropoulos-Karakostas (2002) 31–39.
[128] Scholars disagree about how extensive and permanent agency arrangements tended to be; see Cohen (1992a) 138–46 and Harris (2013).
[129] Harris (1988).
[130] Harris (2001) 272–73.
[131] Manning (2007).

been established in any formal way, but it is far less certain that this affected Athenians' ability to do business. Financiers' liabilities were limited in both the *apophora* system and in trade finance.

Nor can slavery itself be blamed. Early American writers on slavery asserted (without adducing evidence) that slavery was unprofitable or that "the soul of commerce is the spirit of enterprise and this is ever found wanting in communities where slavery exists." This view of the world can be traced back to Adam Smith ("slaves are very seldom inventive, and all the most important improvements...have been the discoveries of free men") and culminated in Phillips's notorious study of Negro slavery.[132] More recent research, based upon detailed analysis of company and plantation accounts, leads to quite different conclusions: slave-based agriculture in America was 35 percent more efficient than family farms and the purchase of a slave was generally a highly profitable investment yielding attractive returns.[133]

All these explanations for Athens's limited industrial development have been made more cogently and with more supporting evidence than has been cited here. Their common flaw, though, is a fatal one: they try to explain something that did not happen. Athens did not fail to build large companies. The average size of a factory today is 10 to 15 employees.[134] To our certain knowledge, Athens hosted several larger than this: Lysias's claim (12.19) that his shield workshop employed 120 slaves might be an exaggeration, but if we halve the number it is still a very large factory, and we hear of another in the same line of business 20 years later with at least 65 slaves (Dem. 36.4).[135] Demosthenes cannot have been stretching the truth too far when he claimed that one of the workshops he inherited employed "33 or 34" slaves and the other, 20 (Dem. 27.9), or he would have been laughed out of court. Pantainetos seems to have had about 30 slaves employed in processing ore (Dem. 37.4, 17, 31). Aristophanes's portrayal of Cleon, especially in the *Knights*, is generally taken to mean that he inherited a tannery, or at least funds that a forebear had made from tanning (*Eq.* 44);[136] if so, his wealth suggests it was a large enterprise. Anytos, rich enough to have been accused of bribing a jury, might have owed his wealth to a similar business ([Arist.] *Ath. pol.* 27.5; Xen. *Apol.* 29).[137] The real question is a much more interesting one: "Why did some firms in Athens grow large, while many remained very small?"

---

[132] Olmsted (1862) Cairns, (1863); Smith (1999) II. 270; Phillips (1918).

[133] Fogel and Engerman (1974) 193, 195.

[134] Australian Bureau of Statistics, Business Operations and Performance, 2000–2001; Eurostat (2012).

[135] Sargent (1925) 97–98; Davies (1971) 433–34.

[136] Van Driel-Murray (2008) 491.

[137] Davies (1971) 40–41.

More promising in this respect are the links between technology, slavery, division of labor, and firm size that have been addressed by many historians in attempts to explain industrial development. Engels held that "It was slavery that first made possible the division of labour between agriculture and industry, and thereby also Hellenism, the flowering of the Ancient World."[138] Glotz argued that without machines it was impossible to develop a "useful specialisation of labour." Because slavery meant there was no appetite for replacing men with machines, "the absence of machinery is at once the cause, and, to a certain extent, the effect of industrial slavery."[139] More recent scholars echo these views, which are best summarized in the syllogism:

- Machinery facilitates the division of labor.
- The division of labor promotes firm growth.
- Therefore machinery promotes firm growth.[140]

The notion that increased mechanization leads to larger firms is a little counterintuitive. The chief reason for introducing machinery to a workplace is usually to reduce labor. The adoption of robots clearly does not increase overall employment, nor does machinery necessarily increase the number of tasks into which work can be divided. Machine-driven mass production often results in many people performing the same tasks in parallel. Mechanization will only increase firm size if it leads to an increase in market share; if all competitors use the same machinery, it will not enable any one of them to grow at the expense of the others.

The ancients were far from unaware of the advantages of division of labor. Xenophon says (*Cyr.* 8.2.5): "It is of course impossible for a man of many trades to be proficient in all of them. One man makes men's shoes, another women's. And in some places, one man supports himself by only stitching, another by cutting, another by only shaping the uppers, and another by doing none of this but only assembling these things."[141] There is plenty of evidence from vase paintings (cited in Chapter 3) that potteries were also organized into separate tasks, such as throwing, painting, kiln management, and even turning the thrower's wheel. By classical times there was specialization within metal processing (Chapter 4), with different smiths working with iron, bronze, silver, and gold; many other crafts were defined by a narrow range of output, such as *artopoios* (loaf-maker) or *lophophoros* (crest-maker). Bronze statues were cast in discrete pieces by multiple individuals, sometimes operating

---

[138] Engels (1972) 121.

[139] Glotz (1926) 206; the premise that slavery reduces the economic incentive to save labor is, of course, nonsense.

[140] Hopper (1979) 103; Harris (2002a); Bresson (2007) ch. 7; Wilson (2008) 393–95.

[141] Finley (1973) 135 emphasises that the focus here is on quality rather than production cost, but other passages in ancient sources are clearly concerned with maximising productivity (e.g., Pl. *Resp.* 369–71).

from several different workshops.[142] The titles of marketplace vendors in Aristophanes show that retailers too specialized in particular foodstuffs or garments. Any failure to organize work into discrete tasks cannot have come from ignorance of the benefits.

These benefits, best articulated by Adam Smith, are very real. Smith, whose famous pin factory occupies the whole of the first chapter of *The Wealth of Nations,* starts with the observation that "The greatest improvements in the productive powers of labour...seem to have been the effects of the division of labour."[143] His pin factory has 10 people allocated among, perhaps, 18 tasks and producing 48,000 pins in a day, or 4,800 each, compared with a sole, unskilled, operator who "could scarce, perhaps, with his utmost industry, make one pin in a day, and certainly could not make twenty." Smith attributes this remarkable productivity gain of between 240 and 4,800 times to three effects of the division of labor: an increase in dexterity from practice, less "sauntering" (downtime moving between tasks), and labor-saving machinery. He is quite specific about the impact of dividing labor tasks: in terms of practiced dexterity, he suggests that a skilled smith who was not used to making nails could make about 200 to 300 in a day, one who made them regularly but not exclusively might get to 800 to 1,000, and one who made only nails could make 2,300. Specializing in just one step takes it up to the 4,800 times level. The first two improvements clearly come from practiced skill in being a smith and in making nails, not from division of labor. It is the last two that are of interest (Table 1.1).

TABLE 1.1 **Impact of Division of Labor**

| *Skill and Focus* | *Nails per Day* | *Impact of Division of Labor* |
| --- | --- | --- |
| Non-smith | 1–20 | — |
| Smith who does not make nails | 200–300 | N/A (impact is smith skill) |
| Smith who makes nails and other objects | 800 | N/A (impact is expertise in nails) |
| Smith who only makes nails | 2,300 | 2.9× |
| Smith who only does one or two stages in nail-making | 4,800 | 2.1× |

We do not know what proportion of a general smith's time making nails and other objects was spent specifically on nails, so we cannot measure how much specialization had increased in moving to nails only (which raised daily output 2.9 times), but we can test the value of moving from making all of a nail to specializing in one-tenth of one with Experience Curve analysis. The Boston Consulting Group (BCG) established that in any enterprise, unit costs

---

[142] Treister (1996) 329–30.
[143] Smith (1999) 1.

fall by a constant percentage each time accumulated experience doubles.[144] How much costs fall depends on the economics of specific businesses or activities. Rules of thumb (never to be trusted against firm-specific analysis) suggest that indirect costs tend to fall by around 30 percent for each doubling, direct manufacturing labor by 6–8 percent, and raw material costs seldom by very much at all. On that basis, if they start at the same time and each step takes a similar amount of time, a member of a team of 10 who concentrates on one or two steps will always have 10 times the experience in a particular step than an individual doing all the steps by himself, so his unit costs should be between $(1 - 0.6^{10} = 54\%)$ and $(1 - 0.08^{10} = 43\%)$ of the non-specialist's. In other words, specializing in one or two tasks increases productivity between 1.9 and 2.3 times, just as Smith had claimed. (We should pause to admire the accuracy of Smith's estimate, made almost 200 years before experience curve effects were properly measured!)

Despite the excellence of Smith's observation, it only goes a little way to explaining firm size. Division of labor into discrete tasks increases productivity and (provided the increased output can be sold) explains enterprise growth up to the minimum size required for efficient production.[145] It does not explain any more than that. In particular it does not explain how firms can grow to greater than this minimum efficient size. There is no obvious reason why there would be more job descriptions in a Toyota factory employing 5,000 people than in a Rolls-Royce one employing 500—probably fewer, as Toyota's volumes and market position might mean that it would be more economic to use robots for painting and welding and some assembly tasks than at Rolls-Royce. There are four principal job descriptions in a McDonald's franchise: cashier, cook, shift manager, and store manager.[146] McDonald's scale cannot be attributed to the productivity benefits of division of labor; rather it involves *multiplying* labor within job descriptions as more franchises are opened up. Some of the world's largest employers have very few job descriptions; the armed forces and the Catholic Church are obvious examples. Nor is it plausible to attribute the massive size of firms like Xstrata or Facebook to better application of division of labor or machinery than others in their industries.

The nature of the product and the number of discrete steps involved in making it set the limit to the benefits of task specialization and define the smallest efficient size, but tell us no more than that. In Nicias's mine-slave rental business, claimed by Xenophon to number a thousand men, everyone's job was the same (Xen. *Vect.* 23–24). The industries Bresson cites that employed large numbers in single establishments, such as shields, knives, and

---

[144] Henderson (1998a) 9–23.
[145] Coase (1937) 386–405.
[146] http://www.bestjobdescriptions.com/company-profiles/mcdonalds (accessed Feb. 16, 2012).

beds, might have had longer production chains than, say, potteries, but not by much. If this was the only factor, Lysias's shield factory would have employed 8 slaves, not 120.[147] Division of labor does nothing to explain why potteries never seem to have operated with more than one team, while shield factories employed perhaps a dozen. As Thompson points out, "four workers dividing the tasks can turn out more shoes than four men who do the entire job individually, but it is hard to see how eight teams of four could turn out proportionally more than a single team of four."[148] Once a firm has exhausted the benefits of division of labor (in the case of the pin factory, Smith thought the optimum number of workers was about 10), then if it is to grow to a size larger than the minimum required for efficient production, it must capture a larger share of the market than competitors who can achieve equal productivity levels by matching its factory layout. We are looking for a different dynamic than simple division of labor.

A broader concept of the forces leading to industry consolidation has been developed by recent historians of the Industrial Revolution, who point out that the rise of the factory as large employer was not an 18th-century phenomenon, but it did become more pervasive as mechanization increased. The technological, organizational, and quality-related factors behind the rise of the factory are correlated and hard to untangle, but there can be little doubt that technology changed the relative costs and benefits of moving people and information.[149] A reduction in the price of manufactured goods reduces the value of working at home and co-location allows for better control of production processes, worker training, the dissemination of best practice, and the ability to experiment. The factors at work in this consolidation are on the one hand, fixed costs and consequent economies of scale, and on the other, information that rewards supervision of the labor effort (whether that effort is exploited or willing).[150] Together they provide factories with enough advantage to grow at the expense of craft shops, and it is this advantage that leads to industry consolidation and the emergence of large firms. More generally, the link between technology and firm size derives from technology's potential to provide some firms with a competitive advantage, enabling them to win market share and grow at the expense of others. As we shall see in the next section, limited technology is indeed an important reason why small firm size was typical in ancient times, because it eliminated the possibility of a competitive advantage based on superior production economics and of barriers to entry based on machinery costs or proprietary technology. Both are important determinants of industry structure today. In classical Athens,

---

[147] Efficient production of shields required a team of about eight workers—see Chapter 4.7.
[148] Thompson (1982b) 74.
[149] Geraghty (2007); Mokyr (2002) 121–30.
[150] Marglin (1974–1975) versus Clark (1994).

firms that employed more people than required for a single efficient production chain had to find other ways of achieving and maintaining a competitive advantage.

### 1.3.3 THE THEORY OF COMPETITIVE ADVANTAGE

While the importance of competition seems obvious enough, the implications are easy to overlook; even Darwin lamented, "Nothing is easier than to admit in words the truth of the universal struggle for life, or more difficult—at least I have found it so—than constantly to bear this conclusion in mind."[151] We have noted that, in order to grow to more than the minimum efficient size for a production process, a firm must achieve greater market share than competitors. To do this, it must possess some form of economic advantage. The potential for advantage among current competitors, and against potential new entrants in the form of barriers to entry, typically determines the level of industry concentration and the benefits or risks facing individual firms attempting expansion. This makes it a reliable predictor of industry structure: sectors where some firms can achieve competitive advantage will become concentrated among a few firms who succeed in doing so; sectors where competitive advantage is not possible will remain fragmented unless the number of competitors is restricted by other factors such as regulation or location. These are the central theoretical concepts we shall use to analyze manufacturing enterprise in Athens, and the remainder of this chapter explains how they are applied.

Business strategy, or the science of deploying assets in such a way as to maximize returns, has only received serious attention in commerce and academia over the last few years. It owes much to the pioneering work of The Boston Consulting Group (BCG), founded in 1963 by the late Bruce Henderson, which introduced a number of well-known heuristics (including the Experience Curve, referred to in the previous section, and the famous "dogs and cows" Portfolio Matrix) in order to help clients choose and implement profit maximizing strategies. Today most large firms employ strategy practitioners (as opposed to planners, who typically work within narrower conceptual boundaries), and many other consulting firms offer strategic advice. Professor Michael Porter of Harvard Business School, himself the founder of the consulting firm Monitor, has written numerous books and articles summarizing the state of knowledge of competitive business theory. Many of the examples that follow, while reflecting the same approach as written work by Henderson, Porter, and others, are drawn from the author's own

---

[151] Darwin (2007) 47.

work with BCG colleagues over many years in research for clients and for educational programs.[152]

Competitive advantage is central to business strategy. Simple microeconomics tells us that in a state of equilibrium, the least profitable or "marginal" competitor will be making just enough profit to stay in business. In a typical business, the stay/exit decision is made by investors, so the marginal competitor's returns will be equal to the minimum returns investors require, known as the cost of capital (Fig. 1.1).

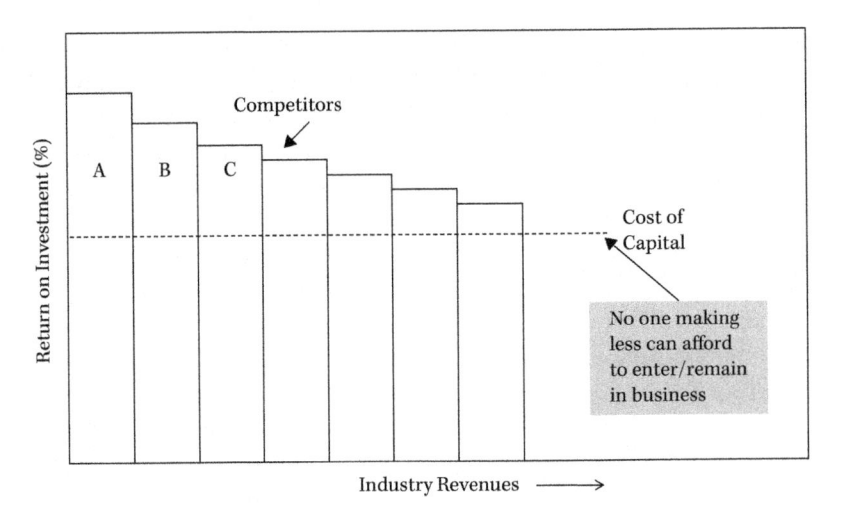

FIGURE 1.1. Competitive Economics

Returns on capital are defined as (Revenue − Costs) ÷ Net Investment, so, to exceed this minimum acceptable return, a firm must have an advantage over the marginal competitor in one of the three components: Revenue (price realization), Costs of Production, or Asset Utilization.

In some businesses, advantage is only possible in one component. Products with a strong brand derive a *revenue advantage* through being able to command a higher price for their product than competitors. In some cases this is justified by known product superiority, but not always. Consumers are often willing to pay a much higher price for certain brands of bleach or pet food than for other brands, although these decisions are unlikely to reflect a very informed judgment. All that matters is their belief that the price premium is worth paying. They are less willing to pay a premium for sliced white bread or whole milk, presumably recognizing that they cannot tell the difference between brands, so price tends not to be a source of advantage in those

---

[152] Porter (1980) provides an excellent overview of the theory. Henderson (1998b) is especially interesting for the analogy Henderson draws between business competition and the Darwinian struggle for survival.

industries. The brand leader may choose not to exploit customers' preferences for his product by maximizing price but by selling more product at the competitor's price point, so gaining volume and lowering indirect costs per unit of output. In practice most brand leaders do a little of both, taking some of the brand benefit in price realization and the rest in increased volume and reduced unit costs. Price premiums for the leading brands in certain industries such as wine, *haute couture*, jewelry, and perfumes can be so large as to make any cost differences almost irrelevant.

In other industries, firms compete on the basis of *cost advantages*. In commodity mining, all output has the same market value, so profit depends on cost position, which reflects ore grade, ease of extraction, and distance from shipping ports. A given mine's profit is determined by its costs of product delivered into market compared with those of the highest cost competitor needed to fill market demand, which sets the industry price level. Figure 1.2 shows how the profitability of a given mine can be directly measured from its position on the cost curve.

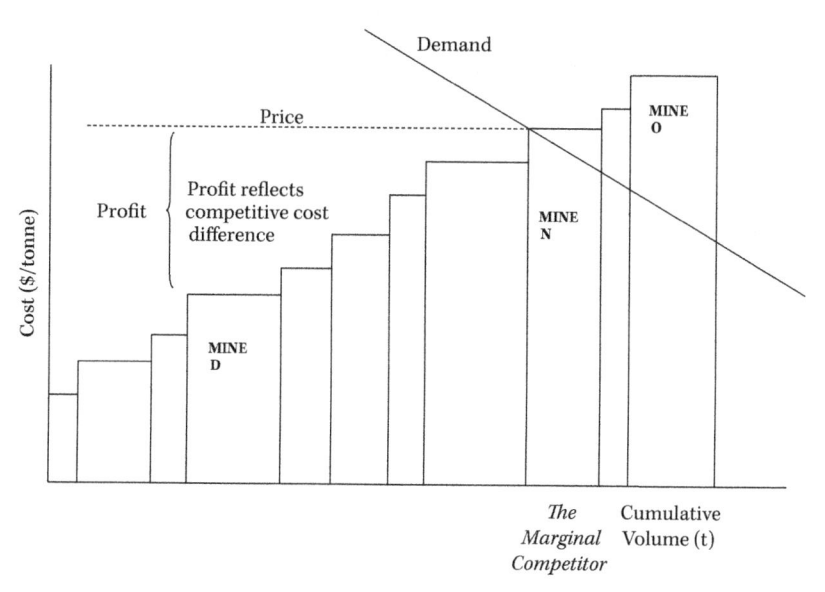

FIGURE 1.2. Cost Advantage Example: Commodity Mining

Cost advantages can stem from economies of scale. Unit costs decline rapidly with volume in many process industries, so that a large brewery, for example, will have much lower costs per liter produced than a small one. The same applies in the automotive industry. In general, when economies of scale are to be found in an industry, some competitors will expand their operations to achieve them. The lower costs that result mean they can reduce prices while remaining profitable. Small competitors who want to survive must differentiate their product so as to realize prices that make up for their higher cost structure—a task that becomes increasingly difficult as their cost disadvantage grows and they have less margin to spend on innovation or product promotion. As a result, while we regularly find premium "boutique" breweries and specialty sports car manufacturers emerging, their strategic positions are seldom robust enough to prevent failure or takeover in the long run. In some industries, such as jet engine manufacture, the world only seems to have room for a handful of competitors.

Limits to the number of people who can be employed in a single production line do not necessarily mean there is no economic value in greater scale. In some industries today, very large companies run parallel production lines (breweries, for example) or operate out of a number of small-scale production units, as many companies do in businesses where transport costs are high relative to product value, such as construction materials, bulk packaging, and dairy products. The value of scale in such cases is achieved through sharing corporate costs, in, for example, marketing, procurement, or research and development. Organization economists have defined an important benefit of scale as reducing the cost of transactions by carrying out more activities in-house.[153] In short, there can be a competitive advantage in owning multiple production units, each of modest size.

Some companies succeed on the basis of *asset utilization*. Technical innovation can enable certain products to be made in much lower-cost facilities than before. Steel mini-mills radically reduced the level of investment needed for producing reinforcing steel bars and mesh. Another way of reducing investment levels is in faster asset turn. In the 1990s, Walmart's stock replenishment system meant it could operate with a much lower investment in inventory per unit of sales than its competitors, and it was able to use this advantage to reduce prices and win market share.

It is possible to change an industry by introducing new elements. Before White Castle and McDonald's, hamburgers for takeout were very much a mom-and-pop business with little scope for advantage. Standardized product and cooking processes, along with heavy expenditure on advertising, rewarded scale and enabled the market leader to make much more than its cost of capital for many years. It is also possible for firms in weak positions to play by a different set of rules; Dell's distribution system enabled it to sell computers at better net prices than it could have realized against stronger competitors in conventional channels. At any given point, however, the rules of the game are clear, and some firms are equipped with a better chance of winning than others.

While different industries typically offer different bases for economic advantage, competitors can sometimes achieve advantage on more than one dimension. A large brewer can achieve cost advantage through economies

---

[153] Arrow (1962); Williamson (1970; 1975); Teece (1998).

of scale in processing, purchasing, and overheads, as well as revenue advantage through spending large sums on promotion and advertising. A successful strategy is one that delivers and exploits these advantages and turns them into superior returns to owners. Companies that do this well earn significantly more than their minimum income needs. Companies that do not tend to struggle to survive.

Although business leaders have a tendency to attribute business success to their own skills and those of their staff—have you ever read an annual report that does not include a comment on the lines of "Our greatest asset is our people"?—management's ability to overcome a weak competitive position is, in practice, very limited (Fig. 1.3), and an advantage derived from superior management can easily be overturned as people retire or change firms or competitors improve their own management skills:

Profitability/Competitive Position Relationship

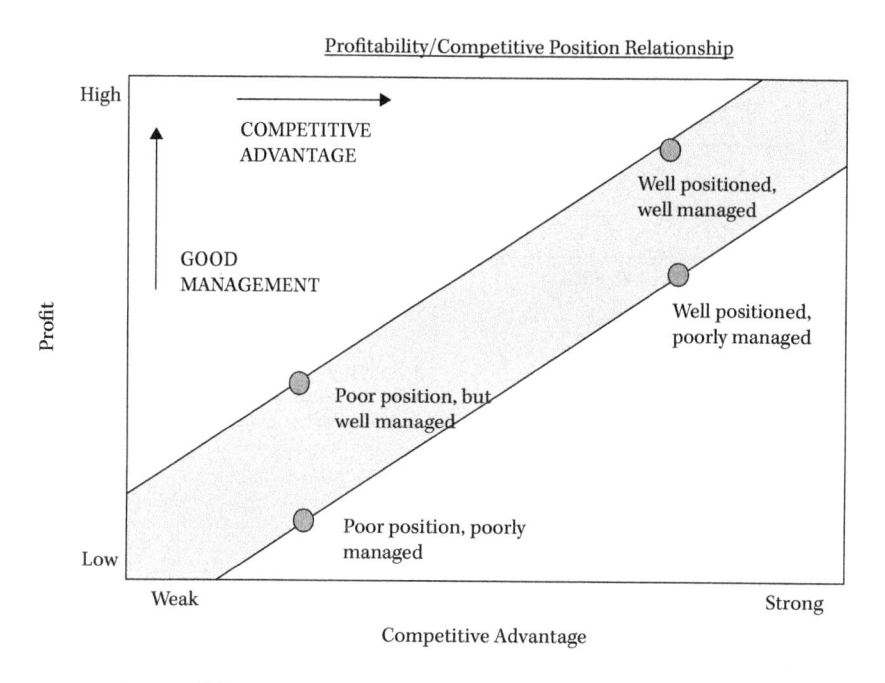

FIGURE 1.3. Impact of Management

Not all industries offer significant scope for competitors to gain advantage over each other. In some, production costs are the same for all, assets are negligible, and the product is hard to differentiate. Corner shop retailing is an example, as are many other service industries such as hairdressing, lawn-mowing, and certain types of financial advice. The private guards businesses that keep an eye on offices at night or provide extra security at major events employ unskilled staff to carry out simple and observable duties over a defined time period. It is not possible for one firm to do this consistently at lower cost than any other could. Some large employers of guards are able to win more work and realize slightly higher prices through developing a prestige brand and reputation, but the benefits tend to be small and largely outweighed by the costs of additional management complexity and a more formal overhead structure.

We may therefore simplify what is really a spectrum into two classes of industry: those in which competitive advantage enables significant differences in profitability between competitors and those where it does not (Fig. 1.4).

### Industry A

Small reward for leadership

### Industry B

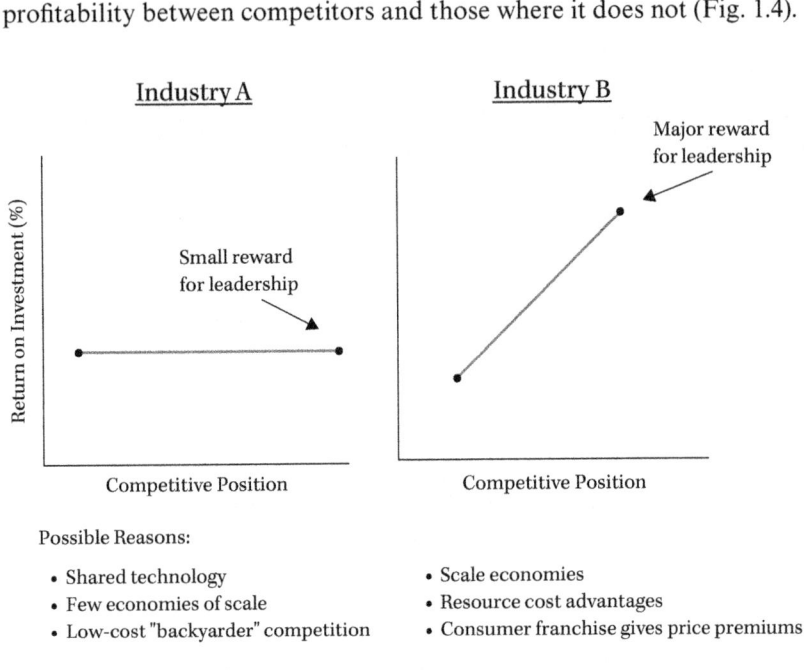

Major reward for leadership

(Return on Investment (%) vs Competitive Position)

Possible Reasons:

- Shared technology
- Few economies of scale
- Low-cost "backyarder" competition

- Scale economies
- Resource cost advantages
- Consumer franchise gives price premiums

FIGURE 1.4. Capacity to Gain a Structural Advantage

In businesses that offer the possibility of attractive returns, incumbents are sometimes wary of being seen to make excessive profits, as this will invite new competitors who might act aggressively and reduce prices and profitability for all. Microeconomic theory predicts that equilibrium is reached when additional volume coming on stream reduces prices just enough to make an equivalent amount of industry capacity redundant because the costs of that capacity are then higher than the new (lower) price (Fig. 1.5; cf. Fig. 1.2).

It is not always possible for new competitors to enter an industry. Barriers to entry are forms of competitive advantage that involve certain economic benefits being available to some or all incumbents that are not available on the same terms to new entrants. Though strictly a subset of competitive advantage, they are sufficiently important in determining industry structure to warrant special attention. Typical barriers are:

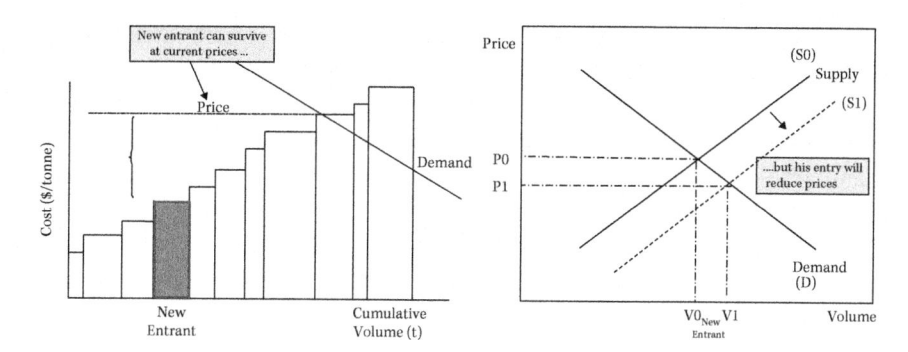

FIGURE 1.5. Impact of New Entry

  i. Supply-side economics (returns to scale in processing, purchasing, or technology)
  ii. Demand-side benefits of scale (brand promotion, network effects)
  iii. Switching costs for customers
  iv. Access to capital
  v. Incumbency (privileged access to critical inputs such as raw materials, experience, location, technology)
  vi. Access to distribution
  vii. Government restrictions or licensing.[154]

The first three barriers are based on normal competitive advantages. These attributes help certain companies succeed against both current and new competitors and can be so strong that a new entrant (who is usually in an especially weak competitive position) simply cannot survive. Capital is only a barrier if financial markets are inefficient. The last three can be seen as to do with endowment: whether by luck or judgment, some firms find themselves in a position that new entrants are simply physically or legally unable to challenge.

As with competitive advantage, industries differ in the extent to which they offer barriers to entry. In businesses where brands matter (confectionery, cereals, and perfume are examples), new entry is often difficult and costly. At the other extreme, it is relatively easy to set up a kebab shop or to offer one's services as a personal trainer. Large-scale manufacture can clearly provide at least a capital barrier to those without ready access to finance. Small-scale, job-shop operations such as cabinet-making and specialty foods require skills readily available in the labor market and little capital, and are therefore easier for a newcomer to enter than are manufacturing processes

---

[154] Porter (2008) 80–82.

with a high degree of technological automation that require a large amount of capital and expertise.

At this stage the reader is probably wondering what possible relevance these contemporary business examples can have to the far less sophisticated manufacturing and marketing processes in ancient Athens. Later chapters show that the framework is timeless, although the advantages available to manufacturers of particular products change over time, often as a result of technical innovation. Some of the industry analyses that follow show how later developments altered competitive dynamics and industry structures along with them.[155] To apply the concepts to the classical world, we must make four adjustments, all stemming from the limited quantity of fixed assets in ancient production systems:

1. Because external capital was not required for many businesses, the entry/exit decision (Fig. 1.1) depended on an individual craftsman's decision on how to spend their time, rather than the cost of capital. In these circumstances, the net income below which a self-employed person will decide to cease operations is the point at which he or she can do as well or better in another occupation, or by doing nothing at all. If a working citizen cannot get enough income out of a productive enterprise, after paying all expenses, to support the household at a minimum acceptable level, they will look for an alternative way to spend their time. Similarly, if they can do better in another occupation they will tend to choose to. Thus the "marginal competitor" is one who finds it only just worth continuing and would exit if income declined. Where external investment is required, as in the case of a workshop run by a slave for an investor, the owner specifies the cost of the capital in the form of the *apophora* and if this is met, so are the owner's return objectives. If, however, the workshop is unable to cover its costs after paying the *apophora*, the owner and foreman must either agree a lower *apophora* or cease operation.
2. With limited technology, production costs consisted largely of labor and raw materials. Labor came at a capital cost determined in the market for slaves that reflected their productive potential and the costs of maintenance were the same for all slaves, so there was little advantage to be had through lower labor costs per unit of output.[156] Most raw materials were available at around the same prices to all, so little advantage was possible there either. Reduced costs through economies of scale were rare, again because of limited technology.

---

[155] See, for example, Chapter 3.5.
[156] See Chapter 9.1 for an analysis of returns on investments in slaves.

3. The absence of fixed assets also meant no advantage was achievable through superior asset turns. Asset-turn advantages generally stem from technological innovation reducing investment required; in classical workplaces, assets consisted almost entirely of slaves and inventory, and we hear of no innovations that increased their productivity in such a way as to bring about an important reduction in investment needs. The minimum labor force and inventory required for a defined level of production were the same for all competitors, although in sectors like perfumery, some competitors might choose to hold extra stock in order to compete on the basis of a wider product range. This is not an asset-turn advantage but rather a revenue advantage at the expense of a *dis*advantage in asset turns.[157]

With no advantage possible in production costs or asset turns, *the only source of competitive advantage in ancient manufacturing was in product differentiation.*

4. The absence of fixed assets also limited the range of barriers to entry. The only barrier based on competitive advantage stemmed from product ("brand") preference—type ii in the list of entry barriers above. Barriers based on a large inventory requirement—type iv—and regulatory or locational pre-emption—types v to vii—were still possible.

These factors determined both the size of enterprises in a given industry and their profit potential.

### 1.3.4 COMPETITIVE ADVANTAGE AND INDUSTRY STRUCTURE

In 1981, BCG developed a matrix that predicts the structure of an industry from the number of potential sources of advantage it offers and the value of these advantages (Fig. 1.6).[158]

Where there are only a few ways of getting an advantage, the industry will tend to be concentrated among a few large firms. If the advantages available are substantial (examples are scale in brewing and ore grade, extraction costs, and access to ports in commodity mining), the strongest competitors will make returns significantly in excess of what is required to keep them in business. This is referred to as an Oligopoly. If the advantages are slight, as is the case in full-price airlines and the pulp and paper industries, all firms will tend to make long-run returns that are close to the cost of capital (Stalemate).

---

[157] Inventories of valuable raw materials might have been higher than necessary in some instances, but the analysis in Chapter 9.1 suggests they were seen as a store of value, so Athenians might not have been concerned to minimize this form of working capital.

[158] Lochridge (1998) 56–59. The position of the ovals within each box in Figure 1.6 reflects the relationship between returns and competitive advantage shown in Figure 1.3.

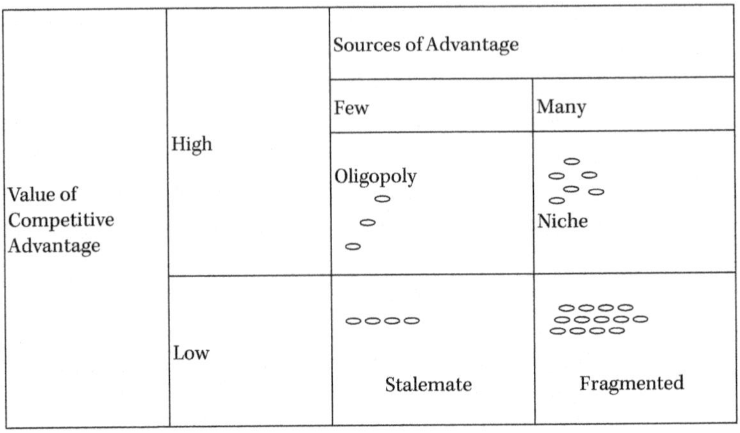

|  | | Sources of Advantage | |
|---|---|---|---|
|  | | Few | Many |
| Value of Competitive Advantage | High | Oligopoly<br>○<br>○ ○<br>○<br>○ | ○ ○<br>○ ○<br>○ ○<br>○<br>Niche |
|  | Low | ○ ○ ○ ○<br><br>Stalemate | ○ ○ ○ ○<br>○ ○ ○ ○ ○<br>○ ○ ○ ○<br>Fragmented |

FIGURE 1.6. Competitive Advantage and Industry Structure (1)

When there are multiple ways of getting advantage through differentiating the product or service, the industry will contain a much larger number of competitors. If the advantages are substantial, then some will be able to make very good returns by defining and owning a profitable Niche and may become quite large; if not, then everyone will make just about enough to stay in business but will tend to remain small-scale (a Fragmented industry).

In applying this framework to manufacturing in classical times, the fact that the only source of sustainable advantage was product differentiation enables us to simplify it considerably. Barriers of entry are important, as it is impossible to build an enterprise larger than the minimum required for efficient production if new competitors can easily enter and win market share. Such barriers could either derive from effective product differentiation by current competitors or from endowment factors such as location and regulation. Combining these concepts gives us the matrix and segment descriptors in Figure 1.7.

When there are no barriers to entry (right-hand side of chart), manufacturing must remain the province of the sole craftsman, possibly helped by other family members and a slave or two. These are traditional "crafts." In some ("Niche") segments, the product could be differentiated and a high degree of skill was especially valued. Craftsmen who excelled in these skills could make very good returns indeed, while weaker performers would just about get by. In other segments all products were seen as similar, so everyone would make a similar and not very attractive living. On the left-hand side of the chart, manufacturing was by large slave gangs, enjoying barriers to entry based either on the differentiation of their product or on some regulatory or locational limitation on competition. Quite unlike traditional crafts in ownership, employment arrangements, and competitive behavior, such workplaces can

|  | | Barriers to Entry | |
|---|---|---|---|
|  | | Yes | No |
| Potential for Differentiation | High | Oligopoly | Niche |
|  | Low | Stalemate | Fragmented |

FIGURE 1.7. Competitive Advantage and Industry Structure (2)

legitimately be referred to as "factories" and their sectors as "industries," on the basis of common parlance. Owners of businesses in differentiated industries could expect good returns if their differentiation was strong enough to block new entry as well as to outperform current competitors. Other barriers to entry in classical Athens included regulation in dirtier industries such as tanning and (probably) dyeing, and the preemption of critical locations in the primary processing of agricultural and mining products. In these cases, profitability depended on the effectiveness of the barrier: the number of competitors the regulations or topography permitted and their potential output relative to demand, and the cost to a customer of transporting their product to be processed at the next nearest location. Figure 1.8 shows the labels applied in this book to different types of manufacturing operations and how returns are related to competitive advantage in each segment.

There is an important historical dynamic at work in Figure 1.8 that is central to the history of industry development. All businesses start as Undifferentiated Crafts. In some cases, such as artistically formed and decorated products, consumers can develop preferences for particular types of output. The result is that these become Differentiated Crafts, and craftsmen whose output is considered superior to their peers will charge more for their work. In others, like simple furniture and commodity pottery, products are indistinguishable and offer no potential to differentiate. These segments will remain Undifferentiated Crafts, with participants surviving on the minimum acceptable ("subsistence") income.[159] Differentiated Crafts were the first sectors to emerge from the *oikos*, as shown in the next chapter.

---

[159] See Figure 1.1 above. Note that "subsistence" is here defined as in that diagram: the minimum income needed to make the activity worthwhile.

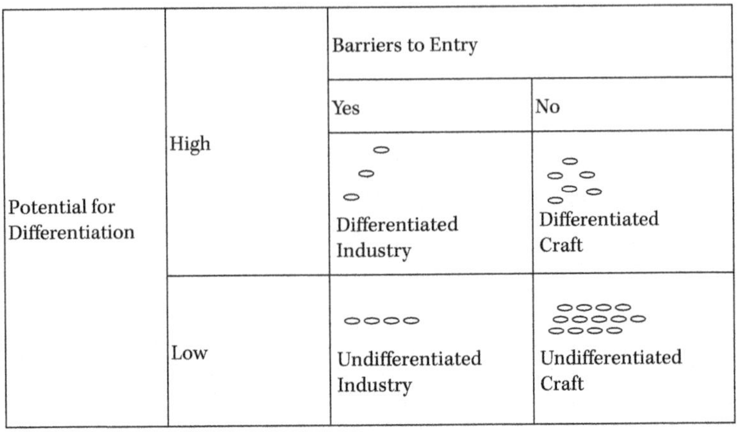

44 { Poiesis

| Potential for Differentiation | | Barriers to Entry | |
|---|---|---|---|
| | | Yes | No |
| | High | ○ ○ ○ Differentiated Industry | ○ ○ ○ ○ ○ ○ Differentiated Craft |
| | Low | ○○○○ Undifferentiated Industry | ○○○○ ○○○○○ ○○○○ Undifferentiated Craft |

FIGURE 1.8. Competitive Advantage and Industry Structure (3)

Except where barriers to entry mean that any firm in the sector starts with a large market share (Undifferentiated Industry), for a firm to employ several workers, competitive advantage must be translatable to the whole workshop rather than the individual craftsman. If a particular goldsmith is admired for his jewelry or a cobbler for his bespoke shoes, he might be able to make an excellent living by charging premium prices but will not be able to expand, since customers are not interested in buying items made by other hands. Some product groups have a more transferable brand image than others; a reputation for making excellent knives can be seen to rely on the quality of raw materials, the initial design, and the consistency of the production and quality control processes, all of which can be attributed to a workshop rather than an individual craftsman. As a result, the advantage can transform the business from Craft to Industry and it will start to concentrate (Differentiated Industry). Small players lacking this advantage might struggle on at subsistence level, but if the larger concerns keep price premiums modest, smaller ones will tend to go out of business or be absorbed by larger ones. Reliability can also provide a basis for differentiating the output of large firms: merchants depending on the reliable supply of ceramic containers meeting a defined specification would have preferred to place their business with a few large workshops with the capacity to absorb production glitches rather than trusting to the spot market or dealing with dozens of small craft shops (Chapter 3). Similar considerations apply to sourcing components for the boat building and construction industries (Chapters 6 and 7).

### 1.3.5 APPLYING THE COMPETITIVE ADVANTAGE FRAMEWORK

The nature of competition in a manufacturing segment is determined by the resources required to make the item (supply) and the considerations that affect the buying decision (demand). For supply, literature tells about the size of certain firms, while the material quantities and labor required to make a given item can be estimated from archaeology and the expertise of modern craftsmen. For demand, Aristophanes shows the selling process for some items, but this is of limited value. Characterizing the considerations that the Athenians brought to their purchases of some items must often rely on a judgment about the relative importance of price, quality, uniqueness, and other factors for each product. In general, this does not require great leaps of imagination: someone buying a shield for their own use probably placed a high value on the reputation of the shield-maker for reliable quality; someone buying an undecorated ceramic plate for use by slaves in the kitchen would be unlikely to care about anything except price. The interaction of these supply and demand factors in a competitive setting reveals whether the segment is likely to have been concentrated or fragmented, which can be tested against whatever facts we have about firm size from literature or vase painting, and can be contradicted by new evidence.

It is important to emphasize that we are not claiming that the ancients applied any such framework. Industries take shape irrespective of how their participants describe what is going on, and, very often, in ways quite contrary to what they intend. Economic outcomes are not social constructs. They are real and they determine business success. The analysis here aims to discover what actually happened and makes no assumptions about the mental processes or aims of agents. Rather the assumption is that the microeconomic forces that shape industries today also shaped those in ancient times—a falsifiable hypothesis that makes a reasonable starting point until proved wrong.

Chapter 3 demonstrates how the model works in detail by applying it to the pottery industry. It is the most detailed of the industry analyses that follow, both because pottery is relatively well documented and because it illustrates some central elements of competitive theory: the instability of returns for undifferentiated product, the impossibility of growth without competitive advantage or barriers to entry, and the potential to achieve stable and attractive returns through differentiating a product or service. There is evidence that several hundred Athenians were engaged in the industry at any one time, probably many more if part-time and seasonal work is included. Despite this, the largest potteries we know of employed no more than a dozen slaves. Competitive analysis shows that small firm size can be fully explained as a rational response to the lack of barriers to entry and the inability of any one competitor to gain an economic advantage over others. To put it another way, the economics of production meant that observed firm size was consistent with intelligent profit maximization.

The theory of competitive advantage is used to describe the structure and performance of each industry analyzed in subsequent chapters: mining, metals, and armor (Chapter 4); textiles, clothing, and footwear (Chapter 5); woodworking (Chapter 6); construction and monumental sculpture (Chapter 7);

and food, drink, and cosmetics (Chapter 8). In each case, the analysis shows how different segments can be classified in the matrix presented in Figure 1.8 above. Chapter 9 considers manufacturing from the angle of different status groups and explores their various motives for participating in different forms of industry and crafts. Manufacturing was clearly a very common pursuit among all status groups, and a methodology for quantifying participation is set out in the Appendix. Before turning to the structure of industries in classical times, Chapter 2 explores the supply and demand factors that had led to their emergence from the *oikos* in the first place.

2 }

# Industry Formation

Athenians of the classical period acquired most of their manufactured possessions from third parties. Even the richest did not have many of the goods they needed made for them by their own slaves, and Hippias the Sophist was looked on as very odd for making all his own clothes and paraphernalia (Pl. *Hp. Mi.* 368b). A few hundred years earlier, such manufacturing for sale was rare in Greece among either rich or poor households. This chapter elucidates the microeconomic forces behind the transformation from a rural subsistence economy to an urbanized one in which manufacturing for sale featured heavily, and draws on Homer and Hesiod for their different perspectives.

Our focus here is not on the overall pace and change of development, nor on the social and institutional changes that accompanied or caused it, but on the microeconomic factors that underpinned it. Readers seeking more information on other aspects of ancient Greek economic development will find it in the texts cited.[1]

Enough is known from literature and the research of experts in relevant technologies for us to be able to assess how costs would have behaved with variations in volume or utilization (supply factors) and to consider the choices confronting purchasers (demand factors), which together explain how third-party manufacture became established in general. Closer analysis of four different products shows that differences in the sequence and extent of their development can be attributed to differences in the nature of their underlying supply and demand. These forces differed in their impact and timing for each product and by region, but were in essence the same forces as those that determined the structures of industries once they had formed, which is the principal theme of this book. Further, the decisions of each Athenian *oikos* in classical times as to whether to make or buy the products it needed continued to be governed by the same criteria. The economic imperatives behind the formation of manufacturing businesses that are explored in this chapter are therefore central to understanding what happened later.

---

[1] See especially Finley (1954); Will (1957), (1965); Hanson (1995); Tandy (1997).

## 2.1 Early Manufacturing

The story of manufacturing goes back a long time. The first physical evidence of manufacture is a collection of stone tools found in the Olduvai Gorge that were used by *Homo erectus* between 1,200,000 and 1,100,000 years ago.[2] The pieces took several distinct shapes, each suited to different purposes such as heavy- or light-duty butchery, woodworking, hide scraping, nut cracking, wood grinding, grass cutting, or acting as missiles. A million years later, Neanderthal man started using tools made of other materials, including wood for long spears and, less commonly, bone.[3] In more recent times, obsidian, a form of volcanic glass rock, was collected over several centuries from two sites on the island of Melos for use as a household tool, although any trade in it was probably opportunistic.[4]

Formal trade between remote communities can be traced to around 3,500 years before classical times. Early agriculture was based on nucleated human settlement, with farmers living close to their fields and working intensively on small farms, their herds perhaps owned in common and collectively moved to different pasture at different seasons.[5] Farming risks and limited trade promoted efforts at collective self-sufficiency within a defined region, and, at times of peace, settlements tended to rely on emigration to ensure the adequacy of local resources. Over time, the boundaries of this self-sufficiency expanded and exchange took place over increasingly large areas. By around 4,000 BCE, local coping mechanisms were at full stretch, so more distant exchange developed and tokens were introduced.[6] Around 3,750 BCE, central control structures emerged, and in many civilizations centrally administered exchange took the place of independent household buffering strategies.[7] This formalization often took the form of a palace system of which ancient Greece's best-known examples were the Mycenaean and Minoan palaces.[8] These palace systems took many forms, but in general the rulers and their court captured a region's agricultural surplus, used much of it for themselves,

---

[2] Leakey (1971).

[3] Klein (1989) 165–66.

[4] Torrance (1986) 135–221; Atkinson (1904); Bosanquet (1904); Renfrew (1972) 455, 473–74; Renfrew (1973) 180.

[5] Farmers may have moved their livestock to high ground in summer, but the separation of pastoral and arable land reduces manure and fodder in low lands, and it is not necessarily the case that transhumance was as widely practiced in ancient Greece as it has been in more recent times (Halstead (1987)).

[6] O'Shea (1989).

[7] Halstead (1987) 77–87; a similar process of increasing formalization of trading networks and specialization of production was noted in a study of North Alaskan cultures between 980 and 1780 CE (Minc and Smith (1989)).

[8] Palace systems featured in many civilizations, including Pharaonic Egypt, Imperial China, Mughal India, and the Incan Empire.

and redistributed part of it.[9] Large segments of the rural economy, however, seem to have been unaffected and developed their own production establishments and practices independent of the palace.[10] The region around Nestor's palace at Pylos, for instance, seems to have had a pottery industry for which the palace was the largest customer, but it only bought a small part of the region's production.[11] The palace system coexisted with the peasant economy and influenced it to a greater or lesser extent but was not generally an alternative to it.

By the time of the Trojan War, the major palaces in Greece were in decline. The eastern Mediterranean suffered a major economic contraction, probably connected with unrest and financial catastrophe in Egypt.[12] The years 1100 to 800 BCE saw the lowest living standards in Greece for around a thousand years, together with a fall in population and a steep decline in production and trade, especially of metals: bronze was scarce, iron a luxury, and precious metals almost unknown. Agriculture reverted to subsistence farming.[13] Even then, there remained rich estates with some degree of control over local serfs, which shouldered at least some of the responsibility for directing neighborhood affairs in such a way as to avoid crises or minimize their effects through managing production, redistribution, and storage. As recurring surpluses enabled Greece to urbanize, responsibility for these strategies was taken on by the *polis* or city-state. Urban populations can manage the risk of shortage initially through such means as extending their frontiers, cultivating larger areas, intensifying land use, colonizing new sites, and expanding trade, but eventually need permanent institutions. A large urban population cannot cope with wide price variations and, to manage prices, it is necessary to influence supply.[14] By classical times, Athens had introduced laws on grain trading and legal status for contracts and officials (*sitones*) to oversee the security of the food supply in the way palaces and feudal lords had done formerly.[15]

Manufacturing data from the Dark Age are scarce. The commonest find, coarse pottery, is typically in the form of containers that do not always provide unambiguous data about their contents.[16] Other finds are mostly fine pottery, ornaments, and figurines for temples, although the population must have continued to make and use clothes, shoes, basic tools, and weapons. Yet

---

[9] de Blois and van der Spek (1997) 56–60; Pullen (2007); Halstead (2011).
[10] Chadwick (1973) 70.
[11] Clarke (1961) 148; Starr (1961) 48; Palmer (1963); Knappett (2001) 80–95; Whitelaw (2001) 51–79.
[12] Markoe (2005) 18–19.
[13] Starr (1977); Morris (2007) 211–41.
[14] Jongman and Decker (1989) 114–22.
[15] Garnsey and Morris (1989) 98–105.
[16] Dietler (2007) 241–76.

it was this period that saw the beginnings of a manufacturing sector that was a prime feature of Greek cities by the time of the Persian invasions.

The pace and nature of the change in different parts of Greece have been the focus of many historians and archaeologists. Millett summarizes the critical conditions for development as increasing land under cultivation, greater non-agricultural employment, and increased labor productivity.[17] Fascinating but contrasting descriptions of how agricultural conditions and status competition affected development have been offered by, among others, Finley (1954), Will (1957), (1965), Snodgrass (1980), van Wees (1992), Rihll (1993), Hanson (1995), and Tandy (1997). Insights into knowledge transfer from the East have added color and movement.[18] The introduction of coinage to Athens in the middle of the sixth century must have accelerated market exchange in the city.[19] Our concern here is not with the specific features of the change but with the general economic forces behind it. The remainder of this chapter examines the economics of manufacturing's journey from the *oikos* to the marketplace.

The approach adopted here is based on the premise that the economic rationality of outcomes does not depend on the economic sophistication of decision-makers. Rather we take as our premises the two incontrovertible facts that (i) classical Athens was home to a great many enterprises of different shapes and sizes that were making goods for sale, and (ii) a few centuries earlier, this type of activity was rare or unknown in the Greek world. The question addressed here is "What were the economics of this transformation?" It is possible that some of the terms we find useful to evaluate transactions (supply, demand, market price, elasticity, and so on) were absent not only from the ancient vocabulary but from the ancient mind.[20] It is also possible that exchange, particularly exchange involving coinage, carried a great range of symbolic meanings, some of which had nothing to do with commercial intent or actually militated against it.[21] Our concern here is with outcomes, not intentions, and adds to the growing body of empirical research that has identified outcomes in ancient economic affairs that are no different from those commercial rationality would predict, irrespective of the stated or tacit intentions of the agents.[22] Outcomes are facts; if they make economic

---

[17] Millett (2001) 27–29.

[18] Guthrie (1935); West (1971; 1997); Momigliano (1975); Burkert and Pinder (1992); Kim (1993).

[19] The first minting of coins in Athens was around the middle of the century, but imported coins were probably in use before then. Caradice and Price (1988) 29; Snell (1995) 1494; Thompson (2003) 68.

[20] The case has been made strongly by Finley (1973, 1985b,c), Millett (1991), Meikle (1995a,b), and Cartledge (1998), though, as noted in Chapter 1.3 of this volume, it has been rather overstated.

[21] Seaford (2004); von Reden (1995); Kurke (1999, 2002); but see Kroll (2000).

[22] Research by Cohen (1992a, 2000), Morris (2002), Harris (2002a, 2006b), and Christenson (2003) provides evidence of behavior compatible with, and predictable from, the principles of commercial rationality.

sense, the point is significant and should encourage greater recourse to the tools of economic analysis to understand them.

Ancient Greece would be described today as a "two-speed" economy. Subsistence agriculture, even under the palace system, remained subsistence agriculture for those doing the work, though their ruler might offer them some protection and food security. And even in the darkest of ages, rich houses survived and commanded the loyalty of local regions. Both rich and poor households could make some show of self-sufficiency. Before the transition to outsourced manufacturing, palaces and rich estates were largely self-sufficient because the manufactured product they consumed was generally made from their own materials by owned or commissioned labor. The poor were largely self-sufficient because, after the costs of subsistence, they had little left to exchange for purchased goods. Both worlds were turned upside-down by the economic forces that came into play in the first half of the first millennium BCE. The following account of the change draws on Homer to illustrate important aspects of the economy of the rich and on Hesiod for that of the poor.[23]

## 2.2 Homer and the Households of the Rich

Homer's heroes were the wealthy owners of private estates. Their homes were in walled towns where women lived and worked, while many of the male slaves and laborers lived on and managed the farms in the surrounding countryside; these smallholders had an obligation to supply their master with meat and produce but otherwise seem to have operated quite independently.[24] The household of a rich landowner included all his dependents, slave and free, together with all his physical possessions. The difference between slavery and freedom was overshadowed by common allegiance to the central authority.[25] A rich family's own productive output was supplemented, though not entirely replaced, by the labor of slaves. The key measures of wealth were land, slaves, herds and flocks, and treasures, typically acquired through war or exchange of gifts, like the foodstuffs, jewelry, urns, and tripods found in Odysseus's storeroom (*Od.* 2.337–42). Forced seizure was a normal and valid mode of production.[26] With these assets and an adequate complement of slaves an estate could

---

[23] The society Homer describes is thought to represent the early centuries of the first millennium rather than the time of the Trojan War he wrote about (Finley (1954)). His poems can be seen to reflect elements of both the eighth century BCE (Morris (1986) 129) and the middle of the sixth (Snodgrass (1998)). See also Parry (1971). For our purposes, it is enough that he was referring to a pre-classical society.
[24] Van Wees (1992) 49–50, 54, 281–82; Lane Fox (2006) 25–28.
[25] Mele (1976) 115–55; Garlan (1982) 36–38.
[26] Rihll (1993) 91–104.

be genuinely self-sufficient in all the products it required for a comfortable life, though still at risk of famine from natural disaster, like everywhere else.

Most manufacturing took place within the *oikos*. It is likely, for instance, that the prize of ore offered by Achilles (*Il.* 23.826) was to be smelted at the winner's home rather than taken to a local smelter, as a rich estate would be expected to do most of its own metalwork. Tasks were shared around between masters and slaves, even in the wealthiest households. Penelope had 50 slaves and still made textiles herself. Princess Nausicaa does the family laundry (*Od.* 6.57–59), while Odysseus prides himself on his skill in constructing his own bed (*Od.* 23.183–201) and makes his raft like a skilled carpenter (*Od.* 5.249–50). Eumaeus, formerly noble but now a swineherd, is still "a god" and "the leader of men" (*Od.* 15.301, 351). But all this activity was for one's own family unit, unlike the despised hired laborer.

Homer's choice of metaphors confirms how familiar his listeners were with manufacturing: in successive books of the *Iliad*, we hear that a falling corpse is like trees felled by builders (16.482–84), the tug of war over Patroclus's corpse is like the tanning process (17.389–93), and dancing is like a potter's wheel (18.600–602). Homer's audience was used to watching products being made to a far greater extent than we are today: how many modern writers would expect readers to appreciate an action better by comparing it to a General Motors assembly line? Homer reflects a world in which crafts took place largely at home, in full view and with the participation of owners, slaves, and neighboring peasants.

Homer loved to praise the work of especially gifted craftsmen. We hear about the excellence of the manufacture of Sarpedon's shield (*Il.* 12.294–97) and of the entry to Odysseus's storeroom (*Od.* 21.43–45). Tychius was "much the best of leatherworkers" (*Il.* 7.221); and Phereclus son of Tecton "knew how to make all kinds of intricate objects with his hands" (*Il.* 5.60–61). One of the characteristics Athena had to take on as a beautiful mortal was being "knowledgeable about splendid workmanship" (*Od.* 13.289, 16.158). The lyric poets echoed Homer's respect for well-made luxury objects. Pindar speaks of a golden goblet being the most prized of possessions (*Ol.* 7.1–2) and describes the marvels of a richly painted jar (*Nem.* 10.37). Praise fits a successful athlete like a well-made sandal (*Ol.* 6.9). Alcaeus gives a fulsome description of the gleaming greaves and corselets in a well-equipped armory (*Fr.* II. 19). Anacreon praises at length a vase depicting Aphrodite (*Fr.* 12) and wrote poems giving instructions to a poet, a painter, and a vase decorator (*Odes* 18 and 28). Sappho goes a little overboard when she claims the chief usher at her wedding will have feet seven fathoms long, shod by ten cobblers with the hides from five bulls (*Fr.* 154), but this is at least confirms that the basic processes of manufacturing were familiar to her audience.

This respect for skill made for honorable exceptions to an estate's self-sufficiency. When Homer introduces a craftsman into his stories, he tends to be highly skilled and itinerant. Nestor summons a goldsmith with his bronze tools (hammer, anvil, and tongs) to help prepare an offering to Athena (*Od.* 3.425–27; 432–25).[27] Eumaeus asks why one would invite anyone from a long way away unless he had some special skill the household lacked (*Od.* 17.382–85). It is clear that by Homer's day, possibly as early as the time he was describing, some craftsmen had taken their skills and implements away from the rich agricultural household and became independent migrant tradesmen who, to take metals as an example, might be looking for ores, servicing ore owners, or teaching their trade, as well as making objects.[28] Many moved between major temple-building sites.[29] The special skills of independent craftsmen gave them a particular status in the social hierarchy.[30] They were free, and practicing a craft for income was a good option for the free poor who lacked sufficient landholdings for subsistence—far better than the servile condition of paid peasants or the itinerant laborers (*thetes*) who found irregular slave-like work in the home or, more usually, in the fields and were typically paid in food and clothing. The products of these independent craftsmen, being of an excellence few estates could match with their own resources, formed the principal—often perhaps the only—exception to self-sufficiency on wealthy estates.[31]

What might have caused this form of self-sufficiency to break down?

One cause was oversupply. Some households may have chosen to create and store surpluses deliberately; on this account, farm production was primarily for the estate's own subsistence and secondarily to generate a surplus for exchange. In the same way, exchange would be applied first to supplementing deficiencies in the estate's own production and second to acquiring products the estate could not make ("treasure").[32] Even without intention, it was inevitable that home output of some products on a wealthy estate would occasionally exceed consumption, perhaps after an exceptional harvest or if, for whatever reason, household labor was misaligned with household demand for a period—an in-house capacity to make arms and weaponry, for example, might not be fully required in times of peace. This would also lead the household to seek opportunities to exchange surplus products for different ones, from a neighbor initially, later perhaps from further afield. Whether or not this process was planned at first, in time some rich households might

---

[27] It is possible that this goldsmith was part of Nestor's household, but he still had to be summoned for a specific task.

[28] Forbes (1964–72) VIII.85.

[29] Morgan (1990) 31, 34–41, 55, 80, 82, 138–89, 206, 262 n. 39.

[30] Finley (1954) 55.

[31] Even though there is little direct evidence in the poems—and few estates had their own supply of ores—Finley (1954) 61 is probably broadly correct to claim that Homeric estates were self-sufficient (van Wees (1992) 52, 221).

[32] Van Wees (1992) 223–25.

54 { Poiesis

choose to specialize rather than redeploy their resources, deliberately overproducing certain items or crops in order to exchange them for others they were less proficient at producing. By the end of the Bronze Age, some parts of the Mediterranean had established themselves as specialist producers of wine or olive oil, and undoubtedly the same thing would have happened at the household level among landed estates. Top-class craftsmanship required specialists; the excellent ladies of Phaeacia focus on particular tasks—and the men on sailing (*Od.* 7.103–11)![33]

In addition to the quality benefits noted by Homer, specialization for exchange reduces unit costs by increasing utilization. Unless by chance an estate's requirements match the annual output of an exact number of specialists, there will be some underutilization of labor. Specialized slaves are a fixed cost, so underutilization increases costs per unit. Unit costs can be minimized by making products for exchange with neighbors (Fig. 2.1).[34]

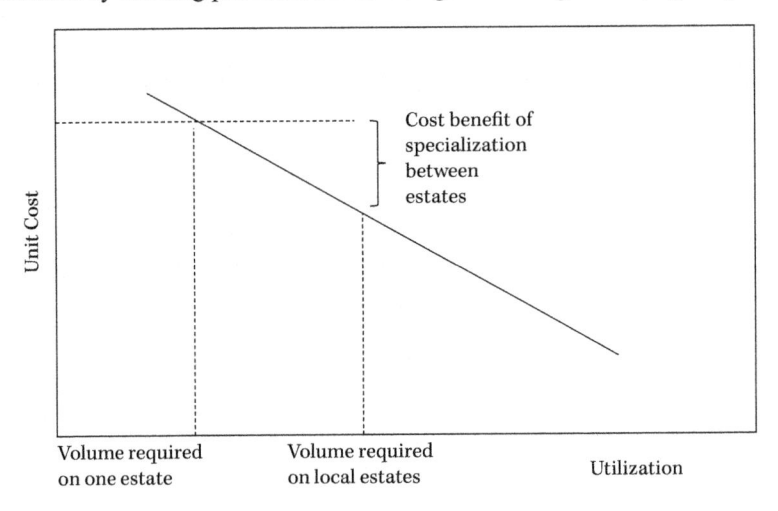

FIGURE 2.1. Specialization and Unit Costs

When not required on a particular activity, a non-specialist worker can be redeployed, and his costs go with him. A specialist only achieves his lowest-cost position when fully occupied at his specialized task (Fig. 2.2).

---

[33] Bucher (1893) identified specialization by material (*Berufsspaltung*, literally "splitting of professions") as the second stage of industry development, the first being labor operating outside the home or *Produktionsteilung* ("division of labor"; cf. Weber (1947)), but specialization by materials almost certainly occurred before labor left the *oikos* and is likely to have been a condition of craftsmen achieving sufficiently recognized skills to operate independently. Homer's "specialists" needed a wide range of skills even within one job description: a *tekton* was carpenter, mason, sculptor, and builder; a *chalkeus* worked a variety of metals and composites into a wide range of goods; and a *skutotomos* tanned, designed, cut, and stitched a broad set of leather products from saddles to shoes.

[34] There was a comparable widening of exchange boundaries among poorer rural communities to secure food (Halstead (1987) 77–87; O'Shea (1989)).

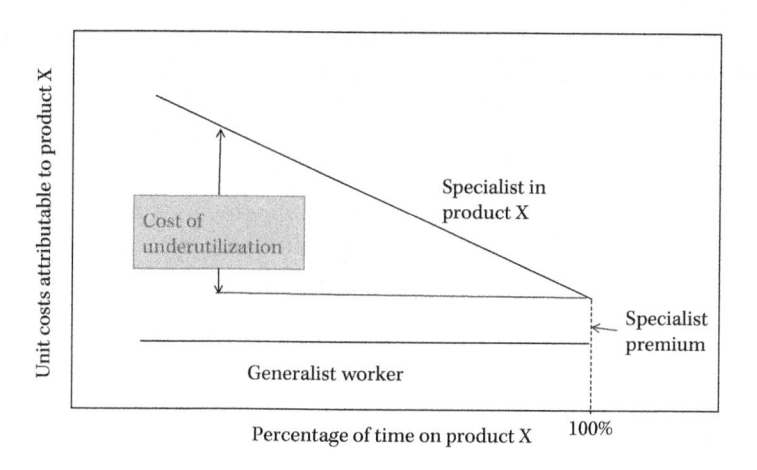

FIGURE 2.2. Specialist and Generalist Unit Costs

The more an owner chose to employ specialist expertise in particular areas, the less flexible his labor force became. If the skill was in making a product that took the expert less than a year to supply for the whole household, and if this expert could not be readily redeployed to other tasks (perhaps for reasons of pride as much as skills), there would begin to emerge a serious opportunity cost. The most productive course would be for him to make surplus products the estate could exchange with guests and neighbors, enabling other estates also to have a labor force more attuned to their needs or particular capabilities. In time, these specialists would establish a customer base of their own, enabling them to operate independently.

The same considerations apply to resources other than labor. If the minimum unit of production requires access to raw materials that for the same degree of effort can be accessed in quantities much greater than one household needs, then there will be savings from aiming the production at a larger market than the household itself. Obsidian collectors on Melos almost certainly shared their spoils with their neighbors, and so would collectors of other metal ores.[35] Similarly, if complex or costly equipment is needed, it is sensible to share it between as many people as are required to use its full capacity. An in-house perfumer would have a great deal of inventory that he might never get through. An in-house metalworker would have equipment that might sit unused most of the time and a large investment in ores. The household's living standards can be increased by specialization and exchange. As discussed in section 2.4 below, the cost-reduction benefit of increasing the utilization of specialized labor and assets is one predictor of the sequence and

---

[35] Renfrew (1972) 455, 473–74; Renfrew (1973) 180; Torrance (1986) 5, 135–221.

extent of industry formation: the more specialized the resources required to make a product, the faster that product will come to be exchanged.

While the mobility of Homer's craftsmen had much to do with quality considerations, supply economics might have been of equal importance. If your skill was a rare one and you wanted to maximize your income, it would be harder among a handful of neighbors, whose appetite for your skilled output and willingness to pay for it would have been finite, than by offering your work to rich households further afield. Mobility provided an opportunity to keep busy while extracting maximum prices for your work. The more specialized the skill, the more it would benefit from access to larger markets (Fig. 2.3).

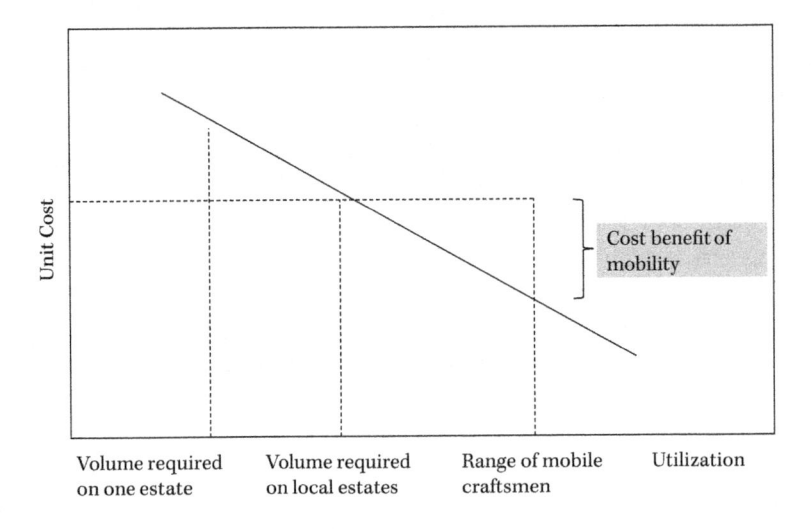

FIGURE 2.3. Value of Mobility

Let us consider how this would have evolved in practice, again taking the example of simple metalwork, which changed very little over three millennia (Ill. 2.1).

Finley believed that the need to acquire ore was the one thing that prevented full self-sufficiency. The acquisition task, "whether by trade or by raid, was a household enterprise, managed by the head, or it would be larger in scale, involving many households acting cooperatively."[36] A rich household might include skilled metal tradesmen among its slaves in order to find ore or source it from other miners and to acquire and maintain the tools to make a range of metal products. This demanded a considerable amount of specialized human resource. On a large estate, especially in time of war when arms and armor were needed, this resource might be kept busy. At other times the

---

[36] Finley (1954) 64, 75–76.

ILLUSTRATION 2.1. Blacksmith—Homeric or early C20?

equipment, the working capital (raw ores), and possibly some specialized elements of the labor force would be underutilized. Many households might be so rich that this waste did not matter to start with. At some point, for some of them, it would have. An excess of heirs, a loss of wealth following conflict, a desire to spend more heavily on other items, or the simple need to redeploy the labor force to fill important gaps in other areas might all have triggered some deliberation about whether the in-house option was best for a particular craft, especially the more specialized ones where underutilization is most costly. The beneficiary of this thinking was the traveling craftsman. Because he keeps busy all year round, he can charge a price very much lower than the cost of keeping an underutilized specialist. (Note that for the purpose of the following analyses, cost movements are assumed to be directly reflected in prices over time as competition emerges.) His income is derived from several customers, each of whom can be charged much less than the cost of maintaining a specialist slave, even if the craftsman's own living standard is much higher. The costs of his equipment and inventory acquisition are similarly shared between several customers. He can afford a large store of raw materials (probably cheaper to buy or easier to find in bulk) because his larger customer base will get through them more quickly. As Figure 2.4 illustrates, these lower costs ($S0 > S1$) mean that he can supply (a) more product at the original price ($V0 > V1$) or (b) the same amount of product at a lower price ($P0 > P1$).

The traveling craftsman's lower costs, and the lower prices he can offer, mean that a householder offered a traveling alternative will probably come to the view sooner or later that it is best to stop employing his own metalworking specialists and rely instead on visiting craftsmen (though at first he might continue to source his own ores). The more this happens, the more the independent specialist's utilization increases, driving his costs down further. When one craftsman in an area is fully occupied, other

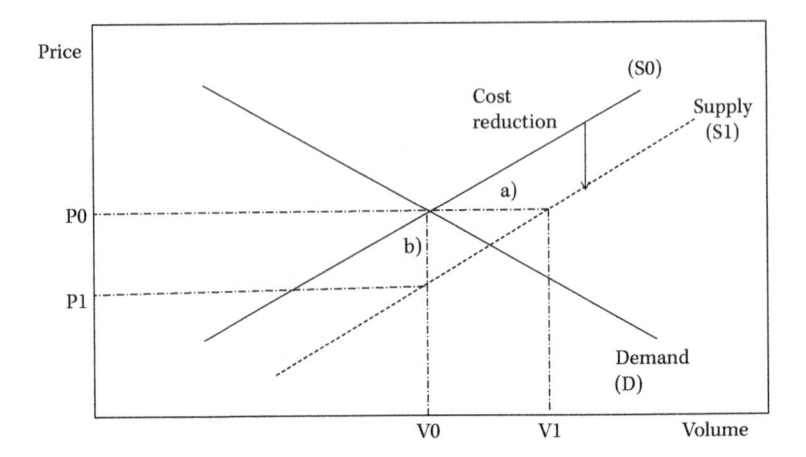

FIGURE 2.4. Impact of Cost Reduction on Supply

people will see the opportunity and set up in competition. This might reduce costs still further through commercial rivalry or intelligent collaboration and will in any case reduce margins and hence prices. Each decline in price brings more volume as more estates find the commercial proposition attractive and become customers. Critical factors in this decision are the extent to which labor, raw materials, or equipment are hard to redeploy into other uses and the sensitivity of specialist costs to utilization.

As product costs fell with increased utilization, better-quality items would have became affordable to more people. "*Demiourgos*" or "worker for the people" (*Od.* 17.383) implies a much wider customer base than the landed gentry. An excess of heirs and increasing fragmentation of landholdings would have created a class of households that had enough wealth to exchange for goods they wanted but not enough to maintain a permanent capability to make all those goods at home. In the meantime, war and mineral discoveries would have enriched some soldiers and peasants. As the costs of purchased products declined and they became more affordable to these groups, increased demand would have resulted in increased volumes, reducing costs still further. Much research has explored how, when, and why this middle class came into being, but it is unlikely that a substantial market for outsourced manufactured goods could have developed if it had not.

Facilitating these increases in demand was the emergence of currency for exchange; an itinerant operator would not find it useful to be paid in cows or for dozens of clients to give him clothes and food. Coinage is only a short step from the way the gift economy actually operated anyway; gifts included "fees, rewards, prizes and sometimes bribes," and "no one ever gave anything…without proper recompense."[37] On this basis, the precise point at which coinage became widespread is not of great significance: in Mesopotamia in the fourth millennium BCE, when human beings first began to produce written records of their activities, it was not to write history, poetry, or philosophy, but to do business.[38] As exchange became more common in ancient Greece with the onset of large-scale colonization, standardized tokens probably started to be used for simple reasons of convenience, but coinage should be seen as only a stage in the gradual monetization of Greek society—a particular manifestation of an evolving mindset, rather than a radical leap in economic development.[39] If anything, the introduction of formal coinage from the East in the sixth century would have reinforced the distinction between the largely self-sufficient wealthy and those who had to work for a living.[40] Economically, what matters is that simplification of the means of exchange would have increased demand by making it easier for more people to buy products made by others.

Increasing wealth also meant a growing number of these new customers could afford "the very best" and would tend to choose it, their domestic resources being unable to match the quality and innovations of the specialists. This search for quality shifts the demand curve for the products of specialists to the right (D0 > D1), so that (a) customers will pay more for a given quality product than before (P0 > P1) and (b) more customers would buy at a given price than before (V0 > V1) (Fig. 2.5).

This combination of the demand curve shifting to the right (D0 > D1) as more people sought and could afford better goods than they could make at

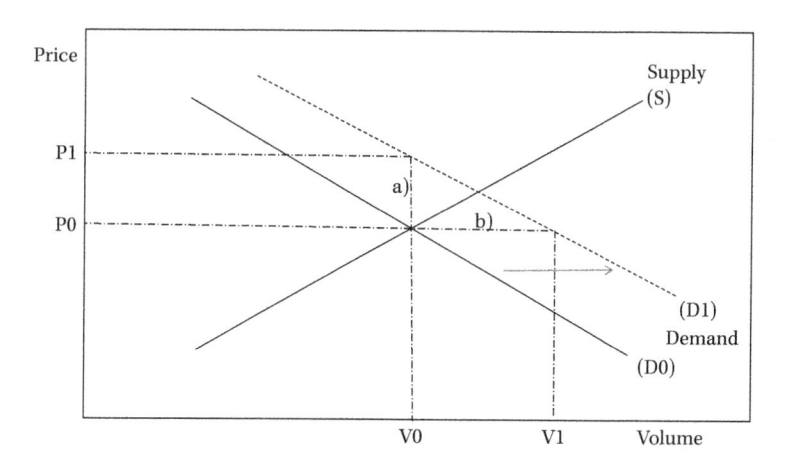

FIGURE 2.5. Increased Demand for Quality

---

[37] Finley (1954) 68.
[38] Ferguson (2008) 28.
[39] Murray (1980) 223; Kim (2001) 7, 19–20.
[40] Seaford (2004).

60 { Poiesis

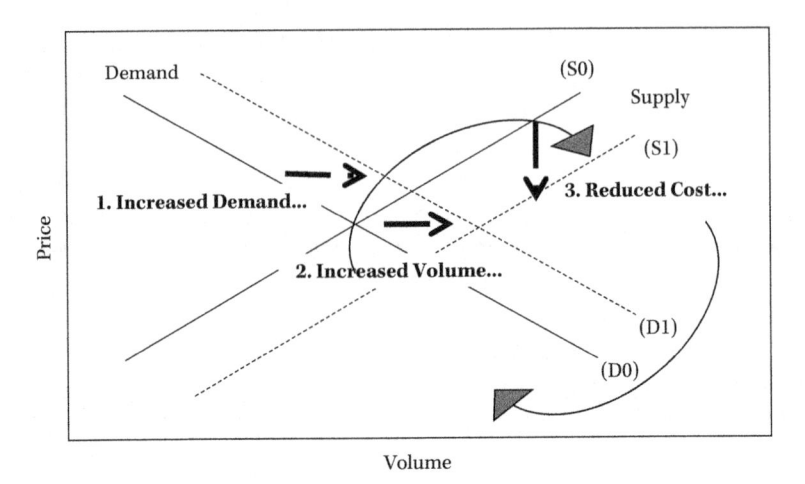

FIGURE 2.6. Demand-Supply Interaction

hom and the supply curve shifting downward through increased utilization and competition (S0 > S1) created a virtuous circle. Price reductions brought in more customers and that in turn elicited more supply and reduced prices still further (Fig. 2.6).

While the traveling craftsman was more cost-efficient than the in-house option on all but the very largest estates, the model was still capable of improvement. Visiting the client might bring good entertainment, but time spent traveling could not be spent producing, and periods when one client's work had to be left for a while in the course of the production process could not be spent on work for other clients. It would be much more efficient to stay in one place and work continuously. If all your business came from a handful of customers, you could afford to visit them. As more households with increasing wealth decided they wanted certain products, but not in sufficient quantity to make them in-house or to expect a traveling craftsman to come to them, the conditions were established for a fixed site. For this to happen, the craftsman needed people to come to him. In the first instance it would probably not have been the richer estates. It might have been difficult for them to cede the principle of self-sufficiency in the first place by having recourse to travelers; it would have been much harder to go to someone else's workshop, or even to send a slave there. Over time the established rich came to use fixed workshops, but it is more likely to have been the middle class, with its new purchasing capacity, that gave them their first work. Only when prices fell very much lower than those offered by the travelers would the rich have been tempted to patronize such establishments. All jobs, however small, could be carried out there without interruptions to production, maximizing utilization and minimizing costs. As density of demand increased, the savings from not traveling grew much faster than the benefits of covering a wider territory. This result was visible by the time of Hesiod, who speaks of small-town workshops as places to lounge in (*Op.* 493). Their anvils, a familiar sight on vases, were noted by Herodotus (1.68). Again increased utilization reduced costs; craftsmen with fixed sites would be able to charge less per unit to achieve a certain level of income, and competition would have ensured they did (Fig. 2.7).

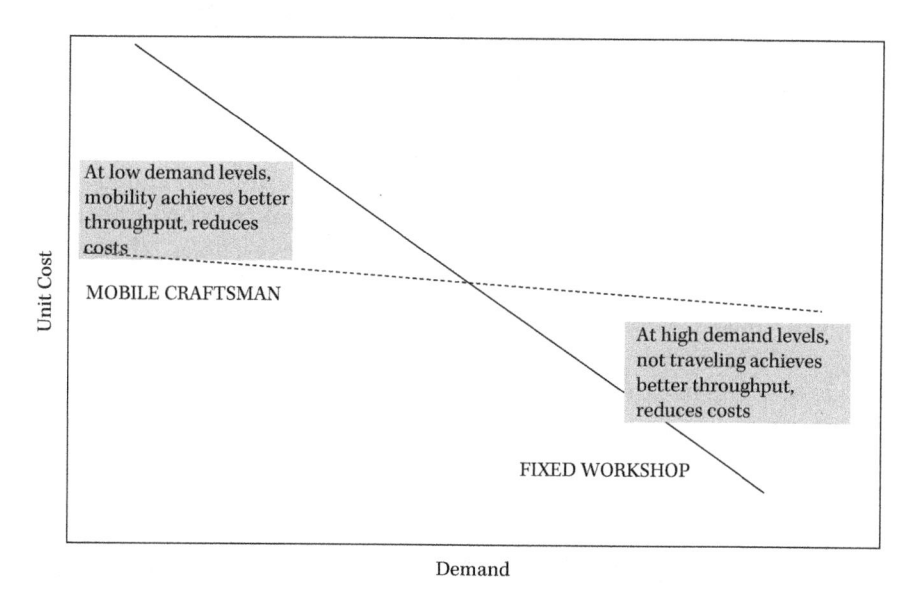

FIGURE 2.7. Advantage of Fixed Workshops

## 2.3 Hesiod and the Peasant Economy

So far we have concentrated on the wants and needs of the rich and the emerging middle class—still very much a minority in the Dark Age of Greece. We must also consider the contribution of peasant households in the shift to manufacturing for exchange.

While references to crafts in Homer and the lyric poets were generally incidental to their themes, Hesiod was consciously trying to describe the realities of rural life. He shows each household as being responsible for its own survival and organizing its affairs in order to be as independent and self-sufficient as possible. His own community of Ascra was a cooperative one, and, though obligations were informal, balanced reciprocity among a small group of neighbors provided some insurance against shortages. Debt was a form of reciprocity owed to neighbors who helped you out (*Op.* 349–51, 353–55, 394–404). He emphasizes the benefits of storage (299–303, 477–78, 576–77), spare equipment (432–34 plough; 455–57 timber for wagons), and savings (361–69), but there is no evidence of managed overproduction—certainly not enough to reflect the direction of a strong leader in the community.[41] There was some exchange of goods at the margin, perhaps leading to a degree of specialization within a community (as suggested by the presence of workshops), but exchange outside a narrow circle would have carried counterparty risks and was probably not extensive.

Status in this peasant community depended on self-sufficiency (*Op.* 293–319). While a rich estate could produce all its own requirements through the labor of the landlord's family, retainers, and slaves, and buy special products from expert purveyors, the poor had to content themselves with whatever they had the time and skill to make at home. In addition to items for home use (clothes, furniture, utensils), grains, grapes, and olives all required some degree of processing, which would have normally been done on or near the farm by the farmer or by a group of neighbors pooling resources. There were also craft specialists: blacksmiths (493–95), potters, and carpenters (25–26), although it is not clear if they practiced these crafts year-round or just between busy times in the fields. There was evidently a labor market—Hesiod recommends bringing in extra labor and selecting the most experienced workers during the planting season (441–47)—and these peasant laborers or *thetes* would have come from households with more people than land to support them, who might well have secured some of their subsistence from exchanging goods they manufactured in the rest of the year. Their engagement was almost certainly seasonal and impermanent, indicating a preparedness to work for other free men occasionally—though not in a permanent arrangement—that seems to have endured to a limited extent in classical Athens.

There is little evidence that third-party manufacture in Hesiod's day went beyond the occasional exchange of goods for food. It is conceivable that landowners hired *thetes* to manufacture products at just those times of year that they themselves were busy in the fields, but unlikely. At the bottom of the social hierarchy, slaves (*dmoes*) were now more a part of the community and less isolated than they seem to have been in the Bronze Age, but again there is no clear evidence that their owners typically employed them in manufacturing. In general, Hesiod and his fellow villagers seem to have relied upon their own labor as much as possible and only rarely turned to craftsmen for specialized products.[42] For the wealthy it was a desire for exceptional quality that led to outsourcing; for peasants it was the only way to get something you could not make yourself—and to afford it you needed a farm that produced more than your family wanted to consume and store.

Though Hesiod provides a clear picture of many aspects of life in a rural community, he gives no clues as to how far a typical household engaged in

---

[41] Edwards (2004) 117.
[42] Edwards (2004) 85.

production for sale or exchange. More specific descriptions of how ancient peasant economies worked have generally been based on observing contemporary ones and drawing out the implications of their overriding imperatives, the avoidance of scarcity and management of risk. A common conclusion is that, even if individual hazards cannot be predicted, societies develop coping mechanisms, including storage, sharing, reciprocity, mobility, and diversifying the subsistence base. The variability of growing seasons leads naturally to storage and exchange, and the way in which this is managed underpins the cohesion and survival of village communities.[43] As a proxy for how this might have worked in practice in ancient Greece, we might consider a more recent and well-documented community, thought to have some of the same characteristics—Russian peasant households at the start of the twentieth century.[44]

The primary model for a Russian peasant farm with no hired labor was 20 to 30 percent agriculture and 10 to 20 percent craftwork, with the rest of the household's labor capacity devoted to festivals and leisure. In a non-wage economy, and one in which no one can go bankrupt, the household's economic decision concerns the trade-off between family labor and living standards in order to maximize income per day worked, so if prices go up, daily income can be maintained by working less, giving rise to an inverse supply curve.[45] Crafts were the obvious way to increase income once you had applied all the labor that could be productively used on your farm, but the evidence shows that each landed household made about the same amount of the items it needed (presumably clothing, vessels, furniture, and agricultural implements) and did not use time freed up from farming to increase non-farm output and income. In fact those with smaller farms simply worked less in total (Table 2.1).

TABLE 2.1 Farm Size and Allocation of Labor—Vologda district[a]

| Sown Area (desyatinas)[1] | % Time in Agriculture | % Time in Crafts |
|---|---|---|
| 0 | 10.3 | 41.9 |
| 0.1–1.0 | 21.7 | 22.8 |
| 1.1–2.0 | 23.0 | 21.9 |
| 2.1–3.0 | 26.9 | 19.8 |
| 3.1–6.0 | 28.1 | 13.7 |
| 6.1–10.0 | 41.6 | 11.1 |

[a] Chayanov (1986) 101.

[1] A desyatina is an area slightly larger than a hectare.

---

[43] Childe (1954); Pearson (1957); Renfrew (1982); Halstead and O'Shea (1989a) 1–7; Halstead (1989b) 68–80.
[44] Chayanov (1986) 224–26.
[45] Net income per day worked = (Gross Income - Raw Material Cost)/Number of Days Worked.

The decision is not driven by profit-maximization, but a subjective judgment by the head of the family about the appropriate balance between living standards and leisure. The choice varies with life-stage but generally does not result in more labor than is required to provide for basic needs, including farm reinvestment and prudent storage.

Analysis of income options facing these households shows that the best was to start a business employing others if you could (Table 2.2).

TABLE 2.2 Annual Income per Consumer—Vologda district[a]

| Employment | Annual Income/Consumer (roubles) |
| --- | --- |
| Agriculture only | 78.3 |
| External employment | 56.6 |
| Independent craft | 66.3 |
| Craft using hired labor | 148.9 |

[a] Chayanov (1986) 102.

The problem in a peasant society was that there was no market to trade in: if every household made its own basic needs (or exchanged products with a neighbor or two to secure food their own land could not supply), no one would want your manufactured product or have the spare means to pay for it. Nor would it be easy to find a regular supply of craft labor unless your community happened to own more slaves than it could use in agriculture. If a free man could operate successfully and independently as a craftsman, he would surely have chosen to do so, rather than share the fruits of his labor with someone else. The initial impetus for the development of markets must have come from the decisions of rich and middle-income households, served initially by mobile craftsmen and then, as demand grew, from fixed workshops. Despite the same economic incentives, peasant households were held back by local demand and supply constraints. Only when regular surpluses enabled the development of larger communities with active product and labor markets could one quit subsistence agriculture and venture into manufacturing with confidence.

New political settlements and urbanization changed all this. From the social disruptions that went with Dark Age poverty emerged strong, stable oligarchies that commanded wars and kept internal peace but did not extort excessive taxes—the "optimality band" for economic development.[46] By 700 BCE, new independent *poleis* had started to form, expand, and acquire the territory of their neighbors. Coinage was introduced, probably from Lydia in the late seventh century (Hdt. 1.94), and arrived in Athens in around 550 BCE.[47] Shipping networks took shape with a multiplicity of vessel types, indicating

---

[46] Jones (1988).
[47] Caradice (1988) 29; Snell (1995) 1494; Thompson (2003) 68.

some degree of trade specialization and interdependence among markets.[48] Increased population density tends to improve productivity;[49] just as today, tradesmen in a small community are typically more multi-skilled and less expert than those serving a larger market. By providing a large market for manufactured product, urbanization meant crafts offered the poor a stable income opportunity, a process that was reinforced by strong commercial infrastructure, including market regulation, commercial laws, treaties, and shipping networks, and inspired by international example and competition.[50] Manufacturing replaced agriculture at the center of urban economies and artisans came to be ranked above peasant farmers.[51] By classical times, the overwhelming bulk of manufacturing in Athens was private, a large and growing proportion was for sale to third parties, and, while traveling craftsmen continued for centuries in rural areas, on major construction projects, and in supporting armies on campaigns, workshops in cities were on fixed sites.

## 2.4 Empirical Evidence

This economic narrative is logical and consistent with the limited information we can glean from literature and archaeology. To assess its empirical validity, its predictions can be tested against what we know about the development of specific manufacturing sectors. Disregarding the contingencies that affected the timing and rate of change in different places and times, the essential economic causality behind industry formation can be summarized as follows:

1. Overproduction, perhaps involuntary at first, leads to exchange and specialization, initially among neighboring estates. The resulting increase in utilization reduces the costs of the specialist and makes third-party manufacture more attractive, especially for products where a high level of craftsmanship is valued (making the labor force less flexible and the cost of underutilization high) or where other dedicated resources such as raw materials or equipment are best accessed in quantities that exceed the needs of one household.
2. Mobility increases the utilization and reduces the costs of specialized craftsmen and resources.
3. As wealth spreads, outsourcing increases, creating a virtuous circle of increasing volumes and falling costs, facilitated by simplification of the means of exchange.

---

[48] Osborne (2007) 300.
[49] Apolte and Gradalski (1992).
[50] Ober (2010).
[51] Calhoun (1926) 21–30.

4. Once demand has developed sufficiently, a fixed workshop increases a craftsman's utilization and reduces his costs still further.
5. Peasant households can only participate in this growth by increasing their craft output when local product and labor markets have developed sufficiently. Urbanization is a critical enabler.

In this analysis, there are three supply factors at work. The most important is *utilization of skilled labor (S1)*, a costly resource to train, support, and replace. Second is *utilization of investments (S2)*. An in-house perfumer would have a great deal of inventory that he might never get through. An in-house metalworker would have equipment that might lie unused most of the time and a large investment in ores. The importance of each factor depends on the *size of the cost benefits* that derive from scale and utilization *(S3)*.[52] The cost of different elements of supply (labor, materials, equipment, etc.) decline at different rates with volume, so the impact of growth on total unit costs varies between products according to the composition of their cost structure. Products with cost compositions that, in aggregate, decline most steeply per unit with volume increases would be especially prone to early outsourcing.

Two demand factors are important. First is the *demand for specialists (D1)*, for luxury items like cosmetics and perfumes and rare textiles, or products in which the quality of workmanship was especially valued; since the times Homer wrote of and probably long before, decisions by the rich that they could best satisfy their wants by purchasing from specialists were enough to establish the viability of independent craftsmen. Second, the emergence of *less rich customers (D2)* increased demand for the work of independent traveling craftsmen and led to more of them deciding to set up in a permanent site as a larger customer base made it increasingly economic to do so. This factor was ultimately critical in the spread of manufacturing for exchange among the poor, but it was only in larger communities that manufacturing for sale became widely practiced.

Not all industries emerged from the *oikos* at the same rate and to the same degree. This model implies that industries will tend to develop faster when the following circumstances apply:

1. Production involves either or both of:
    a. specialized labor capability or resources that are not readily applied to other purposes within the household (*S1, S2*), or
    b. products of a nature or quality that cannot easily be supplied to meet only the needs of a single household as a result of investment (*S2*) or quality requirements (*D1*).

---

[52] This is a question of degree rather than a separate factor, but it is a sufficiently important differentiator to warrant separate consideration.

2. There are significant cost savings to be made through increased utilization (*S3*).
3. The products are wanted by people of more modest means who find it impractical to make them at home (*D2*).

We can test these predictions against the development of four of Athens's most important manufacturing sectors.

## 2.4.1 METALWORKING

As we have seen, metalworking fills all the conditions and is an archetype of industry formation. The diverse specialist skills required, together with the need to source and store ores, would have made the in-house option increasingly expensive relative to the third-party alternative (*S1, S2,* and *S3*). The industry quickly took many forms: mining might be a large-scale business organized by the state, a seasonal occupation for local villagers, or a full-time enterprise conducted by people migrating between sites.[53] Some metalworking was organized centrally, some by temples, and some by private commission.[54] There was a long tradition of local metalworking in temporary kilns at Olympia for festivals; tripods were made on site from about 700 BCE and figurines before that.[55]

Meanwhile, the emergence of a middle class who could not afford a specialized slave or the ore acquisition and storage process would have reinforced the trend to purchased products and encouraged the establishment of fixed workshops; metal armor and jewelry would have been important components of an increase in living standards. While some of this increased demand was for relatively standard items, other products offered the opportunity for highly skilled craftsmen to display their virtuosity—a difference that showed up in industry structure. By classical times the metalwork business had multiple guises offering different opportunities for employment and income, including large factories making knives, minting coins, and making large bronze sculptures; individual craftsmen making bronze armor and ornamental jewelry; and general smiths making and repairing simple utensils. This is the subject of Chapter 4. There were as many segments to the metalwork business as could benefit from specialization.[56] Little metalwork took place in a typical home.

---

[53] Raber (1987) 297–313.
[54] Treister (1996) 11–16.
[55] Morgan (1990) 138–39.
[56] Differences in the set of competitors are commonly used to identify the boundaries between industry segments.

## 2.4.2 LEATHERWORK

In deciding whether to buy leather products or make them at home, the rich householder would have been confronted with much the same choice as in regard to metals. Should he keep his (often underutilized) leather slave(s) or buy product made elsewhere and reduce or retrain his labor force? Though there was less to worry about in terms of equipment and inventory than in metals, over time the superior economics of the busier independent craftsman would tell (*S1, S2,* and *S3*). For shoes, the quality demand factor (*D1*) was probably important, not least with the emerging middle class (*D2*): it is hard to make excellent shoes if you only make one or two pairs a year. Better to spend your time doing what you are good at so you can afford better-made shoes than your own products. In classical Athens, depictions show that much shoemaking was a bespoke craft, practiced by individual cobblers with the assistance of a slave or two, but at least one owner had several leatherworking slaves, and there was probably a high-volume, lower-cost segment as well (see Chapter 5). Because leatherworking skills differed little between different products, segments tended to be defined by price-quality point rather than product range. Tanning did not need to be located close to makers of leather goods, and classical Athens restricted its activity for reasons of amenity. A desire to confine the unpleasant effects to certain locations might well have led neighboring estates to share tanning facilities long before urbanization.

## 2.4.3 COSMETICS AND PERFUMES

In the case of cosmetics and perfumes it was principally demand factors that were at work (Chapter 8). A rich man willing to spend enough money on acquiring the right slaves and equipping them with a large and expensive inventory far beyond his own household's needs could have ensured his *oikos* was self-sufficient (despite *S1, S2,* and S3), but he might have had a difficult time persuading the ladies of the house that they were not occasionally missing out on the latest scent or eyeliner (*D1*). It was not only a question of ingredients, but mixing skills—or at least the appearance of them; the difficulty of ensuring your own employees can keep up with the latest trends and professional know-how without being part of a wider professional community is one that exercises corporations employing professional lawyers today and would certainly have influenced decisions on how to source cosmetics and perfumes. Buying in from independent experts in the craft would have solved this problem as well as being much cheaper in terms of labor and investment, and explains why by classical times cosmetics and perfumes were largely bought from specialist suppliers, though often distributed by individuals perceived to be endowed with some esoteric knowledge.[57]

---

[57] Lys. *Fr.* 38; Hyp. 3; Ar. *Eccl.* 841; Reger (2005) 253–72.

## 2.4.4 TEXTILES

The three industry sectors described above all possess features promoting third-party manufacture. Metalworking offers many opportunities for specialization and a correspondingly wide set of incentives and opportunities for independent manufacturers. Leatherworking had similar supply factors but fewer opportunities to create specialized segments beyond those based on price and quality. It was demand for luxury items and the cost of inventory that made cosmetics and perfumes a business for investors in classical times even though, to meet the expectations of buyers, the products would generally go to market through individual retail intermediaries. Despite these differences of emphasis, all three businesses made the transition from *oikos* to market relatively quickly because they all displayed the characteristics that the supply-demand model predicts would promote manufacture for exchange. The case of the textile industry (Chapter 5) is rather different. Most women could spin and weave, and to the extent that a household's women could make enough for all its members, there was no need to buy day-to-day clothing from third parties (no $S$ factors or $D2$). Only if the workmanship required was of very high quality, or if the cloth to be worked was very rare ($D1$), would there be an incentive for such households to seek external supply. This reflects exactly the nature of much of the industry we find in classical times, when textiles continued to be produced principally at home and for home consumption, although shortages of (usually female) household labor ensured there was a thriving market for purchased everyday clothes as well as for fine textiles made from specially imported fabric.[58] The economics of production and the difficulty of displaying rare skills in a field everyone could compete in meant there was no benefit in forming large workshops, and most independent practitioners were sole operators.[59] The large weaving establishments that we know existed were probably an opportunistic use of underemployed females in a brothel or a large slave gang after the harvest.[60] The dirtier processes such as fulling and dyeing were probably carried out by (male) third parties for reasons of amenity, just as tanning was, and might similarly have been shared among estates from an early date.

That ancient industry formation and subsequent industry structures appear to have followed a pattern predictable from elementary microeconomics is not to suggest that every Greek made a rational calculation on a regular basis and started to buy product in as soon as it became profitable to do so. Some newly rich households might have been especially risk-averse and have favored saving resources rather than spending them on

---

[58] Carr (1999) 163–67.
[59] Bresson (2007) 198; Harris (forthcoming) 13.
[60] Davidson (1997) 85; Cahill (2002).

third-party product. There would be many reasons for an estate to retain a favorite slave even if his or her output was poor value compared to external alternatives; one reason might simply be the owner's pride in having a lot of slaves. Some outsourcing decisions might have been triggered by the deaths of slaves whom it was difficult to replace. Nevertheless, the overall sequence of the emergence of products manufactured for sale must have reflected the cumulative effect of these individual decisions. Whether or not the ancients addressed these problems consciously, whatever language they used, and whatever the hesitations and delays that occurred along the way in particular cases, the outcome of this decision process was clearly consistent with practical economics and tended toward optimizing resource efficiency in supplying household needs. As demand grew and volume increased, costs declined, bringing more customers into the market in a self-reinforcing process, and manufacturing industries, peopled by craftsmen or slave gangs, took shape. Such a radical change in lifestyle meant the process was a slow one, and many sectors probably only took off some time after they could have made an effective business case for customers to buy from them. The reasons the ancients might have resisted making these optimizing decisions for some time after the economic solution became obvious would themselves constitute an interesting subject for study and might highlight important cultural differences between societies.

## 2.5 Supply and Demand in a Competitive Market

Before applying competitive analysis to the various manufacturing segments of classical Athens, it will be helpful to relate the competitive forces that shape industry structure to those identified here as driving industry formation. The economic element of the make or buy decision facing households deciding to outsource for the first time is a simple comparison of costs for any given perceived value of a product (Fig. 2.8).

For low-value products, the in-house option was likely to be cheaper than paying the price set by a traveling expert. For products whose perceived value depended on rare skills that were seldom in demand and not often required by a single estate, in-house utilization was likely to be lower and costs higher than the external option. Once any products started to be outsourced, in-house utilization of a specialized skill would fall further and costs would rise for all perceived levels of value ($A > B$), again increasing the relative attraction of outsourcing.

In a competitive market, the relevant comparison is between competing suppliers. Each competitor positions himself somewhere along the perceived value spectrum and, to win business, needs to offer the best value for money within a perceived value band (Fig. 2.9).

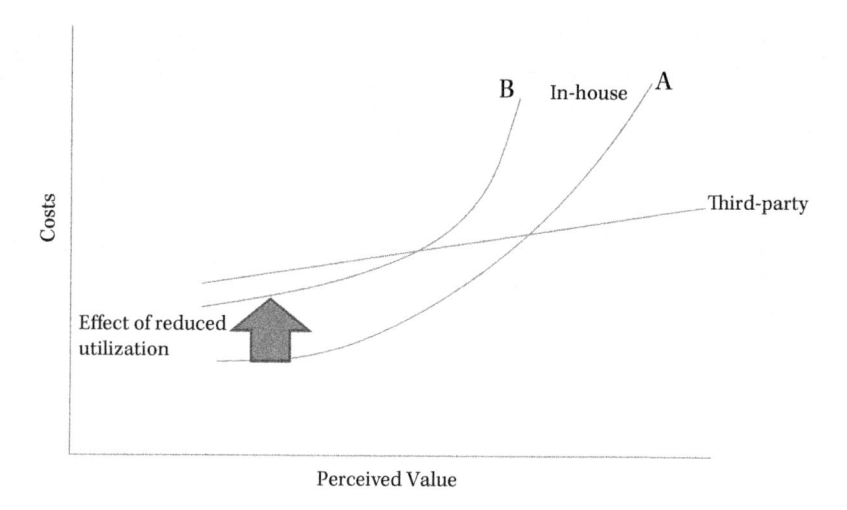

FIGURE 2.8. The Make or Buy Decision

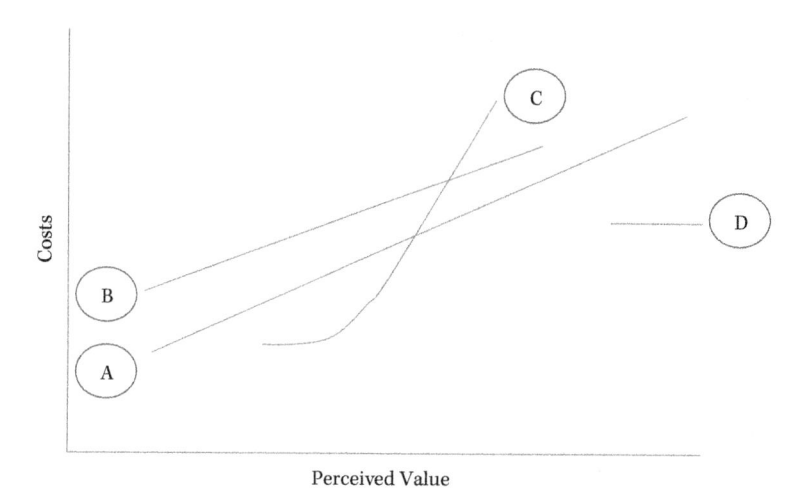

FIGURE 2.9. Competitive Supply

Here the household's motivation is to select the lowest-priced supplier for a desired level of perceived quality. In some cases this perception might reflect genuine differences in material or workmanship, in others it might result from clever promotion or a simple misunderstanding. What matters is the value perceived by the purchaser and the array of possible candidates for supplying it. In this example, A and B compete across most of the quality or value range, their costs rising to meet increased quality requirements. Buyers will tend to source from A, which can afford lower prices at each point. C has a strong cost position in around the middle of the perceived value range, but finds it very expensive to add further value. He will choose to compete with a narrow range for which he has the lowest costs. Customers who want the very best quality at the lowest price will buy from the focused specialist D.

Many products do not lend themselves to competition on the basis of perceived value, as purchasers cannot or do not care to distinguish between items provided they meet minimum standards of functionality. In these cases, Figure 2.9 has no width and the lowest price wins the business. A competitor with a sustainably lower cost position is able to drive other competitors out of business, and the industry will consolidate into a handful of large concerns. Without mechanization, it is difficult or impossible to establish a lasting cost advantage, and such industries generally remained fragmented. The next chapter shows these dynamics at work in the pottery industry.

# 3 }

# The Pottery Industry

This chapter applies the competition framework to the structure of the industry about which we know most, pottery manufacture, and identifies several ways in which Athenians could have created viable pottery businesses, consistent with what can be deduced from original sources. Extensive use is made here of the work of modern archaeologists and researchers and the expertise of contemporary craft potters. I summarize the archaeological data on potteries before analyzing the manufacturing process in some detail to establish what would constitute an efficient deployment of resources around a kiln. The analysis will demonstrate that no single-kiln pottery would have needed more than a dozen workers and most would have had four or five. Furthermore, competitive considerations made it very risky for a business to operate more than one kiln. The lack of natural barriers to entry determined what firms needed to do to succeed, and the industry consisted of a number of full-size workshops with particular specialties and a larger number of kilns operated by the owner with family members or a slave or two, often on a casual basis, making utility ware. Finally I identify changes in industry technology that enabled industrialists in the 18th century to establish much larger and highly profitable pottery enterprises.

## 3.1 The Evidence

### 3.1.1 ORIGINAL TEXTS

"The few literary references to pottery say nothing useful about the industry. What we know or guess comes from the pots themselves and a few inscriptions set up in public by potters."[1] Cook's despair is not strictly justified: literature tells us at least that making pots was a familiar part of ancient life and that they came in a remarkable number of shapes and sizes. Pottery had its own hymn, in which the poet sings for his pots: "may the cups and all the bowls turn out well

---

[1] Cook (1960) 271.

and fetch the benefit of sale, many in the *agora,* many in the streets, and bring a great profit, and for us too who sing for the potters." He ends up blessing or cursing the kilns and their products according to how the owners treated him (Ps-Hes. *Ep. Hom.* 14.3–6). Sophocles was among the first poets to speculate on pottery's origins (*Fr.* 482), and later, it had its own bible—the *Geoponica* gives lengthy advice on the benefits of having potters on a farm and some of the complexities of the manufacturing process such as firing (2.49; 6.3.1–5). One might even say it had its own slice of the Greek language. *Kerameuein,* according to the ancient lexicon, meant to work very hard.[2] Hesiod's description of a fierce rivalry as being "potter vs. potter" (*Op.* 25) had clearly become part of the language by the time Aristotle refers to it (*Rh.* 2.1381b). Plato twice uses the idea of starting to learn pottery by making a *pithos* to describe what we would express as learning to run before you can walk (*Grg.* 514e; *La.* 187b).

We also hear of a very wide range of ceramics. Vessels on sale in Aristophanes's marketplace included the *kados* jar (*Ach.* 549, *Pax* 1202); the funerary *soros* (*Ach.* 691, *Lys.* 600); the *stamnion* for wine (*Lys.* 196, 199); the beaker or *ekpoma* (*Vesp.* 677); a number of small vessels and cups, such as the *kotyliston* (*Ach.* 458), the *skeuarion,* and the *skaphion* (*Thesm.* 402, 758, 633); and ceramic soup ladles (*etnerysis* (*Ach.* 245) or *arystichos* (*Vesp.* 355)).[3] More basic items included the simple *keramos* (*Ach.* 901, 928), the earthen *chutra* (*Ach.* 284; *Eq.* 745, 1174, 1176; *Pax* 923–4; *Lys.* 557), the smaller *chutidron* (*Ach.* 463, 1175; *Pax* 202), *pithoi* or *pithaknai* storage jars (*Pax* 613, 703; *Eq.* 792), stove lids (*pigneus*—*Nub.* 96), *kalpis* jars for water (*Lys.* 358, 400, 539), frying pans (*tagenon*—*Eq.* 929), and chamber pots or *ameis* (*Thesm.* 633, *Ran.* 544a, *Vesp.* 935). Other terms in literature or epigraphy include the *amphora,* the *pelike,* and the *stamnos,* all of which served as containers for wine and other goods. *Hydriai* were designed to carry water which, mixed with wine, perhaps cooled in a *psykter* and ladled out with a *kyathos* prior to making a libation from a *phiale,* might be transferred to one of four basic shapes of *krater,* a *kylix,* a *skyphos,* a *kantharos,* a *mastos,* or a head-shaped single-handed vase, or poured into a conveniently designed "lip" cup or "beard" cup. There were wine jugs (*oinochoai*) and oil jugs or *lekythoi,* and other jars for oils and ointments (*aryballoi, alabastra,* and *askoi*). Women kept their toiletries in a *lekanis* or a *pyxis;* they had special containers for their perfumes and used ceramic implements for rolling wool. The gods had special pottery shapes of their own, with many items such as the Panathenaic *amphora* and the *loutrophoros* water vase being made only for special ceremonies. For weddings there were the *lebes gamikos* or a special *loutrophoros.* Highly decorated ceramics were sought

---

[2] Suidas: "*koinos anti tou katergazesthai.*"
[3] Some of these names are likely to have overlapped each other in application—a source of eternal frustration to archaeologists.

for funerals too, although the top-of-the-line items were vases of *alabastron*. The deceased of more modest means would be commemorated with ordinary *aryballoi, lekythoi*, or *loutrophoroi*, which were suited for other uses as well. There was a special "potters' market" in the Agora.

The remainder of this section explores other sources of information, starting with the pots themselves and covering excavations of the sites of potteries, stamps and graffiti, and vase paintings of active potteries. Of all these sources, only vase paintings and excavations of whole workshop sites (of which there are very few) provide much information about the size of the average workshop, and the former are not altogether to be trusted as a guide to the reality they claimed to depict.

3.1.2 POTS

There is ample evidence, discussed below, that individual potteries typically made many types of pots, ranging from complex decorated items to household crockery and containers. Finds from as early as the Neolithic Age confirm the wide variety of ceramic shapes used for the purposes of everyday life, and this certainly continued into classical times.[4] One workshop excavated in the Hellenistic Agora contained no less than 14 different types of pouring and mixing vessels, 11 shapes of plates and saucers, 11 different forms of bowl, and even 6 of inkwells.[5] Other finds show how various cult activities spawned their own pots. For our purposes it is useful to distinguish three segments: fine ware, utility ware (simple crockery and containers), and other products.

*Fine ware:* It is perhaps telling that Greece appears to have been an exception to the general rule that the first use of ceramics was for functional purposes. None of the pottery finds from the early Greek Neolithic period is identifiable as a cooking pot, while in the late Neolithic only around 30 percent of pots found were used for cooking.[6] In classical Athens the most valuable fine ware was made by noted potters and painters, elegantly decorated and displayed with pride by the master of the house or of ceremonies on festive occasions, sometimes apparently being commissioned to mark a special event (Ill. 3.1).

Athens had displaced Corinth as the leading pottery producer in the second quarter of the sixth century, following an apparent decline in Corinthian quality. In around 530 BCE the innovation of Andocides's workshop in changing from black to red figures helped establish Athens's pre-eminence, which was underpinned by other new techniques such as those of the vase painters Euphronius

---

[4] Richter and Milne (1935) 5–7.
[5] Rotroff (1997) 72–77. For similar discoveries from classical times, see Sparkes and Talcott (1970).
[6] Björk (1995); Urem-Kotsou et al. (2002).

ILLUSTRATION 3.1. Fine Ware

and Euthymides, who competed in developing new ways of foreshortening figures.[7] Scenes ranged from heroic myths to domestic settings and the occasional workshop.[8] Discoveries outside Attica suggest that many fine pieces commissioned for particular symposia in Athens were later sold in export markets, but there is little to suggest that fine ware exports were a major trade.[9]

*Coarse Ware:* Much coarse ware was used domestically. From early times ceramics had been the material of choice for many household objects, such as bowls, dishes, or cooking utensils (Ill. 3.2). It would be a long time before Juvenal described someone being ashamed to be eating off ceramics (*Sat.* III.168). Every Athenian household, rich and poor, would have owned many vessels and dishes that never left the kitchen and would undergo rough usage and need regular replacement.

A typical house contained a few simply decorated mixing bowls, three or four red-figure vases, including one or two special commemorative ones,

---

[7] Moignard (2006) 28; Clark et al. (2002) 40.
[8] Moignard (2002) 69–93; Clark et al. (2002) 5–20.
[9] Isager and Hansen (1975) 37–39; Johnston (1979) 49; Sparkes (1991) 131.

ILLUSTRATION 3.2. Protocorinthian cup

perhaps 40 black glaze cups or vases, and much more undecorated kitchenware for eating from or for storing food.[10] Items sold at market were probably just simple black glazed ware, with more costly products and volume orders supplied at the workshop, although some might come to be resold in the "bazaar."[11] Coarse ware was not signed, and makers did not publicize themselves in epitaphs or dedications. This is only to be expected: there was little credit to be derived from producing a basic plate or jar.[12]

Pottery was associated with trade from early times, both in its own right and as a container for wine, oil, and grain.[13] Early examples from South America show how ceramic exchange strategies develop along a variety of social networks, regardless of the overall state and nature of an economy.[14] Regrettably, finds of containers are not as informative as one might hope. Shipwrecks often hold storage *amphorae* used for transporting wine, oil, or grains (Ill. 3.3), but it is not always easy to be certain of an item's provenance, even with the latest chemical and petrological analysis.[15] Among the more confusing factors are multiple reuse, possibly for quite different contents and destinations, and regular copying of styles within and between regions, reflecting a wide range of possible marketing and innovation strategies.[16]

---

[10] Jones et al. (1962) 88.
[11] Webster (1972) 130; Lawall (2010b) 72–73.
[12] It is probably for the same reason we know the names of many silversmiths but no bronze or iron workers (Burford (1972) 21).
[13] Morgan (1999).
[14] Sillar (1997).
[15] Whitbread (1995); Lawall (1997).

ILLUSTRATION 3.3. Storage *Amphorae*

Even within one region the extent and rate of diffusion of ideas and techniques varied greatly.[16]

*Other objects:* Ceramics had many other applications, such as tiles and statuettes. Roof tiles were among the simplest objects to make. Floor tiles were equally simple but less common and sometimes highly decorated. Lamps were not much more difficult. Ceramics as supposedly curative models of diseased parts of the body became common in Athens in Hellenistic times, but there is little trace of them earlier. Nevertheless we should allow for the possibility that there might have been a small market in classical Athens for certain unusual items of this nature.

### 3.1.3 POTTERIES AND KILNS

Potteries tended to agglomerate near urban areas in order to access a larger market than would be available to a village-based workshop. In Corinth a

---

[16] Lawall (2010b).
[17] Pluciennik (1997) 37–56.

pottery district has been identified two miles west of the temple of Apollo, and Osborne observes "the town clearly offered these potters facilities and a market which they would not have had if working individually in the villages of the territory."[18] In Athens, excellent reddish clay came from beds near Cape Kolias, a few miles south of the city, and from the early Protoattic period we find a site in the Agora with facilities for washing clay and a cleverly designed furnace base alongside residential rooms.[19] This site was abandoned in the third quarter of the seventh century at about the time the other side of the Agora became the main centre of production. Fringe sites, around the Academy, seem generally to have produced to a lower standard. Major pottery sites have been found at the Ceramicus, Colonos Hippios Street, and around Demosion Sema. Colonos Hippios Street featured multiple production sites, principally devoted to pottery, many of them dating from 425 BCE and later. Finds at Demosion Sema include traces of workshops that appear to have specialized in unusual ceramic goods, such as funeral urns. The location of most ancient sites, in or near an urban center, typically on a thoroughfare and in the shade of a wall, is commercially logical but otherwise uninformative.

Kiln-site studies have revolutionized the understanding of *amphora* production in specific locations and of how firing techniques evolved.[20] They are of particular interest in analyzing the economics of pottery production, since their capacity determines the maximum number of people who can be productively employed. Kilns often needed to have their domes rebuilt for every firing, and even the more robust ones might be destroyed by seasonal rains, but some were more durable. The kiln in the House of the Tholos was split-level and clearly a permanent item, as evidenced by the three-centimeter layer of fine clay on the round part of the walls. There are grounds for believing it was used for pottery, given its similarities to the Pentaskouphia tablets from Corinth (see below) and the nearby presence of a basin of the type used for washing clay.[21] The kiln is 1.33 meters in diameter around a central pillar that supports the upper floor, and has an irregularly shaped firing room. The diameters of three kilns discovered in the Metapontum Ceramicus range from 1.0 to 1.2 meters.[22] Papadopoulos identifies a kiln at Torone in Chalcidice of 0.8-meter diameter, though he also notes that a rectangular one at Sindos measured 4.25 by 1.85 meters, an internal area similar to a circle of around 3 meters. He thinks this is unusual: "although larger kilns are known... the most common are small circular updrafts with a temporary dome of clay and

---

[18] Osborne (1987) 117.
[19] Noble (1965) 58; Monaco (2000) 29–32, site AXII.
[20] Eiring et al. (2004) 460.
[21] Thomson (1940) 6–7; Papadopoulos (2003) 126–30.
[22] Cracolici (2003).

conceivably also of turf, stone and wasters."[23] Other excavations and representations seem to support a typical kiln diameter of no more than 1.5 meters. Hasaki analyzed evidence on 296 kilns and found that 41 percent were under 2 meters in diameter and just 26 percent significantly larger; these were rectangular and probably used for architectural and other construction-related ceramics.[24] She concludes that typical diameters of pottery kilns were 1.1 to 1.5 meters.[25] Kiln size was almost certainly constrained by the need for very precise control of temperature and moisture, which becomes exponentially harder as the kiln gets bigger, a problem the Romans addressed with improved arch and flue technology under a well-supported floor.[26]

It is difficult to be certain how many kilns any one workshop contained, especially as rebuildable kilns do not always leave clear traces, but some sites in Athens had more than one kiln, and though these tend to be rectangular, it is possible they were used for ceramics.[27] Analysis of workshop size and kiln space requirements, drawing on archaeological finds and observations of more recent pottery activity in Tunisia, suggest that for two or more kilns to operate simultaneously a workshop needed a floor area of 300 to 400 square meters.[28] Few workshops of this size have been fully excavated in ancient Greece and none in classical times or in Athens, but given the low capital costs involved in building or rebuilding kilns from available clay, it is quite possible that some workshops contained more than one kiln purely for convenience in managing production flows, rather than because they would use the full capacity. For example, it might sometimes be useful to fire up one kiln while waiting for another to cool enough for finished items to be removed, even if both kilns were unused for much of the year. Alternatively, a workshop might have used one kiln for special decorated vases fired alone and the other for less valuable wares. As a result, we cannot take number of kilns as a sound indicator of workshop capacity or labor complement, although it does set a maximum. From the size of the workshops excavated in classical Athens, we can be confident that none had chosen to employ more people than were required to make enough pots to fill two kilns.

### 3.1.4 STAMPS AND GRAFFITI

A large number of pottery items have been found to carry markings on them, including stamp marks and incised graffiti. The practice seems to have

---

[23] Papadopoulos (1992) 219.
[24] Hasaki (2006) 225.
[25] Hasaki (2011) 26.
[26] Peacock (1982) 67; Mattingly et al. (2001b) 77–79.
[27] Hasaki (2002) 233–34.
[28] Hasaki (2006) 225; (2011).

originated in Corinth and Ionia, where markings identified the shipper; until the end of the fifth century only vases shipped west were marked.[29] Marks became common during the fifth century in Athens but faded out, so that in the fourth we find only occasional graffiti. Even so, we have a large sample: although only around 10 percent of *amphorae* have stamps, there were more than 200,000 stamped *amphorae* in collections by 1993.[30]

This wealth of data clearly relates to trade but has proved difficult to interpret. There is little evidence that stamps indicated volumes, and it is no easier to trace a consistent link between a stamp and a vessel's contents. Post-firing graffiti probably designated the purchaser or the consignee.[31] It seems that most were made by or for traders visiting potteries to place orders and that the markings represent different traders, or possibly the traders' customers. The non-Attic characters on Attic vases found in Athens can be explained by the high proportion of immigrant names among potters, but the markings become especially hard to interpret when the pots were destined for export markets.[32] There seems to have been no simple code, and they appear to have been understandable only to trading specialists. If it was a single common system (which scholars deem highly unlikely), it must have been a very complex one.[33]

Recently, scholars have been paying more attention to the archaeological context of finds, but it remains hard to specify the beginning and end dates of many series of stamps and generally impossible to reconstruct the development of a particular workshop, though this might become easier with improved fabric analysis and better integration of stamp studies with quantitative site data.[34] Nevertheless, enough can be learned from pots and their markings for scholars at a recent conference to make convincing cases that, for instance, simple commodity pottery became commercially very important to pioneering seafarers like the Aeginetans, whose soil was too infertile to grow very much; that Thasian wine expanded its range of distribution in a continuing search for more profitable markets; and that large *amphora*-producing sites generally served distant markets, while only a few of the smaller sites did so.[35]

Markings on product made and sold in Athens are easier to interpret. A careful analysis of *amphora* stamps can be used to date buildings.[36] We know that containers for product sold in the Agora carried marks indicating the volume, weight, and price of various commodities, an added detail to the

---

[29] Johnston (1979) 51.
[30] Garlan (1993) 181.
[31] Johnston (1979) 49; Garlan (1993) 182; Eiring et al. (2004) 46; Lawall (2010a) 23–25.
[32] Johnston (1979) 49.
[33] Garlan (1993) 188–89; (2010).
[34] Lang (1956); Johnston (1979); Garlan (1999); Lawall (2001) 534–36; Eiring et al. (2004) 459–60.
[35] Tzochev, Lawall, Panagou (all forthcoming).
[36] Lawall (2009).

picture we get from Aristophanes.[37] We also know the secondhand prices of some items sold at public auction, which at least indicate relativities, if not the price of new products.[38]

### 3.1.5 VASE PAINTINGS

Something of potters' activities and relationships can be learned from signatures on fine vases that reveal the potter or the painter or both. The signing of fine items became very common after 540, but declined after the middle of the fifth century, though it is unclear why; quality remained excellent. Most painters seem to have signed only some of their work, and not always the best. Some, but only very few, vases have two signatures. Sometimes one painter does the major picture and another the rest; sometimes they divide up areas of the vase. Some vases are signed by both potter and painter, revealing who worked with whom at what period.[39]

Unfortunately, knowing the names of participants tells us nothing about the size or operating method of their establishments; the pictures provide more useful information than the writing. The layout of workshops on vases is constrained by the size of the vase, but in general we see a covered area where the potters and decorators work and an open space for the kiln. An Attic lip cup from mid-sixth-century BCE Germany shows a potter standing and a young wheel-turner seated.[40] The earliest extant representation of an Athenian potter or pottery on a vase dates from about 530 BCE.[41] Corinthian votive tablets dating from 575–550 BCE show that kilns were usually beehive-shaped with a small tunnel for the fire-box.[42] A black-figured *pinax* shows an igloo-like kiln, a little higher than the stoker's waist. From the shape, it looks as though its diameter would be about the same diameter as the kiln in the House of the Tholos—a little less than 1.5 meters. The largest of the kilns shown on the tablets still appears to be less than 2 meters in diameter; the rest are much smaller, confirming the typical kiln size deduced from archaeological discoveries.

A picture on the shoulder of a *hydria* in the Leagros Group (520–510 BCE, Ill. 3.4) shows unpainted *pithoi*, suggesting the same workshop would make both decorated and undecorated ware, but this may be artistic license and represent vases being produced in different workshops.[43] Cook suggests that there might have been some differentiation between workshops according to

---

[37] Lawall (2000) 77–82.
[38] Amyx and Pritchett (1958) 163–307.
[39] Webster (1972) 11–13.
[40] Boardman (2001) 143, fig. 176.
[41] Beazley (1944).
[42] The Pentaskouphia tablets in the Staatliche Museen, Berlin, F 871–72; Boardman (2001) 141 fig. 173.1, 3; Louvre MNB 2858, in Schreiber (1999); Hasaki (2006) 222.
[43] Beazley (1956) 362/36.

ILLUSTRATION 3.4. Pottery Workshop on the Leagros Hydria

product: "How far workshops specialised in one or more of these (coarse ware) lines we do not know, but it is natural to suppose that the coarser products were more suited to larger establishments."[44] Other scholars doubt there was much specialization: Stissi contends that fine ware came from workshops that also made coarse ware—even tiles and terracotta statues.[45] Webster includes the possibility of lamps and says that even a specialist in large vessels might have quite a broad range: "it is certainly possible that a single workshop from 570 to 500 produced Tyrrhenian *amphorae*, Mannerist pots, Nicosthenic *amphorae* and *kyathoi*."[46] Arafat and Morgan suggest that "certain workshops seem to have specialised in particular kinds of vessel, but this should be set against a background of diversified production."[47] A large number of different types of pots have been excavated from single workshops. Twenty-nine units from what appears to be a single workshop (the Dikeras Group 270–260 BCE), for example, represent eighteen different types of pots, and the fourteen items attributed to the Shark group (275–240 BCE) have seven different shapes.[48]

## 3.2 Industry and Workshop Size

Several scholars have tried to estimate the numbers employed in making fine ware in total and in individual workshops. From commonality of

---

[44] Cook (1960) 271.
[45] Stissi (1999).
[46] Webster (1973) 296.
[47] Arafat and Morgan (1989) 317.
[48] Rotroff (1997) 72–77.

vase making and painting styles, Webster estimates that in the late sixth and early fifth centuries there were around 200 painters supported by 50 potters and "others" working on fine ware in about 10 workplaces in the Ceramicus, in close proximity to other craftsmen, including bronze workers and stonemasons.[49] Cook argues that two-thirds of all pots have been assigned to one of fewer than 500 workshops and that, allowing for duplication, assigning the rest would not take the total above 500.[50] Assuming a 25-year working life, this would mean 125 active painters in each year to cover a century. More bizarrely, from an estimate of 40,000 red-figure vases from a period of 130 years, Cook derives 13,000 painter-years, or 100 painters active in each year. These premises seem very unlikely. There were probably far more than 40,000 red figure pieces made. The best painters almost certainly worked full-time, and, complex and beautiful though some pieces are, they are unlikely to have taken anything like four months to paint as Cook implies; many were stylized copies, and there are only so many brushstrokes one can get on a vase. The time needed to shape and decorate a vase would have been measured in days, not months. New finds of vases by known painters indicate that individual output might be much higher than was believed.[51] Cook's errors would tend to cancel each other out, so perhaps his conclusion on total painter numbers is reasonable; it is certainly consistent with Snodgrass's view that "it is doubtful whether fine pottery employed more than five hundred at its peak"[52] and justifies Francotte's astonishment at how Athens's reputation in classical times was founded on so small a workforce.[53]

These estimates of fine ware potters and painters only tell part of the story. An estimated 500 potters to serve a smaller community in Bronze Age Mycenae would translate to well over 2,000 for Periclean Athens, and the use of pottery was unlikely to have diminished.[54] To determine typical firm size we must rely on excavations of entire workshops and inferences from vase paintings. From her analysis of workshop size and kilns, Hasaki concludes that the prevalent mode of ancient Greek production was four to six people, using one or two kilns.[55] Based largely on vase paintings, other scholars have come to a similar conclusion. Few vases show more than two or three workers, though the Leagros *hydria* from the end of the sixth century shows a manager, a painter, a craftsman shaping the pot, and five

---

[49] Webster (1973) 127–45; classification based on Beazley (1944).
[50] Cook (1960) 274ff.
[51] Oakley (1992).
[52] Snodgrass (1980) 128.
[53] Francotte (1900–1901) 77: "quelques générations d'artistes et un petit nombre d'ateliers ont suffi pour acquérir à la cité une gloire immortelle."
[54] Whitelaw (2001).
[55] Hasaki (2006) 225; (2011) 26.

ILLUSTRATION 3.5. The Caputi Hydria Showing Four People Painting

others (though they were not necessarily all workers), and a red figure *hydria* from about 460 BCE shows four people painting (Ill. 3.5).[56] Noble suggests there was probably a range of sizes of pottery workshops, from the sole practitioner, perhaps with an assistant to turn the wheel, to a maximum of around 12 workers, though he thinks four to six was typical.[57] Arafat and Morgan propose an average of around six people, perhaps centered on an extended family.[58] Bolkestein agrees that "more than 12 or 15 labourers would never have been united in one workshop."[59] Davies thinks there were "at most five."[60]

It is important to remember that numbers based on vase paintings might be understated: the vase itself constrained the number of figures that could be shown, and, to the extent paintings were likely to have concentrated

---

[56] Noble (1965) 72, n. 2 (Leagros *hydria*); 54, n.19 (Caputi *hydria*).
[57] Noble (1965) xiv.
[58] Arafat (1989) 323.
[59] Bolkestein (1958) 50.
[60] Davies (2004) 44.

on the better-known workshops, they might have been depicting naturally boutique operations and not ones dedicated exclusively to churning out large volumes of commodity product (if there were such workshops). Webster says of the eight figures on the Leagros *hydria* "we may think of this as a minimum" and suggests the average was between 10 and 20, though it is not clear how he arrives at this conclusion: of the eight figures the *hydria* depicts, the seated youth appears to be a customer, and it is far from clear what the roles of several other characters are.[61] Green thought the Caputi *hydria* represented metalworking, despite lacking the conventional metal-shop image of Hephaestus, and we know the metal industry contained some larger enterprises, such as that inherited by Demosthenes (27.9).[62] One expert suggested to me that in the third century BCE, potteries may have had as many as 40 workers, but he acknowledged that the evidence was not strong.[63]

One of the reasons that definitive size estimates are difficult is probably that it was a seasonal industry even for permanent establishments, both because of drying conditions and because of the demands of agriculture on the labor force; there are likely to have been many days of operation with a labor force somewhere between the peak on the one hand and the minimum or seasonal closure on the other. Many workshops would have aimed to operate year-round, but would have been stymied from time to time by seasonal weather conditions. Part of the difficulty in defining typical size may also stem from the fact that the workforce was mobile. In the late sixth century, Oltos painted for at least four potters. There were roving painters, emerging and apprenticed painters, special arrangements for rush orders, painters called in for special tasks, and pots brought in from neighboring shops to be decorated.[64]

Rather than relying on uncertain inferences from vase paintings, the next section analyzes the production process to determine how many workers can be efficiently deployed around one furnace. It shows that no workshop with one or two kilns of the commonly observed diameter would need more than a dozen people in total, and, for most product ranges, six or seven is more than adequate to throw and fire pots. The number of painters would vary, but most workshops probably had no specialized decorators at all and few would have had more than one or two for any period of time.

---

[61] Webster (1972) 41.
[62] Green (1961); (Daremberg (1886) 1127, fig. 304).
[63] Professor John Oakley at the American School of Classical Studies at Athens, August 21, 2007.
[64] Burford (1972) 94; Cook (1960) 272.

## 3.3 Labor Force

### 3.3.1 THE PROCESS OF MAKING POTS

The earliest surviving pots come from Japan, China, and Korea, some dating back as early as 12,000 BCE. The potters' wheel, invented in the fourth millennium BCE, was operated by hand and useful for smooth, quick coiling but initially too light for throwing a heavy pot.[65] Later improvements in design reduced friction and increased weight and momentum. The flywheel that governed rotation speed seems to have been introduced about 1,000 years later in the Middle East and China and spread rapidly. In the Greek world, Minoans were using updraft kilns to make decorated earthenware pots from 2,500 onward—a simple technology but more advanced than those applied until very recently in Africa, India, and among Native Americans, all of whom used open fires, which make heat control very difficult.[66] By classical times in Greece the process and the products had become far more sophisticated. Minoan colored slips were introduced for decoration before 1700 BCE, and complex firing technologies exploited the color-changing properties of oxygen when applied to heated clay.[67] Surfaces could be made so smooth that fine lines could be drawn with a single-hair brush. In fact, "a modern potter could have operated and collaborated with his craft associates around an ancient workshop rather comfortably."[68]

A detailed description of the process for manufacturing pottery by hand has 29 steps.[69] We shall content ourselves here with describing the four main steps of the process—clay preparation, shaping and throwing, decorating, and firing—in order to establish the likely deployment of labor in the largest potteries. The following description is based on interviews with practicing potters and conservationists as well as the work of specialists in ancient ceramics.

#### 3.3.1.1 Clay Preparation

Today clay is a global business with approximately 30 types and multiple variants available through wholesalers, differing in color, texture, and moisture content. All clays are based on silica, alumina, and water, but vary in their content of such minerals as iron oxide, lime, magnesia, potash, quartz, and feldspar. These variations result in different plasticity, porosity, and vitrification properties, so that specific clays suit different applications or the personal preferences of the potter. The prime requirements in any potter's

---

[65] Roux and de Miroschedji (2009) 155–73.
[66] Herrold (2007).
[67] B. Cohen (2006).
[68] Hasaki (2012a) 255.
[69] Clark (1994) 128–63; cf. Richter (1959) 305–10; Leeuw (1999).

clay are that it be malleable, easily worked into shapes, and able to retain those shapes under most conditions. Richter observes that "there are as many different types of clay as there are human beings."[70] Clay that stays with the parent granite following the local volcanic activity that created it is known as "primary" clay, clay that is washed downstream and ground into finer particles is called "secondary," and clay that is more contaminated still is "tertiary" and redder in color. Attic potters had ready and convenient access to a large supply of reddish-brown tertiary clay from beds just south of the city and other sites not far away.[71] It was extremely malleable and, importantly for their decorative achievements, contained iron as an impurity.[72]

To prepare clay it is mixed with water and allowed to stand so that heavy impurities drop out. It must be soaked to a moisture level that will enable easy shaping and predictable shrinkage. A consistent mix requires an understanding of the deposit and its different layers, as well as good judgment as to the right amount of moisture to suit the production process. A rule of thumb among potters today is that preparing the clay takes as long as throwing the pot.

### 3.3.1.2 Shaping and Throwing

In classical Greece, most forming was done on the potter's wheel, though a few experts might have practiced freehand forming. Some cooking ware, such as the *hydria* and the *kados*, was formed by hand, and the inside was then beaten out with a paddle and anvil in order to achieve a thinner wall than a thrown pot—but the wheel dominated, especially with the innovation of using coils of clay to build the spinning pot to the right height. The steps to form a pot on a wheel are:

1. Wedge or beat the clay by cutting it in half and reforming it multiple times to remove air bubbles, make it homogeneous, and get the right consistency. (A large lump of clay can then be used to form several objects.)
2. Place the clay on the rotating wheel. Center, hold firm, then use one's thumbs to form the required cylinder shape.
3. Allow to harden.
4. Replace on the wheel; polish and shave off unwanted clay.
5. Smooth with a wet sponge.
6. Fix handles and foot in place with clay slips.

Some potters might have driven the wheel themselves, although there appears to be no evidence that foot-operated treadles were used in classical times in

---

[70] Richter (1923) 2.
[71] Jones (1986) 21–30.
[72] Noble (1965) 5–8.

Greece or elsewhere.[73] The absence of a kick wheel would have constrained the activity of one of their hands, and in some Attic depictions we see the turning being done by a young boy, quite possibly an apprentice.[74] It is a reasonable conjecture that there was more than one type of wheel: light and fast for forming delicate vessels and slower and heavier for large ones, which were much harder to shape and required more momentum; the latter would often be formed in sections and then bound together with a thick slip of clay. Precision was essential in forming these sections, and the potter had to allow for the natural shrinkage of clay (typically 9 percent in throwing and 0.5 percent in firing). After shaping, a pot would be left to dry to leather-hard consistency for at least 24 hours before decorating and firing.

Mats or potsherds might be placed on the wheel to shape the base. Sometimes molds of fired clay were used to form pots, which was efficient for standard shapes. Corinth seems to have used molds in one of the earliest known examples of an attempt at mass production.[75] Surviving pieces suggest their use was rare in Athens, though this might reflect a survivorship bias in favor of better-quality handmade pieces. Even though experts seem to agree that the use of molds did little to increase production speed, and there is limited evidence of their use in Athens, it was probably economical to use them for high-volume, low-value markets, and some potters probably did so.[76]

### 3.3.1.3 Decorating

Early Egyptian ware from 4000 BCE or earlier had two rather mottled colors, and vases with two clearly identified colors were produced by the Phoenicians in the eleventh century.[77] In around 800 BCE, simple linear human figures began to appear among the geometric designs on Attic pots.[78] The essence of Attic ceramic decorations was the color changes that the addition and withdrawal of oxygen during the firing process could create through its effect on iron in the clay. Athenian potters used this in different ways to create black and red figure pottery and to lend distinctive color and sheen to coarse ware. Black figures were created by applying a black glaze to their shapes, which remained black while the background turned red. Potters found a way to enhance some black figure designs with glaze lines in relief. In about 530 BCE, the potter Andocides (or a painter working with him) reversed the process. By applying black glaze to the pot around the figures instead

---

[73] Noble (1965). It seems likely that the wheel in Jeremiah 18.3 is hand-operated, and the potter in Isaiah 41.25 is using his feet to beat the clay.
[74] Hasaki (2012b) 258–59.
[75] Wilson (2008) 396.
[76] Finley (1965a) 31.
[77] Markoe (2005) 28–29.
[78] The history of Athenian ceramic design is drawn principally from Arias et al. (1962).

of using it to depict the figures themselves, and filling in details on figures with a relief line, he created red figure designs, which came to displace black figure ones.

The glaze itself was a clever invention. It was composed of small-particle clay, usually from the same source as the body of the pot, with potash of soda added for alkalinity so as to ensure it melted at about 900°C. It was normally applied by dipping and pouring, though in fine ware it was sometimes applied with a brush. Some of the simplest pots might be banded and left undecorated, just being dipped in a black glaze en route to the kiln—a simple task taking a few seconds. As the glaze evaporated it would produce a thick, smooth finish, which could be painted over if required.

The task of the painter of a fine vase was a complex and highly skilled one. Creating figures by painting their outlines is not an easy task. Glaze lines had to be added carefully to each figure, other shapes and colors painted in, and, often, words added. And all without being able to know for certain what shades of red and orange would come out of the kiln! A close examination of the Caputi *hydria* suggests that apprentices might learn their craft on the palmette ornamental zones, possibly graduating to background figures before finally being entrusted with the main depiction.[79]

### 3.3.1.4 Firing

This is the most scientifically complex step of all, involving precise timing and temperature control, possibly with the assistance of gold and silver, a step which, we see from vase paintings, was generally managed by two people.[80] Athens's fame in vase painting relied on an ability to avoid firing mishaps, manage the changing colors, and apply sintering glazes.

It has been established that the ancient Greek gloss was attained by a single firing in three stages—a process tailored specifically for Attic clay that must have been the result of many years of experiment and error.[81] The first or "oxidizing" stage takes the temperature from ambient to 800°C, slowly at first to allow the clay to finish its drying gently and avoid the risk of deformation from a sudden loss of moisture. Typically the temperature is raised at around 100°C an hour until it reaches 350°, then heating is accelerated to reach 800°C an hour or so later. Clay becomes "inert" (cannot be broken down again to its original particles) at about 650°C. During this part of the heating process the pot and its slip (glaze) become a brighter red. For this first stage, heating vents are open to allow maximum oxygen flow. In the second or "reducing" stage after 800°C, the vents are closed and damp wood is inserted to reduce the quantity of free oxygen. The temperature continues to rise but

---

[79] Hasaki (2012b) 258.
[80] Tonks (1908) 421.
[81] Richter (1923) 44; Binns and Fraser (1929); Schreiber (1999) 55.

more slowly until it reaches 950°C. The reduction in oxygen turns the iron oxide in the body and the slip from red to black. By 900°C, the alkali and black iron in the slip start to melt and become vitreous, producing a shiny surface. At 950°C, the temperature is reduced again but the atmosphere kept damp until it cools to about 800°C, by which time the slip has become an impervious glass film. At this point vents are reopened to allow enough oxygen in to clear the atmosphere and to be absorbed by the black iron oxide of the porous clay body and return it to its original state of red iron oxide. The surface under the vitrified slip, being protected from contact with the oxygen, remains black, which becomes lustrous as it cools. Much could go wrong, especially in the final stage: if too much air were let in, the whole vase turned red, while if the kiln were damped too much, the pot lost its shape.[82] Other problems were sagging rims and dents in the glazing incurred during the leather-hard stage. Even strong drafts within the kiln could deform objects. Accidents included explosions, typically caused by air bubbles or imperfect drying, which could destroy all the vessels in the kiln. For this reason, an especially finely decorated vase would sometimes occupy the kiln by itself.

A common variation is pre-firing. This involves putting the pottery through the first stage of firing, up to about 350°C, then removing it from the heat for the rest of the firing to be done later. Further smoothing could be done before the final firing, which could be much more rapid, as the first (slow) stage was already done. It would not reduce the total time each piece needed to be in the kiln, though it might have been a convenient way of managing production flows by enabling one and a half batches of material to be fired in a 12-hour working day. Pre-firing in Athens was probably irregular and only used for coarse ware.[83]

Complex though they are, few of these tasks require skills that cannot be quite readily acquired. Wheel turning and general laboring duties could have been undertaken by anyone available. Clay preparation and kiln management required experience that could be picked up from working with an expert for a few months. There is no doubt Athens's best potters were highly skilled in the originality and precision of their work, but most people can achieve a reasonable level of proficiency in most basic pottery shapes with a few months' concentrated effort. Even painting was open to anyone to learn, though success would have come to few. With low capital costs and clay and wood being available to all at (presumably) the same price, this was clearly an industry lacking barriers to entry, which has an important bearing on industry structure.

---

[82] Burford (1972) 72.
[83] Richter (1923) 44.

### 3.3.2 STAFFING NEEDS

Two variables determine the maximum efficient labor force of a pottery establishment: how many items its kilns can fire in a working day, and the number of people it takes to shape enough items to keep the kilns full. The initial analysis assumes that no pottery workshop operated more than one kiln at a time, which is consistent with most of the archaeological evidence. Later we will examine why this might well have been the case.

The number of pieces a typical kiln might take varies with the items to be fired, and physical remains suggest several types of items were involved in each kiln firing. Estimates vary widely; Richter suggests about 15 items, including a few small dishes, was typical, though this seems very low. Hasaki's reconstruction puts it at 150 medium-sized vessels.[84] It is possible to calculate the maximum number of pots of any given size that can be put through a kiln in a day if we know the volume it could hold, how long the cycle time is, and how many hours a day it operates. The archaeological evidence suggests a typical kiln had diameter of 1.5 meters or less, and many were quite a bit smaller. Height was between 1 and 1.5 meters. For simplicity we will consider batches of a single type of product, though this seems to have been unusual.[85] To determine how many items could fit on the floor of a kiln involves the mathematical problem of "circle-packing," which has no standard solutions, so the estimates that follow are derived from physical modeling, using the following methodology:

1. Identify different groups of common ceramic items with contrasting sizes and shapes (e.g., short and wide, tall and thin, medium, small ornaments, etc.).
2. Calculate the average dimensions of each group, based upon samples in a museum collection.[86] Increase to allow for shrinkage.
3. Draw a circle on paper to represent the floor of the kiln. Select coins and calculate their size relative to the size of the circle.
4. Establish for each coin size the number of such items that can fit together without overlapping in the area representing the floor of a kiln.
5. Check the reasonableness of the outcome by calculating the area of unoccupied space on the kiln floor in relation to theoretical total capacity. (The result is normally in the range of 30–50 percent).

---

[84] Hasaki (2012b) 260.
[85] Richter (1923) 31; based on Plate VIII, 19b in Antike Denkmäler I.
[86] The Classical Collection of the Ian Potter Museum at the University of Melbourne was used. All measurements are available on the Museum's website: http://www.art-museum.unimelb.edu.au/ (accessed 02/05/2010).

6. Extend the range of the model and interpolate other sizes by plotting observations on logarithmic graph paper, from which results for intermediate sizes can be read.

TABLE 3.1 **Kiln Capacity (Floor Area)**

| Shape | Sample Size | Average Size (cm) Height | Average Size (cm) Width | Maximum Items on Floor Trial/Interpolation | Maximum Items on Floor Theoretical Maximum | Implied Wastage (%) |
|---|---|---|---|---|---|---|
| Short, squat | 2 | 15.3 | 37.9 | 8 | 15.7 | 49 |
| Large, wide | 3 | 38.4 | 32.5 | 11 | 21.4 | 49 |
| Plate | 1 | 5.5 | 21.9 | 28 | 47.0 | 41 |
| Large, tall | 3 | 40.8 | 17.0 | 52 | 78.0 | 33 |
| Medium | 8 | 25.0 | 15.3 | 59 | 96.6 | 39 |
| Small | 12 | 10.8 | 13.2 | 74 | 128.5 | 42 |
| Ornament | 1 | 3.1 | 6.8 | 330 | 481.5 | 31 |
| Tall, thin | 10 | 16.7 | 6.1 | 400 | 596.5 | 33 |

The results of these calculations are summarized in Table 3.1. Where estimates are involved, the intention has been to err on the side of overstating the number of items that could be accommodated in one firing so as to identify the largest plausible labor force needed to fill the kiln.

An efficient workshop would employ enough people to keep the kiln working at capacity. If it takes about as much time to prepare the clay as to throw the pot, for each potter a well-specialized workshop will employ one clay preparer. There will also be someone to turn the wheel, making two assistants per potter. The firing process seems to have required two people. The maximum size of an efficient workshop is therefore three times the number of potters required to produce enough product to fill the kiln, plus two kiln operators and, in some cases, a painter or two. (If there was a manager/foreman, he would almost certainly be a potter as well.) The critical variable is how many potters it takes to fill the kiln.

For an experienced potter, throwing a vase or dish of a particular shape is a simple task and can be done in a matter of seconds. A contemporary potter can make a shaped vase in two and a half minutes and a plate in 30 seconds.[87] In January 2010, I observed a traditional potter in Rajasthan, using a single ball of clay and with a single hand-spin of a heavy wheel, form three ornamental vases of different shapes, each about 25 centimeters high and 15 in diameter, one with a separate lid, in just over two minutes. For our estimates

---

[87] For much of the detail on craft pottery production, I am indebted to Mr. Ian Gregory of Ansty in Dorset, England.

of how much of a potter's time it would take to fill the kiln we will conservatively assume a lower degree of skill, as shown in Table 3.2.

TABLE 3.2 Forming Labor Required to Fill a Kiln

| Items | Capacity | Minutes per Item | Minutes to Fill Kiln |
| --- | --- | --- | --- |
| Short, squat | 8 | 20 | 160 |
| Large, wide | 11 | 15 | 165 |
| Plate | 392[a] | 0.5 | 196 |
| Large, tall | 52 | 5 | 260 |
| Medium | 59 | 3 | 187 |
| Small | 74 | 2 | 148 |
| Ornament | 330 | 1 | 330 |
| Tall, thin | 400 | 1 | 400 |

[a] Plates might take up a little less than 10 cm each of vertical space, including separating slips, so it is assumed they might be stacked 14 high, allowing 392 on a floor that takes 28.

On this basis, a potter working alone with just a clay-preparer, a wheel-turner, and two furnace operatives could throw enough of most items in an eight-hour day to fill one kiln floor, implying a workforce of five or six at most. Molds probably made little difference, but might have accelerated the production of simple vases somewhat. Even if a workshop specialized in thin items such as perfume bottles and ornaments (for which there is no archaeological evidence), it would not need more than two potters or eight workers in total unless the items were stacked.

Some Byzantine cups and vases show traces of the supports they were fired on and rods that were inserted in the kiln sides to support a second level, and there is evidence of simpler stacking arrangements in late classical times.[88] Many furnace finds contain stacking rings, including several from the Athenian Agora.[89] They are made from clay, "small, crudely and quickly formed, and expendable."[90] Though most of these are from Roman or Byzantine periods, some have been identified as dating from archaic or classical times. A find at the Ceramicus of Metapontum of over 1,800 pieces of kiln supports excavated in 11 dumps and mended from many fragments includes a group going back to the sixth century, so they are likely to have been used in classical Athens as well.[91] They seem to have been used to prevent pots sticking to the kiln floor or touching each other when stacked.[92] Because the black

---

[88] Papanikola-Bakirtzi (1999) 222–23, figs. 1, 2; Naumann et al. (1975) figs. 4–7, pl. 56.1.
[89] Kalogeropoulou (1970) 430, figs. 3, 4.
[90] Papadopoulos (1992) 216.
[91] Cracolici (2003).
[92] Voigtländer (1986) 638–41.

glaze Athens used did not stick, the Athenians were able to stack some items, and some pots carry the marks of the feet of the vessel that was placed to be fired on top of them.[93] Plates, tiles, open bowls, and cups would probably have been stacked several high.[94] A kiln in the cemetery at Rhodes contained vases placed next to each other with alternate ones inverted—a strategy that seems aimed more at minimizing the risk of damage than saving floor space.[95] It seems likely that other vases and narrow-necked items were stacked rather haphazardly in a hemispheric pile, a few items high in the center and just one on the periphery.[96]

Here again we are looking to identify the largest possible labor requirement, so we will assume an improbably high degree of stacking, and assume open-topped cups and bowls were stacked up to near the top of the kiln, perhaps having been fired to the bisque stage first, while other small or medium-sized vases were piled in layers, possibly with some form of separators. Vases are typically higher than their base (Table 3.1) so there would be fewer of them lying on the floor than if they were standing up; they might have been stacked about three high on average (perhaps five or six at the peak of the hemisphere). The net effect of these considerations implies an average load of perhaps twice as many items as the single-level configuration (Table 3.3).

TABLE 3.3 **Stacked Kiln Capacity**

| Items | Maximum—One Level | Stacked—Number of Levels | Number Stacked | Time Required (minutes) |
|---|---|---|---|---|
| Short, squat | 8 | 2 | 16 | 320 |
| Large, wide | 11 | 2 | 22 | 330 |
| Plate | 28 | 14 | 392 | 196 |
| Large, tall | 52 | 2 | 104 | 520 |
| Medium | 59 | 2 | 108 | 324 |
| Small (cups) | 74 | 6 | 444 | 888 |
| Ornament | 330 | 3 | 990 | 990 |
| Tall, thin | 400 | 2 | 800 | 800 |

While most products remain well within the compass of a day's production for an experienced potter, we can see how a workshop that chose to concentrate its efforts in particular groups of smallish items that could be made rapidly could theoretically get enough material into a single firing to warrant employing two or three potters and up to a dozen workers in all. It is

---

[93] Papadopoulos (1992); (2003) 259.
[94] Hampe and Winter (1962).
[95] Papadopoulos (1992).
[96] Cook (1986) 64, figs. 2, 3.

unlikely, though, that any workshop did specialize exclusively in tall, thin objects which it stacked as high as possible. At the rate of production implied in Table 3.3, a single kiln could have supplied a tall, thin vase or ornament to every citizen's household in Athens every 40 days! Archaeological finds show that potteries usually fired small and large items together, an eminently sensible way of optimizing furnace capacity.[97] Nevertheless, we should allow for the possibility that some workshops might have specialized in producing large volumes of plates, cups, and small ornaments and were staffed accordingly, which would mean a workshop of just under a dozen workers to a firing, the largest most historians suspect.

The next question is whether a pottery might do more than one firing in a day. Cycle time for a kiln from its cold state to removing fired items was seven to eight hours; three to four hours made up the first stage, bringing items to bisque state at about 350°C and then taking the temperature to 800°C for oxidation. Reducing to 950°C took another two hours; soaking to 800°C and then cooling to 250°C before finished items could be removed took one to two hours each.

If a full cycle from cold takes over seven hours, it is doubtful that there was more than one full firing in a typical day. Even though items could be removed (with tongs) at 250°C, more cooling time would have to elapse before a new batch could be inserted for the slow heating first stage of the cycle. We do not hear of pottery shops working especially late hours, as would be necessary to achieve two full cycles. Small increments could be made by increasing hours, although flexibility is limited by the nature of the cycle so that increased capacity would have come in large lumps of hours rather than in small stages. Nor would it have fitted what we know of Athenian household arrangements. The master would have had to neglect family duties, and slaves are likely to have had other work to do in the household. Nevertheless, we should allow for the possibility that, at least in summer, workshops might get in two full firings between sunrise and sunset. More likely they would manage their production in such a way as to get more than one. For example, in a 12-hour day, they might do three slow prefirings to 350°C. On another day when the kiln had completed its first full cycle of the day and cooled to about 250°C, items that had been prefired to bisque state could be put in and brought very quickly through the rest of the stages, making for a cycle time of around four hours. In this way a single kiln might increase its requirement of potters and assistants by firing over a 12-hour working day. In such a case, the probable level of market demand for especially thin items makes it even less likely that many workshops could have maximized output in a way that would require more than three potters and a maximum complement of 12.

---

[97] Sparkes and Talcott (1970) 383–99.

Decoration meant some workshops might have had a larger complement at times. In one shop in the middle of the fourth century, decoration was divided between two painters and another had as many as nine in one period.[98] This was probably rare and temporary. In any event, fine painting took longer than the rest of the process, so it would not require much other labor to supply several painters. As shown in section 3.4 below, it would be surprising if many individual artists whose work had its own following would choose to work together for the same master for long periods.

For workshops that made a wider range of product and were not focused on maximizing kiln throughput by stacking small objects, the analysis suggests that not everyone in a full team might have been occupied all day. Most kiln requirements could be easily satisfied with less than one day's shaping and throwing, so the potter, the wheel-turner, and the clay-preparer might well have had other things to do. The master would have had to spend time with customers and suppliers. If the potter was a citizen, he might make enough simple objects to fill a kiln and still carry out his affairs in the assembly or law courts. Some potters may have decorated their products—not necessarily sophisticated, high-quality painting, but pretty, stylized patterning which could increase the appeal of certain items. Simple, repetitive painting and a little relief work might mean two or three potters could be fully engaged in providing enough product to keep the kiln at capacity. In this case, though, with the potters occupied in decorating, no labor is required to prepare clay or turn the wheel, and these two occupations would be idle while the potters were painting, so the workshop still would only need five or six people most of the time. Wheel-turners seem to have been young boys, probably the sons of slaves who would also have a life and other tasks to attend to outside the workshop and were probably there to learn the potter's trade.[99] One assumes the spare time of clay preparers was spent fetching clay and wood, helping break and rebuild the kiln, handling drying items, and, quite possibly, doing a bit of simple decorating themselves. It appears that even apart from seasonal considerations, much activity in a typical pottery would have been of a part-time or casual nature.[100] Thus citizen potters would have attended to civic duties, slaves would have been given other tasks, and even full-time working metics might have spent time on other ventures, including selling their wares.

### 3.3.3 JUSTIFYING A FULL-TIME TEAM

A full-time establishment of between five and 12, including an owner potter, was not a cheap enterprise. The cost of maintaining a slave and his family

---

[98] Webster (1972) 128, 23.
[99] Hasaki (2012b) 258–59.
[100] Arafat (1989) 326–47.

was between 300 and 400 *drachmae* a year, excluding the costs of buying and replacing the slaves in the first place.[101] If we allow for some expenditure on clay, wood, and paints, and an income for the owner and his family, it is likely a workshop of a dozen people needed annual revenues of at least 5,000 *drachmae* to be viable. If climatic conditions allowed the pottery to operate for nine months of the year, six days a week, which is very optimistic, this amounts to over 21 *drachmae* of product sold each working day. From epigraphy, *oxides* (small sauce dishes) and *oxybapha* (even smaller ones) seem to have sold at the rate of 7 per obol (42 per *drachma*) and about 15 per obol (90 per *drachma*) respectively.[102] At these prices, a pottery of 12 workers producing these small, simple, undecorated or black-glazed products would have had to produce around 900 of the former and 1,900 of the latter to cover its basic running costs. If the tiny items were densely stacked, this might have been physically possible in one firing, but only just, and there would have been quite a lot of damage in the stacking and firing process. Twelve workers would almost certainly require two kilns to be viable.

We also have secondhand prices for some large containers such as *phidaknai* (jugs—4 to 11 *drachmae* each) and a *kardopos* (kneading trough—two *drachmae*).[103] These data provide important confirmatory evidence that prices are consistent with relative kiln capacity usage, shown in Table 3.1.[104] With small vases selling at two or three to the obol, similar revenue would be derived from a kiln full of them as from one containing just one large *amphora*. Red figure *hydriae* are worth about 30 times as much as small vases and about half as much as a large *amphora*. In these cases the physical constraints of the kiln would have come into play. A kiln filled with these larger items required less shaping time than small ones did, and the break-even point for a five-slave enterprise was probably around 8 to 10 *drachmae* per working day, so this might also have been feasible.

However astutely a potter selected his product range, viability depended on being sure of selling all his output, and, in the case of household utility products, this is where the absence of competitive advantage and barriers to entry told. It was not possible for one workshop to achieve sustainably lower costs than its competitors. Everyone was applying the same processes on the same equipment; if one workshop was more efficient than another for a time, the second could always improve its operations to erase the difference. Clay, wood, and other inputs were readily available to all at the same price. Labor had an active market: slaves were bought and sold each day, and we know

---

[101] See Chapter 9.1.
[102] Johnston (2006) 22–23.
[103] Amyx (1958) 283.
[104] Amyx (1958) 279 attributes higher prices on these larger items to their "utility." It seems much more likely that it reflected their cost in kiln space.

from literature that the value of any special skills would be reflected in a premium price for the slave asset, negating any net benefit to the employing potter.[105] The products were hard to differentiate from one another, so household items would have been bought on price, whether by an intermediary reseller or by the end-user. Any modest premium for simply decorated items would have been quickly competed away. Other factors would conspire to keep commodity pottery prices low, including marginal pricing by workshops whose main business lay in fine ware but which used the extra kiln space for coarse ware, random entry into the market by individuals or by rich households finding extra work for slaves, and the fact that any large purchaser would have been able to elicit very competitive bids from would-be suppliers. Prices would tend to stabilize at a point where enough craftsmen found their net income worthwhile to be able to meet total demand; in other words, it was as much as they could earn in another way that was no less congenial (see Fig. 1.1 in Chapter 1).

The situation was made still less attractive by the fact that there was no limit to how many people could try to compete in the marketplace. Anyone could start a pottery at home alone or with a slave or two and their unit costs would not be much more than a fully staffed workshop. Most people have enough dexterity to make a reasonable shallow bowl with some instruction and a few hours of practice. With more work and modest aptitude, quite complex vase shapes are within the compass of many amateur potters. Almost all citizen households had at least one slave, and in many cases it would have been the slave who learned the technique first. Some slaves were probably bought for their skills in pottery. Clay preparation and fire management involve some expertise, but are teachable. Clay could be bought, a kiln constructed, and a simple wheel made or purchased. The output would be good enough for the household's own use and perhaps some neighbors could be persuaded to buy a few pieces, especially if you bought other products from them. You might set up a stall in the Agora for a day or two to try to move your wares or sell to an intermediary. The casual craftsman would never have been commissioned to make the vessels for Alcibiades's birthday party or entrusted with the containers for a major shipment of oil or wine, but could quickly learn enough to produce acceptable glazed or undecorated household utensils or tiles.

A particular source of instability would have been seasonal production by households with a large complement of slaves. Pottery has some important characteristics that make it suitable for irregular bursts of activity. It is seasonal (climate affects drying), it requires little fixed investment, different parts of the process can be separated in time, and the skills for making simple ceramics are not hard to acquire and retain. In short, it was a good way for a

---

[105] Compare Dem. 27.9 with Xen. *Vect.* 4.14–5. See also Chapter 9.5.

large household to keep its slaves occupied when they were not required for other activities. A large slave workforce that has just finished the harvest needs something to do; making pots brings in some income to the household and is not time-critical.[106] In fact, there is no real constraint on how many people might be assigned on a temporary basis to throwing pots, as they could build work-in-process inventory that could be fired by one or two specialist slaves long after the potters had gone off to do something else. Large but casual *ergasteria* of this sort would probably not have been common or continuous enough to have had a major impact on the dynamics of the industry, and, given the opportunistic nature of their engagement, would have been happy to take normal industry prices or rather less. It might nevertheless have been an important and rational way of balancing the activities and finances of wealthier households and would explain why there might sometimes have been more than a handful of people employed in potteries as some suggest. Of course, this made life harder still for the individual craftsman.

There were many reasons individuals might choose to become a potter, despite these challenges. Some citizens had no land and would have struggled to survive on military pay or irregular state handouts, even after Pericles introduced payment for attending court. Some might just have felt they had a real aptitude for shaping or painting. Metics might be looking for a more lucrative and less precarious existence than trade. Whatever the motivation, we should expect that at any given time a number of citizens, metics, and freed slaves would be entering the industry or trying to secure enough volume to expand their operation into a full-scale, full-time effort. With no ability to differentiate their output, they would have had to try to win business through underpricing competitors. Each time a new workshop added capacity and forced prices down in order to sell its products, existing competitors would have had to choose between giving up volume and meeting the lower price level. Some would decide to exit the business, resulting in a constant churn of marginal participants, as shown in Figure 3.1.

New capacity shifts the supply curve from S1 to S2. With no change in demand, volume will increase a little but price will fall from P1 to P2. Original prices (P1) were set by the forces of competition at the lowest level compatible with keeping enough suppliers in business to meet market demand. When overcapacity occurs, either from increased entry or from a competitor trying to grow, everyone will need to cut prices to win business. As incomes to all competitors at P1 are at the subsistence or minimum acceptable level anyway, whoever loses the sales is certain to retaliate, knowing that if they do not win

---

[106] Based on the numerical assumptions above, the daily income that a slave working at a potter's wheel could bring in to his master might be only an obol or two more than the cost of keeping him. This was less than a skilled slave might bring their master in some other activities but would have been a welcome offset to the cost of keeping a slave wanted for other purposes.

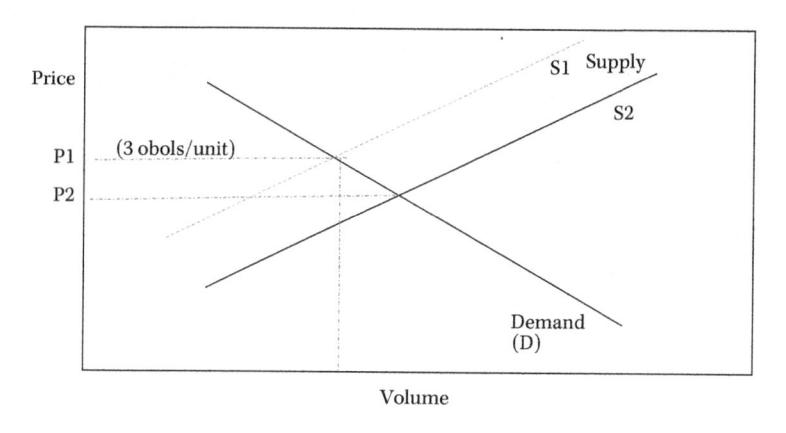

FIGURE 3.1. Impact of Entry and Exit on Industry Prices

the business back, they will be left with the same costs as before but less revenue. As competitors start to exit the industry, the supply curve moves back toward S1 and prices recover. After the price war, everyone will have made less than the usual not very attractive returns in the industry by the amount the war cost them. Where there is a prospect of making outstanding returns from expansion, then the cost of an initial price war might be worth paying, if it drives out competitors and keeps them out; in this case, the lack of potential for advantage or barriers to entry means there is no value in a price war, only short-term losses. Underneath the apparent stability of the industry, careers were made and broken, financial comfort came and went.

As many entrepreneurs in all ages have found, if you have no control over the price your products will fetch, a simple volume strategy will run into regular periods of unsatisfactory income and cannot achieve sustainable growth. Household utility pottery in classical Athens was a naturally fragmented industry fitted for small workshops operated by the owner with help from a slave or family member or two. This low-cost, low-risk operation could at least supply the household's own needs and might make a modest net income from occasional sales to third parties. To justify its costs and provide a return to the owner, a full-time workshop had to sell everything it made at reasonable prices, which meant it had to differentiate its output.

## 3.4 Bases for Differentiation

We have no information from original sources on how industry participants competed, but we do know of two segments, fine ware and shipping containers, which would have provided a basis for differentiating a workshop's output from its competitors', and we may speculate about a third—niche products.

### 3.4.1 FINE WARE

The most obvious way to differentiate pottery was as fine ware. Pots could be shaped or painted with a degree of skill and originality quite different from the commodity ware that any workshop could produce and could compete on the basis of individual potters' or painters' excellence in their craft. The best pieces were targeted at wealthy purchasers (individuals or the state), and there is no evidence of any stable and well-defined wholesale relationships.[107] Some of the best work was probably done on commission, the art commemorating a special event or person. Several names from the Athenian elite have been found on vases and some of the book scrolls, and the words shown as coming from figures' mouths might have been specially requested by customers. Votaries brought specially shaped *loutrophoroi, kylixes,* and *amphorae* for sanctuaries. Exports consisted of both new and secondhand product, presumably consignments made up by traders from a mixture of what was available in the secondhand market and orders placed with potters.[108] The letters SMI on many pieces that ended up in Etruria are probably the abbreviated name of a major exporter on that route. Etruria was an important market and one of very few for which Athenian potters made a special style of vase—the Nikosthenic *amphora*.[109]

Over and above individual commissions and sales of select product to enthusiastic customers, decorated vases were also purchased in large quantities by the state and by sanctuaries for public and religious buildings and events.[110] The quadrennial contract for 1300–1700 *amphorae* to celebrate the Panathenaic Games would have kept a workshop quite busy for the full four years. It would probably have fashioned smaller items that went into the kiln alongside the contracted vases to increase revenue, but as it seems to have been a competitive contract, this potential for additional income was probably reflected in the tender price.

It was not only the decoration that could make a vase precious. Innovative and complex shapes were also treasured. The skills were not always separate; many leading potters were also painters, like Nearchus, Tleson, and Exekias. Douris painted an *aryballos* he had signed as potter and continued as a painter for the next 30 years or more.[111] Euphronius, by contrast, had been a greater painter in 515 BCE, but after about 500, perhaps as a result of failing eyesight, he became a potter exclusively and worked with about 10 different painters over the next 30 years. Fine pottery seems to have been a tradition in some families. Ergotimus, maker of the François vase, a volute

---

[107] Cook (1960) 273–74; Webster (1972) 23; but see also Vickers and Gill (1994) 77–104 on the role of metals.
[108] Johnston (1979) 49; Sparkes (1991) 131.
[109] Webster (1972) 60.
[110] Webster (1972) 3.
[111] Webster (1973) 128.

*krater* painted by Cleitius, was followed as a cup-maker by his son and his grandson.[112] Tleson, one of the sons of the Nearchus who may have dedicated a large *kore*, made lip cups and band cups, while another son, Ergoteles (possibly related to Ergotimus) made lip cups. Amasis, a successful potter of the mid-sixth century, had a son Cleophrades who was also a potter, as were Bacchius and Cittus, sons of the Bacchius who owned a fourth-century workshop that concentrated on Panathenaic *amphorae* and black glaze.

Prices for decorated vases in the Ceramicus seem to have reflected the value placed on the techniques of pottery and painting as we would expect, though the evidence is not always clear. Many prices we have are for items whose description we do not know, such as an *aryster*, a *lepastis*, and a *lydion*, and it is quite likely that some names could be applied to several types of pots and that one type of pot might be referred to by several different names. It is not always possible to tell if a pot found carrying a marked price was originally glazed, decorated, or painted, but comparison of pairs of items with the same date and provenance shows that decorated vases sold for considerably more than black-glazed items.[113] A painted vase might typically fetch from three obols to as much as 18, while small black glazed bowls never seem to have fetched more than one and could be as cheap as 25 to the obol.[114] We also have lists of prices from auctions in the Athenian agora, though these are contentious on several grounds, including whether they were high enough to reflect labor costs.[115] Prices that can be matched to specific items are often for secondhand pots from which we can deduce little about the ex-workshop price, especially as we do not know their condition; *amphorae* going at seven to the obol probably had something seriously wrong with them![116] It has also been suggested they might have been asking prices rather than actual selling prices.[117] Ancient writers give us little help; the only prices to be found in surviving contemporary literature are one obol for a *lekythos* (Ar. *Ran.* 1236) and three *drachmae* for a *kados* (*Pax* 1202)—plausible but hard to relate to other prices. Fortunately, our conclusions are not sensitive to even wide variations in these numbers.

In the secondhand market, *hydrias* sold for more than column *kraters*, which in turn sold for more than bell *kraters*, which reflected the relative complexity and height of the pieces (with some variation according to the number of figures depicted). Painting requirements also affected prices: *kraters* carrying up-to-date red-figure designs fetched four to five obols each, while the much larger Panathenaic *amphorae* painted in the traditional technique sold

---

[112] Beazley (1956) 76/1.
[113] Johnston (1979) 32, 34; (2006) 22–23.
[114] Sparkes (1991) 130–31; Johnston (2006) 22.
[115] Jongkees (1951) 261; Johnston (1979) 35.
[116] Amyx (1958) 275–80.
[117] Webster (1972) 2–3.

for around three.[118] While these secondhand prices seem closely related to production costs, it is likely that, at least when new, some products would fetch a premium for a particular artist or potter's skill or reputation that reflected more than time spent. It would also be natural for this premium to erode or vanish altogether in the secondhand market.[119] Few Greeks at this time were collecting antiques!

Provided a workshop's skill was held in sufficient esteem among the buying public, the owner could be confident of selling as much fine ware as it could produce. It would not result in a large workforce, though. The limit to growth in high-quality vases is not the capacity of the kiln, but of the individual craftsmen whose work the market values. Even though a large fine ware piece would typically occupy a kiln by itself because of the risk of another vessel exploding, the amount of time a highly decorated vase would be kept in the kiln would probably be less than the time it took to paint. The amount of time needed for clay preparation, shaping, and throwing is also much less than the likely painting time. In theory, even if the skilled artist did nothing but decorate, one clay-preparer-cum-potter and one assistant to turn the wheel and help mind the fire could provide all the labor needed to turn out pots much faster than they could be painted. Adding only two or three to this complement would enable a pottery to service several painters—for instance, five painters would mean a workshop of not more than about 10 people.

The little we know about these artists suggests that they took full advantage of their celebrity and moved around the market to where the opportunity presented itself. Some had their own potteries, some were employed (though remaining mobile), and some seem to have freelanced. Most probably moved between these modes and acted as potters when there were no painting commissions to be filled. We have noted examples of vase painting showing as many as four people engaged in decorating vases, but we cannot be certain that even these are creating highly decorated product; they may just be adding simple finishing touches to a basic item.[120] We should not be surprised that craftsmen whose work commanded a strong clientele did not sign up in large numbers to work for one or two employers. The reason we know of no large workshops employing multiple noted painters together for a long period is a simple matter of labor market power.

---

[118] Amyx (1958) 278. Of course we cannot be certain how far price relativities in the secondhand market paralleled those of new products; the condition of pieces would have varied, there may have been a glut of certain products being sold by previous owners and a shortage of others, and the data cover several decades.

[119] Johnston (1979) 35.

[120] Cracolici ((2003) Appendix 1) found fingerprint evidence that decorated vases were often handled by several people, mainly in the dipping process (as many as five in some cases) but dipping takes very little time and we certainly cannot conclude that each potter also required several dippers. The

## 3.4.2 COARSE WARE

Much Athenian pottery production was undifferentiated, probably served by family businesses operating casually and seasonally to supplement their income as need and opportunity arose, but having no control over the prices they might receive. Nevertheless there were certain opportunities to differentiate coarse ware that are worth noting.

One opportunity was to be found in wholesale markets. By the early sixth century, the Phoenicians had standardized a wheel-turned, torpedo-shaped *amphora* that became the standard for sea transport.[121] Because these would have been purchased in large quantities by single customers, they offered an opportunity to establish a secure pattern of sales based upon reliability and service. An Athenian reseller of wine or olive oil who regularly needed a large number of reliably robust *amphorae* would be likely to place large orders with one or more individual workshops rather than trust to the vagaries of the spot market. A trader planning to fill spare cargo space with some new and secondhand ware might have regular supply agreements with one or more potteries. A number of marks on vases relate to specific traders or their customers, who would only have placed large, regular orders if they could be assured of reliable supply at acceptable quality.[122]

Similar considerations might have applied to resellers of utility ware in the domestic market. The cheapness of some small household items makes it improbable that all retail customers would be served directly from the workshop and more likely that long-term supply arrangements were agreed between potteries and resellers. A pottery with a strong relationship with a popular shop in the Agora would have had a secure outlet for its products, though it would have had to accept very low prices.[123] In general it seems likely that large, slightly discounted contracts for the supply of commodity product to shippers or resellers would have been an important part of a dedicated pottery's business, helping to reduce volume risk.

## 3.4.3 NICHE PRODUCTS

Although vase paintings and finds in wells indicate that most potteries (or close groups of potteries) made a wide range of different products, including both fine and coarse ware, some ceramic items are sufficiently different from others that they might have constituted specific niche segments served by specialists. Roof tiles are obvious examples, and builders might have placed

---

casual nature of the task would be consistent with items having multiple handlers, and it is likely dipping was done by people with other tasks as well; see also Hasaki (2007).

[121] Docter (1988–90) 143–88.

[122] Lang (1956); Johnston (1979) 49; Garlan (1999); Lawall (2001) 534–46; Eiring et al. (2004) 459–60.

[123] Lang (1956) 15.

regular large orders for them or had permanent arrangements with particular workshops, although some might have chosen to set up their own kilns on site. Hyperbolus, one of the politicians Aristophanes loved to tease, was associated with making or selling lamps (Ar. *Nub.* 607–26; *Pax* 681–92), which might have been a segment that an early mover could dominate, becoming known as *the* place for lamps. Buyers of small terracotta figurines might perceive some potteries to be more effective in adding the right mystical properties to their product than others. Tiny votive cups, small braziers for incense, and decorative tiles for floors or walls were other product areas where specialists might have been able to carve out a distinctive reputation for themselves. Some might have specialized in low-cost vases for weddings or funerals. Having a reputation for excellence in a very specific product line is a reliable way of achieving attractive margins.

### 3.4.4 A SECOND KILN?

Archaeological research on workshop size suggests that some workshops might have contained two kilns, which in turn might have required more than one potter to keep them supplied.[124] The question arises whether a commercial producer (i.e., a continuous full-time operator, not a family business operating seasonally) who had succeeded in differentiating his coarse ware output from one kiln to the point where he had established regular demand at a profitable margin might choose to expand by using two simultaneously. To calculate the size of the largest workforce he might possibly require, we will make three very bold and rather implausible assumptions:

1. Both kilns were used in parallel.
2. There was enough market demand to specialize in small items.
3. Every potter required two full-time people in support—a full-time wheel turner and a clay preparer—even though, as we have noted, they could hardly all be kept very busy and wheel turners were probably apprentices.

On this basis a workshop might require three potters, and adding two operators for each of two furnaces would imply a complement of just over a dozen. The reason this is unlikely lies not only in the implausibility of the assumptions but in the risk-reward equation the workshop owner would confront (Fig. 3.2).

Adding a kiln doubles the number of workers, but, even if the second kiln can be kept as busy as the first, there would be scarcely any reduction in unit costs, since nearly all input costs (slaves, wood, and clay) vary directly in line

---

[124] See above and Hasaki (2002) 231–33; (2006) 225; (2011) 26.

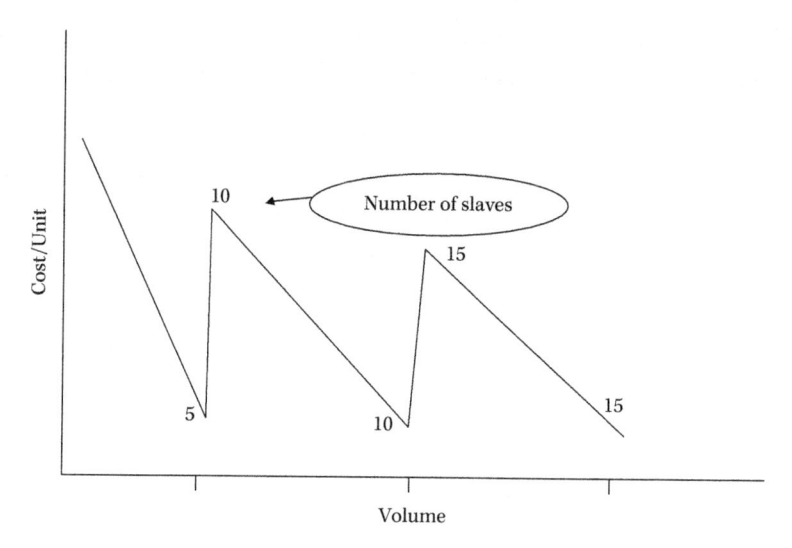

FIGURE 3.2. Pottery Costs and Volume

with output. There are no overheads to be shared except the manager-owner, who was often actively engaged in production, so that managing two workshops without doubling his own labor input might reduce overall productivity. If the second team cannot be kept busy, average cost per unit will increase. To keep these additional productive assets busy and unit costs as low as the first team, the workshop virtually has to double sales. As a result, increasing the number employed with anything less than an ironclad commitment from a customer to buy the whole of the second kiln's product at an agreed price would be highly risky, and one can understand if Athenians chose not to do it. It is possible that some potteries used their relationships with merchants or resellers or relied on their distinctive reputation with customers to operate a second kiln, but few large customers would want to commit for longer than necessary, as it would mean forgoing opportunities offered by cyclical low prices in the industry. In short, it made little sense for an owner to construct a permanent second kiln or acquire a second full team. In practice, when demand was good, a furnace could be readily built and the addition of a second potter might not need the full complement of support, especially if it was for only a limited period; two furnaces could probably be managed by three slaves rather than four on a short-term basis, and there seems to have been enough slack among clay preparers and wheel turners for some sharing to be possible there. And of course if we relax the extreme assumption about kiln content and accept the more likely scenario that the kilns were used for a range of items of medium or large size, including perhaps highly decorated vases fired by themselves, then a single team could have comfortably kept two kilns operating (Table 3.2).

One family offers an interesting case study. The two sons of Nearchus, Tleson and Ergoteles, both became potters but seem to have chosen to operate their own workshops. Had there been serious benefits accruing to a larger permanent operation, they would surely have combined forces to expand their father's workshop. On the basis of the second son's name, Webster suggests that Nearchus might have married the sister of another well-known potter, Ergotimus.[125] In this case the sons might have inherited a pottery each but still chose to keep them separate, seeing no advantage in achieving scale through combination.

In order to explore how demand and supply factors determined the structure of the pottery industry, we have defined product and market segments in static terms. As in many other industries, the apparent stability of the overall picture would have disguised considerable activity and change. New talents would emerge. Recognized stars would change workshops or set up on their own. Major scheduled contracts would be won or lost. Large orders from rich customers would arrive unpredictably, and perhaps sometimes on unusual terms. Traders and rich individuals might change allegiance. The best craftsmen would go blind or go off to war or die. Nevertheless we can be confident that the essential structure of the industry, split between small family businesses and full-scale workshops with specific competitive strengths, would remain unchanged until something happened to change the competitive dynamic.

## 3.5 Subsequent Changes in Competitive Dynamics and Industry Structure

The pottery industry evolved slowly, and it was not until the Industrial Revolution that major changes in technology altered the economics of competition in favor of large companies. After classical times, ceramics lost ground first to metals and later to glass in drinking vessels and utility ware, but population growth meant volumes were relatively steady.[126] Demand for manufacturing premises seems to have been healthy: a general purpose workshop in Delos could be rented for 41 *drachmae* a year in 279 BCE, 95 *drachmae* in 207, and 109 *drachmae* in 179.[127] Premises adapted for pottery cost more, even though workshops remained small—a master and a slave or two were still the most typical operators.[128]

---

[125] Webster (1972) 9.
[126] Treister (1996) 326–27.
[127] Vial (1984).
[128] Ehrenberg (1974); Walbank (1981) 162–63; 87.

Italy had been a good customer for Greek ceramic products, whether new, secondhand, or in the form of containers. It soon became an important producer. Etruscan pottery flourished long before Rome dominated Italy, and distinctive Italian *amphorae* were being made there in the fourth century BCE, by which time Apulia was home to painters whose work survives in sufficient quantities for them to be have been given identifiers, like The Painter of the Berlin Dancing Girl and The Boston Ready Painter.[129] Rome itself was a center for good-quality black-glazed ware in the third century, but the business withered, perhaps as a result of the disruptions of the Punic wars.[130] The best fine ware always came from outside Rome: Arretium was known for its tableware and Modena and Pollentia for their vases. Campania, too, became a major producer. Nine million black-glazed *amphorae* were exported from Naples to Gaul alone between 200 and 50 BCE; some of these utilitarian, mass-produced, unsigned items were shipped empty alongside others filled with wine and oil.[131] Third-century CE Egypt had a large domestic container industry.[132]

Under the Roman Empire, forming technology changed little except for the increasing use of molds. Potters still used the simple wheel. Kilns were better designed and larger; some might have catered to 30 to 40 people. There appear to be two types of reasons for this expansion in unit size compared with classical Athens. First, it became common for large olive- or wine-growing estates to have quite large potteries annexed to them. Some continued to purchase product from independent local craftsmen, but others exploited their own clay with their own slaves or leased the slaves and resources to an entrepreneur-foreman, usually to make containers for transporting and storing produce.[133] Rome's imports of Spanish oil alone required 55,000 *amphorae* a year, and total consumption of oil in the empire needed almost six million.[134] As a result, large potteries were often set up near olive groves in second-century Africa, Spain, and Italy to make containers for oil, and their size depended on the volume of exportable product under single ownership. Much of the coarse ware business came to be dominated by consular families who between them employed many thousands of slaves.[135] There were also large factories for bricks and common vases, often owned by emperors or members of the elite and with strong selling arrangements in place, probably based on monopoly control of the local clay resource. A boom in large-volume pottery production started in Augustus's

---

[129] Beazley (1947).
[130] Morel (2007) 485–510.
[131] Morel (1988) 305–56.
[132] Cockle (1981) 87–95.
[133] Green (1986); Kehoe (2007) 562–63.
[134] Garnsey and Saller (1987); Harris (2007).
[135] Louis (1927) 187.

time and seems to have lasted 200 or 300 years before the industry reverted to low-status independent potters working on rich people's farms.[136]

The second basis for large-scale operations appears to have been the export potential of the pots themselves. *Terra sigillata*, technically identical to Attic black glaze but fired to a red finish, was produced in large quantities in Italy under the Empire.[137] Workshops in Arretium employed perhaps 50 or 60 people working alongside each other.[138] Six hundred potters' workshops dating from the first century CE have been discovered at La Graufesenque in Southern France. The product was "Samian" red terracotta ware, patterned with *sigillae* (stamps).[139] It was not the fine ware that was made by specialists in late Iron Age France, but it was clearly in demand.[140] Designs were modeled on Arretium's and exported all over Western Europe, probably at the expense of Arretium's own potters.[141] Firing was at 1000°C in a wood-fired kiln that took up to 40,000 vases at a time and was probably only used every two to three weeks. Graffiti on the ware show potters' names and the order in which items went into the kiln. Vases were stacked on floors supported on columns above the fire, according to a space-saving formula: the bottom of the kiln held plates and other small, flattish items like *canastri, catini, mortari*, and *pannai*; the middle level held larger bowls and pots, including *licusai, inbratori, vinari, atramentari*, and *catili*, and the third and top level was filled with little vases and *acitabili*. There seems to have been some specialization among potters but many made more than one type. What does seem clear is that there was a ready market for their product at prices they were content with. Demand in classical Athens had been fragmented, embracing multiple types of pots in a relatively small market so that no particular line lent itself to the economies of permanent large-batch production. Pots seem to have been standardized internationally (it is not possible for a layperson to tell if a simple pot from Herculaneum was thrown in Italy, France, or Turkey[142]), so big export markets provided an opportunity to reduce costs by using molds. Potters probably shared the tasks of selling and monetary exchange (it would have been very inefficient not to) and they certainly shared kilns. They did not, it appears, see any benefit in combining ownership or management of their own workshops. Potters were free artisans, and they each tended to take their unfired work to two or three different kilns in lots of 5, 10, or 20 items. There is no evidence of cooperative groupings or of competition between furnaces.

---

[136] Alcock (2007) 682.
[137] Jackson and Greene (2008) 511.
[138] Pucci (1973) 311–15.
[139] Marichal (1988).
[140] Andrews (1997) 57–75.
[141] Favoretto (2010).
[142] This was well demonstrated at the *Life and Death in Pompeii and Herculaneum* exhibition at the British Museum 03/28/13 to 09/29/13; visited 07/17/13.

A kiln was a service business and did not take ownership of the products it fired; it was probably run by a potter. The efficient size of one part of the production chain had altered but the industry dynamics had not; despite the captive market, kiln owners do not seem to have expanded their businesses; we know of no major pottery entrepreneurs in Roman times any more than we do in classical Athens.

Not much changed in early China either. Potters had been active in Jingdezhen, China, since the second millennium BCE, and by the time of the Han Dynasty (second century BCE to third century CE) they had established a reputation for glazed blue pottery. In the fourth century a Jingdezhen craftsman named Zhao Kai was known as the "the master of porcelain making." It was in truth some 500 years later under the Tang Dynasty that the earliest forms of blue and white porcelain were produced, and techniques were continuously refined through the Middle Ages. Kaolin clay was brought into use around 1300 CE. Fame and export markets grew, and the industry's achievements and techniques were recorded by learned scribes like Jiang Qi and Song Yingxing. Even so, technology remained fairly basic. Jingdezhen's porcelain-firing kiln combined the dragon-shaped kiln popular in the south of China and the U-shaped kiln of the north into an egg shape. Improved techniques of form-making, press mold forming, trimming, and glazing were introduced, and while the perfection and luster of finished items improved with innovative exploitation of the chemistry of clay, the basic production system did not, and production units remained small. Describing the process of "kneading clay, fashioning vessels, applying under glazes," the Jingdezhen government's website notes that today's techniques are the same as those recorded in the Song, Yuan, and Ming Dynasties (960–1694 CE).[143] One might add "and in classical Athens."

Technology and industry structure in Europe also evolved slowly. It was not until the 11th century that high-temperature firing was developed in the Ruhr Valley and the 16th century before a higher bench and a flywheel were introduced to improve the operation of the wheel.[144] From the 13th to the 16th centuries, potters in the Saintonge area of France were exporting their fine wares all over Britain and northern Europe. In the 17th century a switch to high-quality coarse ware brought a major volume increase, but the principal production unit remained the household, moving resources in and out of pottery according to prices and opportunity costs and negotiating for space with kiln owners as needed.[145] Outside Europe, China, and Japan, even more primitive technology prevailed. All over the world, much pottery remains a craft industry today, a largely rural activity serving local and tourist markets with

---

[143] http://eng.jdz.gov.cn/Brief/introduction/201112/t20111201_122542.htm; accessed 03/02/2013.
[144] Bryant (1994).
[145] Musgrave (1997) 89.

utility or roughly decorated ware, though the large-scale enterprises that have appeared since the Industrial Revolution now account for the vast bulk of global production. It was only in the 20th century that one could say with any confidence that the greater part of ceramic production was industrial, and it was Josiah Wedgwood and his competitors in the 18th century who triggered this radical transformation of the industry. The reason large manufacturers have come to be the dominant commercial form in more recent times lies in changes to production processes and in the nature of market demand that enabled competitive advantage in a way that ancient technology did not. It is informative to explore what made this industrialization possible.

The history of pottery in England was unremarkable before the 18th century. A study of large-scale imports around Southampton in medieval times indicates that a wide variety of items came to the port but were not distributed inland—exactly as one would expect: consumers near a small port purchased imports to make up for the narrowness of the range available locally.[146] Domestic English pottery went through several changes between the 14th and 17th centuries. The highly decorated styles of the late Middle Ages were abandoned in favor of simple functionality and plain incised lines.[147] Before long the superior robustness and glaze of ceramics from the Rhineland attracted demand in England, whose potters began to copy German techniques and multiplicity of shapes while also introducing new product lines such as majolica floor tiles and ceramic stoves. By the end of the 15th century, the climate was receptive to new goods, culture, and lifestyle, and the rewards for innovation increased as consumer appetites and spending power grew.[148] This increased demand did not, however, lead to much change in industry structures at first; even when making luxury goods for the rich, production remained within the domestic system until new technology changed production economics and created the self-reinforcing shift toward urban employment.[149]

A vital element in the development of the industry in the 18th century was the technology of heat control.[150] By separating the firing floor from the hovel, using under-floor flues and pyromatic beads for measuring heat, it was possible to operate much larger ovens than traditional kilns. This made expansion possible without the cost penalties and management complexity

---

[146] Brown (1997) 97–104.

[147] Hundsbichler (1986) 210–14; Dyer (1989) 204–5; Gaimster and Nenk (1997) 173–77.

[148] Gaimster (1997) 188; De Vries (2008). Prior to the factory system, growth in disposable income tended to derive from increased hours worked by the family rather than from increased wage rates, which remained low (Becker (1965); Thirsk (1978; 173–75)).

[149] Thirsk (1978) 148–70.

[150] For a useful summary of technological developments in ceramics in the time of Sir Josiah Wedgwood, see Stoke-on-Trent City Council website: www.stoke.gov.uk/ccm/museums/museum/2006/gladstone-pottery-museum/inf. Accessed 9/8/2007.

of multiple small kilns. It was accompanied by a number of innovations that reduced processing costs or increased productivity through speeding up the process. These included a string-controlled throwing wheel, a coal-fired slip kiln instead of drying in the sun, suspending lead oxides in a fluid so as to allow dipping instead of the application of powder, and casting glazing slips before applying them.[151] Power from windmills and watermills to grind flint for glazes was in general use in the early 18th century, soon to be replaced by steam pumping engines that reduced labor input and greatly facilitated the task of manipulating new, heavier wheels.[152] Wedgwood sought the advice of the best scientists of his time and was a respected scientist himself, inventing a pyrometer and being elected to the Royal Society in 1783.[153] He laid out his factory to make production flows as efficient as possible and reduced costs still further through his successful campaign for and investment in the Grand Trunk Canal, which could deliver raw material for a penny and a half per ton, compared with 10 pence for horse transport. His factory used flock to make white glazed stoneware inexpensively and plaster of Paris molding to make more elaborate shapes. With the techniques he mastered, he could copy stunningly complex pieces like the Portland Vase, yet he also found new low-cost ways to achieve high-quality decoration on his famous jasper ware and cream ware by using engraved copperplates.[154] As a result he was able to supply high-quality product at prices far lower than had been possible before, generating demand among the moderately well-off that he and a handful of others were best placed to supply. By using the latest technology, his costs would be lower than others in the industry. Because a big factory with sophisticated equipment has a high proportion of fixed costs, the more he grew his sales, the lower his costs became. At the prevailing price level, set by the economics of low-technology production, he and his large competitors could make excellent profits (Fig. 3.3).

While competitors were catching up, not only was Wedgwood able to generate cash to keep investing in growth, which lowered marketing costs for each unit of sales, but his products were securing a brand following that enabled higher prices. He was also building barriers to entry. Newcomers as well as current competitors had to match his capital investment and fight for market share against an established and reputable brand. Thanks to new processing technology, expansion had become an extremely attractive proposition for enterprises with the resources to afford a high level of technical capability such as Wedgwood and a few other majors of the time, including

---

[151] Wedgwood learned the use of lead oxides from Spode, who introduced it in 1779, four years before Wedgwood did.
[152] Rempel (2006).
[153] Mokyr (2009) 133.
[154] Engraved copper plates were first used by John Sadler in 1750.

Spode, Crown Derby, Royal Worcester, and Royal Doulton. Technology had altered the economics of the business, providing significant competitive advantage to those who invested in productivity and product development. Those who could achieve an advantaged position made very good returns, and the more they grew, the better their returns—an outcome that was denied to their Athenian predecessors by the economics of the technology they used.

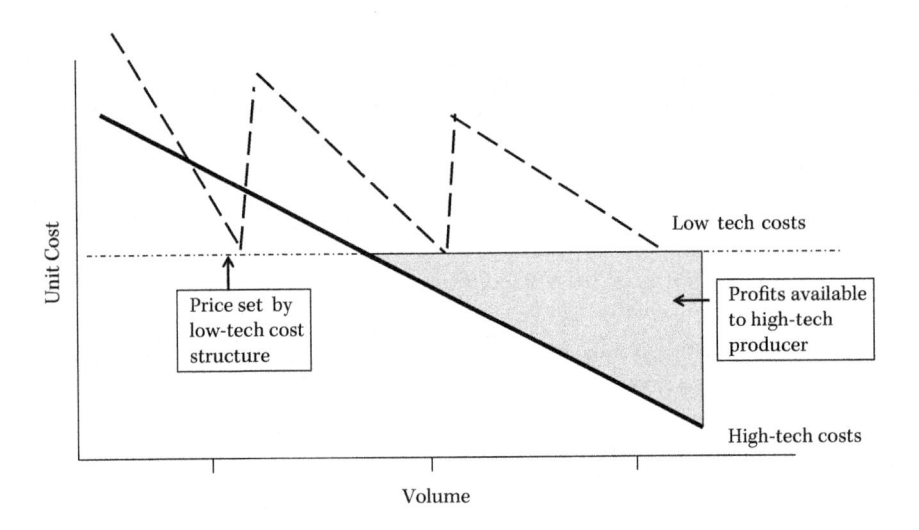

FIGURE 3.3. New Pottery Costs and Volume

## 3.6 Summary

This chapter has looked at pottery in all the stages of industry evolution. Table 3.4 shows how competitive forces produced different economic opportunities at different times (note that—for this instance only—the vertical axis has reverted to "Potential for Competitive Advantage" rather than for differentiation alone, to embrace later changes and their impact on relative cost position).

Before the Industrial Revolution, much pottery was a craft business, as it remains today in the artisan segment. The best you could do was to find a reliable market that would take all the product your kiln could produce, and staff up accordingly. Differentiation of product or reliability was the difference between subsistence-level or casual income for the lone operator and the ability to generate a consistent surplus from the work of five or more people. It was only when new markets emerged and the Industrial Revolution added the potential for cost advantages through scale and technology to the potential

TABLE 3.4  **Pottery Industry Structure**

|  |  | Barriers to Entry | |
| --- | --- | --- | --- |
|  |  | Yes | No |
| Potential for Competitive Advantage | Yes | **Differentiated industry:** Contracted containers  Specialist product niches? (Tiles, lamps, ornaments...)  **Roman Empire/Medieval France:** Cooperative arrangements for major export markets  **Industrial revolution:** Large corporations differentiated by scale, high-technology as well as mass market product design. | **Differentiated craft:** Complex shapes  Highly decorated ware |
|  | No | **Undifferentiated industry:** **Roman Empire:** Integrated production on large agricultural estates | **Undifferentiated craft:** Uncontracted commodity pottery (the "citizen craftsman") |

for differentiation that the optimal size of a pottery facility changed, with the result that the great majority of ceramics today comes from large enterprises marketing their own designs rather than from craft shops.

The limited number of applications of ceramics made for a relatively narrow set of possibilities for competitive advantage and a clear path to change. The next chapter examines metals, the multiple forms and applications of which make for much more diverse competitive sets.

# 4 }

# Mining, Metals, and Armor

Metalwork was probably a more important part of the ancient economy than ceramics.[1] Apart from some use in reinforcement for very large buildings, metals were used principally for making tools, arms, statues, and coins, together with some furniture and decorative art.[2] As we saw in Chapter 2, the economics of specialized metalwork led ancient Greek metalworkers to be among the earliest trades to separate from the *oikos*. As supply and demand in different segments of metal processing evolved, the industry began to take a multiplicity of forms and to offer a variety of opportunities for employment and income. We found large establishments, organized by the state or privately owned; smaller, local, often seasonal, village workshops; craftsmen moving between new construction projects; and the traditional sole craft expert.[3] In classical Athens we find lone craftsmen, large factories, and a wide range of simple products likely to have been made by generalists, perhaps casual smiths. This chapter considers the evidence relating to supply and demand in each segment and suggests the likely bases of competition and their impact on industry structure. It identifies the competitive advantages and barriers to entry that enabled firms in some segments to grow, and discriminates between highly skilled work and simpler operations. Segments considered are: mining, ore processing, general metalwork, jewelry and ornaments, coinage, bronze armor, shields, and knives.[4]

## 4.1 Mining

Mines played a vital part in the success, perhaps the very existence, of classical Athens, and the industry provides a well-documented instance of how

---

[1] Snodgrass (1980) 128; Vickers and Gill (1994) 33–54.
[2] Notable architectural examples are the lintels of the Propylaea, which were supported by iron girders, and iron clamps under the architraves in the temple of Olympian Zeus at Acragas.
[3] Raber (1987) 297–313.
[4] Athenian shields were made chiefly of wood, but are addressed here alongside other martial equipment. Monumental bronze sculpture is addressed in Chapter 7.2.

Athenians liked to invest their capital in productive enterprise. The mines near the port of Laurium were exceptionally large and deep, and their ores had a remarkably high silver content.[5] Their output underpinned the Athenian economy, providing the material of coinage, ingots to be processed and sold, and income to the state treasury from leases and taxes. "It is far more true that the battle of Salamis was won in the mines of Laurium than that the battle of Waterloo was won on the playing fields of Eton."[6] It also represented easily the largest production activity in classical Athens, using complex material-processing technologies on an "industrial" scale.[7] Archaeologists have found mine galleries, facilities for ore processing, and smelting workshops, all testifying to the size of the operation.[8]

The mines at Laurium were probably opened in around 520 BCE or a little earlier. It has been estimated that by the time of the decision to spend some of the proceeds on building Themistocles's "wooden walls" against Persia, the city's reserves included 100 talents (about 2.5 tons) of silver, which might have represented around one year's income from the mines.[9] We do not know what share of mining output the city received, but the total production must have been much larger than this and it must have taken several decades to reach this rate of extraction. Laurium might have produced as much as 20 tons of silver per annum in the fifth century and the early part of the fourth.[10] Recent numismatic studies suggest that the mines were closed only briefly after each of the Persian and Peloponnesian Wars.[11] More than 20,000 slaves absconded from Laurium during the Peloponnesian War between 413 and 409 BCE (Thuc. 6.97.7). We do not know how many actually worked underground, but there can be little doubt mining was the reason they were there.

Although galleries, roof-propping, and ventilation techniques date back to the Bronze Age, much mining in Greece was open cast with short adits, the rest being in narrow shaft mines that were not very deep and could be worked with chisels and other simple tools such as iron picks and hammers.[12] Prospecting was simple, relying on surface evidence and a "follow your lode" approach.[13] Laurium presented a different challenge: by 350 BCE there were

---

[5] Rihll (2001) 120; 134.
[6] Bromehead (1945) 89.
[7] Rihll (2001) 115; Rihll and Tucker (2002) 284.
[8] Treister (1996) 185–88.
[9] Picard (2001) 5–6. Some scholars have made the case for this or a higher number (e.g., Rihll and Tucker (2002) 277–78; Samons (2000) 204 n.153), but mining income might not have been as central to the state's finances as is sometimes supposed. It is not mentioned in Pericles's summary of state revenues (Thuc. 2.13) or in Xenophon's *Poroi* (except to introduce the idea of renting out public slaves) and comes in about the middle of the list of state income sources in Ar. *Vesp.* 658–59.
[10] Conophagos (1980) 341–54; Isager and Hansen (1975) 44–45.
[11] Kroll (2011b) 17–18; contrast Mussche et al. (1975). It is possible that some of the coinage made shortly after each war was reminted, but unlikely that silver mining stopped for long.
[12] Davies (1935) 20, 35–36; Forbes (1964–72) VII. 193–94; Healey (1978) 100.
[13] Forbes (1964–72) VII.146.

2,000 shafts, some as deep as 110 meters, requiring airshafts and galleries. Initially, pillars of good ore were left standing as roof supports and reinforced by packing excavated holes with dross; as exploitation progressed, timber props for the shafts helped cause the deforestation of Attica.[14]

Mining is a well-documented example of how Athenians chose to invest their money. In the fifth and fourth centuries, fixed-term mining leases were sold by the *Poletai* in the presence of the Council of 500.[15] It seems that a decline in mining productivity in the second part of the fourth century led the state to encourage more investment by selling more mining leases.[16] At its peak in the 340s, it was selling around 150 new three-to-seven-year mine leases each year, but the number declined as fewer people found the investment attractive.[17] It appears that mining leases were sold for periods of up to 10 years and priced according to their term at five *drachmae* per *prytany* (10th of a year), with mines that had been worked for a long time going for less.[18] Operators bore all the costs and seem to have owned the silver, though it was subject to state taxes.[19] At the end of the lease, whether it had been successful or otherwise, the asset expired, which is presumably why they were not included in an assessment of assets for *antidosis* (Dem. 52.17–19).[20] Some lessees mined their own ores, using their own slaves or leased ones. Miners would judge by eye whether their ores were rich enough in lead (and hence silver) to bring to the surface and whether they needed to be washed or could be smashed and sent straight for smelting.[21] There was no limit to how many claims an individual might buy.

From early times, Attica's rich and powerful had been involved in mining. Direct or indirect mining interests have been attributed to the sixth-century tyrant Peisistratus and leading politicians and generals including Themistocles, Miltiades, Cimon, Thucydides, Nicias, and Alcibiades.[22] Records for the years 343/42 and 333/32 BCE show that 19 percent of mine leases were purchased by the "elite," who constituted less than 10 percent of the population.[23] Unsurprisingly, the elite were more likely to be involved in more than two mining leases, while the less prominent ("prosopographic nonentities") often had just one or two. The data suggest that diversified or multiple investments formed quite a common strategy among the wealthy,

---

[14] Rihll (2001) 116–17.
[15] Rihll and Tucker (2002) 284.
[16] Kroll (2011b) 17.
[17] Hopper (1953); (1968); for the apparent decline in mine output in the second half of the fourth century, see Flament (2010); Kroll (2013).
[18] Shipton (1998) 58–63.
[19] Lambert (1997) 258.
[20] Hopper (1953) 205.
[21] Forbes (1964–72) VIII.67; Rihll (2001) 117–18.
[22] Rihll and Tucker (2002) 284–85.
[23] Shipton (2001) 133.

with several owning more than one claim and some involved in land leasing as well. The sparse records offer no strong evidence of any family tradition in mining investment, with the notable exception of Pheidippus of Pithos, whose name appears most frequently in the mine leases. He had a son who followed his mining interests and became a trierarch himself. The infrequency of repeat investments and the absence of mining dynasties can be seen to suggest that mining was not considered exceptionally profitable, which is confirmed by recent attempts to model the economics of ancient mining.[24] Even the most successful might lose everything in later ventures (Dem. 52.3).

Nevertheless we have several examples of successful mining entrepreneurs. Two of the richest men in Athens, Hipponicus at the end of the fourth century (Xen. *Vect.* 4.14) and the metic Callaeschrus in the middle of the third (Dem. 21.157), apparently owed their wealth to mining.[25] Other miners to do exceptionally well were Epicrates, whose mining made 300 talents (Hyp. 4.35), and Diphilus, whose pile of 160 talents was distributed to the people by Lycurgus (Plut. *Mor.* 843D). Demosthenes (53.22) tells how two brothers inherited 45 *mina* each, which, lent at interest, would have brought in the average wage. They chose to invest in mining instead.

Importantly from the point of view of industry structure, the size of investment had no impact on likely success. There was no advantage in being able to buy larger blocks, and an investor who could afford just one small claim would be as likely to get a good return on it proportionately as the largest mining magnate. The individual underground worker was the effective operating unit, whether working for himself or as part of a large team. Slave costs (purchase or lease, plus maintenance) were the same for all. They all used the same process and the same tools. The only technical innovations at Laurium, the waste-removal system and the beneficiation of silver ore through washing, were available to all operators through third parties.[26] Even in the third contract, when the shafts were deep and extraction harder, there would be no advantage from operating in large teams and no reason why a team of 10 miners would extract proportionately more silver than a team of one or two. As a result, the economics of mining were independent of firm size; success depended on the quality and accessibility of the ore grade, and there is no evidence that Athenians attempted any sophisticated geological analysis before bidding for claims—if they had, surely the state, as vendor, would have done more to price different blocks according to their expected productivity. An investor's only consideration would have been the relative attractiveness of the likely outcome from buying a claim compared with other investment

---

[24] Osborne (1985) 115; Davis (2014) 270–71.
[25] Rihll and Tucker (2002) 286.
[26] White (1984) 34; Christesen (2003) 41; see next section.

options—a calculation in which mining started to lose its relative appeal as more seams were exploited after the middle of the fourth century.

These are the economic reasons why for most of human history, the scale of individual mining operations has reflected political decisions rather than economic ones. The Romans and later European civilizations made few improvements to mining technology other than using a waterwheel or Archimedes's screw to operate below the water table—the challenge that led to the first modern application of the steam engine. Ventilation remained poor, galleries narrow, and the work hard.[27] When large mines under single ownership emerged, they belonged to temporal rulers rather than the major players in a competitive industry. California, Victoria, and the Transvaal were all initially exploited by lone adventurers. It is only recently that advances in exploration technology, economies of scale in processing, and the increased importance of bilateral negotiations in market access and commodity pricing have rewarded larger enterprises and encouraged industry consolidation.

When mining booms, so does the mining services industry. A number of Athenians derived income from contract labor. According to Xenophon (*Vect.* 4.5), "everyone" involved in the mining industries employed as many slaves as they could and said they needed more. Nicias was a large employer of mining slaves for lease to claim-holders—so many that his slave foreman received a talent a year.[28] A large mining entrepreneur, Sosias, had sufficient claims to want to hire a thousand slaves from him. Philemonides had 300 slaves in the mines and Hipponicus 600 (*Vect.* 4.14–15). These numbers are not supported by anything we can find in the Attic orators or the *Stelae*, but even if they are very much exaggerated, they still suggest there was considerable income to be derived from buying slaves in bulk and contracting them out to mine lessees.

The impressive scale of mining infrastructure makes it tempting to conclude that it was an activity in which only those with substantial resources could participate. We have seen that this is not the case for the extractive activity, either as owner or miner. The next section shows that the existence of large companies in further processing cannot be explained simply by the level of investment required or economies of scale either.

## 4.2 Ore Processing

In the Bronze Age, silver-bearing ores were smelted and fabricated from a raw state and manufacturers were only able to smelt ores that contained a

---

[27] Louis (1927) 204.

[28] But see Chapter 9.1 on the *apophora*. Unusually, this slave-foreman seems to have been an employee.

high level of argentiferous galena (silver) or cerussite (lead). The introduction of elementary processing technology, probably soon after 600 BCE, changed the nature of the silver-mining industry.[29] Ores are first ground on large mortar stones, then hammered into chips and any obvious dross disposed of. The crushed ore is washed in a basin called a *katharisterion*, so that the argentiferous lead sinks and the dross floats away, leaving galena and cerussite; the material is reduced by about 60 percent by weight in the process. The sludge is dried, pressed into pellets and sent for smelting. This purification process enabled smiths to work with the product of poorer deposits and greatly increased the number of claims out of which people could earn a living. Even so, Athenian technology was relatively crude; slagheaps (*scoria*) were exploited in Roman times with better beneficiation techniques (Strabo 9.1.23), and when the mines were reopened in 1864 the remaining dross still yielded 81.5 ounces of silver per ton![30]

Processing was a simple operation, requiring just a few strong but not very expert slaves to grind and wash the ore and prepare it for smelting. Because transporting unprocessed ore is costly relative to the product's value, ores were processed as close as possible to the mines.[31] Some lessees would have used their own slaves to process their ores, or, in some cases, might have done it themselves. Others chose to outsource this activity for a fee, called an *apergastra*. Laurium had little water, so at first many workshops were set up close together in the Bertsekas valley with their own washeries, and probably at Thorikos and Demoliaki as well. Once wells were dug to enable workshops to be nearer to major mining sites, each major site set up its own; miners operating in new areas must have built them or made arrangements with processing entrepreneurs to invest alongside them. Complete workshops have been excavated, including a large one near the theater at Thorikos, which contained crushing tables, grinding mills, storage buildings, dumps, residential quarters, and underground cisterns for waste water.[32] It seems to have been an administrative center and home to mining slaves and their families, who might have worked on local farms. Other sites seem to have been just for processing.

Smelting appears to have taken place at some of these sites. The smelting of *silver* is a complex business requiring specialized skills, as it involves separation of components as well as modifying the ore's properties.[33] It is quite likely that when Laurium started being mined in earnest, processing expertise was imported from areas whose mines were close to exhaustion.[34]

---

[29] Rihll (2001) 118; Rihll and Tucker (2002) 280.
[30] White (1917).
[31] Kakovoyiannis (2001).
[32] Conophagos (1980) 375–89; Jones (1982) 179; Jones (1984–85) 120, Fig. 34; Treister (1996) 185.
[33] Rihll (2001) 119–21; Rihll and Tucker (2002) 276–79.
[34] Davis (2014) 262.

The lead reduction process involves two steps: a fusion of the ore material with lead in a carbon-rich environment, followed by the separation of silver from the lead in an oxygen-rich environment. Cerussite was smelted directly, but galena needed cooking with charcoal before smelting. Furnaces took the ores to 800°C, at which point lead oxide reduces to metallic lead, so that silver-bearing stannum would flow out through a hole near the furnace top and the slag could be skimmed off. There followed the more difficult process of cupellation, which reduces the stannum to lead oxide and then to ash, leaving behind a bubble of silver. Excavated workshops around Laurium contain five or more adjacent smelting furnaces, but no cupellation furnaces have been found. They are likely to have consisted of holes in the ground lined with a refractory material such as bone ash, and as such were not very durable. Fanned by bellows, the temperature in these pits had to exceed 800°C to stop lead oxide forming and aborting the process, but remain below 950°C, or too much silver would be burnt off.

Processing could be a large business. We know one processor, Pantainetus, employed 30 slaves (Dem. 37.4), though they might not have all been in the same workshop. The assets of Timarchus's father, Arizelos of Sphettos, included two workshops (*Aeschin.* 1.101).[35] Diotimus was heavily involved in mining, both as registrant and lessee, and owned workshops around Laurium and Thrasymos; together these investments were enough to enable him to afford a trierarchy, guarantee ships for Chalcis in 340 BCE, and donate a large number of shields after the battle of Chaironea, for which he was crowned by the city.[36] Processing operations were consistently profitable enough to be mortgaged (IG II/III² 7593). Pantainetus's workshop and 30 slaves were mortgaged twice and eventually sold for just over 20,000 *drachmae* (Dem. 37.10–13; 31), a price per slave almost double that of Demosthenes's own bed- and knife-makers (Dem. 27.9). It is unlikely that the slaves themselves were much more skilled than Demosthenes's, so the price might well reflect a premium for the defensible nature of the income stream. We must ask of what this defensibility consisted. What was it that enabled workshop operators to build large and profitable workshops without being challenged by competitors or new entrants?

Rihll argues that processing was by its nature a large-scale operation, requiring significant investment and offering economies of scale, making it hard or impossible for a small operator to compete effectively.[37] She is surely right in concluding that large businesses were protected by barriers to entry, but we may question her explanation. Scale in itself cannot provide a barrier to entry unless participation requires a very large upfront investment. There

---

[35] Davies (2004) 43.
[36] Davies (1971) 163–65.
[37] Rihll (2001) 115; Rihll and Tucker (2002) 284.

is no inherent reason why a new entrant could not start with one basin and one furnace; it would be enough to carry out all the operations and would only be a problem if scale economies meant that the small new entrant's unit costs were much higher than the larger incumbent's. This cannot have been the case. Investment in facilities appears significant by the standards of the time, but only amounts to using slave labor to construct simple facilities from raw materials, most of which were commonly available (plaster, cement, bone ash, iron, and charcoal, for instance) or could be purchased from local craftsmen (bellows, containers, ropes).[38] Someone who could afford a mining lease could certainly afford the materials, and if he could afford a slave to do the processing, the slave could also construct the facilities. In either case they would cost the same amount in exchange or slave labor for all sizes of competitors. If the facilities were durable, the amount of slave and material time involved in building them (depreciation cost) would have quickly become trivial in relation to operating labor, and if they were not, they would be a variable cost of production. In either case the direct cost per unit of throughput would be the same for all. Nor is it accurate to suggest the large incumbent would enjoy economies of scale. These are properly defined as reductions in unit costs resulting from spreading fixed (indirect) costs between more units of output. In most ancient businesses, including this one, with few if any resources other than the owner or supervisor devoted to indirect functions like administration, recruitment, and marketing, almost all costs would have varied directly with volume, including rebuilding equipment. The nature of advantage or barriers to entry enjoyed by large over small ore processors needs another explanation, and one is provided by the way many location-specific businesses work today.

The barrier to entry stems from the cost of transporting unprocessed ore compared with processing it on site and leaving the dross behind. The ratio of silver to other material (about 1:250)[39] meant that transport economics favored processing and cupellation near the mine. The first processor to establish an operation near to a mine site would expect to capture all the local business if his pricing was reasonable, he was seen to do an effective job in recovering silver, and he expanded his capacity to meet demand. New entrants would find it hard to attract business once local customer relationships had been established. Over time, as the infrastructure grew, new facilities were added, and operating history and relationships became more established, it would seem still less sensible for an ore owner to entrust his materials to a new entrant. It is likely that the move to build wells near important adits was a pre-emptive investment by miners and ore processors to block new competitors; once their

---

[38] List of materials drawn from Davis (2014) 261.
[39] A typical ore had 20 percent lead content (Conophagos (1980) 27), which in turn was about 2 percent silver (Rihll (2001) 120; 134).

workshop was in place, they could be sure of capturing adequate volume at good prices. Pricing might allow for very attractive margins, constrained only to the level above which customers would choose to ship the product further afield or process it themselves. A logical industry structure would consist of a number of local monopolies with their boundaries roughly defined as a function of transport costs. Similar dynamics operate today in location-sensitive businesses such as airport hubs, stevedoring, or waste disposal, which often require regulation to ensure competition.

## 4.3 General Metalworking

Smelting of other metals was far less complex than silver.[40] Without cupellation, successful smelting only requires managing time and temperature. Smelting furnaces were of three types, batch, in-and-out, and periodic kilns. They were simple cylinders, smaller than pottery kilns, as they needed to reach higher temperatures, and without any internal divisions or externally projecting stoking channels—remarkably similar to traditional kilns in West Africa today.[41] Furnaces operated at set temperatures with three control zones to keep the temperature even, which required extra heat around the door and the end. Cycle times for most smelting operations were about five hours. *Mercury, tin,* and *lead* are especially easy to smelt—campfire temperatures are all that are needed—but these metals are too soft to be of much use in tools or weaponry. *Copper* is harder and requires higher smelting temperatures (950–1100°C) and purpose-built furnaces. The ideal furnace for smelting copper was between 20 and 40 centimeters in diameter, with up to 6 tuyères and airflow of 250 liters a minute through each. After an hour and a half of preheating, such a furnace would operate with an ore to fuel ratio of 2:1.[42] Sometimes the load was brought up to heat from cold, sometimes added to a heated furnace. Whether it was left to be cooled after smelting would depend on whether it was to be forged, in which case the smith would probably work on the smelted metal while it was still very hot. *Bronze* with less than 10 percent tin content can be cold-worked but tends to become brittle and crack. To overcome this, smiths often annealed the metal by heating it to just below melting point and cooling it slowly, sometimes "quenching" it with water, which enabled it to be hammered without cracking. Products of this technique have been found that date from the 13th century BCE in Cyprus. From the same period, there is literary evidence of a commercial firm established to supervise bronze production in the Levant.[43] The Greeks

---

[40] Descriptions of furnace technologies are drawn from Trinks et al. (2004).
[41] Papadopoulos (2003) 209; Hasaki (2012b) 265.
[42] Bamberger (1985) ch. 1.
[43] Ugarit Text 2101; 2056; see Markoe (2005) 12 n.2.

were relatively slow movers in *iron* and *steel*. Iron was probably the last ore to be smelted, as the required temperature was highest (about 1500°C), much higher than copper or bronze.[44] Iron smelting in Athens dates from the tenth century BCE and grew steadily through the Dark Ages. As in so many areas, the technology was imported from the Near East, but, like the rest of the world until very recently, technology in Athens remained centuries behind Chinese developments.[45] Most early processes in Europe and Africa involved smelting iron ore in a bloomery, where the temperature is kept low enough so that the iron does not melt. This produces a spongy mass of iron called a bloom, which is hammered to drive out the impurities and consolidate the metal into a bar of wrought iron, ready to be worked in a forge—a task requiring strength and some apprenticeship but no exceptional skill or dexterity.

Except in the case of silver and metals like wrought iron that were often imported part-processed, smelting was typically undertaken by the smith who was planning to work the metal. End-use fabricators in businesses like general metalwork, jewelry, knife manufacture, sculpture, and armor would have smelted ore as part of their operations. It was not until Roman times that smelting was undertaken as a separate intermediate stage in the metal processing chain. In classical Athens, smelting must be considered as part of the relevant fabrication segment. Though archaeological finds of metals do not match the richness of pottery, we can still identify metalworking sites through the remains of their furnaces and from casting pits. Six workshops from the classical period have been found in and around the Agora, together with a number of pits that might have been used for casting large public statues.[46] Four casting pits have been identified in the Ceramicus.[47] Bronze products of Athens's metal workshops that have been found include vessels—handled jugs, *hydriai, calpide,* and *oinochoai*—mirrors, jewelry, and abundant statuettes.[48]

Specialization of metalwork increased dramatically in a few centuries. Homer's Hephaestus works gold, silver, bronze, and tin, sourcing his own ores

---

[44] Forbes (1964–72) VIII.194–98.

[45] Chinese metalworkers were making cast iron by around 500 BCE (Elvin (1973) 298; Pomeranz (2002) 43–68). In about 300 BCE, while the Greeks were still struggling to produce consistent iron output by replacing bloomer hearths with more efficient shaft furnaces, the Chinese invented a steel-making process similar to the Bessemer oxidation system but preceding it by around 2,000 years. In around 500 CE they came up with a version of the 1863 English invention, the Siemens regenerative process (Dunlop (1981) 60; Teresi (2002)). The state of technology in classical Greece could not attain the level of precision in mixing carbon needed to make consistent quality steel, even though it was achieved in Tanzania only a few centuries later (Schmidt and Aver (1996)).

[46] Mattusch (1977) 348–59; (1988) 220–27; (1989) 27–39; see Chapter 7.2.

[47] Zimmer (1990) 34–38.

[48] Snodgrass (1980) 201. There seems to have been a decline in the production of these statuettes in classical times, while the market for bronze vessels and mirrors continued to grow.

and using the same tools for each, but by the fifth century, smiths had started to buy from prospectors or mine smelters and specialize by material: bronze, copper, iron, or precious metals.[49] In classical Athens most workshops bought in imported ore or ingots and specialized in one metal. Some operators specialized by product as well: one of Demosthenes's factories made knives or swords (27.9), while Pistias made breastplates (Xen. *Mem.* 3.10.9). As representatives of those likely to lose business by the peace of Nicias, Aristophanes brings on stage individual manufacturers of helmets, trumpets, breast plates, and spears (*Pax* 1209–1264). A specialist rosette gilder was engaged for the Erechtheum building effort.[50] Coinage was made by public slaves, and some metal products were made in large workshops, but the vase images we have of metalworking in Athens are typically of goldsmiths and makers of ornaments working alone; lone smiths forging their material on an anvil and quenching it in cold water, perhaps assisted by a slave; or individual minters making silver into coins.[51] The only surviving vase clearly showing more than two or three people with a metal furnace includes a life-size statue of a man and might depict a bronze sculpture operation.[52]

Important though it might have been, specialization is not an adequate explanation of industry structure. It does not explain why a factory specializing in knives might employ over 30 slaves while a craftsman specializing in gold jewelry might work alone. Not all products would have required a narrow specialization among fabricators; many craftsmen would have been able to produce a wide range of products, and some might have chosen to do so. Table 4.1 shows some of the metal products mentioned in Aristophanes. Those in the left-hand column are simple to make, do not require specific expertise beyond smelting and forming, and, provided minimum quality standards are met, the purchaser will not care who the manufacturer was. Those on the right are ones for which there is literary evidence of some specialization, or a special word to describe the manufacturing activity. We have no evidence to go on for those in the middle, but analogy with those on the right suggests they might have been specialized as well.

As with pottery, the nature of much of the metalworking industry was determined by the lack of barriers to entry or potential for an advantage in production costs. For some products there might have been family traditions

---

[49] Increased specialization seems to have coincided with the advent of iron, which required special heating conditions and continuity and flux to remove impurities, rather than simply removing them by hammering as with copper, and demanded more specialized skills and equipment (White (1984) 36).

[50] Kuznetzov (1990) 27–44.

[51] Examples include: Burford (1972) pls. 29 and 30; Boardman (1975) Figs. 81, 101. (2001).

[52] Oddy and Swaddling (1985); the Berlin Foundry Cup, F2294, in the Staatliche Museen, Berlin (Boardman (1975) 262.2; (1989) 401.1; (2001) 256.1); Mattusch (2008) 16.1–3; see also description in Mattusch (1980) 54–56.

TABLE 4.1 **Metalwork Specialization**[a]

| Probably Unspecialized | Probably Specialized | Specialized |
|---|---|---|
| ***Household utensils***: Sieve *koskinon* (*Nub.* 373); skewer *obeliskos* (*Ach.* 1007; *Nub.* 178; *Vesp.* 354, 363); meat hook *kreagra* (*Eq.* 772; *Vesp.* 1154); tripod *tripous* (*Eq.* 1016); scale-pan *plastinx* (*Pax* 1248; *Ran.* 1378). ***Agricultural items:*** Pitchfork *sminye* (*Nub.* 1486, 1500); *thrinax* (*Pax* 567); shovel *ame* (*Pax* 299, 426); sickle *drepane* (*Pax* 1200, 1203; *Ran.* 576); shackles *pedai* (*Vesp.* 435); horse bit *chalinos* (*Pax* 155); crow bar *mochlos* (*Pax* 299, 307; *Lys.* 428, 432–33). ***Other Household:*** Bathtub *puelos* (*Eq.* 1060; *Pax* 843); brazier *eschara* (*Ach.* 888); lampstand *luchnouchos* (*Ach.* 938); tray *skaphe* (*Eq.* 1315); *kaneon* (*Thesm.* 822). | ***Weapons:*** Arrowhead *akis* (*Pax* 443); javelin *akontion* (*Pax* 553); spear *doru* (*Ach.* 1118, 1188, 1194; *Pax* 353, 356; *Lys.* 50, 985, 1151; *Ran.* 1015; *Vesp.* 1081); spearhead *logche* (*Ach.* 1226; *Thesm.* 826; *Ran.* 1015); dolphin (naval weapon) *delphis* (*Eq.* 762); axe *pelekus* (*Thesm.* 560); trident *triaina* (*Nub.* 566; *Eq.* 839); war trumpet *salpinx* (*Pax* 1240). | ***Jewelry***: Ring *daktylion* (*Eq.* 947, 951; *Thesm.* 425); necklace *hormos* (*Lys.* 408; *Vesp.* 677); mirror *katoptron* (*Thesm.* 140); tiara *stleggis* (*Thesm.* 556). ***Ornaments:*** Statuettes/ Statues *agalma* (*Nub.* 306). ***Armor:*** Helmet *kranos* (*Ach.* 584, 1103; *Pax* 1128); *pelex* (*Ran.* 1015); breastplate/ corselet *thorax* (*Ach.* 1132; *Pax* 1224); greave *knemis* (*Ran.* 1015). ***Knives and swords: xiphos*** (*Ach.* 342; *Pax* 553; *Lys.* 156, 632; *Thesm.* 140); *machaira* (*Ach.* 849; *Eq.* 412, 489; *Pax* 947, 1017; *Thesm.* 694; *Nub.* 1063-66); *xiphomachaira* (*Thesm.* 1127); *xiphidion* (*Lys.* 53); *xuron* (*Thesm.* 219). ***Coins*** (*passim*). |

[a] This list and similar ones in this book are drawn from material distributed by E. M. Harris at the Beyond Self-Sufficiency conference, Durham, July 2011.

that were not shared with outsiders, but apprentices could contribute quickly to a workshop's output and apprenticeships appear to have been generally available. It is likely that anyone of moderate intelligence, physical strength, and dexterity could find a teacher and learn to make at least simple, utilitarian objects in metal. The three main sources of cost advantage—superior processing technology, access to lower input costs, and the effect of economies of scale on fixed costs and asset utilization—are as absent in ancient metalwork as they are in pottery. Processing consisted of smelting and hammering, using the same tools as Homer's smiths: anvil, hammer, tongs, and a furnace slightly smaller than a typical potter's. Raw material could be bought from third parties at whatever the going price was. Slaves could be purchased, their price reflecting their aptness for the work and any prior training.[53] For most products, one or two people could carry out all the work, so there was no benefit in several being located together. Many Athenians would have been able to learn to make and mend a wide variety of simple kitchen items and agricultural tools according to customer demand and market opportunity, and would not have been disadvantaged in competing in these simple products with larger workshops.

---

[53] For variations in the capital costs of slaves, see Chapter 9.5.

It was this ability to respond to a variety of demands, none of which would keep him busy for very long, that enabled the lone village blacksmith to survive well into the 20th century, serving a geographically defined customer base with a wide range of products and repairs. His demise can be attributed to the ability of larger concerns to satisfy demand with more standardized products made at lower cost through the use of capital equipment, especially in materials handling, and greater purchasing power—a process accelerated by massive reductions in the costs of transporting materials and finished product. Where this is impractical, as in the case of shoeing horses, new technology has enabled farriers to become mobile again, in a strange reversal of the developments described in Chapter 2.

Again as with pottery, it was possible for a sole craftsman to earn a modest and unstable income without specializing. A hoe sold for three *drachmae* and a basic drill for five *drachmae* and one obol;[54] allowing for materials, this would probably have represented a reasonable return on labor, provided you could sell your products. For income security and greater rewards it was necessary to differentiate your output to make it more attractive to purchasers. Differentiation meant specialization: narrowing your range of products so as to be considered exceptionally good at a subset of them. In some of these the specialization enabled the development of large workshops, in others it did not. Whether you could expand depended on the nature of the differentiation. If the reason customers sought out a particular product was their regard for the craftsmanship of one man, he might be able to charge good prices but would not be able to grow his workshop. If, on the other hand, the work was the product of the labor of several people, whose individual contributions could not be distinguished but whose collective end product was seen as especially desirable, then this brand effect could be extended to a large workshop. This important distinction, rather than the mere fact of specialization, explains the wide range of enterprise sizes we find in the metal industry. The following sections draw on archaeological and textual information to show the likely structure of each of the major specialized segments of the metalworking and armor industries.

## 4.4 Jewelry and Ornaments

From the earliest days of Mediterranean civilization, jewelry was an important adornment for both men and women. Necklaces, rings, pins, cross-shaped pendants, crowns, brooches, and very fine beadwork have been found in Minoan and Mycenaean palaces dating back to the middle of the second millennium BCE.[55] Phoenicia specialized in jewelry in the Bronze Age,

---

[54] Thompson (1971) 8.
[55] Chandra (1979) 24; Hughes-Brock (1998) 260.

and a vast array of luxury items from that period were found in the palace complex at Kamid el-Loz.[56] Specialties included miniature-scale granulation and filigree work using gold and plated silver, often inset with glass or semiprecious stones such as lapis lazuli or cornelian. Faience (molded vitreous paste) was used to create ornaments in Tyre as early as the 13th century BCE. By classical times, it seems men wore fewer ornaments, though they might use rings and pins, while women decked themselves out with a variety of necklaces, pendants, earrings, and other items, often made of gold and inset with brightly colored stones like amethysts or garnets. Much of the earliest jewelry had been inspired by oriental designs, and in the fourth century these influences reasserted themselves with more delicate filigree work on necklaces and chains.

Microscopic examination of surviving products provides some insight into manufacturing techniques.[57] Minoan finds show that the precious metals were hammered into shape before being set with either uncut or polished stones. More commonly, gold or silver was melted into a convenient-sized lump or sheet to be worked with simple tools of metal, wood, or bone. It could then be inlaid, plated, painted, or embellished with granulation (tiny spheres of metal) or filigree. Very thin sheet gold needs a filler of clay or plaster to add weight and help shaping. Wire-drawing was unknown before the seventh century CE, so thin strips of metal were cut and hammered into shape or twisted by hand to make wire for pendants. Beaded wire was produced as early as 700 BCE by rolling a circular strip under the edge of a sturdy device so as to create indents. For soldering, the Greeks used electrum, sometimes with copper added, as it had a lower melting point than the items to be joined. All the same, to avoid the risk of fusing the piece into rigidity by soldering, chains were usually made by twisting the links through each other. For pierced work, patterns would be scratched in the metal and small holes punched which the craftsman then enlarged with different-sized awls.

Gem cutting seems to have been very efficient. Most of the gems used were quite soft and could be worked with sand (or even flint) and were usually smoothed by grinding between two flat stones.[58] To shape them or make holes, they would be drilled with a bow drill whose wood or metal point was coated with an abrasive. By the Iron Age, the drill was fixed horizontally so items to be worked could be pressed against it. To ensure the snug fit of inlaid gems, metal workers must have worked closely with lapidaries.[59]

Glass was also used for jewelry. By Strabo's time, Alexandria was home to a large number of glassblowers (7.58), and before this glass came from a few

---

[56] Markoe (2005) 14; 203.
[57] Ogden (1992) 41–55.
[58] Ogden (1992) 54.
[59] Chandra (1979) 23.

specialist centers; from the Bronze Age onward it was shipped in the form of ingots or beads, and by the fifth century it was traded extensively around the Mediterranean.[60] Ingots could be shaped by pressing in a mold (or rotating between two molds) so as to form luxury drinking vessels.[61] Perfume bottles were made by heating rods of colored glass around a sand-based stick.[62]

The Bronze Age had seen large workshops of goldsmiths and silversmiths, usually employed by a palace or temple, and they were to re-emerge in Hellenistic times, but there is no evidence of them in Athens. To the contrary, vases seem to indicate that they operated in teams of no more than two or three, presumably a craftsman and his slaves.[63] This is consistent with our understanding of the high degree of skill required and the fact that some of the better items appear to have been customized. Making a fine ornament or piece of jewelry might take between a few hours and several days and was a task for one person.[64] High-quality customized jewelry is a naturally differentiated craft, which would remain fragmented because the reputation of one practitioner would not translate to a gang. We would expect the most expert to make a very good income, but they would not be able to expand beyond the capacity of their own hands.

It would be dangerous to conclude, however, that the sole practitioner and slave was the only—or even the dominant—business model. It is not always possible to tell how much skill and effort went into making particular objects, and it is very unlikely that every piece of jewelry Athenians wore was customized, so the diligent expert painstakingly applying his craft on the finest materials might not account for a very high proportion of output. Inferior craftsmen working with cheaper materials might have found a market among those with less disposable income. Incomes in Athens were rising, and more residents and migrants might well have sought to invest their new wealth in decorating themselves, their families, or their houses without being able to afford this painstaking expert. If there was sufficient demand for lower-quality products, the economics would have been attractive: product could have been made for stock and a large workforce kept busy without waiting for the next customer. Stock was expensive; it is quite likely that customers of the top jewelers paid for the raw materials before the craftsman bought them, but much less likely that all decorative items were ordered on this basis. Scale would spread the costs of acquiring expensive raw materials over a larger volume and possibly bring purchasing discounts. Accurate forecasting of manufacturing needs was important for controlling investment

---

[60] Stern (2008) 520–21; Markoe (2005) 206–8.
[61] Lierke (1998) 198–202.
[62] Reger (2007) 479.
[63] Dovatur and Nejchardt (1980) 75; Snodgrass (1980) 214.
[64] Ogden (1992) 55.

in working capital, another advantage of making for stock. The reputation of individual craftsmen would matter less to these customers, and it would be the workshop that would build a name for reliable value. Mass-production methods had been devised to create spaces in gold and silver that would hold stones tightly and to make statuettes and small pendants at low cost by covering a metal plate with a layer of wax and then hammering an impressed copper-alloy die onto it—a technique still used in India today, and one that requires almost no skill once a craftsman has sculpted the figure for the die. [65]

It is plausible then to suggest that there might have been one or more large workshops making jewelry or ornaments that were not of the quality that an expert with a very large raw materials budget might achieve, but might nevertheless be attractive to quite a large number of customers. On the other hand, there is no strong literary or archaeological evidence to support it. A large workshop of this type is not mentioned by the orators (as far as we know; the functions of slave assets are not always clear), and the first site generally recognized to be a large mass-producer of ornaments was Capua in the first century CE.[66] It is important to remember, though, that archaeology can currently tell us very little about what was made in an excavated furnace and less about how many people worked there, and, for reasons discussed in the previous chapter, vase paintings are not to be taken as an accurate representation of workshop headcount. It is conceivable that future finds, or reinterpretations of past ones, will suggest Athens might have seen several workshops of a dozen or more slaves making jewelry or ornaments for the modestly well-off.

## 4.5 Coinage

The first Athenian coins were minted from imported silver in the mid-sixth century BCE, during the time of Peisistratus, a few years after Aegina and Corinth had initiated the practice in Greece.[67] Early coins carried no indication they came from Athens. There appear to have been only one or two dies used per issue, suggesting volumes were small.[68] Toward the end of the sixth century, coins in circulation were recalled and new ones issued with symbols representing the city, reflecting the increased importance of the coinage outside the *polis*'s own borders.[69] Initially the reverse depicted a Gorgon

---

[65] Snodgrass (1980) 128.
[66] Campbell (2007) 271.
[67] Seltman (1924); Kroll (1979); Kroll and Waggoner (1984). The fact that coinage commenced under the tyrants makes the thesis that it was a weapon in the democratization of the *polis* (Kurke 1999, 2002) rather unlikely—see Kroll (2000). For the economic impact of the introduction of coinage, see Chapter 2 pages 50, 59.
[68] Kroll (1981) 22.
[69] van Alfen (2012) 88, 90–91.

ILLUSTRATION 4.1. The Finest of All Coins

(a symbol of Athena whose aegis traditionally displayed one), and soon afterward coins were marked with Athena herself in profile on the obverse and her owl on the reverse (Ill. 4.1), the famous tetradrachm, the "finest of all coins among Hellenes and foreigners everywhere" (Ar. *Ran.* 721–23) that was to be the dominant coinage of the Eastern Mediterranean for several hundred years.[70] Some time before or around 415 BCE, Athens asserted the primacy of its coinage for trade within the Delian league by insisting that the coins of all other members be overstruck with the Athenian design.[71] Many states stopped issuing their own currency, while Athens's output grew.[72]

Some years after the mines at Laurium were discovered, Athenian tetradrachms were being produced in "staggering quantities"—perhaps five million coins a year.[73] Volumes continued to rise during the fifth century, and although output dipped when Laurium closed for some years toward the end of the Peloponnesian War, the impact does not seem to have been as great as once thought.[74] Even then it was Athenian coinage that was used to pay the Persian-financed fleet of Sparta (Thuc. 8.5.5; Xen. *Hell.* 1.5.7) and the tribute Sparta received from "freed" members of Athens's empire (Plut. *Lys.* 16). The popularity and ubiquity of Athens's coinage invited high-quality imitation from the Near East, and in 375–74 BCE Athens was forced to respond with legislation.[75]

---

[70] Humphrey (2006) 78; Sayles (2006).
[71] Meiggs (1972) 167–73; Kroll (2011a) 229–59; a similar foreign coin replacement program was carried out at a profit by state-owned mints in the Hellenistic period: Treister (1996) 382.
[72] Figueira (1998) 74–77.
[73] Picard (2001); Kroll (2009) 195–96.
[74] Kroll (2011b) 3.
[75] Rhodes and Osborne (2003) 25; Ober (2008) 220–25.

In some cities, coins were directly molded, but this was rare before 300 BCE and the technique was not used in classical Athens. Instead, buttons of refined silver were broken into grains, weighed to the current standard (4.37 gm for most of the classical period), placed in an egg-cup-like holder, heated to liquefaction, and then poured into a mould to create a blank or "flan." This was then placed onto the obverse die, which was usually fixed in a hollow in an anvil of heavy wood or metal to keep it in place and prevent it from expanding under pressure.[76] When partially cooled, the metal was struck manually with the reverse die. Dies were hand-carved, making each batch unique.[77] One obverse die, set into the anvil, could be used to make between 10,000 and 15,000 coins, depending on workers' experience, metal composition, and blank size. The reverse, which gave the direct hammer blow, would need to be replaced perhaps three times as often.[78]

The structure of coin manufacturing is uncontroversial. It was a state enterprise, manned by public slaves. The case seems established beyond doubt by the scholiast to Aristophanes (*Vesp.* 1007) and by a law sanctioning punishment for the public coinage tester if he failed in his duties.[79] The mint required a permanent workforce, so was unattractive to citizens, and, with such valuable material on site, slaves brought the added benefit that they could be kept honest through torture. The state's "clip"—three or five *drachmae* per *mina* minted—would more than pay for the slaves' upkeep. While melting silver and punching it were simple tasks, carving the images in the dies must have required considerable skill and experience, which was probably supplied by a senior slave or a private craftsman on contract. Consistency of output suggests that, if carving was outsourced, the same individuals were regularly selected, perhaps through long-term agreements.[80]

It is extraordinarily difficult to estimate how many slaves were engaged in the work. Minute differences in design resulting from the hand carving of dies indicate how many different dies were used in a period, but estimating total coinage output during a typical year with any accuracy is difficult, as the start and end of the period can seldom be specified precisely. Estimates of the average life of a die are also necessarily imprecise and affected by imponderables such as molecular stress and treatment in use.[81] Combining these uncertainties leads to a production range of between one and nine million coins per year![82] On top of that we are left with the challenge of estimating the rate of production per slave.

---

[76] Rihll (2001) 128; Faucher et al. (2009).
[77] Metcalf (2012) 5.
[78] Humphrey (2006) 80; Kroll (2009) 196.
[79] Hill (1899) 130; Kraay (1976) 74; Martin (1991) 21–27; Lewis (1997) 7; Chappell (2009) 396.
[80] Kroll (2009) 195–96.
[81] Ponting (2012) 12–30.
[82] Flament (2007) 57–120; Kroll (2009) 198.

Even on extreme assumptions, we can be certain the Athenian mint was not a very large employer. At the estimated average life of 15,000 coins per obverse die and 5,000 per reverse one, 9 million coins require 600 of the former and 1,800 of the latter;[83] if it took a full day to carve each face, we are looking at a task requiring no more than seven or eight craftsmen. The task of stamping coins was simple and repetitive. Even with a considerable amount of the "sauntering" Adam Smith abhorred, a slave might be assumed to stamp an average of at least one a minute, or perhaps 500 in a day. Add a handful of people to manage the crucibles and material handling and we can be confident that, even at its very peak, fewer than 80 people were employed in the Athenian mint; more conservative projections of coin output and more optimistic ones of labor productivity suggest it was closer to 20 or 30, and often fewer.

## 4.6 Bronze Armor

The armor of Athenian hoplites gradually took shape from the eighth century, accumulating additional items of body protection until it reached the full panoply of shield, spear, short sword, breastplate or cuirass, bronze helmet, neck and cheek guards, greaves, and a "curtain" at the bottom of the shield. It was up to the user which items he selected from this array. The full panoply became quite common during the second Persian invasion, but people soon began to discard parts of it again.[84] Works of art show great variety in the body armor of hoplites beyond the shield and spear that everyone carried, and for every fully armed warrior there are several with only part of the equipment.[85] Cuirasses are a good example: in paintings and friezes, they are usually worn by mythological figures, while hoplites wear corselets or nothing on their chests. Nevertheless, they continued to be worn by distinguished men and given as a form of military decoration in classical times (Plut. *Alc.* 7.5). Bronze cuirasses were quite rare, even among mercenaries, and replaced during the latter part of the sixth century by a leather corselet, sometimes covered or partly covered with bronze scales. The bronze helmet evolved too; it was originally lined with felt, but over time was often replaced altogether by a separate felt hat or *pilos*.[86] Other variations included whether or not to wear greaves (in some cases, it seems people might have just worn one), and the wealthy might add accoutrements such as arm protectors or ankle guards. Overall the trend was toward mobility rather than solidity in armor design, but there were countless

---

[83] Fourcher (2009); Kroll (2009) 196.
[84] van Wees (2004) 47.
[85] Snodgrass (1967) 37; Anderson (1970) 21.
[86] Anderson (1970) 31–35.

variations on that theme. Compared with Sparta's standardized red tunics, Athens's troops must have looked very motley.

In many places, just as today, military procurement was the business of the state, which often owned manufacturing operations. This was certainly the case in classical Sparta and in Syracuse, which produced 140,000 shields and 14,000 cuirasses (Diod. 14.43.2).[87] State-owned manufacture became more widespread still under Alexander and his successors; artillery and fortification were the major areas of state-driven technological development in Hellenistic Egypt.[88] In Athens, the state did not own armor workshops, but it almost certainly had stores in which to keep large quantities of armor and weaponry for various purposes, such as helping arm another *polis* (Diod. 17.8.5) or supplying certain categories of its own citizens.[89] Athens's basic state provision was a shield and a 2- to 2.5-meter spear for second-year military trainees (*ephebes*—(Arist). *Ath. pol.* 42.4). War orphans were given a panoply (Pl. *Menex.* 4g). Men elevated to hoplite status for the Sicilian campaign had their arms and equipment supplied by the state, but otherwise each man bought himself the best armor he could afford, which explains the lack of standardization.[90] Aristotle favored an infantry of the middle-class who could afford their own armor, arguing that the state's major challenge was to ensure they outnumbered the poorer "naked" citizens and avoided upsetting them (*Pol.* 1297b.16–28). Aristophanes's prices for bronze work—1,000 *drachmae* for a breastplate, 50 for a helmet and 60 for a trumpet (*Pax* 1200–39)—are obviously exaggerated, but if the two sides of a breastplate involved 10 man-days of labor (as I suggest later in this section), and a skilled slave cost about a *drachma* a day to lease and maintain, then, allowing for raw materials and a profit margin for the owner, it would not sell for much less than 20 *drachmae*. The assessed cost of 30 *drachmae* that the men on Salamis were required to arm themselves to (IG I³ 1) amounted to around a month's wages in public employment but probably allowed for little beyond the basics of a shield and a spear.[91] A full panoply would cost between 75 and 300.[92] The wealthiest citizens might be able to afford a full set of armor, but others could not. For the very poor, a javelin was 3 *drachmae* and a bow and arrow 15. Even rowers had some light armor and could be very effective in it, defeating the Spartans at Sphacteria in 425 BCE.[93]

---

[87] Caven (1990) 93–97.
[88] Robert and Robert (1976); Baatz (1979; 1982).
[89] Treister (1996) 223.
[90] Gomme et al. (1970) on Thucydides 6.43.
[91] Early in the third century, a shield cost 20 *drachmae* (Jones (1997) 187).
[92] Trundle (2004) 125.
[93] Van Wees (2004) 52.

Despite the challenges many of its customers faced in being able to afford its products, arms constituted a major business. The largest workshops we know of in Athens made shields (next section). The industry's multifaceted commercial side was represented by the large number of specialists in Aristophanes's *Peace* (1209–64). The variations in what constituted a set of armor for different customers makes it impossible to know how many items were wanted in Athens, but we might imagine that in time of war it might amount to at least 1,000 full-set equivalents a year, possibly many more.[94] Five hundred or more young men would want their first armor each year, and presumably others needed to replace items as they wore out or their designs were superseded. In 412 BCE, the Athenian production effort was able to equip 1,500 Argives in hoplite armor in addition to filling domestic demand (Thuc. 8.25).

Making this armor was a time-consuming occupation. Cuirasses came in two parts, which were fastened together by thongs along the wearer's sides; smelting and molding bronze into a large plate for the front or back might take two workers three to five days, using the lost wax system and with several dippings in a silica solution during this process.[95] After smelting, the face of the plate was laid against some yielding material such as pitch, and the back was beaten (*repoussé*) into shape with the appropriate tools. The plate was then turned over and the ornamentation finished off by chisels and etching devices. In many cases the bronze sheet was so thin that it must have required extraordinary patience, judgment, and skill not to pierce it accidentally. The celebrated Siris bronze shoulder plates were made in this manner. Each figure shows a warrior defeating an Amazon, and there are two small lions at the top, which probably held rings for fastening to the cuirass.[96] A vase painting shows the delicate process of shaping helmets and they would probably take a similar amount of time to form and line.[97]

If we assume that a full panoply of cuirass, greaves, anklets, arm guards, chin guard, and helmet required around four times as much work as just the cuirass, a craftsman working full-time with a slave would not be able to produce many more than 15 full sets of armor, or pieces requiring equivalent time, in a year, even if the molds for some pieces were reused.[98] If Athenian consumption was around 1,000 full-set equivalents, which seems conservative,

---

[94] Of course the manufactured total would be very unlikely to come to a whole number of panoplies, some items being considered more essential than others. For the purpose of the analysis, what matters is the total labor requirement, whatever the product mix.

[95] For a description of this process, see Chapter 7.2.

[96] Treister (1996) 117–19.

[97] Ashmolean Museum; Burford (1972) pl.31.

[98] For these estimates the author is grateful for the experience and expertise of Mr. Rodney Broad, Meridian Sculpture Founders Pty. Ltd., Melbourne. See also Clark et al. (1980).

there must have been between 60 and 100 people involved in bronze armor production.[99]

Upmarket body armor was designed according to the individual's measurements and in response to particular orders.[100] Socrates's insistence that the good fit achieved by the craftsman Pistias justifies a higher price (Xen. *Mem.* 3.10.9) suggests that in armor the individual craftsman's contribution was clearly identified and it was this individual reputation that mattered. An admired craftsman could not grow his operation beyond his own production capacity, as his reputation would not transfer to his slaves, and scale brought no cost advantages while carrying some utilization risk.

As in the case of jewelry and ornaments, though, we must ask whether there might have been some large operations making less customized armor for the less well-off. The process could have been speeded up by using molds, which is what the workers appear to be doing in a painting on the Berlin Foundry Cup. The full figure of a man in metal on the vase is generally taken to be a male statue but might be a mold for a panoply of armor; at any rate the same molds could have been used for armor and for life-size statues.[101]

ILLUSTRATION 4.2. Berlin Foundry Cup: Molds for a Statue or Armor?

---

[99] The nature of the manufacturing process means that there would have been few or no direct exports of customized bronze armor, although visitors to Athens might have taken the opportunity to commission some items for themselves.

[100] The "well-made" thoraxes Pistias shows Socrates are more likely to have been recently completed commissions than stock.

[101] F2294 in the Staatliche Museen, Berlin (Boardman (1975) 262.2; (2001) 256.1; Mattusch (1980) 54–56; (2008) 16.1).

We also hear of Leocrates, a bronze worker (Lyc. *Leoc.* 58) who, before going into self-exile, sold a number of slaves for 3,500 *drachmae* to his brother-in-law, who then sold them to another brother-in-law. (Lyc. *Leoc.* 22–23). It is not certain from the text that these slaves were themselves bronze-workers (and if they were, they might well have been sculptors), but we should allow for the possibility that some larger bronze workshops specialized in mass-produced items of armor. They would not have commanded the prices a Pistias could get, and might have only really found much demand in lesser accessories such as greaves, where fit was not so important, or among those only concerned to maximize body coverage at a minimum price, but the opportunity was probably there, especially in wartime, and it would be surprising if no one seized it. Prices would be low, but competitive advantage over the bespoke craftsman would come from cost savings from product standardization (making for stock so as to keep throughput constant and manage working capital) and division of labor. Over time a brand might develop a reputation for affordable protection.

As with jewelry, subsequent changes in the structure of the industry were due to political strategies rather than to a change in competitive dynamics. The Romans saw metal as providing a vital military advantage over the rough weapons and flimsy protective clothing of barbarians.[102] War-making capacity increased rapidly between 200 BCE and 200 CE, and ordnance factories were established in all provinces under the Empire, with Syracuse and Minturnae and Rome's Vicus Actionum Ferrarium hosting the most celebrated armorers, or *fabrii ferarii*.[103] This consolidation was clearly due to state provision of armor; the fact that most Athenians had to buy their own encouraged a much more diverse and customized industry, but might still have allowed room for large private workshops making standard sizes for the less well-off.

## 4.7 Shield Manufacture

We know of two shield factories, both with a large complement of slaves. The first belonged to the orator Lysias and his brother Polemarchus, sons of the wealthy Cephalus of Syracuse, who, according to Lysias (12.4), was invited to Athens by his friend and reciprocal host Pericles, although another tradition only says he had had been banished from Sicily by the tyrant Gelon ((Plut.) *Lys.* 1). When Cephalus died, his sons fled Athens and lived in Thurii in southern Italy, but their pro-Athenian stance during the Sicilian campaign upset the locals and they returned to Athens, where they started making shields. Lysias and his brother could afford special expensive liturgies (12.4), so it must have

---

[102] Elton (1996) 10.
[103] Corpus Inscriptionum Latinarum, VI.9185, 1214.

been a successful business, and Lysias claimed that when the Thirty Tyrants came to seize their goods in 404 BCE, the workshop contained 700 shields and 120 slaves, of whom they took the best (Lys. 12.19). Lysias was claiming compensation and had reason to exaggerate, so it is quite possible that his figure included slaves employed mainly for other purposes, including domestic service, or the numbers may simply have been "rounded up." Nevertheless, for the case not to have been laughed out of court, the workshop must have been a very large one. We also hear of a shield workshop owned since before 380 BCE by the freed slave and banker Pasion (Dem. 36.4).[104] We do not know if he bought the workshop that had belonged to Lysias and Polemarchus or that of a competitor. Nor does Demosthenes tell us the number of slaves employed in Pasion's factory, though if they did truly bring in revenue of one talent a year as he says (36.11), analogy with other examples suggests there were at least 60 of them, possibly 80 or more.[105]

In Homeric times, and for much of the archaic period, Greek shields were typically made of several layers of bull hide, usually embellished or reinforced with a metal boss and rim.[106] In the early Iron Age, armor became much lighter and shields were typically made of leather or wickerwork. By the classical period, though these lighter "Boeotian" shields persisted, most Athenians were using the *hoplon*, more commonly known by the generic name *aspis* (Ar. *Ach.* 58, 279, 539, 1122, 1140; *Eq.* 846-47, 856; *Lys.* 52, 185, 188, 190, 560, 627; *Nub.* 989; *Pax* 336, 438, 1274-75, 1298, 1303; *Vesp.* 17).[107] It was made of wood and typically circular, around one meter in diameter and between one and four centimeters thick, hollowed out to be deeply concave. The surface was covered in bronze, often highly decorated, and it was fitted with a leather or cord handgrip (*antilabe*) and bronze strap (*porpax*) on the inside. The wearer would put his arm through the *porpax*, grasp the *antilabe* at the shield's rim, and rest the upper rim on his shoulder. The preferred size depended on the strength of the bearer's forearm. The bronze sheets covering the face of the shield added little to the shield's strength and might have been primarily for decoration or identification; vases suggest all hoplites had their own shield designs (Ill. 4.3), and those of the elite like Nicias (Plut. *Nic.* 28.5) or Lamachus (Ar. *Ach.* 964-65, 1124, 1181) were especially noteworthy.[108]

As a people with a proud track record for innovation and the creative adaptation of materials, the Athenians of this period seem to have rather let

---

[104] Davies (1971) 430.

[105] Based on nominal returns on slave assets before depreciation of 30 percent (see Chapter 9.1), the capital value of the slaves would have been 200 *minae*. At 3 *minae* per slave, which is typical in manufacturing, this implies around 67 slaves.

[106] For a comprehensive overview of the development of ancient Greek armor, see Snodgrass (1967).

[107] Van Wees (2004) 47.

[108] Sekunda (1986) 21.

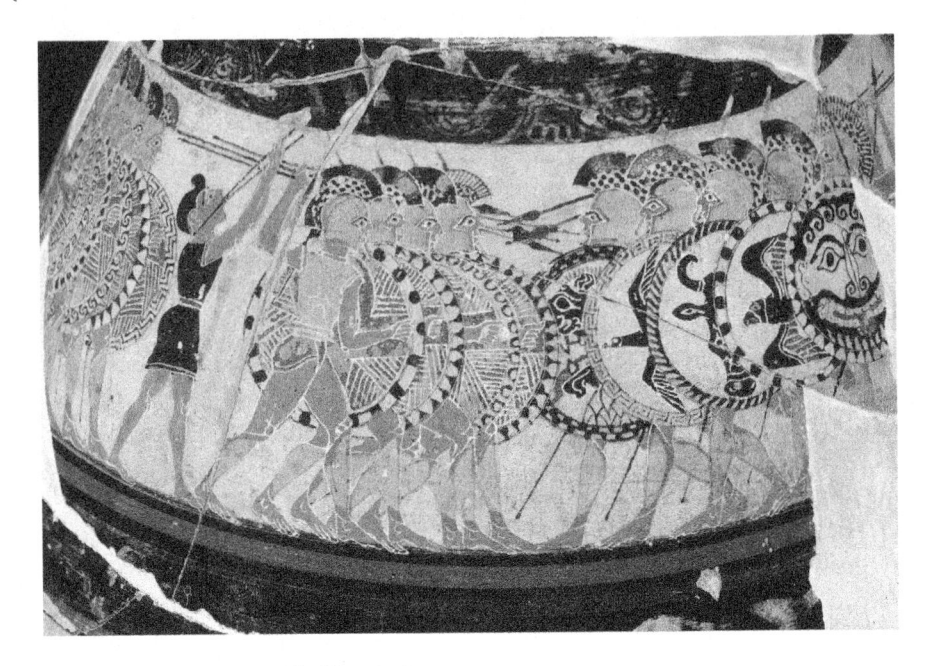

ILLUSTRATION 4.3. Hoplite Shields in Action

themselves down when it came to shields. The items were very cumbersome and heavy—estimated at 16 pounds, which is too heavy for most people to carry in one hand for long.[109] In fact "so great was the effort needed just to hold their equipment that when hoplites became worn out or lost concentration they instinctively dropped their shields."[110] Hanson may be exaggerating, but Cleonymus's "cowardice" in throwing his shield away might not have been as exceptional as Aristophanes makes out (*Vesp.* 19). Even though the weight could be rested on the bearer's shoulder, they were so unwieldy that the first group of Plataeans escaping from the Spartan siege in 429 left their shields behind for the second group to bring (Thuc. 3.22.3). Nor did the great weight provide much durability. Brasidas's shield fell apart on impact at Amphipolis (Plut. *Mor.* 219c), and Xenophon describes the battlefield at Coronea as littered with broken shields (*Hell.* 2.4).[111] On the positive side, some men could at least manage the weight of their shields to the extent of being

---

[109] Van Wees (2004) 48.
[110] Hanson (1989) 67.
[111] This was after an encounter in which the two foes thrust their shields against each other rather in the manner of a rugby scrum (Xen. *Hell.* 4.13.19; cf. Thuc. 4.96.2), but this happened at a late stage in the battle and was probably not a normal fighting tactic. More commonly, soldiers would run towards the enemy until they were close enough for hand-to-hand combat with spears (*eis doru*—Xen. *Hell.* 4.3.17; 7.1.31; Eur. *Phoen.* 1377–85); see Bowie (1990) 221–29.

able to fall and get up three times (Xen. *Hell.* 5.4.33), and they were useful for carrying the injured away from battle (Xen. *Hell.* 6.4.13; Theophr. *Char.* 25).

Manufacturing these items was not particularly complex, but required physical strength and some skill. With today's powered machinery and using glued wood prepared for turning, it takes between three and four hours to form the shape of a hoplite shield.[112] The Athenians would have worked with glued strips as well, since there are few trees thick enough to form a one-meter shield. Ancient gluing technology using animal proteins was very effective, with some glues still remaining firm after 2,000 years or more, though they were not waterproof, which is why paintings show hoplites protecting their shields from the elements. The time taken for turning depends to a large extent on whether the strips of wood have been shaped and planed in advance into approximately the right curvature for a shield before being glued and set on the lathe. This can reduce turning time by about 80 percent, so it is reasonable to expect that experienced shield makers in Athens would have used this technique. It would take a carpenter over an hour to shape and plane each of the 30 or so strips of wood that make up a shield. This and gluing them together might take five days per shield. It would have taken at least three people to lift the shaped and glued wood onto the lathe, and the turning power could have been supplied by four people walking in a circle on a simple carousel. Turning the wood with human power only would take 14 to 16 hours if pre-shaped.[113] Once the shield was formed, the leather or cord strap and the handgrip would be attached to bolts on the inside of the shield and the surface covered with bronze. The first task was a simple one. One slave could probably cut and fit the straps for several shields in a working day. The second was a bigger job. It might take three days to create a sheet of bronze the right size and perhaps two more to hammer it into shape on the shield, including the awkward rim configuration and points to fix the straps. Finally, the bronze would be decorated with hammer-work or paint, or perhaps both.

Translating these tasks into labor requirements, turning the wood would have been the major part of the operation, requiring four people working over about two days or eight man-days.[114] Five man-days went into shaping and planing, and perhaps another five into the bronze surface. Allowing two more days for fitting straps, decorating, materials handling, and any downtime, we have around 20 man-days per shield, which implies that if 120 slaves were really employed in the workshop full-time, they could produce six shields a

---

[112] This description of the manufacturing process and estimates of time requirements were supplied by Manning Imperial of Redan, Victoria, Australia, manufacturer of historical artifacts, including hoplite shields.
[113] Estimate supplied by Mr. Kevin Beasley of Melbourne, Australia, an experienced pattern-maker familiar with the hoplite shield. It would have taken about 10 days working from a solid block.
[114] Manning Imperial.

day collectively, or around 2,000 in a working year for slaves. A shield sold for 20 *drachmae*, or about 1 *drachma* per man-day, in the early third century. Even at lower fifth-century prices, this would have enabled Lysias and Polemarchus to support the slaves, purchase raw materials, and leave a profit margin.[115]

If one workshop could make about 2,000 shields in a year, it is interesting to consider how many such workshops there might have been in Athens. Most commentators agree that at the start of the Peloponnesian War Athens had between 30,000 and 35,000 adult male citizens (see Appendix), many of whom might have been engaged in battle and would need a shield, and many of whose shields would need replacing afterward. In the fourth century, shields were also given to young military trainees in their second year ((Arist.) *Ath. pol.* 42.2). Pasion donated 1,000 shields (Dem. 45.85) and Chairedemus and Diotimus gave 880 (Dem. 18.116). Some slaves and metics might also have required shields in certain campaigns. If we say each citizen bought one every five years, and male slaves and metics every 10 (which seems on the high side), then even allowing for some production for other uses such as display, dramas, and athletic contests, it is hard to believe peak demand would have exceeded 10,000 shields a year. If so, an establishment with 120 slaves would have had a market share of 20 percent or more. If demand was much lower than this, as is likely, it might have been a monopoly. Even if Lysias was exaggerating and his factory only made half as many, we are almost certainly looking at a leading competitor in a concentrated industry.

This workshop is a fine example of why the notion that workshop size depends on the scope for division of labor is not useful. We have seen how the work could be divided into four or five tasks, one of which, powering the lathe, required four people at a time. This explains why a well-organized factory would operate in teams of six to eight and why we do not find individual *aspidopoioi* among Aristophanes's tradesmen. It does not explain why Lysias's workshop might have had 20 such teams and Pasion's a dozen. In bronze armor, the need for customization and the lack of scale benefits in production led to a partly fragmented industry structure. The shield industry was much more concentrated, and its strong, stable returns were well known (Dem. 36.11). This reflects an equilibrium state of a relatively concentrated industry in which advantaged competitors can sustain good returns for a long time. So what constituted that advantage?

As usual, there was no potential for cost advantage. The capital and maintenance costs of slave labor would have been the same for all. Purchased materials (wood, bronze, cord, and leather) could also be purchased by any competitor at, presumably, the same price. All had access to the same technology, and, because it was a process requiring little but continuous labor

---

[115] Jones (1997) 187.

input, there were no economies from high throughput. A small (one-team) competitor's costs per shield are likely to have been the same or very similar to those of an enterprise with multiple teams.

There was certainly a capital barrier to achieving very large scale. At three *minae* each, a typical rate for slaves skilled in a craft, 120 slaves would cost six talents. To this must be added the cost of lathes, cutting tools, and hammers and an investment in wood and ores as working capital. The investment brought with it a lot of mouths to feed, and a competitor could not run the risk of underutilization while building market share. This explains why a new entrant might not have plunged in with a greenfield investment on the scale of Lysias's or Pasion's, but it does not by itself explain what might have deterred smaller concerns from starting up, winning some market share, and then expanding by reinvesting their profits, given that their unit costs would be very similar to those of the market leader. It is unlikely many entrants would have been deterred by the complexity of the operation. A degree of expertise was required to maneuver the heavy blocks and turn them to the right thickness, although crude calipers meant it was not necessary to rely entirely on an experienced eye.[116] The need to manage the workforce in teams, especially in turning, might have made staffing and managing such a workshop more difficult than in most industries, but Athens had a market for skilled slave labor and supervision.

The most likely explanation for the concentrated nature of the shield industry is that purchasers were choosy about the manufacturer's reputation. Even though shields were not very reliable, they were intended to save your life. Despite their tendency to crack, or perhaps because of it, purchasers would be keen to buy from an organization that had a good reputation and track record. Though shields varied in size according to the bearer's strength, a simple classification on the lines of small, medium, or large was probably enough to meet the market need for variation. The 700 shields confiscated from Lysias's workshop by order of the Thirty Tyrants (Lys. 12.19) show that, unlike Pistias's body armor, shields were made for stock. A reputation for quality in shield manufacture would be attributed to a particular workshop, it not being easy to ascribe special virtue to one particular craftsman when the work had to be done in teams and products were sold from a large finished goods warehouse. This made it possible for an owner to expand his operation without diluting his brand.

This brand effect must have been the real barrier to entry. A small entrepreneur setting up on his own, even with the same technology as a large competitor, would have found it difficult to attract customers—"Surely you didn't buy your shield from Whatshisname?" One way would be to acquire a going

---

[116] Ulrich (2008) 445.

concern already known to have the expertise, which is probably how Lysias and Polemarchus entered the business and Pasion and Phormion two or three decades later (it may have been the same workshop). Lysias and Polemarchus would have had extra credibility if Pericles did bring Cephalus to Athens in order to establish a shield-making business, especially if they inherited or repurchased their father's old workshop. If the story is untrue, one can see why Lysias made it up!

## 4.8 Knives

Demosthenes inherited two factories, one of which employed 32 or 33 slaves making items called *machairai* (27.9).[117] It is not clear whether the word should properly be translated as knives or swords or some form of dagger, but in any case the items were made of iron that was smelted and wrought into shape by craftsmen with hammers and sharpening tools and then fitted with handles. Demosthenes's possessions include "ivory, iron, and wood" worth 80 *minae* and "gall and copper" worth 70 (§10). The wood and at least some of the ivory must have related to his other factory, which made furniture, but the iron, gall, and copper would have been for knife-making, and some of the handles may have been ivory.

The reason this manufacturing segment became concentrated was almost certainly the same as that for shields: demand for reliable quality without customers being able to attribute a special capability to an individual craftsman. Whether these items were designed for fighting or to be used as eating utensils (or possibly both), quality mattered. As any soldier or cook knows, there is a very large difference between a good sharp knife and a poor one. As in the case of shields, there is likely to have been a tendency for purchasers to concern themselves with perceived product quality, so the manufacturer's reputation would constitute both a source of advantage for the workshop and a barrier to entry for new competitors. Importantly, purchasers would not have known or cared much about individual craftsmen engaged in specific steps of the production process; the reputation for quality would attach to the workshop as a whole, so it could expand beyond the minimum labor division needed to make a knife efficiently (which is almost certainly less than 32!). As with shields, products might vary slightly but could still be made for stock rather than after receiving a customer's order. Even if handles were customized, blades could be made according to an efficient production schedule. The same customer preferences for dealing with reputable brands that encouraged concentration in the shield industry would have affected knife-making,

---

[117] The economics of both Demosthenes's businesses are discussed in detail in Chapter 9.1.

and probably similar businesses making sharp weapons and tools such as arrowheads, spears and spearheads, axes, and tridents (Table 4.1 above). The fact that some of these different products appear to have been made by different workshops despite the obvious overlap of skills, processes, and raw materials indicates that a narrow specialization was an important component of a reputation for quality—a common phenomenon today, not least in armaments—for instance, Purdey, Colt, and Wesson. There was also a capital barrier to entry; Demosthenes's raw material inventory relating to this operation was worth about two years' income for a craftsman.

## 4.9 Summary

The competitive advantage framework shows the diversity of the metals and armor industries in classical Athens (Table 4.2).

TABLE 4.2 **Metals Industry Structure**

|  |  | Barriers to Entry | |
|---|---|---|---|
|  |  | Yes | No |
| Potential for Differentiation | Yes | Differentiated industry:<br>Shields<br>Knives, swords, etc.<br>*Volume producers of copied ornaments, statuettes, jewelry*<br>*Volume producers of low-cost items of armor* | Differentiated craft:<br>Jewelry<br>Ornaments<br>Bronze armor |
|  | No | Undifferentiated industry:<br>Coinage<br>Ore processing and silver smelting | Undifferentiated craft:<br>Simple domestic and agricultural tools<br>Basic repair work |

*Note: Italic font* identifies business forms for which there appears to have been an economic opportunity, but for which there is limited or no evidence in classical Athens.

Critical determinants of the structure of metals segments were:

1. Whether customers perceived a difference between the output of different manufacturers.
2. Whether this customer preference was for the work of a specific individual or extended to a workshop as a whole.

Very simple operations, such as stamping coins from dies someone else had made, or making and repairing crude implements for house, field, or garden, failed on the first count. Much of the unspecialized metalwork segment remained fragmented and open to casual participation in much the same way as retail commodity pottery. Ore processing and silver smelting enjoyed entry barriers through pre-empting critical locations. Coinage was consolidated because it was a state-owned monopoly—perhaps the most effective barrier to entry of all.

Whether the differentiable segments became large or remained the domain of the individual craftsman and a slave or two depended on the second determinant. If the preference was specific to the individual craftsman, the operation was limited to that individual's output. If it became a "firm brand," the workshop could grow as large as competing brands allowed. In the cases we know of (shields and blades), this consolidation process was helped by two factors. A workshop could make product for stock, thereby smoothing production flows and keeping staffing levels in line with average demand. This is significantly lower risk than employing labor that has nothing to do except when a customer comes along. Second, the more the businesses grew, the more capital they would have had tied up in equipment, molds and, especially, raw materials. To the extent market credibility became associated with a certain critical mass of operations, matching this investment would have constituted a formidable barrier to new entrants. Similar considerations suggest the likely emergence of large metal workshops molding cheap decorative pieces and off-the-shelf items of body armor.

Although the economic importance of metals continued to grow, the only segments that became significantly more consolidated in the Hellenistic and Roman periods than they were in classical Athens—jewelry and armor in Eastern empires and armor under Rome—were centrally directed and not the result of market forces. As in the cases of pottery in the previous chapter and—even more plainly—textiles in the next, metal industry structures would only change with major advances in technology.

5}

# Textiles, Clothing, and Footwear

Textiles, clothing, and footwear (TCF) are usually grouped together in modern national statistics and for industry policy. From an economic point of view, their chief common features are the employment of large numbers of people in unskilled or semiskilled jobs, and a consequent vulnerability to the lower labor costs of competitors in developing countries. In classical Athens, the TCF grouping covers a range of business models: the spinning and weaving of textiles and clothing was a quite different physical activity from processes like scouring, fulling, and dyeing, and a cobbler's shop had little in common with a tannery. This chapter describes the business structure and operations of the principal stages in the two main product groups. Some inferences are drawn from what is known about the industry in other regions and periods where data specific to classical Athens are inadequate and such analogy seems plausible.

## 5.1 Textiles and Clothing

Perhaps because of a natural human interest in the public appearance of our forebears, and because making clothes has been a major activity in all human societies from earliest times, textiles and clothing have received a degree of attention from historians out of all proportion to the survival of remains, which of course are very few and far between.[1] Our main sources are descriptions of clothing in literature, vase paintings of people and certain process stages, statues, and finds of pieces of equipment such as loom weights, combs, beaters, carding tools, and spindle whorls. There has been no shortage of scholars trying to make sense of all this, and the resulting large and fast-growing body of research provides a good basis for understanding the different ways Athenians participated in textile production.

Although the standard Athenian dress was simple (Ills. 5.1 and 5.2), Aristophanes's marketplace saw plenty of clothes for sale. There were woolen

---

[1] For the early history of textiles see Barber (1991; 1994).

shirts; tunics for men and women; women's girdles; robes; and a wide range of cloaks, including the *chlaniskon*, the *himation*, the smaller *himatidion*, the *chlaina*, the rough *katonake*, the *peplos*, and the frog-green *batrachis*.[2] You could buy secondhand clothes there too (*Ach.* 412, 415, 432). Some footwear was made of textiles or basket weave rather than leather, including slippers such as the *persika*, the *hypodema*, or the *peribaris*.[3] Veils, hairnets, and headbands were also for sale.[4] Hawking homemade ribbons seems to have been a common way for a poor widow to support herself (Dem. 57.31–35). Other items could be very expensive:[5] a large cloak might sell for 16 or 20 *drachmae* (*Eccl.* 413; *Plut.* 984), almost a month's wages, and fine women's cloaks could fetch anything from 30 to 200 *drachmae*. Even the cheapest cloaks purchased for slaves by the state cost between 7 and 10.5 *drachmae*. A good winter cloak could cost as much as a year's worth of grain, and it was apparently possible to pay 1,000 *drachmae* for a dress—enough to support two or three families for a year.

Textiles had many applications besides clothing.[6] Sheets were known to Homer (*Od.* 13.73, *Il.* 9.661), but there is no evidence they were used in the sixth or fifth centuries. The Athenian bed was usually covered with a mattress (*tule*), stuffed with a filling (*pleroma*), probably of straw, with a mat (*psiathos*) on top. Over this went fleeces or skins (Pl. *Prt.* 315a; Ar. *Aves* 120–23; *Nub.* 8–10; *Ran.* 1478). Pillows were widely used (*Ach.* 1090; *Vesp.* 676), and extreme luxury was having multiple pillows for head and feet along with perfumed bedclothes (Athen. 6.255c; 2.48c). Outside the bedroom, soft furnishings included loose covers and decorative hangings of wool or linen, with designs woven, embroidered, or painted that could be wonderfully complex and delicate. Curtains with curtain rings for drawing seem to have been common (Theophr. *Hist. Pl.* 4.2.7; Athen. 12.571d), and cloth was hung in front of shelving to form simple cupboards. Other items such as sacks or bags, mats, and rugs were often made from wool or linen but could be of woven reeds.[7]

---

[2] Woolen shirt: *ouloi erion*—*Ran.* 1066; tunic for men: *chiton*—*Eq.* 881, 886; *Lys.* 48, 150; tunic for women: *orthostadion*—*Lys.* 45; women's girdle: *strophion*—*Thesm.* 139, 251, 643; purple robe: *halourgis*—*Eq.* 967; cloaks: *chlaniskon*—*Ach.* 519; *Pax* 1002, *Lys.* 1190; *himation*—*Ach.* 1139; *Nub.* 54, 179, 497, 856, 987, 1498; *Lys.* 1093; *Thesm.* 214, 250, 568, 656, 1181; *himatidion*—*Lys.* 401, 470; *chlaina*—*Lys.* 1156; *Thesm.* 142; *Ran.* 1459; *Vesp.* 677, 737, 1133; *katonake*—*Lys.* 1151, 1155; *peplos*—*Eq.* 1180; *batrachis*—*Eq.* 1406.

[3] *Persika*—*Nub.* 151; *Thesm.* 734; *hypodema*—*Thesm.* 263; *peribaris*—*Lys.* 45, 47, 53.

[4] Veil: *kalymna*—*Lys.* 530, 532; hairnet: *kekruphalos*—*Thesm.* 138, 257; headband: *mitra*—*Thesm.* 257, 941.

[5] Markle (1985) 296; Thompson (1971) 15; Carr (1999) 163–66; Adesp. fr. 516.

[6] Pritchett and Pippin (1956) 203–10; Richter (1966) 117–21; Andrianou (2009) ch. 3.

[7] Sack, bag: *sakos*—*Ach.* 822; *thulakos*—*Eq.* 370; mat: *riphos*—*Pax* 348, 699; *stibas*—*Pax* 348; rug: *stroma*—*Ach.* 1090, 1136; *Nub.* 37; *Lys.* 936, 1189; *Vesp.* 1213; *Ran.* 543a.

ILLUSTRATION 5.1. Menswear (Modeled by Demosthenes)

The chief fiber used was wool, which was widely available in Athens both domestically and as a commodity that a number of metics seem to have been engaged in trading, so those without their own sheep could buy from specialist vendors (*eranopolai*). Garments were also made with linen from flax, which might have been imported: we hear of no linen industry, and there is no evidence of linen production in mainland classical Greece, although it was plentiful in Asia and on Samos. Temple offerings continued to be wool, and non-wool clothing like cotton imported from Egypt (Hdt. 3.106) tended to be rare and costly. After Athens conquered Aegina there seems to have been a change in local dress from Doric to Ionian styles (Hdt. 5.88) and perhaps from wool to linen and then back again to wool (Thuc. 1.6.3). The late-fifth-century tomb of a member of Alcibiades's family might have contained imported silk.[8]

Textiles had entered the world of traded goods in two stages: trade in raw wool and the development of processing and reselling markets. Towns along some of the trade routes, especially on the coast of Asia Minor, took

---

[8] Hundt (1969) 66–70.

150 { Poiesis

ILLUSTRATION 5.2. Ladies' Wear (Modeled by Athena)

to buying wool from passing ships, fabricating garments and exporting them on the same route.[9] Cyprus, Megara, and, most of all, Corinth had become known for their textile exports.[10] The island of Amorgos produced a very fine cloth based on a rough raw material processed by specialist slaves. Lydia was a favored source for Athens, and Milesian wool was especially famous for its quality (Athen. 12.540; Plin. *HN.* 29.33, Plut. *Alc.* 23.3). The city's wealth had prompted Cyrus to make a separate peace (Hdt. 1.141, 143, 169) and made her "the cynosure of Ionia" (5.28).

Athens seems to have exported few textile products, and the focus of the analysis here is on domestic production for resale. Textile processing has four principal steps: scouring, spinning, weaving, and finishing. The spinning and

---

[9] Even in the sixth to twelfth century CE, the town of Tinnis was totally dependent on textiles—Hordern and Purcell (2000) 363.

[10] Cyprus was an attractive capture for Egypt, which extracted a tribute from it (Hdt. 2.182); it was later able to supply Xerxes with 150 ships (Hdt. 7.90). Megara seems to have been known for salt (Ar. *Ach.* 760) and smocks (Xen. *Mem.* 2.7.6) and to constitute enough of a threat to Athenian production to encourage thoughts of an informal trade war (Ar. *Ach.* 521–28). The wide spread of Corinth's colonies and pottery indicate they made good commercial use of the naval power Thucydides praises (1.13).

weaving activities are closely aligned, and the scouring and finishing processes share important common features.

### 5.1.1 SPINNING AND WEAVING

The nature of the spinning and weaving process, cultural traditions, and a number of literary references support a conventional view that it was essentially a home-based business dominated by women making clothing for their own household, but there are good reasons to believe there was more manufacture for sale—and more types of business operation—than this picture suggests. In particular, finds of loom weights in apparently "industrial" quantities need another explanation and one that is compatible with the competitive dynamics of an industry in which differentiation was limited and hard to achieve.

The *spinning* process draws wool fibers into yarn using a distaff and drop spindle.[11] Conical lumps of clay or "whorls" are attached to the fiber to provide momentum. Spinning speeds depend on the weight of fiber that can be attached to the spinning whorl. The shortest fibers, perhaps four grams per whorl, could be spun at around 35 meters an hour; longer ones (8–18 gm per whorl) might reach speeds of 40–50, and very long ones (which were rare) could be spun by an experienced worker at 100 meters of thread an hour.[12] A large two-ply cloak might require up to 200,000 meters of thread and more than a person-year of spinning. Most garments would have been quicker to make, and a large household might use more than one person to spin the wool for each item. The spun wool is stored on bobbins prior to weaving.

*Weaving* brings two batches of spun yarn together at right angles to form cloth. The ancient Greeks used an upright loom with weights of pyramidal, discoid, or biconical shapes, sometimes marked with glaze or an identifying stamp. Athens appears to have used discoid loom weights through most of the fifth century, when they were replaced by conical ones, probably introduced from Corinth, which had been using them for some time by then. Pyramidal weights were popular and commonly used in Athens. Bronze Age Egypt had used floor looms, but most looms in classical times were upright (vertical), to be replaced later by the Roman horizontal loom. Greek looms were about 2.5 meters wide, with two timber uprights, a cloth beam across the top, and a fixed rod below. They were typically erected near courtyards, where there was good light. Setting up the spun threads on the loom might take a week, but once this was done, weaving would only take a few days for most items, although complex hangings would involve more weaving time,

---

[11] Except as specified, technical details on textile processes are from Forbes (1964–72) IV and Barber (1991) 107.

[12] Carr (1999) 164; Martinson (2007).

mainly resetting different colored threads on the loom. It typically took 10 spinners to keep a single loom fully supplied with yarn.[13]

The technology that the Athenians derived from the Levant or Egypt was primitive and static. Techniques have hardly changed in the last 3,000 years in the Eastern Mediterranean, and there were certainly no significant advances in weaving between the Bronze Age and the introduction of the horizontal loom and an improved cross-press in Roman times.[14] Technology development for hand-spinning has been equally unimpressive: the low-whorl drop spindles shown on Athenian vases are identical to those used in some peasant societies today.[15] Before the Industrial Revolution, India led the way in textiles. Drawing out the fibers with multiple high-speed spindles in a series accelerates spinning and was introduced in India in around 500 BCE, but there is no strong evidence that it was adopted in Greece.[16] Nor does Greece appear to have been familiar with the relatively simple techniques of using parallel fibers or crosswise carding.

The conventional picture of textile manufacture as a domestic business dominated by women is plausible, though inadequate. Unlike metallurgy, all the process stages of textiles are very straightforward, and only the scouring and finishing stages are physically demanding. Women had played a major role from the earliest times. There is evidence from early Assyria of women making cloth for sale as well as clothes for the household. They appear to have owned the products they made, and men took them to market.[17] In the palace at Mycenae the work was organized in six process steps, all done by women.[18] In the time of which Homer tells—possibly as late as the seventh century—all of these tasks were still being done at home, in a rich man's home by his family and slaves and by the womenfolk in the houses of the poor. The luxury clothing that often formed a part of hospitality or friendship gifts was typically made by the women in the giver's household, as were the garments the whole household wore (*Od.* 15.101–8; *Il.* 24.229–35). Women spun and wove, while the heavy, smelly business of fulling usually fell to men. Women often did the final dyeing, though that was not particularly pleasant either.

Not only could nearly all the work be done by women, but there were cultural reasons why it should be. Homer's assumption that all women from

---

[13] Wild (2008) 470–71.
[14] White (1984) 39.
[15] Barber (1991) 68.
[16] The Muslim spinning wheel was adopted in India in the 14th century and further increased spinning speeds by a factor of six—Habib (1982) 80.
[17] Barber (1991) 281–89.
[18] Barber (1991) 284–85. The steps are *plektia* (plaiting), *talasia* (spinning), *alakateia* (working the spindle), *histeia* (working the loom beam), *onucheia* (plucking), and *rhaptria* (sewing). This rigid division of labor does not seem to have persisted in classical times.

princesses to paupers could spin and weave continued in classical times (Xen. *Oec.* 7.6; *Mem.* 2.7.5).[19] The image of a virtuous woman was closely linked to the goddess Athena, patroness of weaving. Penelope was a role model, though weaving had much more sinister connotations in the hands of other women like the Fates, Circe, and Medea. According to Herodotus, it is the good, decent women who weave and spin; sluts and slovens do not (4.34.1; 5.12.3). This was not strictly true: "weaving cloth is a perpetual occupation for all classes of Athenian women. The Archon's wife does it while her husband presides over the court, and prostitutes do it during slack times at the brothel."[20] Finley saw the positive side: "Denied the right to a heroic way of life, to feats of prowess, competitive games, and leadership in organized activity of any kind, women worked regardless of class."[21] Women were the housekeepers but would still have had plenty of time on their hands that they could devote to textile production. There were various tasks that men could do and women could not, ranging from fighting, voting, attending legal cases, and participating in various festivals to heavy physical tasks around the home; women had fewer alternative occupations. Spinning wool and making clothes were obviously useful ways to spend that time. When rebellious women control the government of Athens, they still expect to have to make clothes for the otherwise idle men (Ar. *Eccl.* 654). Under the ancient Cretan law of Gortyna, divorcing women could take their weaving and spinning gear with them (1 Cr. IV.72).

Sociological considerations have made textile work a major occupation for women in many societies over millennia: "If the economic role of women is to be maximized...the economic activity must be such that it can be carried out concurrently with childcare"—in other words the work must be dull and repetitive, not needing concentration, easily interrupted and resumed, safe with children around, and home-based![22] This certainly applied to spinning, although weaving required more concentration and fewer interruptions.[23] Women's textile work was a vital element of household income in revolutionary France, with a deputation of Women of the Third Estate petitioning the king in October 1789: "To prevent so many ills, Sire, we ask that men not be allowed, under any pretext, to exercise trades that are the prerogative of women—such as seamstress, embroideress, *marchande de mode,* etc."[24] Greater employment opportunities for women resulting from increased trade

---

[19] The first of these texts might have described an idealized community (Purves (2010) 199–216), but the *Memorabilia* seems intended as a realistic portrayal of life in Athens.
[20] Matyszak (2008) 25.
[21] Finley (1954) 78.
[22] Brown (1970) 1073–78.
[23] Nixon (1999) 561–67.
[24] Quoted in Gay Levy et al. (1981) 19.

in clothing helped maintain household incomes in England at the time of the Industrial Revolution.[25]

The economics of domestic female labor were irresistible. The women were maintained in the house anyway, so from an economic point of view, the labor that went into domestic production had a marginal cost of zero and, despite the large differences we have noted in spinning productivity, no amount of efficiency or specialization could make outsourcing a lower-cost option. Women seem to have dominated textile production for sale as well. At least two-thirds of the women whose occupations are identified in the lists of people making dedications were *talasiourgoi*, or wool-spinners, and they all came from the industrial area of Athens. There were no similar concentrations of occupations or residence among the men.[26] Most sellers of clothing in Aristophanes were women who appear to have produced their wares themselves (e.g., *Ran*. 1349–51).[27] The only wool-spinner among Timarchus's gang of slaves was a woman who seems to have specialized in fine garments (Aeschin. 1.97). The fabric she worked, *amorgina*, was probably a specially fine and diaphanous type of linen and might have required special weaving dexterity.[28] This was a natural occupation for a lone operator and ideally suited to widows and spinsters.[29] We cannot conclude that independent spinners all worked with special cloth so as to be sure of steady demand and returns to labor that would not be achievable for plain items, but slaves working under an *apophora* arrangement probably did, as otherwise the income accruing to the foreman and investor would be very uncertain.

All this suggests textile manufacture was a fragmented industry employing almost exclusively women and producing little for exchange except especially fine garments.[30] Three considerations show this picture is too simple: abundant evidence for male weavers, the improbability that many households achieved exact self-sufficiency for long, and finds of large weaving sites.

We know of many male weavers. There is a famous depiction of women at a loom by the Amasis painter, but they are thought to have been weaving the gigantic *peplos* for Athena.[31] In fact, most depictions of weavers in antiquity, including the one nearby that is attributed to the Taleides painter, show men, though these are from other places and times.[32] Plato's *hyphantes* seem to be

---

[25] De Vries (2008) 86–107.
[26] Schaps (1979) 19; Betalli (1982) 261–63. The dedications to which these inscriptions relate had been thought to have been made by manumitted slaves, but Meyer (2010) provides good reason to think that they were made by metics—see n.67 below.
[27] Hordern and Purcell (2000) 258.
[28] Richter (1929) 27–33; Linders (1972) 20; 45; 62; Barber (1994) 189–206; Fisher (2001) 233–34; *Amorgina* was prominent among offerings of women's clothing to Artemis Brauronia (Ar. *Lys*. 150; 735–37).
[29] Harris (forthcoming) 13.
[30] Francotte (1900–1901) I. 78.
[31] New York Metropolitan Museum 31.11.10; Barber (1992) 103–18.
[32] Exhibit 47.11.5; see also Boardman (1974) 212; Barber (1991) 290–92.

masculine (*Phaed.* 87b–c, *Grg.* 490d, 517e, *Resp.* 370e, 374b). Specialist tailors Demeas of Collytus (capes) and Menon (cloaks) were men (Xen. *Mem.* 2.7.7), and Helicon and Acesas of Cyprus were celebrated male weavers (Athen. 2.48b). One of Timarchus's slaves was a "man skilled in pattern-making"— almost certainly a weaver.[33] Theophrastus (*De Lapid.* 68) and Pollux (7.78) talk of male clothing retailers, and many of the garments for sale in Athens are thought to have been woven by men.[34] Fullers, almost certainly men, may have sold garments too.[35] When Aristarchus complains he is hard up because of the war and has to accommodate 14 relatives, Socrates tells him to put the relatives to work making and selling clothes (Xen. *Mem.*2.7.3–6). There is no question that these relatives, male and female alike, have the skills or can acquire them rapidly.[36] Socrates's advice is startling, not because it would mean men making clothes but simply because they are free citizens of a class that is not used to working for a living at all.[37]

Carr has estimated what it would take for a household to be self-sufficient.[38] She assumes the citizen family needs a total of six adult and four child tunics each year and three other cloaks. This would require 40 m² of cloth to be spun and woven. Allowing 3,000 meters of thread for each meter of cloth gives 120,000 meters of thread to be spun, perhaps 200,000 if the garment is two-ply. With long fibers and a spinning rate of 100 meters an hour (about as fast as possible and requiring threads of rare length), the household would need to spend 2,000 hours a year spinning—at today's work rates, a full-time job for one person. If the fibers were short, which would have been more likely, it might take twice as long. If the cloth was a mixture of linen (say 14 m²) and wool (26 m²), spinning time would be 1,560 hours for the first and 2,500 for the second. Adding time for weaving takes the total toward 5,000 hours a year, or almost three full-time jobs. As a result, the availability of female labor in a home had a very important impact on living standards. A household of six required at least two full-time textile workers. More than that, and the household could earn from its surplus; with fewer it would have to purchase clothing from third parties or seldom wear new clothes. This was one reason unattached women were valued and often taken in by relatives. From the point of view of textiles, a household of six with one man, three women, and two children would be profitable; one with three men, two women, and a child would be a net buyer of clothes and furnishings. Even without precise demographic data on household composition, we must conclude that a great many

---

[33] Fisher (2001) 233–34.
[34] Thompson (1982a) 217–19.
[35] Ehrenberg (1951) 181–82.
[36] Millett (2000) 33.
[37] Betalli (1982) 261–63.
[38] Carr (1999) 163–67.

households would not have been self-sufficient at some stages during the family's life cycle, and that the amount of trading in textiles was more prevalent than the traditional picture allows.

Finally there is the question of workshop size. If products are fairly standard, as everyday Athenian dress was, and most customers are capable of making the product themselves or had someone at home who could make it at zero marginal cost, there is evidently little basis for either barriers to entry or product differentiation. This explains the typically fragmented structure of the textile industry everywhere prior to power-operated looms.[39] Yet finds of loom weights and other durable equipment show there were several places where large numbers of textile workers were engaged. A house in Pylos contained a large number of spindle whorls.[40] At Olynthus, 43 rooms in 35 houses seem to have been used for weaving and some houses had combined to share workshops that contained several looms.[41] Forty-one weights and a spindle whorl were found in the House of Many Colors. Several other houses had more than 40 loom weights, and one had 133. There have been similar finds in Athens too. Room 9 in House C in the industrial district contained 20 loom weights, a whorl, and a fragment of a brazier, probably for heat or light but possibly for the drying stage of the dyeing process. Room 7 in C4 in the south Areopagus had 9 weights, Building Z more than 100 spread between 20 rooms, and Ceramicus Building 23 had 146 in 8 rooms.[42]

What are we to make of this challenge to the laws of competition? Why would anyone take the risk of acquiring and maintaining a large number of slaves who made products that could be matched at any time by any household or desperate widow willing to accept any price to supplement their income? Three explanations seem plausible. The first is that they had found a basis on which to compete. In the fifth century, Olynthus was considered a poor place (Delian League quota-lists show its contribution was the lowest of all confederation members), so it might have competed on cost, but this had changed by the fourth century, and in any case, cheap labor cannot produce cheaper products than labor with no effective cost at all.[43] Athens and other states would have commissioned large quantities of garments for public slaves or for drama festivals, but it is not clear why these would have been sourced from Olynthus rather than locally.[44] A possible explanation is that Olynthus had developed an export market for fine woven cloth, which seems to be supported by the fact that the weights were of an unusually careful

---

[39] An exception to this fragmentation in textiles was the supply of ropes and sails for boat building (see Chapter 6.3).
[40] Coleman and Abramowitz (1986) 32; 62; 74–75; 90; 102.
[41] Robinson and Graham (1938); Robinson (1946); Cahill (2002) 169–79; 250–52.
[42] Knigge (2005) 201–8; Tsakirgis (forthcoming).
[43] Cahill (2002) 284.
[44] Cf. Records of the Epistatai of Eleusis (329/28–327/26 BCE).

design.[45] It is conceivable that Olynthian textile manufacturers had superior access to excellent cloths or dyes, so a largish production house might establish a barrier to entry and even a premium position based on its brand or designs. It is unlikely, however, that this explains the situation in Athens: if she had an important export trade in fine cloth, it is surprising that it is not mentioned by historians.

There were other ways to differentiate textile products. Vases often show rugs and hangings, and these might have been specialist segments in which a workshop could develop a strong brand and expand accordingly. Ptolemaic Alexandria specialized in luxury tapestries (Athen. 5.196–97), and specialist producers were sufficiently common in Tarsus a few centuries later to form a "dangerous rabble" (Dio. Chrys. *Orat.* 34.21). Some products could only be made in large workshops, including large garments for cult purposes such as Athena's *peplos* for the Panathenaic festival and the sails and ropes for Athens's fleet (see Chapter 6.3), but again we cannot conclude that all large weaving establishments for which we have evidence were engaged in these specialist segments.[46]

An alternative hypothesis recalls the dynamics of the pottery industry. A rich household with a large number of female slaves might well find it sensible to provide proportionately large facilities for spinning and weaving to be used during times of the day when they were not busy on other tasks or when the whole household was in town after the harvest. These large workshops would not have been set up primarily for commercial purposes but would bring in some marginal contribution while conforming to the cultural image of a virtuous household in which everyone was engaged in doing something clever and useful. This is what Aristarchos was doing when he borrowed the funds to buy wool to keep his household profitably occupied (Xen. *Mem.* 2.7.11) and is likely to account for some of the larger finds in Athens.

A third explanation relates to less virtuous households. Prostitutes would have had plenty of time to kill between clients and were expected to continue to make money for their pimp/owner/husband when they had their clothes on. Spinning and weaving would have been ideal occupations for prostitutes just as they were for child minders, and several vases show men with large bags of money approaching a woman who is spinning.[47] A woman excuses her poor productivity in weaving as the result of having just entertained three sailors (Strabo 7.6.20). Epigrams in the Anthologia Palatina (6.48; 283–85) show the interchangeability of textile manufacture and prostitution in the ancient mind. *Ergazesthai* ("to work") carried the same double meaning as "to be a

---

[45] Cahill (2002) 179.
[46] Barber (1992) 103–11.
[47] Davidson (1997) 85; 86–90.

working girl" today, and an *ergasterion* could be a brothel as well as any other type of workshop.

These last two explanations are consistent with what we know about the structure of textile activities in Athens, which otherwise seems to consist of individual practitioners, and with the fact that despite the huge consumption of textiles, teams of textile slaves never feature in lawsuits. Large workshops making textiles for sale are more likely to have been casual and opportunistic extensions of a household or brothel's general activities than a purposeful allocation of investment resources to a dedicated profit-maximizing enterprise. It was not possible to differentiate a product that almost any household could make, nor to offer them at lower cost than the labor of otherwise unemployed women in a household, so there was no basis for winning consistent enough business to justify a large workshop on commercial grounds.

Developments in later antiquity owed more to changes in supply or purchasing than to entrepreneurial innovation. Owners of the wool-clip might seek to add value to it, as happened in Memphis in the third century BCE when it imported a factory system of textile production from Syria or Palestine, and under the Roman Empire when large estates supplied the raw materials to their own large workshops, making products for sale as well as for the estate (Varro *Rus.* 1.2.21).[48] When large textile works reappeared in Egypt 400 years later (Ox. Pap. 22.23410), it was probably because purchasing patterns had changed; market demand was higher than in classical Athens, as it was in Rome, not least because slaves' clothing was purchased and probably made to bulk orders. In the meantime, artisans continued to make a good living out of luxury and customized clothes, shoes, and headgear, and many families continued to make their own clothes when they had the resources to do so.

It is a mistake to conclude that the fragmented nature of ancient textile industries reflects an especially backward economy. Bresson contends that the Athenian industry was highly productive.[49] Hordern and Purcell take strong exception to Finley's unfavorable comparison to the Middle Ages: "'Where are the cloth-halls, the Guildhalls and Bourses?' demanded Moses Finley. When they are not forthcoming, the case for the irremediable primitiveness of the ancient economy is found proven, and variations of social organization are converted into a major qualitative difference in economic complexity."[50] In fact, a true comparison does not support Finley's point anyway. Modern research shows that to speak of "large-scale production" and "capitalist methods" in connection with the famous cloth-making centers of Flanders and north Italy is to give an entirely false impression of the structure of the

---

[48] Loftus (1999); Drinkwater (2001).
[49] Bresson (2007) 198.
[50] Hordern and Purcell (2000) 359; Finley (1973) 137.

industry.[51] Before the advent of much larger, power-operated looms, textile manufacture was a naturally fragmented business even in relatively developed societies. The clothing industry in China in the Middle Ages remained home-based, even when selling was concentrated in the hands of a few merchants and raw materials were sourced centrally from other traders.[52]

Even after the Industrial Revolution, though spinning mills became larger, weaving remained small-scale. There was a major discontinuity in the spinning industry's costs when watermills were harnessed, Arkwright's Spinning Jenny was developed, and mechanized high-speed spindles were used in series; as a result, quite unlike the ancient world, textiles was the first industry to industrialize in Massachusetts after the War of Independence, when Samuel Slater brought Arkwright's technology over from England.[53] The low costs achieved, together with other employment opportunities for women, changed the equation for households considering whether textile-making was the best use of the household's female labor. The extent of the change in production costs can be seen in Britain's trade policy: before mechanization, she erected trade barriers against low-cost Indian textiles; once she had mechanized her own industry, she demanded free trade.[54] Despite these innovations, textile manufacturing remains relatively labor-intensive today. A large part of the value chain relates to the brand—either as a general quality mark or as a fashion label—and brand owners often outsource manufacturing to low-labor-cost countries.

## 5.1.2 SCOURING AND FINISHING

The heavier-process steps consolidated more rapidly, although it is hard to tell when. Scouring and finishing (fulling and dyeing) were of a nature that encouraged outsourcing and offered barriers to entry, but the archaeological record offers only dubious evidence of large establishments before Hellenistic and Roman times.

*Scouring* involves washing, cleaning, and beating the fiber prior to spinning. It is not clear how clean the wool was that was sold at market in Athens, and preparation of wool for spinning was depicted as a home craft on Greek vases, but it is likely that imports had been at least partially scoured, if only to allay buyers' concerns about net weight.[55] For those working with their own wool or who had purchased unclean material, scouring was a physically demanding and dirty job, after which the prepared wool was weighed and put

---

[51] Bridbury (1982) 11.
[52] Elvin (1973) 195.
[53] Rosenberg (2007) 7.
[54] Monaghan (1999) 167–72.
[55] White (1984) 39.

in a basket (*kalathos*). The scoured wool was then combed and formed into cylinders by twisting it over the thigh, sometimes using a thigh cover called an *epinetron*.[56] This "carding" process breaks up clumps of fiber and aligns the individual fibers so that they are more or less parallel with each other. It might take several weeks to card a batch of fiber for spinning, and the task was tedious but not unpleasant.

After the cloth is woven the wool is cleansed and whitened by *fulling*. The most effective solution requires ammonium salts, and before the discovery of fuller's earth this involved standing ankle-deep in tubs of stale human urine and treading vigorously.[57] Fullers would then "felt" the cloth by matting the fibers together to give it strength and increase waterproofing, which was especially necessary for cloth made of short staple wool, as most of the Attic clip was. The cloth would be thoroughly rinsed to get rid of the smell before dyeing. Similar processes were used to have garments cleaned, and heavy laundering was probably a part of the fuller's job.[58] Unsurprisingly, fulling was a job for men (IG.I³ 554, 616, 905; Xen. *Mem.* 2.7.6; Aeschin. 1.124, Lys. 23.2).

*Dyeing* could be applied to spun wool or the original fleece (which resulted in the best color uptake) but more commonly to the finished cloth.[59] Once the dye had been prepared, the material to be dyed was immersed in the solution, then removed, the excess squeezed out, and the cloth left to dry. Dyeing was considered a normal part of a household's budget, though Lysias's estimated cost of 100 *drachmae* per person per year (32.20) must be an exaggeration. Dyes were made from a range of animal and plant material, mixed in cold and hot water with mineral fixing agents or "mordants." The Phoenician cities of Tyre and Byblos had been active in the textile and garment trades in the late Bronze Age, exporting murex, the famous "Tyrian" purple dye made from crushed sea snails, and making and selling dyed garments.[60] Pliny describes how the murex shells were broken and their glands extracted and heated for 10 days in a large vat containing hot water (*HN*. 9. 60–65). Murex stains on *amphorae* found at Sidon and Sarepta date back to the 13th century BCE and murex harvesting was still a large industry in Roman times, but there is no evidence of it in Athens, and it is likely that the Athenians used other vegetable and animal dyes, which would have been prepared in similar ways.[61]

---

[56] Heinrich (2006).

[57] Wilson (2003) 442–46.

[58] The physical demands of laundering had been recognized in Egypt around 1200 BCE: "The washerman's day is going up, going down. All his limbs are weak, [from] whitening his neighbors' clothes every day, from washing their linen." From the Nebmare-Nakht, an exercise for student scribes: Andrea and Overfield (2004) 23.

[59] Halleux (1981).

[60] Markoe (2005) 13–14; 216.

[61] Alcock (2007) 683.

An important motive for outsourcing these trades was amenity. The unpleasant smells involved mean that it was probably environmental factors as much as the more masculine nature of the tasks that led to the fixed independent sites for which there is abundant evidence in later periods.[62] In the Roman Empire, private fulleries were found only in wealthy (spacious, airy!) houses; the rest were huge establishments situated near aqueducts and regulated by a special law.[63] A large number have been found at Timgad in Roman Africa, and it seems fullery workers may have had exclusive use of the nearby baths![64] These Roman examples are informative, and Athens may have operated on similar lines with families whose houses were not exceptionally large choosing to outsource in order to avoid the stench that would result from having their slaves do the work in their home. Herodotus (4.14) mentions a specialist fuller in Scythia, Lysias (3.16) refers to a fuller named Molon, and Ehrenberg seems to have assumed a thriving fulling industry in classical Athens as a matter of course.[65]

Similar considerations apply to dyeing, though the smell of the process was usually less noxious (especially if murex was not used), which explains why some households did their own (Plut. *Per.* 1–2). Nevertheless, effluent could still be a problem and was sometimes toxic, which might have prompted at least some households to outsource. Independent dye houses would have had the additional advantage of access to innovative ingredients that individual households might have struggled to source. It is possible they formed a simple supply chain, with some groups acquiring the dyestuffs and others specializing in particular cloths or colors.[66] One would expect these houses to have competed on the basis of their distinctive range of colors or colorfastness; households who could afford it would look for better dyes and more consistent output than they could achieve at home.

Job titles of people making votive dedications suggest dyeing was specialized by around 330–320 BCE, but physical evidence from classical Athens is limited and there have been no significant finds of murex to indicate large dye houses.[67] This archaeological silence is not definitive: vegetable and animal dyes are hard to trace, and it is not easy to separate fulling and dyeing sites: both require stalls with tubs for treading cloth; only some dyeing

---

[62] The impact of such factors on location is well illustrated in the case of the tanning of leather (see section 5.2.1 below).
[63] Forbes (1964–72) IV.88; Kehoe (2007) 564–67.
[64] Wilson (2001) 287–91.
[65] White (1984) 39; Ehrenberg (1951) 181–82.
[66] Monaghan (1999) 168.
[67] Lewis (1968) 368–80. The text was originally interpreted as commemorating the gifts of slaves thanking the gods for an acquittal under the *dike apostasiou* or for being allowed to start living outside the home, while a more recent reading suggests the matters related to the *graphe apostasiou* and were to do with non-payment of the *metoikon*. (Koehler (1878) 172–77; Wilamowitz-Moellendorff (1887a,b); Cohen (2000) 130–54; Meyer (2010) 80.)

establishments had heaters under the tubs.[68] Vessels and pressing equipment were simple and small-scale, and might have had other household uses when there was no cloth to be treated.[69] Recent finds of baths used for fulling in Iron Age Philistine cities, as well as murex stains at various sites around the Aegean from a similar period, suggest new discoveries might still change the picture in classical Athens.[70]

## 5.2 Footwear

On the face of it, tanning and shoemaking seem to have much in common with textiles. The technology is quite simple; part of the process is strenuous, dirty, and smelly; raw materials were often sourced from a farm; and products were often made specifically for members of the immediate household. The reason leatherwork was commercialized relatively quickly, while textiles were not, reflects differences in the nature of the work. Leatherwork required physical strength in making the final product as well as in tanning; cutting, piercing, and stitching leather without machinery is physically demanding. It may have been possible for women to carry out these tasks, but they were not seen as part of a woman's education or as relevant to their identification with Athena. It would not have taken much time anyway; one or two people could tan enough hides and turn them into shoes and other leather needs for a large estate in just a few days a year. Better to outsource this, as we saw in Chapter 2, and for the female labor force to focus on the more diverse range of products and applications offered by clothing and hangings. Another attraction of not doing one's own tanning was avoiding having the smell of the process hanging around the home for weeks.

### 5.2.1 TANNING

The production of leather goods starts with the preservation of raw hides.[71] Simple curing results in an unstable product that is not water-resistant, so the ancients applied tannins extracted from tree bark or oak gall skins.[72] In classical times, the process began with beating the skin to make it supple; it was then depilated and soaked in tannin-rich vegetable oils before being stretched and scraped on a beam. No Greek tannery has been excavated, but a Roman one in Pompeii has a receival room, a pit for vegetable tanning, and a workshop for preparing solutions, which contains a range of implements for

---

[68] Wilson (2001) 273.
[69] Monaghan (1999) 167–72.
[70] Mazow (2010).
[71] The description of the process and archaeological finds here are from Forbes (1964–72) V.48–63.
[72] Van Driel-Murray (2008) 485.

scraping and cutting. The work was strenuous, the smell appalling, and the waste water foul. In Homer, tanning seems to have been chiefly a home-based industry, though there were some specialists like Tychus, who made Ajax's shield with the hides of seven bulls (*Il.* 7.219–23). The rich had their shoes and horse gear made by slaves at home from animals on their estate, while the poor did their own tanning and made leather goods from the hides of their own animals. By classical times, commercial tanning had become quite a substantial industry, and, it seems, a profitable one. Cleon's father owned a tannery (Ar. *Eq.* 44) and left him a large inheritance. Anytos, apparently another tannery heir (Xen. *Apol.* 29), was rich enough to be accused of bribing a jury ((Arist). *Ath. pol.* 27.5).[73]

Van Driel-Murray observes that, despite the wealth of tanning families like those of Anytos and Cleon, few tombstones commemorate tanners, while many identify shoemakers.[74] The reason is not far to seek. These shoemakers were independent craftsmen; tanning operatives were slave gangs whose owners did not necessarily seek to be known primarily by the nature of their investment. Nevertheless, the wealth of tannery-owning families suggests that the tanning industry in Athens was one in which either better-than-average margins were available or establishment size was large, probably some combination of the two. What forms of advantage or barriers to entry would produce such an outcome? Tanning is essentially a materials-handling operation and costs depend entirely on handling productivity, so only significant advances in materials-handling technology based on the application of power would give large tanneries a worthwhile cost advantage over small ones. It is also hard to differentiate product quality.

One source of attractive profitability that has been suggested was forward integration into shoemaking.[75] This certainly became the pattern later, but the only real evidence for this in classical times is the scholiast to Plato's Apology, who says Anytos's tannery sold shoes.[76] Leather hides were sold in the Agora (*bursa*—*Eq.* 136, 369, 892; *Pax* 753; *Vesp.* 38; *skutos*—*Eq.* 868, *Pax* 669) and some simpler thongs (*himas*—*Ach.* 724) might have been sold directly by tanners, but, as the next section describes, shoemaking was a quite different activity, requiring specific training and expertise. Aristophanes's occasional mocking association of Cleon with shoes can be explained as simple extrapolations of the basic joke about descent from a tannery-owner; the much-cited reference to turning Cleon's hide into shoes (*Ach.* 299) is more than matched by multiple lines in the *Knights* associating the Paphlagonian with every kind of process and product of the tanning industry but shoes (*Eq.* 48; 59; 104; 136;

---

[73] Davies (1971) 40–41.
[74] Van Driel-Murray (2008) 491.
[75] Forbes (1964–72) V. 60.
[76] Scholiast on Pl. *Ap.* 18b.

203; 315; 379; 449; 963–64). We see how easily Athenians conflated different leather-based specialties such as *neurorraphoi* (stitchers) and *skutotomoi* (cutters) with *bursopolai* (sellers of skins; *Eq.* 738–40). The economic rationale for forward integration is unconvincing anyway; the notion that a competitive advantage can be extended from one industry to an adjacent one in the supply chain through vertical integration and clever transfer pricing is a common one, but simple arithmetic shows it is incorrect. If the nature of tanning was such as to allow high margins, tanners could realize them by selling to leatherworkers without entering the finished product market themselves. Conversely, if the true source of profit was in making end products, shoemakers would do better without putting part of their resources into tanneries.

A more likely explanation is that the unpleasantness of the work and a probable limitation on sites underpinned tanning's profitability. The first might mean a lack of willing new entrants to such an unpleasant business, just as the shoemaking trades in India belonged to the untouchable class. Probably more important would have been public amenity. Many cities throughout history have regulated where tanneries could be located. Boston, Massachusetts, still has a Leatherworkers District. Originally the site of tanneries (segregated from residential areas because of their smell), it became the hub of a large shoe manufacturing cluster. The archaeological evidence suggests that Athens achieved the same result, with its tanneries clustered in one district, Cydathenaion. This was at least partly enforced by regulations; one from 440–420 BCE prohibited tanning and soaking hides in the Ilissos near Heracles's shrine (IG.1³ 257).[77] The Ilissos flowed through the centre of Cydathenaion, which remained the tanning district of Athens right through the Roman and Byzantine periods up until the Ottomans in the 16th century CE—a longevity suggesting the city insisted on keeping it in one place.[78] A spot near the temple of Hercules would have been a convenient site for treating the hides of sacrificial animals, but the "odeurs nauséabondes et la pollution des eaux" made it desirable to banish the practice from the temple surrounds.[79]

Location restrictions would have provided an important barrier to entry and might have raised prices above a competitive level by artificially restricting supply. Entrepreneurs who got established in a permitted area could set prices without fear of new entry. Restricted site licenses can be the source of exceptional levels of profit in certain environmentally sensitive businesses today such as waste disposal and the cleaning of chemical vessels, and similar limits on competition might well have provided a privileged position for tanneries in classical Athens.

---

[77] Sokolowski (1962) 19.4.
[78] Hughes (2010) 104.
[79] Billot (1992) 155–56.

## 5.2.2 SHOEMAKING

The principal application of tanned leather—and the only one about which we have much information—was shoes. Leather footwear included sandals, shoes, and boots with or without straps.[80] The standard Athenian shoe or sandal consisted of a flat sole, a broad band across the front of the foot, and a thong attached an inch or two from the front of the sole that came up between the toes and was knotted round the ankle to four smaller thongs attached to the sides of the sole (Ill. 5.3). Most of the foot was left bare.[81] The leather might remain in its natural color or be dyed red, white, vermillion, scarlet, saffron, green, or black and could be embellished with fancy borders. The precise design varied over time—to the point where it has been used for dating sculptures[82]—but the essential structure and componentry endured.

ILLUSTRATION 5.3. Ancient Sandal with Decorative Cut

---

[80] Sandal: *embas*—Ar. *Nub.* 858; *Eq.* 321, 869, 871, 875; *Vesp.* 1157; shoe: *kattymata*—*Ach.* 301; *hypodema*—*Thesm.* 262; boot: *kothornos*—*Lys.* 657; *lakonikae*—*Vesp.* 1158, 1162.
[81] Cosgrove (2000) ch. 2.
[82] Morrow (1985).

The shoes of richer women might be decorated with embroidery, gilt, or pearls.[83] The *kothornos* had a raised platform sole and is thought to have been introduced for actors. Heavy-duty versions might be strengthened with hobnails. A pair of sandals or boots typically fetched between four and six *drachmae* a pair, sometimes as much as eight (IG.II² 1672.105; Ar. *Plut.* 983).[84] Indoors the Athenians wore slippers. Many women probably owned nothing else. Some might have been made from soft leather, but the popular *persikai* (Ar. *Nub.* 151; *Thesm.* 754) were usually of basket weave, and others like the *peribaris* (*Lys.* 45, 47, 53) might have been made from some type of cloth.

Many other leather items were on sale in Aristophanes's Agora, including garments for agricultural workers, goatskin cloaks, and containers such as wine skins, flute cases, panniers, quivers, spear cases, crest cases, and knapsacks. Rowers could buy oar-port covers and thongs for their oars, soldiers could get chinstraps for their helmets, horsemen could buy whips, and farmers could get yoke straps. Domestic leather goods included bellows, pouches, dog-skin caps, and dog leads.[85]

Vase paintings and epigraphy suggest that shoemaking was a bespoke operation, requiring just one craftsman and a handful of assistants. A relief dedicated by a cobbler named Dionysius and his children shows a young man working on a sandal and a small boy cutting leather at a cobbler's bench, while an old man reaches for sandals on a peg.[86] A sixth-century *kylix* shows a shoemaker using a half-moon knife and an *amphora* depicts a customer standing on a table while leather is cut round his foot, indicating that shoes were made to measure.[87] Literature supports this view: Plato uses shoemaking as an archetypal example of a craft needing specialized training and continual practice (*Resp.* 601c; *Meno* 90c), and asking for a refit was common (Ar. *Lys.* 416–19).

It seems to have been considered a rather sedentary occupation (Ar. *Plut.* 162), allowing plenty of time for philosophical conversation. Diogenes Laertius (2.122–23) tells how Socrates used to sit and converse with a shoemaker named Simon in his shop on the edge of the marketplace. It enabled

---

[83] Yue and Yue (1997).

[84] Thompson (1971) 17.

[85] Leather agricultural garment: *diphtheria*—*Nub.* 72; goat-skin cloak: *sisyra*—*Nub.* 10; *Ran.* 1459; *Vesp.* 737; wine skin: *molgos*—*Eq.* 963; *askos*—*Ach.* 549, 1225, 1235; *Thesm.* 733; flute cases: *sybene*—*Thesm.* 1197; 1215; panniers: *kanthelos*—*Vesp.* 170; quiver: *pharetra*—*Eq.* 1272; spear case: *elutron*—*Ach.* 1120; crest case: *lopheion*—*Nub.* 751; *Ach.* 1109; knapsack: *gylion*—*Ach.* 1097, 1138; *Pax* 527; oar-port cover: *askoma*, *Ach.* 97; *Ran.* 364; thong for oars: *tropoteros*—*Ach.* 549; chinstrap for a helmet: *phorbeia*—*Vesp.* 582; whip: *mastix*—*Thesm.* 933, 1125, 1135; yoke strap: *lepadnon*—*Eq.* 768; bellows: *rhipis*—*Ach.* 888; pouch: *peridion*—*Nub.* 923; dog-skin cap: *kynee*—*Nub.* 268; dog lead: *himas kyneios*—*Vesp.* 231.

[86] Agora I 7396; Camp (1986) 146–47, Fig. 126.

[87] Ashmolean Museum: Burford (1972) pl. 3; Fine Arts Museum of Boston: Forbes (1964–72) V. Fig. 13.

him to address a young audience, youths not being allowed into the Agora (Xen. *Mem.* 4.2.1; Diog. Laert. 2.13.122; cf. Plut. *Mor.* 776b). Diogenes names 33 Socratic dialogues known as *skutikoi logoi* or "leather cutters' talk," and claims Simon was the first to write one. For the Cynics he was a model for self-sufficiency and freedom of speech (*parrhesia*—*Soc. Epist.* 8) and the true heir to Socrates (*Soc. Epist.* 18.2).[88] Even though Simon is not mentioned by Plato or Xenophon, archaeological finds seem to support Diogenes: traces of a shop in the southwest corner of the Agora have been found, including a large number of hobnails and ivory eyelets for laces as well as the base of a pot labeled "Simonos."[89] Socrates would have approved the application of *techne* and the apolitical life represented by Simon. Zeno tells a similar anecdote about Crates the cynic sitting in a shoemaker's shop reading philosophy (Diog. Laert. 6.91).

All this suggests shoemaking was a small craft business engaged in by sole operators with, at most, a handful of assistants, working in their own premises and tailoring shoes to fit customers who came into the shop. Seen in this way, shoemaking shares many features with bronze armor in terms of the ordering process and the difficulty of transferring the reputation of an individual to a large workshop, and we have seen how that tended to remain an industry of lone craftsmen. Nevertheless, we are entitled to wonder whether this was the full story: were every Athenian's shoes custom-made by skilled craftsmen or might there also have been businesses making shoes for stock? Forbes suggests there was not enough volume in particular sizes to make for stock, but he is almost certainly mistaken.[90] If each non-slave male bought a pair every five years and women and slaves never bought leather shoes at all (which seems absurdly conservative, given the likely conditions underfoot) this amounts to over 10,000 pairs of shoes for adults a year. Even with the fine gradations of today's footwear market, this would mean thousands in some sizes and hundreds in others. As the Athenian shoe did not have an upper, any given shoe could accommodate a wide range of foot sizes with comfort, so an Athenian cobbler whose production concentrated on one or more of the most popular sizes would have been able to find plenty of off-the-shelf customers.

We know of one example of a sizable gang of leatherworking slaves, and, given the sparse nature of the literary sources, it would be unwise to assume there were not more. Aeschines describes Timarchus as owning a number of working slaves, including nine leatherworkers and their overseer (1.97). How can we reconcile a large team with a bespoke craft? Again what matters is whether they could sell enough of their output to cover their costs. There is no suggestion that Timarchus's income from these slaves was subject to the

---

[88] Malherbe (1977).
[89] Thompson (1960) 234–40; Sellars (2003).
[90] Forbes (1964–72) V.63.

vagaries of the market. It is conceivable that the individual slaves guaranteed their own *apophora*, but this seems unnecessarily complex and makes the overseer redundant. It is more likely that the *apophora* was guaranteed by the overseer, which was the typical model.[91] No overseer would take on this obligation on behalf of himself and nine others without a great deal of confidence that their output could find a buyer at a reasonable price. Nor would any owner be likely to invest in an *apophora* that had a good chance of not being paid. With most shoes selling at four to six *drachmae* a pair, and assuming that leather accounted for a third to a half of the final price and the nine shoemakers and their overseer cost around a *drachma* a day each to maintain, including the payment to the owner, they might have broken even at a collective production of four or five pairs a day. If they sold less, the overseer would have a problem.

Specialization is one possible explanation for the shoemakers working together, but not a convincing one. Xenophon used shoemaking to illustrate the benefits: "One man makes men's shoes, another women's. And in some places, one man supports himself by only stitching, another by cutting, another by only shaping the uppers, and another by doing none of this but only assembling these things" (8.2.5). Timarchus's nine leatherworkers might have specialized in different types of shoe or other leather products (there were 82 words for footwear in classical Greece, reflecting a wide range of styles, origins, and materials[92]), but this type of specialization would tend to attract different labels such as *humantopoios* (sandals), *persikopoios* (slippers), or *neurorraphos* (stitcher/cobbler), so perhaps the specialization was in the form identified by Xenophon, by process step. Chapter 1 has shown that this is a weak explanation of enterprise size, and it certainly seems inadequate here. It is difficult to see how cutting and stitching layers of leather for a sole and thongs, making eyelets, and then attaching the thongs and eyelets to the sole can be divided into more than four or five different activities. Xenophon only identifies four sub-tasks. A sole was simply not large enough for several people to work on it at once. Almost certainly, if the shoemakers were busy, several of them would have been doing the same thing at the same time, and nine is not the solution to an equation optimizing the division of shoemaking labor. It is possible that Timarchus's team was making other things than shoes, such as leather corselets or thongs for armor or agricultural gear—*skutotomoi* just means leather workers—but the same considerations apply. If anything, such products involved fewer steps and would have been still less divisible. And we may question just how much productivity benefit accrues from such specialization as they might have achieved. It is conceivable that the division of labor meant that nine slaves would produce more than nine times as much as one in

---

[91] See Chapter 9.1.
[92] New Pauly (2003) 13.403.

a given period, but not much more: the tasks were not so different that worker focus would have more than a marginal impact on productivity. Such cost advantage as it did bring is unlikely to have been large enough to encourage smaller shoemaking concerns to risk expansion.

It is conceivable that there was some demand advantage from working together. If shoes were made to measure, a customer who had been fitted would expect to collect his shoes fairly quickly. A single shoemaker can only accommodate one customer at a time, but once he has finished that customer's shoes, he needs another order to keep going. He is likely to have periods when he is overloaded, possibly leading to customer dissatisfaction, and other periods when he has no work. A larger workforce is able to manage such peaks and troughs better and will also attract custom from being known to have the capacity to respond quickly to orders at all times. Hotelling's Law explains that ice-cream sellers tend to gather at one end of the beach so they can steal each other's customers, but another common reason for reseller co-location is so that customers know where to find them.[93] An establishment where customers can be sure to get what they want rapidly might have an advantage in attracting business compared to a lone shoemaker.

Though this is possible, it is hard to believe that Timarchus's team was made up of Simons, each engaging in light philosophical banter while loyal customers queued to have their feet measured. If they were, it is hard to see why they would need an overseer or how their overseer could make sure they were productive enough to pay the *apophora* as well as their own living expenses.[94] It is much more likely that they were making standard products for which there was a steady demand. These could have been basic leather products that did not require customization, like whips, thongs, oar tethers, chinstraps, dog leads, or wine skins, for instance. It might have been possible to establish a regular trade in some of them to a reseller or boat builder who would take all of a workshop's output. It is also quite possible that they were making standard-size shoes. It seems ready-made shoes were on sale in the Agora.[95] The shoes that Sausage-Maker gives Demos (Ar. *Eq.* 871) were clearly not made to measure and probably lacked the fancy finishing in the illustration above. Standard shoes made for stock would have fetched a much lower price than bespoke items, but would be cheaper to make, as they carried no costs for measuring, fitting, or involuntary downtime. The skills and strength required made the business less vulnerable to new entry than basic textiles or ceramics, and producers known for reliable quality might have been able to develop a consistent retail market among the less well-off. In fact, leather

---

[93] Hotelling (1929).
[94] A slave's living expenses tended to fall on the manager-foreman, not the owner—see Chapter 9.1's analysis of Demosthenes 27.
[95] Thompson (1971) 17.

workshops of several slaves making off-the-shelf products for specific leather market niches, including shoes, may have been quite common. There would still have been room for the independent craftsman without the skills to be a bespoke shoemaker to make a living in basic leather goods, but it would not have been a very attractive or stable source of income.

In recent times, shoemaking consolidation has been based on technological advances in cutting and stitching machinery, which have reduced a large workshop's costs well below those of the lone craftsman, together with a heavy investment in branding. Like textiles, however, it remains a very labor-intensive industry, with the result that leading brand owners now outsource all or most of their manufacturing to low-labor-cost countries.

## 5.3 Summary

TCF activity in Athens comprised numerous segments with very different characteristics (Table 5.1).

TABLE 5.1 Textile Clothing and Footwear Industries

|  |  | Barriers to Entry | |
|---|---|---|---|
|  |  | Yes | No |
| Potential for Differentiation | Yes | Differentiated industry: *Standard shoes and leather goods?* | Differentiated craft: Bespoke shoes Fine garments Tapestries |
|  | No | Undifferentiated industry: Tanning *Scouring, fulling, dyeing?* | Undifferentiated craft: Simple garments Basic leather goods |

*Note: Italic font* represents business forms for which there appears to have been an opportunity, but for which there is limited or no evidence in classical Athens.

Except for tanning in classical times, and fulling and dyeing probably sometime afterward, TCF manufacturing was largely of the traditional craft type, conducted in the home by slaves, metics, and free alike. Skill alone did not provide a barrier to entry in textiles; all women and many men could spin and weave. The specialist fine cloth and tapestry segments were probably the only ones to offer attractive returns. Leatherwork skills were less widespread, but the role of assistants shown on vase paintings indicates a natural apprenticeship path and there is no doubt that if the occupation was seen to be highly profitable, more craftsmen would have found ways to learn the skills and compete away the higher margins. The only way for an individual to achieve good price realization was customizing products for a loyal clientele—a loyalty that could be achieved partly through good conversation.

Large leatherworking teams making large-volume, specialized products, including standard shoes, might also have succeeded, provided they had secure reselling arrangements. The greater opportunity for a large workshop in both segments was where environmental considerations limited the number of operating sites, as in tanning and perhaps in fulling and dyeing. Restricted supply would have meant attractive prices and secure revenues that would grow with the market, enabling risk-free and highly profitable trading.

From textiles and footwear we turn to woodworking, which provided quite different bases for successful expansion.

# 6 }

# Woodworking

Although few wooden objects survive from antiquity, several sources allow us to reconstruct ancient woodworking activity. The 1991 discovery of wooden artifacts with the body of the Neolithic "Iceman" in the Alps showed that humans were selecting different woods for different purposes according to their intrinsic properties 5,000 years ago. By the Iron Age, improved design and stronger composition of tools had increased the repertoire of wooden products far beyond traditional uses as fuel and in weaponry, and wood had become the main material in land transport, ships, and structural features of buildings, as well as in furniture and other household objects.[1] In Homeric times, Odysseus was using an adze, an auger, and a chalkline to make his bed (*Od.* 13.195–98) and the poet can refer to the action of a strap drill and assume his listeners will understand (*Od.* 9.384–46). Woodworking tools were sufficiently well known to be mentioned in lyric poetry (e.g., Leonidas 6.205.204), and Pliny attributed the invention of most of them to the archaic sculptors Daidalos and Theodorus of Samos (*HN.* 7.198). For classical times, surviving texts specify wood types and their uses; depictions of wooden items on vase paintings and in reliefs can provide reliable insight into the techniques and tools that must have been used;[2] and inscriptions carry the names of roofing components.[3]

A wide range of woods was available around Athens, including beech, oak, chestnut, fir, lime, maple, poplar, pine, and walnut.[4] Each had properties that suited it for different applications, although in many instances the difference in product performance would be slight and it is likely that the choice depended on price and availability. The enormous demands of constructing Athens' fleet and supporting the structure of mines and major buildings meant she became increasingly dependent on importing large timber; wood for her ships came from the northern end of the Aegean, and cypress wood for

---

[1] Ulrich (2008) 439–40.
[2] Examples include bentwood on a fifth-century Athenian *klismos* (Richter (1966) 33–37, fig. 175) and lathe turning in a seventh-century Etruscan relief (Steingräber (1979) 340–41, pl. 44).
[3] Caskey (1910); Hodge (1960) 116–27.
[4] Meiggs (1982) ch. 7.

construction beams was typically sourced from Crete or Carpathos.[5] Timber became Athens's principal import after grain.

The technology of carpentry has changed very little over the centuries other than in the gradual sophistication of tools and the introduction of nonhuman power to work them.[6] Ancient carpenters used a full range of hand implements for cutting, boring, smoothing, and measuring: axes, saws, drills, planes, hammers, chisels, borers, knives, screwdrivers, files, compasses, rules, calipers, framing squares, levels, and plummets.[7] Multiple adaptations suited various purposes: saws included the two-man crosscut, bow saws, large and small frame saws with tensioning devices, and small handsaws. Chisels and gouges came in a wide range of sizes, shapes, and strengths according to the nature of the wood and the hole or groove to be made; the strongest were of iron with tempered cutting edges, and the shape that could penetrate deepest, especially in hardwoods, was the mortising chisel. There were multiple drill types too, but most consisted of a flat diamond-shaped point at the end of an iron rod that could be spun in either direction by a thong and bow device. Such devices could also drive small lathes, capable of turning furniture components such as table legs, the handles of agricultural tools, or small wooden containers (Aesch. *Fr.* 57; Pl. *Phlb.* 56b).[8] Other furniture was finished by bending: Theophrastus identifies the most pliable woods (*HP.* 5.6.2; 7.3.4), which were probably seasoned to prevent splitting (Plin. *HN.* 16.192, 222) and bent into shape with steam (*HN.* 16.227). Glue (Arist. *Metaph.* 1652a; Ar. *Eq.* 463) made from animal or fish cartilages was used to apply veneers. Fir took glue well, so was suitable for veneering, whereas oak did not.

Joinery was especially well developed. Nails were not used very much, partly because they had to be purchased from a bronze or iron smith but also because they tend to damage wood over time. Screws could not be made in quantity before the 18th century, so the principle was only applied in jewelry bolts and agricultural presses. The most common joining technique was mortise and tenon, essential for assembling wooden furniture and in joining heavy architectural beams.[9] Other joints included corner, miter, tongue and groove, half-lap or saddle, or, more simply, wooden dowels and tenons (*gomphos*; Ar. *Eq.* 461–62), the choice depending on likely stress and wear and, in some applications, aesthetics.

For many wood products, limited technological development and the common availability of materials made for a fragmented industry like pottery.

---

[5] The wood for the 200 ships Themistocles had built in 483 BCE probably came from southern Italy—Meiggs (1982) 121–30.
[6] Richter (1966) 122–29.
[7] Ulrich (2008) 445–47.
[8] Cf. Roman applications in Pugsley (2003) 67; 79; 108.
[9] Ulrich (2008) 451–53.

Nevertheless, as with metalwork, the numerous applications of wood result in a variety of specialized business segments, each with their own supply and demand conditions and each offering scope for differentiation. We have seen how one wood industry, shields, required teams of at least six slaves (Chapter 4.7) and how the importance of reputation meant a competitor could capture a large market share. This chapter starts by analyzing supply and demand in the highly differentiable furniture segment, then examines the scope to differentiate other wooden products, and concludes with a section on the shipbuilding industry. The application of wood in large-scale construction projects is treated in the next chapter.

## 6.1 Furniture

Athenian house furniture was very scanty by our standards, consisting merely of a few couches, chairs, tables, and chests.[10] Nevertheless, keeping 50,000 or more houses supplied made it a large business. Much furniture was of plain design and cheap materials, but there were also high-end couches, tables, thrones, and chests that could be true luxury items and real works of art, decorated with inlay (often of ivory) and sometimes set with gems or colored glass and covered with fine mattresses, rugs, and pillows.[11] Trying to define the furniture a typical house contained is not easy, although several sources shed some light. Furniture is often listed in epigraphic records of confiscations and temple inventories as well as being represented in a number of vase paintings. The items pictured are never named on vases, and names in texts are seldom accompanied by any descriptions, so the challenge is to match the words to the pictures. Many scholars have made thorough and detailed attempts to do so, but a great deal of uncertainty remains about exactly what form of chair, couch, or bed a dozen or more words refer to.[12] From the point of view of manufacturing, what matters is the nature of the tasks involved in making them, so the overview that follows concentrates on materials and complexity of manufacture and on the potential to differentiate a workshop's output.

One of the earliest items of furniture recorded was the *throne* (*thronos*), the seat of nobles and gods. Homer's *thronoi* were high, very dignified (*Od.* 5.251, 422), gleaming (*Il.* 18.422), and well wrought (*Od.* 1.31). In classical Athens, most were in temples and public buildings for use on ceremonial occasions and unlikely ever to have been found in ordinary homes. One was confiscated

---

[10] Tucker (1907) 64–66; Rostovtzeff (1941) II.1203–4.

[11] Richter (1966) 125–26; Rostovtzeff (1941) II.1203–4.

[12] See especially Ransom (1905); Richter (1926); Pritchett and Pippin (1956); Richter (1966); Boardman (1990); Andrianou (2009).

from Alcibiades's house, but his co-offenders in the mutilation of the herms (Thuc. 6.27–28) did not seem to own anything similar.[13] Unlike other articles of furniture, *thronoi* only came in luxury versions and would have been made exclusively by highly skilled craftsmen. Vase paintings show several variations, including Egyptian-style animal feet, though these lost favor after the mid-fifth century. Turned legs with palmette engravings were common at around that time, but the legs became longer and ultimately metamorphosed into rectangular shape. Many thrones had a back and armrests, but the addition of solid sides was mainly for cult and votive purposes. In the Hellenistic period, side panels became highly decorated and were copied by Roman, medieval, and Renaissance emperors and monarchs.[14]

For more common items for sitting or lying on, we have a range of labels, including *kline, klinidion, skimpous, skimpodion, chameuna, krabbatos, askantes*, and *stibas*, all of which have been translated as both "*bed*" and "*couch*."[15] Dining rooms appear to have had several couches, three being typical but some houses had many more.[16] Fifteen out of 25 men's rooms excavated at Olynthus might each have held five couches, and there might have been nine in one house in Megara.[17] Pictures of feasts typically show two men on each couch, invariably accompanied by a small side table. In mythological scenes the nuptial bed can be referred to as a *kline*, and they may have been used as beds in classical times; in small houses residents probably slept in the dining room anyway. *Klinai* do not seem to have been ideal for lying on, though, and most people would have slept on rugs on the floor.

Whether for feasting, sleeping or simply lounging, couches were designed to accommodate a relaxed posture. They consisted of a frame (*enelaton*) generally of wood but sometimes of bronze or iron (Thuc. 3.68.3), four legs (*podes*), and a set of thongs (*tonoi*) to be covered with a mattress. At least one end curved upward, sometimes both. One Milesian *kline* seems to be designated in the Attic Stelae as *amphikephalos* or "two-headed," though the word might actually be *amphiknephalos*, meaning "two-pillowed" (Poll. 10.36).[18] The first reading is more likely and probably indicates a head or armrest, which in some cases were detachable and fitted into the couch with dowel pins. The question of precisely what is being referred to in texts is compounded by the fact that the names of these heads or armrests were also used to represent the main items themselves: thus one meaning for *epiklintron* in the Lexicon

---

[13] Pritchett (1953) 255ff; Stela II, 145, 236; Pritchett and Pippin (1956) 217–20.
[14] Richter (1966) 13–33.
[15] *Kline* seems to have been the most common term for a bed/couch in classical times, though it was not used by Homer, who uses a number of other names, such as *lechos* (*Il.* 1.609), *lektron* (*Od.* 8.258), *demnia* (*Il.* 24.644), and *klintes* (*Od.* 18.190).
[16] Robinson (1946) 350; Murray (1990) 149–52.
[17] Robinson (1938); Studnickza (1913) 173.
[18] Pritchett and Pippin (1956) 229.

is "couch," while Pollux (6.9; 10.34) clearly uses the term to mean an armrest.[19] Similarly, *anaklintron* sometimes seems to stand for a couch rather than just the upsweep at one end, while an *anaklisis* is a comfortable chair with a back as well as the back itself.[20] From a manufacturing point of view, whatever the correct terminology for different items, it was clear that making *klinai* typically involved making a head and armrests and attaching them to the main item, either permanently or through an interlocking dowel pin. Other variations concerned the legs and the finishing. Like *thronoi*, couches could have either turned or rectangular legs, with the latter becoming more popular during the fourth century.[21] They might be carved in the shape of animal legs and feet and could be very elaborate. The best pieces might be finished by polishing with skate skin (Plin. *HN*. 9.40; 19.87; 23.108) or cedar or juniper oil (*HN*. 16.197). The most highly regarded *klinai* were from Chios and Miletus, examples of which were among the treasures of the Parthenon (IG. I³ 343–45; 351) and in Alcibiades's house.[22]

Different forms of couch were used for different purposes, such as the small version or *klinidion*, the *skimpous*, a simple pallet bed (Pollux 10.35; scholiast to Ar. *Nub*. 234), and a low couch or *chameuna*. Most of these variations were in the direction of simplicity and low cost, but we know of a *chameuna* selling at twice the price of a Milesian bed, so all except the *skimpous* probably came in luxury versions as well.[23]

*Klinai* often had alongside them a *footstool* (*threnus, hypopodion*, or *sphelas*; Ill. 6.1), probably to help users climb up or down (Hom. *Il*. 14.240) as much as to rest the feet, which were usually curled up on the couch. Odysseus had one thrown at him (*Il*. 17.462). Some footstools were boxlike and had no legs, while the legs of others were perpendicular at first, giving way in the fourth century to curved legs, often with lion paws. Tops remained plain but some had curved sides, which were rare and expensive.[24]

*Chairs* offer another rich field for interpretation. *Klinter, klismos, klisia*, and *prosklintron* all designate easy chairs with backs, but any distinction intended by the different terms is obscure to us. The most common chairs used by women had backs and were occasionally designed for reclining on like chaises longues.[25] A Greek invention, they were light, easy to move, and elegant. It was uncommon for chairs to be decorated, but, as with thrones and couches, legs could take a range of shapes and fashions changed over time.[26] *Stools* (*diphroi*), deriving originally from Egypt, were still more practical

---

[19] Ransom (1905) 48, n. 2; 109; 111.
[20] Robert and Robert (1950) 46 n. 2.
[21] Richter (1966) 52–62.
[22] Pritchett and Pippin (1956) 228–29.
[23] Pritchett and Pippin (1956) 231.
[24] Richter (1966) 49–52.
[25] Pritchett and Pippin (1956) 230.
[26] Richter (1966) 33–37.

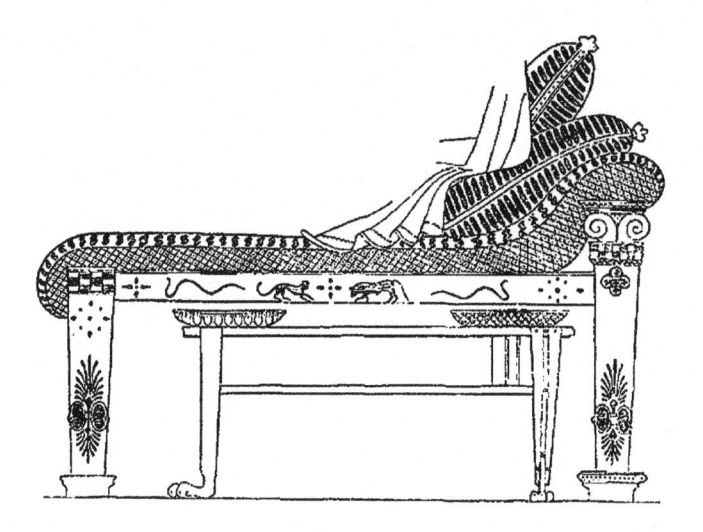

ILLUSTRATION 6.1. Couch and Small Table

and light and distinguished from *klinteres* by having no back ((Plut). *Lyc.* 9). Some had three legs instead of the usual four, but leg shapes varied less than for chairs. Sitting on one was still a sign of inferiority (Athen. 5.192e–f), just as it had been for Odysseus (Hom. *Il.* 20.259).[27] The ultimate in seating portability was the folding stool, or *diphros okladias*. Like today's camp stool, and with the same crossed-legs folding mechanism, it was used mainly for visiting, but even so it could be decorated and embellished to become a luxury item; several were listed in the Parthenon Treasures (e.g.: IG. I³ 343). Other stool configurations included boxlike pieces with geometric decorations and ones with plain rectangular seats.[28]

*Bathron, thranos, thranidion,* and *ikria* all mean *"bench,"* although there are instances where they are used as footrests or to help someone get up from a couch. Some had backs, generally perpendicular ones. They often refer to the seat of those engaged in philosophical discourse (Pl. *Prt.* 315e) and of pupils in schools (*Prt.* 325e). Benches in theaters and sanctuaries were made of stone, but those for indoor use in private houses were generally of wood. Alcibiades seems to have had several; some were listed with his chairs, some with beds, and some with miscellaneous wooden items.[29]

*Tables* are less confusing. No wooden tables survive, though some table feet in bronze and marble have been preserved that are likely to have been for outdoor use.[30] The Greeks had few possessions to dispose on surfaces, so

---

[27] Richter (1966) 38–43.
[28] Richter (1966) 43–47.
[29] Pritchett and Pippin (1956) 215; 217.
[30] Richter (1966) 63–72.

a *trapeza* was only used for meals. Vases show them in banquet scenes, laden with food, but as most food was taken on the couch by diners, they became light and portable so that they could be removed once the food had been distributed (Xen. *Anab.* 7.3.21: *Symp.* 2.1; Men. *Kekr.* 2). The table most frequently pictured in the fifth century was small and rectangular, with two legs at the corners of one end and a single leg centered at the other end, but there were numerous variations.³¹ There is no compelling evidence for round tables before the first century BCE; there might have been some round luxury ones, but they were normally rectangular.³²

Indoor tables could be very precious. They might be carved and inlaid with ivory (Athen. 2.49a; IG. I³ 343, 357), or coated with silver (IG. XI.199A.82–85). Herodotus (9.82.2) mentions gold and silver tables among the possessions of Xerxes. Sicily was famous for its tables, probably for their elaborate decoration. They could be very expensive: in the first century BCE Cicero paid half a million sesterces for a table of Mauretanian citrus wood and ivory, a hanging table of King Juba was sold for 1.2 million sesterces, and a table from the estate of the Cethegi went for 1.3 million, the price of a large estate (Plin. *HN.* 13.92-93). At the other end of the price range were the *eleos*, or simple kitchen table, and the *phatne*, which might have been a small table, but was possibly a manger-like chest.³³

*Chests*, *boxes* and *caskets* also enjoyed a wide range of names, including *kibotos, kibotion, larnax, chelos, phoriamos*, and, most commonly, *kiste*. Archaic chests were simple, with flat lids, and were fastened by tying a string between a knob on the body and one on the lid, a design that goes back to Homer (*Od.* 8.438–40). Some scholars suggest that the form reached Greece from Egypt via Crete, but it is more likely that such an obviously useful item was invented locally. Large chests were used for clothes, which were easier to fold than to hang, and might be scented with citrons. A small chest (*kibotion*) might contain jewelry, money, precious scent bottles, or papyrus (Poll. 10.61).³⁴ Many chests were probably simple and functional, but considerable elaboration was possible. By the fifth century we find lions carved on the feet and decorations on the sides. The fourth century saw rectangular feet and gabled or arched lids, often brightly decorated in terracotta, stucco, or wood.³⁵ They were generally made of wood, but precious ones might be made of bronze (IG. II/III² 3869) or gilded wood like some in the Parthenon (IG. I³ 78) and later inventories (IG. II/III² 4321; 4403); the lid was attached with

---

[31] Illustrated in Richter (1926) figs. 195–205; *trapeza* originally meant four-footed, and we also read of a *tripous* and a *tetrapous*.
[32] Pritchett and Pippin (1956) 242–44.
[33] Pritchett and Pippin (1956) 243–45.
[34] Pritchett and Pippin (1956) 225.
[35] Richter (1966) 72–78.

metal hinges.[36] The *koite* was a special type of chest, normally used for carrying food (Poll. 10.91).[37]

Whether or not the Athenians had *cupboards* is debated. Interpreting the word *thyros* (entrance) in its compounds *dithyros* and *tetrathyros* as meaning "door," and drawing on some puzzling fifth-century reliefs from Locris Epizephyrioi, a case can be made that the cupboard or cabinet appeared in Greece as early as the fifth century BCE, but the words are more likely to refer to top-opening chests than versions of the Roman *armarium* or cupboard as we would know it.[38]

There was not much other storage required. Wine was kept in *amphorae* on the floor, and vases and cups were commonly hung on pegs, but sometimes stored on shelves in the kitchen.[39] Shelving was also used in shoe shops and perhaps in other commercial concerns.[40] Most evidence for sideboards (*engutheke* or *kulikeion*) is Hellenistic, and none are seen on vases of the classical period. Cooked food probably went straight from the outdoor oven or brazier to the couch or table.

It appears there were at least three forms of *lampstand* (*lychneion*): a stand ring of metal or terracotta that might be simple or ornate; a tripod, wall bracket, or upright with an arm from which the lamp was suspended by chains or thongs; and a spike which went through the central hole of a circular lamp, with a ridge at a short distance from the top on which the lamp would rest, with some kind of flat base to allow the spike to stand upright. These last two types of lampstand were made of wood and sold for about one obol.[41] There were luxury versions in, for example, marble.[42]

Table 6.1 summarizes the principal characteristics of Athenian household furniture from a manufacturing point of view; products where fine sourcing or craftsmanship could be displayed are shown in bold. The Table shows the potential to differentiate products according to the quality and complexity of their manufacture. Many items came in luxury and simple versions, and there would have been a wide range of quality and price points between the two extremes. The most valuable ones demanded not only choosing the best timber from the correct wood, balancing function and aesthetics, but also advanced skills in the more complex aspects of woodwork. The quality of the joinery would have an important impact on the look and durability of the item, and the best joints required exceptional accuracy in measuring, cutting, and planing, as well as understanding how the direction of the grain affected

---

[36] Deonna (1938) 242–44.
[37] Budde (1940) 5; the word can also mean couch, especially in lyric poetry—Ransom (1905) 109.
[38] Studnickza (1908) 165, but see also Richter (1966) 79–80; Pritchett and Pippin (1956) 221–25.
[39] Thompson (1971) 7.
[40] Richter (1966) 78; Mus. Fine Arts, Boston 01.8035. Ashmolean Museum 563.
[41] Pritchett and Pippin (1956) 240–41.
[42] Beazley (1940) 22–49.

TABLE 6.1 Furniture Manufacturing

| Broad Descriptor | Greek Names | Materials | Principal Components | Embellishments | Luxury Versions? |
|---|---|---|---|---|---|
| Throne | *Thronos.* | Usually wood*<br>Precious inlays | Seat<br>Back and arm rests common but not universal | **Leg shape**<br>**Feet carving**<br>**Panel decorations/inlays** | Essentially a luxury item |
| Bed/couch | *Kline, klinidion, skimpous, skimpodion, krabbatos, chameuna, askantes, stibas* | Usually wood<br>Sometimes bronze or iron. | Frame<br>Thongs<br>One or two headrests at end of frame, sometimes detachable | **Leg shape**<br>**Feet carving**<br>**Scrolled headrest**<br>**Inlays** | Highly decorated versions became increasingly common in the fourth century |
| Footstool | *Threnus, hypopodion, sphelas.* | Wood | Box | Legs (straight, curved or none)<br>Side panel decoration | Apparently rare |
| Chair | *Klinter, klismos, klisia, prosklintron* | Wood | Long frame with back | **Leg shape** | Limited |
| Stool | *Diphros* | Wood | Seat<br>Three or four legs or none (boxlike)<br>Legs sometimes crossed for folding | **Panel decorations/inlays** | Probably quite common |
| Bench | *Bathron, thranos, thranidion, ikria* | Stone or wood | Long flat top<br>Legs | Unknown | Unlikely |
| Dining table | *Trapeza, tripous, tetrapous* | Light wood, often maple (Cratinos ap. Athen. 2.49a; Pollux 10.35) or citrus<br>Sometimes metal, esp. for outdoors | Rectangular top (sometimes round?)<br>Three or four legs | **Leg shape**<br>**Feet carving**<br>**Inlays**<br>**Precious metal covering** | Increasingly common |
| Simple table | *Eleos, phatne* | Wood | Top and legs or box | Unknown | Unlikely |
| Chest, box, casket | *Kiste, kibotos, kibotion, larnax, chelos, phoriamos, koite* | Wood<br>Possibly ivory or bronze | Rectangular box with top-opening lid | **Leg shape**<br>**Feet carving**<br>**Panel decorations/inlays**<br>**Gilded wood** | Common |
| Lampstand | *Lychneion* | Wood, metal, terracotta | (Wood): wall bracket or flat base with spike | Unknown | Probably limited |

*The woods most used for furniture included beech, birch, cypress, ebony, juniper, and walnut, the choice often depending on aesthetics or cost. Palm, poplar and citrus were commonly used as veneers (Meiggs (1982)). Cedar was preferred for work exposed to the elements (Theophr. HP.5.55.2).

*Source:* Ulrich (2008) 450–51.

the join. The legs of luxury couches, beds, and heavy-backed chairs had to be shaped by turning on a lathe. Bending wood panels was similarly challenging, as was forming the thin sheets of more valuable wood that were used as veneers. Additional skills required for the most expensive items included inlaying ivory or precious metals and relief carving. At the other end of the spectrum, some of the simpler items of furniture, like side tables, shelves, and chests, could be made to fit a tight budget. Many could be assembled with a basic saw, hammer, and nails with very little expertise or supervision. Wooden furniture for sale in Aristophanes's Agora included tables, stools, chests, pallets, beds, and couches, and it is unlikely they were all luxury versions.[43] The possible variations in wood quality and workmanship would have enabled manufacturers to select a point on the perceived value axis (Fig. 2.9 in Chapter 2) at which they felt most able to compete, and industry structure would have reflected this proliferation of price points.

Carpentry is not well suited to the sole operator, as it is invariably useful to have assistance in carrying, measuring, and aligning the timber. Even the smallest furniture workshops would have had a slave or two, working alongside the owner. Each workshop's success and ability to expand would depend on producing to a quality standard that was demanded by customers and perceived as better value than its competitors. Some successful ones might build a much bigger business, like the establishment Demosthenes inherited that employed 20 slaves making *klinai* (27.9).[44] Exactly what these *klinopoioi* were making is, of course, unclear, though it was clearly some form of couch. We can deduce that it was a luxury line from Demosthenes's list of his "passive" assets, which included a considerable amount of ivory as well as wood (27.10).[45] Although ivory work could be very delicate, either as perforated open work (*ajouré*) or with the background cut away (*champlevé*), the carving skills were essentially similar to woodwork. Demosthenes's assets do not include fabrics, so it seems his workshop made and embellished the frames (and presumably attached the thongs) while the mattress and soft furnishings were bought elsewhere, or perhaps made in the home of the purchaser by his family and female slaves. Depending on the complexity of carved decoration, 20 slaves might turn out 100 or more beds a year, and this workshop must have had a large share of the top-end luxury couch market.

---

[43] Table: *trapeze—Ach.* 1090, 1158; *Nub.* 177; *Eq.* 1165; *Pax* 1032, 1059, 1193; *Ran.* 518; *Vesp.* 1216; stool: *diphros—Eq.* 1164; *okladia—Eq.* 1384; chest: *kibotos—Eq.* 1000; pallet: *askantes—Nub.* 633; bed: *lechos—Thesm.* 1122; couch: *skimpous—Nub.* 254, 709; *kline—Ach.* 1090; *Nub.* 694; *Lys.* 733; *klinis—Thesm.* 261, 796.

[44] The economic performance of both of Demosthenes's workshops is explored in Chapter 9.1.

[45] The Romans generally used ivory in the form of thin plates affixed to a wooden surface, and this technique was known in archaic Greece: archaeologists have found a set of six appliqués of cows (to be applied to furniture) made by three different people, probably before 530 BCE (Koch (1986)).

As in the case of knives and shields, reputation for excellence of workmanship that could not be ascribed to an individual craftsman would have enabled a workshop like this to capture market share that enabled it to grow beyond its minimum efficient size. Luxury furniture was a fashion item and probably often bespoke. Customers would not commit large sums to workshops that lacked a reputation for good-quality materials, design, and workmanship. In this case, the need for a large inventory of costly raw materials was another important reason for industry concentration. Ivory was an especially expensive commodity. Elephants had become extinct in Syria during the eighth century, and it could only be obtained from North Africa or, more rarely, Asia.[46] Demosthenes's inventory of "ivory, iron, and wood" was worth 80 *mina* (27.10); the iron and perhaps some of the ivory was for his other factory, which made knives, but even so, the amount tied up in ivory and wood for couches was substantial and would have constituted a formidable entry barrier for anyone trying to start up in luxury couches. The barrier of investment in costly raw materials combined with a premium for perceived product excellence offers a basis for a sustainable and profitable business with significant market share. Demosthenes might well have been right in attributing its failure to his guardians.

There might have been several workshops of a similar size to Demosthenes's, specializing in different product ranges or decorative styles. *Thronoi* would certainly have been made in specialist workshops, and so would top-end tables, chairs, chests, and footstools. There would have been other workshops that offered less expensive furniture, and many households would have made their own. Based on prices of goods confiscated from the mutilators of the herms in 414 BCE, Pritchett and Pippin estimate that an entire house would not cost more than 500 *drachmae* to furnish, or 650 including ceramics and soft furnishings—perhaps about the same as one luxury couch.[47] They go on to speculate that low prices resulted from low demand. In this instance, their premises are dubious and their grasp of economics weak. The constant stream of new arrivals in Athens, even if as foreigners they could not own land, would want to furnish a house (or at least a room). For long-term residents, fashions changed and, if the typical Athenian house was completely refurnished only every 30 years on average, that would suggest annual demand for over 10,000 items, not an especially small market and one likely to have employed several dozen people in manufacture, even if most purchases were simple and functional. As to economic causality, low demand for a specific product may result in lower prices for that product than for preferred alternatives, but low demand for a category overall increases the cost of supplying it, so that customers have to pay a *higher* price to keep producers in business.

---

[46] Markoe (2005) 196–97.
[47] Pritchett and Pippin (1956) 210–11; Jones (1997) 191.

If the prices Pritchett and Pippin cite really were low in relation to the work involved (which we may never know), it is probably because secondhand prices for inexpensive, readily obtainable goods do tend to be low. In fact, it is not clear how low these secondhand prices were. They point to *klinai* as selling for between six and eight *drachmae* apiece. Unless a large amount of inlay work was required, as it was in Demosthenes's business, an efficient workshop might not require more than three or four man-days to saw and join the frame and attach thongs. With common raw materials, these prices would have easily covered costs. In any event, prices for good-quality furniture must have been high enough to give full-time carpenters enough to live on—or to pay for dedicated slaves.

## 6.2 General and Specialized Woodworking Segments

Like simple furniture, several of the wooden items in Aristophanes's Agora only required basic carpentry and offered little scope for brand preference, such as a chopping-block, a ruler, a broom, a door-bar, a walking stick, a figwood dog collar and a phallus pole.[48] For these wooden items, as with commodity pottery and basic clothing, many households might make their own, and the business would only offer manufacturers subsistence rewards and no scope for growth without serious risk; on the other hand, if a market was well developed, it would have been reasonably stable in terms of volume and pricing and, provided skills were kept up, open to casual engagement. Basic wooden items for sale were probably made by small concerns earning a subsistence amount or by occasional producers looking for some extra income.

To earn a higher income, or to be able to run a profitable workshop with several slaves, a competitive advantage was necessary. There would certainly have been products other than furniture that would lend themselves to differentiation. One segment that required fine craftsmanship was the making of musical instruments, like the double-flute (*aulos*—*Ach.* 554, 752; *Nub.* 313; *Pax* 531) or the lyre (*lyra*—*Nub.* 1355; *Eq.* 990; *Thesm.* 138, 969; *Ran.* 1304). There might have been a large market for flutes; Athens was home to a number of flute girls, a trade one step up from streetwalking.[49] The orator Isocrates's father was a flute-maker and seems to have left his son comfortably off. Pseudo-Plutarch describes Isocrates as employing slaves to make flutes (*Isoc.*1), implying a concern of some size. He and others might have owned quite large workshops, based on a reputation for excellence in making

---

[48] Chopping-block: *epixenon*—*Ach.* 318, 355, 359, 366; ruler: *kanon/peches*—*Ran.* 799; broom: *korema*—*Pax* 56; door-bar: *kleithron*—*Lys.* 264; *mochlos*—*Thesm.* 415; walking stick: *tribonia*—*Vesp.* 31; figwood dog collar: *kloos*—*Vesp.* 897; phallus pole: *phallos*—*Ach.* 243, 260.

[49] Davidson (1997) 73.

instruments. If a modern analogy holds and brand strength was confined to one instrument, then flutes, lyres, and drums might all have been dominated by different workshops or small groups of rival workshops, just as Stradivarius, Steinway, Fender, and Yamaha are leaders in different instruments today. Some of the best instruments also contained more expensive materials: flutes could incorporate metal and bone, and lyres might have a tortoiseshell sound box, possibly creating an investment hurdle for new entrants as well as the brand one. Wooden dramatic masks (*skeuopoiema—Eq.* 232) probably constituted another specialized segment that demanded creativity and artistry, and there might well have been others.

Some larger items are also likely to have been made by specialized workshops. There is little known about how commercial cartage operated in ancient times, but a variety of commodities needed transport: agricultural products on their way to and from primary processing, stone for building sites, imported shipments from the Peiraeus to the city, and the home contents of individuals moving house or being ostracized. Carts (*hamaxa*—Ar. *Eq.* 464) required some skill in making, not least planing the axle and fitting the felloes (usually made of springy ash) to the hub of the wheel (usually split-resistant elm).[50] The need for reliable vehicles would have provided an opportunity for certain workshops to develop a brand and a loyal customer base. Some of the agriculturalists and quarrymen might have had their own carts but other users would not have needed one for more than a few hours at a time, so there was probably a transport service industry, perhaps sometimes offered by the manufacturers themselves. Military vehicles like the chariot (*harma*—*Eq.* 968; *Pax* 901; *Vesp.* 1427) and the war chariot (*polemistros*—*Nub.* 28) would also have lent themselves to brand loyalty and price premiums. Similar considerations might have applied to wooden industrial equipment such as looms (*antion*—*Thesm.* 822; *kerkis*—*Ran.* 1316) and to stage machines (*mechane*—*Pax* 307).

In addition to product-specific expertise, a factor driving consolidation in these latter segments was the bulk of the finished product and the need to deploy a large team for efficient manufacture. This was certainly the case for preparing building timbers.[51] Wood, usually mountain pines or silver fir, was used in all major building projects as wall and door frames, floors, roof beams, and, often, part of the foundations. Before the second century BCE, when masonry vaults were used to roof some buildings, large buildings like temples and state assembly houses had all-wooden roofs, generally built on the prop-and-lintel system, which set a heavy ridge pole on vertical supports, fixed directly on the building's columns or walls or placed on crossbeams. This is clearly quite a different segment from furniture and other forms of

---

[50] Ulrich (2008) 451.
[51] Ulrich (2008) 456–57; see also Chapter 7.1.

woodwork. The skills required for the accurate framing and joining of these massive beams so that they could support their own weight through all climates was quite different from the delicate joinery of a piece of furniture. The need to maneuver the timber necessitated large teams: ridge beams could be over 20 meters long and disproportionately wide in order to support other rafters and sheathing. The task was clearly one for a gang of slaves operating under the direction of a skilled joiner with experience in large construction projects. Similar teams would have been involved in assembling the hulls and building some of the larger wooden components of boats.

## 6.3 Boatbuilding

For most of the fifth and fourth centuries, naval construction was one of Athens's largest employers, building triremes for the war against Xerxes and then to control Athens's maritime empire and fight the Peloponnesian and later wars. As early as the fifth century CE, the Byzantine historian Zosimus was lamenting a lack of information about how triremes were built (*Hist. Nov.* 5.20), but we know enough about their composition to be able to tell what was involved in their construction, especially for the trades of carpentry and textiles. In addition to the (often confusing) words of ancient poets and historians, we have two main sources of data on the warships the Athenians built: excavations of dockyards provide evidence of the physical dimensions of the ships, and naval lists identify the different items of componentry and gear each ship carried. These enable us to estimate, though with some uncertainty, how many people were involved in hull fabrication and assembly and how much of the work was probably carried out by specialist suppliers. The focus of the analysis here is on the trireme, but other warships and trading vessels built locally by private contractors would have been supplied by the same industries.

### 6.3.1 THE TRIREME: DEVELOPMENT AND CONFIGURATION

It has become fashionable in management literature to cite the classical Greek trireme[52] as a model of the benefits of speed and flexibility in hostile engagements, but the ships that fought at Salamis and in later wars were the culmination of several centuries of development. Thucydides (1.4) says it was Minos who owned the first navy. Many depictions on Bronze Age vases show vessels with a ram on the prow, propelled by oar and sail and steered

---

[52] "Trireme," the term commonly used for these boats, is a Latin one; the Greeks called them *triereis*. Both mean "three oar," but the Roman ship was configured quite differently from the Greek one.

by another oar in the stern. Most appear to have had between 30 and 50 oarsmen. They were decorated with a painted wheel near the prow, probably developed in the Geometric period (900–700 BCE), which evolved into an eye.[53] The earliest written reference to boats in Greek comes from Nestor's tallies of the crews to fight at Pleuron (*Il.* 2.494–759).[54] Homer uses ships' timber as imagery for something heavy (*Il.* 17.742–44), crashing down (*Il.* 13.390–91; 16.482–84), and well fitted (*Il.* 15.410–12). His ships vary in size: he regularly mentions a crew size of 20 (*Il.* 1.309; *Od.* 1.280; 2.212; 4.778), which seems to have been normal for dispatch vessels and was the size Tim Severin chose in 1984–85 to re-enact the voyages of Jason and Odysseus.[55] Each of Achilles's 15 ships was manned by 15 men (*Il.* 16.169), but the Boeotians were credited with 120 per ship (*Il.* 2.509), which must have included non-rowing passengers. Elsewhere in the Odyssey (8.36) we hear of 52, close to the expected number for the 50-person *pentecontor* that was the most common warship of the Archaic age. Thucydides (1.10.4) gives the range of ship sizes of ships of this period as between 50 and 120 men, all serving as both fighters and rowers, just as Philoctetes's crew in Sophocles's tragedy were all archers. There is unlikely to have been room for 120 people rowing, and the *pentecontor* was able to carry a large number of non-rowers, so the likely interpretation is that these ships were rowed by around 50 men at a time and could carry 50 or more others and they all shared rowing duty.

It was probably the Phoenicians who developed a ship with rowers on two levels. Fragments from an eighth-century relief at the Assyrian capital of Nineveh depicting the fleets of Tyre and Sidon have been interpreted as showing two- and three-level warships, fitted with rams.[56] Depictions from the Archaic Age typically show one row of oarsmen, but some have two; the geometrically decorated Toronto bowl from Corinth in the Royal Ontario Museum shows 19 oarsmen on one level and 20 oar ports below, although this might be a naïve artist's attempt to show both sides at once. There are two similar paintings in the National Museum at Athens, but the earliest mention we have of a multi-level ship (*polyzugos*) in literature is in the second half of the sixth century.[57] Thucydides (1.13.2) attributes the invention of the trireme to the Corinthians, which would place it in the first part of the seventh century, before Corinth's sea power diminished. He says they were uncommon before the Persian Wars (1.14), when most fleets consisted of *pentecontors* and smaller boats. He is probably underestimating the rapidity of the trireme's dispersion as well as mistaking its origin; according to Herodotus (7.89–95), Xerxes's fleet of 1,207 ships included 307 triremes from his Greek allies and

---

[53] Morrison and Williams (1968) 9–11; 18–37.
[54] See also Ventris and Chadwick (1956) An. 1; An. 610.
[55] Welsh (1988) 30–32.
[56] Casson (1995) 57–58.
[57] Williams (1958) 125.

another 150 from Cyprus. His best sailors were the Phoenicians, who were starting to dominate sea trade all over the Mediterranean with a taller trireme of their own design (Hdt. 6.114).[58] By Herodotus's time, *"naus"* (ship) had come to mean "trireme," with *pentecontors* and *tetracontors* (40 rowers) specified as such. It seems triremes had largely replaced *pentecontors* across the Eastern Mediterranean by about 500 BCE, and they remained the fighting ship of choice for many years.

New models were introduced: the *tetreis* (four oars) and the *pentereis* (five). Diodorus Siculus (14.42.2) attributes both to Dionysus of Syracuse, though Aristotle gave credit for the former to the Carthaginians (Plin. *HN*. 27.7). By the middle of the fourth century, the Phoenician navy was sailing *pentereis* with 270 oarsmen, and by the time the Punic wars began in the late second century BCE they had become the Phoenician ship of the line.[59] Ptolemy IV Philopator is said to have had a ship built of "forty oars."[60] These figures make the assumption that the numeric indicator referred to levels of rowers clearly untenable. Some experts question whether the prevailing skill level could have managed to build even a sound three-level boat.[61] On the other hand, excavations of boat sheds give the maximum length of a trireme and show it would have been impossible to have fitted the 170 rowers in less than three straight lines on each side. Some inferred that there might have been three men to each oar, while others attempted to show how three levels of rowers could be arranged. In 1861 Napoleon III had a three-level ship built that was so slow and unstable it was abandoned after one very short voyage. Much of this speculation was thrown into further disarray by the lists from fourth-century naval stores; they show each trireme was allocated 200 oars, of which 30 were spares—clearly one man per oar—and, more confusingly, that oars were all about the same length. "Tri-" had to have some bearing on the three classes the 170 rowers were divided into (62 *thranites*, 54 *zygians*, and 54 *thalamians*), but the differences in oar lengths were only a few centimeters and the numbers of oars of any given length do not match the numbers in each class, so the three groups cannot each have been placed at a different distance from the water. The most probable explanation seems to be that the *thranites* were seated on an outrigger, level with and outside the *zygians* on the top deck, with the *thalamians* on a level below (Ill. 6.2). The Lenormant relief found near the Erechtheum shows just such a configuration.[62] Rather than specifying three levels, trireme probably meant three thole pins (*triskalmoi*) in one *metron*—a rowing space measured lengthways along the

---

[58] Markoe (2005) 90.
[59] Markoe (2005) 90–97.
[60] Welsh (1988) 34.
[61] Morrison et al. (2000) 8–24.
[62] Brouskare and Binder (1974) 176 fig. 379.

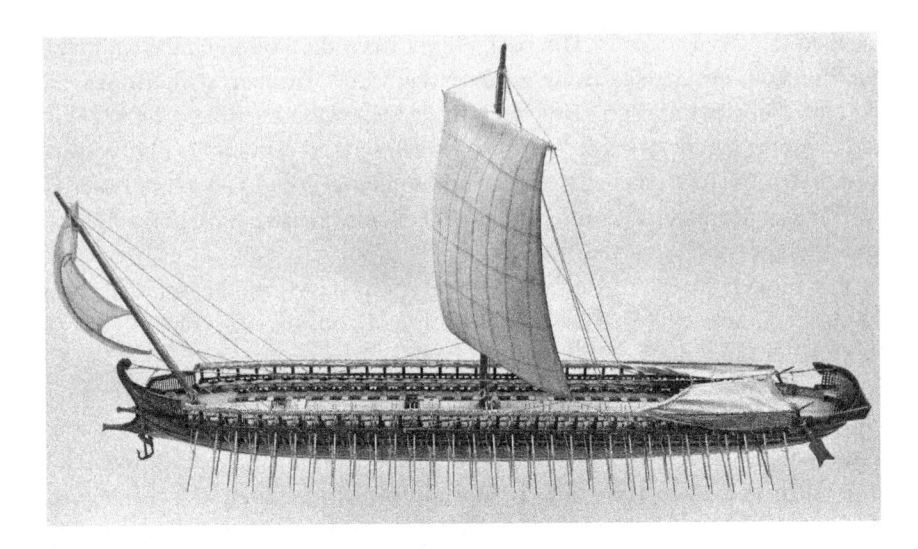

ILLUSTRATION 6.2. Trireme with Full Deck (Model)

ship that on a single-level ship with no outrigger would only accommodate one rower.[63] Rowers on different decks held their oars at different angles to the water, so length varied only with position in the ship; if they were sitting in straight lines, the oars in the widest (middle) part, had to be a little longer, as anatomists observed, noting that the longest human fingers, like oars, were the middle ones (Arist. *Part. an.* 4.10; Galen *De Usu Pulsuum.* 1.24).[64] A recent reconstruction showed this was feasible.[65] The Persian ships at Salamis seem to have had a single deck over the whole length of the ship (*katastroma*; Hdt. 5.33), which enabled them to carry more non-rowing troops or *epibatai* than the Athenians, who were still using the bow and stern platforms of Homer's time. Aeschylus, possibly a participant at Salamis, speaks of a poop deck (*selma*—*Pers.* 358), and in the *Agamemnon* (182–83) it serves as the "proud" seat of the gods. Sometime after the battle of Eurymedon but

---

[63] Morrison (1968) 155.

[64] It is quite possible that the Phoenician triremes, taller and with no outriggers, were actually on three levels; we have no evidence on oar length to determine this.

[65] In 1985–87 a Peiraeus shipbuilder, financed by banker and writer Frank Welsh and using evidence from underwater archaeology and the expertise of historian J. S. Morrison and naval architect John Coates, reconstructed an Athenian trireme and named it the *Olympias*. The project is described in Welsh (1988), Morrison and Coates (1986), and Morrison (2000). The reconstruction used modern chemicals, oxyacetylene torches, power-operated winches, and computer simulation. The result was probably not exactly like a trireme, but it confirmed Morrison's hypothesis about how the three sets of rowers were configured and it certainly matched the original's reputation for speed and flexibility. Crewed by 170 volunteer oarsmen and oarswomen with no experience of rowing as part of such a huge team, *Olympias* achieved 9 knots (17 km/h or 10.5 mph). It could go from 0 to 6 knots in 30 seconds from a stationary start or after a 90° turn and was able to execute a 180° turn in one minute in an arc no wider than two-and-a-half ship-lengths. Unsurprisingly, teamwork and coordination among the

before the Peloponnesian War, Athens adopted full decks but still does not seem to have increased the numbers of *epibatai*.[66]

The ram was still the prime attack method (*Pers.* 334), as vase paintings show it had been from at least the sixth century.[67] An alternative tactic was to disable the enemy by getting up speed, shipping oars, and grazing along the side of the enemy ship before its crew could get their oars out of the way.[68]

### 6.3.2 RESPONSIBILITY FOR BUILDING TRIREMES

There is considerable uncertainty about how much of the cost of constructing, operating, and maintaining Athens's fleet was borne directly by the state and how much by liturgiasts. In 483, according to Herodotus (7.144), Themistocles argued that 100 talents of state income from the mines of Laurium should not be distributed to the populace as had been proposed but spent on ships. Pseudo-Aristotle explains that one talent was lent to each of the hundred richest men in Athens, and if the people didn't like the result, the recipients were to pay their talent back. Each built one trireme (*Ath. pol.*22.7). A likely interpretation is that the recipients were expected to cover the full construction costs, with the talent as the state's contribution.[69] Alternatively, they might have been expected to meet operating costs: we do not know what rowers were paid in the Persian War, or if they received anything at all beyond their rations.[70]

The system of private contributions to Athens's naval capability became formalized and trierarchs were appointed by the hundred each year, probably by their demes (there is no evidence of a central register).[71] Except in the case of the commanders of the sacred ships *Paralos* and *Salaminia*, who were public officials, formal appointment was by the *strategos*, who probably had limited discretion—despite the threat of imposing a trierarchy as a punishment

---

rowers turned out to be vital. Conditions were cramped and smelly. Blades came within 30 centimeters of each other, making it very hard to avoid clashing (Morrison (2000) 231–74). Team leaders noted that successful operation demanded "a capacity for tolerance and mutual respect, which it is difficult to imagine existing other than in a democratic society." (Welsh (1988) 205; 209).

[66] Munro (1902) 326.

[67] Debate about whether sails were necessary to generate enough speed to use the ram effectively reached a crescendo in the pages of the London *Times* in 1975 and became known as the Great Trireme Controversy. The (still unstable) consensus seems to be that ramming was only possible in very calm water and probably unmanageable under sail.

[68] Morrison (1968) 281–82.

[69] Aperghis (1997–98).

[70] It is notable that the rowers were to be citizens and resident aliens, not slaves. The ancients appear to have been very circumspect about manning their navies. The Carthaginian army was composed almost entirely of mercenaries, but the navy only included citizens—Markoe (2005) 97.

[71] Gabrielsen (1994) 68–75.

in Aristophanes (*Eq.* 912–18)! It was legitimate for a nominee to find a substitute, and some were able to get exemptions, usually on the grounds of other liturgical service. In 430 BCE, 400 trierarchs were nominated to command 300 ships. In 354, 1,200 were nominated when the fleet only had 340 triremes and no more than 400 ships in total.

Again, it is not certain what these trierarchs were responsible for. It cannot have been the cost of campaigns; in the Peloponnesian War pay was one *drachma* per day plus rations (Thuc. 3.17.3; 6.8.1; 6.31.3), and was topped up as needed.[72] Hanson estimates that having two-thirds of the fleet at sea for the eight sailing months would have cost 1,600 talents—a massive sum and twice the amount of the tribute Athens received from the Delian League, but one that can be almost entirely explained by pay for 170 rowers on each boat.[73] On this basis, ships probably cost as much to run and maintain each month as to build—perhaps more according to IG. I$^3$ 363, which puts the cost of the 440 Samos campaign at 2.3 talents per month for each ship. Athens was not only able to fund these costs during campaigns, but for weeks or months of training before any engagement (Plut. *Cim.* 11.2–3; (Xen.) *Ath. pol.* 1.19–20; Thuc. 1.80, 142.6–7; 2. 84–86, 89; Xen. *Mem.* 3.5.18).[74] There were other costs too: ships at sea needed cleaning every five days or so; the hulls became waterlogged (Thuc. 7.12) and they were brought onshore to dry. They also needed constant repair (Xen. *Hell.* 1.5.10–11).

A plausible explanation offered by Gabrielsen is that the state supplied the hulls and equipment and employed *treiropoioi* to construct them. The state also paid crews' wages. The obligation of the trierarchs was to provide timber, pitch, paint, and labor to maintain the ships. Major repairs seem to have been managed and financed by public officials and then charged back to the trierarchs on a per capita basis.[75] Even if this is not correct, and trierarchs did actually pay some or all construction costs, the work was almost certainly managed by the state. There does not seem to be a great deal of sense in allocating responsibility for the complex task of getting a ship built to a different group of people each year, whether or not they are financing the work, so it seems safe to assume that building warships was a state-run industry, employing contractors and their slaves. The scale of the enterprise can be gauged from an incomplete list of 63 names of individual shipbuilders from the later part of the fourth century.[76] Besides an understanding of naval architecture and the ability to manage a team

---

[72] It seems normal for service pay not to have been paid at once (Ar. *Eq.* 1366–67); half of it was retained until the return home, probably to discourage desertion (Thuc. 8.45).
[73] Hanson (2005) 262.
[74] Pritchard (2010) 18–19.
[75] Gabrielsen (1994) 136–7; 144–45.
[76] Schmidt (1931); Miltner (1931) 947–52.

of joiners, an important skill these men must have had was purchasing. Imported woods had to be sourced, quality-checked, and delivered on time, and locally fabricated components had to conform to specification and be bought at the right price.

## 6.3.3 MANUFACTURING: THE HULL

The largest physical construction was the wooden hull. Themistocles's father showed him wrecks lying aground around the Peiraeus in an attempt to discourage him from entering public life (Plut. *Them.* 2), but there are none there now, and although finds of sunken boats are increasing rapidly, most are remote from Athens and are merchant rather than fighting ships. Buoyant wooden ships not laden with cargo seldom come to rest on the seabed for divers to find in later ages. We can, however, deduce ship size from the fourth-century boatsheds excavated at the Peiraeus, which replaced Phaleron as Athens's main harbor (Hdt. 2.154).

Homer mentions no dockyards, though good natural harbors were highly prized. Ships were probably drawn up on beaches along shallow grooves and packed around with stones to keep them upright (*Il.* 2.153). Athens, on the other hand, was very proud of her docks, which were "as beautiful as the Parthenon," and sabotage was a major concern (Ar. *Ach.* 916–21; Dem. 18.132).[77] Five hundred special guards were appointed to protect them ((Arist). *Ath. pol.* 24.3) under the control first of *neoroi* (IG. I³ 127; IG. I³ 154) and then *epimeletai* (IG. I³ 382). The Peiraeus sheds, of which traces remain, were probably built on the foundations of yards partially destroyed in 404 BCE by Sparta; they were "falling down" in 399 BCE (Lys. 30.22) rather than razed to the ground. They underwent a major rebuild in the 340s, interrupted by the war with Philip and completed by Lycurgus (Plut. *Lyc.* 7.).

The sheds were built on unfluted columns and roofed in pairs with occasional solid walls between them, probably for fire protection. They averaged 37 meters in length and 6 meters in width, and we can assume boats fitted quite snugly within them with a little space all around, giving a probable length of 35 to 36 meters. With up to 30 rowers in a line on each side, this length fits with Vitruvius's statement (*De Arch.* 1.2.4) that each rower should have two cubits (about 90 centimeters) of space. As the widest point had to allow for a beam projecting from either side of the boat to strike the enemy ship after the ram slipped past, the hull itself was probably around four meters wide. This is compatible with the trenches, channeled about three meters wide and partly built up with stone, that slope gently to the water for hauling ships—a task that almost certainly involved pulleys and possibly rollers. Research

---

[77] Com. Adespot 340 (Edmunds).

indicates that the draught of a trireme was about 1.15 meters, and the sheds show its height above the waterline was about 2.1 meters.[78] The absence of any larger sheds, even when Athens's fleet included *pentereis,* implies that they were of similar length and width, though evidently configured differently.[79]

The hull was built as a shell, with the outer hull constructed first and the ribs fitted in later and stretched with windlasses.[80] The quality of the joins was critical, as Odysseus had reason to observe as he fled Calypso's island (*Od.* 5.360–64). Homer describes how cords rotted after nine years at sea (*Il.* 2.135; cf. Aesch. *Suppl.* 124–25), which suggests the ship's planks were bound together with rope of papyrus or hemp, but he also knew of a mortise and tenon system using dowel pins (*Od.* 5.243–48).[81] In classical times, the edges of the planks were joined by mortise and tenon—thousands of joints were needed for each hull—and individual strakes were joined at the edges to one another with a tenon held in place by a dowel.[82] Scarf joints were used for the longitudinal joins, perhaps reinforced by nails. By classical times, pitch was used to make the ship's joins watertight (Ar. *Eq.* 310) and probably applied before each sailing. It was used liberally on a third-century BCE Carthaginian auxiliary ship now on display in Marsala (Lilybaeum), and the export of pitch was prohibited in Athens in wartime (Ar. *Ran.* 364).[83] Ships would still rot if they were out at sea too long (Thuc. 2.94) and needed to be dried out to be kept in good condition and to maintain their swiftness (Xen. *Hell.* 1.5.10). The fleet became waterlogged at Syracuse after being at sea for 18 months (Thuc. 7.12). To make it easier to bend, hull planking would not have been fully seasoned, though the timber for the crosstrees would have been.

A wide range of different woods was used: fir for the fastest ships—Macedonian silver fir when it was available—and pine for slower, sturdier ones that were used as merchant ships or for troop transport (IG. 1³ 21; Xen. *Hell.* 1.1.36).[84] Keels were made of oak to withstand wear and tear on beaches, while ribs might be of pine for lightness (Theophr. *HP.* 5.7.2). Larch and plane were used for interior fittings (Pl. *Leg.* 705c), and cutwaters and catheads were made from ash, mulberry, or elm.[85] The ships were light enough to be carried

---

[78] Morrison (1968) 285–86.

[79] Morrison (1968) 181–83.

[80] Fields and Bull (2007) 8; this process, inefficient as it was compared with building on an internal frame, was also used by the Romans centuries later (Garnsey (1987) 60).

[81] McGrail and Kentley (1985); Mark (2005) 25–39.

[82] Ucelli (1940); Ulrich (2008) 15.

[83] Frost (1976); Markoe (2005) 97.

[84] The theoretical maximum achievable speed of a trireme was 25 kilometers an hour (kph), and the lightest, fastest boats were said to achieve speeds of up to 21 kph for short journeys. Making the 345-kilometer journey from Athens to Lesbos in under 24 hours in 427 BCE (Thuc. 3.49.2–4—an average of around 14 kph) was evidently exceptional and bears comparison with today's motor ferry that takes over 10 hours (Hellenic Ferries Timetable 2012; excludes time in port). A more normal cruising speed was 8–9 kph—Cotterell and Kamminga (1990) 258–59.

[85] Morrison (1968) 279–303; Welsh (1988) 109–10.

ashore by 140 men, less than the number of rowers (IG. 1³ 24). Naval and other construction requirements quickly led to the deforestation of Attica and much of the rest of southern Greece, so by the end of the fifth century most woods were imported from Macedon, Thrace, and even the Levant.[86] The 1980s reconstruction had to use thicker rib tenons for the trireme than those found on the Carthaginian ship at Marsala, evidence of the higher-quality timber in ancient boats.

### 6.3.4 MANUFACTURING: COMPONENTS

While the hull and the ship are easily conflated in our perceptions of shipbuilding, it is important to remember that most parts of the ship are removable and often were removed. Between expeditions and during winter months, triremes' equipment was stored separately from the hulls—the wooden parts (oars, masts, etc.) in the ship sheds and the hanging parts (sails, ropes, cables) in special arsenals (*skeuothekai*). In 347/346 Eubulus's plans for the revival of the Athenians' naval power included the construction of a new arsenal that was designed by the architect Philon and completed in the time of Lycurgus.[87] The building's fame preceded its 1988–89 discovery, thanks to praise from Strabo (9.1.15), Pliny (*HN*. 7.12), Plutarch (*Sulla* 14.7), Cicero (*De Or.* 1.14.62), and Valerius Maximus (8.12)—all written after Sulla's forces had destroyed it in 86 BCE. Vitruvius (7.12) names Philon as the author of a treatise on temple symmetry and one on this arsenal. It was built between the Hippodameian Agora and the ship sheds, northeast of the deepest recess of the gulf of Zea, with its axis running from southwest to northeast, a direction that allows the proper ventilation of its internal space and that Philon considered an important element of the design. The size of the building gives a good idea of the sheer bulk of the equipment stowed there: it was 18 meters wide and 130 meters long, with entrances on both its narrow sides and two colonnades of piers that divided its inner space into three aisles. The central aisle extended the whole length and height of the building, while the side aisles were each separated into 34 compartments with lofts and wooden shelves.

Homer's vocabulary tells us a great deal about the components of ships, with multiple references to sails, masts, and oars. Ships had rowing thwarts and probably no deck. There seems to have been one sail, sewn from small rectangles of cloth and controlled by shrouds and leather halyards. There were three types of mooring rope, *eunai, peismata,* and *speira,* and three others: *hyperai, kaloi,* and *podes*. There was a raised footing for the mast, a place to stow it, a crossbeam, and an *aphlaston* or decorative tail or horn at

---

[86] Meiggs (1982).
[87] Dragatses and Dorpfield (1885) 64–68.

the stern.[88] New gear shown in the longships that dominated in the Archaic Age included forestays, backstays, crow's nests, and various additions to the stem and stern posts.[89] Catheads for raising and dropping anchors appeared, robust rams developed from the stem post, and paintings of fierce animals proliferated. Herodotus describes the Athenian ships that fought in the Persian campaign as fitted with oar ports (*kalamia*—5.33) and the Homeric *aphlaston* (6.114) and carrying a ram (*embolos*—1.166).[90] The navy lists identify a large range of wooden items. The most numerous were the oars, with one for each of the 170 rowers and 30 spares. A trireme also needed two steering oars (*pedalia*—IG. II² 1606.74; 1611.23).[91] There were two masts, the mainmast, *histos megas*, and the smaller *histos akateios* or "boat mast" (IG. II² 1604.48), invented around the middle of the first millennium and set forward of the mainmast.[92] Until the end of the fifth century we hear only of single sails attached to the mainmast; subsequently boat sails appear (Ar. *Lys.* 63–64; Xen. *Hell.* 6.2.27), rigged on the boat mast. (For battle, triremes left the mainmast and sail on shore and used the boat sail if they needed to flee.) The sailyards attached to each mast (*keraiai*—Aesch. *Eum.* 557) were probably made from a single piece of wood. Cutwaters were fastened to the front of the keel as reinforcement. Wooden platforms for boarding and disembarking (*parexeiresiai*—Thuc. 4.12) protruded from each end of the ship.[93] In front were the *epotides*, the projecting ends of a beam laid across the bow to strike the prow of an enemy ship in a head-on engagement after the rams had grazed past each other. These could play a vital role in battle; having reinforced its own beams Corinth broke Athens's (Thuc. 7.34). Each ship also carried two ladders (*klimakes*—IG. II² 1611.28), two or three poles for fending off (*kontoi*—IG. II² 1609.90), and two chocks for keeping the vessel upright on a beach (*parastatai*—IG. II² 1604.34).

The quantity of largely imported wood and the associated profusion of carpentry tasks make it very unlikely that all these items were manufactured

---

[88] Sails: *histia*: e.g., *Il.* 1.433, 434, 480; *Od.* 2.426; 3.10–11, 15.291; masts: *histoi*—*Il.* 1.434, 480; 23.852, 875; oars: *eretmai*—*Od.* 4.782; *kope*—*Od.* 9.489; shrouds: *protonoi*—*Od.* 12.409–10; halyards: *epitonoi*—*Od.* 12.422–23; rowing thwart: *zuga*—*Od.* 9.98–99; 12.20–22; mooring ropes: *eunai*—*Il.* 1.436; *peismata*—*Od.* 6.268–69; *speira*—*Od.* 5.318; other ropes: *hyperai, kaloi, podes*—*Od.* 5.260; raised footing for the mast: *histopede*—*Od.* 12.178–79; place to stow mast: *histodoke*—*Il.* 1.434; cross beam: *mesodme*—*Od.* 2.424–25 = 15.289–90; decorative tail: *aphlaston*—*Il.* 15.716–17.

[89] The longship shown on the Kleitias vase in the Louvre was probably typical (Beazley (1956) 76–78).

[90] Markoe (2005) 90.

[91] Aeschylus refers to this steering mechanism in both the plural (*Ag.* 802) and the singular (*Ag.* 663), which suggests it might have been two pieces joined by a connecting bar. Aristotle used it as an example of how the lever principle can enable a small device to shift a large mass (*Mech.* 550b25).

[92] Casson (1995) 70; 242.

[93] The scholiast to this passage of Thucydides thought the *parexeiresiai* were on board the ship, but is almost certainly wrong.

in the dockyards. The Punic ship at Marsala has markings on the wooden components to facilitate assembly from prefabricated parts, and it is likely that Athens used this technique too.[94] Hulls would have been built near the sea for obvious reasons, but wooden components, including oars and masts, are more likely to have been made by specialized workshops and delivered according to a project manager's timetable. The workshops that won these supply contracts must have had the manpower and skills to meet precise specifications with very large pieces of timber, and would have kept winning business if they met quality and delivery demands. It would probably have been the same workshops that supplied the construction industry (Chapter 7) and pit-props for Laurium. The docks would have been home to large facilities for sawing, bending, and fitting planks for the body of the ship—tasks that demand large teams—and for assembling components. These long-term semiskilled tasks were exactly the type that citizens avoided where they could and were almost certainly carried out by slaves, while the naval architects, overseers, and those responsible for the more complex tasks would have been contractors of any status—citizen, metic, or slave.

Another important supply industry was textiles, in the form of sails, ropes, and defensive curtains. Sails were made of linen by specialist *histiorraphoi*. A few triremes, presumably the faster ones, had special light sails (IG. II/III² 4280.415), which cost 150 *drachmae* more than the standard ones (IG. II/III² 4280.671). The ropes for a trireme were made from papyrus and hemp, bound with pitch. The first items mentioned in naval lists were the *hypozumata* or "swifters"; each ship had four (IG. II² 1631.671), of which two were probably spares. Plato compares the *hypozumata* to the sinews in a body (*Leg.* 945c) and to light holding the heavens together (*Resp.* 616b–c), and their most probable purpose was to bind the hull. The dimensions of the ship, with its length nine times its breadth and ten times its height, meant it required strong reinforcement to prevent the keel "hogging" or bending upward in the middle.[95] A rope around and under the hull would have made beaching and launching very hard, so it was probably bound around the outside along the length of the ship. Fitting the binding rope was a strenuous exercise requiring several men.[96] Exporting them from Athens was another capital offense.[97] There were also leather halyards (*himantes*) and five types of light ropes for working the sails:[98] *podes* at the bottom of the sail; *hyperai* or braces at the end of the sailyard; *kaloi* or brailing ropes, a Phoenician invention to keep the main sail taut to the mast;[99] bunt lines called *kalinoi* attached at right angles to the *kaloi*; and

---

[94] Frost (1976).
[95] Welsh (1988) 112–15.
[96] Morrison (1968) 285.
[97] Coates (2005).
[98] Morrison (1968) 299–301.
[99] Wachsmann (1995) 331.

*ankoinai* or mast shrouds.[100] They carried four much heavier ropes or *schoiniai* (IG. II² 1611.254; IG. II² 1611.393), the heaviest pair (about 14 centimeters in diameter) for the anchor and the lighter ones (10 centimeters) for mooring the stern.[101] Triremes were also equipped with various coverings made of linen or fur, including the *katablemata*, a defensive covering over part of the ship, the *hypoblemata* or floor covering, and the *parablemata* or *pararrumata*, side shields. Here again it would have been practical for only certain items to have been made in the docks, perhaps some of the sails and the heavier ropes and deck coverings, with others supplied to order by independent workshops. As with wooden gear, components could have been made for stock and brought to the site for assembly as the ship's construction advanced.

Ships required metal and leatherwork as well as carpentry and textiles. Rams (*chalkomata*—Diod. Sic. 20.9; Plut. *Ant.* 67.3) were made of bronze, and probably came in two parts that were lashed to the hull. There might have been smaller additional rams beside the main one.[102] There were two iron anchors (*ankuras*) per ship (IG. II² 1609.114; 1611.259; 1627.449). Leather items included oar port fittings to keep water out (*askomata*), straps used as tightening devices on the *hypozumata* (*entonoi*—Ap. Rhod. 1.367–69), and halyards (*himantes*; Hom. *Od.* 2.46 = 15.291).

The final task was to paint the ship with symbols and monsters that would bring glory to the owner and strike terror into the enemy. The only ship's name we hear of before the fourth century was the *Argo*, but the naval lists from 377 to 322 BCE contain about 300. They included heroes, divine epithets (but not the proper names of gods and goddesses), abstract concepts like justice and peace, and places important in Athenian history; these names were probably written or symbolized in paint too, almost certainly by specialist painters.[103] A handful might have been enough to paint a year's output of new vessels but many more would have been engaged in repainting. Some were probably skilled freelancers responding to special requests from trierarchs and their captains; others might have made their whole career painting ships.

Table 6.2 lists the principal items that went into making a trireme.

In selecting component suppliers, the contractor would look for establishments that had a proven ability to meet specifications, quality standards, and deadlines. These would tend to be workshops of a size that could absorb volume fluctuations, rather than an individual who could only work on one thing at a time and might struggle to fill a new order quickly. It is unlikely, for instance, that leather gear for a new trireme would come from retail purchases of the oar port covers (Ar. *Ach.* 97; *Ran.* 364) and oar-thongs (*Ach.* 549) on

---

[100] *Podes, hyperai,* and *ankoinai* had all been known to Homer (*Od.* 5.260–62; 10.32–33).
[101] Morrison (1968) 301–3.
[102] Morrison (1968) 280.
[103] Schmidt (1931); Miltner (1931) 947–52; Casson (1995) 350–55.

TABLE 6.2 **Principal Components of a Trireme by Trade**

| Woodwork | Textiles | Other |
|---|---|---|
| **Main body:** | **Sails:** | **Metal:** |
| Hull planking | Main sail | Ram |
| Ribs | Boat sail | Anchors |
| Cross-beams | **Covers:** | **Leather:** |
| **Components:** | Floor | Oar port fittings |
| Mainmast; boat mast | Defensive (top and sides) | Straps |
| Steering oars | **Ropes:** | Halyards |
| Boarding platforms | Swifters | Painting |
| Cutwater; catheads | Six types of light rope | |
| Horn | Anchor cables | |
| Cross beam behind ram | Mooring cables | |
| **Movable gear:** | | |
| Oars | | |
| Ladders | | |
| Fending poles | | |
| Chocks | | |

sale in the Agora. These retail products were probably replacements, or for private boats. Naval contractors would have chosen to order from larger carpentry, metalwork, leather, and textile workshops, underwriting their sustainability and reinforcing their reputation advantage. The wood and textile workshops that won these supply contracts must have had the manpower and skills to meet precise specifications with very large pieces, and would have kept winning business provided they met quality and delivery demands.

### 6.3.5 SHIPBUILDING AND SUPPLYING INDUSTRIES

Athens built her navy with extraordinary speed. Just before the battle of Marathon in 490 BCE, she had 50 ships (Hdt. 6.89) and they were probably not all triremes. Soon afterward, she sent 70 ships to Paros. At Artemision in 480, Athens commanded 147 ships (Hdt. 6.32), of which 20 belonged to the Chalcideans (7.1). For the battle of Salamis later that year, she had 200 ships of her own and 53 from allies (7.14).[104] Otherwise the busiest period for shipbuilding in Athens was probably the 15 years leading up to the Peloponnesian War, 446–31, during which time the fleet increased in size from 200 to 300 ships. On top of the 100 additional ships, old ones had to be replaced after a life of around 25 years or if they were destroyed in battle. During this 15-year period, Athens would have had to replace at least 120 of its older ships as well as building 100 new ones, making about 15 new boats a year,

---

[104] A fourth-century copy of Themistocles's decree of 480 BCE, establishing Athens's naval preparations for the Persian invasion, states that women and children are to be evacuated to Troezen, while the men (citizens and metics) man 200 triremes, each carrying 10 *epibatai* and 4 archers, a total complement of almost 40,000! (Jameson (1960)). Some scholars considered this a forgery, but though it has been edited, it is probably genuine enough (Lewis (1961) 61–66; Burn (1962)).

plus replacements for sinkings, though these would not have been high at this relatively peaceful time. This chimes with Diodorus Siculus's estimate (11.43.3) that Athens built 20 ships a year after 480 BCE.

To estimate the size of the industry, it would be helpful to know just how much a trireme cost to build. There is no simple answer to this, because many components like timber and papyrus were imported and must have varied considerably in price from time to time.[105] Scholars have tended to assume a number of around one talent, perhaps drawing a dubious conclusion about the exact nature of Themistocles's invitation to the 100 richest citizens in 483, based on Pseudo-Aristotle 22.7 (see 6.3.1 above). It is also likely that ships were much cheaper to build at that time than later—not only did the ships built to fight the Persians not have complete decks, but there was significant cost inflation over the classical period.[106] Nevertheless, the sum might be a reasonable average: fourth-century compensation for a lost hull was 5,000 *drachmae*, and the original cost is unlikely to have been less—or very much more, though it is not clear if this includes fittings. Boeckh suggests the hull and the equipment each cost one talent, which is conceivable but not well supported.[107]

Assuming that the cost to build a ship was one talent, Hanson deduces that each new trireme required 6,000 man-days and that between 10,000 and 20,000 people at a time might have been engaged in "building and repairing the hulls and rigging" of Athens's fleet.[108] (A *drachma* a day seems to have been the going rate for free labor for much of the period, and adding the *apophora* to the daily cost of maintaining a slave would not come to much less than a *drachma*).[109] Hanson's calculation seems to make no allowance for purchased raw materials or off-site workshops. The cost to the boat shed of imported timber and papyrus must have accounted for a significant part of a boat's cost. Other raw materials would have to be sourced by workshops supplying the shipbuilder with wooden, textile, and other componentry. For any trireme cost, the number of people working at the dockyards making the hull and assembling the ship depends on the relative cost of raw materials to labor and the proportion of labor actually deployed around the hull (Table 6.3). Raw material costs are likely to be small relative to labor; even with today's lifting machinery and powered tools, labor can account for as much as 30 percent of total shipbuilding costs, and the industry is dominated by countries with low labor costs.[110] In

---

[105] Gabrielsen (1994) 139–40.
[106] Loomis (1998) 257 quantifies wage inflation between 450 and 432 BCE at 50 percent. After a dramatic fall in the crisis of 412–403, there was a further increase of 100 percent between 403 and 330.
[107] Boeckh (1886) 196–210.
[108] Hanson (2005) 260.
[109] Webster (1973) 46–47; Stewart (1990) 65. See also Chapter 9.1.
[110] McQuilling Services (2007).

TABLE 6.3 **Man-Days per Trireme at Hull:** *Assuming a trireme costs one talent to build*

|  |  | Raw Materials (% of total cost) | |
|---|---|---|---|
|  |  | 25 | 45 |
| Percentage of Labor at Hull | 67 | 3,015 | 1,809 |
|  | 50 | 2,250 | 1,350 |

ancient times the proportion would have been much higher. One estimate puts it at between 54 and 68 percent of costs.[111] Allowing for assembly work to be done in addition to constructing the hull itself, one might expect that at least half the labor force worked at and around the hull. The calculations can only be imprecise, but nevertheless suggest some caution about Hanson's figures. Assuming, for instance, that raw materials amounted to between 25 percent and 45 percent of the total cost, and that between one-third and one-half of the labor was conducted off-site, gives between 1,350 and 3,015 as the number of man-days required to build one hull and fit the components.

Translating these into the number of slaves making the hull and fitting components suggests that between four and eight slaves could construct a trireme in a year, with slightly fewer occupied full-time in component industries. (Of course, they almost certainly worked in larger teams and completed the work more quickly, and master shipbuilders might also have supervised more than one build at a time, but this does not affect overall numbers.) At the rate of 20 new ships a year, shipbuilding might have occupied about 400 people in total, including supplying industries, and perhaps a few hundred more in repairs and maintenance of older ships. On this basis, even an annual output of 200 triremes would not require more than about 2,500 people working on those tasks at the shipyards and about 2,000 upstream. We might suspect that the total cost to build a trireme was more than a talent or that labor cost less than a *drachma* a day, but, even with very conservative estimates of labor productivity, these adjustments cannot bring us anywhere near to Hanson's estimate.

There were other tasks to keep trireme builders busy (though not enough to explain Hanson's arithmetic). Cleaning ships every five days when they were close to home would have employed several dozen more slaves, possibly from the gangs who built the ships. Furthermore, shipbuilding gangs were not confined to triremes. Athens's ability to raise production quickly (though undoubtedly helped by the use of imported labor) suggests some spare capacity. It is likely that independent shipbuilders making commercial vessels would be contracted to make triremes for the state when it needed to increase production.

---

[111] Peck (2001) App. 2.

Some of these independent shipbuilders might have been quite substantial. They must certainly have had good access to investment capital or have been able to sell a ship before building it. There would have been some smaller, less well-organized concerns as well that might be making smaller trading or fishing boats or working on maintenance jobs. One can assume their viability would have been based on respect for the master's long association with boats and permanent presence in the docks area, but the business would have been unstable and not very rewarding financially. These marginal competitors would only be called in to make warships when demand was running too high for the established industry leaders to cope. This downmarket segment of the industry provided some useful flexibility. If a dearth of large contracts continued for long, the larger enterprises could turn to making smaller commercial boats and force some of the less robust competitors out of business.

The structure of Athens's main boatbuilding industry was very simple: triremes were built primarily by contractors and slaves, under the direction of a skilled naval architect (of any status) and foreman (probably a slave) engaged by the state.[112] Private ships would be built by private contractors and their slave gangs, sometimes on commission and sometimes opportunistically; these same gangs would have been available to help build, clean, and repair triremes when more capacity was needed. These hull and assembly operators, public and private, were also major customers for several of Athens's industries and provided an opportunity for wood, textile, metal, and leather workshops to grow large if they could achieve a good track record for quality and delivery. The number of woodworkers employed in larger wood workshops must have numbered several hundred, possibly a thousand or more, as these larger workshops would supply not only ship components but structural timber for public buildings, high-quality furniture, and other specialized segments where product quality or reliability of delivery mattered.

### 6.4 Summary

The multiplicity of wood products used by the Athenians, and the wide range of skills that could be deployed in making them, gave rise to a multifaceted industry structure (Table 6.4).

Basic woodworking skills were readily acquired, and undoubtedly many home handymen would have made simple wood products, including simple furniture, for themselves and their neighbors and sometimes for sale. To make more than a subsistence living as a sole craftsman one would have to be very good. Some highly skilled individuals might have developed a loyal following, perhaps in carvings or furniture, for clever work and original designs

---

[112] In some instances, these might have been the same person.

TABLE 6.4  **Woodworking Industries Structure**

|  |  | Barriers to Entry | |
| --- | --- | --- | --- |
|  |  | Yes | No |
| Potential for Differentiation | Yes | Differentiated industry: Luxury furniture *Mass-market furniture* Musical instruments *Transport vehicles* Dramatic masks and equipment *Industrial machinery* *Boat component suppliers* Carpentry workshops Bronze workshops Textile workshops Dye houses Rope workshops Leather workshops | Differentiated craft: *Customized carvings* *Boutique furniture* Naval architect/project manager Boat design painter |
|  | No | Undifferentiated industry: Ship hull and assembly | Undifferentiated craft: Basic furniture Household utensils |

Note: *Italic font* represents business forms for which there appears to have been an opportunity, but for which there is limited or no evidence in classical Athens.

and a uniqueness not to be obtained from larger outfits. Larger enterprises did not depend on the skill of an individual craftsman and, for some special items, would have to carry an inventory large enough to make new entrants think twice. Given the volume of demand, it is quite probable that some basic furniture was made in medium to large workshops, their appeal to purchasers being based on reliable value. Competition between these workshops, and with some individual craftsmen, would take the form illustrated in Figure 2.9.

Other segments were highly specialized, and purchasers would have tended to concentrate their buying on one or two workshops known to be expert. Musical instruments, dramatic equipment, and looms are likely examples, although we only have a recorded instance of the first. The other way was to supply major contracts such as those provided by boat builders. The common view that Athenian industry benefited from the building programs on land and sea because of the extra and consistent demand they generated is true, though oversimplified. The business people who benefited most were those who succeeded in the competition to become preferred suppliers to the programs. Trireme makers wanted reliable wooden components, and workshops known to be good at providing them promptly to order would win and maintain a good share of new business. The same applied to suppliers of textile, metal, and leather componentry.

The effect on the woodworking industry structure of demand from boatbuilding was supplemented by demand from other public construction projects. The next chapter shows how these projects also shed light on the structure of various quarrying, stone-working, and sculpturing industries.

7 }

# Construction Industries

This chapter deals with two of the more remarkable manufacturing achievements of classical Athens, public buildings and monumental statuary, and includes a brief and rather speculative analysis of private housing and common infrastructure. The public building program probably did as much as literature to establish the splendor of Athens's cultural achievements in the minds of succeeding generations, and although it was a public monopoly whose workings are well documented, the fact that it occupied such a large number of skilled people of all status groups makes the way it operated a matter of central importance to understanding manufacturing in Athens. There are many overlaps in skills and techniques between general stonemasonry and sculpture, between marble and bronze statuary, and between bronze statues and other parts of the metalworking industry, but the focus here is on what public contracts tell us about private manufacturing. We know too little about the business of private house construction to be sure how it worked, though it almost certainly involved do-it-yourself householders, specialist tradesmen, and some privately owned slave gangs.

## 7.1 Public Buildings

Despite data limitations, we can rely on two incontrovertible facts about Athens's public building programs: they drew on a very large number of skilled people for varying periods, often at unpredictable times, and they worked well. Problems in delivering public projects are a favorite butt of today's satirists but are absent from Aristophanes, which tells us much about the probable structure and conduct of supply industries. The cost and timetable of public works depended on the presence of specialized craftsmen.[1] When the long walls were rebuilt by Conon in 395/94 BCE, the project could not begin until labor had been imported from Thebes, Boeotia, and elsewhere (IG II² 1656–64; Xen. *Hell.* 8.9–10). We do not hear of such delays in

---
[1] Burford (1965) 30–34; Beard (2003) 117–53.

the Periclean program even at its height. Even though four large temples were built in the 30-year period from 450 to 420 BCE, we hear of no recurrent or lasting shortages of labor, materials, or finished components.[2] There is no doubt the works attracted craftsmen from overseas, but the projects could not have been carried out so smoothly if they depended entirely on foreigners arriving in Athens at short notice. Nor would it have been very sensible of the *polis* to continue to spend a large amount of public funds on tradesmen who left after each project, taking a good portion of their earnings with them. Stimulating the local economy and making more income available to citizens, either through temporary employment or through the multiplier effect on the local economy from payments to other residents, are generally considered to have been major objectives. The metics who made up a large proportion of the workforce on public projects must have resided in Athens for spells in which there was no public work for them to do and, like other residents, must have found work in these downtimes that meshed seamlessly with public labor needs.

In classical times, both new buildings and maintenance of defense structures were overseen by committees accountable to the *demos* for the use of public funds and managed by supervisors or architects. The requirement for accountability involved detailed recordkeeping, and surviving epigraphy casts an important light on how the projects were managed and staffed. Meier (1959, 1961) has identified and analyzed 87 pre-Augustan inscriptions concerning wall-building and maintenance, of which 25 relate to Athens and 14 to the fifth and fourth centuries (mostly to the long walls at the start of the fourth). Feyel (2006) conducted a very detailed analysis of five major public buildings, including two in Attica in the classical period, the Erechtheum at the end of the fifth century and the temple at Eleusis toward the end of the fourth. The main focus of this section is on Feyel's work, as that suggests how these massive but irregular building projects fit with the rest of Athens's manufacturing activities; data relating to the construction and maintenance of other buildings and the city walls are drawn upon where relevant.

Before the fifth century, most public buildings had been financed by aristocrats or tyrants, and, even when the state started to provide funds, private finance continued to play an important role, often in the form of liturgies. Themistocles restored the temple at Phyla (Plut. *Them.* 1.4) and paid for the shrine to Artemis Aristoboule.[3] Cimon planted the Agora with greenery and embellished the academy (Plut. *Cim.* 13.7), and Telemarchus of Acharnai built the sanctuary of Asclepios and Hygeia (IG. II[2] 1649–50). On the island of Ioulis, even the city walls were built from a private donation.[4] Such initiatives must

---

[2] Intriguingly, only once in Plutarch (*Per.* 13.7–8) do we hear of an industrial accident. They seem to have been quite common in Rome (Gourevitch (2011) ch. 3).

[3] Plutarch (*Them.* 22) observes that he should have asked the assembly first.

[4] Meier (1959) no. 38.

have been quite common, as Lampon proposed an amendment to stop private altars being put up in the Pelargicon (IG. I³ 78). Some religious establishments financed their own projects (IG. I³ 64).[5] Demes also had their own buildings, which were the responsibility of their chief magistrate, the *demarch*.[6]

For projects financed by the *polis*, a sophisticated system of management and accountability was established. With no regular state budget, Athens's decision to invest in public buildings was a decision to spend accumulated state wealth or how best to use current income from mining, taxes, booty, and tribute. Pericles's program was largely funded by the resources of the Treasurers of Athena, with only a minor contribution from allied tribute.[7] Constructing magnificent buildings was clearly a more productive way of transferring funds to the populace than a dole payment, but ensuring cost-effectiveness demanded active oversight (IG. II² 463). Magistrates called *kolakretai* had been responsible for allocating public funds from at least the seventh century until Cleisthenes transferred the control of finances to a new body, the *apodektai*, of whom there were 10, one for each tribe, or *phyle*. At that point the *kolakretai* had only to provide for the meals in the Prytaneium (Ar. *Vesp*. 693; 724 with scholion), until Pericles introduced pay for jurymen, when the *kolakretai* took over responsibility for that as well. They allocated funds to some specific works during the fifth century, including several religious ones (IG. I³ 36; 395; 435A–F), but they are not mentioned in any literature or inscription after 411 BCE, so it seems the office was abolished then and their remaining functions assumed by the *apodektai*, who received all the income from ordinary taxes and distributed it to separate branches of the administration according to the resolutions of the council (*boule*) or assembly (*ekklesia*). To initiate public projects, the *boule* considered proposals (*probo ulemata*), and submitted approved ones to the *ekklesia*, sometimes adding its own refinements (IG. I³ 35; IG I³ 78).[8] Sometimes the *ekklesia* took the initiative and passed motions on such matters as financing (IG. I³ 52) or a new bridge (IG. I³ 79) without prompting by the *boule*. An approving vote was required in both bodies before a project could proceed. At that stage the contracting arrangements were defined, including the number of separate contracts to be offered.

---

[5] Boersma (1970) 3–8.

[6] Projects could not be classified for governance or management according to the building's end use; many buildings were multipurpose and acted as a temple, cult-center, offering-site, treasury, and meeting place.

[7] Kallett-Marx (1989) 254–63; contrast, e.g., Merritt (1954) 210–11; Meiggs (1963) 14; Hammond (1975) 161. The traditional view that much of Pericles's program was funded by an allocation of income from the Delian League relies on a weakly supported interpretation of the fate of the surplus of the *Hellenotamiai* based on IG. I³ 49, as well as a too literal reading of Plut. *Per.* 12.2.

[8] Glotz (1968).

Major projects were supervised by a commission of overseers (*epistatai*), which might include members of the *ekklesia*. Some buildings, typically sanctuaries, had permanent commissions for maintenance, on the lines of the ten *teichopoioi* who, in conjunction with two public stewards (*epimeletai* or *tamiai*), were responsible for the condition of the city walls (IG. I² 343.90).[9] In other cases, commissions were appointed to serve for one year at a time and had a secretary and sometimes an assistant. They were responsible for agreeing on the general design with the "architect" and submitting it to the *boule* (IG. I³ 35), which sometimes asked for a preliminary sketch (*syngraphe*) or wax models (*paradeigmata*) of particular features like rosettes and set up a special commission to judge entries (IG. I³ 64); more commonly, projects were very broadly defined and it was up to the commission to select detailed drawings. The commission also set the architect's payment (IG. I³ 64), oversaw the works (IG. I³ 52), managed the budget, and reported back to the *boule* on completion (IG. I² 372–74). Transparent recordkeeping was of the highest importance, and contract arrangements were inscribed in stone (e.g., IG. I³ 24; 35; 45; 84).[10] Walls needed regular repair and maintenance, and this too was managed transparently;[11] one inscription detailing the arrangements for managing the repair and maintenance of a part of the city's walls (IG. II² 463) says it has been prepared for anyone who wants to know how the finances were managed.[12]

In the seventh century, when Athens began building temples from stone instead of wood and mud bricks, it used limestone first, then marble from the quarries at Penteli and Hymettus.[13] Quarrying techniques probably derived from Egypt; quarrymen drilled narrow channels around the desired block and then split it out with wedges—a simple task but one requiring some care and practice.[14] Two types of pick were used, a light one for careful extraction with minimal waste and a heavier one for faster, less precise extraction. Wedges were initially of wood, but by classical times were made of iron, though wood continued to be used for levering chiseled blocks from the rock bed. Columns were generally dressed on-site to reduce transport costs. Volumes were huge—even in the Archaic Age, it has been estimated that 270 tons of marble were being shipped each year for construction projects. The Parthenon required 100,000 tons of stone and, even though some was recycled from a previous temple on the site, the continuing Periclean program meant that new Mount Pentelicon quarries had to be exploited

---

[9] Meier (1961) 46.
[10] Davis (1948) 488.
[11] Frederiksen (2001) 41–49.
[12] Meier (1959) no.11; cf. Hedrick (1999) 413–14.
[13] Lawton (2006) 9; Malacrino (2010) 16.
[14] Rockwell (1983) 142–55; Waelkens et al. (1988) 11–16, (1990) 47–72.

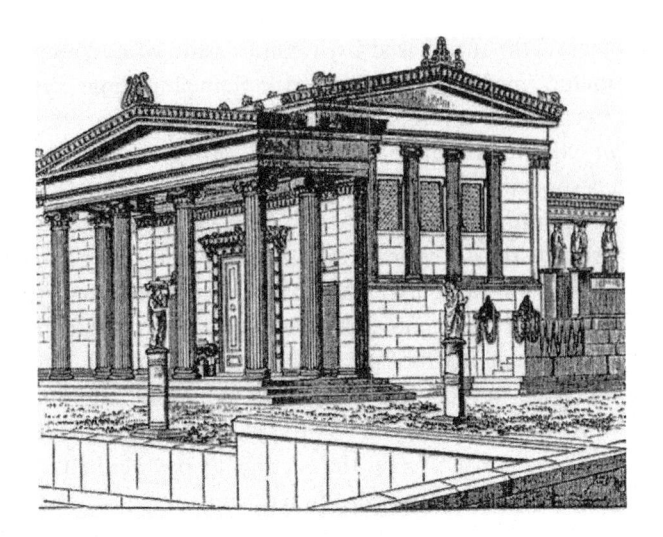

ILLUSTRATION 7.1. The Erechtheum (Artist's Reconstruction)

each year from 439 to 432 BCE.[15] The building program was far more extensive than the major sites that capture our attention, and the pace of development was scarcely interrupted during the Peloponnesian War, which saw the completion of the Temple of Athena Nike, the restoration of several smaller sanctuaries in the city or on the fringes, and new buildings, including a new *bouleterion*, the Erechtheum (Ill. 7.1), the Temple of Hephaistos, the Stoa of Zeus Eleutherios, and the sanctuary of Asclepius.[16] Only the last was privately financed. Burford's estimate that there might have been between 30 and 50 people continuously employed in quarrying for much of the mid- to late fifth century is probably conservative.[17]

From the fact that public building accounts do not include a cost for stone, one may infer that the two major quarries were owned by the state. There is no evidence that the state owned quarrying slaves, however, and any cost attributable to the resource would have been dwarfed by quarrying labor.[18] The work was almost certainly carried out by gangs of slaves belonging to citizens or metics who had preempted the commercial opportunities by being first to establish their operations in the best quarrying sites.[19] Stanier

---

[15] Snodgrass (1983) 22; Burford (1969) 189–91; Palagia (2006a) 132.
[16] Miles (1989) 230–33.
[17] Hurwit (2004) ch. 8; Burford (1963) 32–33. Based on supplying the Parthenon alone over a five-year period, this estimate suggests about one ton could be extracted and dressed per man-day, which seems ambitious.
[18] Burford (1969) 189–91.
[19] Snodgrass (1983) 20; Osborne (1985) 105; Lalonde et al. (1991) 62 and n.30; Korres (1995; 2000); Malacrino (2010) 33–36, 39. This industry structure was echoed in Roman brick production, with owners leasing out their clay pits to *officinatores* (Helen (1975)).

estimated that quarrying accounted for almost half the total costs of building the Parthenon, although Korres maintains that the cost of fluting the columns would have come to more.[20]

Loading the wagons for transporting the material would have been a strenuous and slow process. Some blocks were too large to be borne on wagons (one statue at Delos was made from a 23-ton block and had a 34-ton base) and had to be dragged along the ground, but even over a distance like the 48 kilometers from Corinth to Athens, transport costs were typically less than half of quarrying costs.[21] We may infer an important link to agricultural production: up to 100 pairs of oxen were used to transport materials every day for public buildings in midsummer, a time when they would not be needed on farms and the roads were not muddy, and again it is likely that the slaves, beasts, and wagons were owned or leased by private transport entrepreneurs or quarrying operators.[22]

As "chief builder," the architect was accountable to the *ekklesia* or the *boule* for project delivery. Architects might be assigned responsibility for total project oversight and on smaller projects would report directly to the *boule* rather than to a dedicated board. We know of one case in which the architect and a sanctuary overseer constituted the project board with a one-year term (IG. I³ 52). An architect replaced the *teichopoioi* on the walls commission in 307/4 and was responsible for a whole section of the wall rather than individual tradesmen being engaged by the commission.[23] Some projects had two or more architects.[24] The Olympeion, built in the sixth century, had four: Antistates, Callaischros, Antimachides, and Posinos. Philocles, an architect of the Erechtheum, was succeeded by Archilochus. Callicrates appears to have been the sole architect of the temple of Athena Nike, but he worked alongside Iktinos on the Parthenon, where it was Pheidias who directed the art work and Carpion who wrote the project up (Vit. 7. *Praef.* 12).[25] There are no firm data on how roles were allocated, but a reasonable conjecture is that Iktinos was responsible for the design, helped by Carpion as his junior, while Callicrates managed the project. An architect was appointed for the construction of the Arsenal in the Piraeus in 347 BCE, after the design, attributed to Euthydemus and Philon, had already been chosen (IG. II² 1668).[26] The (unnamed) architect's task was to explain the model and

---

[20] Stanier (1953) 68–72; Korres (2000).
[21] Burford (1969) 189–91; Coulton (1974) 1–19.
[22] Salmon (2001) 200–1; Burford (1963) 33 suggests the figure might have been between 500 and 1,000 yokes if the transport season was only two months long.
[23] Meier (1961) 46; Pleket (1963) 443.
[24] Boersma (1970) 7.
[25] Shear (1963) 375–424; Gruben (2001) 173.
[26] The view that it was "Philon's Arsenal" might stem from the fact that he wrote a treatise describing its architectural features that was well known in antiquity.

the measurements to the hired tradesmen who would actually do the work (*hoi misthosamenoi*).

A chief responsibility of the architect was to hire specialist subcontractors, especially for the decorative elements, giving them more or less discretion according to their skill level and the overall requirements of the building.[27] The structural design belonged to the lead architect, who was probably involved in developing it. It could not be subcontracted, because there was no effective way of transmitting it; there is little evidence of architectural drawings before the fourth century (though there must have been some notation for communicating and copying ideas).[28] To implement it as designed, he had to be involved in managing it on-site, where he would mark out the space and specify the size and number of blocks required, with the details of assembly and decoration often left to the specialists.[29] He would need a very good understanding of stone construction and experience in such tasks as contracting labor, specifying materials, designing and approving subcontracted sections, procurement, expediting, and project accounting.[30] It seems the career steps involved were cumulative: the first was to demonstrate mastery of a trade, working to the plans and designs of others. Those showing a high degree of skill would get the opportunity to create their own designs. These project masons, sculptors, and painters would design friezes, statues, and pictures that they and others would execute, working within the architect's overall framework. The third and final step was to be a master contractor and take responsibility for a total project, which included commissioning the work of master tradesmen and designers and ensuring they had adequate semiskilled and unskilled support. You could be described as an architect at any of those stages if you were in charge; even supervising the removal of a statue fell within the scope of "*architectein*" (Ar. *Pax.* 305). Training for broader project responsibilities took the form of a further apprenticeship. Two of the architects working on the Erechtheum earned only the skilled labor rate of one *drachma* a day, which suggests they were assisting in managing affairs on-site while also learning about building design from a more experienced and senior architect.[31] They might have been slaves, though as they were paid through the project accounts they were clearly not owned by the state. Some architects are known to have been citizens, but it would have been a risky career path for a free man, as it reduced the opportunities to practice one's craft and to keep one's client base.

---

[27] Hurwit (1999) 166–68.
[28] Sensenay (2011) 10–15; Rojas (2012); Coulton (1977) 114; Hurwit (2005) 135–45.
[29] Webster (1973) 147.
[30] Haselberger (1997) 77–94.
[31] Shear (1963) 422 n. 317.

Preserved financial accounts give details of expenditure on other workers for the Parthenon (IG. I³ 436–51), the Erechtheum (IG. I³ 474–79), and the Telesterion at Eleusis (IG. I³ 386–87), and we have similar though less-detailed records for the Propylaea and for statues, including those of Athena Promachos, Athena Parthenos, and Hephaistus.[32] The first side of the Parthenon stele includes payments to quarrymen and carters as well as builders, as materials were brought to the site and the foundations put in place; next come payments to woodworkers, evidently for scaffolding and roof beams; column builders and decorators are paid next, and finally the record shows receipts from the sale of surplus materials.[33] Feyel's analysis of recorded expenditure on the Erechtheum (Ill. 7.1) in 409/8 and 408/7 and on the temple at Eleusis around 80 years later offer an insight into how the workforce was recruited and managed. The first includes the names of 123 people employed on the project, their tasks, and their remuneration, and the second identifies 185 or 186 workers, only naming some but including the status group and tasks of most of them.[34]

The status group most represented is metics, who constitute a little under half the identifiable workforce in both projects.[35] Experts discern quite diverse techniques, reflecting the different regions from which some of these workers hailed, although the records nominate the urban demes where they were based in Athens.[36] Eleven of the workers at Eleusis were aliens without rights of long-term residency.[37] Various explanations have been put forward as to why significantly fewer citizens than foreigners can be identified in both cases, none very satisfactory. It cannot have been because they were more likely to be absent or killed in war, as Randall proposes, because metics bore that burden equally.[38] The very fact that they remained in Athens throughout the Peloponnesian War until they were expelled by the Thirty Tyrants at the end of it demonstrates their commitment and loyalty.[39] The suggestion that it was because citizens preferred other ways of making a living, such as lending (Francotte) or paid civic duties (Glotz), has an element of truth, but not all citizens had funds to lend and none could depend entirely on state pay.[40] As discussed in Chapter 9.2, contributing on an occasional basis to public

---

[32] Rhodes and Lewis (1996).
[33] Cuomo (2008) 18.
[34] The comprehensive provision of names in the Erechtheum accounts has been variously explained as being to make it harder for opponents to cancel the project (Davis (1948) 485–89), to demonstrate the meticulousness of those responsible for spending public funds (Wittenburg (1978) 72–73), or because resources were especially tight at that period in Athens's history (Feyel (2006) 16).
[35] Feyel 320; 325; Davies (2001b) 223.
[36] Stewart (1990) 151; Feyel (2006) 342–48; 367–68.
[37] Feyel (2006) 325.
[38] Randall (1953) 199–210; challenged by Gauthier (1976) 59–62.
[39] Gauthier (1972) 111–18.
[40] Francotte (1900/01) I. 196; Glotz (1926) 210–11.

buildings, either as suppliers or craftsmen, was an attractive income opportunity for those with the time, the need, and the capability. Citizens and metics appear to have performed similar tasks, most being stonemasons or carpenters, although metics feature more strongly as suppliers of materials and as specialist tradesmen.[41] Few citizens were engaged as general (unqualified) laborers, though some metics were. Slaves were almost exclusively confined to general labor and the major trades of stonemasonry and carpentry. They seem to have worked in teams of between four and six, managed by their master.[42] The records offer no support for the view that many of the labor force were public slaves, and it is intrinsically improbable. With no regular state budget and with unpredictable demands on its finances, the *polis* wisely chose not to own a large number of slaves, and the ones it did own were used for work in continuing demand that citizens found unacceptable, like sewage removal, or where there was an advantage in being able to ensure the compliance and integrity of employees through torture, such as weights inspectors, coinage manufacturers and assayers, public record keepers, public executioners, and, most notably, the police force of captured Scythian archers.[43] These circumstances did not apply to the trades required in the building program, with the possible exception of quarrying the building blocks and moving them to the site, which would have been unattractive to citizen-laborers, but there is no reason to believe that the slaves involved belonged to the *polis*. The building data show that slaves were typically employed on a more continuous basis than the free, most of whom seem to have been engaged for one-off tasks, which is consistent with what we know about citizens' attitudes to paid labor.[44]

Industry dynamics, rather than inherent limitations of capability, explain why slaves were engaged primarily for unskilled tasks. Previous chapters have identified workshops employing highly skilled slaves, including knife-making, luxury furniture, and shoemaking. Slaves with these skills would not be sent to work on a public building if their normal workplace was busy. The slaves that were sent to perform general laboring duties would have come from workshops that demanded a lower level of individual capability, such as tanning or shield-turning. If the workshop was a large one and tasks were reasonably interchangeable, this would probably cause little disruption. In smaller enterprises, particularly those with low and volatile income streams, the private operation might have been suspended while the whole workforce went to work on a public building—constituting the teams of four to six under their master.[45] The lack of continuity would not affect their skills,

---

[41] Feyel (2006) 323–24.
[42] Feyel (2006) 324.
[43] Bradley and Cartledge (2011) 60–61.
[44] Feyel (2006) 332–40; for citizens' attitudes to paid work see Chapter 9.2.
[45] Feyel (2006) 324.

as they were continuing to exercise them on the public project; in fact it might have helped promote their capabilities in the private markets they normally serviced. Skilled owner-craftsmen might take on specialist tasks in the public work themselves and leave their workshop in the care of one or more slaves. Some slave gangs might have been employed chiefly in agriculture and put to work as laborers on public buildings only seasonally.

There were three forms of payment arrangement: some workers were on contracts, some were paid for specific tasks (IG 1³ 475. 206–44), and some for time spent, the last being an arrangement that seems to have been peculiar to Athens.[46] Some of the free labor force did piecework between contracts, while a few, apparently the construction elite, worked exclusively or almost exclusively on contract. Those paid most in total were the contracted workers, and they are likely to have been those whose labor or skills were required through the whole project and working in areas where error or delay would have been especially damaging. Piece-rates were paid for narrowly defined outputs such as material supply or engraving, while those who did simple and repetitive tasks received the daily rate of one *drachma* a day, whatever their social status.[47] Different projects evidently managed procurement differently: 35 suppliers of materials are identifiable at Eleusis against just three for the Erechtheum.[48] In contrast to the other three temple projects analyzed by Feyel (Epidaurus, Delphi, and Delos), very few workers on the Attic projects earned more than 100 *drachmae* in total, and those that did were primarily engaged in decoration or sculpture. In the face of irregular work requirements and constrained funding, having only a few people on contracts was a logical strategy; the bulk of the work could be allocated on an as-needed basis and bid for by people who would fit it in with, or use it as a temporary substitute for, their normal business operation, thereby keeping costs down. The project managers of medieval cathedrals took a similar approach.[49]

Plutarch (*Per.* 12.6–7) names a wide range of crafts employed in the Periclean building program: *carpenters, molders, bronze smiths, stonemasons, dyers, gold-workers, ivory-workers, painters, inlayers,* and *embossers*. Variations in the composition of the workforce obviously depended on the design of the building, and it is unwise to rely too heavily on the precision of terms in Plutarch or the relevant epigraphy, but we can be confident that nearly all those involved came from private sector manufacturing businesses in Athens or elsewhere. Whatever their status, there is no doubt that the

---

[46] Feyel (2006) 429–38; 441–67. We have no sound data on payment arrangements for work on Athens's walls, but elsewhere it was done by independent artisans, employed on piecework with or without their slaves (Meier (1959) nos. 33; 58; 98; 104; 186; 270; Pleket (1961) 169–70).

[47] Stewart (1990) 66. In this way the owners of slaves received an effective *apophora* of around two obols a day (a typical rate) above the cost of maintaining them.

[48] Feyel (2006) 385–94.

[49] Feyel (2006) 469–518.

craftsmen engaged on major building works were skilled at their trade, either as independent artisans or implementing the designs of master craftsmen and artists, which indicates that they must have come from private enterprises in which they had learned their trade and where they continued to work when not engaged on public buildings—in other words, they must have come largely from active workshops, owned by citizens, freed slaves, or metics, which could be suspended while they carried out a public contract.[50] In many other cities, public building programs were few and far between, so the labor force was an itinerant one who would have left town once the project was complete. Athens's larger market and more consistent supply of public works meant that even the metics would remain and carry out their trades in the private sector between public contracts.

"*Stonemasons*" had the most work to do on a building, shaping, smoothing, and fitting the blocks and columns. They accounted for around 40 percent of identified trades at the Erechtheum.[51] There appears to have been a standard process for construction, beginning with the external colonnade, as this was complex to align and determined the height of the much simpler inner part or *cella*, which only involved piling up blocks of stone.[52] Gaps were probably left in the colonnade to allow access for those working on the internal structures; even if the other columns were monolithic, these gaps would eventually be filled by columns made of piled drums. An estimate based on surface area suggests that the number of masons required on the Periclean building program peaked at around 1,000 a year, possibly more.[53] Marble statuary was another large employer: based upon the cost of two half-size figures carved in relief, it can be estimated that a life-size statue in the round took around eight man-months to construct, and many temples had dozens.[54] There was little to distinguish masons, sculptors, and Plutarch's "*molders*," who designed and realized the friezes, bases, and capitals of public buildings as well as some of the statuary that might form an important part of project costs. All three trades would include master designers and journeyman carvers, sometimes as a team from one workshop, sometimes individually, and they all worked with the same tools: hammers and variously shaped chisels, punches, and drills. When there was no public building work to be done, there were numerous other markets for them to serve, making statues for the private or cult markets, carving funerary monuments, or maintaining and repairing the city's major buildings, walls, roads, and drains.[55]

---

[50] Loomis (1998) 232–39.
[51] Feyel (2006) 385–94.
[52] Burford (1963) 28–30; Younger and Rehak (2009) 44–45.
[53] Salmon (2001) 202.
[54] Younger (2009) 48–50.
[55] Burford (1963) 25 suggests that the work of fluting columns was so specialized that it must have been conducted by itinerant specialists traveling from one temple project to the next, but it is difficult to see why fluting would have been beyond the capability of a typical skilled sculptor.

Socrates's father, Sophroniscus, might have been a master mason. Socrates was a member of the hoplite class and reasonably well-off, even though he did not earn anything from his teaching. He may have found sponsors, but it is also possible that his father owned a substantial masonry-cum-monumental sculpture operation from which he inherited the income.[56]

"*Carpenters*" accounted for 20 percent of the Erechtheum workforce and made up the largest category at Eleusis. It is hard to be definitive about their contribution to public buildings, as wood is a poor material for preservation, but it is likely that it consisted of roof beams, tables, couches, altars, and wooden statues. Sourcing the smaller items would have presented few challenges since, as we saw in the previous chapter, Athens was home to a large number of carpenters who could carry out the work in the course of their normal business. Supporting beams present a different challenge in handling and precision, but large carpentry workshops were already supplying the boat-building and mining industries. "*Ivory-workers*" used similar techniques to carpenters and were probably interchangeable with the most skillful of them (see Chapter 6.1).

Another substantial employment category was metalwork. A stonemason might play more than one role, moving between, say, sculpture and fluting, but metallurgists were specialized.[57] Chapter 4.4 found that there were probably two segments in the decorative trades that Plutarch describes as "*gold-workers... inlayers and embossers.*" One consisted of highly skilled craftsmen in small establishments, inlaying and embossing various types of metal, ivory, or precious stones to their own designs, and often making products to the order of particular customers. The other comprised larger workshops employing several slaves to produce standard products in volume for the general retail market. Both designer-craftsmen and artisans who worked on other people's designs would be needed on a public building, and it seems they were paid the same rate, despite the opportunity cost of the former probably being much higher; skilled tradesmen known for their design capabilities and the quality of their workmanship would have enjoyed premium prices for their output in the commercial marketplace, while journeymen or slaves implementing the simpler designs of others would not have earned more than a basic wage. Pay parity on a public project reflects the value Athens placed on equality, and would have been facilitated by the honor of being known to have made a personal sacrifice for the public good, as well as the opportunity for self-promotion.

The distinction between creative artists and those who implemented their designs also held among "*bronze smiths.*" This industry, discussed in the next section, included workshops employing several slaves to make large statues

---

[56] Hughes (2010) 65–66.
[57] Feyel (2006) 372–83.

according to a predetermined design, often copied from famous works. On public buildings it is likely that the architect engaged a master craftsman to design appropriate statuary and oversee its realization, using his own slaves or ones hired specifically for the purpose.

Before modern chemical analysis was applied to ancient monuments, Plutarch's reference to *"dyers"* and *"painters"* was one of the few indications that these imposing white blocks of marble and the statues adorning them had originally been decorated in the brightest of colors.[58] The contribution of *"dyers"* was to statues rather than the building proper; cult figures might be clad in brightly colored garments. It is unclear why Plutarch does not mention textile manufacturers, without whom there would have been nothing to dye. It is likely that the clothing for statuary, being outsize and presumably made of high-quality and hard-wearing cloth, was either made in large specialized workshops (perhaps ones that made sails, which also needed massive looms) or woven as part of a sacred rite, like Athena's *peplos* (Chapter 5.1.1).

TABLE 7.1 **Sources of Contract Workers**

| Craft or Trade[a] | Supervisors/Masters/Designers | Laborers/Subordinates |
| --- | --- | --- |
| Quarrying and Cartage | Slave supervisor | Teams of dedicated quarrymen and haulers |
| Architect | Master mason, following apprenticeship to an experienced architect | Apprentices: expert masons (status unknown) |
| Masons, moulders | 1. Craftsmen-owners or supervisors of large workshops<br>2. Lone craftsmen | 1. Slaves from large monumental sculpture workshops<br>2. Gangs of mobile building workers |
| Gold-workers....inlayers and embossers | 1. Craftsmen-owners or supervisors of large workshops<br>2. Lone craftsmen | Slaves employed in large workshops, implementing standard ornamental designs |
| Bronze smiths | Craftsmen-owners or supervisors of large workshops | Slaves employed in large bronze workshops, doing the physical work on large statues |
| Carpenters, ivory workers | Craftsmen-owners or supervisors of large workshops | Slaves employed in large workshops, probably supplying the boat building industry as well |
| Dyers | Textiles would have been made and dyed off-site in specialist large-scale establishments or as part of a ritual | |
| Painters | Master craftsmen, probably hired as individuals or in small teams | Painter's assistants, probably supplied by painters |

[a] From Plut. *Per.*12. 6–7.

---

[58] Webster (1973) 147–48; Gruben (2001) 115; Brinkmann, Wünscher et al. (2007); Brinkmann (2008).

The technique of painting made important strides in depth and representation during the fifth century, to the point where painters could be seen as no less accomplished than architects and shipbuilders (Pl. *Grg.* 463–65).[59] The leading painters were top craftsmen and well known to the public, some, like Apollodoros and Zeuxis, gaining their reputations initially for their work on public buildings and statuary. Praxiteles used a painter called Nicias to paint his sculptures. Highly regarded painters who came from overseas to work on Athenian buildings included Polygnotos of Thasos and Agatharchus of Samos. These artists would often have worked alone, with assistants preparing their equipment and colors, but there may also have been teams of slave painters who would work together on plain surfaces or standard scenes, probably outlined for them by a master painter.

Table 7.1 summarizes the likely source of skilled workers for the public building program. Each project attracted a few foreign workers, either invited for a special skill or arriving in Athens in the hope of finding work, but by far the bulk of contract workers must have come from local operations.

## 7.2 Monumental Statues

Surprising though it may seem, one of the world's earliest crafts, and one that in every generation has enabled individual artists to find fame and fortune through their creative genius, was also a major employer and an important source of income for hundreds, perhaps thousands, of Athenians in classical times.[60] The freestanding statuary and deep relief work required for the Periclean building program occupied a large number of stone carvers and metallurgists for much of the fifth century. The reason is to be found in the way these technologies facilitated the division of roles between creative artist and journeyman. To appreciate how this could occur, it is important to consider how technologies developed to meet changeable but growing demand.

Marble and bronze were the principal materials used for Athenian statues, generally marble for architectural sculptures and bronze for freestanding works.[61] Other materials included clay, wood, limestone, iron, silver, gold, and ivory and various combinations of them, sometimes embellished with precious stones, enamel, glass, copper, or tin.[62] By 500 BCE, Athenian sculptors had abandoned clay, wood, and limestone, finding them duller and less durable than other materials, and marble, using styles adopted from Egypt

---

[59] Webster (1973) 148.
[60] For prehistoric sculpture, see Conard (2003; 2009).
[61] Palagia (2006a) 119.
[62] Penny (1993); Lapatin (2001) 7–21; Lawton (2006) 2–7; Palagia (2006a) 122–23, 125. Statuary in the temple of Demeter and Kore in Corinth was made of terracotta—Bookidis (2010).

in the seventh century, was used throughout the classical period for architectural statues, building, and reliefs.[63] Athens had originally sourced its marble from the Cyclades, which was also where the best sculptors came from at the start of the classical period, but she soon had her own skilled sculptors and source of materials; most of the marble for the sculptures of the Periclean building program came from nearby Mt. Pentelicon. It continued as the building stone of choice through the classical period, but its role in statuary was increasingly challenged by bronze, which displaced marble in the fifth century as the leading material for freestanding monumental works and remained preferred for statues through Roman times, probably because of its versatility and human-like appearance (Dio Chrys. *Orat.* 28.3). Gold and ivory continued to be used in statues of special cult significance like the Athena Parthenos, with gold foil used as a particular enhancement. Faces and hands might be of ivory and eyes inlaid with glass to bring out a sparkle; embossed silver-gilt wigs completed the effect.

Archaeological finds are constrained by the durability of materials. The only artifacts surviving from the Dark Ages are small, unpretentious votive bronzes and terracottas. Bronze statues are sometimes depicted on vases and coins, but most of the originals have been lost. Around 30 life-size bronze works have been recovered, mainly from shipwrecks, but only one is properly signed.[64] There are not many early copies that survived, either, and finds represent less than 10 percent of the statues mentioned by Pliny. Pausanias described 33 statues at Argos and 50 are shown on coins, but only one copy of all these pieces has been identified.[65] The greater durability of marble has left more original examples to corroborate what the texts tell us; we know, for example, that the northwest corner of the Agora was full of marble herms (monumental stones dedicated to Hermes and placed in front of buildings for good luck) and of equestrian statues in bronze with marble bases on which dedications were inscribed. Copies of some famous marble statues survive, though they tend to be much smaller and less detailed than the originals and possibly made from old columns, bases, or basins. There are examples of statues with votive dedications on them (e.g., IG. II² 3109) and of decrees commissioning statues (IG. II² 555) or providing honors for sculptors (IG. II⁴ 514). Some gravestones carry the name of the artist who made them.[66]

Much Athenian public sculpture was closely aligned to the architecture of public buildings, which combined the closely balanced system of verticals and horizontals of the Doric style, in which sculpture was placed on metopes or in pediments or on gable corners, and the looser Ionic style, in which

---

[63] The Egyptians preferred harder granite and basalt.
[64] By Boethus (this piece is mentioned in Pliny *HN.* 34.84).
[65] Stewart (1990) 24–26.
[66] Stewart (1990) 22–23.

freestanding statues can fit "almost anywhere" and decorate any part of the building.[67] Relief sculpture was common in important buildings, and Greek relief work was much deeper than the typical one centimeter in Egypt, where the technique originated, so Athenian artists were able to build multiple layers of background perspective.[68] In the sixth century, the exteriors of Athenian temples started to display figures and epic narrative scenes carved on metopes and friezes.[69] Freestanding public statuary consisted principally of honorific pieces commemorating an individual or a particular achievement, building on a long tradition in Athens, where Antenor had portrayed the tyrannicides in 510 and probably undertook similar public commissions for the Alcmaionids.[70] A statue of Conon celebrated his role in the battle of Cnidos in 394 and others portrayed victors at ritual games. In the later part of the fourth century statues honoring individuals like Philip and Alexander appeared in the Agora (Paus. 1.9.4). To guard against *hubris*, these statues could not be more than life-size, and only triple games victors were shown in action.

Private commissions for tombs and funerary ornaments tended to become increasingly elaborate, and restrictions on ostentatious display were introduced by Solon in 594/93; some years later, perhaps by Cleisthenes (Cic. *De Leg.* 2.64–65); and by Demetrius (317–307). These regulations seem to have been less rigorously enforced during the Peloponnesian War and in its aftermath; 6,000 gravestones have been found in Athens dated between 430 and 317 BCE, representing a minimum demand of almost 60 pieces a year, which made Athens the largest private market for sculpture in western history.[71] From the third century onward, portraits and tombs accounted for most sculpture other than cult images and consisted largely of images of rulers or private benefactors, often with a finely judged nod to patriotism.[72]

Evidence of workshops is not as informative as we might wish. Stone sculptures did not require a permanent installation, and craftsmen could work anywhere they could set up the block to be worked on.[73] As a later writer put it, sculptors "exported only their own hands and tools for working stone and ivory; others provided the raw materials while they plied their craft in the temples…" (Philostr. *VA* 5.200). Nevertheless, the residential and industrial zone southwest of the Agora was host to several sculpture workshops in the fifth century, and excavators named one street "Street of the Marbleworkers." Plutarch's "herm-carvers' quarters" (*De Gen.* 10.580d–f) may have been there or close by. Much early production in bronze was itinerant, with independent

---

[67] Stewart (1990) 4.
[68] Konstam (1984) 81–83.
[69] Tanner (2006) 161.
[70] Mattusch (1988) 88.
[71] Webster (1973) 57.
[72] Lippold (1950); Akerstrom (1981) 7–34; Stewart (1990) 60–64; 43.
[73] Hasaki (2012b) 267.

sculptors working on-site and using temporary casting pits for statues for major building projects. The earliest bronze workshops found near the Agora date from the fifth century, but a red figure *kylix* by the Foundry Painter suggests that production dated back to archaic times.[74] A large foundry discovered on the southwest slope of the Acropolis was probably for public statuary. Fixed workshops were fully established by the early fifth century, probably because of the need for secure storage of precious raw materials and work in process. Six workshops from the classical period have been found in and around the Agora, together with a number of pits that might have been used for casting large bronze statues.[75] Four such pits have been identified in the Ceramicus.[76] The area just outside the southeast corner was active in metalwork until the third century CE. One statue-making site, known as the workshop of Mikion and Menon, was in production for 200 years from around 475 BCE.[77] Collaboration between workshops was evident from archaic times, perhaps even internationally: the 1.63-meter-high bronze Vix *krater* from Laconia, found in a Celtic burial site and probably made before 530 BCE, seems to have been assembled from components brought in by sea from a number of different workshops, all working from a common model.[78] In classical times, versions of the huge statue of Athena Promachos have been identified as coming from five different workshops.[79]

The lives and works of statue makers were well documented, with the result that we probably know the names of more of them than of any other craftsmen—even potters and painters.[80] Douris of Samos, Xenocrates, Strabo, and Pausanias all wrote on sculptors and their works. Book 34 of Pliny's *Natural History* concerns marble statues and Book 36 bronze. Statue bases from Hellenistic Rhodes carry signatures of both sculptors and founders.[81] Sculptors also liked to document their techniques, including Theodorus of Samos (around 550 BCE), the fourth-century artists Euphranor and Silanion, and Polyclitus, whose *Canon* gave very precise proportions for each element of the human frame.[82] Lysippus explained how to produce an idealized body by reducing the proportions of the head and arms to make the statue seem taller, and Xenocrates based his guidance to practitioners on Lysippus's particular qualities of balance, rhythm, and discernment. Pheidias was the most

---

[74] Berlin 2294; Hoppin (1973) I. 454; Mattusch (1980) 54–56; (2008) 16.1.
[75] Mattusch (1977) 348–59; (1988) 220–27; (1989) 27–39; see Chapter 4.3.
[76] Zimmer (1990) 34–38.
[77] The name of the first owner, Mikion, was found inscribed on a bone stylus and that of the last, Menon, on some black-glazed dinner ware (Lawton (2006) 17–19).
[78] Shefton (1989) 219; Herfort-Koch (1986) 70–73.
[79] Niemeyer (1960) 37–55; Tölle-Kastenbein (1980) 70–71.
[80] See, for example, the fourth-century prosopography in Stewart (1990) 277–94.
[81] Blinkenberg (1902–14) T 11.
[82] Stewart (1990) 21, 35; Linfert (1990) 240–97.

distinguished sculptor of the fifth century—as wealthy as 10 other sculptors (Pl. *Meno.* 91d)—and from the fourth century the historical record includes Demetrios of Alopeke, Euphranor (also known as a painter—Plin. *HN.* 35.128–29), Bryaxis, Lysippos, and Xenocrates, as well as Praxiteles, the most famous of all. Praxiteles's sons, Cephisodotus and Timarchus, also achieved a reputation of their own, and the family undertook six trierarchies in the 10 years between 334 and 325. Prominent artists founded schools: sons succeeded fathers (Pl. *Prt.* 328a) and apprentices their masters.[83] Ageladas, a sculptor from Argos, taught Myron, Pheidias, and Polyclitus. Myron taught his son, Pheidias taught Agoracritus, and Polyclitus taught seven others.

Despite this extensive documentation, the artists who achieved fame and fortune comprised only a small proportion of those employed on monumental statues, and there is substantial evidence that statues were made by large gangs and most of the work involved in carving stone or casting bronze was carried out by anonymous individuals who had served an apprenticeship but were not given responsibility for creating original designs. The Foundry Painter's *kylix*, discussed in Chapter 4.6, shows six people working on a small nude and a much larger figure which might be a statue or a mold for a suit of armor.[84] Both would have used the same techniques, and the spatial constraints of the vase mean that the true number of workers might have been higher. Lycurgus (*Leoc.* 58) describes how, before going into self-imposed exile, the bronze-worker Leocrates sold a number of slaves for 3,500 *drachmae* to his brother-in-law, who then sold them to another brother-in-law, Timochares (*Leoc.* 22–23).[85] He does not specify what these slaves did, but, unless they were much more expensive than knife-makers (Dem. 27.9), the sum represented at least 10 industrial slaves, and even the rich would have found it convenient to make sure such a large gang had something useful to do, so they almost certainly were engaged in some form of production.

A wealthy bronze smith like Leocrates would have needed a large team if he was to make statues that were life-size or larger. As in architecture, the creative artist conceived the "big picture" in terms of size, shape, angles, and proportions, and left it to experienced journeymen to produce the finished article. Aristophanes was familiar with this distinction: journeymen smiths (*Av.* 488–89) and jewelers (*Plut.* 617–18) were inferior to true artists (though hard-working and a great deal better than sycophantic politicians).[86] In Roman times, the distinction remained: Horace (*AP.* 32–35) commiserates with a craftsman who has only been entrusted with the nails and curls of a figure, and Lucian (CE 120–180) claimed he switched to rhetoric because no

---

[83] Hasaki (2012a) 182–83.
[84] Mattusch (1980) 54–56; (2008) 16.1.
[85] See Chapter 4.6.
[86] Treister (1996) 234.

matter how good a sculptor he became, he would still be a laborer (*Somn.* 9). Trade associations were formed in Argos and Sidon in the first century BCE, and it is unlikely they represented master craftsmen or artists.[87] It is consistent with this need for a large team that the labor component in a Hellenistic bronze portrait accounted for 2,000 of the 3,000 *drachmae* the object cost (IG. II² 555).[88]

Another reason work was done in teams was the sheer size of some works. Many statues were simply too large to have been made by one man. Sculptures on the Parthenon had to be supported by iron brackets and frames.[89] It is inconceivable that all the carving and forming in the 69 known works of Pheidias was done by the artist himself. His bronze figure of Athena Promachos could be seen from ships at sea, and his workshop at Olympia, which still exists today, measured over 18 meters by 12 in floor space and was 13 meters high.[90]

The analysis of the building program in the previous section confirms the team-based nature of the business. Classical Athens offered regular but intermittent employment on public projects, and the program could not have worked so successfully if it depended entirely on importing foreign workers when required. Many of the 53 marble workers required on the Parthenon in one year must have been working locally in private industry. Other cities' demands were much more sporadic: Epidauros invested in a project that took four people 18 months in around 380 BCE, and then purchased no more public sculpture for the next 50 years. The result was a mobile workforce based around major sites of demand—specifically, the major religious centers like Olympia, Delphi, and Delos.[91] In Athens, the work was more regular and traces of permanent workshops show the local workforce found continuing opportunities in the private market. Even when there was plenty of public work being commissioned, relying on it offered an unsteady career with no security of employment, an itinerant lifestyle, and total dependence on winning tenders and competitions.

The nature of the work and the skills required by laborers differed between metal and stone, as becomes evident when one examines the respective techniques, and these differences determined the nature of the relevant slave gangs.[92] In metals, flat sheets were forged and small objects could be solid cast or formed by hammering sheets of metal over a wooden core, but

---

[87] Charneux (1992) 335–43; Wilsdorf (1952) 170.
[88] Dillon (2007) 73 and fig. 58.
[89] Palagia (2006a) 120.
[90] Heilmeyer et al. (2007).
[91] Feyel (2006) 320; 325.
[92] The process for shaping other metals was similar to that for bronze, and the carving of wood, ivory, and other stone was similar to that for marble, with any differences reflecting the specific qualities of the material.

considerations of weight and material cost made hollow casting the chosen method for statues.[93] At its simplest, the solid lost wax technique, used in Greece from as early as 900 BCE, involves forming a clay mold directly from a wax model, heating the mold to melt the wax and harden the clay, and then pouring molten metal into the empty mold.[94] More sophisticated was direct lost wax hollow casting in which the wax model is built over a clay core, sometimes supported with armatures. The model is covered with clay and heated so the wax can be removed, and the remaining clay forms the mold for pouring the metal into. The technique that came to dominate by the middle of the fifth century, indirect lost wax hollow casting, was more sophisticated still. A clay model is formed and then surrounded with more clay, generally of a pliable nature (rubber is used today). The external clay mold is removed, reassembled, and lined with wax. When the mold is removed from the wax model, the wax is given some finishing touches to conceal joins and imperfections and strengthening armatures are added as needed. It is covered with a "slurry" of clay or plaster into which vents or runners are inserted to allow wax and gases to escape. The mold is then heated to 600–650°C to melt or burn off the wax and placed in sand, where molten metal is poured into it. When the metal has cooled and is removed from the mold, finishing details are applied with sharp tools or sanders, and a wax glaze can be added. Large statues often came in several pieces to be fitted or soldered together at this stage.[95] The final step is to patinate the work by cleaning it thoroughly, correcting color blemishes chemically, or by vigorous rubbing and waxing.[96] Unlike direct casting, this indirect technique has the advantage, vital to a manufacturer of anything other than unique works, of allowing the original molding to be used many times. The only task requiring artistic creativity and technique is forming the original mold; everything else can be done by unskilled laborers. Even portrait sculptures were constructed by putting a customized head on a standard body.[97]

The Greeks learned stone carving from Egypt.[98] It had quite different labor demands. It began with unskilled or semiskilled labor working under direction and was finished by the artist assisted by experienced and dexterous associates. To procure marble for building blocks or sculpture from the quarries at Mt. Pentelicon, narrow channels were drilled in the rock surface

---

[93] Mattusch (2008) 422; Hasaki (2012b) 462.
[94] This description of casting processes is derived from Clark (1980), Stewart (1990) 33–42, Mattusch (2006) 211–15, and Hasaki (2012b) 262–65, and discussions with a contemporary manufacturer of decorative sculpture, Mr. Rodney Broad of Meridian Sculpture Founders Pty Ltd., Melbourne.
[95] Mattusch (2006) 215.
[96] Konstam (1984) 161.
[97] Mattusch (2006) 234.
[98] Palagia (2006b) 244.

around the desired block, which was then split out with pick-hammer wedges.[99] Dressing with a punch could approximate the shape of the finished object and reduce the amount that had to be transported to the workshop, a technique called "quarry-bedding." Many pieces were shaped to within a centimeter of their final form while still in the quarry, although this does not appear to have been the norm in classical times; the Parthenon accounts show most of the carving was done at the construction site.[100] In the workshop, further roughing out with drills, wooden mallets, and iron chisels or punches took place before detailed modeling began. Technique varied with the material: granite required vertical blows and marble oblique ones.[101] A modern sculptor's manual tells novices to "block out" the stone with a drill, then "peck gently away at the stone with tools at right angles to the surface, removing layer after layer."[102] Classical sculptors' modeling tools consisted of mallets applied to differently shaped iron chisels, of which the most basic were flat ones, for detailed work and for smoothing surfaces, and claw chisels, invented in about 500 BCE, for trimming rough surfaces. The fifth century saw an increased number of specialized tools for making surface textures to give the effect of fabric or hair.[103] Early sculpture in limestone had required little preparation other than simple sketches scratched on the side of the block to guide the carving, but marble needed more precision. The limited strength of iron tools meant going very slowly, eroding the stone rather than cutting it, and more complex figures required a sketched grid or matrix.

Drilling technology was used at every stage in stone work: quarrying, modeling, forming eyes, ears, nostrils, and hair, carving relief outlines, undercutting reliefs, making channels between figures and their drapery, and creating grooves. Holes for attaching ornaments, separately worked parts, or limbs that had been broken off were sometimes made by hammering piercing tools into the stone, but more often by drilling. It was an operation for one or two men in which the drill bit was rotated with a strap or bow and could be used to make a hole at any angle or moved along a line to dig a channel— the "running drill," an innovation of Callimachos in the late fifth century.[104] Stone statues were finished by smoothing and polishing with a rasp (invented in the mid-sixth century) and with abrasives, usually made from sand, emery, or pumice. Paint was mixed with oil and wax to give the item a sheen.[105] Both stone and bronze statues of gods might be gilded with thin gold leaf pressed

---

[99] Lawton (2006) 25–33.
[100] Palagia (2006b) 247–49; Younger (2009) 48.
[101] Hasaki (2012b) 267.
[102] Konstam (1984) 34.
[103] Stewart (1990) 33–42; Palagia (2006b) 251–61.
[104] Lawton (2006) 25–33.
[105] Later, Punic wax was used to make marble more translucent (Vit. *De Arch.* 7.9.3–4).

onto a glued surface or forced into grooves as an *appliqué*, or by heating the statue and pouring molten metal onto it. An optional final step in both technologies was *kosmesis*, adorning the piece with fabrics and jewels. In contrast to bronze work, where only mold-forming varied between pieces, each carver had to work to follow the artist's specific intentions.

Several important differences between the two technologies affected workshop structure:

(i) Large bronze pieces required a team to move the materials around between process steps. Stone only needed to be moved at the beginning and end of the process.

(ii) For metals, much of the work involved tending the furnace and handling materials, and artistic creativity was only required in designing a mold, which could be used several times. By contrast, all workers in stone made a direct contribution to a piece's final appearance, even when working to someone else's design.

(iii) Bronze work had several stages that could work in parallel, with different pieces at each stage at any point in time. This facilitated specialization and maximized the utilization of the master craftsman/designer. Only a handful of people could work on a marble statue at the same time.

(iv) Molds lent themselves to the copying in metal of any model likely to find a buyer, and reuse of molds made mass production in bronze possible without the forming labor needed to make an original piece. The precise technique used for copying works in stone is not known, but it seems workshops made casts in clay and used calipers to triangulate measures and mark them on the new piece of stone.[106] This made the task simpler, but the total labor requirement would have been the same as the original, and there seems to have been no wholesale copying in marble.

On this basis one would expect to find several bronze workshops employing at least half a dozen slaves to do the physical work and some larger ones making copies. Leocrates might have owned one of these. Large gangs of bronze-worker slaves under one owner might have operated more than one casting pit in parallel, not necessarily on adjacent sites. Marble workshops, by contrast, might consist of only a master and slave and could only grow as fast as the master could find workers he could rely on to execute forming work without his constant supervision. The reason bronze came to dominate fourth-century statuary might well have been relative labor economics. For original items, it could use less skilled labor, or labor that could be more

---

[106] Palagia (2006b) 264–65.

quickly trained, and was therefore less constrained by the need to find or develop skilled craftsmen. At least as important was the greater ease with which copies could be made. Copies of a bronze nude male by Polyclitus of Argos were in many later Greek and Roman homes.[107]

Despite these differences, there was clearly some interplay between the two technologies—at least at the level of the master craftsman or artist. Some applications in marble clearly use the techniques of bronze workers.[108] Leading sculptors were seldom associated with specific materials, and some craftsmen worked with several in combination. Pheidias's reputation was based on his versatility and technical virtuosity as much as his artistry.[109] The techniques he was master of included chryselephantine, acrolithic, bronze, and marble, and his two chief pupils, Agoracritus and Alcamenes, also worked in both marble and bronze.[110] He probably invented the technique of unscrolling ivory into thin sheets and chemically softening them so they could be worked and molded like wood; previously a large ivory figure had to have its parts carved separately and attached to wooden cores that were then painted or gilded.[111] The fifth-century sculptor Alcamenes, a contemporary from Lemnos, is credited with the bronze statues of Hephaestos and Athena in the Hephaesteion and about a dozen large marble pieces in Athenian temples, including statues of Hecate and Hermes Propylaeus. Polyclitus was similarly versatile.[112] Lysippus, whose 50 known works were all in bronze, seems to have been something of an exception.

The more complex requirements for copying stone did not prevent the best marble sculptors from accumulating considerable wealth. It might well have been the copying of admired pieces that enabled leading "brand-name" artists like Praxiteles to expand their workshops far beyond their own production capability.[113] Gravestones also became more standardized, enabling marble workshops to grow more rapidly by being able to employ less-skilled workers who carried out repetitive copying tasks on the same matrices.[114] Added to this were the price premiums available for the best work. The price of a completed 2-foot-high figure commissioned for the Erechtheum was 60 *drachmae*, while fourth-century funeral monuments

---

[107] Spivey (2013) 39.
[108] Stewart (1990) 151.
[109] Stern (2008) 531–32; Plutarch (*Per.* 13.4) suggests Pheidias supervised the entire building program, but recent research shows he was only involved in a few buildings and his role was much less important than Plutarch implies (Hurwit (2005)). The story that he died in prison is probably incorrect (Himmelmann (1977)).
[110] Palagia (2006a) 125.
[111] Lapatin (1997) 663.
[112] Mattusch (2006) 226.
[113] Starr (1977) 77, 83–84.
[114] Lawton (2006) 17–19; 25–33.

could cost up to 12,000 *drachmae*, and it is highly unlikely they required 200 times as much material and labor.[115] The risk of owning masonry slaves was reduced by the availability of public building and maintenance jobs for general masonry workers, and the annual cleaning of statues was probably also entrusted to the craftsmen responsible for the original finish.

The distinction between artist and laborer meant that the laws of competition in monumental statues worked quite differently from other industries. Previous chapters identified a number of trades in which a highly skilled craftsman could not build a large business because the skills were seen to reside in him alone and his reputation would not transfer to a gang of slaves. Bespoke shoemaking, bronze armor, and the forming and painting of high-quality pottery were notable instances. Large slave gangs were typically found in differentiated trades, where the contribution of an individual to the finished item could not be isolated, such as shield- or knife-making and luxury furniture. In statuary, differentiation was very clearly associated with a particular individual, but in order to deliver his product he had no choice but to employ several slaves.

## 7.3 Private Housing and Infrastructure

Residential Athens consisted mainly of simple houses in narrow streets.[116] Men spent little time at home, and do not seem to have worried too much about their accommodation; many of the houses in classical Athens were not very large by the standards of the period (about 150–200 m$^2$) and of plain construction, though a few rich families lived in much larger homes with more rooms and sometimes a second story.[117] Most large houses were some distance from the centre of the city, and Demosthenes announces with pride that the houses of the rich near the Agora were indistinguishable from those of the poor (3.25; 23.207). Houses in Egypt and Italy in the early days of the Roman Empire were larger than classical Greek urban dwellings had been, and even the poorer habitations had more sophisticated plumbing, drainage, roofs, and foundations.[118] Urban planning for residential areas near the city was apparently not a concern of the *ekklesia*, except in the case of the Peiraeus, in which residential zones were incorporated in the original layout by Hippodamos.[119] Elsewhere, the houses destroyed by the Persians in 480 BCE

---

[115] Stewart (1990) 66–67; even allowing for inflation, the difference cannot be attributed to input costs.
[116] Except where otherwise stated, the description of private houses is based on Jones (1975), Camp (1986) 177–81, Goette (2001, ch. 1), and Tsakirgis (2009).
[117] Shear (1973) 147–49; Canlas (2010) 35.
[118] Morris (2010b); Alston (1997) 25–39; Wallace-Hadrill (1994).
[119] Webster (1973) 156.

were rebuilt on the original pattern, with no attempt to develop a more thoughtful system of streets and intersections.

Several dozen private dwellings have been excavated, mainly to the south and southwest of the Agora. The foundations and lower walls consisted of rubble set in clay, on top of which the upper walls (above one foot from the ground) were of sun-dried mud bricks covered in stucco. There were no standard house formats, but they seldom contained more than six rooms and often as few as four, based around a courtyard that provided light, though some, generally further from the city center, would be rather larger (Ill. 7.2). There were few external windows and only one or two doors. The main room, the *andron*, was used for entertaining and often faced south; it might have a mosaic floor of pebbles embedded in a lime mortar and a slightly raised border on which couches were placed. Other rooms are harder to identify, though drains indicate bathrooms, piles of pots suggest kitchens, and loom weights probably come from the women's quarters. The roof was made of clay tiles supported by wooden beams and boards, and if it was lost, exposure to the rain made walls revert to mud and made the site hard to clear. As a result, new houses were often built on top of earlier ones. Most courtyards had wells, originally bored 12 to 15 meters deep, but by the fourth century the water table had sunk and most domestic water came from rain captured in cisterns. Clean drinking water was fetched from public fountain houses fed by fresh springs. Some controls over private development were enforced by the *astunomoi* in the fourth century and possibly earlier. No windows were allowed to open onto the street, and overhanging balconies or open drains were forbidden. Pollux (3.9.30) cites several instances of balcony owners being fined.[120]

Houses were rebuilt approximately every 30 years and cost between eight and 10 years of subsistence food for one person, but even so were not considered an important part of a household's assets.[121] There is nothing in the surviving literature to suggest there was a vibrant private building industry in Athens, and we hear of no entrepreneurs in residential development or owners of gangs of laborers working on private buildings. The simplicity of the typical house and its ease of construction suggest that many people would have built their houses themselves, probably with the help of some slaves and preferably a neighbor or two who had done it before. This is consistent with the wide array of construction material and equipment available in the Agora, including bricks, brick molding frames, timber, ladders, block and tackle, roof beams, panels and tiles, doors, door-bars, and bathtubs.[122] Specialized

---

[120] Andreades (1931) 130 n. 2.

[121] Morris (2010b) 30–50; Höpfner, Schwander, et al. (1994) 150; Nevett (2000); Davidson (1997) 179.

[122] Bricks: *plinthos*—Ar. *Pax* 100; *Ran.* 621; brick molding frame: *plaisipon*—*Ran.* 799; timber: *hyle*—*Ach.* 273; *Vesp.* 301; ladder: *klimax*—*Nub.* 1486; *Pax* 69; block and tackle: *trachilea*—*Lys.* 722; roof beam: *dokos*—*Nub.* 1496; roof panel: *kalathiskos*—*Thesm.* 822; roof tile: *keramos*—*Nub.*

ILLUSTRATION 7.2. Luxury Private House: An Illustrated Reconstruction

builders would have sourced these items directly from a manufacturer, and the simplicity of most houses makes it likely the retail trade existed to serve a do-it-yourself construction and maintenance market.

There was probably some contracted activity as well. The houses of the wealthy, especially the few two-story stone structures, would almost certainly have been built by practiced specialists. Some householders with too few male slaves (or good-natured friends) would have paid for trusted, experienced, and well-supervised labor if they needed to build a new house or rebuild an old one. The *polis* may also have contracted private slave gangs for some buildings for common use such as *oikemata* (cubicles in public spaces for daytime sexual activity) and the principal nighttime brothels. The *astunomoi* managed these sites on behalf of the *polis*, keeping prices to no more than two *drachmae* a night (some working girls were named after their price, like Obole and Didrachmon) and organizing lots if more than one man wanted the same girl;[123] they might also have hired gangs to build and maintain these sites.

---

1127; door: *thura*—*Ach.* 127, 403, 864, 988, 1189; *Nub.* 132, 133, 509; *Pax* 1023; *Lys.* 161, 309, 1070, 1216; *Thesm.* 481; door-bar: *kleithron*—*Lys.* 264; *mochlos*—*Thesm.* 415; bathtub: *puelos*—*Eq.* 1060; *Pax* 843.
   [123] Davidson (1997) 118–19.

There was also an opportunity for private contractors in residential infrastructure. To build one large drain in the industrial district west of the Areopagus, each householder was made responsible for his own section.[124] The shoddy workmanship that resulted from this worker-bee approach suggests that the rather better infrastructure on other common property was probably undertaken by a contractor engaged by the *polis* and supervised by the *astunomoi* or *hodopoioi* to ensure a more acceptable outcome ((Arist.) *Ath. pol.* 50.2, 54.1).[125] Who these contractors were is not known, but it is unlikely that the state owned enough slaves to undertake all the construction and maintenance tasks the city needed. It would have been open to entrepreneurial citizens or metics to assemble a team of building slaves, probably under a supervisor with expertise in masonry or woodwork. These teams could expect a regular flow of work on minor public construction or maintenance projects and private housing.

## 7.4 Summary

Though the operating context of the businesses analyzed in this chapter differs in important ways from most of the others in this book, the nature of competition took forms we have seen in previous chapters. Table 7.2 shows how they fall within the competitive advantage framework.

With the exception of the freelance architect/project manager and a few sole skilled practitioners of crafts, all the businesses in construction and statuary meet our definition of an industry in that they enabled the profitable

TABLE 7.2 **Construction Industries Supply Structure**

|  |  | Barriers to Entry | |
| --- | --- | --- | --- |
|  |  | Yes | No |
| Potential for Differentiation | Yes | Differentiated industry:<br>Sculptors and their workshops<br>Bronze statue designers and their workshops<br>Painters and their gangs<br>Suppliers to construction projects<br>  Carpentry workshops<br>  Textile workshops<br>  Dye houses<br>  Ornament and jewelry workshops | Differentiated craft:<br>Architect/project manager<br>Sole craftsmen<br>  Masons<br>  Carpenters<br>  Jewelers<br>  Smiths |
|  | No | Undifferentiated industry:<br>Quarrying and cartage | Undifferentiated craft:<br>General laborers |

---

[124] Boersma (1970) 10.
[125] Young (1956).

employment of gangs of slaves. Many of the individual craftsmen were metics, not sufficiently established in Athens (or perhaps lacking sufficient distinctive talent) to have their own slave workshop but able to make a living with their hands when there was not enough public contract work for them to do. Some of the master craftsmen who had graduated to project management and architectural design may have had slave workshops of their own and engaged them on projects for which they were responsible.

There were two forms of competitive differentiation among construction industries. In some trades (sculpture, bronze statues, and complex painting), the differentiation comes from the perceived skills of the master artist, who needs a large team to help execute his designs. In the others (supplying industries), it reflects affordable reliability of the type that made for success in supplying the boat building industry (Chapter 6.3) and pottery containers (Chapter 3). The temporary volume security offered by public projects had to be replaced by other work if workshops were to maintain their size and profitability. Between major construction projects, some gangs of stonemasons, bronze workers, and painters might have found recurrent work maintaining public buildings and infrastructure, but most of them must have competed in the private sector for at least some of the time between public contracts, possibly including work on private housing.

The quarrying and cartage industry was clearly undifferentiated in that, provided a team was well managed, its output would be no better or worse than that of any other. It is another example of a business that could be built by preemption (cf: Chapter 4.2—ore processing; Chapter 5.2.1—tanning). The first entrepreneurs to set up an operation in a prime quarrying site could secure the best sites, acquire and train a large team, and install efficient processes for managing tasks so as to be able to deliver marble at an on-site cost that new entrants could not compete with. They would be hard to dislodge, unless they priced so high as to invite competition. If competition did emerge, it would be simple enough to reduce their prices and make it unattractive for new entrants, who would have setup costs to take into account—notably the cost of acquiring and training a slave gang. The same would have applied to the business of carting quarried material to building sites.

So far, we have considered relatively impersonal manufactured objects for which the word "consumption" is used metaphorically. The next chapter applies the same principles to goods that were actually ingested or applied to the skin.

8 }

# Food, Drink, and Personal Care

From the construction of boats, buildings, and monuments, this chapter turns to manufacturing of a more intimate nature: converting natural products for use as food, drink, cosmetics, perfumes, and medicines. The smaller scale of the products is reflected in the smaller size of enterprise. A few primary processes conducted on farm are likely to have lent themselves to some consolidation and third-party sales in the way ore processing did (Chapter 4.2), some inns and bakeries sold prepared meals, and some perfume businesses held large, expensive inventories, but in all other respects these businesses were fragmented. Preparing food and drink required little skill and probably provided a scanty living to participants, but was nevertheless an important source of income to many Athenians. Some would have done better out of cosmetics, perfume, and medicine, often owing as much to bravado as to expertise.

## 8.1 Agricultural Products

As in any society prior to the industrialization of agriculture, much of classical Attica's population was involved in the production and preparation of agricultural and forestry products for food, drink, and fuel. Many products were consumed in their natural or raw state, but, simple and limited as agricultural processing was, it provided a livelihood, or at least a source of income, for many Athenians. This section examines what the Athenians ate and drank and how much effort went into transforming these and other agricultural products before final sale to consumers.

### 8.1.1 THE ATHENIAN DIET

In developed economies today, food goes through several stages from paddock to plate. After harvest or slaughter, products undergo primary processing before being shipped to manufacturers, who carry out further processing and packaging before selling to retailers or food service establishments (sometimes through more than one level of wholesaler or distributor) and finally to consumers. For prepared meals, there can be several intermediate processing steps, carried out by different companies. In ancient times, most food products reached the consumer raw or at the primarily processed stage, to be cooked or baked at home. Of the foodstuffs for sale in the Agora or local markets, much was fresh, some had been simply processed, and the rest was prepared for instant consumption. Harris lists 12 terms describing people involved in food production and 20 for vendors of raw and cooked food.[1] All of the former category are primary producers (farmers, herdsmen, or fishermen) except three bakers and one miller. The only processed products the resellers deal in are cheese, sausages, wine, salt fish, and bread.[2] The rest sell a splendid range of fresh vegetables, herbs, grains, pulses, meats, and honey.

Limited processing did not condemn the Athenians to a dull or unhealthy diet. Like other civilized people, the ancient Greeks took their food very seriously. The first cookbook was produced in the fifth century by the renowned chef Mithaecus of Sicily and was well known at Athens, where fresh ingredients went far beyond the traditional Mediterranean Triad of cereals, olive oil, and wine.[3] Table 8.1 shows the main elements of the Attic diet and the degree of processing involved for these and for non-food rural products.

Prime cuts of red meat were generally eaten only at festivals, reflecting a traditional association with sacrifices, and were either distributed to the citizenry or sold in the Agora.[4] At other times, there was sausage, haggis, savory

TABLE 8.1 **Agricultural Processing**

|  | Unprocessed | Processed | Food Service |
|---|---|---|---|
| Food and drink | Meat<br>Fish<br>Vegetables<br>Herbs<br>Fruits | Salted fish<br>Salted meats<br>Sausages<br>Cheeses<br>Olive oil; crushed olives<br>Wine; vinegar<br>Grains | Soups and<br>stews<br>Cakes and<br>pastries |
| Non-food | Wood for fuel<br>Flowers | Flax (?)<br>Charcoal<br>Soap<br>Wool<br>Wreaths; garlands |  |

[1] Harris (2002a) App. I. 88–97.
[2] Baker: *artokopos*—IG. II² 11681; Pl. *Grg.* 518b; *artopoios*—Xen. *Mem.* 2.7.6; *Cyr.* 5.3.39; *sitopoios*—Thuc. 6.22; Pl. *Grg.* 517e; miller: *mulothros*—IG. II² 10995; IG. III³ 68a1–2; (Arist.) *Ath. pol.* 51.3; Dem. 45.33; 53.14; vendors: cheese: *turopoles*—Ar. *Ran.* 1368–9; *Eq.* 854; *Lys.* 23.6–8; sausages: *allantopoles*; Ar. *Eq.* 143, wine: *oinopoles*—Theophr. *Char.* 30.5; salt fish: *tarichopoles*—IG. II² 1557 68–71; Theophr. *Char.* 6.9; bread: *artopoleslis*—IG. I³ 546; IG. II² 1556 30–2; (Arist.) *Ath. pol.* 51.3; Ar. *Vesp.* 238; *Ran.* 858.
[3] Davidson (1997) 5.
[4] Thompson (1971) 24.

mince, and blood sausage to be had, along with a wide variety of fowl and game.[5] Some of the foodstuffs available were later to characterize Roman luxury.[6] Aristophanes (*Ach.* 875–80; 1104–16) exaggerates the benefits of peace by listing the foodstuffs that reappear with a resumption of trade, including ducks, geese, coots, francolins, jackdaws, wrens, diver birds, martens, thrushes, chaffinches, and doves.[7] Other "delicacies" included fox, badger, cat, hare, water snake, and locust.[8] More conventional livestock like goats, sheep, oxen, and pigs could be bought on the hoof and fattened and killed at leisure.

Fish was popular and commonly used for flavoring. Fish paste was a way of enhancing taste, through the practical application of the *umami* (deliciousness) sensation that was common to many cultures from early times, though only recognized and explained scientifically in the 21st century.[9] *Opson*, originally a descriptor of any central ingredient of a dish, came to mean "fish." Homer's heroes ate no fish because it was too degenerate (Pl. *Resp.* 404b–c), and conspicuous expenditure at a fish market was a sign of great self-indulgence (Ar. *Ran.* 1065–7). A greedy person was called a "fish-eater" (*opsophagos*). Most people could afford to buy small salt fish to add flavor, and sprat, anchovy, pilchard, and mackerel were all for sale in the Agora alongside various minnows, but for those on the average income a meal of large, whole finfish and seafood for a family might cost several days' wages (Amphis 30).[10] Two mullets cost 10 obols, an octopus 4, and barracuda from 8 to 11 (Antiphanes 50). Other expensive items included tuna, sea bass, plaice, sponge, sea urchin, and squid.[11] Those who could afford to indulge themselves found a feast with 8 sea bass and 12 gilt-heads could set them back 100 *drachmae* (Eupolis 153). Whether these prices were typical and how far they might have been extreme examples or exaggerated for rhetorical or comic effect we cannot know for certain. Prices would in any case have varied with the season and with the day's catch.

---

[5] Sausage: *allas*—*Eq.* 143, 144, 148, 161, 179, 201, 208, 432, 1242, 1246; haggis: *gaster*—Ar. *Nub.* 409; savory mince: *muttotos*—*Ach.* 174; *Pax* 247, 273; blood sausage: *chorde*—*Ach.* 1041.

[6] Thurmond (2006) 263–71.

[7] Duck: *nassa*; goose: *khan*; coot: *phalaris*; francolin: *attagos*; jackdaw: *koloios*; wren or plover: *trochilos*; diver: *kolumbos*; marten: *iktis*; thrush: *kichle*; chaffinch: *spinas*; dove: *phatta*. A similar list of envied foods appears in *Pax* 1003–5.

[8] Fox: *alopex*; badger: *pictis*; cat: *ailuros*; hare: *lagos* or *lagodion*; water snake: *enudris*; locust: *akris*.

[9] Lehrer (2007) 59–60. The first *umami* receptor was discovered in 2000 (Chaudhuri), the second in 2002 (Nelson et al.).

[10] Sprat: *phalerikos*—*Ach.* 901; anchovy: *trichidis*—*Ach.* 551; *Eq.* 662; pilchard: *aphye*—*Eq.* 645, 649, 666, 672; mackerel: *skombros*—*Eq.* 1008; small, salted fish: *epanthrakides*—*Ach.* 670; *tarichos*—*Ach.* 967, 1101; *Eq.* 1246; *Pax* 563; *Ran.* 557; *Vesp.* 491.

[11] Tuna: *thunnos*—*Eq.* 312, 354; sea bass: *labrax*—*Eq.* 361; plaice: *psetta*—*Lys.* 115, 131; sponge: *spongos*—*Ach.* 463; *Ran.* 482, 487; sea urchin: *echinos*—*Ach.* 879; squid: *teuthis*—*Ach.* 1156; *Eq.* 929.

The wide range of vegetables, herbs, fruit, and grains available at market would have gone a long way to compensate for the irregular consumption of meat and the costliness of fresh fish. Vegetable vending was a common trade for women (Ar. *Ach.* 478; *Thesm.* 387, 456; *Ran.* 840), and Athenians could buy cucumbers, onions, cress, radishes, celery, beans, beets, leeks, and sprouts.[12] Herbs included garlic, cloves, chervil, pennyroyal, oregano, saffron, anise, mustard, coriander, thyme, silphium, lavender, and hellebore.[13] The fruits on offer were similarly diverse: olives, figs, gourds, apples, pomegranates, sage-apples, acorns, and nuts.[14] To make your own bread or porridge you could buy grain in various forms, including barley, corn ears, barleycorns, bran, or husks.[15] Eggs, honey, milk, and salt were common consumption items.[16]

These untransformed products account for a large proportion of the food recorded as being on sale. Several non-food products of rural Attica were also sold unprocessed, like fuel wood and flowers. All were taken to market directly by pastoralists, horticulturists, and (in the case of fish, nuts, and probably flowers) hunter-gatherers. In short, a large part of the Athenian demand for rural produce did not involve any form of manufacturing.

### 8.1.2 PROCESSING

Curtis identifies four sets of reasons to process food: to preserve it, to transport it, to make it edible and to make it taste better.[17] Processing for preservation purposes tended to involve very little transformation. *Figs* were simply dried; *honey* was turned into a syrup;[18] *vegetables, fruit,* and *nuts* could be

---

[12] Brock (1994) 339; cucumber: *sikuos*—*Ach.* 520, 1001; onion: *krommuon*—*Ach.* 550, 1099–1100; cress: *kardamon*—*Nub.* 234, 236; *Thesm.* 616; radish: *rhaphanis*—*Nub.* 981; celery *selinon*—*Nub.* 982; bean: *kyamos*—*Eq.* 41; *Lys.* 537; *phaselos*—*Pax* 1144; beet: *teutlon*—*Pax* 1014; leek: *geteion*—*Eq.* 677; *prasos*—*Ran.* 62; sprout: *kaulos*—*Eq.* 824.

[13] Garlic: *skorodon*—*Ach.* 164, 521, 550, 761, 813; *Eq.* 494, 600, 946; *Pax* 258, 502, 1000; *Thesm.* 494; *Ran.* 554, 987; *Vesp.* 679; clove: *aglitha*—*Vesp.* 680; chervil: *skandix*—*Ach.* 478, 480; *Eq.* 19; pennyroyal: *glachon*—*Ach.* 874; oregano: *origanon*—*Ach.* 874; saffron: *krokos*—*Nub.* 51; anise: *annethon*—*Nub.* 982; *Thesm.* 486; mustard: *napu*—*Eq.* 631; coriander: *koriannon*—*Eq.* 676, 682; thyme: *herpillos*—*Pax* 168; silphium: *silphion*—*Eq.* 895; lavender: *iphyon*—*Thesm.* 910; hellebore: *helleboron*—*Vesp.* 1487.

[14] Olive: *elaia*—*Ach.* 550; fig: *sukon*—*Pax* 575, 1145, 1249, 1324; *Vesp.* 303; gourd: *kolokunte*—*Nub.* 327; apple: *melon*—*Pax* 1001; *Lys.* 856; *Vesp.* 1268; pomegranate: *rhoa*—*Pax* 1001; sage-apple: *sphakos*—*Thesm.* 486; acorn: *phegos*—*Pax* 1137; nut: *karya*—*Vesp.* 5.

[15] Grain: *sitos*—*Ach.* 258; barley: *alphita*—*Nub.* 176, 788; *Eq.* 857, 1009, 1104; *Pax* 368, 477, 636; *Thesm.* 420; *Vesp.* 300; corn ears: *stachus*—*Eq.* 393; barley corns: *krithe*—*Eq.* 1101; *Pax* 1322; bran: *achuron*—*Ach.* 508; husks: *kyrebia*—*Eq.* 254.

[16] Egg: *oon*—*Lys.* 856; honey: *meli*—*Ach.* 1041, 1130; *Pax* 252, 253; *Thesm.* 1192; *Vesp.* 676; milk: *pyos*—*Vesp.* 710; salt: *hals*—*Ach.* 521, 760, 814, 831, 1099; *Nub.* 1237.

[17] Curtis (2008) 370–72.

[18] Dried figs: *trasia*—*Nub.* 50; *ischas*—*Eq.* 755; *Pax* 634; honey syrup: *siraion meli*—*Vesp.* 878.

pickled or fermented in vinegar, grape juice or honey;[19] *milk* was turned into cheese by adding fig juice or rennet.[20] Catering to the huge demand for *salted fish* was not much more complex. It involved filling a container with alternate layers of fish meat and salt and adding weights to force water out and replace it with salt—a technology that advanced little over the next several centuries and could be applied with only minor modification to other products, including meat and vegetables.[21] Specialty stores, *tarichopoleia*, sold processed fish products, and fish merchants adopted specific titles, such as *tarichopoles* (salt-fish dealers) and *garopoles* (fish sauce dealers), probably indicating their major product lines rather than an exclusive focus. It is noteworthy that all these descriptors involve selling; how much processing took place in Athens is uncertain. Greeks certainly imported salted fish from the Black Sea and, in the case of Corinth at least, from the Punic areas of Sicily and Spain.[22] Nevertheless, it is reasonable to assume that at least some of the local catch was salted in Athens. In Roman times, fish vendors attempted to differentiate their product by promotional messages on *amphorae*, emphasizing variety and quality, though the commonality of salting technology and the aleatory nature of fish procurement suggest the advertising message was not justified by real product differences.[23] Salt procurement lends itself to large-scale operation, not least in cartage, while fishing has all the variability of output one would expect in a hunting activity, so one might hypothesize that the local industry consisted of salt-gatherers purchasing the day's catch from fishermen and vying to establish a reputation for their salted offerings—a form of competition not unlike the way fresh fish wholesalers operate today.

Some products underwent greater transformation before sale. Grains, olives, and grapes were often processed before arriving at city markets, the purpose in these cases being to reduce cartage and storage costs by disposing of parts that will not be consumed.[24] For this reason primary processing tends to take place near the farm and scale reflects local farm output. As well as threshing to eliminate the chaff before transport, many *grain* crops, including barley and most common forms of wheat, require pounding to release the grain before it can be milled. For this the Greeks always used simple mortars

---

[19] Curtis (2008) 384.

[20] Cheese: *tyros—Eq.* 771; *Pax* 368, 1129; *Ran.* 559; *Vesp.* 676, 683; cheese curdled with fig juice: *opia—Vesp.* 35. For the process: Arist. *Hist. An.* 522a22–b6.

[21] Curtis (2008) 385–86.

[22] Curtis (1991) 115.

[23] Surprisingly to our era, there seems to have been much less attempted differentiation by vendors of wine or olive oil (Curtis (1991) 90–96 and correspondence with the author).

[24] Crushed olives: *stemphylon—Nub.* 45; olive oil: *elaios—Ach.* 35, 1128; *Nub.* 56; *Thesm.* 420; *Vesp.* 702; vinegar: *oxos—Ach.* 35; *Ran.* 620; vinegar with brine: *oxalme—Vesp.* 331; wine: *oinos—Nub.* 417, 1123; *Eq.* 85, 95, 102, 355; *Pax* 1323; *Thesm.* 420; *Vesp.* 676. The most expensive of these commodities was olive oil, selling for three to four times the price of wine, which cost one obol for a pint and a half (Hesychius *Lexicon*); Amyx (1958) 176.

and pestles (*haletribanos*—Ar. *Pax*: 259, 265, 269, 282). By the fifth century, millers had replaced the cumbersome and inefficient Neolithic saddle quern with the hopper.[25] Instead of the miller having to reset his crushing stones for each small batch, the hopper fed grain through a hole in the upper stone while the miller ground it by turning the stone backward and forward with a wooden lever.[26] Combining this automatic feed with rotary action was an important technical breakthrough but did not reach Greece until the first century BCE. There was still no use of animal or water power.

Much of the *wine* Athenians drank was imported, as can be seen from containers found in Athens originating from wine exporting regions. Thasos's viticulture was advanced and well managed, and Chios was known for dry (*austeros*) and sweet (*glucazon*) wines as well as for its blend of the two (*autokratos*). Wines from Mende were also well regarded, as were those from Lesbos in the fourth century. Ancient wine could be "black," white, or amber and was sometimes flavored with salt water, herbs, perfumes, or honey to offset the high tannin content. Aging was prized, though vintage variability was not a concern.[27] The most common drink for Athenians was a rather undistinguished wine produced locally from small, unspecialized holdings, purchased in measures of three half-pints (*tricotylos*). It was probably a little stronger than we are used to—about 15–16 percent alcohol, rather than 12–13 percent—but generally drunk diluted with about five parts water to two of wine. Moderation in drinking was encouraged by use of flat vessels (Pherecrates *Fr.* 235); deep drinking cups were clearly for getting drunk, especially the Spartan *kothon*—the word *kothonizein* meant to go on an alcoholic binge.[28] Some wine was bought for home consumption, while those not in the symposium class might go down to their local bar or *kapeleia*, which also sold vinegar and, importantly, torches. Teetotalers like Demosthenes (6.30; 19.46; Lucian. *Dem. Enc.* 15) were rare. A sixth-century attic *amphora* has been interpreted as portraying a method for separating must from marc so as to make either white or red wine.[29] Despite this sophistication, grapes were crushed by feet throughout antiquity.[30]

*Olives* were harder to crush and required a simple pestle or a stone roller in a shallow basin (Ill. 8.1), and then pressing to extract the juice. Pressing equipment was one area in which technology developed quite rapidly in antiquity, although here again classical Greece was not an innovator.[31] A *skyphos* from

---

[25] Curtis (2001) 227–33.
[26] Curtis (2008) 373–79.
[27] Davidson (1997) 40, 42–43.
[28] Davidson (1997) 41–42, 46–47, 67.
[29] Curtis (2001) pl. 22.
[30] Curtis (2008) 380.
[31] Curtis (2008) 387.

ILLUSTRATION 8.1. Ancient olive press

the sixth century shows a simple, labor-intensive press operated by a lever with one end set into a wall, and many of the settings in which presses have been found suggest they dealt with multiple types of product.[32]

Presses were made more effective by adding weights (generally in the form of bags of stones) and by the introduction of a winch to pull down the crushing beam. The rotary design of the *trapetum* press and the Hellenistic introduction of the screw made pressing more efficient still, though screw-presses were probably only used for the most precious liquids.[33] Most of these innovations postdated classical Greece and enabled large-scale Roman olive oil production to become a major contributor to economic growth.[34] In classical Greece, the scale of pressing operations appears to have remained relatively small, with little specialization among installations—a phenomenon that has been attributed to laws making it difficult to build large rural estates in Attica, though these laws did not prevent the pragmatic sharing of resources.[35]

Even with primitive technology, primary processing often lends itself to cooperative activity among neighboring farms. Equipment is underutilized year-round except at harvest times, so it makes sense to share primary processing facilities such as mills and presses among a group of farms and, as in ore

---

[32] Boston Museum of Fine Arts 99.525; Foxhall (2007) 138.
[33] Curtis (2008) 380–83.
[34] Hitchner (2002) 71–81; (2005) 207–21.
[35] Jameson (2001); Foxhall (2007) 177.

processing, for the area of this sharing to be a function of cartage costs from producers in the region. The price a processor can charge cannot exceed the point at which outlying farms will be able to access alternative facilities more cheaply or justify their own investment in processing, or a joint investment with nearby farms. Stability is achieved when the region is served by a number of primary processing centers, each with its own geographically defined catchment.

Grain mills and olive presses are likely instances. Even these limited devices were often shared between neighboring farmers, and some may have made a living operating them on behalf of a group of farms.[36] While cooperative arrangements may have been the norm, it is quite possible that some mill and press owners turned it into a profitable business, though one limited to a defined territory and a short season each year. The massive investments in machinery and in agronomic research and development made by agribusiness today, and the accompanying economies of scale, extend the size of catchments that can be served efficiently from a central point and provide an economic case for consolidating primary food production that simply was not there in ancient times, whatever the impact of land-holding laws.

There were several *non-food* agricultural products that offered Athenians an income. *Beeswax* (*keros*—Ar. *Nub.* 149, 150) was used for treating wood. *Flax*, a grain processed by threshing and milling to make food additives or to make linseed oil for preserving wood, was also the source of linen, though it is not certain that it was grown in Attica. Rural sources of income open to all included weaving *garlands and wreaths* of flowers for special occasions and making *baskets* from reeds and twigs.[37] Some collectors would have made their own floral decorations or baskets, some would have had them made up by the women of their household, and some might have sold to specialists who chose not to collect their own materials. Slightly more complex to make was *charcoal* (*anthrax*—*Ach.* 34, 214, 348, 891; *Nub.* 97; *Pax* 440). Production of charcoal in districts with abundant wood dates back to very ancient times, and the Greeks probably applied the method still used today in Africa and India, which involves heaping billets of wood on their ends so as to form a conical pile, with vents at the bottom and a hole at the top to act as a flue.[38] The pile is covered with wet turf or clay and firing begins at the bottom of the flue, and gradually spreads outward and upward until the billets become charcoal. An alternative method involves a pit of about a meter square, packed with poles about 10–15 cm. in diameter.[39] In each case, a typical batch might

---

[36] Foxhall (2007) 216.
[37] Garland: *stephanos*—*Ach.* 551, 1091; *Nub.* 255, 256, 625; *Eq.* 221, 502, 968, 1227; *Lys.* 604; *Thesm.* 401; *Vesp.* 677, 702; violet garland: *iostephanos*—*Eq.* 1323, 1329; wreath: *stemma*—*Pax* 947; harvest wreath: *eiresione*—*Eq.* 729; myrtle wreath: *myrrhine*—*Vesp.* 861.
[38] Emrich (1985) 296.
[39] Rihll (2001) 32–33.

burn for about two days (Theophr. *HP.* 9.3.1–3), although we hear of larger ones that might go for a month or more. Skill helped, because the higher the yield, the less time a burner would have to spend in order to achieve a certain level of income.[40] In England before the Industrial Revolution, charcoal making was the domain of professional colliers. In Athens, it was a trade open to anyone prepared to keep an eye on a fire for long periods. When charcoal is "activated" or extremely porous, it can be mixed with aromatic oils and herbs to make an effective *soap* (*rhymma*—Ar. *Lys.* 377). Some charcoal gatherers might have made soap; others might have sold their charcoal to cosmetics workshops for the same purpose. A charcoal-gathering slave in Menander (*Epitrep.* 380) pays his owner an *apophora,* indicating a regular income. *Pitch* (*pitta*—*Ach.* 190; *Ran.* 364) was a by-product of charcoal making with its own commercial value, not least in boat building.

### 8.1.3 FOOD SERVICE

Before the introduction of home refrigerators in the early 20th century, limitations to preserving food meant that households would purchase their groceries for only one or two meals at a time.[41] There were no supermarkets or general stores, because resellers would not take the risk of carrying a large inventory of miscellaneous perishable foodstuffs, and so would choose to specialize in a product for which there was predictable demand. As a result, there was no scope for processors to supply standard processed product to be sold in large quantities through retail outlets under a consumer brand, as food companies do today. Food reselling was naturally fragmented, largely the domain of individual stall holders or hawkers (the latter especially at times of festivals). Most food purchased was either to be consumed fresh (vegetables, honey, meats) or to be transformed at home (flour, herbs, and spices). The only items for home consumption that had undergone more than very basic processing before sale were common foodstuffs (high demand) that required a lot of work to make at home (difficult supply), like cheese, wine, and bread, or that were best processed in bulk, like salt fish.[42]

There was also a ready-to-eat segment: prepared food that could be eaten on the run or taken home or to festivals for an immediate meal. There seem to have been two principal types of food involved: bakery products, and soups and stews. An *artopolion* (Ar. *Ran.* 112, 857–58; *Lys.* 458; *Vesp.* 238) sold not

---

[40] Depending on the rate of combustion, charcoal to wood yield today is about 60 percent by volume and 25 percent by weight. It is extremely doubtful that Athenian charcoal burners would have achieved anything similar.

[41] Refrigeration technology had been around since the early 19th century but seems to have had little impact on food reselling until the home refrigerator was developed and marketed by General Electric in 1911.

[42] Harris (2002a) App. I. 88–97.

only bread but Boeotian rolls, scones, and a dozen different types of cakes and biscuits.[43] Prepared soups and stews included vegetable soups, broths, and casseroles.[44] No doubt some of these concoctions took full advantage of Athens's diverse fresh produce markets and followed many different recipes using many different flavorings, but we hear nothing to suggest they were especially highly regarded or seen as superior to typical home cooking. Without such differentiation, margins would have been low.

Ready-to-eat food could be purchased from taverns (*kapeleia*) as well as from stalls and hawkers. These wine and vinegar wholesalers had integrated forward into retailing and then branched out by serving snacks (Ar. *Plut.* 426, 1120: *Ran.* 549–53).[45] The take-out snack industry remains very fragmented today. A good part of the volume has been captured in the last 50 years by fast-food chains leveraging technology, standardization, and the power of mass advertising, but every city remains well served by independent cafes, sandwich bars, and cake shops, with new ones constantly starting up, not altogether dissimilar to the taverns and the individual purveyors in the Agora.

## 8.2 Cosmetics, Perfumes, and Medicines

It might appear surprising that the cosmetics, perfumes, and medicines business is included here as an important industry in its own right, but it was by no means a small part of domestic Athenian commerce. For classical Athens, we have enough information to posit that there were at least two main segments, one customized and making up proprietary formulations, often with obscure and sometimes secret ingredients, and one offering standard concoctions to the mass market. There is evidence that both segments were served by workshops containing several slaves as well as by individual formulator-resellers.

The business had been established in mainland Greece since the Mycenean period and has a long pedigree: the use of cosmetics and perfumes is generally held to have originated in the East in historical times, although archaeologists have found fragments of red and black pigments at Neanderthal sites that were not used in objects found in graves, suggesting they may have been

---

[43] Bread: *artos*—*Nub.* 1383; *Eq.* 282, 778; *Pax* 120, 853; *Lys.* 1207; Boeotian roll: *kolix*—*Ach.* 872; cake: *itrion*—*Ach.* 1092; *pyramous*—*Eq.* 277; *elater*—*Eq.* 1183; *popanon*—*Thesm.* 285; *kollabos*—*Pax* 1196; *Ran.* 507; fine-meal cake: *amylos*—*Ach.* 1092; *Pax* 1195; flat cake: *plakous*—*Ach.* 1092, 1125, 1127; *Eq.* 1190, 1191, 1219; *Pax* 869, 1359; *Ran.* 507; honey cake: *melittouta*—*Nub.* 507; dried fruit cake: *palasion*—*Pax* 574; sesame cake: *sesame*—*Pax* 869; barley cake: *maza*—*Eq.* 55; *Pax* 1, 3, 4, 565, 853; *Thesm.* 570; *Vesp.* 676; barley scone: *maziske*—*Eq.* 1105, 1166; wheat or olive biscuit: *chidron*—*Eq.* 806; fig-leaf biscuit: *thrion*—*Ach.* 1102; *Eq.* 955.

[44] Broth: *zomos*—*Nub.* 386, 389; *Eq.* 357, 360, 1174, 1178; *Pax* 885; soup: *zomeuma*—*Eq.* 279; lentil soup: *phake*—*Eq.* 1007; pea soup: *pisinos*—*Eq.* 1171; bean or pea broth: *etnos*—*Ran.* 62, 506; casserole: *lopas*—*Vesp.* 511.

[45] Davidson (1997) 53.

used on human skin (though they might have been used on animal hides).[46] Finds in the Blombos cave in South Africa show that *Homo sapiens* was collecting ochre for body decoration in around 100,000 BCE.[47]

By the Bronze Age, the use of cosmetics and perfumes was well established in palaces, attested by finds of containers and jars. Women in frescoes in the palace of Minos are shown wearing bright lipstick, and Helen's domestic entourage included expert preparers of perfumes and cosmetics (*Od.* 4.227–32).[48] Her famously pale skin might have been achieved with the help of white lead, and perfume production was a useful adjunct to olive oil pressing in the palace of Nestor.[49] The practice expanded beyond the wealthy, not least through demand from men (Theophr. *De Od.* 42); when Dareios of Persia was defeated by Alexander at Issos in 333 BCE, he had 14 perfumers on his staff (Athen. 13.607f–608a). The story that Solon forbade men to sell perfumes and ointments was probably fictitious, but for it to have had any credibility, perfume vendors or *muropoloi* (Xen. *Symp.* 2.4) must have been quite prevalent in Athens at the time.[50] Perfumes were associated with extravagance, especially among later stoic philosophers (*luxuria*—Plin. *HN.* 13.1), but in classical Athens, spending time at the perfumer's was quite acceptable (Dem 25.52; Lys. 24.20).

Cosmetics and perfumes form part of the broader field of aromatics, which include incense, body rubs, inhalations, and ointments. The same ingredients can also be used as food flavorings, as with rose oil (*elaion rhodinon*) in the Hippocratic writings. The boundary between many of these items and herbal medicine is never very clear. Medicinal properties can be attributed to distilled scents, rubs, and ointments, as well as to herbs ground in a raw state and consumed with water or wine, like Socrates's final drink of hemlock. Products we consider to be foods (and not necessarily healthy ones) were also used as medicines, including butter and specially prepared salted fish.[51]

Perfumes covered a wide range of price points, value being determined by the rarity and expense of ingredients.[52] Production was technically very simple; it could be done anywhere in the Hellenistic world and probably in most of classical Greece. Odor is concentrated by *enfleurage* (pressing in oil-soaked cloth), maceration (steeping in oil), and expression (squeezing out). The local availability of ingredients determined price: there was a high-end

---

[46] Klein (1989) 166.
[47] Henshilwood et al. (2011) 219–22.
[48] See also Hughes (2005) 233.
[49] Hughes (2005) 25; 107.
[50] Pherecrates, *Fr.* 64 mentions such a decree of Solon's; Plutarch does not, even when he is describing the actions Solon took to improve civic morality (*Sol.* 21), and the story seems belied by subsequent observed practice.
[51] Curtis (1984); (2009) 385.
[52] Forbes (1964–72) III.1–37.

trade to which only very wealthy customers might aspire, consisting of the latest imported ingredients freshly mixed to order by an expert—probably accompanied by mystical mumblings about the properties of the herbs—but the average citizen and his wife would be more likely to buy standard products like *rhodinon muron*, mixed largely from items sourced locally. It was composed of roses, honey, and salt, all available in Athens; an oil-base (*omphakinon*) made from local olive oil (the cheapest was called *chrismata*) or sesame oil (which Theophrastus recommended—*De. Od*. 15–16); *aspalathos* (probably a form of henna) from nearby islands; and *kalamos* or *skoinos* (camel grass), which was imported from Syria in bulk at a low price. A much more expensive scent was *kupros*, which also included *omphakinon*, *aspalathos*, and *kalamos*, but added *kureos* from North Africa, India, Arabia, or Persia, and the expensive exotics myrrh and cardamom.[53] Most recipes were easy to copy and products readily substitutable, making the business easy to enter and open to fraud.[54]

The clues archaeology and literature provide into how the business was conducted in ancient times are limited and mainly relate to the Hellenistic and Roman periods. Finds of *unguentaria* (perfume flasks) have been used to try to identify perfume shops, but it is not certain that perfume was the main use of these sites, as the range of container shapes and sizes makes it unlikely that they all held perfume. Alexandria had been exporting perfumes to Greece for a long time (*De Od*. 38), perhaps based on convenience of trade routes, and the Ptolemies encouraged the planting of aromatic trees (Plin. *HN*. 12.42–99).[55] By then, the perfume business had become large-scale, making a single product for a huge market and exploiting economies in purchasing, process (yield), quality control, and expertise.[56] Storing materials of such value in one place made it vulnerable to pilfering, as Pliny noted: "At Alexandria where frankincense is worked up for sale—good heavens! No vigilance is sufficient to safeguard the Officinae. A seal is put upon the workmen's aprons, they have to wear a mask or a net with a close mesh on their heads, and before they are allowed to leave the premises they have to take off all their clothes" (*HN*. 12.18).

From Italy, by contrast, there is evidence of small-batch production, which would allow the flexibility needed for the regular changes of formulae needed to serve a limited market. A painting from the House of the Vettii in Pompeii shows perfumery equipment, including a hammer, a rack, a basin, a wedge-press, a storage cabinet, and several large pots and containers, and we know that a wedge press was installed in the first or second century CE in a

---

[53] Reger (2005) 260–72; cf. Ar. *Pax* 526.
[54] Reger (2005) 253–60.
[55] Fraser (1972) 143.
[56] Rathbone (2007) 707.

perfumery in Paestum that had been operating for four or five hundred years without one. By the second century CE, Southern Italy was home to large Alexandria-type perfumeries.[57] Classical Athens may have used smaller-scale technology; there is no evidence for more than a handful of slaves being employed in one enterprise in the perfume and cosmetics business.[58]

Theophrastus's lengthy exposition *Concerning Odours*, from around 300 BCE, covers a large range of technical matters, including mixing techniques, the medical properties of certain plants, and how to make perfumed wines. His description of the technique of mixing ingredients for scents is insightful: "The more numerous and the more various the perfumes that are mixed, the more distinguished and the more gratifying the scent will be...in perfumes of this class the aim and object is not to make the mixture smell of some one particular thing, but to produce a general scent derived from them all. That is why every day they open the vessel and remove each time that perfume whose scent is overpowering the other, adding at the same time smaller quantities of the less powerful scents, while some perfumes are added" (*De Od.* 57). The work is descriptive rather than a production manual of the sort Dioscurides produced on medicines four hundred years later, and provides little information on the manufacturing process that would help derive predictions about industry structure. His descriptions include an analogy with wool processing (*De Od.* 17), a technology Theophrastus would have learned from his father, who was a fuller (Diog. Laert. 5.36), but no clues as to labor deployment or process steps.

Contemporary writings offer two contrasting pictures. Both the metic lists and the market scenes in Aristophanes indicate sole operators offering individually prepared medicines, incense, and perfume, and they seem to have operated in a special place in the Agora (Ar. *Eccl.* 841).[59] We also hear of two workshops employing several perfumery slaves, so the industry must have embraced both forms of operator, each with its own basis of competition.

The first account is the story of Aeschines trying to extract himself from ruinously expensive debt by refinancing his maritime loan against the security of a new perfume business (Lys. *Fr.* 38). It is unclear how much of this new finance was to be used to acquire stock rather than slaves, but if it was for stock only, we would expect the loan to be described as such. What is clear is that Aeschines was expecting to start a perfume business, and that it was the *apophora* from slaves involved in the operation that was to cover interest costs. Even if perfume skills were exceptionally highly valued and this was reflected in their mortgage price, it would have required more than one or

---

[57] Louis (1927).
[58] Brun (2000) 277–308; Reger (2005) 266; Reger (2007).
[59] Metic lists: Meyer (2010); medicine: *pharmakon*—Ar. *Eq.* 906; *Thesm.* 561; *kukeon*—*Pax* 712; incense: *libanotos*—*Vesp.* 861; perfume: *muron*—*Ach.* 1091; *Nub.* 51; *Pax* 169, 526; *Lys.* 47, 944, 947.

two slaves to service what seems to have been a substantial amount of debt. Perfume manufacture at that time in Athens was evidently seen as a business in which several slaves might be profitably employed in one establishment.

The second example provides some of the improbable comedy that occasionally enlivened Athens's law courts. According to a speech of Hyperides (3) on behalf of Epicrates, written between 330 and 324, Athenogenes, an Egyptian resident in Athens, owned three perfume businesses, one of which was managed by the slave Midas and his two sons. Epicrates took a fancy to one of the sons and bought the three slaves for 40 *minae*. Before the sale was complete, Athenogenes mischievously convinced a lady called Antigone to seduce the evidently bisexual Epicrates and persuade him that a condition of the deal was that he free all three slaves. She succeeded but Athenogenes then dropped this condition and Epicrates, taken in by the double bluff, paid up the 40 *minae* with the slaves still enslaved. On taking over the business, Epicrates found it had undisclosed debts amounting to the huge sum of five talents. Athenogenes claimed he had not known of the debts (§19) that were incurred by Midas (§20); but "if a slave does something useful, the benefit goes to the master (§22)." By a converse logic, slaves were not responsible for debts they had incurred and Epicrates, now their owner, was.

Interpreting this story is fraught with risk. Hyperides seems to base much of his case on his client's naïveté, and Cohen cites it as a typical example of "unprofitable masculinity"; it would have been unmanly for Epicrates to have understood his own business dealings.[60] The sexual motivation means that the transaction might not have borne much relation to true values, even apart from the fraudulent transfer of debt. It is quite likely that a lust-crazed Epicrates simply paid far too much. Nevertheless, we can draw some tentative conclusions about the principal factors of production: labor and raw materials.

Forty *minae* is an extraordinarily high price for three slaves, however skilled. More typical values are three or four *minae* each. Mixing perfumes probably required a long apprenticeship and the mixing process relied on individual experience and judgment (Theophr. *De Od.* 37), so one would expect a slave expert in perfume (*murepsos*) to be highly valued, especially if their concoctions were appreciated in the marketplace.[61] But how much? For Epicrates to earn a "normal" return on the investment each slave would have had to generate an annual *apophora* of four *minae* in total, around five times the amount per slave Demosthenes expected. It is conceivable that some of the amount was for stock, but this does not seem to be normal practice in Athenian acquisitions, and stock is dealt with separately in this passage.

---

[60] Cohen (2002) 101–6.
[61] IG. II² 11688.

The slaves were doing so well (someone had lent them five talents!) that one might have expected them to have bought their own freedom by now, but of course the more they were earning for their owner, the more they would have to pay to buy themselves.[62] Whether the most expert slave could continually generate returns of the level implied here, though, is highly doubtful; however hard and costly it might be to train new experts, the potential rewards would certainly have attracted other entrants and brought prices down. A shortage of capacity might explain a very high valuation of ready-trained slave assets at a point in time but would not be sustained for long in the face of more entrepreneurs importing specialist slaves or having locally acquired ones trained. Skilled manufacturers from outside Attica would also come to compete in such an attractive market and receive the full price set by the local demand-supply imbalance, not reduced by transport costs. We can conclude that the prices mentioned in the speech (if truly paid by Epicrates) must either reflect a serious but temporary skill shortage or, much more likely, the checkbook idiocy of a besotted pedophile. Importantly, however, the story confirms that perfumery in classical Athens was seen as a business in which a group of slaves was able to attract large revenues and provide their owner with a bankable *apophora*.

While Theophrastus emphasized skills, from an economic point of view he was drawing attention to a substantial investment in inventory of herbs and spices and containers. The procurement process was complex and costly. To be able to offer a wide range of formulations, it was necessary to carry a wide range of ingredients, for many of which a good price probably depended on acquiring them in much larger quantities than one household would use in a long while. Some would have been perishable. The high-end trade was a fashion business—Pliny (*HN.* 13.1) describes fashion changes among scents and their places of origin—so it would have been necessary to keep up to date with new ingredients and mixtures, which increased the required investment and the frequency with which major acquisitions of new inventory had to be funded.

The cost and risks of acquiring and holding a variety of valuable and rare ingredients would constitute not only a barrier to entry for those without capital but an incentive to expand: the same bulk purchase could supply multiple dispensing experts whether or not they were co-located. Keeping up with new mixtures and fashions and experimenting with novel formulae would also be more easily achieved within a community of experts than by a sole

---

[62] Cohen (2000) 154. It is possible that this problem would have been reduced over time if the slaves were to capture more of the benefit of their own superior economics in the form of improved conditions or living allowances, especially if they were *choris oikountes* (living independently); valuable rare skills tend to confer bargaining power irrespective of formal status considerations. This would reduce their capitalized value while simultaneously increasing their capacity to pay.

operator working for one master. If owning individual perfume slaves was profitable and the incremental working capital investment to supply multiple slaves negligible, it is likely that there were a number of operations carrying a large and costly inventory for several reseller-dispensers. It is significant that Athenogenes owned three perfume businesses; even if this was because he had three apparently trustworthy slaves to run them, his investments would have enjoyed significant economies in sourcing common ingredients in bulk and from supplementing each others' stocks (all of which belonged to the owner; see Dem. 27.10 and Chapter 9.1 of this book). This strategy would never lead to complete market consolidation, as some customers would always choose an individual expert or range or proprietary mixture rather than the market leader, so a skilled individual with a narrow range and a good sales patter could find customers and make a good living alongside larger concerns. Products known to be from those large workshops would have been subject to stronger price competition than the customized concoctions of sole practitioners.

For specialist *muropoloi* to operate successfully probably required some standardization of product so that consumers knew what they were getting.[63] Ingredients for these standardized products would probably have been sourced in bulk and blended for resale by larger enterprises, and resellers would include both slaves from the perfume-making operation itself selling directly to the public and individual traders buying from the makers at wholesale prices and selling in retail quantities, possibly with a different description and novel curative claims. Being found out was the only barrier to setting up in the business in a small way with a narrow but well-differentiated and promoted product range, perhaps using ingredients sourced from the same importer-wholesalers, but still claiming special properties for proprietary concoctions. Other individuals would have offered less common products, competing on the basis of personal reputation and the genuine novelty of their formulations. Some of these niche competitors would have been able to charge very high prices, not least if they made convincing claims about medicinal effects.

This dichotomy between big business and individual formulators has remained a feature of the plant extract business throughout human history. Most perfumes now come from large companies sourcing rare ingredients in bulk and investing heavily in research and development and in the mass media promotion of their brands, but much of the rest of the aromatics and body rubs industry is fragmented, localized, and reliant on lore and tradition as much as on science. The cosmetics industry is also relatively consolidated but includes a staggering number of niche brands as well as major houses.

---

[63] Harris (2002a) App. I. 94.

Medicinal applications are especially prone to fragmentation—consider the enthusiasm for patent medicines as recently as the early 20th century, or the number of manufacturers represented on the shelves of health food shops today. Natural medicines and aromas still sell in large quantities despite the economic power of the pharmaceutical industry, and will continue to do so until that industry is known to have a cure for everything and a way of standardizing doses of natural ingredients without reducing their effectiveness.

## 8.3 Summary

Table 8.2 summarizes the likely structure of the industries covered in this chapter.

Food processing in Athens was essentially an undifferentiated business. The output of primary processes is undifferentiated as they result in a standard transformation. Any special value of the primarily processed product normally accrues to the owner of the raw material.[64] There is no evidence from classical Attica that any such owners (who must properly be considered agriculturists rather than manufacturers) differentiated their estate wines or oils in the way we are familiar with today. It is likely that some primary processing operations served multiple farms in one region; depending on tolling arrangements and ownership, they might have generated good returns if the region's output was high relative to minimum efficient capacity, but

TABLE 8.2 **Other Industries Structure**

|  |  | Barriers to Entry | |
| --- | --- | --- | --- |
|  |  | Yes | No |
| **Potential for Differentiation** | Yes | Differentiated industry:<br>*FD:* —<br>*CPM:* Importer-wholesaler (possibly with owned resellers) | Differentiated craft:<br>*FD:* Well-known chefs<br>*CPM:* Retail dispensers and formulators (*muropoloi*) |
|  | No | Undifferentiated industry:<br>*FD:* Primary processing: olives, grain<br>*CPM:* — | Undifferentiated craft:<br>*FD:* Charcoal, soap, flowers, garlands, baskets…<br>Secondary processing and sale<br>Bakery<br>Soups, stews<br>*CPM:* — |

---

[64] The value growers receive for their products today in most countries depends upon grade of beef, micron-measurement of wool, hardness of wheat, protein content of milk, etc. Primary processing costs and charges differ little if at all between grades of raw material.

were probably mainly cost-recovery cooperatives. Secondary processing was also undifferentiated and fragmented, restricted by limitations in the transport and storage of food. If there was any differentiation achievable by food craftsmen it would be celebrity chefs, but the literature does not suggest such people were commonly found in Athens.

Cosmetics, perfumes, and medicines are not always easy to distinguish from each other, but we can make out two quite different business models, both apparently viable. On the one hand were well-capitalized importers employing several slaves to mix and resell aromatic products, and on the other the *muropoloi* who sourced product directly or from the large importers, offering a narrow proprietary range, their income depending on how convincingly they could promote its special virtues.

* * *

These industries bring our analysis of Athenian industry structures to an end. There may be important segments that have not been addressed, but it is likely that they would relate to one of the industries covered and behave like one of the other segments in that industry. There was also a considerable number of service industries wholly or largely dependent on manufacturing, including acquiring and shipping raw materials, reselling, transport, and financial services, but they would form a subject for another book. The final chapter of this one considers the part manufacturing played in the lives of different groups of Athenian residents.

9 }

# Athens's Manufacturers

This chapter addresses manufacturing from the point of view of the participants. First it will be useful to summarize the likely structure of industry segments, as these define the types of activity in which people from different social groups took part (Table 9.1).

Davies identifies manufacturing as the first of five factors that transformed the Athenian economy from almost total dependence on agriculture in the early sixth century to one with multiple sources of wealth in the classical period.[1] It offered an investment opportunity for the wealthy, a path to riches for citizens, metics, and a few slaves, a daily occupation for tens of thousands of slaves, a means of subsistence for thousands of citizens and metics, and an opportunity for extra income—or avoidance of expenditure—for many others.[2] The review of industries in previous chapters showed the roles played by different groups in different types of manufacturing operation, which are summarized in Table 9.2.

Manufacturing formed part of the investment portfolio of many distinguished citizens. A large part of this chapter is devoted to a single speech of Demosthenes: his case against his guardians throws an important light on how the *apophora* system worked and how Athenians thought about investment in industry. For many other citizens, metics, and freed slaves, manufacturing was a necessary part of life; in some product segments, master craftsmen could build industrial enterprises employing several slaves, while in others they could earn an excellent income from their crafts, but if demand attached to them personally it could not be translated to a larger operation. Less distinguished craftsmen earned a subsistence income, either because their output was considered inferior to others and sold for less or because they made products whose quality did not matter to consumers, provided they met minimum functional requirements, so they had to compete on price

---

[1] Davies (1981) 38. The other new sources of wealth he identifies are: rents (due largely to metic demand and the geographic spread of landholdings—49–53), lending against property outside Attica (55–58), maritime and personal loans (60–65), and bribes or booty (66–68).
[2] For quantifying methodology and assumptions, see Appendix.

TABLE 9.1 **Industry Structure Overview**

| Sector | Subsector | | | |
|---|---|---|---|---|
| | Industry | | Craft | |
| | Differentiated | Undifferentiated | Differentiated | Undifferentiated |
| Pottery | Trade containers<br>Niche products (e.g., lamps) | — | Decorated<br>Large, complex | Basic crockery |
| Mines, Metals and Armor | Shields<br>Knives, swords etc.<br>*Volume producers of copied ornaments, statuettes*<br>*Volume producers of low cost items of armor* | Coinage<br>Ore processing and silver smelting | Jewelry<br>Ornaments<br>Bronze armor | Simple domestic and agricultural tools<br>Repair work |
| Textiles, Clothing, and Footwear | *Off-the-shelf shoes* | Tanning<br>*Scouring*<br>*Fulling*<br>*Dyeing* | Fine garments<br>Tapestries<br>Bespoke shoes | Simple garments<br>Basic leather goods |
| Woodworking | Luxury furniture<br>Musical instruments<br>*Other furniture*<br>*Transport vehicles*<br>*Dramatic masks and machines*<br>*Industrial machinery*<br>*Boat component suppliers* | Ship hull and assembly | *Customized carvings*<br>*Boutique furniture*<br>Naval architect/project manager | Basic furniture<br>Household utensils |
| Construction | *Workshops of sculptors, bronze statue makers and painters*<br>*Building suppliers in wood, bronze, leather, rope, and textiles* | Quarrying and cartage | Architect/project manager<br>Skilled tradesmen | General laborers |
| Food | — | Primary processing (olives, grain) | Chef | Bakery<br>Soups and stews |
| Cosmetics and Perfumes | Importer-wholesalers | | Retail dispensers and formulators | — |

Segments in *italics* are hypotheses based on supply and demand dynamics but lacking primary evidence.

TABLE 9.2 **Roles in Manufacturing**

| | Industry | Craft |
|---|---|---|
| Owner | Rich citizen<br>Metic<br>Freed slave | Citizen<br>Metic<br>Freed slave |
| Manager | Freed slave<br>Senior/trusted slave | Owner (citizen/metic/freed slave)—often in practice the lady of the household |
| Labor | Slave gang | Owner, family, and slave(s) |

against many with equal skills. Some might work full-time at trades like this, while others might use them to fill idle time and supplement income between various civic, military, and agricultural activities. Despite legal restrictions, women from all status groups were active investors, workshop managers, producers, and marketers, and dominated some large segments. Resident foreigners and freed slaves might operate as craftsmen, supervisors, or workshop owners. Slaves participated in two quite different ways; domestic slaves attached to small households would assist the master or mistress in the home workshop, while industrial slaves operated in large businesses, and the margin they generated for their owner after their upkeep defined their market value. The remainder of this chapter tries to fill out this picture.

## 9.1 Citizen Investors

Manufacturing was one of several investment choices available to rich citizens. Others included buying or leasing land in Attica or new overseas territories, lending against land, commerce or maritime trade, and acquiring a mining lease. Many citizens invested in more than one asset class, perhaps following the advice of Hesiod to diversify (*Op.* 678–80). Returns on different investments reflected their relative risk (Fig. 9.1) and rather than naive "piecemeal opportunism," diversification strategies seem consistent with modern financial theory.[3]

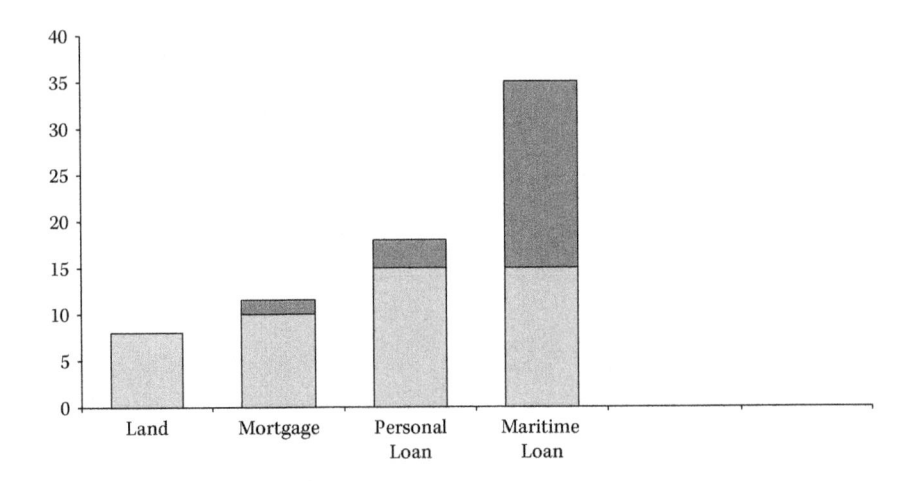

FIGURE 9.1. Investment Returns (1) (%)

---

[3] "Piecemeal opportunism"—Millett (2000) 31; versus "expressive rationality"—Christensen (2003) 39, 53; diversification strategies—Thompson (1982b) 75–76.

The option with the lowest risks and returns, *land ownership*, was an active occupation and not simply a matter of collecting rents. The standard plot size was small, and poorer citizens worked their own lands, while those who owned several plots would employ gangs of slaves and hire extra labor seasonally, probably including citizens without farms of their own. Politics and geography made it difficult to own large estates in Attica, but public land could be leased, and the restrictions themselves must have led to attractive returns to those with land to rent out, given new demand from metics and *choris oikountes* slaves as well as younger siblings in citizen families.[4] Overseas real estate could also provide good returns, and many wealthy Athenians took advantage of it.[5]

There was evidently an active market in land, though Finley and others deny it.[6] Estates confiscated from those who profaned the Mysteries or from the Thirty Tyrants were quickly sold off. Davies describes an extended family that consolidated its domestic power base over several generations through intermarriage, marriage with neighbors, judicious adoption of relatives, and cunning funeral arrangements. A scion of this family, Theopompus, broke the mold, married out of the family and deme, and set about acquiring his relatives' shares of the family holdings through employing the best lawyers to exploit the inheritance and adoption laws and making bargains with suborned co-litigants whom he later betrayed. Some of the properties were sold off or acquired to be let out or used as security on another investment.[7] This shady behavior certainly confirms that increasing private landholding in a conventional manner was difficult, but land was evidently tradable, and a modest investment in real estate would have formed part of most citizens' portfolios.[8]

The notion, drawn from the investment profile of aristocrats in later societies, that the elite favored investment in land over commerce is not supported by the literary or prosopographic evidence.[9] In fact, the majority of estates included commercial and manufacturing investments, and it is more likely to have been the less rich who tended to invest in land, as it carried less risk and could involve lower capital investment or leasing costs. Analysis of mining leases also supports a view that the riskier form of investment was actually preferred by those who could afford a loss and that, in contrast to mining, the elite's involvement in leasing public land was much *lower* than their population share. From an admittedly small sample, it appears that the "liturgical class" (either liturgiasts themselves or the descendants or forebears of one), accounted for 35 percent of the money invested in silver mines but only

---

[4] Davies (1981) 40.
[5] Foxhall (2002) 214.
[6] Finley (1973) 116, 141; (1981) 62–76; Millett (1991) 177, 232–34.
[7] Davies (2002) 201–9.
[8] Walbank (1982) 95–97.
[9] Kron (1996) 154, iii, xiii.

14 percent of that paid to lease public land.[10] For the wealthy, land was a possible source of income, but only one of several, and a hard one in which to accumulate much beyond one's inheritance without leaving Attica.

*Mining leases* are not included in the comparison of returns in Figure 9.1 because the investment provides too great a range of possible results (including the possibility of a dud lease) to compare directly with other options, and it would in any case be wrong to assume a risk-neutrality on the part of the ancients that does not apply to ourselves. Chapter 4 told how a number of citizens did very well from owning them, but, as with gambling in our own society—and often with venture capital for that matter—mathematically expected returns from Attic mining might have been lower than the cost of the lease plus extraction, but investors were prepared to risk a small portion of their assets in the hope of an outstanding return. This sits well with the fact that few investors owned multiple leases and there were few families of multiple mining investors.

*Lending money* was an important source of income for those with capital, and while some loans were among friends (*eranoi*) and did not carry interest, some certainly did.[11] Francotte asserts that a citizen's favorite use of capital was lending, and it was by no means only against real property.[12] Previous chapters have cited many loans to individuals against the acquisition of manufacturing slaves or raw materials: Timochares borrowed against his metalworkers (Lyc. *Leoc.* 23), and Pantainetus's ore processing facilities and slaves seem to have been largely or wholly debt-funded (Dem. 37.4). Mantias and his son funded their mining interests with debt (Dem. 40.52). For his perfume business, Aeschines borrowed from friends at 1.5 percent per month (Lys. fr. 38). Aristarchus borrowed funds to acquire the raw materials for making clothes (Xen. *Mem.* 2.7.11–12), and Athenogenes to buy stock for his perfumery (Hyp. 3.6.9–10).

*Maritime loans* were popular. Voyages usually involved a round trip, and the law prescribed that return journeys include a delivery of grain to Athens. Contracts specified the route and timing, and interest was charged according to the length of voyage and its danger, which often depended on the time of year. A typical two- to three-month journey such as Athens to the Bosporus and back might return 20–30 percent (Dem. 24.23), while a shorter, one-way voyage like Sestos to Athens might be worth 12.5 percent (Dem. 1.17). One loan of 3,000 *drachmae* for a voyage from Athens to the Bosporos via Mende or Scione was at the rate of 22.5 percent if the return from Pontus was before mid-September and 30 percent if later (Dem. 35.10–14). The lender's security for loans for a voyage might be either the cargo or the vessel, although

---

[10] Shipton (2001) 133–34; see Chapter 4.1.
[11] Millett (1991) 160–78, 235–40; Cohen (1992a) 44–46; (1992b); Harris (1993).
[12] Francotte (1900–01) I.213.

security in this context is a misleading term. The hypothecated goods would not be available in the event of default caused by piracy or shipwreck, so they only served to secure the borrower against a trader welshing after a successful trip, although it was also possible for the lender to get recourse to real property in case of default (Dem. 35.10–14). In other respects, these loans acted as a form of insurance for the trader by allowing him to risk someone else's money, the premium being the high rate of interest on the loan. Many such loans were syndicated, which enabled more specialized and informed opinion to be brought to bear on risk and investors to diversify into multiple shared risks rather than take on a few large ones. The volume of Athens's overseas trade, the likelihood that few traders could afford to finance their own voyages (or would choose to take all the risk themselves), and the frequency with which maritime loans appear in legal contests all suggest many of the better off Athenians indulged in these high-risk, high-return investments. Some borrowers were citizens too. Historians have tended to underestimate the importance of citizens to Athenian foreign commerce, often preferring to believe that the business was largely left to metics, but in fact, of the merchant captains (*naukleroi*) and traders (*emporoi*) mentioned in forensic speeches, we can identify 15 citizens against 14 metics.[13] There is no suggestion in the sources that borrowing terms differed according to status.

*Direct investment in manufacturing* provided another investment option. Aristophanes associated well-known figures like Cleon, Hippolytus, and Nicias with the ownership of productive enterprises, and Isocrates and Demosthenes inherited significant wealth from workshop owners. The standard model of investment in a workshop was to entrust the management of it to a slave, who would then pay the owner a certain amount per slave per period, a sum known as an *apophora*. The owner received a fixed payment, provided the business could pay it (a form of preferred dividend rather than the variable returns normally accruing to equity), while the slave-foreman would take the profit and loss on the business. In many cases, this allowed the slave to buy his freedom; in some that ended up in court, the business failed, sometimes through fraud.

Exactly how the *apophora* system worked is not made explicit in the sources and has not been very convincingly elucidated by historians. *Apophora* means the payment of what is due, a tax or a tribute.[14] To bring (*pherein*) an *apophora* meant to achieve a profit (Arist. *Pol.* 1264a32) while to fulfill (*telein*) an *apophora* was to pay a war tax, both implying a due return, but to understand how investment in Athenian manufacturing compared with other options, we need to determine exactly what this return allowed for and who was

---

[13] Isager and Hansen (1975) 72. Engen (2011) is an excellent example of reluctance to accept a significant trading role for citizens; see my review (Acton (2012)).

[14] Liddell and Scott (1940), citing Hdt. 2.109; Plut. *Thes.* 23.

responsible for which costs and assets. Fortunately, the main principles can be deduced from Demosthenes (27), which also sheds light on the financial returns on investment in industry and the non-monetary value the Athenians placed on certain types of assets.

Demosthenes's father died when he was a boy, leaving a legacy worth about 14 talents, including two factories (§4).[15] Demosthenes senior had been considered one of the *kaloi kai agathoi* (leading citizens) by Theopompus (*Fr.* 297), but his wife, daughter of a certain Gylon who betrayed Athens and fled into exile, only came with a dowry of 5,000 *drachmae* and, soon after the marriage, a substantial financial liability resulting from her father's disgrace. She was very protective of the young Demosthenes, restricting his exercise, but probably also encouraging his ambition.[16] In this speech, Demosthenes is suing one of his guardians, Aphobus, the nephew of Demosthenes senior, for not looking after his inheritance.[17] He complains that, after allowing for interest being paid to another guardian and dowries for his sister and mother, Aphobus's stewardship has left him with only 14 slaves and 30 *minae* (§6) instead of the 14 talents worth of assets he started with. Aphobus had done well out of the family; on his uncle's death he married Demosthenes' mother (§5), and it has been calculated that he received a total of 10 talents from the Demosthenes estate.[18]

This inheritance featured three items which Demosthenes describes as *energa* (§§7, 10), usually translated as "productive capital," the first two of which have been analyzed above in the context of their respective industries:

1 A knife (sword?) factory with "thirty-two or thirty-three knife makers, worth five or six *minae* each, none worth less than three *minae*, from which (he) derived net income of thirty *minae* a year."
2 A luxury furniture (beds, couches?) factory, which had "furniture makers twenty in number, pledged for forty *minae*, who brought (him) in twelve *minae* net (a year)." Demosthenes senior had taken these slaves as security for 40 *minae* he had lent to Moeriades.
3 A talent "lent at a *drachma* (a month), whose yield each year came to more than seven *minae*."

Demosthenes's guardians initially managed the workshops themselves and later appointed a freed slave named Milyas to be foreman (§19).[19]

---

[15] In this section, all numbers in this format indicate a paragraph in Dem. 27.
[16] Sealey (1993) 96–98.
[17] There are three speeches against Aphobus in Demosthenes's name, of which at least the third (29) is considered unauthentic—Thür (1977).
[18] Schaefer (1885) 266–67.
[19] The economic status of these workshops is explored in Chapters 4.8 and 6.1, respectively.

Finley is highly critical of Demosthenes's economic awareness and uses the speech as an instance of his contention that the well-educated Athenian neither understood nor cared about financial matters: "This represents a remarkable conception of 'capital' and it becomes all the more remarkable when one pursues in detail the actual claim on the guardians, which ignores amortization and depreciation and assumes unchanging figures for annual production, rate of profit and income."[20] He was correct in noting Demosthenes's failure to allow for asset depreciation, but his concern about unchanging rates of return is based on a fundamental misunderstanding of the nature of such investments. Under the *apophora* system, the risk and the profit of the business belonged to the foreman and, provided the factory remained solvent, the owner's income was unaffected by the business's performance. That the sum was a fixed amount per slave in this case is confirmed by Demosthenes's arguments that when half the knife-making slaves were sold he should have continued to receive half the income (§18–19), and that the income from the (vanished) furniture-making slaves should have continued at the previous rate (§29), despite the fact both businesses were obviously failing. If the arrangements had been different and Demosthenes was taking an equity risk on factory profits, then in the interests of plausibility one would have expected him to propose an average income figure or to say the sum was "sometimes as much as X" or "never less than Y," which is the way he usually deals with variable numbers. In the absence of marked and measurable inflation in the economy as a whole, a rate fixed for the duration of the arrangement is perfectly sensible.[21]

Demosthenes gives enough information to enable us to calculate the yield (annual income divided by net assets) on each investment.[22] He is vague about the number (32 or 33) and value (5 or 6, not less than 3 *minae* each) of the knife-making slaves. He might have been inclined to exaggerate a little here, but 32 at an average value of 4 *minae* is the most commonly accepted inference for his capital investment in slaves, so an investment of 128 *minae* gives a return of 30, or about 24 percent. If they were really worth 5 *minae* on average, then the return is just under 20 percent; if he was exaggerating and the true average value was closer to 3 *minae*, then the return was about 31 percent. The furniture enterprise seems to have been doing just as well: if we assume that the value of the security is the market value of the slaves, then 40 *minae* worth of slaves brings in 12 *minae* a year—a neat 30 percent return. The yield on the loan is 12 percent, which is also the rate Demosthenes assumes the guardians'

---

[20] Finley (1973) 166.

[21] Elsewhere (36.37) Demosthenes provides further evidence that the *apophora* was a fixed sum: the four slaves operating Pasion's bank paid the owner a talent a year, irrespective of changes in revenues or profits.

[22] With all values unchanged in all periods, yield and return on investment are identical.

ill-gotten gains would be reinvested at (§23), indicating it was a typical rate for loans with a modest degree of risk.

On the face of it, these returns are surprising. Demosthenes appears to be saying that there were opportunities to make a return of 30 percent on capital investment in industry, but his father had still chosen to leave a large amount of his "productive capital" on loan at 12 percent. And presumably, if Demosthenes expected jurors to see this as normal behavior, other Athenians were known to pass up similar opportunities. The risk-return paradigm posits that in a rational market, the higher the risk on an investment, the higher its return. Although the terminology would have been strange to the Greeks, the concept was not. Demosthenes praised Apollodorus's wisdom in choosing a shield workshop rather than a bank that was earning much more; the shield enterprise was *ktem' akindunon* (a riskless business) while the bank produced risky revenues from other people's money (36.11). Yet in the case of his own factories, Demosthenes seems to be expecting such high returns from his investment in industry that either industrial investment was seen as very high-risk, or the Athenians were not rational in their appraisal of it.

The simplest explanation for such a high level of returns is that Demosthenes was exaggerating his inherited income (as he had a motive to do in this case). This is consistent with his complaint that the factories had made no money during his childhood, but it is unlikely that he would take the risk of projecting a state of affairs that the court would see as untypical or fabricated. Another possible explanation is that Demosthenes senior's factories enjoyed such competitive advantages against other competitors and new entrants that, while others in these industries might only make a modest return approximating their cost of capital, the returns of the Demosthenes businesses were much higher. This is possible but also unlikely: two other texts refer to similar, unvarying returns on the deployment of slaves for productive purposes in situations where such advantages were not available.

In retaliation for a case brought against him by Demosthenes and Timarchus for corruption on an embassy to Philip of Macedon, of which he was narrowly acquitted, Aeschines charged Timarchus with being unfit to participate in the rights and duties of a citizen. Of the four grounds that might sustain such a charge, maltreatment of parents, military cowardice, prostitution, and squandering an inheritance, Aeschines accused Timarchus of the latter two.[23] The inheritance that he had been forced to sell included about a dozen slaves, including "nine or ten craftsmen of the art of shoemaking, each of whom brought him a payment of two obols a day and the supervisor of the workshop brought him three" (Aeschin. i.97).[24] The craftsmen had a capital value of four *minae* a head and the supervisor six *minae*. To determine the income they generated, we need to estimate

---

[23] Fisher (2001) 4–6.
[24] See Chapter 5.2.2.

how many days slaves would work in a year. Few free craftsmen appear to have worked full-time.[25] Citizens employed on public works seem to have had a working year of no more than 200 days, with much of the rest being devoted to at least 60 public holidays, attending festivals, and performing various other civic duties, including participating in legal proceedings. Slaves did not enjoy these privileges and obligations, and Xenophon's calculations (below) assume 360 days a year for mine slaves. Evidence from construction projects at the temple of Eleusis and at Delos shows laborers being paid for 360 days a year.[26] A very conservative 250 days would give an income to Timarchus of around 80 *drachmae* per year from each slave and 360 days would produce over 120, giving returns on capital of between 20 and 30 percent.[27] The same returns accrue on the supervisor.

Xenophon was thrilled to discover a new way of resourcing the state: "A truly remarkable thing about the city is that it watches many people getting rich, but does not imitate them. We who are interested in these things heard long ago that Nicias the son of Niceratus owned a thousand slaves in the silver mines. He hired them out to Sosias the Thracian at one obol net per day and on condition that he kept the number the same. Hipponicus had six hundred slaves and hiring them out brought him in one *mina* net per year; Philemonides had three hundred who earned him half a *mina*..." (*Vect.* 4.14–15). Given continuing demand and abundant capital, the state ought to get into this business: "If you start with 1,200 slaves, then from the income they bring in, in five or six years you will have at least 6,000, and then if they each bring in one obol net per day, revenues will be 600 talents a year. If you set aside 20 slaves for the city's own purposes, then they will become 40. When the total gets to 10,000, revenues will be 100 talents a year" (*Vect.* 4.23–24). We can calculate the returns from this reinvestment strategy: in order for 1,200 units to grow to 6,000 in five or six years through compound reinvestment requires a yield in excess of 30 percent a year.[28] Based on these two examples, Glotz concludes that "below 25% the income from industry is on the low side; above 30% it is rather high."[29]

In a normal competitive market, outstanding investment opportunities do not last very long. If people perceive that they can increase their wealth by investing in particular assets at the going price, they will acquire such assets; competition results in all such opportunities being taken up as they emerge, increasing the amount investors will bid for them (their capital value). If, after allowing for risk, a knife factory's yield was significantly higher than the yield on a loan, and the skills were easily teachable, other slaves would be trained,

---

[25] Glotz (1926) 283.
[26] Francotte (1900-01) II.13–17; Bourget (1929) Inscription 2940; IG. II² 1672.105.
[27] For comparison, Demosthenes's knife-makers were supposed to bring in about 100 *drachmae* each per year and the furniture-makers just 60.
[28] 30 percent would achieve it in a little over six years and 35 percent in about five and a half.
[29] Glotz (1926) 283.

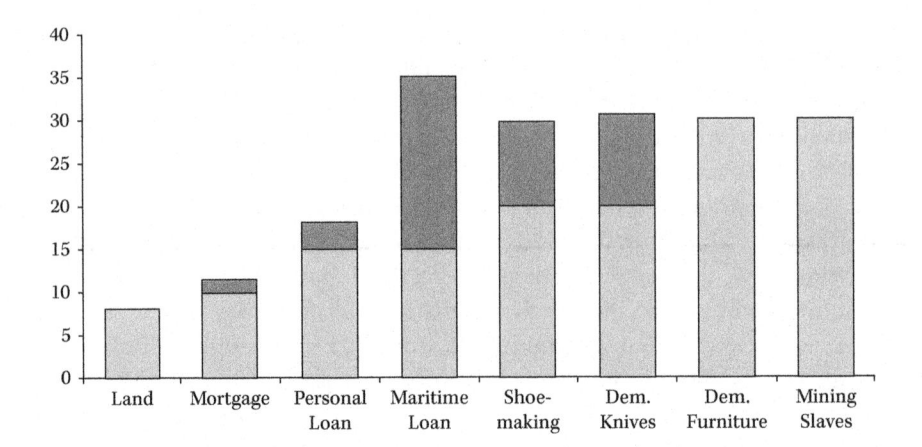

FIGURE 9.2. Investment Returns (2) (%)

and this new capacity would reduce prices and trim returns. If the business depended on skills that could not be easily duplicated, the price of trained slaves would be bid up, also reducing the returns available to investors. If the original owner is sensible enough to value his asset at market rates (his opportunity cost) rather than his historic cost, he will be aware his returns have gone down too. This instability is a feature of investments; in the language of shareholder value analysis, exceptional returns tend to "fade" toward the category mean. There is no indication of such instability in any of the texts we are concerned with, and it is therefore legitimate to assume that the numbers given by Demosthenes reflect a state of equilibrium, that the yields implied are typical and sustainable, and that he might well be right in claiming that nonpayment of the *apophora* during his childhood was due to his guardians' incompetence or dishonesty.

If we rank these returns from manufacturing alongside other investment alternatives, their magnitude suggests an extraordinarily high degree of risk (Fig. 9.2). In a rational investment market, we would expect returns on investment in industry to exceed the risk-free loan rate (for which we will take as surrogate the return on land, which seems to have been around 8 percent) by an amount that reflects the market valuation of the higher risk, including any premium necessary to compensate for possible aversion to taking up the opportunity (for example, if it meant changing one's way of life in an unappealing manner). Investment premiums, reflecting intangible attitudes to risk and lifestyle, cannot be known to us with any degree of certainty, but it would be surprising if they were as large as those implied in these numbers. For a typical business with an established customer profile and proven manufacturing capability, today's financial markets seldom add more than 5 percent to the risk-free cost of capital.[30] The

---

[30] The rate on government bills is typically used by investment analysts as a measure of the interest available on risk-free investments (i.e., it only takes account of the time value of money).

premium for maritime loans in Athens could be much higher, but the comparison is indirect, as maritime loans were not time-based, and in any event, the Demosthenes factories can hardly be thought to involve risks comparable to the storms, piracy, and fraud that seagoing traders faced on each voyage. Here Demosthenes seems to be looking at a premium of around 20 percent. Must we then conclude that citizens, metics, and freed slaves had strong non-financial reasons to avoid investing in industry and chose not to pursue these commercial opportunities unless they offered extraordinarily high returns?

Before coming to this conclusion, we should look closely at Demosthenes's numbers. Within the overall ownership-management framework of the *apophora*, the question of who pays for what is not one that has received much attention. Xenophon clearly assumed that no costs at all attach to the owner, and, given the low cost of leasing the slaves in the case he cites, he might be right. In other cases, the owner might have carried some of the business's costs or assets. Both Demosthenes and Xenophon describe the owner's returns as *ateles*, which is conventionally translated as "net." The lexicon gives four groups of meanings: (i) *Unending*: unaccomplished (Homer, Xenophon, Sophocles); incomplete, unfinished (Thucydides, Aristotle); imperfect (Aristotle, Lucian); unending (Plato); indeterminate (Aristotle); (ii) *ineffectual* (Pindar, Plato, Aristotle); uninitiated or unmarried (Plato); (iii) *free from tax or tribute* (Herodotus, Aristophanes) or *not costly* (Sophocles, Pausanias); and (iv) *net*.[31] The only references for this last definition are the passages at issue from Demosthenes and Xenophon, so we need to draw our conclusions from the figures rather than the label. Did the returns put forward by Demosthenes reflect all the costs and assets he carried on behalf of the business?

One substantial expense was the maintenance cost of slaves. Slaves had been bought and raised at their master's expense and they had to be fed, clothed, and taken care of.[32] Surprisingly, no scholars seem to have formed a view on who paid these costs under an *apophora* arrangement, but there are many estimates of what such costs would amount to. Original sources give various accounts of what a man would consume in a day, ranging from half a *choinix* of barley (Thuc. 7.87.2; Plut. *Nic.* 29.1; Diod. Sic. 13.19.4) to two *choinikes* (Thuc. 4.16.1; Hdt. 6.57.3).[33] Aristophanes makes a joke of a dole at the ridiculously extravagant rate of three *choinikes* a day (*Eccl.* 424), and we hear in Athenaeus of records set by trumpeters—a woman who ate four *choinikes* at a sitting (10.415b), and a man who ate six (10.414f). Foxhall and Forbes argue that one *choinix* a day was a standard "distributed" quantity, but really only necessary for active adult males.[34] They prefer an average of

---

[31] Liddell and Scott (1940).
[32] Kyrtatas (2002) 142.
[33] A *choinix* was a little under two imperial pints.
[34] Foxhall (1982) 41–90.

237 *choinikes* of grain per person per year and suggest that grain provided 70–75 percent of daily calorific consumption. Slaves might have had a lower entitlement, but if they were earning income in a physically demanding role, a prudent owner might not have chosen to undernourish them.

At the time Demosthenes was speaking, wheat cost around 5 *drachmae* per *medimnos* (48 *choinikes*), so a *choinix* a day would cost about 40 *drachmae* a year.[35] Presumably, part of the slave diet consisted of more expensive commodities than grain, and there were additional costs for clothing, lodging, and fuel. On that basis, Glotz estimates the cost of supporting a slave and his family (a total of three adult equivalents) as 280 *drachmae* a year at the end of the fifth century, rising to around 450 late in the fourth.[36] Ober estimates the cost of subsistence food alone at 80–90 *drachmae* per adult, which is consistent with Glotz's calculations.[37] We may infer that it was probably of the order of 350–400 per family at the time of which Demosthenes was speaking. The standard rate of pay on state projects of a *drachma* a day might well have been calculated as the subsistence income for a small family. It is also consistent with Jones's estimate that the capital cost of a slave was between 100 and 125 percent of the annual cost of their upkeep.[38] Both Demosthenes and Timarchus's slaves were worth around 400 *drachmae* each.

The responsibility for maintaining industrial slaves may not have extended to a slave family. Many slaves had none, and the wives of those that did were expected to bring in income from spinning, weaving, or prostitution, and even young slave children would have been expected to contribute to their own living costs. Even so, the amounts received by Demosthenes and Timarchus would not even cover the costs of maintaining the slave alone. At 150 *drachmae* per slave per year, slave maintenance in the knife factory would have amounted to one and a half times the *apophora* and in the furniture factory two and a half times. The necessary implication is that maintenance costs fell on the supervisor, whose revenue per slave net of raw material costs must have been enough to cover these costs and the *apophora* before he could make a profit for himself. The owner would only have to maintain his slaves when they were not being leased out. It was to avoid this risk with his 1,000 mining slaves that Nicias apparently paid his supervisor the colossal sum of one talent a year (Xen. *Mem.* 2.5.3).

One cost that was certainly borne by the owner and not the foreman was the cost of replacing slaves. As Finley noted, capital assets depreciate over time as their productive capabilities deteriorate and need to be replaced. One

---

[35] Glotz (1926) 287; Pritchett and Pippin (1956) estimates wheat costs at six *drachmae* per *medimnos*, which seems a little high.
[36] Glotz (1926) 286.
[37] Ober (1989) 131.
[38] Jones (1956) 194.

machine in a factory might last 20 years, another 10. The business owner will need to replace his asset as it starts to fail and eventually ceases to function altogether. To provide for this, he makes a charge against profits each year representing how much further the asset has moved toward the end of its useful life. This is not a cash cost, so in theory this creates a pool of cash, not allocated to owners as profit, which will ultimately fund the replacement of the asset at its original cost.

There is no indication that the Athenians accounted for depreciation in any formal way. They did, however, face the problem that the slaves they owned depreciated fairly fast. They fell sick, aged, died, and ran away. Some probably required continuous maintenance in an unproductive old age or after an accident. Maintaining a slave team would require regular reinvestment. Someone leasing a gang of slaves would expect any that ceased to be productive to be replaced by the owner or would stop paying for them. This is why Sosias insisted that Nicias kept up the complement of the gang he was leasing (*Vect.* 4.23). It is clearly an error in Xenophon's calculations that, though he emphasizes the condition that Nicias "kept the number the same," he never allows for the cost of making good any attrition among the slave cohort. The passage of five or six years among slaves, especially if they were to be employed in mines, would have seen a lot of death, injury, and escape. In the mines at Laurium we find "human vitality sapped by nightshifts, heavy labor for women and children, such complete exhaustion as is quite unknown in the Old World."[39] It would be surprising if any mine slaves lived to retire into a comfortable old age, and even if they did, they had to be replaced at that point. Xenophon understood that replacement of slaves was a cost that fell on the owner, though his calculations fail to allow for it.

The planter Edward Littleton estimated that to maintain a complement of 100 slaves in 18th-century Barbados it was necessary to acquire between 8 and 10 per year.[40] An 8–10 percent attrition rate reflects conditions of very high mortality and very low reproduction (though better than in Brazil, where a slave's life expectancy as recently as the 1850s was 23 years).[41] Industrial and domestic slaves in Athens almost certainly lived longer, and they probably reproduced more. Overall male life expectancy was not more than 44, possibly as little as 40.[42] Assuming they were not fully productive earlier than about the age of 15, allowing for physical limitations and some apprenticeship, and that the last five years of their life were unproductive, we might suggest a good, faithful, and healthy slave could work in his master's workshop for about 20–25 years, which would prompt a depreciation charge against

---

[39] Bolkestein (1958) 35; cf. Diod. 3.13 on Egyptian mines.
[40] Ferguson (2004) 80.
[41] Coale and Demeny (1966); Schwartz (1992) 42.
[42] Bisel and Angel (1985); Morris (2004).

profits of 4 to 5 percent a year. In practice, an owner of a gang of 20 slaves would need to replace his slaves at a higher rate than this. Disease, disability, crippling accidents, manumission, and the temptations of escape would all account for some slaves before their time. This cost would be partially offset by slaves who fathered sons who entered the same occupation, but we have no evidence that this was a frequent occurrence. A prudent owner might provide for depreciation at the rate of 6 percent a year or more.[43]

Of course, this is not to suggest that the Athenians did these calculations explicitly. Clearly Xenophon did not do them at all. What matters is that those seriously contemplating entry into such a business would have been aware that part of the earnings would need to be ploughed back in to renewing the labor force. To put it another way, is it conceivable that intelligent Athenians would continually find themselves having to reinvest a significant part of an *apophora* in order to maintain it without ever taking that experience into account in their future investment decisions? As Christesen suggests, "it is much more likely that…the risk-return balance emerged as a result of experience rather than abstract calculation."[44]

Other than slave replacement and upkeep, the main cost of operations would have been raw materials. In his list of *arga* (non-*energa*) assets, Demosthenes refers to "ivory, iron and wood" worth 80 *minae* and "gall and copper" worth 70 (§10), so it is clear that the owner held the raw material investment. Demosthenes claims that one workshop typically used two *minae* worth of ivory every month and the other more ivory and some iron. Even without allowing for "wood, gall and copper," we are looking at annual raw material costs that amount to well over half the *apophora*, so the cost of using the raw materials must have been borne by the foreman and he must have reimbursed the owner for them as and when they were used. Since the current prices of most commodities were easily ascertained, transfer was probably at cost or at a price negotiated along with the *apophora*. Larger and more expensive pieces of equipment such as looms and lathes might also have been supplied by the owner, though whether this was explicitly reimbursed, perhaps through a higher *apophora*, is not known and probably varied between product segments.

Costs other than slaves and raw materials would have been negligible. They might have consisted of consumables such as oil and nails, and small inexpensive tools. The complexity of arranging for the owner to pay these

---

[43] This appears to be borne out by Demosthenes' guardians themselves, who claimed a *kephalaion* expenditure on these slaves of almost 1,000 *drachmae* over 10 years (§24), or about one and a half *mina* per year per slave. There is no agreed definition of exactly what *kephalaion* means, but annual slave maintenance is likely to have come to more, so it might refer to slave replacement and is compatible with a depreciation rate of just under 5 percent per year.

[44] Christesen (2003) 47.

minor expenses—and the obvious difficulties in trying to audit the expenditures claimed—suggest that these costs were likely to have been carried by the foreman. Further evidence that the person running the workshop was expected to pay all operating expenses as well as the *apophora* is to be found in the guardians' claim they had spent money on the short-team lease of three slaves (§21). In fact Demosthenes voices the suspicion that the guardians had let Milyas pay all such costs, including raw materials, and then kept the *apophora* for themselves rather than passing it through to Demosthenes (§43). Evidently *ateles* is best interpreted to mean that there were no regular financial obligations on Demosthenes as owner other than slave replacement.

The high nominal returns assume the only investment is slaves, but the 150 *minae* worth of inventory should obviously be included in the asset base. The wood and part of the ivory must have related to the furniture factory and would have accounted for most of the 80 *minae*. Some ivory, the iron, and the gall and copper were for knife-making. We might allocate 80 *minae* of raw materials to the knives and 70 to the furniture. Land occupied by the *ergasteria* should also be treated as a component of capital investment. The factories were attached to Demosthenes's house (§24–25), which must have been large enough to accommodate the slave labor force and workshops and was valued at 30 *minae*. More than 50 slaves would take up a large amount of space relative to the needs of a small family and their domestic slaves (if these were separate). There was also the need to store the substantial quantity of raw materials. The wood and ivory for the furniture factory in particular would be bulky. Perhaps an estimate of 40 percent living space and 30 percent (nine *minae*) for each workshop is reasonable. Equipment is unlikely to have been significant. For knife-making, a rebuildable furnace, some simple handling tools, and some whetstones would probably be enough. The furnace would be made of basic materials, and the labor involved in building and rebuilding it would be fully accommodated by costs already attributed to the slaves. The furniture makers used hammers, nails, saws, planes, and chisels, none costly.[45] There is consistent evidence from Aristophanes, Plato, and Xenophon that most sales were cash-on-delivery, so debtors would also be a small item and of concern to the foreman rather than the owner, probably balanced by suppliers with raw material bills outstanding. Finished goods inventory is likely to have been small. Most luxury items of furniture would probably have been delivered and paid for when finished. Knives would have been made for stock, but intelligent production management would have kept finished inventory to a few weeks of demand at most. Cash requirements are also likely to have been small and, as a practical matter, would have had to be dealt with by the foreman.

---

[45] See Chapter 6.1.

Some of the other figures in Demosthenes's abbreviated profit and loss statement also need revision. His valuations of the slaves are troubling. As Davies points out, if we take the 40 *minae* valuation of the furniture team as their true value, then after adding the deposited talent and subtracting the sum from the total for the three *energa* assets of four talents and 50 *minae*, we have a valuation for the knife-makers of 190 *minae*; this could be composed of 8 at 5 *minae* and 25 at 6, but if any really were worth 3 as Demosthenes admits, the sum does not work.[46] And why would Demosthenes choose phraseology that leads the listener to infer a much lower number? Harris argues for a much higher investment valuation for the furniture makers than the 40 *minae* that Demosthenes senior lent to Moriades.[47] He approaches the sum from the other direction and assumes that the average value of the knife-makers was 5 *minae* each, which, added to one talent and subtracting from four talents and 50 *minae*, gives a residual sum of about 65 *minae* for the furniture makers, rather than the 40 in the text. Furthermore, he argues, this is just what we would expect; the 40 *minae* clearly refers to the figure for which the furniture slaves were pledged, and however primitive one might consider the Athenian credit system, their value as security would surely have been lower than their true value in terms of earning potential. Support for Harris's view is found at §27–28, which refer to an additional 500 *drachmae* that Aphobus lent to (and recouped from) Moriades against these same slaves.

Harris's argument is well supported by his analysis of the text and the figures, although there still remains a question as to why, if the average value of a knife-making slave was five *minae*, Demosthenes describes it as "five or six and none less than three," which a skeptical listener would interpret as implying a lower average. A more comfortable reading suggests that the total value of the knife-makers might have been around 155 *minae*, and the furniture makers about 75.

Together these adjustments make a large difference to the initial calculation of returns on Demosthenes's investment (Tables 9.3 and 9.4).

We have arrived at quite a different puzzle from the one we started with. Prima facie, Demosthenes's words suggested that owning factories was a great opportunity to make money and, in an economically rational society, people would have done much more of it. In fact, by adjusting the asset base using numbers provided by Demosthenes himself and recognizing the obvious truth that slaves are not immortal, we find that he would have been better off putting all his money on loan at 12 percent.

We should consider carefully what these adjustments represent. Despite Finley's strictures, a failure to take depreciation into account is scarcely evidence of an uncommercial approach to business. Depreciation was

---

[46] Davies (1971) 127.
[47] Harris (2006a).

TABLE 9.3  Knife Factory—Revised (*minae*)

|  | Original | Revised |
|---|---|---|
| Income | 30 | 30 |
| Depreciation on slaves | — | (9) |
| **Net income** | 30 | 21 |
| **Assets:** Slaves | 128 | 155 |
| Land and buildings | — | 9 |
| Raw material inventory | — | 80 |
| Other assets | — | 1 |
| **Total assets** | 128 | 245 |
| **Yield %** | 24 | 9 |

TABLE 9.4  Furniture Factory—Revised (*minae*)

|  | Original | Revised |
|---|---|---|
| Income | 12 | 12 |
| Depreciation on slaves | — | (4) |
| **Net income** | 12 | 8 |
| **Assets:** Slaves | 40 | 75 |
| Land and buildings | — | 9 |
| Raw material inventory | — | 70 |
| Other assets | — | 1 |
| **Total assets** | 40 | 155 |
| **Yield %** | 30 | 5 |

only recognized as an expense by the UK tax system in 1878, long after the Industrial Revolution and after the "nation of shopkeepers" had come to dominate world trade.[48] The analysis has also assumed that the slaves spent all their time in the factory. It is apparent from Aristophanes's plays that there was no firm distinction between domestic and industrial slavery. When Plato observes that "one who supervises many slaves in his own service is rightly concerned with the income coming to him from them" (*Leg.* 846d), the word he uses is *oiketai,* conventionally taken to refer to slaves engaged on household tasks. When listing his *arga* assets (§10), Demosthenes nowhere mentions domestic slaves, but he describes the workshop slaves as being left "in the house" (§24). Complaining of the present state of his finances, he says he has just "14 slaves and 30 *minae*" (§7). Is it fanciful to suggest that 14 might have been the proportion of the original 52 or 53 factory slaves whose activities centered on the Demosthenes home and family rather than their workshops?

---

[48] Macve (1985).

If so, how was this reflected in the *apophora*? Did the foreman pay for these "reserves," only called into the production team when needed, or was there an understanding, perhaps a widespread convention, that industrial slaves would be available to work in the owner's home at certain times?

Raw material inventory seems large, and there was enough for several months' production. It is informative that the materials are not included in the *energa* assets. Evidently Demosthenes and his audience did not see these as investments in the business, any more than he saw his own house as a factor of production. They are both simply elements in calculating wealth, and the categorization reflects the indivisibility of home and *ergasterion* in the Athenian mind. The fact that these assets were earning nothing does not seem to have been a concern. Here we do have evidence of behavior that is not economically rational; a profit-maximizing approach would have caused inventory to be minimized and taken into account in the investment analysis. Far from minimizing it, Demosthenes seems proud of the amount. And if he had factored it into the analysis, a profit-maximizer would have closed the business, liquidated the stock, and lent the proceeds at 12 percent.

Economically irrational though it might seem, this behavior is understandable. Francotte observes that "aux époques primitives, l'accumulation des métaux précieux est l'une des formes de richesse."[49] In fact this attitude is also relatively common today. Stock is a major outlay for small businesses and often a major element of value when the business comes to be sold. Once an owner has made the initial investment, his financial concerns center on getting enough cash flow for his income needs while still being able to replenish his stock, which is considered a form of saving. Antique dealers, jewelers, and secondhand booksellers are familiar examples, and it seems Demosthenes senior was another. He also owned 80 *minae* worth of silver, also classified as *arga* (§10) and apparently unconnected with the factories.

In other words, both of the factors that make factory ownership seem financially unattractive, slave depreciation and working capital, bring quite different advantages when seen from an owner's perspective and are rational within an easily recognizable paradigm. It can also be shown that with some reasonable allowance for the non-economic value Demosthenes might have placed on these items, returns converge around the levels we are expecting. For instance, if 20 percent of the cost of slaves reflects personal use and the raw material inventory is considered purely as a store of wealth, then the yield of the knife factory is about 15 percent and that of the furniture factory 12 percent, just the sort of returns to risk one would expect. Again, it is not being suggested that Demosthenes or his contemporaries did these

---

[49] Francotte (1900–01) I.88.

calculations, only that had they not implicitly understood matters in this way, their investment choices might have been different.

A review of Demosthenes's other inherited *arga* (inactive) assets throws more light on Athenian investment preferences. The full list after the two sets of raw material is (§9–10):

- House: 3,000 *drachmae* (*dr*).
- Furniture, jewelry etc: 10,000 *dr*.
- Silver: 80 *minae*
- Maritime loan: 70 *minae*
- Bank of Pasion: 2,400 *dr*.
- Bank of Pylades: 600 *dr*.
- Demonides (loan): 1,600 *dr*.
- Miscellaneous small loans at no interest: one talent.

The maritime loan seems out of place here. Clearly it was "commercial"—as noted above, such loans tended to pay very high returns and involved taking considerable insurance risk. Yet it is not included in the *energa* (productive) assets. Perhaps *energa* had an active meaning—capital that the owner has put to work directly rather than as a passive loan or savings—but that raises questions about the *energa* talent lent at 12 percent. We must also wonder why the deposits with Pasion and Pylades were included here and not in the *energa* assets along with that talent. Was it because they were non-interest-bearing? Harris argues that banks never paid interest on loans, though other scholars believe they did and specifically refer to these loans to make the point.[50] If they did not bear interest, why does Demosthenes say explicitly that the miscellaneous talent was non-interest-bearing without saying anything about these deposits? And what about the loan to Demonides? Lent on the same terms as the *energa* talent, the three sums in question would have provided an adequate income for a whole family.

The way Demosthenes describes his income suggests that if the loans bore interest, it was not very much. When he adds up his *energa* assets of four talents and 50 *drachmae*, he ascribes to them an expected income of 50 *minae* (only a slight exaggeration; 30 from knives, 12 from furniture, and 7 from the deposited talent make 49). But when he sums his other assets (eight talents, 46 *minae*) he makes no reference to income. If there was any income generated from this asset group, it must have been incidental. It is probably safer to see the list as not producing reliable income at all, the maritime loan being considered a large bet whose outcome was uncertain and not a source of regular cash.

---

[50] Harris (1993) 102–7; Bogaert (1968) 347–48; Isager and Hansen (1975) 95.

It would be of great value if we could compare Demosthenes's statement of assets with those of contemporaries other than Timarchus, but unfortunately we can deduce little about manufacturing from other examples we have. Ciron's estate included income generating slaves and furniture worth 1,300 *drachmae* (Isaeus. 8.35), but we cannot separate them or tell how much income the slaves generated or how. Their value suggests there were not more than two of them, three at most, so they were certainly not part of a Demosthenes-type operation and might well have generated their income by providing personal services or assisting their master in a craft. Stratocles's list of assets (Isaeus. 9.42–43) makes no mention of slaves. Nevertheless, we can take a view on just how well-off Demosthenes senior had been as a result of his investments. The 49 *minae* of stated income must be offset by slave replacement needs, after which he would have been deriving between 35 and 40 *minae* a year from his industrial activities and his loan, which would keep him in some style, especially if the costs of buying and maintaining a good domestic slave force were already covered. If this was the full extent of his wealth, he could certainly have undertaken the occasional liturgy but would have struggled to afford many trierarchies. It is notable that the orator never refers to such public benevolence on his father's part. Davies suggests that this might be because some of the senior Demosthenes's wealth was hidden (*aphanes*), and that it was in order to maintain this invisibility that the guardians agreed to the maximum rate of tax being levied on a sum slightly higher than the claimed value of the estate (§7)—they wanted to avoid a tax audit.[51] This is plausible, but it is unlikely that the hidden amount would have represented a very substantial degree of wealth. Certainly the debts resulting from his father-in-law's disgrace would have been a good reason for Demosthenes senior to conceal his wealth, but the underlying premise of the case makes it unlikely that the deceased estate was very much greater than the sums his son is claiming.

The son himself was a great deal better off. Davies lists two full trierarchies and three joint ones; multiple liturgies; several public gifts, including one of a talent and another of rather more; some major arms purchases on behalf of the city; two chorus productions; and a ransom of prisoners from Philip. His last trierarchy was in 353 and his last liturgy in 341, his beneficence thereafter being confined to irregular, special-purpose activities on behalf of his fellow citizens. This does indeed look like someone who preferred to keep his wealth *aphanes,* perhaps because much of it derived from slightly dubious payments for settling public cases in particular ways. It was certainly not from his inherited industrial investments that the orator became "the richest man in Athens" (Din. 1.111). On the other hand, there is no suggestion in the whole of

---

[51] Davies (1971) 125–27.

this family history that industry was an unacceptable form of wealth generation or an inappropriate inheritance for a truly distinguished Athenian. Even though the investment in the furniture factory was originally made by Moriades, the Demosthenes family seems quite as happy to be deriving income from it as from more conventional loan interest, despite the concomitant need to tie up a large amount of funds in working capital. As far as we know, the knife factory was a deliberate investment choice by Demosthenes senior.

The preceding analysis is necessarily imprecise and cannot be taken as exactly representing the economics of investing in all forms of industrial activity in classical Athens. It does, however, demonstrate that one apparent piece of evidence that classical Athenians were not economically rational and motivated beings can equally well be interpreted as showing that they thought about the returns needed from enterprise in very much the same way as many small business owners do today, and that their implicit approach to determining the equilibrium rate of return from industrial investments was not all that different from ours. Direct investment in manufacturing was as an investment option with defined characteristics, including a (theoretically) steady income, access to the services of a group of slaves outside working hours and, for some products, the need to accumulate and store wealth in the form of raw material inventory. As a result, investment in manufacturing was a feature of city life throughout antiquity, and a number of well-known Athenian citizens—including at least Aeschines, Anytos, Aristarchus, Demosthenes, Epicrates, Hyperbolus, Isaeus, Isocrates, Cleon, Cleophon, Leocrates, Lysias, and Timarchus—did make such investments or benefited from ones they inherited.[52] This is no surprise: investors in industry were, by definition, people with access to money.

Not all *ergasteria* of the rich were examples of profit-maximizing investment strategies. We have seen how undifferentiated products could accommodate casual participation without offering more than subsistence rewards for time spent and how some wealthy owners might have employed their slaves in weaving or commodity pottery when they were not busy with the harvest. Philocrates owned multiple properties outside the city, a house in the city deme of Melite and two *ergasteria* next door to it—a combination that was probably common and implies quite large workshops, since they were separate from the residence.[53] Pimps might have operated similar *ergasteria* to keep their employees earning when upright.

There was a vital distinction between owning craftsmen-slaves and working in an *ergasterion*. It is clear for reasons of time availability, let alone any status concerns, that politicians and professional orators would not engage

---

[52] In calling such investment "rare," de Ste. Croix (1981) 124 is plainly mistaken; contrast Burford (1972) 119.
[53] Osborne (1985) 53.

physically in the manufacturing process, and it is reasonable to assume that, unless driven by a special artistic zeal, other citizens would choose to avoid it if they had less demanding sources of income; but even the most distinguished citizens were comfortable owning teams of manufacturing slaves, whether inherited or acquired.[54] Any aversion was not to the fact of making money or the source of it; it only concerned the dignity of the specific activity. The manufacturing businesses open to profit-seeking investors were permanent, dedicated, specialized businesses with the predictable and comfortable margins offered by competitive differentiation and barriers to entry. Unless something went wrong, they could be relied upon to provide an *apophora* or meet the costs of servicing a loan and constituted a sensible component of an investment strategy. Other manufacturing roles were open to the citizen looking for income and lacking investment capital, but he had to get his hands dirty.

## 9.2 Citizen Craftsmen

An Athenian citizen's life was rich and varied. As Rihll and Tucker put it: "Most free men spent some of their time providing for themselves and their families, generally as farmers. Most spent some of their time on management of their slave(s) and the rest of their household. Most spent some of their time on what we would call leisure pursuits, such as chatting with friends in public places and taking physical exercise in public gyms. Most spent some of their time on religious observances, such as performing purification rituals for their dearly departed and going to the theater (which was more of a holy day than our secularized holiday, but no less entertaining for that—comedy and satire, as well as tragedy, were invented for these religious festivals). Most of those who had a voice in the political system of their place and time spent some of their time on it, formally in meetings and informally talking with friends. In all these cases an ancient might consider what he was doing as 'work': survival meant not just having enough food to eat, but also preserving the community."[55]

There is one thing we can be sure of among all these activities: for most citizens, manufacturing was not so much one of a range of investment options as a means of survival. There were precious few other ways to supplement their income or reduce their outgoings as many needed to, and several manufacturing sectors offered the potential for casual engagement compatible with civic duties. Over a quarter of the citizenry had no land (Dion. Hal. *Lys.* 34) and would have needed an income to keep themselves and their family.

---

[54] de Ste. Croix (1981) 125.
[55] Rihll and Tucker (2002) 18.

Most farms were too small to produce a sellable surplus that could cover non-food expenses—a problem exacerbated by generations of inheritance, the infrequency of agricultural land changing hands, and perhaps by the concentration of multiple land parcels in the hands of a few.[56]

There was a limited range of income options for citizens, many of them coming through the *polis*, including service in the military or navy in time of war, being selected by lot to hear legal cases, and carrying out other political duties for which the state paid a basic allowance. Military pay consisted of board (*sitos*) and cash (*misthos*), with plunder a third, and often the most valuable, component. Pericles introduced pay for hearing trials at the rate of two obols a day, which Cleon raised to three (Plut. *Per.* 9.2–3; (Xen.) *Ath. pol.* 27.3; Pl. *Grg.* 515e; Arist. *Pol.* 1274a). The courts sat between 175 and 225 days a year, but the lottery system for selection to the panel of judges meant it could never be a reliable source of income.[57] Attending the assembly was originally worth one obol; by the time of Aristophanes's *Ecclesiazusae* it was three (308–9), and in Aristotle's time as much as nine (*Ath. pol.* 62.2). With the Assembly meeting at least 40 times a year, this could contribute significantly to a poor citizen's sustenance, but the fact that it was paid at all suggests that, compared with pursuing a craft, many saw civic duties as dull and not worth forgoing income for.[58] The *polis* provided few permanent employment opportunities for citizens. With the exception of councilors (five obols a day for the period of appointment) and specific bureaucratic roles in tax-collection or regulating the market or port, state civilian employment was usually through public building works and tended to be sporadic and casual, though it provided plenty of work for craftsmen of all status levels for much of the classical period. Architects and project managers were typically the only salaried citizens engaged in public works, others being hired by the day. Other long-term administrative posts in the state's gift were invariably allocated to slaves.

There was also a system of public handouts. The disabled (*adunatoi*) were beneficiaries of a special fund. Cleophon introduced the *diobolon*, intended to be a daily dole of two obols (which could only support a very modest lifestyle at best), but it was probably only affordable irregularly and in short bursts. The theoric fund, created in the fourth century after the *diobolon* had been abandoned, tied dole payments to attending festivals and the theater, so was not a permanent income source for the poor. While this might seem a "bread and circuses" approach to preventing social discontent, the logic of these handouts was simple. Citizens would find it hard to devote time to the democratic institutions Athens prided itself on if they needed to work

---

[56] For contrasting views on land distribution, see Foxhall (2002) and Hanson (1995).
[57] Markle (1985); Hansen (1991).
[58] Scholion to Dem. 24.20; Harris (2006c) 103–20.

full-time earning a living. Public handouts made it more likely that poorer citizens would have the leisure to enjoy their democratic rights, but most households still needed other sources of income.

Craft manufacture was one of the few acceptable ways for a citizen to supplement his income. Personal services such as grooming and prostitution were the province of slaves. A few citizens might make a living on the stage (which had the added attraction that even chorus members were exempt from military service), but it would be a precarious and part-time occupation. Both trade and banking needed capital or credit. Long-term paid employment in an *ergasterion* owned by someone else was socially unacceptable. Isaeus bewails the lot of the free man compelled to accept paid employment (5.39), Isocrates equates hired employment (*thetia*) with slavery (14.48), and the dead Achilles compares being a prince among the dead with the worst imaginable condition for a free man, not having control over one's own work (*Od.* 11.489–91). A character in Menander observes that it is better to be a slave with a good master than to live a base life as a free man.[59] Such status concerns about working for another citizen were not peculiar to the ancients but, along with assertions about leisure facilitating the virtuous life, have tended to be strongest in slave-owning societies.[60]

Few citizens were constrained from engagement in industry by a lack of capital. With no economies of scale in production or capital barriers to entry in many industry sectors, even a poor citizen could compete on equal terms with other craftsmen, building a business on his own labor, supported by one or two slaves. It is quite likely that all 5,000 or more citizens with no land, and as many again with small or unproductive farms, were engaged in some form of production.[61] Land holders too would have been looking for employment, and income during the summer months before harvest time and pursuing a craft would have been an attractive option for many of them.[62] Many potteries probably only operated during the summer, in which drying conditions were better anyway.

Self-employment in a craft was more than socially acceptable for citizens; it was seen as positively praiseworthy. Hesiod defined work as good, not least because it helps you to get rich: "Work is not a disgrace at all, but not working is a disgrace. And if you work, the man who does not work will quickly envy you when you are rich" (*Op.* 298–316). Xenophon approved of manufacturing for income: "By manufacturing one of these commodities, namely groats, Nausicydes keeps not only himself and his family, but large herds of swine and cattle as well, and has so much to spare that he often takes on expensive public duties as well and lives in luxury by baking bread, Demeas of Collytus by

---

[59] Cited by Schopenhauer (2007) 51.
[60] The antebellum Southern States are a good example: Schiedel (2002).
[61] Harris (2002a) 70.
[62] Jameson (2002) 170.

making capes, Menon by making cloaks, and most of the Megarians make a good living out of smocks" (*Mem.* 2.7.6). Contemporary observers, including Aristophanes, Thucydides, Plato, and Aristotle, all portray poorer citizens making goods for market through their own labor supported by any slaves they had. Xenophon's Socrates observes that "those who can afford it buy slaves so that they may have fellow-workers" (Xen. *Mem.* 2.3.3). A disabled craftsman appeals for state support because he cannot afford a slave assistant (Lys. 24.6). Many fathers of famous men were craftsmen: Sophocles's father was a carpenter or a smith;[63] Cephalus, the statesman and envoy to Chalkis, was the son of a potter;[64] Cleophon's forebears had made lyres (Andoc. 1.146); the Hyperbolus family was involved in lamps (Ar. *Eq.* 1302–15); and Isocrates's father made flutes ((Plut.) *Isoc.* 1). Being employed in your own business might be considered essential for self-respect, and the small craftsman, working alongside whatever slaves he could afford, might have been the normal type of citizen.[65]

Previous chapters have identified the crafts open to the lone craftsmen as distinct from slave-workshops (see Table 9.1). In crafts that offered the potential for differentiation, those able to establish a reputation for superior work could earn a premium for their labor and might make a very good living. They would be likely to operate full-time, not only to maximize their income but also to maintain their skills and keep their customer base. Some of these small craft shops would grow to employ several slaves and become a vehicle for citizen investment rather than direct participation, but this was only possible if the brand reputation could attach to a workshop rather than an individual craftsman, as it could in the case of, say, knives, but not in customized armor. Lyre- and flute-making also appear to have produced significant wealth for their owners, so they may have made the transition. Cleon and Anytus clearly earned money from tanneries, but it is equally clear that neither of them were practicing tanners. We do not know when these businesses ceased to be operated by members of the owning family and became simply income-producing assets for subsequent generations, but by classical times, most such slave-based businesses were already in place, and the ordinary citizen who could not afford to buy one was largely confined to working at a craft.

Those without the skills to make a product customers specifically sought out, or who chose not to work full-time, could earn a modest income either by producing cheaper versions of premium items or by operating in segments where products were indistinguishable, like commodity

---

[63] Attributed to Aristoxenos in *Life of Sophocles I*.
[64] Scholion to Ar. *Eccl.* 81. An earlier Cephalus, possibly related, is satirized as a potter in the same play (248–53).
[65] Humphreys (1970) 14, 16, 21; Bolkestein (1958) 65.

pottery, clothing, simple woodwork, and basic metal tools and utensils. Some would have had to work at these occupations full-time to survive, especially the landless and those unfit for military or administrative service, but it was an important characteristic of undifferentiated craft work that it could be practiced casually. Prices, reflecting subsistence income for the full-timer, would be the same for all products that met the basic standard. This would have especially suited those with land to be cared for, or who chose to spend time and earn money on civic duties rather than in a workshop. Importantly for Athenian democracy, large markets for simple undifferentiated products made casual engagement possible.

This link between earning income from undifferentiated crafts and democratic participation is a crucial one. Pay for public duties would not have persuaded people to take time off from their craft activity if that would have meant long-term damage to their business. If industries had been so concentrated and customers so demanding that the only way to earn any income in manufacturing was full-time work, democratic participation must have suffered. Pericles stressed the compatibility of crafts with civic duties (Thuc. 2.40.2). Aristotle defined an Athenian citizen as "one who shares in the administration of justice and in the holding of office" (*Pol.* 1275a), and the Athenian assembly was populated by "lamp-merchants, turners, leather-dressers and cobblers" (Ar. *Eq.* 738–40) and not just the idle rich (cf. Xen. *Mem.* 3.7.6). Many of these people would have been small farmers during the winter and served in the military in summer, but in town they were identified by their craft occupations.

Previous chapters have described how developments in technology eventually provided the barriers to entry and returns to scale that led to the consolidation of industry structures. In this sense, the history of technological development is also the story of the decline of the individual craftsman. Athenian democracy flourished at a time when there was still scope for the sole operator to make an adequate living on a part-time basis in many fields that subsequently came to be dominated by large concerns demanding full-time employment and the indignity of working for someone else. The ability to combine income earning and political participation became more and more difficult as industries evolved, and a participatory democracy on Athenian lines simply could not exist in a developed economy today.

## 9.3 Women

Despite a façade of seclusion and legal incapacity, women played a major role in Athenian manufacturing. They made investment decisions, managed factories, made items for sale, and often took those items, or items that others in their household had made, to market. The restricted status of women has formed one of the elements that some historians cite to argue that economic activity in Athens was so different from our own that comparison is meaningless, but in manufacturing at least, women had as much influence on investment, supervision, and output as in subsequent societies, and they dominated some segments, including prepared foods, simple textiles, and floral arrangements. Female management of household finances, including productive investments and exchange of goods and coin with other parties, is common in many less-developed societies. In fact, a case can be made that it is only since the Industrial Revolution, when the rewards for success in industry became large, visible, and envied, that women became largely alienated from the management of production.

Poorer women still collected water alongside slaves (Ar. *Lys.* 327–31), but since slavery had relieved the better-off of some of the household duties that had taken them outside the home in archaic times, such as shopping and fetching water, it was considered quite unusual for well-bred women to be seen in public (Lys. 1.4–10). There was a specific women's marketplace (*gynaikeia agora*), where some historians conjecture they could buy and sell away from the public gaze, but in general their business was in the home, not the marketplace, and even there some were separated from the rest of the household by a bolted door (Xen. *Oec.* 7.3; 7.22).[66] In some homes, women were secluded on an upper floor in their own *gynaikon* or *gynaikontis* away from the main rooms and visitors (Euphiletus in Lys. 1). This was probably unusual—weaving requires light, so women weavers, including the wives and daughters of citizens, must have used the central courtyard—but it does indicate a male ideal of female propriety as secluded and inactive, far from reality though that was in most households. Outside the home, women played a leading part in some religious activities and held some of the highest offices, including priestess of Athena, but in secular matters they were severely constrained. They were not able to enter contracts in their own name, and widows were attached to family assets so that if there was no male heir, she would marry a suitable family member, who, if already married, was expected to get a divorce.[67]

Pragmatic as always, the Athenians found ways of accommodating legal restrictions when convenient. Men could represent the interests of their wives so that they were able to protect themselves within the law (Lys. 32). The problem of women and freed men not being able to act as bankers because they could not own land as security was overcome by an extraordinarily

---

[66] This might refer only to slave women.

[67] Divorces were normally initiated by men, although a divorced woman's dowry would revert to her. Alcibiades's wife Hipparete tried to turn the tables by divorcing him, but it ended in ignominious failure and she was dragged home by her husband (Andoc. 4.14–15).

unconvincing legal fiction when Pasion's freed slave married his widow in order to keep the bank within the *oikos*. In one intriguing instance, a woman organized a group of people to make an *eranos* loan (a loan among friends). As lead-syndicator, she was responsible for getting the loan back, but as a woman she lacked the status to seize the secured asset. This was readily solved with the help of a male associate.[68]

A high level of female influence was an inevitable demographic consequence of the social custom of late marriage for men and early marriage for women; there were many widows, and they held the purse strings. Our division between the workplace as a sphere of production and the household as a sphere of consumption was entirely absent from classical Athens.[69] The *oikos* was the economic unit that owned assets and generated income for an Athenian family, and the limited rights of women did not disqualify them from managing it. The comic poet Pherecrates suggested that before slavery, women did all the work.[70] Xenophon observes that "the wife has primary responsibility for managing the household" (*Oec.* 7.35–43). Ischomachus's wife runs their entire household by herself: she manages their slaves "like a queen bee," plans the household's consumption, manages the stores, and is charged with increasing the value of slave assets through training (Xen. *Oec.* 7.32). Aristotle takes issue with Plato's claim that men and women can do the same work, on the grounds that women have households to run (*Pol.* 1264b). A more scurrilous version of the same sentiment holds that escorts are for pleasure because they can sing and dance and keep up a good conversation, concubines are for sex, and wives are for bearing children and looking after the household assets (Dem. 59.107–26).

Female control of the household's assets and staff included managing the productive output of all its slaves and keeping the female members of the *oikos* and underutilized males busy in various ways, including manufacturing products for sale, especially but not only clothing. Rich citizens' wives and widows would have played a major role in investment decisions, and many investments in slaves or working capital for a manufacturing operation would have been made by women, or at least with their interested involvement.[71] For women of the households of poorer citizens, metics, and freed slaves, the *oikos* was the *ergasterion* and, very often, the lady of the house was the foreman. They worked in the family workshop, supervising slaves and producing goods themselves. In general, they would have contributed less in differentiable segments where their husband's skill was specifically valued by customers, although a certain Artemis did the gilding for her helmet-maker husband

---

[68] Harris (2006b) 333–46.
[69] Harris (forthcoming) 3.
[70] Long (1978) 381.
[71] The fact that no mining leases are held in women's names is more likely to reflect their legal status than that women avoided mining investments.

Dionysius (SIG. 1177) and we know of a female cobbler (IG. II² 1578.5) and a metalworker (or possibly a potter).[72] Pliny (*HN* 35.136) mentions a number of painters' daughters who became artists themselves. These are thought to have been exceptions, and most of the highly skilled trades seem to have been carried out by men. The extent of female ownership of workshops is unclear: scholars agree that a vase painting showing a woman on a raised dais is at least evidence that there were women craftworkers, but not about whether the dais suggests proprietorship [73] Some suggest it was a compositional necessity and says nothing about ownership, while others question whether women were qualified to own large workshops of the type depicted, but in fact the amount they were allowed to own was quite large and certainly enough to cover most day-to-day business activities.[74] It is significant that both the Erechtheum and the temple at Eleusis listed a woman as a material supplier.[75]

Besides managing the household's output, many citizen women had to work for a living themselves. Here they often played roles that were quite independent of any male relatives, generally in undifferentiated crafts and often to do with food or textiles.[76] Not only were these seen as typically feminine occupations, they also allowed intermittent involvement and could be taken up or dropped as other demands such as childbearing allowed. Many women in Aristophanes operate places of refreshment or sell bread, porridge, vegetables, garlic, figs, and garlands.[77] Epigraphy shows women selling sesame (IG. II² 1561.27), salt (IG. II² 12073), and honey (IG. II² 1570.73). The literature seldom makes explicit the social status of the women, and many of them would have been metics or slaves or freedwomen, but it seems clear that the bread and vegetable sellers in the *Wasps* are citizens' wives, as was Lysistrata's army of tradeswomen. Textiles were commonly sold by women and often manufactured by the vendor (Ar. *Ran.* 1349–51), and 31 out of 42 identified professions of female metics making dedications were woolworkers or *talasiourgoi*—a far higher concentration in a single trade than among men.[78] Selling ribbons seems to have been another major sector, and one which required little labor

---

[72] Green (1961) 73–75, referring to the Caputi *Hydria* (note below).
[73] The Caputi *Hydria*: Daremberg and Saglio (1896) 1127, fig. 304; Beazley (1942) 376.61; Hasaki (2012b) 256.
[74] Venit (1988) 270; Beazley (1944) 13; Richter (1923) 71; Cohen (1992a) 106–9.
[75] ER 64 and EL 22 in Feyel (2006) 328.
[76] Vegetable selling references are to Euripides's mother and may not be quite true. There is a male vegetable seller at *Vesp.* 680.
[77] Landlady/bar owner: *kapeleides*—*Plut.* 426, 1120; *pandokeutriai*—*Ran.* 549–53; vendor of bread: *artopolis*—*Ran.* 858, Xen. *Cyr.* 5.3.39; of porridge: *lekythos*—*Lys.* 457, 562; of vegetables:— *skandika*—*Ach.* 478; *lachanopoletriallachanos*—*Thesm.* 387; 456; *arouraia*—*Ran.* 840; of garlic: *skorodopandokeutriartopolis*—*Lys.* 458; of figs: *ischadopolis*—*Lys.* 564; weaver of garlands: *stephaneplokousia*—*Thesm.* 446–58.
[78] Meyer (2010) 80; Schaps (1979) 19; cf. Glotz (1926) 217.

TABLE 9.5 **Women's Roles in Manufacturing**

|  |  | Barriers to Entry | |
|---|---|---|---|
|  |  | Yes | No |
| Potential for Differentiation | Yes | Differentiated industry: Investor Supervisor | Differentiated craft: Support husband's work; oversee slave assistance; help sell output (Rarer) Practice craft |
|  | No | Undifferentiated industry: Investor Supervisor | Undifferentiated craft: Supervise household resources to earn additional income Manage small workshop in husband's absence Make own products (flowers, food, clothes) for sale |

or skill (Dem. 57.31). There were some things women did not do: Pherecrates (*Fr.* 70) says no one has seen a woman fishmonger or butcher, and they are not attested as selling books or armor.[79]

While the need to earn was a reality of life for many women, it was not seen as honorable.[80] Euxitheos knew that his mother's past as a wet-nurse was an obstacle to his being granted citizenship (Dem. 57.31–35), despite the fact that wet-nursing was the most common occupation on the gravestones of citizens' wives and daughters.[81] A wife not earning income was probably something of a status symbol, but there is little doubt that economic necessity bound a large proportion of the female population, including the citizenry.

Women might operate in several segments simultaneously. The doyenne of a household with investments in slave workshops might have to supervise those workshops in the absence of her husband or a freed slave and would still be expected to keep her domestic slaves occupied weaving and spinning. A poorer woman might split her time between assisting her craftsman-husband, making her own flower arrangements or soups, and taking products to market. Table 9.5 shows the roles women played in different types of manufacturing business.

## 9.4 Foreign Residents

Metics (foreigners with permanent rights of residence in Athens) had diverse origins and motivations. Some were Greek and some barbarian; some had chosen to migrate to Athens for the commercial opportunities it offered, while some had been brought in as slaves and earned their freedom, which

---

[79] Brock (1994) 340–41.
[80] Schaps (1979) 18.
[81] Brock (1994) 337.

gave them the same status as freeborn metics.[82] An alien (*xenos*) who had stayed for a certain period of time in Attica had to register as a metic and enroll in one of the demes under the auspices of a *prostates* or guardian, or they were liable to be sold into slavery. Aliens without metic status had to pay a *xenika* tax and could appear before the *dikai emporikai* (and before that tribunal was established in 350 BCE there were probably similar arrangements in place), but they could only bring a lawsuit if a treaty had been signed with their home town. There is little evidence to support the theory that there were citizens at Athens whom other cities had appointed on a permanent basis to look after the legal interests of their aliens; any such *proxenoi* arrangements were probably temporary and ad hoc, but might nevertheless have been quite common.[83] As a result, there would have been very few unregistered aliens who could not put themselves in a position to secure their entitlements in commercial dealings if they needed to, but their restricted legal status and the threat of slavery if they overstayed their welcome meant they operated almost exclusively as traders. Anyone wanting to establish themselves in manufacture at Athens would almost certainly have registered as a metic.[84]

Registering did not bring many privileges beyond the right to stay. Metics were not considered members of their demes and had no political rights or capacity to hold public office (Arist. *Pol.* 1275a). They could not marry a citizen, and they had less protection under the law, with no capacity to bring private lawsuits except before the *polemarch*, whose jurisdiction was more circumscribed than the jury-courts. They received no allowances or social benefits but were still liable for military service and fought in the army, especially in local campaigns, and as rowers (Xen. *Vect.* 2.1). They could not own land, so their ability to borrow was restricted by not being able to offer real estate as security. They were subject to the *metoikon*, an annual tax not based on income or assets but simply a charge for the right to live and do business in Athens. This put them at a cost disadvantage compared with citizens, so to make the same net income they would have to work longer hours or more productively.

Despite the drawbacks, the fact that so many foreigners chose to live in Athens is testimony to the economic opportunities it offered; their rights were at least protected more there than in many other places, and their contribution was recognized and rewarded.[85] Athens was the labor exchange of the Greek world, and people from other parts of Greece saw being a metic in Athens as a privilege.[86] Nicias used this to motivate metic rowers before the

---

[82] Garlan (1982) 79.
[83] Wallace (1970); Isager and Hansen (1975) 69.
[84] Gauthier (1972) 122; Levy (1988) 53–61; Cohen (2000) 72.
[85] Whitehead (1977) 11–13.
[86] Burford (1972) 59.

battle at Syracuse (Thuc. 7.63). Pseudo-Xenophon noted that Athens treated metics well because they were useful for trade and in the fleet (*Ath. pol.* 1.11–12); Xenophon proposed that those who offered capital and services to the city should be rewarded with property in the form of a small parcel of land and a house, even though property rights were strictly confined to citizens (*Vect.* 2.1–6). Naturalization increased significantly after 411 BCE, and by 406 the Athenians were "accepting any individual who would serve aboard their warships."[87]

It is safe to assume that virtually all metics would have been directly involved in some form of commercial activity, since they needed to make a living.[88] Foreigners made up most of the traders frequenting the Peiraeus, ranging from major investors with the ability to finance an entire ship and its cargo to modest dealers who shared voyages and arranged finance for their own moiety of the cargo while the master contractor insured the ship itself.[89] Among one group of lenders who financed Athenian foreign commerce through maritime loans, there were 12 metics and aliens but only seven citizens.[90] Many voyages were probably self-financed (and not represented in the literature because self-financing would give rise to fewer disputes), but many of the ship owners would also have been metics. Isocrates (7.32) and Demosthenes (27.61; 34.51) emphasized that lending to these traders was of prime importance for the development of the city.

The fact that the highest proportion of metics settled in urban demes is indirect evidence of the importance of their contribution to manufacturing. Many were entrepreneurs, trained in metalwork or other trades. Some had special expertise in crafts such as armor, stonemasonry, shipbuilding, pottery, and ornaments. Undoubtedly a large number of manufacturing enterprises, large and small, were set up and run by metics, and they would have employed many manufacturing slaves. Manumitted slaves who had been assigned metic status are sometimes thought to have performed lower-status work than foreign metics. Some scholars have argued they had continuing obligations enshrined in the law that governed slavery, the *dike apostasiou*, which obliged the former slave to continue to live in his original master's home, work for him, and even provide him with slave-children.[91] The evidence for this is very slight, and the practice seems inconsistent with temporarily freeing slaves in order to sell them to another owner, who would not want to be encumbered by any preexisting obligations in the way Epicrates was.[92]

---

[87] Cohen (2000) 19; 67.
[88] Harris (2002a) 70.
[89] Cartledge (1998) 27–28.
[90] Isager and Hansen (1975) 69.
[91] Harpocration's *Lexicon* s.v. "apostasiou"; cited in Westermann (1945) 95; see also Wilamowitz-Moellendorff (1887a, b).
[92] See Chapter 8.2.

A list of names and votive offerings from the late fourth century throws some light on metic activity.[93] From 110 of these dedications, Harris has identified the occupations of 98 individuals, including 26 in craft or industry, 35 in retail, 13 in agriculture, and 12 in other activities.[94] If these grateful metics are representative, the numbers indicate that more than a quarter of all long-term foreign residents of Athens were engaged in manufacturing. Some metics had the wherewithal to acquire a slave-factory from the time of their arrival, as Cephalus may have done, while others might earn enough in Athens to acquire one, as the freed man Pasion did. Some freed slaves might have continued as factory supervisors for their old master, worked for a new one, or started up on their own account. The majority, lacking investment capital, would have set up and run craft operations. Some brought special skills to the large and vibrant market that was Athens. Many of the potters well enough known for their names to have been preserved sound non-Attic, like Amasis, Chachrilion, Brygos, and Douris.[95] As many metics had come to Athens specifically to practice their craft and fewer could afford casual engagement (especially as they had to pay the *metoikon* tax and were ineligible for paid civic duties), it is likely that proportionately more metics than citizens were successful at differentiating their craft output and looked to manufacturing for more than a subsistence income. Like Athens's women, these foreign residents, both migrants and freed slaves, played various roles in all manufacturing segments, as shown in Table 9.6.

TABLE 9.6  Role of Metics and Freed Slaves in Manufacturing

|  |  | Barriers to Entry | |
|---|---|---|---|
|  |  | Yes | No |
| Potential for Differentiation | Yes | Differentiated industry<br>Investor<br>Supervisor | Differentiated craft<br>Probably common |
|  | No | Undifferentiated industry<br>Investor<br>Supervisor | Undifferentiated craft<br>Probably less common |

## 9.5 Slaves

Analysis of ancient slavery has tended to focus on its social implications, but it had important economic consequences.[96] Athens was a true slave

---

[93] Lewis (1959) 208–38; 37 (1968) 368–80; Meyer (2010).
[94] Harris (2002a) 70.
[95] Webster (1973) 128.
[96] Weidemann (1997) 31.

economy to an extent matched by few others; production, distribution, and consumption in the city were all highly dependent on slaves.[97] While a few were owned by the state, such as the Scythian archers, or by temples like Eleusis, most belonged to private citizens. As Bresson puts it, "on achetait donc un esclave comme aujourd'hui on achète une machine," reflecting a similar sentiment in Aristotle (*Pol.* 1255b).[98] By classical times, slaves and their families accounted for well over a third of Athens' population, possibly two-thirds: scholars generally estimate there were between 70,000 and 120,000 in the fifth century and perhaps over 200,000 by the end of the fourth.[99] Breeding was encouraged, and while Sparta depended entirely on this to maintain the number of helots (Xen. *Oec.* 7.9.5; Pl. *Meno* 82a–b; Lys 13.18; Dem. 53.19; Pherecrates fr. 183; Arist. *Pol.* 1255a), slave reproduction in fourth-century Athens was well below the replacement rate, and the vast majority of slaves were probably "barbarians," who were being imported at the rate of at least 3,000 a year.[100] Sparta's helots were a racially identifiable population who often served in the military and could be freed as a result (by the state, not by a master), but were never accepted into positions of any status; Athens's more diverse slave population lived more diverse lives, some becoming wealthy and influential, some becoming a central and trusted part of a respectable family, and some living and dying in the mines.

Where these slaves came from is unclear. The first of P. G. Wodehouse's ill-advised broadcasts from Berlin in June 1941 began: "Young men, starting out in life, have often asked me 'How can I become an Internee?' Well, there are several methods. My own was to buy a villa in Le Touquet on the coast of France and stay there till the Germans came along. This is probably the best and simplest system. You buy the villa and the Germans do the rest."[101] The system for becoming enslaved in ancient Greece was rather less easy to follow. The general assumption that slave-owning societies achieved that position through military superiority is surely correct, but there were few major wars that delivered a large contingent at once, let alone a steadily increasing flow as large as the one classical Athens absorbed.[102] There would have been organized raids to acquire slaves, but these do not seem to be been sufficiently common to have been a major source and would have invited competition and retaliation.[103] Only in the plays of Aristophanes were many

---

[97] Cohen (2000) 130.
[98] Bresson (2007) 197.
[99] Gomme (1933); Finley (1952) 57; Hansen (1986) 29.
[100] Isager and Hansen (1975) 32–33.
[101] McCrum (2004) 267.
[102] Garlan (1982) 20.
[103] Rosivach (1999) 155 n. 105.

Athenians enslaved for debt.[104] In some cities, like Halicarnassus, enslavement was a legal penalty, but again the numbers would have been small. Some people sold their children into slavery—the Thracians (Hdt. 5.6) and the Phrygians (Philostr. *Ap. Ty.* 7.12) were reputed to have done so, and some rich Orientals might have sold their slaves' children—but if the practice was prevalent we would surely have heard more about it. Nor is there any evidence that the trans-Saharan slave trade was active before the second century CE.[105] The rapid but steady increase in slave numbers in Athens during the fifth and fourth centuries, few of them apparently captured in Athens's own battles, suggests an equally rapid increase in enslavement around the Aegean and Black Seas, but the mechanisms for supplying this trade must have been diverse and almost certainly included colonization.[106]

Despite the sourcing puzzle, there was a very active market in slaves, and it priced each slave individually. Epigraphy gives a range of prices between 72 and 360 *drachmae* (IG. I³ 421, 422, and 430); Demosthenes's slaves varied from 300 to 600 (Dem. 27), and other texts mention 125 (Dem. 53.1), 180 (Xen. *Vect.* 4.4–16), 200 (Dem. 41.8) and 300 (Hyp. 3.2). At the very top of the scale, we hear of two for 3,000 (Dem. 59.29), and Xenophon gives a range of 50 to 1,000 (*Mem.* 2.5.2). Athenians obviously felt they could put a value on what they were buying. The market was well organized: it took place on the first of the month, in a fixed place, with transactions agreed through open bidding or private negotiation.[107] There was a sales tax on slaves, and their prices were advertised on "whiteboards" (Hesychius. s.v. *en leukomasi*).[108] Deals included warranty clauses (Hyp. 3.15; Pl. *Leg.* 916a). We may infer, first, that slaves were so readily bought and sold that gang owners could treat them as a variable cost and adjust capacity to demand and, second, that the capital value of a slave took account of expected earning power so that returns on investment were the same for very good (expensive) slaves as for deservedly cheaper ones.

The high ratio of slaves to citizens can be attributed to the demands of agriculture or military service on smallholders, combined with the mentality among citizens that associated paid employment with humiliation.[109] The

---

[104] The idea that slave numbers grew after Solon's reforms to debt bondage is not compatible with recent evidence: debtors still worked for their creditors, though this was not deemed to be slavery, so Solon's decrees could have had little impact on the demand for slave labor—Harris (2002b).

[105] Ferguson (2011) 130.

[106] Rihll (1993) 94–105; Lewis (forthcoming).

[107] First of the month: Ar. *Vesp.* 169–71 plus schol; schol to Ar. *Eq.* 43; in a fixed place: Harpocration s.v. *kukloi*; Poll. 7.1, Men. Sik. 315; auction: fr. 273; Ar. Fr. 339; private negotiation: Theophr. *Char.* 17.6.

[108] A grant of *ateleia* (tax immunity) to a merchant in Cyzicus at the end of the sixth century (SIG³4) explicitly excluded this tax.

[109] Cohen (2000) 141–42.

ratio seems to have risen from just over 2:1 to more than 5:1 during the classical period, and it is hard to imagine this could be accounted for by an increase in domestic duties or personal services. Silver mining could not have accounted for a very large part of the increase, agriculture would not have needed more labor, and there was little advance in further processing of farm produce, so much of this rapid growth must have come from Athenians' desire for manufactured goods. The city had the wealth to acquire the necessary additional labor input, and the growth in slave numbers in classical times almost certainly marked a rise in manufacturing.

There has been some debate among economic historians about whether slavery depressed wage rates for the free.[110] Finley's observation that wage-earners do not seem to have objected to competition from slaves is true, but rather than indicating an uncommercial approach, it merely shows that they were seldom in competition with each other.[111] Though they only undertook paid labor if there was no alternative, and even then would avoid committing themselves for very long, the employment of free men offered several advantages.[112] They could be engaged for exactly the period needed without a contract with their owner or any maintenance obligations, and they were, by definition, willing workers who would not run away. In general, when deciding whether to employ slaves or freemen, the Athenians seem to have taken the sensible option. If a permanent, year-round establishment was needed, they used slaves. If not, they kept their labor costs variable by leasing slaves or by the casual employment of freemen. In public works, there may have been direct competition, but the official philosophy of paying all workers the same rate simply presented free men (if they were good enough to get hired) with a temporary and respectable opportunity they could take or leave according to their circumstances.

It is important to distinguish three quite different manufacturing roles for slaves: an extension of domestic duties in a household of modest means; a member of a gang of slaves, usually but not necessarily co-located in a workshop; and the foreman charged with day-to-day management of a gang. In terms of desirability, the worst lifestyle would fall to a slave in a mine, where the labor was hard, the working conditions appalling, and life expectancy short, but many large workshops were probably little better. To work at a craft, often beside your master, would have been vastly preferable. Running a business on behalf of the owners and being able to keep profits after the *apophora* was best of all, especially as it offered the prospect of manumission.

---

[110] Oertel (1925); Erb (1937–1938).
[111] Finley (1973) 79–80.
[112] Cohen (2002) 142.

The largest contingent of the slave population was probably *domestic* slaves, although this is to draw a sharper distinction between domestic and industrial slaves than the Athenians did.[113] They certainly outnumbered mining slaves, even though the latter have been estimated at as many as 30,000.[114] Rich Athenians might have had as many as 50 slaves, and many might have owned a dozen or more.[115] Aristotle's friend Mnason was said to have 1,000 (Athen. 6.264d). Apparently a very poor man could not afford a slave (Lys. 24.6; Arist. *Pol.* 1252b12), but it is likely that only very few citizens were in this position. Lysias elsewhere contradicts himself by saying "everyone" has a slave (5.5), and Demosthenes expects all dicasts (jurors) to have one (45.86). Aristotle defines the Athenian nuclear family as "a man, his wife and their slave" (*Pol.* 1252a–b). Not known to have been especially rich himself, he still seems to have had at least five male slaves and seven female ones; Theophrastus had nine, Stration seven, and Lycon 13 (Diog. Laert. 5.11–16). All Aristophanes's peasants have at least two slaves (*Nub.* Strepsiades; *Pax*: Trygaeus), and some have three (*Pax*: Choristes; *Eccl.* Chremes; *Plut.* Chremyles) or four (*Ach.* Dicaeopolis; *Eq.*: Demos). The rich have up to eight on display and possibly more offstage (*Vesp.* Bdelykleon; *Ran.* Pluto). While dedicated slaves provided all the labor in mining and in large workshops, the contribution of domestic slaves to small-scale craft production should not be underestimated. In Homer and Hesiod, practicing a craft for a living was the province of serfs and a way for them to achieve independence from working for a master, and from the earliest times slaves almost certainly did much of the work inside the *oikos* that later became the production of goods for sale. By the classical period, it is safe to assume that any slave-owning *oikos* making goods for market would have employed its slaves in production, perhaps working alongside the master when he was around and continuing on their own or with other family members when he was at court, attending a play, or otherwise engaged.

The segments these domestic-craft slaves worked in reflected the occupations of their owners. Their ability to deputize for an absent master would have been lower in crafts where the master had a special skill that was sought out—custom shoemaking or decorating pots, for example. Here the slave's work would have been looking after the workplace, acquiring and preparing raw materials, and perhaps selling the output. In other cases, it might be the slave who possessed a rare skill and did most of the work, and in some small workshops, the master might have contributed nothing at all to the production effort. Sometimes individual slaves would be sent off to bring in an income for the *oikos* on their own: a charcoal-burner slave in Menander refers

---

[113] French (1964) 156; note that Demosthenes (27.24) describes the manufacturing slaves he inherited as having been left to him "in the house."
[114] Lauffer (1956) 916.
[115] French (1964) 139.

specifically to his *apophora* (Men. *Epitrep.* 380). Female slaves were occasionally employed in workshops but more usually in the home, and often making clothes.[116] Few households could afford not to have their slaves doing something useful, and clothing and simple pottery were obvious outlets.

More visible, but not necessarily larger in overall output, were the *gangs of slaves* owned primarily for their manufacturing capability. The suggestion by those keen to trivialize Athenian economic competence that a business should be considered insignificant because it was operated by slaves "abrogates plain meaning."[117] A slave workforce managed by slaves or recently freed men was the normal system for dedicated workshops. In addition to the fact that few citizens would enter long-term employment arrangements, slaves had advantages as employees. They were exempt from political and military duties and had no option but to report for work each day. They had to concentrate on their work, as there was nothing else that would provide security for themselves and their families. Some could be motivated by expectations, others at least by fear. Slaves were more reliable than citizens for confidential matters, not least because they could be tortured. They showed little respect for citizens unless it suited their master, and might be prosecuted for *hubris* as a result (Dem. 21.47). On the other hand, as we saw in the analysis of Demosthenes's investments, they represented a capital outlay and their maintenance was a fixed expense to the enterprise, independent of their productivity. Death, disease, and debility were costly risks. Webster calculates that it would only take about a year working at a craft to buy freedom at the average price of 174 *drachmae* for a slave.[118] He bases this calculation on the *drachma* per day slaves earned building the Erectheion and assumes slaves gave one obol to their master, spent two on food, and saved three. This almost certainly understates the slaves' cost of living (what about clothing? family members?) and might understate the *apophora*. It is more likely that many simple slave craftsmen could not buy their freedom at all.

The industrial slaves most likely to achieve wealth and freedom through manufacturing were gang *supervisors* or foremen. In theory, slaves in Athens had no rights at all: they could not own anything without their master's consent, and they had no legal protection against ill treatment. Yet, as we saw in Chapter 1, these limitations do not seem to have prevented them from carrying out considerable business activity; in Cohen's words, "legal adaptation surmounted such incapacity."[119] Owners of large businesses without the time, inclination, or knowledge to carry out day-to-day management became very dependent on slaves or former slaves. Demosthenes's factories were run by

---

[116] An alternative occupation was that of prostitute, with the owner as pimp.
[117] The suggestion is Millett's (1991) 310 n. 40; contradicted by Cohen (2000) 140.
[118] Webster (1973) 46–47.
[119] Cohen (forthcoming) 9.

*apeleutheroi* or freed slaves (27.19); Timarchos's team of shoemakers had a slave as leader, or *hegemon ergasteriou* (Aeschin. 1.97); the slave Midas managed Athenogenes's perfumery works (Hyp. 3). It had become a common way of doing business.[120] Slaves would save the profits they made and eventually use them to buy their freedom. This was an attractive system for the capitalist too; the slave took the risk on the business and the owner received a steady income without personal effort, followed by the possibility of a capital sum on manumission and sometimes a willingness on the part of the freed slave to continue to work in the same enterprise.[121] The system led to a proliferation of business enterprises, as freed slaves left their masters and went into business on their own account and the cycle started again. The main risk to the owner was that the foreman was given so much discretion he might abuse the owner's trust. Moschion took advantage of his master Comon (Dem. 48.14–15), and Cittus and his accomplices were accused of appropriating the enormous sum of six talents from their masters (Isoc. 17.11–12).

Xenophon approved of making your slaves rich; it made them less liable to defraud their master (*Oec.* 7.14.7). Demosthenes provides many examples of rich slaves in service businesses, including Pasion, who ran a bank for his owners, then started his own (36.43–48); Xenon, Euphron, Euphrainus, and Callistratus, who ran Pasion's bank under a lease (36.43); and Phormion, who took over the bank (36.4) and accumulated enough wealth to make large maritime loans (49.3). Lampis owned and operated a commercial firm that made loans, received payments for others, exported grain, and made a legal deposition (34.5–10); Zenothemis too seems to have done well out of maritime cargoes and litigation (32.4–9). As today, riches seem to have been easier to come by in banking than in manufacturing: "If Pasion had been bought by a skilled artisan, he would not be nearly so rich" (Dem. 45.71–72). The slaves running workshops might achieve eventual freedom but rarely the same conspicuous wealth.

Some of these slaves lived in their own homes (*choris oikountes*), including, it seems Lampis, Aristarchus, Timarchus's shoemakers, Midas, and the charcoal-gathering slave in Menander.[122] Scholars have taken this as evidence that they had been freed, but there is no evidence of manumission and it would have suited masters to allow slaves who could make a living independently to set up on their own without freeing them.[123] In this way they had a continuing obligation to the owner, who could still motivate them with the promise of freedom and control them by keeping their property. The slave

---

[120] Cohen (2002) 103.

[121] The notion that this was a requirement is probably wrong (Cohen (2000) 142).

[122] Lampis: Dem. 34.37; Aristarchus: Pritchett (1953) stele 6.21, 31–46; shoemakers: Aesch. 1.97; Midas: Hyp. 3; slave: Men. *Epitrep.* 378–80.

[123] Davies (1981) 41–49; Todd (1993) 192–94; Cohen (2002) 130–54.

could operate more freely, and the master could keep the net income without worrying about maintaining the slave and his dependents. It was the *apophora* system without the middleman.

While slaves who enjoyed these positions of responsibility and the income and chance of freedom they brought are well documented, they would have formed only a tiny fraction of the slaves engaged in manufacturing. From the names we have of slaves who enjoyed such arrangements, it appears that these privileges and opportunities were chiefly or only available to Greek-born slaves rather than barbarians, who were in any case more likely to have been put to work in fields, mines, and brothels. By far the majority of slaves in manufacturing, Greek or not, would have been engaged in basic laboring tasks, either on the shop floor of large industrial operations or assisting their masters in crafts such as shoe-making, pottery, or carpentry.

\* \* \*

This analysis of the propensity of different social groups to participate in manufacturing is a first step in a challenge that no one has yet seen fit to take up: estimating how many people of each class were engaged in manufacturing and on what basis. Data limitations are daunting, but a tentative illustration of how it might be approached is offered in the Appendix.

# Coda

Chapter One drew attention to the concerns of the great Moses Finley and his many followers about the wisdom of applying modern economic concepts to societies whose value systems and conceptual frameworks differed from our own as much as classical Athens's clearly did. The analyses that followed ignored this stricture, not least on its faulty logic. It is difficult to see how one can hope to develop a good understanding of a society different from one's own if one denies the relevance of some of the most powerful tools we have for understanding how societies work. It is especially problematic when dealing with occupations that dominated the lives of many Athenian residents and affected them all through the quality and cost of their output and their alignment or otherwise with status systems. Can we really believe that, when it came to the fundamental human challenge of making a living, Athenians behaved irrationally? Can this be what a great historian really meant?

Finley's famous passage about M. Jourdain unwittingly speaking prose seems to deduce the absence of what we would consider commercially rational behavior from the absence of a language to talk about it, an obvious non sequitur even if the premise were true.[1] But what are we to make of his addendum to the second edition of his most famous work, in which he says economic models are "the only way to advance our understanding of the ancient economy"?[2] He singles out for praise the work of Hopkins and Pekary on Roman trade and seems unconcerned that they use quite different algorithms and draw opposing conclusions.[3] He borrows from socioeconomic geographers to define what he means by a model: "a simplified structure of reality which presents supposedly significant relationships in a general form...allowing fundamental aspects of reality to appear."[4] The competitive advantage framework might claim to meet this definition. It defines relationships between commercial entities in terms of their relative position in regard to the components of profitability, based on elementary supply economics. It has been used here to explain the size of workshops

---

[1] Finley (1973) 23, quoted in Chapter 1.3.1, with evidence against Finley's premise.
[2] Finley (1973) 2nd ed. 182.
[3] Hopkins (1980); Pekary (1981).
[4] Chorley and Haggett (1968) 22.

where we know them, to suggest their likely size where we do not, and to support hypotheses about the nature and extent of industry participation among different status groups. Unlike the case of Roman trade, there is no question of which variables to include in the analysis; the only ones that matter in this framework are those that determine ease of entry, value for customers, and the unit costs of production. It is quite possible Finley would have embraced the application of these particular microeconomic principles and appreciated their value in making sense of the confused jumble of enterprise forms we find in classical Athens. He would surely have appreciated the light they shed on matters such as slave deployment and asset valuation, where the analysis shows the Athenian approach differed importantly from one driven by perfect economic rationality (though not so much from our own).

Although I have tried to avoid gratuitous attacks on Finleyan orthodoxy, the industry analyses offer little to support a strict interpretation of the Embeddedness Paradigm. To the contrary, the following propositions have been tested explicitly or implicitly and seem to have stood up to scrutiny:

1. The nature of manufacturing industry in classical Athens was determined by supply technology and demand factors. This applies both to the sequence in which products started to be manufactured for sale to third parties in ancient Greece and to the structure of industries in classical Athens.
2. The small size of typical enterprises was consistent with profit-maximizing strategies.
3. The intelligentsia's respect for the contemplative life and contempt for all manifestations of commerce and industry did not prevent people at all levels of society from participating in manufacturing with commitment, enthusiasm, and some success.
4. The participation of different segments of the population in manufacturing reflected rational choices based on the differing economic characteristics of the product segments and their ability to meet different economic needs.
5. When Athenians engaged in commercial activity, they made decisions that were for the most part (but not always) consistent with today's understanding of good (rational, profit-maximizing) business practice.

The conclusions formed are all subject to falsification, but any claim they might make to being the most probable interpretation of events must depend on the logical status of the principles they rest on. If they can explain commercial dynamics in societies as different as classical Athens and the contemporary developed world, they would seem to be more than contingent truths depending on specific observations. In fact, they are true by definition: the Law of Supply and Demand can be presented as $P = f(S, D)$, competitive advantage means that $\pi -$ Cost of capital $= \Sigma$ (Aprice + Acost + Aassets), and the Capital Asset Pricing Model of risk-related investment returns is expressed as $E(Ri) = Rf + \beta i\ (E(Rm - Rf))$.[5] Nevertheless, the reluctance of many historians to work with these tools suggests that the universality of their application is not self-evidently true. And, let's be frank, they do not always apply with full force at once—hence the opportunities for arbitrage in investment markets and the ability of companies in irredeemably weak competitive positions to make excellent profits for short periods, especially with aggressive leadership. Over time, however, the rules tend to apply and outcomes to reflect them. Tautologies are not usually subject to such qualification. Even if economics is truly "a subset of the socio-biology of one species of the primates," we cannot conclude that these laws are simply part of some people's biological makeup.[6] They describe what happens when we undertake business in a competitive setting, irrespective of our genetic predispositions. Perhaps the rules are what Ayer called "necessary truths...independent of experience in that they do not owe their validity to empirical verification," or, less likely, instances of Kant's synthetic a priori.[7] If we found them not to apply, we would be more likely to question our observations than the rules' validity.[8] Whatever their logical status, predictions derived from these rules are readily falsifiable and can be tested against any relevant evidence. It is possible that new evidence will be found to contradict the hypotheses put forward here about how certain industries worked or to show that industry formation did not always reflect supply and demand conditions or that many investors in classical times had a quite different preference set from both Demosthenes and us.

This book has focused on transactions and outcomes, not on the intent behind those transactions. In all the analyses, care has been taken to emphasize that there is no suggestion that classical Athenians did—or even could—describe their activities in the terms used here. It is conceivable, though rather unlikely, that these transactions and outcomes have the appearance of commercial rationality while in fact being motivated entirely by other considerations. A more reasonable conclusion is that when making commercial decisions, humans tend to operate in consistent and predictable ways across

---

[5] P—price; S—supply; D—demand; $\pi$—profitability; Ax—the financial value of an advantage against the marginal competitor in element x; $E(Ri)$—the return on the value of enterprise i; Rm—the market rate of return; Rf—the risk-free rate of return; $\beta i$—a measure of the volatility of the value of enterprise i relative to that of other enterprises.

[6] Alfred Marshall, quoted in Henderson (1981).

[7] Ayer (1971) 109–11; Kant (1968) 50.

[8] Ayer (1971) 102–3; see also Popper (1959).

cultures and eras, and that these ways are captured under the general rubric of microeconomics. Whether or not these laws were understood or articulated by the actors, human behavior converged toward conformity with them. Irrespective of conscious motivation by ancient agents, elementary economic principles are heuristically effective and a source of important historical insight. A leading article in *The Economist* observed that "economics is less a slavish creed than a prism through which to understand the world."[9] I have tried to show that this prism is an especially revealing one that deserves to be more widely used by historians.

Of course Finley was correct to assert that Athenian behavior was not invariably profit-maximizing. Previous chapters have identified many instances in which it was not. Demosthenes seems to have placed a higher value on the benefits of slave ownership than a simple financial calculation would suggest. He also saw working capital as a store of value rather than a cost of investing. Finds of large textile operations in Athens and at Olynthus, and the suggestion by a few experts that some ancient potteries might have contained more slaves than we have shown to be economically optimal, suggest that in at least some areas the Athenians made choices different from the ones that pure profit-maximization would prompt. The error is to conclude that this makes them so different from modern society that they cannot be understood in our terms. Certainly some objectives were sometimes more important to some people than immediate financial gain. These choices are not irrational; they are logical ways of achieving certain objectives and simply show that in Athens, as in all other societies, including ours, commercial motivation was often tempered by other goals. It has been called the economic rationality of the *oikos*, not the bourse, but it is no less rational for that. As Xenophon (*Oec.* 6.4) and Marshall both recognized, economic rationality can and does reflect a conception of what is useful that embraces more than short-term profit-maximization.[10] Economic analysis is a powerful device for revealing what Athenians considered useful.

Our conclusions sit more easily with words of the philosophers and the orators, the latter mostly serious men for whom their own and their clients' business affairs were the stuff of life. They chime with the hordes of characters Aristophanes presents as filled with commercial intent. While Plato and Aristotle argued that a state would be better off without commerce and industry, they knew that was impossible and so argued that economic activity needed managing in new ways. Finley took their dreams literally and painted

---

[9] *The Economist* newspaper, July 18, 2009.
[10] Marshall (1959) 1.

the ancient economy as the sort of non-economy that goes with the ideal polity. In the realm of Finley's imagination no philosophers' intervention would have been necessary: why fear the moral impact of an exchange culture based on *philia*? Certainly some of the factors he emphasized must have affected how manufacturing enterprise was conducted, including status restrictions on who could conduct certain transactions, democratically enforced philanthropy, a different sense of the obligations of friendship, elitist contempt for industry, the absence of some commercial infrastructure, limited evidence of an ability to conceptualize economics, and the fact that business transactions were open to scrutiny in a very public forum. From these social differences, Finley and others deduced that economic behavior must have been recognizably different from that in later societies, especially our own; our analyses have shown that the empirical case for this has not been established. Finley notes what the ancients said; we have examined what they did, and found that his world coexisted with the immutable laws of economics and that his insights serve principally to prove that economic principles operate in even the most unlikely social milieux. More generally, we would put the onus of proof back where it belongs and challenge those who claim economic analysis has no place in the study of certain societies and eras to identify any non–centrally directed societies in history where the simple microeconomic principles enunciated here can be shown to be inapplicable or uninformative.

In terms of historiography, we seem to have come full circle. The original modernist-primitivist debate centered on whether or not there were certain economic laws that led to the emergence of particular types of commercial activity at different periods of history. Menger sought the "exact laws" that could inform historical analysis.[11] Bucher, Weber, Polanyi, and Finley in their different ways also sought economic rules that explained social development. The rules they were looking for were grand laws of social behavior and macroeconomic settings that could explain or describe discontinuities in economic history. The rules we have applied deal with individual decision-makers and the microeconomics of individual decisions, and we have found them to display a remarkable continuity in their relevance to how commercial businesses actually work. The perspective they provide is, perhaps surprisingly, quite compatible with the views of some of the historians who most influenced Finley. They bear out Weber's suggestion that there were real markets in slaves and land, and the distinction made here between industry and craft echoes his analysis of the twofold role of slaves in manufacturing.[12] Polanyi's concern that markets would destroy the livelihood of smallholders also seems to offer an accurate assessment of the typical effect of technical advances on industry

---

[11] Menger (1985) 38.
[12] Weber (1891).

economics. The Athenian economy was in a primitive state compared with the world Bucher knew, but we have shown that this was not attributable to the institutional framework of the *oikos* so much as to the state of technology and its impact on the economics of production: technology limitations meant that a major source of competitive advantage (low unit costs resulting from large-volume production and high asset utilization) was scarcely to be found anywhere before the Industrial Revolution; large-scale mechanization changed this and provided the basis for more industries to become concentrated as some competitors became newly advantaged.

Perhaps the most important insight generated by the analysis is the apparent relationship between the availability of certain opportunities for earning an income and the social structures it facilitated. Limited technology resulted in abundant opportunities for the lone craftsman, and it was possible to earn at least part of one's income from manufacturing in a way that was compatible, both in dignity and time-requirements, with being an active participant in a democracy of nominal equals. Each society at a point in time will provide different opportunities to small and unsophisticated competitors according to the state of technical development. Manufacturing in classical Athens can be characterized by the extent to which one could earn a good income while still attending to civic duties, or a rich household could open and close a large slave workshop on a seasonal basis without being disadvantaged against dedicated incumbents. The evolution of competitive advantage means that opportunities to do the same in any manufacturing business today are vanishingly few. This makes for a curious inversion of the Embeddedness Paradigm; rather than society determining the nature of the economy, it was the undeveloped nature of the micro economy that enabled the Athenian lifestyle and values.

No one should treat the analyses here as definitive. It should be possible to refine them without discovering new primary sources by, for example, more fully testing the propositions that among sole operators differentiated crafts offered better incomes than undifferentiated ones and that only businesses with entry barriers lent themselves to commercial investment. It may also be possible to quantify how far the inherent profitability of certain segments was reflected in the price of dedicated slaves. The information gathered here on labor input for various goods can be improved and related more thoroughly to what is known about the cost of labor, selling prices, and consumption volumes, so as to build a fuller financial profile of the manufacture and sale of certain products. The demographic analysis in Chapter 9 and the Appendix takes a representative population for two centuries and adduces evidence drawn from the whole period; more granular analysis might reveal how the structure of certain industries and the demographics of participation evolved.

Beyond the potential to use this approach to developing more and better insights about ancient Athens, similar analyses of other places and times might address some intriguing questions, for example:

- The relation between different forms of government and income opportunities for citizens.
- The structure and conduct of manufacturing in highly commercial societies such as 11th-century Venice, Renaissance Florence, and Reformation Holland.
- How manufacturing industry was structured in radically different advanced cultures, such as the Moghul, Han, Incan, Persian, Ottoman, etc., both overall and in relation to specific industries.
- Case studies from different periods and societies of the emergence and development of particular industries in the context of competitive supply and demand factors.
- How changes in competitive advantage and industry structure resulting from the Industrial Revolution affected social and political institutions.
- How colonization affected competitive advantage and industry structure in particular industries and how this in turn affected colonization policies.

I should dearly like to see the results.

# ATHENIAN CURRENCY

1 talent = 60 minae
1 mina = 100 drachmae
1 drachma = 6 obols

**Indicative values:**

Subsistence (single person): 150–200 *drachmae* p.a.
Standard wage on public projects: 1 *drachma*/day
Wealth: top 5% – over 1 talent.
Liturgiasts (over 3 talents) – top 1%

*Note: Many sophisticated attempts have been made to restate Athenian values in today's currencies, but they quickly become irrelevant with inflation and exchange rate movements. These values are provided in order to give a sense of relative wealth and purchasing power as they mattered to Athenians of the time.*

# APPENDIX

# QUANTIFYING MANUFACTURING PARTICIPATION

Quantifying the level of participation by different status groups in different manufacturing segments is challenging, given data limitations. It is attempted here for two reasons: first, to set out a methodology that might encourage better-informed historians and subject experts to contribute their expertise to the task (there is certainly more quantifiable material available than this book has been able to capture) and second, to demonstrate that, even on apparently conservative assumptions, manufacturing played a vital role in the lives of most Athenian residents. Recognizing the sheer quantity of human effort devoted to manufacturing and its importance as a source of subsistence for so many Athenians provides a rather different perspective on the city than the conventional one of assemblies, law courts, temples, festivals, theater, and lots of philosophizing. Even the vendors in Aristophanes's Agora are only the final stage in what was often a dirty, dangerous, and laborious value chain. A true depiction of most of the city would owe more to Hieronymus Bosch than to Raphael. The very substantial size of the manufacturing sector that resulted from the growth in population, wealth, new products, and expectations of increasing living standards becomes evident as soon as we start to quantify it.

The two analytical approaches outlined here depend on answers to two very different questions:

- *Supply analysis* asks what proportion of Athenian income needs was likely to have been earned through manufacturing. This can be approached at a macro level by estimating living standards for different status groups and the proportion accounted for by other sources, such as farm surpluses, state pay, and distributions or trading activity. Differentiating manufacturing income from earnings from other commercial activities is tricky, but we know that Athens cannot have been a nation of shopkeepers reselling imported goods: we have far too much archaeological and textual evidence of local manufacture for that, and besides, many of the products covered in previous chapters are expensive to transport relative to their value, so if they were being imported in volume, it would have been an open invitation to local craftsmen to make a local product

that could be sold profitably at much less than the landed price of an import. We must also include manufacture for home consumption; applying labor to replace external purchases is economically equivalent to applying labor to be able to afford them.
- **Demand analysis** calculates how much labor was required to make the goods Athenians consumed or exported, less what they imported. Here again, the examples show my best estimates but are put forward principally in the hope that subject experts will take the time and trouble to improve on them.

## A.1 Supply Analysis

Supply analysis can be applied at different levels of detail, and its accuracy improves with data segmentation. This illustration of the methodology is at the gross level of half a dozen population groups and a single point in time (around the middle of the fourth century, where much of the data come from). For greater accuracy, the population should be divided into as many segments as can be identified as having different propensities to participate in manufacturing, and data should be analyzed as a time series, since the relative importance of different sectors and the way in which they were configured evolves over time, as might the level of engagement of different population groups.

There is considerable debate about the size of Athens's population during the fifth and fourth centuries. Numbers undoubtedly changed considerably at every level. Pericles's Law of 451 restricting the citizenship to those whose parents were both of citizen status almost certainly reduced the numbers of citizens, and war and plague would have reduced them further. Detailed analysis of sources including representative assemblies, public positions, the numbers involved in military campaigns, and miscellaneous textual references suggest that there might have been up to 60,000 adult male citizens at the start of the period, at least 25,000 throughout, and about 30,000 living in Attica in the second half of the fourth century, with a few more overseas.[1] It is also useful to distinguish those citizens who had significant wealth and those who lacked land, as both factors influenced participation in manufacturing. Determining how many citizens might be rich enough to invest in manufacturing is far from simple. Ober points out that Greek writers had no clear concept of a middle class, but typically speak of the "wealthy" and the "poor." This distinguishes the leisure class from those who had to work for a living, but says nothing about the relative size of each group.[2] Harris suggests about 1,200 people conducted liturgies in the fourth century and

---

[1] Hansen (1986) 65–69; Moreno (2007) 28–31.
[2] Ober (1989) 27–28.

a slightly larger group paid the *eisphora*—a form of wealth tax.[3] Davies argues that the wealth needed for a liturgy was three to four talents and that not more than 300 or 400 citizens would qualify at any one time. He goes on to suggest that the number with net assets of a talent or more was probably around 1,200 and certainly not more than 2,000.[4] A talent was more than enough to be able to invest in or lend against industrial slaves, especially as families with this level of wealth are likely to have been able to feed their household from their own farms, perhaps even selling a seasonal surplus or two. A person who owned property assessed at 2,500 drachmae (a little over 40 percent of a talent) would probably have had land, housing, and four or five slaves.[5] Putting these to work would bring in income of 300 to 400 *drachmae* a year—subsistence income for a whole family. Businesses using local raw materials that could be obtained readily and inexpensively would not have to hold a great deal of inventory unless they chose to, so total investment would not be much greater than the cost of the slaves. It seems reasonable to conclude that the *oikoi* of around 5,000 citizen families had enough funds to invest in gangs of up to half a dozen slaves making product from inexpensive raw materials, and perhaps half that number could afford to own larger workshops and carry quantities of expensive inventory.

The number of citizen-status women might have been slightly higher despite the hazards of childbirth, as they were less often killed in war, and we hear of a large number of widows. Differences in age at marriage and life expectancy meant many households were run by women who had once been widowed, though some married again. As males quickly created a new citizen *oikos* when they came of age and females did not, several households must have contained more than one adult female of citizen status, and the population numbers used here assume females of citizen households outnumbered males by 20 percent.

As a cosmopolitan city with many overseas interests and a leading trading port, Athens was home to many foreigners. Writers of the time spoke highly of the contribution these metics made to the economy, but we have little to go on in terms of numbers. Thucydides (2.31.2) says there were over 3,000 of them by 431 BCE, and the numbers clearly increased in the fourth century. A census at the end of the fourth century gives 10,000, but it might have been higher earlier; some scholars suggest it had declined by as much as 30–40 percent.[6] Including freed slaves, who also had metic status, the number might have been closer to 20,000 adult males for much of the period. Again, we have no numbers for metic women. It seems the majority of immigrants were men, and not all aspiring craftsmen and traders would have brought a spouse with them when they first came to Athens,

---

[3] Harris (1995) 18–19.
[4] Davies (1981) 6–35.
[5] Markle (1985) 295.
[6] Ctesicles (apud Athen. 6.272c); Austin and Vidal-Naquet (1977) 100–101; Harris (2002a); Hansen (1991).

but there is evidence for women arriving as metics, and, despite their inability to marry citizens, some immigrant males would have found a status-compatible wife in the city, as would a number of the freed slaves who had lived longer in Athens.[7] A 3:2 male to female ratio is assumed for immigrant metics and for freed slaves; the numbers would have tended to converge as metic families became established. We have no figures at all for "aliens" who resided in Athens and did not have metic status. As they were not allowed to do business for long, their numbers would only be relevant to manufacturing if they were so numerous as to have an important impact on consumption, which is very unlikely.

Slaves made up by far the largest proportion of residents. A tradition that there were 400,000 slaves at the time almost certainly derives from an arithmetical error by the historian Ctesicles (FHG 245.1), but scholars generally estimate there were between 80,000 and 120,000 in the fifth century and possibly over 200,000 by the end of the fourth, by which time they were being imported at the rate of 3,000 a year.[8] We do not know the proportion of male and female slaves; males seem to have made up the majority of those imported, but numbers would have tended to converge as they bred and the slave population grew. We again assume a male to female ratio of 3:2.

For our purposes, precision is not essential, though it is useful to understand the order of magnitude and relative size of different status groups. The data available are too scanty to differentiate periods easily, so the demographic analysis here uses a "representative" population as shown in Table A1.

First we consider the likely proportion of male residents engaged in manufacturing on a full- or part-time basis. To estimate the number of *citizen investors* in manufacturing we have little to go on but inference from a handful of known examples. The number of investors involved is limited to the number of manufacturing slave gangs. We know of around half a dozen, mainly from lawsuits, and the fact that the *apophora* system continued to thrive suggests there were rather more arrangements that went smoothly. Previous chapters have identified other segments in which gangs were likely to have been able to operate successfully (summarized in Table 9.1), but we do not know how many gangs there were in any one segment. Some industries like shoemaking and bronze armor were probably split between a premium segment served by individual craftsmen and slave gangs owned by citizens like Timarchus (Aesch. 1.97) and Leocrates (Lyc. *Leoc.* 58). If there were fewer than 100 gangs large enough for industrial investment, then a surprisingly high percentage ended up in court. If there were more than 1,000 and the average size was anything like Demosthenes's factories, we might have to revise our estimates of slave numbers. As it seems unlikely that there could have

---

[7] As in South (but not North) America in more recent times, slaves were able to buy their freedom (Ferguson (2011) 132–36).

[8] Sargent (1925); Gomme (1933); Finley (1952) 57; Isager and Hansen (1975) 32–33, 5; Hansen (1986) 29; Jameson (2002).

TABLE A1  **Representative Population Figures**

| Social Group | Adult Males | Adult Females[a] | Total |
|---|---|---|---|
| Investor class citizens | 5,000 | 6,000 | 11,000 |
| Landless citizens | 5,000 | 6,000 | 11,000 |
| Other citizens | 20,000 | 24,000 | 44,000 |
| Immigrant metics | 15,000 | 10,000 | 25,000 |
| Freed slaves | 5,000 | 4,000 | 9,000 |
| Slaves | 90,000 | 60,000 | 150,000 |
| **Total residents** | **140,000** | **110,000** | **250,000** |

[a] All numbers for females are very uncertain and derived from an impression of the likely male to female ratio.

been less than 100 or more than 1,000 such investment opportunities, 500 seems a reasonable estimate.

Some gangs were owned by metics, such as Pasion's shield factory (Dem. 36.11), and some investors would have owned multiple slave gangs or workshops. Some of the gangs would be the property of widows rather than citizens. A preliminary estimate might be that the *oikoi* of 200 citizens and 200 widows and a handful of metics had investments in around 500 manufacturing operations between them. This is admittedly vague, but fortunately the numbers are certain to be small in relation to the total population.

Estimating the level of citizen participation in production involves assessing how many citizens were sufficiently well-off to pursue a rounded lifestyle without working for it, how many needed to ensure additional income, and how many simply had to work as hard as they could in order to make ends meet. *Citizens without land* had few choices to increase their income in peacetime other than through manufacturing, since many of the more intimate forms of personal service were carried out by slaves and trading required some capital—or at least assets to borrow against. Some might have relied on state payments and irregular fees for political duties or on working for other citizens for brief periods at harvest time, but it is likely that manufacturing constituted at least a source of supplementary income for most of them and the livelihood of many. The need to provide wholly for the *oikos*, including basic food, the irregularity and unreliability of state pay, and the absence of alternatives, suggest 50 percent might be a conservative estimate for the engagement of citizens without land working full-time in manufacturing, and perhaps another 25 percent would have done some manufacturing on a less regular basis. Few *citizens with land* would have had been able to devote all their time to manufacturing, nor would they have needed to, as their land would provide some of their basic necessities, though if they were skilled at a craft they might still choose to dedicate themselves to it full-time and generate a much more adequate income. Only a few landed citizens would have earned much from selling a farm surplus, and they would have faced the same constraints as the landless with regard to acceptable alternatives for increasing the *oikos*'s income, which would make part-time manufacture attractive. Others would have been involved as a casual and seasonal supplement to other sources of income, with much of their output directed at home consumption and relying largely on their slaves. We might estimate only 5 percent of landed citizens were full-time manufacturers, leaving their farm to be worked and managed by other members of the household, while perhaps 50 percent were irregular participants.

All *metics* would have been earning a living, but we know many of them were involved in trade, making the percentage who were in manufacturing correspondingly smaller. On one account, 26 of 98 metics (26 percent) making dedications were active in craft or industry, and another interpretation of the same source identifies 24 manufacturing occupations out of 69 (35 percent).[9] Other epigraphy gives 39.9 percent of a metic group as craftsmen and 8.5 percent as industrial entrepreneurs, against 20.9 percent merchants.[10] One category is women (12.5 percent and otherwise unclassified), but we know many of them were craftspeople too. There is certainly some danger of misreading these figures, but they cannot be too far off.[11] Extrapolating them, we might estimate that at least 30 percent of immigrant metics were engaged in some form of manufacturing. For most of these craftsmen it was their reason to come to Athens, so they would have worked full-time.

The metic population also included *freed slaves*. This distinction between immigrants and freed slaves is an important one and is reflected in the illustration here, even though the numerical segmentation of the metic class into freed slaves and immigrants is little more than guesswork. We might expect a larger proportion of freed slaves to have had a manufacturing background than immigrants, as it was a major avenue to freedom, but not all would have; once freed, some would have become engaged in other activities and discontinued their manufacturing work or would have operated part-time or become a passive owner.

For reasons given earlier, it is likely that any foreigners resident in Athens who engaged in manufacturing would have become metics, so *aliens* can be omitted from supply figures, though they still contributed to domestic demand.

By far the majority of residents involved in manufacturing were *slaves*. They not only constituted the large gangs in industries, but each individual craft shop would have had one or more slaves supporting the master and sometimes taking over from him. Even houses with no master probably produced items made by slaves, at least for their own consumption. Very large households would put their slaves to work at manufacturing when they were in town and not required

---

[9] Lewis (1959) 368–80; 26 out of 98—Harris (2002a), App.1.88–97; 24 out of 69—Glotz (1926) 216–18.
[10] Gerhardt (1933).
[11] Davies (1981) 50.

on other tasks. For male slaves, the following estimates of time spent manufacturing are based on factors cited in Chapter 9.5: 20 percent of slaves were for mining, 60 percent domestic, and 20 percent industrial (employed as part of large gangs). Of the 60 percent domestic, perhaps one-third spent all their time making products for the household and for sale, or helping others to do so. (This allows for an average of one full-time manufacturing slave in around 60 percent of citizen households.)[12] Most of the remaining two-thirds of domestic slaves would spend at least some of the year making simple undifferentiated products.

Finer analysis would segment domestic slaves by size of household. In a one-slave *oikos*, the slave would have a number of other tasks, whereas with four slaves, two or three might be available to make goods full-time. Some wealthy citizens owned so many slaves that there would have been nothing else for them to do. Unless their workshop enjoyed a competitive advantage they would not bring in a great deal of income, but would at least contribute the cost of their own upkeep. There is a limit to how many assistants a recognized craftsman can practically use, so in houses where the master was making highly differentiated products for select customers and earning enough money to afford several slaves, he would probably put some of them to work on simpler clothing or pottery products. Larger households might have a number of female slaves making garments and male slaves making household items from ceramics, metal, or wood for most of the year, with other slaves being put to work making products for sale when they were not needed in the fields. For some slaves, making products for the *oikos* or for sale would be one of a range of tasks they carried out to bring in income, alongside personal services such as grooming and prostitution. Envisioning the daily schedule of domestic slaves according to household size will lead to more accurate conclusions.

Table A2 applies these estimates to Athens' mid-fourth-century male population by social group. Uncertainty about the population numbers is of minor importance, as it is the proportions and ratios that are of most interest. We can conceive a vital difference between a city in which, say, 70 percent of citizens were involved in manufacturing and one where the figure was 30 percent. Our understanding is not increased very much by resolving whether it was 70 percent of 25,000 or 35,000.[13] Similar considerations apply to the meaning of part-time; differences in capacity do not matter—a slave's working year was much longer than that of a citizen who observed his civic duties, but it is the proportion of time available for productive work that is of interest. Estimates of the proportion of full-time capacity applied by part-timers in each group are derived from the considerations in Chapter 9: investing took up very little time, and slaves whose

---

[12] One-third of 60 percent of 90,000 male slaves = 18,000 = 60 percent of 30,000 households.

[13] Provided consumption is calculated on the same population basis as supply, the results of demand and supply analysis will covary precisely and their integration will be unaffected.

TABLE A2  **Manufacturing Participation by Adult Males (c. 350 BCE)**

| Social Group | Adult Males | Estimated % Manufacturing Full-time | Number Full-time | Estimated % Manufacturing Part-time (Part-time % of FTE) | Number Part-time | Total Full-time Equivalent (% of total group) |
|---|---|---|---|---|---|---|
| Investor class citizens | 5,000 | — | — | 4 / 5 | 200 | 10 / 0.2% |
| Landless citizens | 5,000 | 50 | 2,500 | 25 / 30 | 1,250 | 2,875 / 57.5% |
| Other citizens | 20,000 | 5 | 1,000 | 50 / 30 | 10,000 | 4,000 / 20% |
| Immigrant metics | 15,000 | 30 | 4,500 | 0.33[a] / 5 | 50 | 4,502 / 30% |
| Freed slaves | 5,000 | 25 | 1,250 | 11[b] / 30 | 550 | 1,402 / 28% |
| Slaves | 90,000 | 60[c] | 54,000 | 32[d] / 10 | 28,800 | 56,880 / 63.2% |
| Total (%) | 140,000 | | 63,250 (45.2%) | | 40,850 (29.2%) | 69,749 (49.8%) |

[a] Owners (one in 300; ignored in capacity calculation).

[b] Includes 50 owners at 5% of capacity.

[c] Assumes one-third of the 60% of slaves that were "domestic" worked full-time at manufacturing (20% of total); added to the 20% of slaves that were "industrial" plus the 20% mining slaves gives 60% of all slaves.

[d] 80% of the remaining two-thirds of domestic slaves, who made up 40% of all slaves.

prime function was different would also have spent little time in manufacturing. For other groups, part-time operation is assumed to be 30 percent of full-time capacity.

No claim is made here that these numbers are especially accurate, and it will be disappointing if they do not lead a number of experts to suggest much better approximations and perhaps undertake more granular analysis. Nor should we expect startling revelations; conclusions should be consistent with our preconceptions, because they are based on the same information. Nevertheless, seeing qualitative impressions presented in a quantitative form can be thought-provoking, and Table A2 presents some points of interest, not the least of which is that almost three adult male residents in four, including more than half of all citizens outside the investor class, had at least some involvement in manufacturing. While this conclusion does not rest on any new data, it surely colors our picture of what life was like for many Athenians. Other points to note are:

1. Only a few rich citizens had any involvement, and that involvement was hands-off. It is consistent with written sources that manufacturing did not feature significantly in the life of the Athenian elite and that, where it did, it was a passive investment option.
2. The tension between the image of the citizen who considers himself superior to manual labor and the romantic vision of the citizen craftsman is partly elucidated by considering the landless and the landed separately.
3. It has always been assumed that manufacturing labor was predominantly provided by slaves, but attempts to quantify the extent of this predominance have been skimpy. On this account, slaves constitute 85 percent of full-time male manufacturing labor and over 70 percent of part-time:
    a. The full-time proportion is no surprise, as the only other full-time workers were poor (or highly skilled) citizens and a handful of metics. The 54,000 full-time manufacturing slaves are divided equally between industrial gangs, mining, and the home, with 18,000 in each. The number of domestic slaves working full-time in manufacturing can only have been much lower than 18,000 if we assume that the typical *oikos* could afford to leave many slaves with nothing to do (or would choose to do so if they could—a form of hubris that usually proves fatal in a slave society). It is likely that almost all the 10,000 or so citizens and metics engaged in crafts full-time used at least one slave to support them, in some cases perhaps two or even three. In larger households, slaves owned for status reasons or that came as part of a slave family would have had little to do; weaving

and spinning for women and perhaps pottery or carpentry for males would have kept them usefully and properly occupied under the supervision of the lady of the house. Whether or not manufacturing was the main motive behind increasing slave imports, it was certainly what many of the new arrivals must have ended up doing, and a sizable proportion might not have had anything else to keep them occupied.

b. The predominance of slaves among part-time manufacturers reflects the fact that few domestic slaves could be allowed to be idle, so manufacturing provided an outlet for most of them, if only for a short time each year. These slaves would have had other duties for some of the time, but few would have been occupied all day and all year round, and most are likely to have been given some textile, carpentry, ceramic, or simple metalwork jobs on occasion.

We have observed that *women* had a central role in various capacities in all types of manufacturing. The assumption that control of *investments* in manufacturing was equally split between men and women may understate the female share, but again the numbers are small. The proportion of females among the *rest of the citizen group* involved in industry was likely to have been higher than males; the women of most citizen households outside the investor class would have been engaged in manufacturing, or supervising slaves who were manufacturing, while their husbands performed other tasks—perhaps in the fields or in the navy or on other state duties. Widows might also have continued to run their late husbands' workshops. On the other hand, few citizen women would have worked full-time at manufacturing; the head of the household had other responsibilities. We might estimate that 70 percent of citizen women were engaged in some way, mainly for a third of their time.

Some *metic* women evidently worked full-time at manufacturing, some having moved to Athens specifically to do so and others earning as much as they could, perhaps while their husbands were busy trading. Forty-six metic women making dedications included 35 weavers and two shoemakers.[14] Many others probably made simple clothing and other items at home on a part-time basis, also estimated here at 33 percent. These estimates are especially uncertain, but the numbers do not really affect the overall picture very much. A few female *slaves* might have been imported specifically for their craft skills, though there is no firm evidence for it and in such a case they would probably have been employed

---

[14] Glotz (1926) 217, corrected by Meyer (2010); cf. Schaps (1979) 19. The figures cannot be extrapolated to suggest that 80 percent of all metic women were weavers or shoemakers; the dedications seem to have marked success in a legal contest (Meyer (2010)), and women with no commercial activity were less likely to be involved in such actions.

in the owner's domestic craft shop rather than as members of a workshop gang. A small house with limited culinary capability does not provide a great deal of housework to be done; there would be plenty of time for female slaves to weave and spin. Chapter 5 showed that in most houses, all the available female labor would be fully occupied trying to keep the household clothed. Some might have earned money for the *oikos* from prostitution, but might still have made clothes or helped in a pottery or carpentry shop at other times. A preliminary estimate is that one-third of all female slaves worked effectively full-time in manufacture and that all but a handful of the rest spent a quarter of their time on it. Clothing demand analysis (section 2.1 of this Appendix) suggests these figures are probably conservative. Table A3 quantifies these estimates.

This table again does no more than put numbers to our preconceptions. Relatively high part-time female participation rates among the citizen class reflect the woman's role in allocating the household's resources, including making the best use of slaves. A critical assumption is that all but 10 percent of slave women did at least some manufacturing, which seems consistent with the evidence and allows for a few to have been earning their keep solely through housekeeping work and personal services.

Table A4 compares full- and part-time participation rates for men and women.

Although on these assumptions a slightly higher proportion of women than men had some involvement in manufacturing (76 percent against 74 percent), more women worked at it part-time, so the proportion of their overall capacity engaged was lower (40 percent against 50 percent). While it is no surprise to find that over half of the available time of the slaves and almost half of that of landless citizens was taken up in manufacturing, it is interesting to note that, excluding the rich, between a fifth and a third of the working capacity of the other status segments was similarly engaged.

No attempt is made here to estimate the participation rates of adolescents and children. Some would have taken formal apprenticeships, and many would have learned trades less formally at home while carrying out other tasks. Many would have helped out, or been encouraged to think they were helping out, in the home *ergasterion*. Some would have found it an interesting, if sometimes dangerous, place to play. In terms of the overall demographics of manufacturing, though, only a few non-adults would have contributed very much to output or to family income.

The final step in the supply analysis is to define the types of manufacturing operation members of these population groups worked in. The considerations of status, opportunity, and economic necessity on which the preceding tables were based tell us nothing about whether the products they made were differentiated or undifferentiated, but do enable us to assign them to industry or craft activities. Table A5 shows manufacturing participation by social group and workshop type.

TABLE A3 **Manufacturing Participation by Adult Females (ca. 350 BCE)**

| Social Group of Spouse | Adult Females | Estimated % Manufacturing Full-time | Number Full-time | Estimated % Manufacturing Part-time (Part-time % of FTE) | Number Part-time | Total Full-time Equivalent (% of total group) |
|---|---|---|---|---|---|---|
| Investor class citizens | 6,000 | — | — | 3.3 / 5 | 200 | 10 / 0.2% |
| Landless citizens | 6,000 | 20 | 1,200 | 50 / 33.3% | 3,000 | 2,200 / 36.7% |
| Other citizens | 24,000 | 10 | 2,400 | 60 / 33.3% | 14,400 | 7,200 / 30.0% |
| Immigrant metics | 10,000 | 20 | 2000 | 33.3 / 33.3% | 3,333 | 3,111 / 31.1% |
| Freed slaves | 4,000 | — | — | 33.3 / 33.3% | 1,333 | 444 / 11.1% |
| Slaves | 60,000 | 33 | 20,000 | 57.0 / 33.3% | 34,200 | 31,400 / 52.3% |
| Total | 110,000 | | 25,600 (23.3%) | | 58,267 (53.0%) | 44,336 (40.3%) |

TABLE A4  **Manufacturing Participation by All Adults (c. 350 BCE) (% of Group)**

| Social Group | Full-time (%) M | Full-time (%) F | Part-time (%) M | Part-time (%) F | % of Capacity M | % of Capacity F | % of Combined Capacity |
|---|---|---|---|---|---|---|---|
| Investor class citizens | — | — | 4 | 3 | 0.2 | 0.2 | 0.2 |
| Landless citizens | 50 | 20 | 25 | 50 | 58 | 37 | 46.1 |
| Other citizens | 5 | 10 | 50 | 60 | 20 | 30 | 25.5 |
| Immigrant metics | 30 | 20 | 0.3 | 33 | 30 | 31 | 30.4 |
| Freed slaves | 25 | — | 11 | 33 | 28 | 11 | 20.5 |
| Slaves | 60 | 33 | 32 | 57 | 63 | 52 | 58.9 |
| Total | 45 | 23 | 29 | 53 | 50 | 40 | 45.6 |

TABLE A5  **Manufacturing Participation by Social Group and Workshop Type** *(Italics denote numbers of part-timers)*

| Social Group | Male Industry[a] | Male Craft | Female Industry | Female Craft |
|---|---|---|---|---|
| Investor class citizens | *200* | — | *200* | — |
| Landless citizens | — | 2,500 *1,250* | — | 1,200 *3,000* |
| Other citizens | — | 1,000 *10,000* | — | 2,400 *14,400* |
| Immigrant metics | *50* | 4,500 | — | 2,000 *3,333* |
| Freed slaves | *50* | 1,250 *500* | — | – *1,333* |
| Slaves | 36,000[b] | 18,000 *28,800* | — | 20,000 *34,200* |
| Total | 36,000 *300* | 27,250 *40,550* | 200 | 25,600 *56,266* |
| Full-time individuals | 57% | 43% | 0% | 100% |
| Part-time individuals | *0.7%* | *99.3%* | *0.4%* | *99.6%* |

[a] Part-timers in industry are owners. We have examples of immigrants (Lysias and Polynices) and freed slaves (Pasion) owning factories but no sound basis for estimating the number of such ownerships. Fortunately, it is likely to have been very small.

[b] This figure is composed of 18,000 in the mines and 18,000 in industrial gangs.

Scholars will surely be able to make the numbers much more robust, but it would be surprising if these observations change greatly through the adoption of alternative assumptions that still fit what we already know.

## A.2  Demand Analysis

Demand analysis involves estimating the annual consumption of products made in Athens, adjusted for net exports, and calculating how long it would take to make them.[15] The equation to find the labor needed to make each product is:

*Annual Labor requirement (FTE) = (((Population × per capita consumption p.a.) + Net Export Volume) × hours per item) ÷ Hours per FTE year*

The total derived for each product segment can be assigned to industry or craft activity and the grand total checked against the results of the supply analysis in Table A5. The knowledge required is product-specific: for each item (as tightly defined as possible) we need to know likely usage, typical product life, and the production process. Critical inputs are expert assessments of consumption (based on literature, epigraphy, and domestic archaeology) and estimates by modern craftsmen of labor requirements. Again, it is a task that rewards fine segmentation—an estimate of how long it would take to make a houseful of furniture will be more accurate if the labor input for different items is specified separately rather than an average estimated for a number of quite different items. Consumption estimates will be differently arrived at for different goods, so there follow four examples of how the methodology might be applied.

## A.2.1 EXAMPLE ONE: CLOTHING (CHAPTER 5)

Carr's analysis of clothing labor requirements showed that, allowing for variation in fiber source and characteristics, weaving and spinning for a typical family constitutes almost three full-time jobs.[16] Her estimate of demand at six adult and two child tunics and three other garments per citizen household per year might be correct but could also be a little understated: the better-off might have wanted more than one garment a year each. It is also difficult to see how a household with a dozen slaves or more could have clothed them all in castoffs from people with such small wardrobes. A detailed analysis would allow for differences in demand according to wealth and status, adding estimates of how much new clothing was purchased or made for other household members and incorporating non-tunic items separately if the labor requirements are very different.[17] Nevertheless, even these rough and understated demand numbers shed some light on the supply analysis. Carr's estimates suggest that well over 100,000 tunic-equivalent items were needed, which would require more than 30,000 full-time spinners and weavers,

---

[15] For most manufactured products other than shipping containers, exports were probably negligible, but it might be important, though far from straightforward, to estimate them in high-value segments like decorated vases and jewelry.

[16] Carr (1999) 163–67.

[17] Exports are unlikely to have figured significantly, as Athens offered neither high-quality raw material nor a surplus of cheap labor.

which is 70 percent of the manufacturing capacity we have estimated for all female residents collectively. This is around the same percentage as the textile-makers made up of metic women making dedications, which suggests that the assumptions that a third of slave women worked full-time at making things and nearly all the rest manufactured for a third of their time might be conservative. It also reinforces the probability that a large amount of spinning and weaving was done by men.

### A.2.2 EXAMPLE TWO: SHOES (CHAPTER 5)

The standard Athenian shoe or sandal consisted of a flat sole, a broad band across the front of the foot, a large toe-thong, and four smaller side thongs. To calculate the number of sandals required per year, it is probably useful to segment the population once more. A poor citizen might only buy one pair a year (remember the streets were stony and rough and leather wears out, especially if worn every day), while others might buy two and the rich four or five. Slaves probably had none, although metics were often quite well-off and probably wore sandals. Women usually wore other footwear. A simple calculation of demand for sandals might be that shown in Table A6.

The time to make a sandal can be disaggregated by process step—for example: measuring the customer's foot, marking out the leather, cutting the leather, and stitching thongs to the sole. Doubling this gives the manpower requirement per pair purchased. With no punching and stitching machinery, the work was physically demanding. If each pair took around one man-day to make, there must have been around 300 cobblers occupied solely in making sandals, an estimate that can be refined by more expert input on unmechanized leatherworking speeds. Similar calculations can be made for women's slippers, boots, and other footwear, most of the latter being relatively low-volume. Quantifying footwear consumption also puts a number on an important component of demand for the upstream tanning industry.[18]

### A.2.3 EXAMPLE THREE: BASIC FURNITURE (CHAPTER 6)

Chapter 6 suggested that this particular component of the woodworking industry must be quite an important one, since refurnishing the typical Athenian house completely every 30 years on average would mean annual demand for over 10,000 items. It is not clear how many houses there were, though we should expect at least 30,000–40,000 homes for people of citizen status (the prevalence

---

[18] Other important applications of tanned leather were saddles, thongs, and sundry other leather items known from Aristophanes (see Chapter 5.2.1).

TABLE A6 **Sandal Consumption C4 Athens (for Illustration Only)**

| Population Segment (Male Residents) | Number | Pairs per Year | Total |
|---|---|---|---|
| Rich citizens | 5,000 | 4 | 20,000 |
| Moderately wealthy citizens | 15,000 | 2 | 30,000 |
| Poor citizens | 10,000 | 1 | 10,000 |
| Metics and aliens | 25,000 | 2 | 50,000 |
| Slaves | 90,000 | — | — |
| Total | 145,000 | | 110,000 |

of widows means the number exceeded that of male citizens) and perhaps another 20,000–30,000 for immigrants, freed slaves, and slaves who were *choris oikountes*. Again some segmentation will be useful. For instance, the number of households likely to be able to afford Demosthenes's luxury couches and equivalent items can be estimated. For basic furniture, households might be segmented into three or four wealth strata, with the higher ones likely to own more furniture and replace them more often, as shown in Table A7.

The likely composition of a typical set of basic furniture will vary for each income level, and a simplified inventory might look like the scenario illustrated in Table A8.

The quantity of each item can then be used to calculate labor needs, as illustrated in Table A9.

The number of hours in a man-year differed with status. Three thousand is a reasonable approximation for slaves and a "full-time" citizen or metic would have put in less. For reasons explained in Chapter 6, much basic furniture would have been made by small, often part-time, craftsmen rather than in slave factories, but much of the labor in a domestic workshop would also have been slaves.[19] We might allow a 2,500-hour year. In any event the assumptions here suggest the full-time equivalent of almost 100 people were engaged in making basic furniture. Many of these might have been making their own and perhaps a few items for neighbors every now and then, while for others it constituted a permanent living.

These estimates can certainly be improved by a deeper understanding of household furniture usage and more technical input into production rate. They should also be looked at in conjunction with other woodwork segments, many of which were dominated by slave gangs, including luxury furniture, hull building, naval supplies, transport vehicles, and looms.[20] We know

---

[19] To assign employment numbers between different enterprise types (craft-shops or factories) is complex. Some products are likely to have been one or the other, but some might be made in both modes, with the products differing in price, quality, and availability, according to customer purchasing power and preferences.

TABLE A7  Basic Household Furniture C4 Athens (for Illustration Only)

| Household | Number | Basic Furniture Items/House | Refurnishing Frequency (Years)[a] | Items per Year |
|---|---|---|---|---|
| Wealthy | 5,000 | 2[b] | 20 | 500 |
| Moderately wealthy | 10,000 | 12 | 20 | 6,000 |
| Modest means | 25,000 | 8 | 30 | 6,667 |
| Poor | 25,000 | 5 | 40 | 3,125 |
| Total | 65,000 | | | 16,297 |

[a] In practice, this average would be achieved by buying a few items irregularly until the full set is purchased over a period, rather than on a single occasion for all items. It is difficult to imagine that data will emerge that would allow a distinction between the average lives of different items.

[b] Wealthy households are presumed to own mainly luxury items.

TABLE A8  Basic Furniture Items per Household C4 Athens (for Illustration Only)

| Household | Chair | Bed/Couch | Stool | Dining Table | Other Tables | Chest | Total |
|---|---|---|---|---|---|---|---|
| Wealthy | | | | | 1 | 1 | 2 |
| Moderately wealthy | 3 | 4 | 2 | 1 | 1 | 1 | 12 |
| Modest means | 2 | 2 | 1 | 1 | 1 | 1 | 8 |
| Poor | 1 | 1 | | 1 | 1 | 1 | 5 |
| Total | | | | | | | |

TABLE A9  Basic Furniture Labour C4 Athens (for Illustration Only)

| Item | Number per Year | Time to Make (Man-Hours) | Total Time (Hours/Year) |
|---|---|---|---|
| Chair | 3,792[a] | 10 | 37,792 |
| Bed/couch | 4,292 | 25 | 107,300 |
| Stool | 1,833 | 4 | 7,332 |
| Dining table | 1,958 | 15 | 29,370 |
| Other tables | 2,208 | 9 | 19,872 |
| Chests | 2,208 | 8 | 17,664 |
| Total | 16,297 | | 219,330 |

[a] Moderately wealthy: 10,000 households buying 3 chairs every 20 years = 1,500 chairs/year, plus modest means 25,000 × 2 ÷ 30 = 1,667, plus poor 25 × 1 ÷ 30 = 625.

Demosthenes's number of luxury bed makers, but we do not know how complex his beds were to make or what his market share was. Different assumptions of his factory's output can be assessed and modified by comparing them with likely demand. For boatbuilding, there is reasonable information on wooden ship components, and the time per ship for each item can be estimated

---

[20] The reasons these were probably industries rather than crafts are given in Chapter 6.2.

as in Table A9. Estimating the total volume of the major wood product categories quantifies demand for wood as well as labor, providing another check on the reasonableness of the assumptions made about each segment.

### A.2.4 EXAMPLE FOUR: CERAMICS (CHAPTER 3)

Here again it is important to segment the analysis into different product groups. Demand for ceramic containers in Athens must reflect Attica's olive oil and (possibly) wine production. There was a significant export trade in decorated vases, though many of the items might have been secondhand. Demand for household utility ware is very hard to estimate, as we are dealing with large numbers of disposable pieces, the durability of which is unknown. Nevertheless anyone knowledgeable and bold enough to make an enlightened guess at how many plates, bowls, and cups the average Athenian would have used can then classify them according to the space they take up in a kiln, as shown in Table A10.

The middle column defines kiln capacity and the right-hand one can be used to calculate how many potters are required—the last three shapes require two or three. The original analysis (Chapter 3.3.2) calculated maximum kiln volumes in order to show that it was very unlikely that any pottery with a single kiln (and few had more) would need more than one potter and a total complement of five or six. The crucial variable to estimate is the percentage of maximum theoretical capacity at which the average kiln would have operated. Realistically, kilns would seldom have been filled to capacity; few are thought to have used stacking very much except for plates and shallow bowls, and few combinations of product allow for a very efficient use of space; a likely rate is in the order of 30–50 percent.[21] Applying this factor to the throwing time, multiplying the result by annual demand for each form (calculated as for furniture in Table A9), and dividing by 60 minutes gives the total man-hours required for household utility ceramics.[22] Highly decorated pots and ones of complex design must be added, but the numbers will be small—a few score painters and master potters at any one time at most.

*   *   *

The number of estimates required for all these calculations, and the lack of firm information on which to base them, are daunting, but plenty of progress

---

[21] Provided both manage their firing sensibly, there is no important difference in productivity between a full-time pottery with four slaves supporting the potter and a workshop operated by a citizen and a slave on an occasional basis; whether the tasks are done in combination by a team of five or in sequence by two people over a longer period, output per man-hour is the same.

[22] Tasks that support the potter (clay preparation and wheel turning) can be assumed to require the same amount of time as the potter. If this is much shorter than seven hours, then the fire managers will be working longer than implied by the calculation, but this does not affect headcount.

TABLE A10  Stacked Kiln Capacity (from Table 3.3)

| Items | Maximum Number Stacked | Throwing Time Required (minutes) |
|---|---|---|
| Short, squat | 16 | 320 |
| Large, wide | 22 | 330 |
| Plate | 392 | 392 |
| Large, tall | 104 | 520 |
| Medium | 108 | 324 |
| Small (cups) | 592 | 1,184 |
| Ornament | 1,320 | 1,320 |
| Tall, thin | 800 | 800 |

TABLE A11  Manufacturing Employment by Social Group and Industry Type

| Sector | Segment | Industry Investor | Industry Metic | Industry Slave | Craft Citizen | Craft Metic | Craft Slave | Total |
|---|---|---|---|---|---|---|---|---|
| Wood working | Basic furniture | | | | x | x | x | x |
| | Naval supplies | x | | x | | | | x |
| | Boat hull and assembly | x | x | x | | | | x |
| | Luxury furniture | x | | x | | | | x |
| Ceramics | Shipping containers | x | | x | | | | x |
| | Domestic utility, etc. | | | | x | x | x | x |
| Total (FTE)[a] | | 20 | 50 | 36,000 | 16,275 | 9,459 | 52,280 | 114,085 |

[a] Sum of male and female capacities from Tables A2 and A3.

is possible. Specialist archaeologists and social historians can improve on all the numbers used here for illustration. The more opinions expressed on each subject, the more likely there is to be some convergence around an estimate most are comfortable with. As the database grows, more cross-checking and refinement by agglomeration, disaggregation, and direct comparison will become possible. One check that would be invaluable is aggregate consumer expenditure based on known and inferred prices against what is known about consumer income. An ultimate goal here might be an equation showing the part manufacturing played in national income and expenditure.

Integrating this demand analysis with supply will present a powerful insight into the structure of Athenian manufacturing activity along the lines shown in Table A11.

# SECONDARY SOURCES

Acton, P. H. 2012. Review of D. T. Engen, *Honor and Profit: Athenian Trade Policy and the Economy and Society of Greece 415–307 B.C.E. Classical Review* 62, no. 1: 210–12.
Andrianou, D. A. 2006. "Late Classical and Hellenistic Furniture and Furnishings in the Epigraphical Record." *Hesperia* 75: 561–84.
———. 2009. *The Furniture and Furnishings of Ancient Greek Houses and Tombs*. New York: Cambridge University Press.
Akerlof, G. A., and R. E. Kranton. 2010. *Identity Economics: How Our Identities Shape Our Work, Wages, and Well-Being*. Princeton, NJ: Princeton University Press.
Akerstrom, A. 1981. *Etruscan Tomb Painting: An Art of Many Faces*. Opuscula Romana 13/1. Stockholm: Swedish Institute in Rome.
Alcock S. E. 2007. "The Eastern Mediterranean." In *The Cambridge Economic History of the Greco-Roman World,* edited by W. Scheidel, I. M. Morris, and R. P. Saller, 671–97. Cambridge: Cambridge University Press.
van Alfen, P. G. 2012. "The Coinage of Athens, Sixth to First Century BC." In *The Oxford Handbook of Greek and Roman Coinage,* edited by W. E. Metcalf, 88–104. New York: Oxford University Press.
———. Forthcoming. "An Overview of Commodities in Long Distance Trade, 500–300 BCE." In *Markets, Households and City States in the Ancient Greek Economy,* edited by E. M. Harris, D. M. Lewis, and M. Woolmer. New York: Cambridge University Press.
Allen, C. 1994. *Plain Tales from the Raj*. London: Abacus.
Allen, R. 2009. *The British Industrial Revolution in Global Perspective*. Cambridge: Cambridge University Press.
Alston, R. 1997. "Houses and Households in Roman Egypt." In *Domestic Space in the Roman World: Pompeii and Beyond,* edited by R. Laurence and A. Wallace-Hadrill, 25–39. Journal of Roman Archaeology Supplementary Series 22. Portsmouth, RI.
Amyx, D., and W. K. Pritchett. 1958. "The Attic Stelai—Part III. Vases and Other Containers." *Hesperia* 27: 225–310.
Anderson, J. K. 1970. *Military Theory and Practice in the Age of Xenophon*. Berkeley and Los Angeles: University of California Press.
Andrea, A. J., and J. H. Overfield. 2004. *The Human Record: Sources of Global History*. Vol. 1, *To 1700*. 5th ed. Boston: Houghton Mifflin.
Andreades, A. M. 1931. *Geschichte der Griechischen Staatswirtschaft*. Munich: Georg Olms Verlag.
Andreau, J. 1995. "Présentation Vingt Ans d'après L'Économie Antique de Moses I Finley." *Annales: Histoire, Sciences Sociales* 50: 947–60.
———. 2002. "Markets, Fairs and Monetary Loans: Cultural History and Economic History in Roman Italy and Hellenistic Greece." In *Money Labour and Land: Approaches to the*

*Economies of Ancient Greece*, edited by P. A. Cartledge, E. E. Cohen, and L. Foxhall, 113–29. London: Routledge.

Andrews, K. 1997. "From Ceramic Finishes to Modes of Production: Iron Age Finewares from Central France." In *Not So Much a Pot, More a Way of Life: Current Approaches to Artefact Analysis in Archaeology,* edited by C. G. Cumberpatch and P. W. Blinkhorn, 57–75. Oxbow Monographs 83. Oxford: Oxbow Books.

Aperghis, G. 1997–98. "A Reassessment of the Laurion Mining Lease Records." *Bulletin of the Institute of Classical Studies* 42, no. 1: 1–20.

Apolte, T., and F. Gradalski. 1992. "Systemic Change to a Market Economy: General Issues and First Experiences in Poland." In *Transforming Economic Systems: The Case of Poland,* edited by M. Kramer, M. Weber, and F. Gradalski, 3–22. Heidelberg: Physica-Verlag.

Arafat, K., and C. Morgan. 1989. "Pots and Potters in Athens and Corinth: A Review." *Oxford Journal of Archaeology* 8, no. 3: 311–46.

Arias, P. E., M. Hirmer, and B. B. Shefton. 1962. *A History of Greek Vase Painting.* London: Thames & Hudson.

Arrow, K. J. 1962. "The Economic Implications of Learning by Doing." *Review of Economic Studies* 29, no. 3: 155–73.

Atkinson, T. D. 1904. "Excavations at Phylakopi in Melos: The Architecture." In *Excavations at Phylakopi in Melos,* edited by T. D. Atkinson, R. C. Bosanquet, C. C. Edgar, A. J. Evans, D. G. Hogarth, D. Mackenzie, C. Smith, and F. B. Welch, 25–69. Society for the Promotion of Hellenic Studies Supplementary Volume 4. London: Macmillan.

Aubert, J.-J. 2001. "The Fourth Factor: Managing Non-Agricultural Production in the Roman World." In *Economies beyond Agriculture in the Classical World,* edited by D. J. Mattingly and J. Salmon, 90–111. London: Routledge.

Austin, M., and P. Vidal-Naquet. 1977. *Economic and Social History of Ancient Greece.* London: B. T. Batsford.

Ayer, A. 1971. *Language, Truth and Logic.* Harmondsworth: Penguin.

Baätz, D. 1979. "Teile Hellenistischer Geschütze aus Griechenland." *Archäologischer Anzeiger* 94: 68–75.

———. 1982. "Hellenistische Katapulte aus Ephyra (Epirus)." *Mitteilungen des Deutschen Archäologischen Instituts, Athenische Abteilung* 97: 211–33.

Bamberger, M. 1985. "The Working Conditions of the Ancient Copper Smelting Process." In *Furnaces and Smelting Technology in Antiquity,* edited by P. T. Craddock and M. J. Hughes, 151–57. Occasional Papers 48. London: British Museum.

Barber, E. J. W. 1991. *Prehistoric Textiles: The Development of Cloth in the Neolithic and Bronze Ages with Special Reference to the Aegean.* Princeton, NJ: Princeton University Press.

———. 1992. "The Peplos of Athena." In *Goddess and Polis: The Panathenaic Festival in Ancient Athens,* edited by J. Neils, 103–18. Hanover, NH: Hood Museum of Art, Dartmouth College.

———. 1994. *Women's Work: The First 20,000 Years; Women, Cloth, and Society in Early Times.* New York: Norton.

Beard, M. 2003. *The Parthenon.* Cambridge, MA: Harvard University Press.

Beazley, J. D. 1940. "A Marble Lamp." *Journal of Hellenic Studies* 60: 22–49.

———. 1942. *Attic Red-Figure Vase Painters.* Oxford: Clarendon Press.

———. 1944. *Potter and Painter in Ancient Athens.* London: G. Cumberledge.

———. 1947. *Etruscan Vase Painting.* Oxford: Clarendon Press.
———. 1956. *Attic Black-Figure Vase Painters.* Oxford: Clarendon Press.
Becker, G. 1957. *The Economics of Discrimination.* Chicago: University of Chicago Press.
———. 1965. "A Theory of the Allocation of Time." *Economic Journal* 75: 493–517.
———. 1968. "Crime and Punishment: An Economic Approach." *Journal of Political Economy* 76: 169–217.
———. 1976. *The Economic Approach to Human Behavior.* Chicago: University of Chicago Press.
———. 1991. *A Treatise on the Family.* Cambridge, MA: Harvard University Press.
Betalli, M. 1982. "Note sulla produzione tessile ad Atene in età classica." *Rivista internazionale per la storia economica e sociale dell'antichità* 1: 261–70.
Billot, M.-F. 1992. "Les Cynosarges, Antiochos et les Tanneurs: Questions de topographie." *Bulletin de Correspondance Hellénique* 116, no. 1: 119–56.
Binns, C. F., and A. D. Fraser. 1929. "The Genesis of Greek Black Glaze." *American Journal of Archaeology* 33, no. 1: 1–9.
Bintliff, J., B. Slapšak, B. Noordervliet, J. van Zwienen, K. Wilkinson, and R. Shiel. 2010. "The Leiden-Ljubljana Ancient Cities of Boeotia Project 2008 Season." *Pharos: Journal of the Netherlands Institute at Athens* 16: 31–60.
Bisel, S., and J. Angel. 1985. "Health and Nutrition in Mycenaean Greece: A Study in Human Skeletal Remains." In *Contributions to Aegean Archaeology: Studies in Honor of William A. McDonald*, edited by N. Wilkie and V. Coulson, 197–210. Minneapolis: Kendall/Hunt.
Bitros, G., and A. Karayannis. 2004. "The Liberating Power of Entrepreneurship in Ancient Athens." *IDEAS*, http://129.3.20.41/eps/mhet/papers/0411/0411004.pdf. Accessed 10/25/2007.
———. 2006. "Morality, Institutions and Economic Growth: Lessons from Ancient Greece." *MPRA*, http://mpra.ub.unimuenchen.de/994/. Accessed 10/25/2007.
Björk, C. 1995. *Early Pottery in Greece: A Technological and Functional Analysis of the Evidence from Neolithic Achilleon Thessaly.* Studies in Mediterranean Archaeology. Jonsered: Paul Åströms Förlag.
Black, E. A., and G. F. Bell, eds. 2011. *Law and Legal Institutions of Asia: Traditions, Adaptations and Innovations.* New York: Cambridge University Press.
Blinkenberg, C. 1902–14. *Lindos: Fouilles et recherches 1902–14; Fouilles de l'Acropole.* Berlin: Walter de Gruyter.
Boardman, J. 1974. *Athenian Black Figure Vases: A Handbook.* London: Thames & Hudson.
———. 1975. *Athenian Red Figure Vases: The Archaic Period.* London: Thames & Hudson.
———. 1989. *Athenian Red Figure Vases.* London: Thames & Hudson.
———. 1990. "Symposion Furniture." In *Sympotica: A Symposium on the Symposion*, edited by O. Murray, 122–31. Oxford: Clarendon Press.
———. 2001. *The History of Greek Vases.* London: Thames & Hudson.
Boeckh, A. 1886. *Die Staatshaushaltung der Athener.* 3rd ed. 2 vols. Berlin: G. Reimer.
Boersma, J. S. 1970. *Athenian Building Policy from 561/0 to 405/4 BC.* Groningen: Wolters-Noordhoff.
Bogaert, R. 1968. *Banques et Banquiers dans les Cités grecques.* Leiden: A. W. Sijthoff's Uitgeversmaatschaappij.
Bolkestein, H. 1958. *Economic Life in Greece's Golden Age.* Leiden: E. J. Brill.

Bookidis, N. 2010. *The Sanctuary of Demeter and Kore: The Terracotta Sculpture.* Corinth Series 18.5. Princeton, NJ: American School of Classical Studies at Athens.

Bosanquet, R. C. 1904. "The Obsidian Trade." In *Excavations at Phylakopi in Melos,* edited by T. D. Atkinson, R. C. Bosanquet, C. C. Edgar, A. J. Evans, D. G. Hogarth, D. Mackenzie, C. Smith, and F. B. Welch, 216–33. Society for the Promotion of Hellenic Studies Supplementary Volume 4. London: Macmillan.

Bourget, E. 1929. *Fouilles de Delphes.* Vol. 3.1, *Epigraphie: Inscriptions de l'entrée du Sanctuaire au trésor des Athéniens.* Paris: Éditions de Boccard.

Bowie, E. 1990. "Miles Ludens? The Problem of Martial Exhortation in Greek Elegy." In *Sympotica: A Symposium on the Symposion,* edited by O. Murray, 221–29. Oxford: Clarendon Press.

Bradley, K., and P. A. Cartledge. 2011. *Cambridge World History of Slavery.* Vol. 1, *The Ancient Mediterranean World.* Cambridge: Cambridge University Press.

Braudel, F. 1969. *Écrits sur l'histoire.* Paris: Flammarion.

Bresson, A. 2000. *La Cité Marchande.* Bordeaux: Ausonius.

———. 2007. *L'Économie de la grèce des Cités: fin VIe-Ier siècle a. C.* Paris: Armand Colin.

Bridbury, A. 1982. *Medieval English Cloth Making: An Economic Survey.* Portsmouth, NH: Heinemann.

Brinkmann, V., R. Wünscher, et al. 2007. *Gods in Color: Painted Sculpture of Classical Antiquity.* Exhibition at the Arthur M. Sackler Museum, Harvard University Art Museums, in cooperation with Staatliche Antikensammlungen and Glyptothek Munich, Stiftung Archäologie Munich, 9/22/07–1/20/08. Munich: Stiftung Archäologie Glyptothek.

Brinkmann, V. 2008. "The Polychromy of Ancient Greek Sculpture." In *The Color of Life: Polychromy in Sculpture from Antiquity to the Present,* edited by R. Panzanelli, E. D. Schmidt, and K. Lapatin, 18–39. Malibu, CA: Getty Publications.

Brock, R. 1994. "The Labour of Women in Classical Athens." *Classical Quarterly* 44, no. 2: 336–46.

Bromehead, C. E. N. 1945. *Geology in Embryo.* Proceedings of the Geological Association. London: n.p.

Brouskare, M. S., and J. Binder. 1974. *The Acropolis Museum: A Descriptive Catalogue.* Athens: Commercial Bank of Greece.

Brown, D. H. 1997. "The Social Significance of Imported Medieval Pottery." In *Not So Much a Pot, More a Way of Life: Current Approaches to Artefact Analysis in Archaeology,* edited by C. G. Cumberpatch and P. W. Blinkhorn, 95–112. Oxbow Monographs 83. Oxford: Oxbow Books.

Brown, J. 1970. "A Note on the Division of Labor by Sex." *American Anthropologist* 72, no. 5: 1073–78.

Brun, J.-P. 2000. "The Production of Perfumes in Antiquity: The Cases of Delos and Paestum." *American Journal of Archaeology* 104, no. 2: 277–308.

Bryant, V. 1994. "The Origins of the Potter's Wheel." *Ceramics Today.* http://www.ceramicstoday.com/articles/potters_wheel.htm. Accessed 8/16/2007.

Bucher, K. 1893. *Die Entstehung der Volkswirtschaft: Sechs Vorträge.* Tübingen: Laupp.

Budde, E. G. 1940. *Armarium und kibotos: ein Beitrag zur Geschichte des Antiken Mobiliars.* Würzburg: K. Triltsch.

Burford, A. M. 1963. "The Builders of the Parthenon." *Greece and Rome* Supplement 10, 23–35.

———. 1965. "The Economics of Greek Temple Building." *Proceedings of the Cambridge Philological Society*, n.s., 11: 21–34.

———. 1969. *The Greek Temple Builders at Epidauros: A Social and Economic Study of Building in the Asklepian Sanctuary during the Fourth and Early Third Centuries B. C.* Toronto: University of Toronto Press.

———. 1972. *Craftsmen in Greek and Roman Society*. Ithaca, NY: Cornell University Press.

Burkert, W., and M. E. Pinder. 1992. *The Orientalizing Revolution: Near Eastern Influence on Greek Culture in the Early Archaic Age*. Cambridge, MA: Harvard University Press.

Burn, A. R. 1962. *Persia and the Greeks*. London: Minerva Press.

Cahill, N. 2002. *Household and City Organization at Olynthus*. New Haven, CT: Yale University Press.

Cairns, J. 1863. *The Slave Power: Its Character, Career and Probable Designs; Being an Attempt to Explain the Real Issues Involved in the American Context*. New York: F. Foster.

Calhoun, G. M. 1926. *The Business Life of Ancient Athens*. Chicago: University of Chicago Press.

Camp, J. M. 1986 *The Athenian Agora: Excavations in the Heart of the Classical City*. London: Thames & Hudson.

Campbell, G. 2007. *The Grove Encyclopedia of Classical Art and Architecture*, Vol. 2. Oxford: Oxford University Press.

Canlas, G. 2010. "Women in the *Oikos*: The Flexibility and Variability of Athenian Households." *Agora, the Undergraduate Journal of the University of British Columbia, Classical, Near Eastern and Religious Studies* 1: 27–35.

Caradice, I., and M. Price. 1988. *Coinage in the Greek World*. London: Seaby.

Carr, K. 1999. "Women's Work: Spinning and Weaving in the Greek Home." In *Archéologie des textiles des origines au Vème siècle*, edited by D. Cardon and M. Feugère, 163–66. Actes du Colloque des Lattes. Montagnac: Éditions Monique Mergoil.

Cartledge, P. A. 1998. "The Economy (Economies) of Ancient Greece." *Dialogos* 5: 4–24.

———. 2002. "The Political Economy of Greek Slavery." In *Money, Labour and Land: Approaches to the Economies of Ancient Greece*, edited by P. A. Cartledge, E. E. Cohen, and L. Foxhall, 156–66. London: Routledge.

Caskey, L. D. 1910. "The Roofed Gallery on the Walls of Athens." *American Journal of Archaeology* 14, no. 3: 298–309.

Casson, L. 1995. *Ships and Seamanship in the Ancient World*. Princeton, NJ: Princeton University Press.

Caven, B. 1990. *Dionysius I, War Lord of Sicily*. New Haven, CT: Yale University Press.

Chadwick, J., M. Ventris, and A. J. B. Wace. 1973. *Documents in Mycenaean Greek*. Cambridge: Cambridge University Press.

Chandra, R. G. 1979. *Indo-Greek Jewellery*. New Delhi: Abhinav.

Chappell, T. 2009. "'Naturalism' in Aristotle's Political Philosophy." In *A Companion to Greek and Roman Political Thought*, edited by R. K. Balot, 382–98. Chichester: Wiley-Blackwell.

Charneux, P. 1992. "Sur un décret des forgerons d'Argos." *Bulletin de Correspondance Hellénique* 116, no. 1: 335–43.

Chaudhuri, N., et al. 2000. "A Novel Metabolic Glutamate Receptor Variant Functions as a Taste Receptor." *Nature Neuroscience* 3: 113–19.

Chayanov, A. 1986. *The Theory of Peasant Economy*. Translated by R. E. F. Smith. Madison: University of Wisconsin Press.

Cherry, J. F., J. L. Davis, and E. Mantzourani. 1991. *Landscape Archaeology as Long-Term History: Northern Keos in the Cycladic Islands from the Earliest Settlement until Modern Times.* Monumenta Archaeologica 16. Los Angeles: UCLA Institute of Archaeology.

Childe, G. 1954. *What Happened in History.* Harmondsworth: Penguin.

Chorley, R. J., and P. Haggett. 1968. *Socio-Economic Models in Geography.* London: Methuen.

Christesen, H. 2003. "Economic Rationalism in Fourth Century BCE Athens." *Greece and Rome* 50, no. 1: 31–56.

Clark, A. J., M. Elston, and M. L. Hart. 2002. *Understanding Greek Vases: A Guide to Terms, Styles and Techniques.* Los Angeles: Getty Publications.

Clark, D. A. 2002. "Development Ethics: A Research Agenda." *International Journal of Social Economics* 29, no. 11: 830–48.

Clark, G. 1994. "Factory Discipline." *Journal of Economic History* 54, no. 1: 128–63.

———. 2007. *A Farewell to Alms: A Brief Economic History of the World.* Princeton Economic History of the Western World Series. Princeton, NJ: Princeton University Press.

Clark M., J. Gore, R. Jordan, et al. 1980. *Sculpture Techniques: A Sculpture Manual.* Melbourne: Victorian College of the Arts.

Clarke, G. 1961. *World Prehistory: An Outline.* Cambridge: Cambridge University Press.

Coale, A. J., and P. Demeny. 1966. *Regional Model Life Tables and Stable Populations.* Princeton, NJ: Princeton University Press.

Coase, R. H. 1937. "The Nature of the Firm." *Economica*, n.s., 16: 386–405.

Coates, J. 2005. "Some Engineering Concepts Applied to Ancient Greek Trireme Warships." 18th Jenkin Lecture. Published online 2006 by the Society of Oxford University Engineers, http://www.soue.org.uk/souenews/issue5/jenkinlect.html.

Cockle, H. 1981. "Pottery Manufacture in Roman Egypt: A New Papyrus." *Journal of Roman Studies* 71: 87–95.

Cohen, B. 2006. *The Colors of Clay: Special Techniques in Athenian Vases.* Los Angeles: Getty Publications.

Cohen, E. E. 1992a. *Athenian Economy and Society: A Banking Perspective.* Princeton, NJ: Princeton University Press.

———. 1992b. Review of Paul Millett, *Lending and Borrowing in Ancient Athens. Bryn Mawr Classical Review*, 2003.04.10, http://bmcr.brynmawr.edu/1992/03.04.10.html.

———. 2000. *The Athenian Nation.* Princeton, NJ: Princeton University Press.

———. 2002. "An Unprofitable Masculinity." In *Money, Labour and Land: Approaches to the Economies of Ancient Greece,* edited by P. A. Cartledge, E. E. Cohen, and L. Foxhall, 100–112. London: Routledge.

———. 2006. *Consensual Contracts at Athens.* Proceedings of the XIVth Symposium of the Society for Greek and Hellenistic Legal History at Rauischholzhausen Castle near Marburg (2003), http://www.isnie.org/ISNIE06/Papers06/01.2/cohen.pdf. Accessed 10/28/2008.

———. Forthcoming. "Overcoming Legal Incapacity at Athens: Juridical Adaptations Facilitating the Business Activities of Slaves." In *Legal Documents in Ancient Societies VI: Ancient Guardianship, Legal Incapacities in the Ancient World.* Proceedings of a conference at the Israel Academy of Sciences and Humanities, Jerusalem, November 4–5, 2013.

Coleman, J. E., and K. Abramowitz. 1986. *Excavations at Pylos in Elis.* Hesperia Supplement 21. Princeton, NJ: American School of Classical Studies at Athens.

Coleman, J. S. 1986a. *Individual Interests and Collective Action: Selected Essays.* New York: Cambridge University Press.

———. 1986b. "Social Theory, Social Research, and a Theory of Action." *American Journal of Sociology* 91, no. 6: 1309–35.

———. 1990. *Foundations of Social Theory.* Cambridge, MA: Harvard University Press.

Conard, N. J. 2003. "Paleolithic Ivory Sculptures from Southwestern Germany and the Origins of Figurative Art." *Nature* 426: 830–32.

———. 2009. "A Female Figurine from the Basal Aurignacian of Hohle Fels Cave in Southwestern Germany." *Nature* 459: 248–52.

Conophagos, C. E. 1980. *Le Laurium antique et la technique grecque de la production de l'argent.* Athens: Ekdotike Hellados.

Cook, R. M. 1960. *Greek Painted Pottery.* London: Methuen.

———. 1986. "The Calke Wood Kiln." In *Ancient Greek and Related Pottery: Proceedings of the International Vase Symposium in Amsterdam, April 11–15, 1984*, edited by H. A. G. Brijder, 63–66. Amsterdam: Allard Pearson Museum.

Cosgrove, B. 2000. *Costume and Fashion: A Complete History.* London: Hamlyn.

Cotterell, B., and J. Kamminga. 1990. *Mechanics of Pre-Industrial Technology: An Introduction to the Mechanics of Ancient and Traditional Material Culture.* Cambridge: Cambridge University Press.

Coulton, J. J. 1974. "Lifting in Early Greek Architecture." *Journal of Hellenic Studies* 94: 1–19.

———. 1977. *Ancient Greek Architects at Work: Problems of Structure and Design.* Ithaca, NY: Cornell University Press.

Cracolici, V. 2003. *I Sostegni di Fornace dal Kerameikos di Metaponto.* Beni Archaeologici—Conoscenza e Technologie. Bari: Edipuglia.

Cuomo, S. 2008. "Ancient Written Sources for Engineering and Technology." In *The Oxford Handbook of Engineering and Technology in the Classical World,* edited by J. P. Oleson, 15–34. New York: Oxford University Press.

Curtis, R. I. 1984. "Salted Fish Products in Ancient Medicine." *Journal of the History of Medicine and Allied Sciences* 39, no. 4: 430–45.

———. 1991. *Garum and Salsamenta: Production and Commerce in Materia Medica.* Leiden: E. J. Brill.

———. 2001. *Ancient Food Technology.* Leiden: E. J. Brill.

———. 2008. "Food Processing and Preparation." In *The Oxford Handbook of Engineering and Technology in the Classical World,* edited by J. P. Oleson, 369–92. New York: Oxford University Press.

Dalton, M. 1959. *Men Who Manage: Fusions of Feeling and Theory in Administration.* New York: John Wiley.

Daremberg, L., and E. Saglio. 1896. *Dictionnaire des Antiquités Grecques et Romaines d'après les textes et les monuments.* New York: Harpers.

Darwin, C. 2007. *The Origin of Species.* London: Folio Society.

Davidson, J. N. 1997. *Courtesans and Fishcakes: The Consuming Passions of Classical Athens.* London: Harper Collins.

Davies, J. K. 1971. *Athenian Propertied Families, 600–300 BC.* Oxford: Clarendon Press.

———. 1981. *Wealth and the Power of Wealth in Classical Athens*. New York: Arno Press.

———. 1998. "Ancient Economies: Models and Muddles." In *Trade, Traders and the Ancient City*, edited by H. Parkin and C. Smith, 225–56. London: Routledge.

———. 2001a. *Hellenistic Economies in the Post-Finley Era*. In *Hellenistic Economies*, edited by Z. Archibald, J. K. Davies, V. Gabrielsen, and G. J. Oliver, 7–44. London: Routledge.

———. 2001b. "Rebuilding a Temple: The Economic Effects of Piety." In *Economies beyond Agriculture in the Classical World*, edited by D. J. Mattingly and J. Salmon, 209–29. London: Routledge.

———. 2002. "The Strategies of Mr. Theopompos." In *Money, Labour and Land: Approaches to the Economies of Ancient Greece*, edited by P. A. Cartledge, E. E. Cohen, and L. Foxhall, 200–208. London: Routledge.

———. 2007a. "Linear and Non-Linear Flow Models for Ancient Economies." In *The Ancient Economy: Evidence and Models*, edited by J. G. Manning and I. M. Morris, 127–56. Stanford, CA: Stanford University Press.

———. 2007b. "Classical Greece: Production." In *The Cambridge Economic History of the Greco-Roman World*, edited by W. Scheidel, I. M. Morris, and R. P. Saller, 333–61. Cambridge: Cambridge University Press.

Davies, O. 1935. *Roman Mines in Europe*. Oxford: Clarendon Press.

Davies, W. S. 2004. *A Day in Old Athens: A Picture of Athenian Life*. Boston: Allyn & Bacon. Available online at http://www.gutenberg.org/etext/4716. Accessed 6/3/2010.

Davis, G. 2014. "Mining Money in Late Archaic Athens." *Historia: Zeitschrift für Alte Geschichte* 63, no. 3: 257–77.

Davis, P. H. 1948. "In the Workshop of the Erechtheion." *American Journal of Archaeology* 52, no. 4: 485–89.

Dawkins, R. 1976. *The Selfish Gene*. Oxford: Oxford University Press.

de Blois, L., and R. J. van der Spek. 1997. *An Introduction to the Ancient World*. Translated by S. Mellor. London: Routledge.

Defoe, D. 1728. *A Plan of the English Commerce*. London: Charles Rivington.

de Long, J. B. 1997. *The Embedded Economy Hypothesis: A Note on Karl Polyani*. University of California at Berkeley. http://www.j-bradford-delong.net/movable_type/2003_archives/002483.html. Accessed 6/23/2007.

Deonna, W. 1938. *Le mobilier délien*. Delos 18.2. Paris: Éditions de Boccard.

Descat, R. 1995. "L'Économie Antique et la Cité Grecque: Une Modèle en Question." *Annales, Histoires, Sciences Sociales* 50, no. 5: 961–89.

de Ste. Croix, G. M. 1956. "Greek and Roman Accounting." In *Studies in the History of Accounting*, edited by A. Littleton and B. Yamey, 14–77. London: Sweet & Maxwell.

———. 1981. *The Class Struggle in the Ancient Greek World from the Archaic Age to the Arab Conquests*. London: Duckworth.

de Vries, J. 2008. *The Industrious Revolution: Consumer Behavior and the Household Economy, 1650 to the Present*. New York: Cambridge University Press.

Dietler, M. 2007. "The Iron Age in the Western Mediterranean." In *The Cambridge Economic History of the Greco-Roman World*, edited by W. Scheidel, I. M. Morris, and R. P. Saller, 241–76. Cambridge: Cambridge University Press.

Dillon, S. 2007. "Portraits of Women in the Early Hellenistic Period." In *Early Hellenistic Portraiture: Image, Style, Context*, edited by P. Schulz and R. von den Hoff, 63–83. Cambridge: Cambridge University Press.

Docter, R. F. 1988–90. "Amphora Capacities and Archaic Levantine Trade." *Hamburger Beiträge zur Archäologie* 15–17: 143–88.

Dovatur, A. I., and A. A. Nejchardt. 1980. *Rabstvo v Attike VI–V vv. do n.e.* (Slavery in Attica in the sixth and fifth centuries). Leningrad: Nauka.

Dragatses, I. C., and W. Dorpfeld. 1885. "Ekthesis peri ton en Peiraiei Anaskaphon." *Praktika* 40: 63–68.

van Driel-Murray, C. 2008. "Tanning and Leather." In *The Oxford Handbook of Engineering and Technology in the Classical World*, edited by J. P. Oleson, 483–95. New York. Oxford University Press.

Drinkwater, J. F. 1978. "The Rise and Fall of the Gallic Iulii: Aspects of the Development of the Aristocracy of the Three Gauls under the Early Empire." *Latomus* 37: 817–50.

———. 1981. "Money-Rents and Food-Renders in Gallic Funerary Reliefs." In *The Roman West in the Third Century: Contributions from Archaeology and History*, edited by A. King and M. Henig, 215–33. Oxford: British Archaeological Report.

———. 1982. "The Wool Textile Industry of Gallia Belgica and the Secundinii of Igel." *Textile History* 13, no. 1: 111–28.

———. 2001. "The Gallo-Roman Woolen Industry and the Great Debate: The Igel Column Revisited." In *Economies beyond Agriculture in the Classical World*, edited by D. J. Mattingly and J. Salmon, 297–308. London: Routledge.

Dunlop, R. 1981. "The Real China Syndrome." *Popular Mechanics*, August, 58–60.

Dyer, C. 1989. *Standards of Living in the Late Middle Ages: Social Change in England c. 1200–1520*. Cambridge: Cambridge University Press.

Edwards, A. T. 2004. *Hesiod's Ascra*. Berkeley: University of California Press.

Ehrenberg, V. 1951. *The People of Aristophanes: A Sociology of Old Attic Comedy*. New York: Schocken.

———. 1974. *Man, State and Deity: Essays in Ancient History*. London: Methuen.

Eiring, J., G. Finkielsztejn, M. K. Lawall, and J. Lund. 2004. "Concluding Remarks." In *Transport Amphorae and Trade in the Eastern Mediterranean: Acts of the International Colloquium at the Danish Institute at Athens, September 26–29, 2002*, edited by J. Eiring and J. Lund, 459–66. Aarhus: Aarhus University Press.

Elton, H. 1996. *Warfare in Roman Europe, ad 350–425*. Oxford: Clarendon Press.

Elvin, M. 1973. *The Pattern of the Chinese Past*. London: Eyre Methuen.

Emrich, W. 1985. *Handbook of Charcoal Making: The Traditional and Industrial Methods*. Commission of the European Communities. Dordrecht: D. Reidel for the Commission of the European Communities.

Engels, F. 1972. *The Origin of the Family, Private Property and the State, in the Light of the Researches of Lewis H. Morgan*. New York: Pathfinder Press.

Engen, D. T. 2007. "The Economy of Ancient Greece." *EH.Net Encyclopedia*, http://www.eh.net/encyclopedia/engen.greece.php. Accessed 3/27/2007.

———. 2010. *Honor and Profit: Athenian Trade Policy and the Economy and Society of Greece, 415–307 bce*. Ann Arbor: University of Michigan Press.

Erb, O. 1937–1938. "Wirtschaft und Gesellschaft im Denken der hellenischen Antike." *Schmollers Jahrbuch* 61: 663–96.

Faraguna, M. 1992. *Atene nell' età di Alessandro: problem politici, economici, finanziari*. Atti della Accademia Nazionale dei Lincei Memorie Series 9.2. Rome: Accademia Nazionale dei Lincei.

———. 1994. "Alle Origini dell' Oikonomia: Dall' Anonimo di Giamblico ad Aristotele." *Atti della Accademia Nazionale dei Lincei* 9, no. 5: 551–89.
Farrington, B. 1944. *Greek Science: Thales to Aristotle*. Harmondsworth: Penguin.
Faucher, T., F. Téreygeol, L. Brousseau, and A. Arles. 2009. "À la recherche des ateliers monétaires grecs: l'apport de l'expérimentation." *Revue Numismatique* 6, no. 65: 43–80.
Favoretto, P. 2010. Aurelle-Verlac, http://www.aurelle-verlac.com. Accessed 1/10/2011.
Ferguson, N. 2004. *Empire: How Britain Made the Modern World*. Harmondsworth: Penguin.
———. 2008. *The Ascent of Money: A Financial History of the World*. Harmondsworth: Penguin.
———. 2011. *Civilization: The West and the Rest*. Harmondsworth: Penguin.
Feyel, C. 2006. *Les Artisans dans les Sanctuaries grecs aux Époques Classiques et Hellénistiques à travers la documentation financière en Grèce*. Bibliothèque des Écoles Françaises d'Athènes et de Rome fasc. 318. Athens: École Française d'Athènes.
Fields, N., and P. Bull. 2007. *Ancient Greek Warship 500–322 BC*. Oxford: Osprey Publishing.
Figueira, T. J. 1998. *The Power of Money, Coinage and Politics in the Athenian Empire*. Philadelphia: University of Pennsylvania Press.
Finley, M. I. 1952. *Studies in Land and Credit in Ancient Athens, 500–200 BC: The Horos Inscriptions*. New Brunswick, NJ: Rutgers University Press.
———. 1954. *The World of Odysseus*. London: Chatto & Windus.
———. 1959–60. "Was Greek Civilisation Based on Slave Labour?" In *Slavery in Classical Antiquity: Views and Controversies*, edited by M. Finley, 53–72. Cambridge: W. Heffer.
———. 1965a. "Technical Innovation and Economic Progress in the Ancient World." *Economic History Review* 18: 29–45.
———. 1965b. "Classical Greece." In *Trade and Politics in the Ancient World*, vol. 1, 1–35. 2nd International Conference of Economic History. Paris: Mouton & cie.
———. 1970. "Aristotle and Economic Analysis." *Past and Present* 47, no. 1: 3–25.
———. 1973. *The Ancient Economy*. Berkeley: University of California Press.
———. 1981. "Land, Debt and the Man of Property in Classical Athens." In *Economy and Society in Ancient Greece*, edited by B. D. Shaw and R. P. Saller, 62–76. London: Chatto & Windus.
———. 1985a. "The Ancient Historian and His Sources." In *Ancient History: Evidence and Models*, 7–26. London: Chatto & Windus.
———. 1985b. "Documents." In *Ancient History: Evidence and Models*, 27–46. London: Chatto & Windus.
———. 1985c. "How It Really Was." In *Ancient History: Evidence and Models*, 47–66. London: Chatto & Windus.
———. 1985d. "Max Weber and the Greek City State." In *Ancient History: Evidence and Models*, 88–103. London: Chatto & Windus.
———. 1986. "Archaeology and History." In *The Use and Abuse of History*, edited by M. I. Finley, 87–101. London: Hogarth Press.
Fisher, N. 2001. *Against Timarchos: Introduction, Translation, and Commentary*. Oxford: Oxford University Press.
Flament, C. 2007. *Le monnayage en argent d'Athènes del'époque archaïque à l'époque hellénistique (c. 550-c. 40 av. J.-C)*. Louvain-le-Neuve: Association de Numismatique Hoc.
———. 2010. "Le monnayage en argent d'Athènes au IIIe siècle av. notre ère." *Revue Belge de Numismatique et de Sigillographie* 156: 35–71.

Fogel, R. W., and S. L. Engerman. 1974. *Time on the Cross: The Economics of American Negro Slavery*. Boston: Little Brown.

Forbes, R. J. 1964–72. *Studies in Ancient Technology*. 9 vols. Leiden: E.J. Brill.

Foxhall, L. 2002. "Access to Resources in Classical Greece: The Egalitarianism of the Polis in Practice." In *Money, Labour and Land: Approaches to the Economies of Ancient Greece*, edited by P. A. Cartledge, E. E. Cohen, and L. Foxhall, 209–20. London: Routledge.

———. 2007. *Olive Cultivation in Ancient Greece: Seeking the Ancient Economy*. Oxford: Oxford University Press.

Foxhall, L., and H. Forbes. 1982. "Sitometreia: The Role of Grain as Staple Food in Classical Antiquity." *Chiron* 12: 41–90.

Francotte, H. 1900–1901. *L'Industrie dans la Grèce ancienne*. 2 vols. Brussels: Société Belge de Libraire.

Frank, R. 1985. *Choosing the Right Pond: Human Behavior and the Quest for Status*. Oxford: Oxford University Press.

Fraser, P. M. 1972. *Ptolemaic Alexandria*. 3 vols. Oxford: Clarendon Press.

Frederiksen, M. W. 1975. "Theory, Evidence and the Ancient Economy." *Journal of Roman Studies* 65: 164–71.

Frederiksen, R. 2001. *Greek City Walls of the Archaic Period, 900–480 bc*. Oxford Monographs on Classical Archaeology. New York: Oxford University Press.

French, A. 1964. *The Growth of the Athenian Economy*. London: Routledge & Kegan Paul.

Fried, C. 1981. *Contract as Promise: A Theory of Contractual Obligation*. Cambridge, MA: Harvard University Press.

Frost, H. 1976. *Lilybaeum*. Atti dell'Accademia Nazionale dei Lincei, Notizie degli scavi di antichità 30, Supplement. Rome: Edizioni Lincei.

Fuller, L. L. 1939. "Williston on Contracts." *North Carolina Legal Review* 18: 1–15.

Gabrielsen, V. 1994. *Financing the Athenian Fleet*. Baltimore: Johns Hopkins Press.

Gaimster, D. R. M., and B. Nenk. 1997. "English Households in Transition c. 1450–1550: The Ceramic Evidence." In *The Age of Transition: The Archaeology of English Culture 1400–1600*, edited by D. R. M. Gaimster and P. Stamper, 171–95. Oxbow Monograph 98. Oxford: Oxbow Books.

Galbraith, J. 1962. *The Affluent Society*. Harmondsworth: Penguin.

Garlan, Y. 1982. *Les esclaves en grèce ancienne*. Textes à l'appui. Paris: Maspero.

———. 1993. "À qui étaient destinés les timbres amphoriques grecs?" *Compte Rendu des Séances de l'Académie des Inscriptions et Belles-Lettres* 137: 181–90.

———. 1999. *Production et Commerce des amphoras anciennes en Mer Noire: Colloque international organisé à Istanbul, 25–28 mai 1994*. Aix-en-Provence: University of Provence.

———. 2010. "Le timbrage amphorique grec a-t-il été une initiative privée? L'exemple 'héracléote.'" In *Analyse et exploitation des timbres amphoriques grecs*. Colloque Athènes. Athens: École française d'Athènes.

Garnsey, P. 1988. *Famine and Food Supply in the Graeco-Roman World: Responses to Risk and Crisis*. Cambridge: Cambridge University Press.

———, and I. M. Morris. 1989. "Risk and the Polis: The Evolution of Institutionalised Responses to Food Supply Problems in the Ancient Greek State." In *Bad Year Economics: Cultural Responses to Risk and Uncertainty*, edited by P. Halstead and J. O'Shea, 98–105. Cambridge: Cambridge University Press.

———, and R. P. Saller. 1987. *The Roman Empire: Economy, Society and Culture*. London: Duckworth.

Gauthier, P. 1972. *Symbola: Les étrangers et la justice dans les cités grecques.* Annales de l'est. Nancy: Universite de Nancy.

———. 1976. *Un Commentaire Historique des Poroi de Xenophon.* Geneva: Librairie Droz.

Gay Levy, D., H. B. Applewhite, and M. D. Johnson. 1981. *Women in Revolutionary Paris 1789–1795.* Urbana: University of Illinois Press.

Geraghty, T. M. 2007. "The Factory System in the British Industrial Revolution: A Complementarity Thesis." *European Economic Review* 51: 1329–50.

Gerhardt, P. 1933. *Die attische Metoikie im vierten Jahrhundert.* Königsberg: n.p.

Glotz, G. 1926. *Ancient Greece at Work: An Economic History of Greece from the Homeric Period to the Roman Conquest.* New York: Knopf.

———. 1968. *La cité grecque.* Paris: Albin Michel.

Goette, H. R. 2001. *Athens, Attica and the Megarid: An Archaeological Guide.* New York: Routledge.

Gomme, A. W. 1933. *The Population of Athens in the Fourth and Fifth Centuries BC.* Oxford: Blackwell.

———, A. Andrewes, and K. J. Dover. 1970. *An Historical Commentary on Thucydides.* Vol. 4, Books V (25)–VII. Oxford: Clarendon Press.

Gourevitch, D. 2011. *Pour une archéologie de la médecine romaine.* Collection Pathographie 8. Paris: Éditions de Boccard.

Granovetter, M. 1985. "Economic Action and Social Structure: The Problem of Embeddedness." *American Journal of Sociology* 91, no. 3: 481–510.

———, and R. Swedberg. 2001. *The Sociology of Economic Life.* 2nd ed. Boulder, CO: Westview Press.

Green, K. 1986. *The Archaeology of the Roman Economy.* London: B. T. Batsford.

Green, R. 1961. "The Caputi Hydria." *Journal of Hellenic Studies* 81: 73–75.

Gruben, G. 2001. *Die Tempel der Griechen.* Munich: Hirmer.

Guthrie, W. K. C. 1935. *Orpheus and Greek Religion.* London: Methuen.

Habib, I. 1982. "Northern India under the Sultanate: Non-Agricultural Production and Urban Economy." In *The Cambridge Economic History of India. Vol. 1, c.1200–c.1750,* edited by T. Raychaudhuri and I. Habib, 76–93. Cambridge: Cambridge University Press.

Haldane, J. 1968. *Science and Life: Essays of a Rationalist.* London: Pemberton.

Halleux, R. 1981. *Les Alchimistes grecs Papyrus de Leyde; Papyrus de Stockholm; Fragments de Recettes.* Vol. 1. Paris: Société d' Édition "Les Belles Lettres."

Halstead, P. 1987. "Traditional and Ancient Rural Economy in Mediterranean Europe: Plus ça change?" *Journal of Hellenic Studies* 107: 77–87.

———, and J. O'Shea. 1989a. "Introduction." In *Bad Year Economics: Cultural Responses to Risk and Uncertainty,* edited by P. Halstead and J. O'Shea, 1–7. Cambridge: Cambridge University Press.

———. 1989b. "The Economy Has a Normal Surplus: Economic Stability and Social Change Among Early Farming Communities of Thessaly, Greece." In *Bad Year Economics: Cultural Responses to Risk and Uncertainty,* edited by P. Halstead and J. O'Shea, 68–80. Cambridge: Cambridge University Press.

———. 2011. "Redistribution in Aegean Palatial Societies: Terminology, Scale, and Significance." *American Journal of Archaeology* 115, no. 2: 229–35.

Hammond, N. G. L. 1975. *The Classical Age of Greece.* London: Weidenfeld & Nicholson.

Hampe, R., and A. Winter. 1962. *Bei Töpfern und Töpfinnerinnen in Kreta, Messenien und Zypern.* Mainz: Römisch-Germanisches Zentralmuseums.

Hancock, W. K. 1958. "Trek." *Economic History Review* 10, no. 3: 331–61.

Hansen, M. 1986. *Demography and Democracy: The Number of Athenian Citizens in the Fourth Century B.C.* Denmark: Systime.

———. 1991. *The Athenian Democracy in the Age of Demosthenes: Structure Principles and Ideology.* Oxford: Blackwell.

———. 2006. *The Shotgun Method: The Demography of the Ancient Greek City-State Culture.* Columbia: University of Missouri Press.

———. 2008. "An Update on the Shotgun Method." *Greek, Roman and Byzantine Studies* 48, no. 3: 259–86.

Hanson, V. D. 1989. *The Western Way of War: Infantry Battle in Classical Greece.* New York: Knopf.

———. 1995. *The Other Greeks: The Family Farm and the Agrarian Roots of Western Civilization.* New York: Free Press.

———. 2005 *A War Like No Other: How the Athenians and Spartans Fought the Peloponnesian War.* New York: Random House.

Hargreaves Heap, S. 1989. *Rationality in Economics.* New York: Blackwell.

Harris, E. M. 1988. "When Is a Sale Not a Sale? The Riddle of Athenian Terminology for Real Security Revisited." *Classical Quarterly* 38, no. 2: 351–81.

———. 1993. Review of P Millett's Lending and Borrowing in Ancient Athens. *Classical Review* 43, no. 1: 102–7.

———. 1995. *Aeschines and Athenian Politics.* New York: Oxford University Press.

———. 2001. Review of A. Bresson, *La Cite Marchande. Bryn Mawr Classical Review,* 2001.09.40, http://bmcr.brynmawr.edu/2001/2001-09-40.html.

———. 2002a. "Workshop, Marketplace and Household: The Nature of Technical Specialisation in Classical Athens and Its Influence on Economy and Society." In *Money, Labour and Land: Approaches to the Economies of Ancient Greece,* edited by P. A. Cartledge, E. E. Cohen, and L. Foxhall, 67–99. London: Routledge.

———. 2002b. "Did Solon Abolish Debt Bondage?" *Classical Quarterly* 52, no. 2: 415–30.

———. 2006a. "Law and Economy in Classical Athens." In *Democracy and the Rule of Law in Classical Athens: Essays on Law, Society and Politics,* 143–62. Cambridge: Cambridge University Press.

———. 2006b. "Women and Lending in Athenian Society: A Horos Re-examined." In *Democracy and the Rule of Law in Classical Athens: Essays on Law, Society and Politics,* 333–46. Cambridge: Cambridge University Press.

———. 2006c. "When Did the Athenian Assembly Meet?" In *Democracy and the Rule of Law in Classical Athens: Essays on Law, Society and Politics,* 103–20. Cambridge: Cambridge University Press.

———. 2013. "Were There Business Agents in Classical Greece? The Evidence of Some Lead Letters." In *Legal Documents in Ancient Societies 1: The Letter: Law, State, Society and the Epistolary Format in the Ancient World,* edited by U. Yiftach-Firanko, 105–24. Proceedings of a Colloquium at the American Academy at Rome, September 28–30, 2008. Wiesbaden: Harrassowitz

———. Forthcoming. "Wife, Household and Marketplace; The Role of Women in the Economy of Classical Athens." In *Donne che Contano nella storia greca,* edited by U. Bultrighini. Convegno di Chieti, May 2–4, 2007, Alessandria. Lanciano: Carabba.

Harris, J. R. 1992. *Essays in Industry and Technology in the Eighteenth Century: England and France*. Guildford: Variorum.

Harris, W. V. 2007. "The Late Republic: The Archaeology of the Roman Economy." In *The Cambridge Economic History of the Greco-Roman World*, edited by W. Scheidel, I. M. Morris, and R. P. Saller, 511–39. Cambridge: Cambridge University Press.

Hasaki, E. 2002. "Ceramic Kilns in Ancient Greece: Pyrotechnology and the Organization of Ceramic Workshops." PhD dissertation, University of Cincinnati.

———. 2006. "The Ancient Greek Ceramic Kilns and Their Contribution to the Technology and Organization of the Potters' Workshops." In *Proceedings of the 2nd International Conference on Ancient Greek Technology*, edited by P. Tasios and C. Palyvou, 221–27. Athens: EMAET Technical Chamber.

———. 2007. Review of V Cracolici, *I Sostegni di Fornace dal Kerameikos di Metaponto*. Bryn Mawr Classical Review, 2007.09.35, http://bmcr.brynmawr.edu/2007/2007-09-35.html.

———. 2011. "Crafting Spaces: Archaeological, Ethnographic and Ethnoarchaeological Studies of Spatial Organization in Pottery Workshops in Greece and Tunisia." In *Pottery in the Archaeological Record: Greece and Beyond; Acts of the International Colloquium Held at the Danish and Canadian Institutes in Athens, June 20–28, 2008*, edited by M. K. Lawall and J. Lund, 11–28. Gösta Enbom Monograph series 1. Aarhus: Aarhus University Press.

———. 2012a. "Craft Apprenticeship in Ancient Greece: Reaching Beyond the Masters." In *Archaeology and Apprenticeship: Acquiring Body Knowledge in the Ancient World*, edited by W. Wendrich, 281–329. Tucson: University of Arizona Press.

———. 2012b. "Workshops and Technology." In *A Companion to Greek Art*, edited by T. J. Smith and D. Plantzos, 255–72. Oxford: Blackwell.

Hasebroek, J. 1928. *Staat und Handel im alten Griechenland: Untersuchungen zur antiken Wirtschaftsgeschichte*. Tübingen: J. C. B. Mohr.

———. 1931. *Griechische Wirtschafts- und Gesellschaftsgeschichte bis zur Perserzeit*. Tübingen: J. C. B. Mohr.

Haselberger, L. 1997. "Architectural Likenesses: Models and Plans of Architecture in Classical Antiquity." *Journal of Roman Archaeology* 10: 77–94.

Healey, J. 1978. *Mining and Metallurgy in the Greek and Roman World*. London: Thames & Hudson.

Hedrick, C. W. 1999. "Democracy and the Athenian Epigraphical Habit." *Hesperia* 68, no. 3: 387–439.

Heilmeyer, W. D., G. Zimmer, and G. Schneider. 2007. "Die Bronzegiesserei unter der Werkstatt des Phidias in Olympia." *Archäologischer Anzeiger* 102: 239–99.

Heinrich, F. 2006. *Das Epinetron. Aspekte der weiblichen Lebenswelt im Spiegel eines Arbeitsgeräts*. Rahden: Verlag Marie Leidorf.

Helen, T. 1975. *Organisation of Roman Brick Production: An Interpretation of Roman Brick Stamps*. Annales Academiae Scientiarum Fennicae, Dissertationes Humanarum Litterarum 5. Helsinki: Suomalainen Tiedeakatemia.

Henderson, B. 1981. *The Concept of Strategy (abridged)*. Boston: Boston Consulting Group.

———. 1998a. "Three Perspectives Reviewing the Experience Curve." In *The Boston Consulting Group on Strategy*, edited by C. Stern and M. Deimler, 9–23. Boston Consulting Group Perspectives. Hoboken, NJ: John Wiley.

———. 1998b. "Strategic and Natural Competition." In *The Boston Consulting Group on Strategy*, edited by C. Stern and M. Deimler, 2–8. Boston Consulting Group Perspectives. Hoboken, NJ: John Wiley.

Henshilwood, C. S., F. d'Errico, K. L. van Niekirk, Y. Coquinot, Z. Jacobs, S. E. Lauritzen, M. Menu, and R. Garcia-Moreno. 2011. "A 100,000-Year-Old Ochre-Processing Workshop at Blombos Cave, South Africa." *Science* 334, no. 6053: 219–22.

Herfort-Koch, M. L. 1986. *Archaische Bronzeplastik Lakoniens*. Boreas Supplement 4. Münster: Archäologisches Seminar der Universität.

Herrold, D. 2007. "History of Ceramics." Ceramics Resource, De Pauw University, http://www.depauw.edu/acad/art/faculty/dherroldweb/pages/histp1.html. Accessed 6/27/2007.

Herzberg, F. I. 1959. *The Motivation to Work*. New York: John Wiley.

Hill, G. F. 1899. *A Handbook of Greek and Roman Coins*. London: Macmillan.

Himmelmann, N. 1977. "Planung und Verdingung der Parthenon-Skulpturen." In *Bathron: Beiträge zur Architektur und verwandten Kunsten für Heinrich Drerup zu seinem 80 Geburtstag von seinem Schülern und Freunden*, edited by H. Busing and F. Hiller, 213–24. Saarbrücken, Germany.

Hirschleifer, J. 1976. *Price Theory and Applications*. Englewood Cliffs, NJ: Prentice-Hall.

———. 1983. "From Weakest-Link to Best-Shot: The Voluntary Provision of Public Goods." *Public Choice* 41, no. 3: 371–86.

———. 2001. *The Dark Side of the Force: Economic Foundations of Conflict Theory*. New York: Cambridge University Press

———, and J. G. Riley. 1994. *The Analytics of Uncertainty and Information*. New York: Cambridge University Press.

Hitchner, R. B. 2002. "Olive Production and the Roman Economy: The Case for Intensive Growth in the Roman Empire." In *The Ancient Economy*, edited by W. Scheidel and S. von Reden, 71–88. Edinburgh: Edinburgh University Press.

———. 2005. "'The Advantages of Wealth and Luxury': The Case for Economic Growth in the Roman Empire." In *The Ancient Economy: Evidence and Models*, edited by J. C. Manning and I. M. Morris, 207–21. Stanford, CA: Stanford University Press.

Hodge, A. T. 1960. *The Woodwork of Greek Roofs*. Cambridge: Cambridge University Press.

Hodkinson, S. J. 1983. "Social Order and the Conflict of Values in Classical Sparta." *Chiron* 13: 239–81.

———. 1988. "Animal Husbandry in the Greek Polis." In *Pastoral Economies in Classical Antiquity*, edited by C. R. Whittaker, 35–74. Proceedings of the Cambridge Philological Society. Supplement 14. Cambridge: Cambridge Philological Society.

———. 2000. *Property and Wealth in Classical Sparta*. London: Duckworth.

Höpfner, W., E. L. Schwander, et al. 1994. *Haus und Stadt im klassischen Griechenland*. Rev. ed. Berlin: Deutscher Kunstverlag.

Hopkins, K. 1980. "Taxes and Trade in the Roman Empire (200 bc–ad 400)." *Journal of Roman Studies* 70: 101–25.

———. 1995–96. "Rome, Taxes, Rents and Trade." *Kodai: Journal of Ancient History* 6–7: 41–75.

Hopper, R. J. 1953. "The Attic Silver Mines in the Fourth Century BC." *Annual of the British School at Athens* 48: 200–254.

———. 1968. "The Laurion Mines: A Reconsideration." *Annual of the British School at Athens* 63: 293–326.

———. 1979. *Trade and Industry in Classical Greece.* London: Thames & Hudson.

Hoppin, J. C. 1973. *A Handbook of Attic Red-Figure Vases.* 2 vols. Washington, DC: McGrath.

Hordern, P., and N. Purcell. 2000. *The Corrupting Sea.* Oxford: Blackwell.

Hotelling, H. 1929. "Stability in Competition." *Economic Journal* 39, no. 153: 41–57.

Hughes, B. 2005. *Helen of Troy: Goddess, Princess, Whore.* London: Jonathan Cape.

———. 2010. *The Hemlock Cup: Socrates, Athens and the Search for the Good Life.* London: Jonathan Cape.

Hughes-Brock, H. 1998. "Greek Beads of the Mycenaean Period (ca. 1650–1100 BC): The Age of the Heroines of Greek Tradition and Mythology." In *Beads and Beadmakers: Gender, Material Culture and Meaning,* edited by L. D. Sciama and J. B. Eicher, 247–71. Oxford: Berg.

Hume, D. 1822. "Of the Populousness of Ancient Nations." In *Essays and Treatises on Several Subjects,* 360–431. Cambridge: J. Jones.

Humphrey, J. W. 2006. *Ancient Technology.* Westport, CT: Greenwood Press.

Humphreys, S. C. 1970. "Economy and Society in Classical Athens." *Annale della Scuola Normale Superiore di Pisa* 39: 1–26.

Hundsbichler, H. 1984. "Nahrung," "Kleidung," and "Wohnen." In *Alltag im Spätmittelalter,* edited by H. Kühnel, 196–270. Graz: Styria Premium.

Hundt, H.-J. 1969. "Über vorgeschichtliche Seidenfunde." *Jahrbuch des Römisch-Germanischen Zentralmuseums* 16: 59–72.

Hurwit, J. M. 1999. *The Athenian Acropolis: History, Mythology, and Archaeology from the Neolithic Era to the Present.* New York: Cambridge University Press.

———. 2004. *The Acropolis in the Age of Pericles.* New York: Cambridge University Press.

———. 2005. "The Parthenon and the Temple of Zeus at Olympia." In *Periklean Athens and Its Legacy: Problems and Perspectives,* edited by J. M. Barringer and J. M. Hurwit, 135–45. Austin: University of Texas Press.

Isager, S., and M. Hansen. 1975. *Aspects of Athenian Society in the Fourth Century BC: A Historical Introduction to and Commentary on the Paragraphe Speeches and the Speech against Dionysodorus in the Corpus Demosthenicum (XXXII–XXXVIII and LVI).* Odense: Odense University Press.

Jackson, M., and K. Greene. 2008. "Ceramic Production." In *The Oxford Handbook of Engineering and Technology in the Classical World,* edited by J. P. Oleson, 496–519. New York: Oxford University Press.

Jameson, M. H. 1960. "A Fourth Century Inscription of Themistocles' Decree." *Hesperia* 29: 198–223.

———. 2001. "Oil Presses of the Late Classical and Hellenistic Period." In *Technai: Techniques et Sociétés en Méditerranée,* edited by J.-P. Brun and P. Jockey, 281–99. Paris: Maisonneuve & Larose.

———. 2002. "On Paul Cartledge, The Political Economy of Greek Slavery." In *Money, Labour and Land: Approaches to the Economies of Ancient Greece,* edited by P. A. Cartledge, E. E. Cohen, and L. Foxhall, 167–74. London: Routledge.

Jameson, M. H., C. N. Runnels, and T. H. van Andel. 1994. *A Greek Countryside: The Southern Argolid from Prehistory to the Present Day.* Stanford, CA: Stanford University Press.

Johnston, A. W. 1979. *Trademarks on Greek Vases.* Warminster: Aris & Philips.

———. 2006. *Trademarks on Greek Vases: Addenda.* Warminster: Aris & Philips.

Jones, A. H. M. 1956. "Slavery in the Ancient World." *Economic History Review* 2, no. 9: 185–99.

———. 1964. *The Later Roman Empire 284–602: A Social, Economic, and Administrative Survey.* 3 vols. Baltimore: Johns Hopkins University Press.

Jones, J. E. 1975. "Town and Country Houses of Attica in Classical Times." In *Thorikos and the Laurium in Archaic and Classical Times,* edited by P. S. H. Mussche and F. Goemare-de Poercke, 63–116. Ghent: Belgian Archaeological Mission in Greece.

———. 1982. "The Laurium Silver Mines: A Review." *Greece and Rome* 29: 169–83.

———. 1984–85. "Laurium: Agrileza 1977–83: Excavations at a Silver Mine Site." *Archaeological Review* 31: 106–23.

———. 1988. *Growth Recurring: Economic Change in World History.* Oxford: Oxford University Press.

———, L. H. Sackett, and A. J. Graham. 1962. "The Dema House in Attica." *Annual of the British School at Athens* 57: 75–114.

Jones, N. 1997. *Ancient Greece: State and Society.* Upper Saddle River, NJ: Prentice Hall.

Jones, R. E. 1986. "Greek Potters' Clays: Questions of Selection, Availability and Adaptation." In *Ancient Greek and Related Pottery: Proceedings of the International Vase Symposium in Amsterdam,* edited by H. A. G. Brijder, 21–30. Allard Pierson Series 5. Amsterdam: Allard Pierson Museum.

Jongkees, J. H. 1951. "On Price Inscriptions on Greek Vases." *Mnemosyne,* 4th ser., 3–4: 258–66.

Jongman, W., and R. Decker. 1989. "Public Intervention in the Food Supply in Preindustrial Europe." In *Bad Year Economics: Cultural Responses to Risk and Uncertainty,* edited by P. Halstead and J. O'Shea, 114–22. Cambridge: Cambridge University Press.

Kahnemann, D., P. Slovic, and A. Tversky. 1982. *Judgment under Uncertainty: Heuristics and Biases.* Cambridge: Cambridge University Press.

Kakovoyiannis, E. 2001. "The Silver Ore Processing Workshops of the Laurium Region." *Annual of the British School at Athens* 96: 365–80.

Kalogeropoulou, A. 1970. "From the Techniques of Pottery." *Athens Annals of Archaeology* 3: 429–34.

Kallett-Marx, L. 1989. "Did Tribute Fund the Parthenon?" *Classical Antiquity* 8, no. 2: 252–66.

———. 1993. *Money, Expense and Naval Power in Thucydides' History 1–5.24.* Berkeley: University of California Press.

Kant, I. 1968. *A Critique of Pure Reason.* London: Macmillan.

Kealey, T. 1996. *The Economic Laws of Scientific Research.* London: Macmillan.

Kehoe, D. P. 2007. "The Early Roman Empire: Production." In *The Cambridge Economic History of the Greco-Roman World,* edited by W. Scheidel, I. M. Morris, and R. P. Saller, 543–69. Cambridge: Cambridge University Press.

Keynes, J. M. 1921. *A Treatise on Probability.* London: Macmillan.

———. 1936. *The General Theory of Employment, Interest and Money.* London: Macmillan.

Kiel, M. 1987. "Population Growth and Food Production in 16th-Century Athens and Attica According to the Ottoman Tahrir Defters." In *Proceedings of the VIth Cambridge Comité Internationale des Études Pré-Ottoman et Ottoman.* Istanbul: Divit Yayıncılık.

Kim, H. S. 2001. "Archaic Coinage as Evidence for the Use of Money." In *Money and Its Uses in the Ancient Greek World,* edited by A. Meadows and K. Shipton, 7–21. Oxford: Oxford University Press.

Klein, R. G. 1989. *The Human Career: Human Biological and Cultural Origins.* Chicago: University of Chicago Press.

Knight, F. 1921. *Risk, Uncertainty and Profit.* Boston: Hart, Schaffner & Marx.

Knappett, C. 2001. "Overseen or Overlooked: Ceramic Production in a Mycenaean Palace System." In *Economy and Politics in the Mycenaean Palace States: Proceedings of a Conference Held on 1–3 July 1999 in the Faculty of Classics, Cambridge,* edited by S. Voutsaki and J. Killen, 80–95. Cambridge: Cambridge Philosophical Society.

Knigge, U. 2005. *Der Bau Z.* Kerameikos 17. Munich: Hirmer.

Koehler, U. 1878. "Phialai exeleutherikai." *Mémoires de l'Académie des Inscriptions et Belles Letters* 3: 172–77.

Konstam, N. 1984. *Sculpture: The Art and the Practice.* London: Collins.

Korres, M. 1995. *From Pentelicon to the Parthenon: The Ancient Quarries and the Story of a Half-Worked Column Capital of the First Marble Parthenon.* Athens: Melissa.

———. 2000. *The Stones of the Parthenon.* Malibu, CA: Getty Publications.

Kraay, C. M. 1976. *Archaic and Classical Greek Coins.* London: Methuen.

Kroll, J. H. 1979. "A Chronology of Early Athenian Bronze Coinage, c.350–250 BC." In *Greek Numismatics and Archaeology: Essays in Honour of Margaret Thomson,* edited by O. Morkholm and N. M. Waggoner, 139–54. Wetteren: Universa Press.

———. 1981. "From Wappenmünzen to Gorgoneia to Owls." *American Numismatic Society Museum Notes* 26: 1–32.

———. 2000. Review of Leslie Kurke, *Coins, Bodies, Games and Gold: The Politics of Meaning in Archaic Greece. Classical Journal* 96, no. 1: 85–90.

———. 2011a. "The Reminting of Athenian Silver Coinage 353 BC." *Hesperia* 80: 229–59.

———. 2011b. "Athenian Tetradrachm Coinage of the First Half of the Fourth Century bc." *Revue Belge de Numismatique* 157: 3–26.

———. 2013. "On the Chronology of Third Century BC Athenian Silver Coinage." *Revue Belge de Numismatique* 159: 33–44.

———, and N. M. Waggoner. 1984. "Dating the Earliest Coins of Athens, Corinth and Aegina." *American Journal of Archaeology* 88: 325–40.

Kron, G. 1996. "Landed and Commercial Wealth in Classical Athens 500–300 B.C." Ph. D. diss. University of Toronto.

———. 2005. "Anthropometry, Physical Anthropology, and the Reconstruction of Ancient Health, Nutrition, and Living Standards." *Historia* 54: 68–83.

———. Forthcoming. "Classical Greek Trade in Comparative Perspective: Literary and Archaeological Evidence." In *Beyond Self-Sufficiency: Households, City-States and Markets in the Ancient Greek World,* edited by E. M. Harris, D. Lewis, and M. Woolmer. New York: Cambridge University Press.

Krugman, P. 1991. *Geography and Trade.* Cambridge, MA: MIT Press.

Kurke, L. 1999. *Coins, Bodies, Games and Gold: The Politics of Meaning in Archaic Greece.* Princeton, NJ: Princeton University Press.

———. 2002. "Money and Mythic History: The Contestation of Transactional Orders in the Fifth Century BC." In *The Ancient Economy,* edited by W. Scheidel and S. von Reden, 87–113. Edinburgh: Edinburgh University Press.

Kuznetzov, V. D. 1990. "The Builders of Erechtheion." *Vestnik Drevnei Istorii* 4: 27–44 (in Russian with English summary).

Kyrtatas, D. 2002. "Domination and Exploitation." In *Money, Labour and Land: Approaches to the Economies of Ancient Greece*, edited by P. A. Cartledge, E. E. Cohen, and L. Foxhall, 140–55. London: Routledge.

Lalonde, G., M. K. Langdon, and M. B. Walbank. 1991. *Inscriptions.* Athenian Agora: Results of Excavations Conducted by the American School of Classical Studies at Athens 19. Princeton, NJ: American School of Classical Studies at Athens.

Lambert, S. 1997. *Rationes Centesimarum: Sales of Public Land in Lykourgan Athens.* Amsterdam: J. C. Gieben.

Lanchester, J. 2010. *Whoops: Why Everyone Owes Everyone and No One Can Pay.* London: Allen Lane.

———. 2012. "Greece vs. the Rest." *New Yorker*, June 18.

Landes, D. S. 1969. *The Unbound Prometheus: Technological Change and Industrial Development in Western Europe from 1750 to the Present.* Cambridge: Cambridge University Press.

Lane Fox, R. 2006. *The Classical World: An Epic History of Greece and Rome.* Harmondsworth: Penguin.

Lang, M. 1956. "Numerical Notation on Greek Vases." *Hesperia* 25: 1–24.

Lapatin, K. D. S. 1997. "Pheidias Elephantourgos." *American Journal of Archaeology* 101, no. 4: 663–82.

———. 2001. *Chryselephantine Statuary in the Ancient Mediterranean World.* Oxford Monographs on Classical Archaeology. New York: Oxford University Press.

Lauffer, S. 1956. *Die Bergwerkssklaven von Laurium.* Mainz: Abhandlungen der Akademie der Wissenschaft in Mainz.

Lawall, M. L. 1997. Review of I. K. Whitbread, *Greek Transport Amphorae: A Petrological and Archaeological Study 1995. American Journal of Archaeology* 101: 176–77.

———. 2000. "Graffiti, Wine Selling and the Re-Use of Amphoras in the Athenian Agora ca. 430–400 B.C." *Hesperia* 69: 3–90.

———. 2001. "Amphoras in the 1990s: In Need of Archaeology: Review of Y. Garlan, *Les timbres amphoriques de Thasos* (Athens 1999); Y. Garlan (ed.), *Production et commerce des amphores anciennes en Mer Noire* (Provence 1999); and N. Conovici, *Histria VIII, Les timbres amphoriques 2. Sinope* (Bucarest 1998)." *American Journal of Archaeology* 105: 533–37.

———. 2009. "The Temple of Apollo Patroos Dated by an Amphora Stamp." *Hesperia* 78, no. 3: 387–403.

———. 2010a. "Socio-Economic Conditions and the Contents of Amphorae." In *Production and Trade of Amphorae in the Black Sea: Acts of the International Round Table held at Kiten, Nessebar and Sredetz, September 26–30, 2007*, edited by C. Tsochov, T. Stoyanou, and A. Bozkova, 23–33. Sofia: Bulgarian Academy of Sciences, National Archaeological Museum.

———. 2010b. "Imitative Amphoras in the Greek World." *Marburger Beiträge zur Antiken Handels-, Wirtschaft und Sozialgeschichte* 28: 45–88.

———. Forthcoming. "Transport Amphoras and Market Behaviour in the Economies of Classical and Hellenistic Greece." In *Markets, Households and City States in the Ancient Greek Economy*, edited by E. M. Harris, D. M. Lewis, and M. Woolmer. New York: Cambridge University Press.

Lawton, C. 2006. *Marbleworkers in the Athenian Agora*. Athens: American School of Classical Studies at Athens.

Laziridis, D. 1952. "Anaskafe kai Ereunai en Abdirois." *Praktika* 260–278.

Leakey, M. D. 1971. *Olduvai Gorge*. Vol. 3, *Excavations in Beds II and III, 1960–1963*. New York: Cambridge University Press.

van der Leeuw, S. 1999. "Exchange and Trade in Ceramics: Some Notes from the Potter's Point of View." In *The Complex Past of Pottery: Production, Circulation and Consumption of Mycenaean and Greek Pottery in the Sixteenth to Early Fifth Centuries BC; Proceedings of the ARCHON International Conference held in Amsterdam 8–9 November 1996*, edited by V. Stissi, J. P. Crielaard, and G. J. van Wijngaarden, 115–36. Amsterdam: E. J. Brill.

Lehrer, J. 2007. *Proust Was a Neuroscientist*. Edinburgh: Canongate Books.

Levitt, S. D., and S. J. Dubner. 2005. *Freakonomics: A Rogue Economist Explores the Hidden Side of Everything*. New York: William Morrow/Harper Collins.

———. 2009. *Superfreakonomics: Global Cooling, Patriotic Prostitutes, and Why Suicide Bombers Should Buy Life Insurance*. New York: William Morrow/Harper Collins.

Levy, E. 1988. "Métèques et Droit de Résidence." In *L'étranger dans le monde grecque: Actes du colloque organisé par l'Institut d' Études Anciennes, Mai 1987*, edited by R. Lonis, 47–61. Nancy: Université de Nancy.

Lewis, D. M. 1959. "Attic Manumissions." *Hesperia* 28: 208–38.

———. 1961. "Notes on the Decree of Themistocles." *Classical Quarterly* 11: 61–66.

———. 1968. "Dedications of Phialae at Athens." *Hesperia* 37: 368–80.

———. 1997. "Public Property in the City." In *The Greek City from Homer to Alexander*, edited by O. Murray and S. Price, 245–63. Oxford: Clarendon Press.

Lewis, D. M. Forthcoming. "The Market for Slaves in the Fifth and Fourth Century Aegean: Achaemenid Anatolia as a Case Study." In *Markets, Households and City States in the Ancient Greek Economy,* edited by E. M. Harris, D. M. Lewis, and M. Woolmer. New York: Cambridge University Press.

Liddell, S. G., and R. Scott. 1940. *A Greek-English Lexicon*. New edition by H. S. Jones. 2 vols. Oxford: Clarendon Press.

Lierke, R. 1998. "The Ancient Glass Pottery Process." *Annales du 14ème congrès de l'Association Internationale pour l'Histoire du Verre*, 198–202.

Lieven, A. 2005. *America Right or Wrong: An Anatomy of American Nationalism*. Oxford: Oxford University Press.

Linders, T. 1972. *Studies in the Treasure Records of Artemis Brauronia Found in Athens*. Stockholm: P. Äström.

Linfert, A. 1990. "Die Schule des Polyklet." In *Polyklet: Der Bildhauer de griechischen Klassic*, edited by H. Beck, P. C. Bol, and M. Buckler, 240–97. Mainz: P. von Zabern.

Lippold, G. 1950. "Die Griechische Plastik." *Handbuch der Archäologie* 3, no. 1.

Loftus, A. 1999. "A Weaving Factory in Third Century Memphis." In *Archéologie des textiles des origines au 5ème siècle*, edited by D. Cardon and M. Feugère, 165–78. Actes du Colloque des Lattes. Montagnac: Éditions Monique Mergoil.

Long, T. 1978. "Pherecrates' 'Savages': A Footnote to the Greek Attitude on the Noble Savage." *Classical World* 71, no. 6: 381–82.

Loomis, W. T. 1998. *Wages, Welfare Costs, and Inflation in Classical Athens*. Ann Arbor: University of Michigan Press.

Louis, P. 1927. *Ancient Rome at Work: An Economic History of Rome from the Origins to the Empire*. London: Kegan Paul.

Macauley, S. 1963. "Non-Contractual Relations in Business: A Preliminary Study." *American Sociology Review* 28: 55–67.

Macve, R. 1985. "Some Glosses on Greek and Roman Accounting." In *Crux: Essays in Greek History Presented to G. E. M. de Ste. Croix on His 75th Birthday*, edited by P. C. Cartledge and F. D. Harvey, 223–64. London: Duckworth.

Maffi, A. 2008. "Lo statuto giuridico delle scuole filosofiche greche nel III sec. A. C." In *Enseignement superieur dans les mondes antiques et medievaux; aspects institutionneles, juridiques et pédagogiques*, edited by H. Hugonnard-Roche, 113–26. Paris: Librairie Philosophique J. Vrin.

Malacrino, C. G. 2010. *Constructing the Ancient World: Architectural Techniques of the Greeks and Romans*. Los Angeles: Getty Publications.

Malherbe, A. J. 1977. *The Cynic Epistles: A Study Edition*. Missoula, MT: Society of Biblical Literature.

Manning, J. G. 2007. "Hellenistic Egypt." In *The Cambridge Economic History of the Greco-Roman World,* edited by W. Scheidel, I. M. Morris, and R. P. Saller, 434–59. Cambridge: Cambridge University Press.

Mark, S. E. 2005. *Homeric Seafaring*. College Station: Texas A&M University Press.

Markle, M. 1985. "Jury Pay and Assembly Pay at Athens." In *Crux: Essays in Greek History Presented to G. E. M. de Ste. Croix on His 75th Birthday*, edited by P. C. Cartledge and F. D. Harvey, 265–97. London: Duckworth.

Markoe, G. E. 2005. *The Phoenicians*. London: Folio Society.

Marglin, S. A. 1974. "What Do Bosses Do? The Origins and Function of Hierarchy in Capitalist Production." In *The Division of Labour: The Labour Process and Class Struggle in Modern Capitalism*, edited by A. Gorz, 13–54. Brighton: Harvester Press.

Marichal, R. 1988. *Graffittes de la Graufesenque*. Gallia Supplement 47. Paris: Éditions de la Recherche Scientifique.

Marshall, A. 1959. *The Principles of Economics*. 8th ed. London: Macmillan.

Martin, T. R. 1991. "Silver Coins and Public Slaves in the Athenian Law of 375/4 B.C." In *Mnemata: Papers in Memory of Nancy M. Waggoner*, edited by W. E. Metcalf, 21–47. New York: American Numismatic Society.

Martinson, K. 2007. "Felt—Myths and Reality." *Interweave Felt Magazine*.

Maslow, A. H. 1943. "A Theory of Human Motivation." *Psychological Review* 50, no. 4: 370–96.

Mattingly, D. J., and J. Salmon. 2001a. "The Productive Past: Economies beyond Agriculture." In *Economies beyond Agriculture in the Classical World*, edited by D. J. Mattingly and J. Salmon, 3–14. London: Routledge.

Mattingly, D. J., D. Stone, L. Stirling, and N. Ben Lazreg. 2001b. "Leptiminus (Tunisia): A 'Producer City'?" In *Economies beyond Agriculture in the Classical World*, edited by D. J. Mattingly and J. Salmon, 66–89. London: Routledge.

Mattusch, C. C. 1977. "Bronze and Ironworking in the Area of the Athenian Agora." *Hesperia* 46: 340–79.

———. 1980. "The Berlin Foundry Cup: The Casting of Greek Bronze Statuary in the Early Fifth century BC." *American Journal of Archaeology* 84, no. 4: 435–44.

———. 1988. *Greek Bronze Statuary: From the Beginnings through the Fifth Century BC.* New York: Cornell University Press.

———. 1989. *An Athenian Foundry: The Production of Bronze Statuary in Greece during the IVth Century BC.* Bulletin of the Metals Museum 14. Sendai: Japan Institute of Metals.

———. 2006. "Archaic and Classical Bronzes." In *Greek Sculpture: Function, Materials and Techniques in the Archaic and Classical Periods,* edited by O. Palagia, 208–42. New York: Cambridge University Press.

———. 2008. "Metalworking and Tools." In *The Oxford Handbook of Engineering and Technology in the Classical World,* edited by J. P. Oleson, 418–38. New York: Oxford University Press.

Matyszak, P. 2008. *Ancient Athens on Five Drachmae a Day.* London: Thames & Hudson.

Mayo, E. 1949. *Hawthorne and the Western Electric Company: The Social Problems of an Industrial Civilisation.* London: Routledge & Kegan Paul.

Mazow, L. B. 2010. "Throwing the Baby Out with the Bathwater: Innovations in Mediterranean Textile Production at the End of the 2nd/Beginning of the 1st Millennium BCE." Paper read at the Conference on Textile Production in the Ancient Near East, April 16, 2010, London.

McCrum, R. 2004. *Wodehouse: A Life.* London: Penguin Viking.

McFadden, D. 2013. "The New Science of Pleasure." National Bureau of Economic Research Working Paper 18687.

McGrail, S., and E. Kentley. 1985. *Sewn Plank Boats: Archaeological and Ethnographic Papers Based on Those Presented to a Conference at Greenwich in November, 1984.* British Archaeological Reports 276. Oxford: British Archaeological Reports.

McKendrick, N. 1982. "The Consumer Revolution in Eighteenth Century England." In *Birth of a Consumer Society: The Commercialization of Eighteenth Century England,* edited by N. McKendrick, J. Brewer, and J. H. Plumb, 9–33. Bloomington: Indiana University Press.

McQuilling Services. 2007. "Tankers." *Shipbuilding,* September 30.

Meier, C. 1993. *Athens: A Portrait of the City in Its Golden Age.* Translated by R. Kimber and R. Kimber 1998. New York: Metropolitan Books.

Meier, F. G. 1959. *Griechische Mauerbauinschriften: Erster Teil: Texte und Kommentare.* Vestigia 1. Heidelberg: Quelle & Meyer.

———. 1961. *Griechische Mauerbauinschriften: Zweiter Teil: Untersuchungen.* Vestigia 2. Heidelberg: Quelle & Meyer.

Meiggs, R. 1963. "The Crisis of Athenian Imperialism." *Harvard Studies in Classical Philology* 67: 1–36.

———. 1972. *The Athenian Empire.* Oxford: Oxford University Press.

———. 1982. *Trees and Timber in the Ancient Mediterranean World.* Oxford: Clarendon Press.

Meikle, S. 1995a. "Modernism, Economics, and the Ancient Economy." *Proceedings of the Cambridge Philological Society* 41: 174–91.

———. 1995b. *Aristotle's Economic Thought.* Oxford: Oxford University Press.

Mele, A. 1976. "Esclavage et liberté dans la société mycénienne." In *Actes du colloque 1973 sur l'esclavage,* 117–55. Besançon: Université de Besançon.

Menger, K. 1985. *Investigations into the Methods of the Social Sciences, with Special Reference to Economics.* Translated by F. J. Nock. New York: New York University Press.

Merritt, B. D. 1954. "Indirect Tradition in Thucydides." *Hesperia* 23: 185–231.
Metcalf, W. E. 2012. *The Oxford Handbook of Greek and Roman Coinage*. New York: Oxford University Press.
Meyer, E. A. 2010. *Metics and the Athenian Phialai Inscriptions: A Study in Athenian Epigraphy and Law*. Stuttgart: Franz Steiner Verlag.
Miles, M. M. 1989. "A Reconstruction of the Temple of Nemesis at Rhamnous." *Hesperia* 58, no. 2: 133–249.
Millett, P. 1990. "Sale, Credit and Exchange in Athenian Law and Society." In *Nomos: Essays in Athenian Law, Politics and Society*, edited by P. A. Cartledge, P. Millett, and S. Todd, 167–94. Cambridge: Cambridge University Press.
———. 1991. *Lending and Borrowing in Ancient Athens*. Cambridge: Cambridge University Press.
———. 1993. "Warfare, Economy and Democracy in Classical Athens." In *War and Society in the Greek World*, edited by J. Rich and G. Shipley, 177–96. London: Routledge.
———. 2000. "The Economy." In *The Shorter Oxford History of Europe: Classical Greece*, edited by R. Osborne, 23–51. Oxford: Oxford University Press.
———. 2001. "Productive to Some Purpose? The Problem of Economic Growth." In *Economies beyond Agriculture in the Classical World*, edited by D. J. Mattingly and J. Salmon, 17–48. London: Routledge.
Miltner, F. 1931. "Seewesen." In *Realencyclopädie der classischen Altertumswissenschaft*, Supplement 5, 906–62. Stuttgart: Pauly-Wissowa.
Minc, L. D., and K. P. Smith. 1989. "The Spirit of Survival: Cultural Responses to Resource Variability in North Alaska." In *Bad Year Economics: Cultural Responses to Risk and Uncertainty*, edited by P. Halstead and J. O'Shea, 8–39. Cambridge: Cambridge University Press.
Mitchell, B. R., and P. Deane. 1962. *Abstract of British Historical Statistics*. Cambridge: Cambridge University Press.
Moignard, E. 2006. *Greek Vases: An Introduction*. London: Bristol Classical Press.
Mokyr, J. 2002. *The Gifts of Athena: Historical Origins of the Knowledge Economy*. Princeton, NJ: Princeton University Press.
———. 2009. *The Enlightened Economy: An Economic History of Britain 1700–1850*. New Haven, CT: Yale University Press.
Momigliano, A. 1975. *Alien Wisdom: The Limits of Hellenization*. Cambridge: Cambridge University Press.
Monaco, M. 2000. *Ergasteria: Impianti Artigianali Ceramici ad Atene ed in Attica*. Rome: "L'Erma" di Bretschneider.
Monaghan, M. 1999. "Dyeing Establishments in Classical and Hellenistic Greece." In *Archéologie des textiles des origines au 5ème siècle: Actes du Colloque des Lattes*, edited by D. Cardon and M. Feugère, 167–72. Montagnac: Éditions Monique Mergoil.
Morel, J.-P. 1988. "Remarques sur l'art et l'artisanat de Naples antique." In *Neapolis: Atti del XXV Convegno di Studi sulla Magna Graecia (Tarento 1985)*, 305–56. Naples.
———. 2007. "Early Rome and Italy." In *The Cambridge Economic History of the Greco-Roman World*, edited by W. Scheidel, I. M. Morris, and R. P. Saller, 487–510. Cambridge: Cambridge University Press.
Moreno, A. 2007. *Feeding the Democracy: The Athenian Grain Supply in the Fifth and Fourth Centuries BC*. Oxford: Oxford University Press.

Morgan, C. 1990. *Athletes and Oracles: The Transformation of Olympia and Delphi in the Eighth Century b.c.* Cambridge: Cambridge University Press.

———. 1999. "Some Thoughts on the Production and Consumption of Early Iron Age Pottery in the Aegean." In *The Complex Past of Pottery: Production, Circulation and Consumption of Mycenaean and Greek Pottery in the Sixteenth to Early Fifth Centuries BC; Proceedings of the ARCHON International Conference Held in Amsterdam 8–9 November 1996*, edited by V. Stissi, J. P. Crielaard, and G. J. van Wijngaarden, 213–59. Amsterdam: E. J. Brill.

Morley, N. 1996. *Metropolis and Hinterland: The City of Rome and the Italian Economy, 200 b.c. to a.d. 200.* Cambridge: Cambridge University Press.

Morris, I. M. 1986. "The Use and Abuse of Homer." *Classical Antiquity* 5, no. 1: 81–138.

———. 1994. *The Community against the Market in Classical Athens.* In *From Political Economy to Anthropology*, edited by C. A. M. Duncan and D. W. Tandy, 52–79. Montreal: Black Rose.

———. 1999. "Foreword." In *The Ancient Economy* by M. I. Finley, ix–xxxvi. Rev. ed. Berkeley: University of California Press.

———. 2002. "Hard Surfaces." In *Money Labour and Land: Approaches to the Economies of Ancient Greece,* edited by P. A. Cartledge, E. E. Cohen, and L. Foxhall, 8–43. London: Routledge.

———. 2004. "Economic Growth in Ancient Greece." *Journal of Institutional and Theoretical Economics* 160: 709–42.

———. 2005. "Archaeology, Standards of Living, and Greek Economic History." In *The Ancient Economy: Evidence and Models*, edited by J. C. Manning and I. M. Morris, 91–126. Stanford, CA: Stanford University Press.

———. 2007. "Early Iron Age Greece." In *The Cambridge Economic History of the Greco-Roman World*, edited by W. Scheidel, I. M. Morris, and R. P. Saller, 211–41. Cambridge: Cambridge University Press.

———. 2010. "Social Development." Stanford University 2010, http://www.ianmorris.org/socdev.html. Accessed 8/25/2011.

Morrison, J. S., and J. F. Coates. 1986. *The Athenian Trireme: The History and Reconstruction of an Ancient Greek Warship.* Cambridge: Cambridge University Press.

———, J. F. Coates, and N. B. Rankov. 2000. *The Athenian Trireme: The History and Reconstruction of an Ancient Greek Warship.* 2nd ed. Cambridge: Cambridge University Press.

———, and R. T. Williams. 1968. *Greek Oared Ships: 900–322 b.c.* Cambridge: Cambridge University Press.

Morrow, K. D. 1985. *Greek Footwear and the Dating of Sculpture.* Madison: University of Wisconsin Press.

Munro, J. A. R. 1902. "Some Observations on the Persian Wars (Continued)." *Journal of Hellenic Studies* 22: 294–332.

Murray, O. 1980. *Early Greece.* London: Harvester Press.

———. 1990. "The Affair of the Mysteries: Democracy and the Drinking Group." In *Sympotica: A Symposium on the Symposion*, edited by O. Murray, 149–61. Oxford: Oxford University Press.

Musgrave, E. 1997. "Family, Household and Production: The Potters of the Saintonge, France, 1500 to 1800." In *Not So Much a Pot, More a Way of Life: Current Approaches* to *Artefact Analysis in Archaeology,* edited by C. G. Cumberpatch and P. W. Blinkhorn, 85–94. Oxbow Monographs 83. Oxford: Oxbow Books.

Mussche, H. F., P. Spitaels, and F. Goemare de Poerck. 1975. *Thorikos and the Laurion in Archaic and Classical Times: Papers and Contributions.* Miscellanea Graeca 1. Ghent: Belgian Archaeological Mission in Greece.

Naumann, R., I. D. Huff, and R. Schnyder. 1975. "Takht-i-Suleiman: 1963–1973: Bericht über die Ausgrabungen." *Archäologischer Anzeiger* 90: 109–204.

Nelson, G., et al. 2002. "An Amino-Acid Taste Receptor." *Nature* 416: 199–202.

Nevett, L. C. 2000. "A Real Estate 'Market' in Classical Greece? The Example of Town Housing." *Annual of the British School at Athens* 95: 329–43.

Niemeyer, H.-G. 1960. *Promachos: Untersuchungen zur Darstellung der bewaffneten Athena in Archaischer Zeit.* Waldsassen: Stiftland-Verlag.

Nixon, L. 1999. "Women, Children, and Weaving." In *Meletemata: Studies in Aegean Archaeology Presented to Malcolm H. Weiner as He Enters His 65th Year,* edited by P. P. Betancourt, P. P. Karageorghis, R. Laffineur, and W.-D. Niemeyer, 561–67. Aegaeum 20. Liège: Université de Liège.

——, and S. Price. 1990. "The Size and Resources of Greek Cities." In *The Greek City from Homer to Alexander,* edited by O. Murray and S. Price, 137–70. Oxford: Oxford University Press.

Noble, J. V. 1965. *The Techniques of Painted Attic Pottery.* London: Faber & Faber.

North, D. C. 1981. *Structure and Change in Economic History.* New York: W. W. Norton.

Oakley, J. H. 1992. "An Athenian Red Figure Workshop from the Time of the Peloponnesian War." In *Les ateliers des potiers dans le monde grec aux époques géométriques, archaiques et classiques,* edited by F. Blondé and J. Y. Perreault, 195–203. Bulletin de Correspondance Hellénique Supplement 23. Athens: École Française d'Athènes.

Ober, J. 1989. *Mass and Elite in Democratic Athens: Rhetoric, Ideology and the Power of the People.* Princeton, NJ: Princeton University Press.

——. 2008. *Democracy and Knowledge: Innovation and Learning in Classical Athens.* Princeton, NJ: Princeton University Press.

——. 2010. "Wealthy Hellas." Version 1.1, May. Princeton/Stanford Working Papers in Classics, http://www.princeton.edu/~pswpc/pdfs/ober/051001.pdf. Accessed 3/21/2013.

——. 2012. "Ober on the Ancient Greek Economy." *Library of Economics and Liberty* (podcast), July 6, 2012, http://www.econtalk.org/archives/2012/08/ober_on_the_anc.html.

Oddy, W., and J. Swaddling. 1985. "Illustrations of Metalworking Furnaces on Greek Vases." In *Furnaces and Smelting Technology in Antiquity,* edited by P. T. Craddock and M. J. Hughes, 43–58. London: British Museum.

Oertel, F. 1925. "Anhang." In *Geschichte der Sozialen Frage und des Sozialismus in der antiken Welt,* edited by R. von Pöhlmann. 3rd ed. Munich: Beck.

Ogden, J. 1992. *Ancient Jewellery.* Berkeley: University of California Press.

Olmsted, F. 1862. *Journeys and Explorations in the Cotton Kingdom of America.* New York: Mason Brothers.

Oliver, G. J. 2007. *War, Food, and Politics in Early Hellenistic Athens.* Oxford: Oxford University Press.

Osborne, R. 1985. *Demos: The Discovery of Classical Attika.* Cambridge: Cambridge University Press.

———. 1987. *Classical Landscape with Figures: The Ancient Greek City and Its Countryside.* London: G. Philip.

———. 1988. "Social and Economic Implications of the Leasing of Land and Property in Classical and Hellenistic Greece." *Chiron* 18: 225–70.

———. 1991. "Pride and Prejudice, Sense and Subsistence: Exchange and Society in the Greek City." In *City and Country in the Ancient World,* edited by J. Rich and A. Wallace-Hadrill, 119–45. London, New York: Routledge.

———. 1992. "Is It a Farm? The Definition of Agricultural Sites and Settlements in Ancient Greece." In *Agriculture in Ancient Greece: 7th International Symposium of the Swedish School at Athens. 16–17 May 1990*, edited by B. Wells, 21–25. Stockholm: Svenska Institutet i Athen.

———. 2007. "Archaic Greece." In *The Cambridge Economic History of the Greco-Roman World*, edited by W. Scheidel, I. M. Morris, and R. P. Saller, 277–301. Cambridge: Cambridge University Press.

O'Shea, J. 1989. "Coping with Scarcity: Cultural Exchange and Storage." In *Economic Archaeology*, edited by A. Sheridan and G. Bailey, 167–83. British Archaeological Reports, International Series 96. Oxford.

Palagia, O. 2006a. "Classical Athens." In *Greek Sculpture: Function, Materials and Techniques in the Archaic and Classical Periods*, edited by O. Palagia, 119–62. New York: Cambridge University Press.

———. 2006b. "Marble Carving Techniques." In *Greek Sculpture: Function, Materials and Techniques in the Archaic and Classical Periods*, edited by O. Palagia, 243–79. New York: Cambridge University Press.

Palmer, L. R. 1963. *The Interpretation of Mycenaean Greek Texts.* Oxford: Clarendon Press.

Panagou, T. Forthcoming. "Patterns of Amphora Stamp Distribution: Tracking down Export Tendencies." In *Markets, Households and City States in the Ancient Greek Economy*, edited by E. M. Harris, D. M. Lewis, and M. Woolmer. New York: Cambridge University Press.

Papadopoulos, J. K. 1992. "Lasana, Tuyeres and Kiln Firing Supports." *Hesperia* 61: 203–22.

———. 2003. *Ceramicus Redivivus: The Early Iron Age Potters' Field in the Area of the Classical Athenian Agora.* Hesperia Supplement 31. Princeton, NJ: American School of Classical Studies at Athens.

Papanikola-Bakirtzi, D. 1999. *Byzantine Glazed Ceramics: The Art of Sgraffito.* Athens: Archaeological Receipts Fund.

Parry, M. 1971. *The Making of Homeric Verse: The Collected Papers of Milman Parry.* Edited by A. Parry. Oxford: Oxford University Press.

Peacock, D. P. S. 1982. *Pottery in the Roman World: An Ethnoarchaeological Approach.* London: Addison-Wesley Longman.

Pearson, H. W. 1957. "The Economy Has No Surplus: A Critique of a Theory of Development." In *Trade and Market in the Early Empires*, edited by K. Polanyi, C. M. Arensberg, and H. W. Pearson, 320–41. Glencoe, IL: Free Press.

Peck, R. 2001. "Athenian Naval Finances in the Classical Period: The Trierarchy, Its Place in Athenian Society and How Much Does a Trieres Cost?" Diss., School of Archaeological Studies, University of Leicester.

Pekary, T. 1981. "Zur Bedeutung des Handels in der Antike. Schwerpunkte und Methoden." In *Aspekte der historischen Forschung in Frankreich und Deutschland*, edited by G. A. Richter and R. Vierhaus, 30–39. Göttingen: Max-Planck-Instituts für Geschichte.

Penny, N. 1993. *The Materials of Sculpture*. New Haven, CT: Yale University Press.

Phillips, U. B. 1918. *American Negro Slavery: A Survey of the Supply, Employment and Control of Negro Labor as Determined by the Plantation Regime*. New York: D. Appleton.

Picard, O. 2001. "Le Découverte des Gisements du Laurium et les Débuts de la Chouette." *Revue Belge de Numismatique et de Sigillographie* 147: 1–10.

Pleket, H. W. 1961. Review of F. G. Meier, *Griechische Mauerbauinschriften: Erster Teil*. *Mnemosyne*, 4th ser., 14., no. 2: 168–71.

———. 1963. Review of F. G. Meier, *Griechische Mauerbauinschriften: Zweiter Teil*. *Mnemosyne*, 4th ser., 16, no. 4: 441–44.

———. 1990. "Wirtschaft." In *Handbuch der Europäische Wirtschafts- und Sozialgeschichte in der Romischen Kaiserzeit*, edited by F. Vittinghof, 25–160. Stuttgart: Speyer.

Pluciennik, M. Z. 1997. "Historical, Geographical, and Anthropological Imaginations: Early Ceramics in Southern Italy." In *Not So Much a Pot, More a Way of Life: Current Approaches to Artefact Analysis in Archaeology*, edited by C. G. Cumberpatch and P. W. Blinkhorn, 37–56. Oxbow Monographs 83. Oxford: Oxbow Books.

Polanyi, K. 1957. "Aristotle Discovers the Economy." In *Trade and Market in the Early Empires*, edited by K. Polanyi, C. M. Arensberg, and H. W. Pearson, 64–97. Glencoe, IL: Free Press.

Pomeranz, K. 2000. *The Great Divergence: China, Europe, and the Making of the Modern World Economy*. Princeton, NJ: Princeton University Press.

Ponting, M. J. 2012. "The Substance of Coinage: The Role of Scientific Analysis in Ancient Numismatics." In *The Oxford Handbook of Greek and Roman Coinage*, edited by W. E. Metcalf, 12–30. New York: Oxford University Press.

Popper, K. 1959. *The Logic of Scientific Discovery*. New York: HarperCollins.

Porter, M. 1980. *Competitive Strategy: Techniques for Analyzing Industries and Competitors*. New York: Free Press.

———. 2008. "Five Forces That Shape Competitive Strategy." *Harvard Business Review* 86, no. 1: 79–93.

Pringsheim, F. 1950. *The Greek Law of Sale*. Weimar: Hermann Bohlaus Nachfolger.

Pritchard, D. M. 2010. "The Symbiosis between Democracy and War: The Case of Ancient Athens." In *War, Democracy and Culture in Classical Athens*, edited by D. M. Pritchard, 1–62. Cambridge: Cambridge University Press.

Pritchett, W. K. 1953. "The Attic Stelai—Part I." *Hesperia* 22: 225–99.

———, and A. Pippin. 1956. "The Attic Stelai—Part II." *Hesperia* 25: 178–328.

Pucci, G. 1973. "Terra sigillata italica." In *Ostia III*, edited by A. Carandini and C. Panella, 311–15. Studi Miscellenei 21. Rome: Università di Roma.

Pugsley, P. 2003. *Roman Domestic Wood: Analysis of the Morphology, Manufacture and Use of Selected Categories of Domestic Wooden Artefacts with Particular Reference to the Material from Roman Britain*. British Archaeological Reports, International Series S1118. Oxford: British Archaeological Reports.

Pullen, D. J., ed. 2007. *Political Economies of the Aegean Bronze Age: Papers from the Langford Conference, 22–24 February, 2007*. Tallahassee: Florida State University.

Purves, A.C. 2010. *Space and Time in Ancient Greek Narrative.* New York: Cambridge University Press.

Raber, P. 1987. "Early Copper Production in the Polis Region, Western Cyprus." *Journal of Field Archaeology* 14: 297–312.

Randall, R. H. 1953. "The Erechtheum Workmen." *American Journal of Archaeology* 57: 199–210.

Ransom, C. L. 1905. *Studies in Ancient Furniture: Couches and Beds of the Greeks, Etruscans, and Romans.* Chicago: University of Chicago Press.

Rathbone, D. W. 2007. "Roman Egypt." In *The Cambridge Economic History of the Greco-Roman World,* edited by W. Scheidel, I. M. Morris, and R. P. Saller, 698–719. Cambridge: Cambridge University Press.

Raychaudhuri, T. 1982. "Non-Agricultural Production: Mughal India." In *The Cambridge History of India,* vol. 1, *c.1200–c.1750,* edited by T. Raychaudhuri and I. Habib, 261–308. Cambridge: Cambridge University Press.

von Reden, S. 1995. *Exchange in Ancient Greece.* London: Duckworth.

———. 2002. "Demos's Phiale and the Rhetoric of Money in Fourth Century Athens." In *Money, Labour and Land: Approaches to the Economies of Ancient Greece,* edited by P. A. Cartledge, E. E. Cohen, and L. Foxhall, 52–66. London: Routledge.

Reger, G. 2002. "The Price Histories of Some Imported Goods on Delos." In *The Ancient Economy,* edited by W. Scheidel and S. von Reden, 133–54. Edinburgh: Edinburgh University Press.

———. 2005. "The Manufacture and Distribution of Perfume." In *Making, Moving and Managing: The New World of Ancient Economies, 323–31 BC,* edited by Z. H. Archibald, J. K. Davies, and V. Gabrielson, 253–97. Oxford: Oxbow Books.

———. 2007. "Hellenistic Greece and Western Asia Minor." In *The Cambridge Economic History of the Greco-Roman World,* edited by W. Scheidel, I. M. Morris, and R. P. Saller, 460–83. Cambridge: Cambridge University Press.

Reinders, H. R. 1988. *New Halos, A Hellenistic town in Thessalia, Greece.* Utrecht: Hes Publishers.

Rempel, G. 2006. "The Industrial Revolution." Western New England College, http://www.ode.state.oh.us/GD/.../DocumentDownload.aspx?DocumentID. Accessed 6/26/2007.

Renfrew, C. 1972. *The Emergence of Civilisation: The Cyclades and the Aegean in the Third Millennium bc.* London: Methuen.

———. 1973. *Before Civilisation: The Radiocarbon Revolution and Prehistoric Europe.* London: Jonathan Cape.

———. 1982. "Polity and Power: Intensification, Interaction and Exploitation." In *An Island Polity: The Archaeology of the Exploitation of Melos,* edited by C. Renfrew and M. Wagstaffe, 264–90. Cambridge: Cambridge University Press.

Rhodes, P. J., and D. M. Lewis. 1996. *The Decrees of the Greek States.* New York: Clarendon Press.

Rhodes, P. J., and R. Osborne. 2003. *Greek Historical Inscriptions 404–323 BC.* Oxford: Oxford University Press.

Richter, G. M. A. 1923. *The Craft of Athenian Pottery.* New Haven, CT: Yale University Press.

———. 1926. *Ancient Furniture: A History of Greek, Etruscan, and Roman Furniture.* Oxford: Clarendon Press.

———. 1929. "Silk in Greece." *American Journal of Archaeology* 33: 27–33.
———. 1959. *A Handbook of Greek Art*. London: Phaidon Press.
———. 1966. *The Furniture of the Greeks, Etruscans and Romans*. Aberdeen: Phaidon Press.
———, and M. J. Milne. 1935. *Shapes and Names of Athenian Vases*. New York: Metropolitan Museum of Art.
Riezler, K. 1907. *Über Finanzen und Monopole im alten Griechenland*. Berlin: Puttkammer & Mühlbrecht.
Rihll, T. E. 1993. "War, Slavery and Settlement in Early Greece." In *War and Society in the Greek World*, edited by J. Rich and G. Shipley, 77–107. London: Routledge.
———. 2001. "Making Money in Classical Athens." In *Economies beyond Agriculture in the Classical World*, edited by D. J. Mattingly and J. Salmon, 115–42. London: Routledge.
———. 2002. "Greek Science in Context." In *Science and Mathematics in Ancient Greek Culture*, edited by C. J. Tuplin and T. E. Rihll, 1–21. Oxford: Oxford University Press.
———, and J. Tucker. 2002. "Practice Makes Perfect: Knowledge of Materials in Classical Athens." In *Science and Mathematics in Ancient Greek Culture*, edited by C. J. Tuplin and T. E. Rihll, 274–305. Oxford: Oxford University Press.
Robert, L., and J. Robert. 1950. *Hellenica: Recueil d'épigraphie, de numismatique et d'antiquités grecques*. Vol. 9, *Inscriptions et reliefs d'Asie Mineure*. Paris: L. Robert.
———. 1976. "Une inscription grecque de Téos en Ionie: l'union de Téos et de Kyrbissos." *Journal des Savants* 3: 153–235.
Robinson, D. M. 1946. *Excavations at Olynthus, Part XII: Domestic and Public Architecture*. Baltimore: Johns Hopkins Press.
———, and D. W. Graham. 1938. *Excavations at Olynthus, Part VIII: The Hellenic House, a Study of the Houses Found at Olynthus, with a Detailed Account of Those Excavated in 1931 and 1934*. Baltimore: Johns Hopkins Press.
Rockwell, P. 1993. *The Art of Stoneworking: A Reference Guide*. Cambridge: Cambridge University Press.
Rojas, F. 2012. Review of J. R. Senseney, *The Art of Building in the Classical World: Vision, Craftsmanship and Linear Perspective in Greek and Roman Architecture*. Bryn Mawr Classical Review, 2012.01.09, http://bmcr.brynmawr.edu/2012/2012-01-09.html.
Rosenberg, C. M. 2007. *Goods for Sale: Products and Advertising in the Massachusetts Industrial Age*. Amherst and Boston: University of Massachusetts Press.
Rosivach, V. J. 1999. "Enslaving Barbaroi and the Athenian Ideology of Slavery." *Historia* 48, no. 2: 129–57.
Rostovtzeff, M. 1941. *The Social and Economic History of the Hellenistic World*. Oxford: Clarendon Press.
Rotroff, S. I. 1997. *Hellenistic Pottery: Athenian and Imported Wheelmade Table Ware and Related Material*. Athenian Agora: Results of Excavations Conducted by the American School of Classical Studies at Athens 19. Princeton, NJ: American School of Classical Studies at Athens.
Roux, V., and P. de Miroschedji. 2009. "Revisiting the History of the Potter's Wheel in the Southern Levant. *Levant*. 41, no. 2: 155–73.
Ruskin, J. 1866. *The Crown of Wild Olive Three Lectures on Work, Traffic and War*. New York: John Wiley.
Russell, B. 1960. *In Praise of Idleness and Other Essays*. New York: Barnes & Noble.

Sahlins, M. D. 1981. *Historical Metaphors and Mythical Realities: Structure in the Early History of the Sandwich Islands Kingdom*. Association for Social Anthropology in Oceania, Special Publication no. 1. Ann Arbor: University of Michigan Press.

Saller, R. 2002. "Framing the Debate over Growth in the Ancient Economy." In *The Ancient Economy*, edited by W. Scheidel and S. von Reden, 251–69. Edinburgh: Edinburgh University Press.

Salmon, J. 2001. "Temples the Measures of Men: *Public Buildings in the Greek Economy*." In *Economies beyond Agriculture in the Classical World*, edited by D. J. Mattingly and J. Salmon, 195–208. London: Routledge.

Samons, L. J., II. 2000. *Empire of the Owl: Athenian Imperial Finance*. Historia Einzelschriften 142. Stuttgart: Steiner.

Sargent, R. L. 1925. *The Size of the Slave Population at Athens during the Fifth and Fourth Centuries before Christ*. Urbana: University of Illinois Press.

Sayles, W. G. 2006. *Ancient Coin Collecting: Numismatic Art of the Greek World*, vol. 2. Iola, WI: Krause Publications.

Schaefer, D. S. 1885. *Demosthenes und Seine Zeit*. Leipzig: Teubner.

Schaps, D. 1979. *Economic Rights of Women in Ancient Greece*. Edinburgh: Edinburgh University Press.

Scheidel, W. 2002. "The Hireling and the Slave." In *Money, Labour and Land: Approaches to the Economies of Ancient Greece*, edited by P. A. Cartledge, E. E. Cohen, and L. Foxhall, 175–84. London: Routledge.

———. 2010. "Real Wages in Early Economies: Evidence for Living Standards from 1800 BCE to 1300 CE." *Journal of the Economic and Social History of the Orient* 53: 425–62.

Schmidt, K. 1931. *Die Namen der Attischen Kriegschiffe*. Leipzig: C. & F. Vogel.

Schmidt, P. R., and D. H. Aver. 1996. "Complex Iron Smelting and Prehistoric Culture in Tanzania." In *The Culture and Technology of African Iron Production*, edited by P. R. Schmidt, 172–85. Gainesville: University of Florida Press.

von Schmoller, G. 1900–1904. *Grundriss der allgemeinen Volkswirtschaftslehre*. Leipzig: Duncker & Humblot.

Schmookler, J. 1966. *Invention and Economic Growth*. Cambridge, MA: Harvard University Press.

Schopenhauer, A. 2007. *Studies in Pessimism, On Human Nature and Religion: A Dialogue*. New York: Cosimo.

Schwartz, S. B. 1992. *Slaves, Peasants, and Rebels: Reconsidering Brazilian Slavery*. Urbana: University of Illinois Press.

Schreiber, T. 1999. *Athenian Vase Construction: A Potter's Analysis*. Los Angeles: Paul Getty Museum.

Seaford, R. 2004. *Money and the Early Greek Mind: Homer, Philosophy, Tragedy*. Cambridge: Cambridge University Press.

Sealey, R. 1993. *Demosthenes and His Time: A Study in Defeat*. New York: Oxford University Press.

Sekunda, N. 1986. *The Ancient Greeks: Armies of Classical Greece, 5th and 4th Centuries BC*. Oxford: Osprey.

Sellars, J. 2003. "Simon the Shoemaker and the Problem of Socrates." *Classical Philology* 98, no. 3: 207–16.

Seltman, C. T. 1924. *Athens: Its History and Coinage before the Persian Invasion*. Cambridge: Cambridge University Press.

Sen, A. 1979. "Rational Fools: A Critique of the Foundations of Economic Theory in Scientific Models and Man." *Philosophy and Public Affairs* 6: 317–44.

Senseney, J. R. 2011. *The Art of Building in the Classical World: Vision, Craftsmanship and Linear Perspective in Greek and Roman Architecture.* New York: Cambridge University Press.

Shear, I. M. 1963. "Kallikrates." *Hesperia* 32: 375–424.

Shear, T. L. 1973. "The Athenian Agora: Excavations of 1971." *Hesperia* 42: 121–79.

Shefton, B. B. 1989. "Zum Import und Einfluss Mediterraner Güter in Alteuropa." *Kolner Jahrbuch Vor- und Fruhgeschichte* 22: 207–20.

Shipton, K. M. W. 1998. "The Prices of the Athenian Silver Mines." *Zeitschrift für Papyrologie und Epigraphik* 120: 57–63.

———. 2001. "Money and the Elite in Classical Athens." In *Money and Its Uses in the Ancient Greek World,* edited by A. Meadows and K. Shipton, 129–44. Oxford: Oxford University Press.

Sillar, B. 1997. "Reputable Pots and Disreputable Potters: Individual and Community Choices in Present-day Pottery Production and Exchange in the Andes." In *Not So Much a Pot, More a Way of Life: Current Approaches to Artefact Analysis in Archaeology,* edited by C. G. Cumberpatch and P. W. Blinkhorn, 1–20. Oxbow Monographs 83. Oxford: Oxbow Books.

Simon, H. A. 1957. *Models of Man Social and Rational: Mathematical Essays on Rational Human Behavior in a Social Setting.* New York: John Wiley.

Smith, A. 1976. *The Theory of Moral Sentiments.* Oxford: Clarendon Press.

———. 1999. *An Inquiry into the Nature and Causes of the Wealth of Nations.* Harmondsworth: Penguin.

Snell, D. 1995. "Methods of Exchange and Coinage in Ancient Western Asia." In *Civilizations of the Ancient Near East,* vol. 3, edited by J. M. Sasson et al., 1487–97. New York: Scribner.

Snodgrass, A. 1967. *Arms and Armour of the Greeks.* London: Thames & Hudson.

———. 1980. *Archaic Greece: The Age of Experiment.* London: J. M. Dent & Sons.

———. 1983. "Heavy Freight in Archaic Greece." In *Trade in the Ancient Economy,* edited by P. Garnsey, K. Hopkins, and C. R. Whittaker, 16–26. Berkeley, CA: University of California Press.

———. 1994. "The Euboeans in Macedonia: A New Precedent for Westward Expansion." In *Apoikia. Scritti in onore di Giorgio Buchner,* edited by B. d'Agostino and D. Ridgway, 87–93. Annali di archeologia e stroia antica, n.s., 1. Naples: Istituto Universitario Orientale.

———. 1998. *Homer and the Artists.* Cambridge: Cambridge University Press.

Sokolowski, F. 1962. *Lois sacrées des cités grecques.* École française d'Athènes Supplement. Paris: Éditions de Boccard.

Sparkes, B. 1991. *Greek Pottery: An Introduction.* Manchester: Manchester University Press.

———, and L. Talcott. 1970. *Black and Plain Pottery of the 6th, 5th and 4th Centuries BC.* The Athenian Agora: Results of Excavations Conducted by the American School of Classical Studies at Athens 12. Princeton, NJ: American School of Classical Studies at Athens.

Spivey, N. 2013. *Greek Sculpture.* Cambridge: Cambridge University Press.

Stanier, R. S. 1953. "The Cost of the Parthenon." *Journal of Hellenic Studies* 73: 68–76.

Starr, C. G. 1961. *The Origins of Greek Civilization: 1100–650 b.c.* New York: Knopf.

———. 1977. *The Economic and Social Growth of Ancient Greece 800–500 b.c.* 4th ed. New York: Oxford University Press.

Steingräber, S. 1979. *Etruskische Möbel.* Rome: Giorgio Bretschneider.

Stern, E. M. 2008. "Glass Production." In *The Oxford Handbook of Engineering and Technology in the Classical World,* edited by J. P. Oleson, 520–47. New York: Oxford University Press.

Stewart, A. 1990. *Greek Sculpture: An Exploration.* New Haven, CT: Yale University Press.

Stinchcombe, A. L. 1959. "Bureaucratic and Craft Administration of Production." *Administrative Science Quarterly* 4: 168–87.

Stissi, V. 1999. "Production, Circulation and Consumption of Archaic Greek Pottery (Sixth and Early Fifth Centuries B.C.)." In *The Complex Past of Pottery: Production, Circulation and Consumption of Mycenaean and Greek Pottery in the Sixteenth to Early Fifth Centuries BC; Proceedings of the ARCHON International Conference held in Amsterdam 8–9 November 1996,* edited by V. Stissi, J. P. Crielaard, and G. J. van Wijngaarden, 83–113. Amsterdam: E. J. Brill.

Stoke-on-Trent City Council. 2006. "The Industrial Revolution and the Pottery Industry." ThePotteries.org. http://www.thepotteries.org/sot/five.htm. Accessed 6/26/2007.

Stroud, R. 1974. "An Athenian Law on Silver Coinage." *Hesperia* 43: 157–88.

———. 1998. *The Athenian Grain Tax Law of 374/3 B.C.* Hesperia Supplement 29. Princeton, NJ: American School of Classical Studies at Athens.

Studnickza, F. K. 1908. *Das Bildnis des Aristoteles.* Leipzig: Teubner.

———. 1913. *Das Symposion Ptolemaios II.* Abhandlung der Königlichen Sachsischen, Gesellschaft der Wissenschaft, Philologisch-historische Klass 30. Leipzig: Teubner.

Tandy, D. 1997. *Warriors into Traders: The Power of the Market in Early Greece.* Berkeley: University of California Press.

Tanner, J. 2006. *The Invention of Art History in Ancient Greece: Religion, Society and Artistic Rationalisation.* Cambridge: Cambridge University Press.

Teece, D. J. 1998. *Economic Performance and the Theory of the Firm: The Selected Papers of David J. Teece.* 2 vols. Cheltenham: Edward Elgar Publishing.

Teresi, R. 2002. *Lost Discoveries: The Ancient Roots of Modern Science—From the Babylonians to the Maya.* New York: Simon & Schuster.

Thirsk, J. 1978. *Economic Policy and Projects: The Development of a Consumer Society in Early Modern England.* Oxford: Clarendon Press.

Thompson, C. M. 2003. "Sealed Silver in Iron Age Cisjordan and the 'Invention' of Coinage." *Oxford Journal of Archaeology* 22, no. 1: 67–107.

Thompson, D. B. 1960. "The House of Simon the Shoemaker." *Archaeology* 13: 234–40.

———. 1971. *An Ancient Shopping Center: The Athenian Agora.* Princeton, NJ: American School of Classical Studies at Athens.

Thompson, W. E. 1982a. "Weaving—A Man's Work." *Classical World* 75: 217–22.

———. 1982b. "The Athenian Entrepreneur." *L' Antiquité Classique* 51: 53–85.

Thomson, H. A. 1940. *The Tholos of Athens and its Predecessors.* Hesperia Supplement 4. Princeton, NJ: American School of Classical Studies at Athens

Thur, G. 1977. *Beweisführung vor den Schwurgerichtshöfen Athens: die Proklesis zur Basanos.* Vienna: Verlag der Österreichische Akademie der Wissenschaft.

Thurmond, D. L. 2006. *A Handbook of Food Processing in Classical Rome: For Her Bounty No Winter.* Leiden: E. J. Brill.

Todd, S. C. 1993. *The Shape of Athenian Law.* Oxford: Clarendon Press.

Tölle-Kastenbein, R. 1980. *Frühklassische Peplosfiguren: Originale.* Mainz: P. von Zabern.
Tonks, O. S. 1908. "Experiments with the Black Glaze on Greek Vases." *American Journal of Archaeology* 12: 417–27.
Torrance, R. 1986. *Production and Exchange of Stone Tools: Prehistoric Obsidian in the Aegean.* Cambridge: Cambridge University Press.
Treister, M. Y. 1996. *The Role of Metals in Ancient Greek History.* New York: E. J. Brill.
Trinks, W., M. H. Mawhinney, R. A. Shannon, R. J. Reed, and J. R. Garvey. 2004. *Industrial Furnaces.* 6th ed. Hoboken, NJ: John Wiley.
Trundle, M. 2004. *Greek Mercenaries: From the Late Archaic Period to Alexander.* New York: Routledge.
Tsakirgis, B. 2009. "Living near the Agora: Houses and Households in Central Athens." In *The Athenian Agora: New Perspectives on an Ancient Site,* edited by J. M. Camp and C. A. Mauzy, 47–54. Mainz: P. von Zabern.
——. Forthcoming. "Whole Cloth: Exploring the Greek Economy through the Evidence for Textile Manufacture and Purchase in Greek Houses." In *Markets, Households and City States in the Ancient Greek Economy,* edited by E. M. Harris, D. M. Lewis, and M. Woolmer. New York: Cambridge University Press.
Tschira, J. 1972. "Untersuchungen im Süden des Parthenon." *Jahrbuch des Deutsches Archäologischen Instituts* 87: 158–231.
Tucker, T. G. 1907. *Life in Ancient Athens: The Social and Public Life of a Classical Athenian from Day to Day.* London: Macmillan.
Tzochev, C. Forthcoming. "The Markets for Thasian Wine." In *Markets, Households and City States in the Ancient Greek Economy,* edited by E. M. Harris, D. M. Lewis, and M. Woolmer. New York: Cambridge University Press.
Ucelli, G. 1940. *Le Navi di Nemi.* Rome: La Libreria dello Stato.
Ulrich, R. B. 2008. "Woodworking." In *The Oxford Handbook of Engineering and Technology in the Classical World,* edited by J. P. Oleson, 439–64. New York: Oxford University Press.
Urem-Kotsou, D., K. Kotsakis, and B. Stern. 2002. "Defining Function in Neolithic Ceramics: The Example of Makriyalos, Greece." *Documenta Praehistorica* 29: 109–19.
Vélissaropoulos-Karakostas, J. 1980. *Les Nauclères grecs: recherches sur les institutions maritimes en Grèce et dans l'orient Hellénisé.* Geneva: Minard.
——. 2002. "Merchants, Prostitutes and the 'New Poor': Forms of Contract and Social Status." In *Money, Labour and Land: Approaches to the Economies of Ancient Greece,* edited by P. A. Cartledge, E. E. Cohen, and L. Foxhall, 130–39. London: Routledge.
Venit, M. 1988. "The Caputi Hydria and Working Women in Classical Athens." *Classical World* 81, no. 4: 265–72.
Ventris, M. G. F., and J. Chadwick. 1956. *Documents in Mycenaean Greek.* Cambridge: Cambridge University Press.
Vial, C. 1984. *Délos Indépendante (314–167 avant J.-C.).* Bulletin de Correspondance Hellenique Supplement 10. Athens: École Française d'Athènes.
Vickers, M., and D. Gill. 1994. *Artful Crafts: Ancient Greek Silverware and Pottery.* Oxford: Clarendon Press.
Voigtländer, W. 1986. "Umrisse eines vor- und frühgeschichtlichen Zentrums an der karisch-ionischen Küste Erster Vorbericht—Survey 1984." *Archäologische Anzeiger* 1986: 622–51.

Wachsmann, S. 1995. *Seagoing Ships and Seamanship in the Bronze Age Levant.* College Station: Texas A & M University Press.

Waelkens, M., P. de Paepe, and L. Moens. 1988. "Quarries and the Marble Trade in Antiquity." In *Classical Marble: Geochemistry, Technology, Trade,* edited by N. Herz and M. Waelkens, 11–28. Dordrecht: Kluwer Academic Publishers.

———. 1990. "The Quarrying Techniques of the Greek World." In *Marble: Art, Historical and Scientific Perspectives on Ancient Sculptures,* edited by M. True and J. Podany, 47–72. Malibu, CA: J. Paul Getty Museum.

Walbank, F. W. 1981. *The Hellenistic World.* London: Fontana Paperbacks.

Walbank, M. B. 1982. "The Confiscation and Sale by the Poletai in 402/01 BC of the Property of the Thirty Tyrants." *Hesperia* 51, no. 1: 74–97.

Wallace, M. B. 1970. "Early Greek Proxenoi." *Phoenix* 24: 189–208.

Wallace-Hadrill, A. 1994. *Houses and Society in Pompeii and Herculaneum.* Princeton, NJ: Princeton University Press.

Wallinga, H. T. 1964. "The Unit of Capacity for Ancient Ships." *Mnemosyne,* 4th ser., 17: 1–40.

Weber, M. 1891. *Die Römische Agrargeschichte in Ihrer Bedeutung für das Staats- und Privatrecht.* Tübingen: J. C. B. Mohr.

———. 1947. *The Theory of Social and Economic Organization.* Translated by A. M. Henderson and T. Parsons. New York: Free Press.

Webster, T. B. L. 1972. *Potter and Patron in Classical Athens.* London: Methuen.

———. 1973. *Athenian Culture and Society.* London: B. T. Batsford.

van Wees, H. 1992. *Status Warriors: War, Violence and Society in Homer and History.* Amsterdam: J. C. Gieben.

———. 2004. *Greek Warfare: Myths and Realities.* London: Duckworth.

Weidemann, T. 1997. *Greek and Roman Slavery.* London: Routledge.

Weintraub, E. R. 2002. *How Economics Became a Mathematical Science.* Durham, NC: Duke University Press.

Welsh, F. 1988. *Building the Trireme.* London: Constable.

West, M. L. 1971. *Early Greek Philosophy and the Orient.* Oxford: Clarendon Press.

———. 1997. *Early Greek Philosophy and the Orient: West Asiatic Elements in Greek Poetry and Myth.* Rev. ed. Oxford: Clarendon Press.

Westermann, W. L. 1945. "Two Studies in Athenian Manumission." *Journal of Near Eastern Studies* 5, no. 1. 92–104.

Whitbread, I. K. 1995. *Greek Transport Amphorae: A Petrological and Archaeological Study.* Athens: British School at Athens.

White, B. 1917. *Silver, Its History and Romance.* London: Hodder.

White, H. C. 1981. "Where Do Markets Come From?" *American Journal of Sociology* 87, no. 3: 517–47.

White, K. D. 1984. *Greek and Roman Technology,* Ithaca, NY: Cornell University Press.

Whitehead, D. 1977. *The Ideology of the Athenian Metic.* Proceedings of the Cambridge Philological Society Supplementary Volume 4. Cambridge: Cambridge Philological Society.

Whitelaw, T. 2001. "Reading between the Tablets: Assessing Mycenaean Palace Involvement in Ceramic Production and Consumption." In *Economy and Politics in the Mycenaean Palace States: Proceedings of a Conference held on 1–3 July 1999 in the*

*Faculty of Classics, Cambridge*, edited by S. Voutsaki and J. Killen, 51–79. Cambridge: Cambridge Philological Society.

Wilamowitz-Moellendorff, U. von. 1887a. "Demotika des attischen Metoeken I." *Hermes* 22, no. 1: 107–28.

——. 1887b. "Demotika des attischen Metoeken II." *Hermes* 22, no. 2: 211–59.

——. 1965. *Antigonos von Karystos.* Reprint. Berlin: Weidman.

Wild, J. P. 2008. "Textile Production." In *The Oxford Handbook of Engineering and Technology in the Classical World,* edited by J. P. Oleson, 465–82. New York: Oxford University Press.

Will, E. 1957. "Aux Origines du Régime Foncier Grec: Homère, Hésiode et l'arrière-plan mycénien." *Revue des Études Anciennes* 59: 5–50.

——. 1965. "Hésiode: crise agraire? Ou recul de l'aristocratie?" *Revue des Études Grecques* 78: 542–56.

Williams, R.T. 1958. "Early Greek Ships of Two Levels." *Journal of Hellenic Studies* 78: 121–30.

Williamson, O. E. 1970. *Corporate Control and Business Behavior: An Inquiry into the Effects of Organization Form on Enterprise Behavior.* Englewood Cliffs, NJ: Prentice Hall.

——. 1975. *Markets and Hierarchies, Analysis and Antitrust Implications: A Study in the Economics of Internal Organization.* New York: Free Press.

Wilsdorf, H. 1952. *Bergleute und Hüttenmänner im Altertum bis zum Ausgang des Römischen Republik: Ihre wirtschaftliche, soziale, und juristiche Lage.* Berlin: Forsch.

Wilson, A. I. 2001. "Timgad and Textile Production." In *Economies beyond Agriculture in the Classical World,* edited by D. J. Mattingly and J. Salmon, 271–96. London: Routledge.

——. 2003. "The Archaeology of the Roman Fullonica." *Journal of Roman Archaeology* 16: 442–46.

——. 2008. "Large Scale Manufacturing, Standardization, and Trade." In *The Oxford Handbook of Engineering and Technology in the Classical World,* edited by J. P. Oleson, 393–417. New York: Oxford University Press.

Wittenburg, A. 1978. *Griechische Baukommissionen des 5. und 4. Jahrhunderts.* Munich: Ludwig-Maximilians-Universität.

Young, J. H. 1956. "Studies in South Attica: Country Estates at Sounion." *Hesperia* 25: 122–46.

Younger, J. G., and P. Rehak. 2009. "Technical Observations on the Sculptures from the Temple of Zeus at Olympia." *Hesperia* 78, no. 1: 41–105.

Yue, C., and D. Yue. 1997. *Shoes: Their History in Words and Pictures.* Boston: Houghton Mifflin.

Zimmer, G. 1990. *Griechische Bronzegusswerkstätten: Zur Technologieentwicklung eines antiken Kunsthandwerkes.* Mainz: P. von Zabern.

# PHOTO CREDITS

2.1 Blacksmith. Stock Photo.
3.1 Fine ware. Niobid Painter (fifth century BCE), (possibly Heracles and the Argonauts) Side A. Orvieto, 460–450 BCE. © RMN-Grand Palais/Art Resource, NY.
3.2 Protocorinthian cup. Gianni Dagli Orti/The Art Archive at Art Resource, NY.
3.3 Storage Amphorae. Museum of Underwater Archaeology, Bodrum Castle, Turkey.
3.4 Pottery workshop on the Leagros Hydria. Attic hydria in the Leagros Group (SH 1717). Staatliche Antikensammlungen und Glyptothek.
3.5 The Caputi hydria showing four people painting. Torno Collection, Milan.
4.1 "The finest of all coins." Athenian Tetradrachm, circa 480–420 BC. Museum of Fine Arts, Lyon.
4.2 Berlin Foundry Cup: Molds for a statue or armor? Kylix, from Vulci (#2620). bpk, Berlin/Staatliche Antikensammlungen und Glyptothek/Ingrid Geske/Art Resource, NY.
4.3 Hoplite shields in action. Museo Nazionale di Villa Giulia. Scala/Art Resource, NY.
5.1 Menswear. Demosthenes, Roman copy of a 280 BCE Greek original by Polyeuctus. Braccio Nuovo, Museo Chiaramonti, Vatican Museums. © Vanni Archive/Art Resource, NY.
5.2 Ladieswear. Statue of Athena, known as the "Medici Athena," copy of a Greek original of about 440–430 BC (marble) (detail), Greek School/Louvre, Paris, France/B. de Sollier & P. Muxel/ The Bridgeman Art Library.
5.3 Ancient sandal with decorative cut, detail. Minerva Tritonia, terracotta statue. Museo Archeologico Lavinium, Pomezia Pratica Di Mare, Italy. © DeA Picture Library/Art Resource, NY.
6.1 Couch and small table. Image of *kline* and table from *Illustrated History of Furniture, from the Earliest to the Present Time*, by Frederick Litchfield, 1893.

6.2 Trireme with full deck (Model). Deutsches Museum, Munich, Germany.
7.1 The Erechtheum (artist's reconstruction). Northwest View of the Erechtheum, ancient Greek temple on the north side of the Acropolis of Athens in Greece. Stock Photo.
7.2 Luxury private house. Reconstructed residential building, Ancient Greece. Color illustration. © DeA Picture Library/Art Resource, NY.
8.1 Ancient olive press. Erich Lessing/Art Resource, NY.

# INDEX LOCORUM

*Abbreviations used in the text follow the* Oxford Classical Dictionary *Third Edition (Oxford University Press, 1996) and are shown here in italics.*
The following abbreviations refer to sources of fragments cited:
**FHG**: Müller, C., and Müller, T. (1853–1883). *Fragmenta Historicum Graecorum.* Paris: A. F. Didot.
**K-A**: Kassel, R., and Austin, C. (1983). *Poetae Comici Graeci.* Berlin: W. de Gruyter.
**Kock**: T. Kock. (1880–1888). *Comicorum Atticorum Fragmenta.* Vol. 3. Leipzig: B. G. Teubner.
**LL**: *Lyra Graeca.* Vol. 1. Ed. D. A. Campbell. (1982). Loeb edition. Harvard University Press, Cambridge, MA.
**LS**: *Sophocles Fragments.* Ed. H. Lloyd-Jones. (1996). Loeb edition. Harvard University Press, Cambridge, MA.

**GREEK AUTHORS**
**Adespota** (*Adesp.*):
Fr. 516 (Kock): 148n5

**Aeschines** (*Aeschin.*):
1. 97: 154, 167, 256, 287, 287n122, 302
101: 122
124: 160
2. 29: 19

**Aeschylus** (*Aesch.*):
Agamemnon (*Ag.*):
182–83: 188
663, 802: 194n91
Eumenides (*Eum.*):
557: 194
Persian Women (*Pers.*):
334: 189
358: 188
Prometheus Bound (*PV*):
109–12, 236, 448–50: 9
715: 10
Suppliant Women (*Suppl.*):
124–25: 192
Fr. 57 (K-A): 173

**Alcaeus** (*Alc.*):
II. 19. (LL): 52

**Amphis**:
Fr. 30. (K-A): 232

**Anacreon** (*Anac.*):
18, 28, Fr. 12 (Anth. Pal.): 52

**Andocides** (*Andoc.*):
1. 133: 5, 5n28, 6, 12
146: 273
4. 14–15: 275n66

**Anthologia Palatina** (*Anth. Pal.*):
6.48: 157
283-85: 157

**Antiphanes**:
Fr. 50 (K-A): 232

**Apollonius Rhodius** (*Ap. Rhod.*):
Argonautica (*Arg.*):
1. 367–69: 196

**Aristophanes** (*Ar.*):
Acharnians (*Ach.*):
34: 237
35: 234n24
58: 139
97: 166n84, 196
127: 226n22
164: 233n13
174: 233n5
190: 238
214: 237
243: 183n48
245: 74
258: 233n15
260: 183n48
273: 226n122
279: 139
284: 74

357

358 { Index Locorum

Acharnians (*Ach.*) (*Cont.*)
  299: 163
  301: 165n79
  318: 183n48
  342: 127
  348: 237
  355, 359, 366: 183n48
  403: 226n122
  412, 415, 432: 148
  458: 74
  463: 74, 232n11
  478: 233, 233n13, 277n77
  480: 233n13
  508: 233n15
  519: 148n2
  520: 233n12
  521: 233n13, 233n16
  521–28: 150n9
  539: 139
  549: 75, 166n84
  550: 233n12, 233n13, 233n14
  551: 232n10, 237n37
  554: 183
  584: 127
  670: 232n10
  691: 74
  724: 163
  752: 183
  760: 150n9, 233n16
  761, 813: 233n13
  814: 233n16
  822: 148
  831: 233n16
  849: 127
  864: 226n122
  872: 239n43
  874: 233n13
  875–80: 232
  879: 232n11
  888: 127, 166n84
  891: 237
  901: 74, 232n10
  916–21: 191
  928: 74
  938: 127
  964–65: 139
  967: 232n10
  988: 226n122
  1001: 233n12
  1007: 127
  1041: 232n5, 233n16
  1090: 148, 181n43
  1091: 237n37, 242n59
  1092: 239n43
  1097: 166n84
  1099: 233n16
  1099–1100: 233n12
  1101: 232n10
  1102: 239n43
  1103: 127
  1104–16: 232
  1109: 166n84
  1118: 127
  1120: 166n84
  1122, 1124: 139
  1125, 1127: 239n43
  1128: 234n24
  1130: 233n16
  1132: 127
  1136: 148
  1138: 166n84
  1139: 148n2
  1140: 139
  1156: 232n11
  1158: 181n43
  1175: 74
  1181: 139
  1188: 127
  1189: 226n122
  1194: 127
  1225: 166n84
  1226: 127
  1235: 166n84
Birds (*Av.*):
  120–23: 148
  488–89: 219
Clouds (*Nub.*):
  8–10: 148
  10: 166n84
  28: 184
  37: 148
  45: 234n24
  50: 166n84
  51: 233n13
  54: 148n2
  56: 234n24
  72: 166n84
  96: 74
  97: 237
  132, 133: 226n122
  149–50: 237
  151: 148n3, 166
  176: 233n15
  177: 181n43
  178: 127
  179: 148n2
  234 and schol: 176, 233n12
  236: 233n12
  254: 181n43
  255, 256: 237n37
  268: 166n84
  306: 127

313: 183
327: 233n14
373: 127
386, 389; 239n44
409: 232n5
417: 234n24
497: 148n2
507: 239n43
509: 226n122
566: 127
607–26: 106
625: 237n37
633, 694, 709: 181n43
751: 166n84
788: 233n15
856: 148n2
858: 165n79
923: 166n84
981: 233n12
982: 233n12, 233n13
987: 148n2
989: 139
1063–66: 127
1123: 234n24
1127: 226n122
1237: 233n16
1355: 183
1383: 239n43
1486: 127, 226n122
1496: 226n122
1498: 148n2
1500: 127
Ecclesiazusae (*Eccl.*):
 81 (schol), 248–53: 273n63
 308–9: 271
 413: 148
 424: 259
 654: 153
 814 (schol): 16n68
 841: 68n57, 242
Frogs (*Ran.*):
 62: 233n12, 239n44
 112: 238
 364: 166n84, 192, 196, 238
 482, 487: 232n11
 506: 239n44
 507: 239n43
 518: 181n43
 543a: 148
 544a: 74
 549–53: 239, 277n77
 554: 233n13
 557: 232n10
 559: 234n20
 576: 127

620: 234n24
621: 266n122
721–23: 132
799: 183n48, 226n122
840: 233, 277n77
857–58: 238
987: 233n13
1015: 127
1065–7: 232
1066: 148n2
1236: 103
1304: 183
1316: 184
1349–51: 154, 277
1368–69: 231n2
1378: 127
1459: 148n2, 166n84
1478: 148
Knights (*Eq.*):
 19: 233n13
 41: 233n12
 44: 8, 28, 163
 48: 163
 55: 239n43
 59: 163
 85, 95, 102: 234n24
 104, 136: 163
 143: 231n2, 232n5
 144, 148, 161, 179, 201: 232n5
 203: 164
 208: 232n5
 221: 237n37
 232: 184
 254: 233n15
 277: 239n43
 279: 239n44
 282: 239n43
 310: 192
 312: 232n11
 315: 16
 321: 165n79
 354: 232n11
 355: 234n24
 357, 360: 239n44
 361: 232n11
 369: 163
 370: 148
 379: 164
 393: 233n15
 412: 127
 432: 232n5
 449: 164
 461–62, 463: 173
 464: 184
 489: 127

## 360 } Index Locorum

Knights (*Eq.*) (*Cont.*)
494: 233n13
502: 237n37
600, 631: 233n13
644–45: 17
645, 649, 662, 666, 672: 232n10
676: 233n13
677: 233n12
682: 233n13
729: 237n37
738–40: 6, 164, 274
745: 74
755: 233n18
762: 127
768: 166n84
771, 772: 127
778: 239n43
792: 74
806: 239n43
824: 233n12
839: 127
846–47: 139
854: 231n2
856: 139
857: 233n15
868: 163
869: 165n79
871: 165n79, 169
875: 165n79
881, 886: 148n2
892: 163
895: 233n13
906: 242n59
912–18: 190
929: 74, 232n11
946: 233n13
947, 951: 127
955: 239n43
963: 166n84
963–64: 164
967: 148n2
968: 184, 237n37
990: 183
1000: 181n43
1007: 239n44
1008: 232n10
1009: 233n15
1016: 127
1060: 127, 226n122
1101, 1104: 233n15
1105: 239n43
1164, 1165: 181n43
1166: 239n43
1171: 239n44
1174; 74, 239n44
1176: 74
1178: 239n44
1180: 148n2
1183, 1190, 1191, 1219: 239n43
1227: 237n37
1242: 232n35
1246: 232n5, 232n10
1272: 116n84
1302–15: 273
1315: 127
1323, 1329: 237n37
1366–67: 190n72
1384: 181n43
1406: 148n2
Lysistrata (*Lys.*):
45: 148n2, 166
47: 148n3, 166, 242n59
48: 148n2
50: 127
52: 139
53: 127, 148n3, 166
63–64: 194
115, 131: 232n11
150: 148n2
156: 127
161: 226n122
185, 188, 190: 139
196, 199: 74
264: 183n48, 226n122
309: 226n122
327–31: 275
358: 74
377: 238
400: 74
401: 148n2
408: 127
416–19: 166
428, 432–33: 127
457: 277n77
458: 238, 277n77
470: 148n2
530, 532: 148n4
537: 233n12
539: 74
560: 139
562, 564: 277n77
600: 74
604: 237n37
627: 139
632: 127
657: 165n79
722: 226n121
733: 181n43
856: 233n14, 233n16
936: 148

944, 947: 242n59
985: 127
1093: 148n2
1070: 226n122
1151, 1155, 1156: 127, 148n2
1189, 1190: 148
1207: 239n43
1216: 226n122
Peace (*Pax*):
  1, 3, 4: 239n43
  56: 183n48
  69, 100: 226n122
  120: 239n43
  155: 127
  168: 233n13
  169: 242n59
  202: 74
  247: 232n5
  252, 253: 233n16
  258: 233n13
  259, 265, 269, 282: 235
  270: 8
  273: 232n5
  282: 235
  299: 127
  305: 208
  307: 127, 184
  336: 139
  348: 148
  353, 356: 127
  368: 233n15, 234n20
  426: 127
  438: 139
  440: 237
  443: 127
  477: 233n15
  502: 233n13
  526: 242n59
  527: 166n84
  531: 183
  553: 127
  563: 232n10
  565: 239n43
  567: 127
  574: 239n43
  575: 233n14
  613: 74
  634: 233n18
  636: 233n15
  669: 163
  681–92: 106
  699: 148
  703: 74
  712: 242n59
  752–53: 11
  753: 163
  843: 127, 226n122
  853, 869: 239n43
  885: 239n44
  901: 184
  923–4: 74
  947: 127, 237n37
  1000: 233n13
  1001: 233n14
  1002: 148n2
  1003–5: 232n7
  1014: 233n12
  1017: 127
  1023: 226n122
  1032, 1059: 181n43
  1128: 127
  1129: 234n20
  1137: 233n14
  1144: 233n12
  1145: 233n14
  1193: 181n43
  1195, 1196: 239n43
  1198–1202: 17
  1200–39: 135
  1200: 127
  1202: 74, 103
  1203: 127
  1209–64: 126, 136
  1224, 1240, 1248: 127
  1249: 233n14
  1274–75, 1298, 1303: 139
  1322: 233n15
  1323: 234n24
  1324: 233n14
  1359: 239n43
Plutus (*Plut.*):
  162: 166
  426: 239, 277n76
  617–18: 219
  983: 166
  984: 148
  1120: 239, 277n76
Thesmophoriazusae (*Thesm.*):
  138: 148n4, 183
  139: 148n2
  140: 127
  142, 214: 148n2
  219: 127
  250, 251: 148n2
  257: 148n4
  261: 181n43
  262: 165n79
  263: 148n3
  285: 239n43
  387: 233, 277n76

Thesmophoriazusae (*Thesm.*) (*Cont.*)
  401: 237n37
  402: 74
  415: 183n48, 226n122
  420: 233n15, 234n24
  425: 127
  446–58: 277n76
  456: 233, 277n76
  481: 226n122
  486: 233n13, 233n14
  494: 233n13
  556, 560: 127
  561: 242n59
  568: 148n2
  570: 239n43
  616: 233n12
  633: 74
  643, 656: 148n2
  694: 127
  733: 166n84
  734: 148n3
  754: 166
  758: 74
  796: 181n43
  822: 127, 184, 226n122
  826: 127
  910: 233n13
  933: 166n84
  941: 148n4
  969: 183
  1122: 181n43
  1125: 166n84
  1127: 127
  1135: 166n84
  1181: 148n2
  1192: 233n16
  1197, 1215: 166n84
Wasps(*Vesp.*):
  5: 233n14
  17: 139
  19: 140
  31: 183n48
  35: 234n20
  38: 163
  169–71 and schol: 283n107
  170, 231: 166n84
  238: 231n2, 238
  300: 233n15
  301: 226n122
  303: 233n14
  331: 234n24
  354: 127
  355: 74
  363, 435: 127
  491: 232n10
  511: 239n44
  582: 166n84
  676: 148, 233n16, 234n20, 234n24, 239n43
  677: 74, 127, 148n2, 237n37
  679: 233n13
  680: 233n13, 277n76
  683: 234n20
  693: 204
  702: 234n24, 237n37
  710: 232n16
  724 and schol: 204
  737: 148n2, 166n84
  861: 237n37, 242n59
  878: 233n18
  897: 183n48
  935: 74
  1007 (schol): 133
  1081: 127
  1133: 148n2
  1154: 127
  1157, 1158, 1162: 165n79
  1213: 148
  1216: 181n43
  1268: 233n14
  1427: 184
  1487: 233n13
Fr. 339 (K-A): 283n107

**Aristotle** (*Arist.*):
History of Animals (*Hist. An.*):
  522a22–b6: 234n20
Metaphysics (*Metaph.*):
  1652a: 173
Nicomachean Ethics (*Eth. Nic.*):
  2.1: 7
On the Parts of Animals (*Part. an.*):
  4.10: 188
Politics (*Pol.*):
  1252a–b: 285
  1252b12: 285
  1255a: 282
  1255b: 282
  1258b, 1259a: 17
  1264a32: 253
  1264b: 19, 276
  1268: 233n14
  1274a: 271
  1275a: 274, 279
  1297b.16–28: 135
Rhetoric (*Rh.*):
  1381b: 74

**Pseudo-Aristotle** ((Arist.)):
Constitution of the Athenians (*Ath. pol.*):
  19.3: 7

22.7: 189, 198
24.3: 191
27.5: 28, 163
42.2: 142
42.4: 13550.2: 228
51.3: 231n2
54.1: 228
62: 271
Mechanics (*Mech.*):
　550b25: 194n91

**Athenaeus** (*Ath.*):
Deipnosophistae:
　**2**. 48b: 155
　　48c: 148
　　49a: 178, 180
　**5**. 192e–f: 177
　　196–97: 157
　**6**. 255c: 148
　　272c: 301n6
　　264d: 285
　**10**. 414f, 415b: 259
　**12**. 511d: 10
　　540: 150
　　571d: 148
　**13**. 607f–8a: 240

**Ctesicles**:
　245.1 (FHG): 302

**Demosthenes** (*Dem.*):
　**1**. 17: 252
　**3**. 25: 225
　**6**. 30: 235
　**18**. 116: 142
　　132: 191
　　257–65: 12n49
　**19**. 46: 235
　**20**. 30–40: 6
　**21**. 47: 286
　　157: 119
　**24**. 6–23: 19
　　20 (schol): 271n58
　　23: 252
　**25**. 52: 240
　**27**: 12, 169n93, 254
　　9: 25, 28, 86, 99n105, 122, 126, 144, 181,
　　　219, 254
　　10: 144, 181, 182, 245, 262, 265, 266
　　18–19: 255
　　19: 254, 287
　　21: 263
　　23: 256
　　24: 285
　　24–25: 263
　　27–28: 264
　　29: 255
　　43: 263
　　61: 280
　**29**. 254n17
　**32**: 19
　　4–9: 287
　**33**. 4: 19
　**34**. 5–10: 19, 287
　　23, 31: 19
　　37: 287n21
　　39: 16n68
　　51: 280
　**35**. 10–14: 252, 253
　**36**: 19
　　4: 28, 139, 287
　　11: 139, 142, 256, 303
　　14: 19
　　37: 255
　　43–48: 287
　**37**: 4: 26, 28, 122, 252
　　10–13: 122
　　17: 28
　　31: 25, 28, 122
　　38. 25–27: 12n49
　**40**. 52: 26, 252
　**41**. 19
　　8: 283
　　31: 19
　**45**. 33: 231n2
　　71–72: 287
　　85: 142
　　86: 285
　**48**. 14–15: 287
　**49**. 3: 287
　**52**. 3: 119
　　17–19: 118
　**53**. 1: 283
　　14: 231n2
　　19: 282
　**56**: 19
　　8, 10: 16n68
　　48–50: 27
　**57**. 31: 278
　　31–35: 148, 278
　**59**. 29: 283
　　107–26: 276

**Dinarchus** (*Din.*):
　1.111: 268

**Dio Chrysostom** (*Dio Chrys.*):
　Orationes (*Orat.*):
　28.3: 216
　34.21: 157

**Diodorus Siculus** (*Diod. Sic.*):
3. 13: 261n39
11. 43.3: 198
13. 19.4: 259
14. 42.2: 187
43.2: 135
16. 41.4: 6
17. 8.5: 135
20. 9: 196

**Diogenes Laertius** (*Diog. Laert.*):
2. 13.122–23: 166, 167
5. 11–16: 285
36: 242
6. 91: 167

**Dionysius of Halicarnassus** (*Dion. Hal.*):
On Lysias (*Lys.*)
34: 270

**Euripides** (*Eur.*)
Phoinissai (*Phoen.*):
1377–85: 140n111

**Galen** (*Gal.*):
De Usu Pulsuum:
1.24: 188

**Geoponica**:
2. 49: 74
6. 3.1–5: 74

**Harpocration**:
Lexicon: 280n91, 283n107

**Herodotus** (*Hdt.*):
1. 94: 64
109: 253n14
141, 143: 150
166: 194
169: 150
2. 154: 191
166–67: 11
182: 150n9
3. 106: 149
4. 14: 161
34.1: 153
5. 6: 283
12.3: 153
28: 150
33: 188, 194
88: 149
6. 32: 197
57.3: 259
89: 197
114: 187, 194
7. 14: 197
89–95: 186
90: 150n9
144: 189
9. 82.2: 178

**Hesiod** (*Hes.*):
Works and Days(*Op.*):
25–26: 74
293–319: 62
298–316: 272
678–80: 250
Theogony(*Theog.*):
139–41: 10

**Pseudo-Hesiod**:
Epigrams of Homer (*Ep. Hom.*):
14.3–6: 74

**Hesychius**:
Lexicon:
314

**Homer** (*Hom.*):
Iliad (*Il.*):
1. 309: 186
433–34, 436, 480: 194n88
609: 175n15
2. 135: 192
153: 191
433: 194n88
494–759: 186
509: 186
5. 60–61: 52
7. 219–23: 163
9. 661: 148
12. 294–97: 52
13. 390–91: 186
14. 240: 176
15. 410–12: 186
716–17: 194n88
16. 169: 186
482–84: 52, 186
17. 389–93: 52
462: 176
742–44: 186
18. 395–405: 10
422: 174
600–602: 52
20. 259: 177
23. 826: 52
852, 875: 194n88
24. 229–35: 152
644: 175n15
Odyssey (*Od.*):
1. 31: 174

280: 186
2. 46: 196
212: 186
337–42: 51
424–25: 194n88
426: 194n88
3. 10–11: 194n88
425–27, 432–25: 53
4. 227–32: 240
778: 186
782: 194n88
5. 243–48: 192
249–50: 52
251: 174
260: 194n88
260–62: 196n100
318: 194n88
360–64: 192
422: 174
6. 57–59: 52
268–69: 194n88
7. 103–11: 52
8. 36: 186
258: 175n15
438–40: 178
9. 98–99: 194n88
384–86: 172
489: 194n88
10. 32–33: 196n100
11. 489–91: 272
12. 20–22, 178–79, 409–10, 422–23: 194n88
13: 73: 148
195–98: 172
289: 52
15. 101–8: 152
289–90: 194n88
291: 194n88, 196
301, 351: 52
16. 158: 52
17. 383: 58
18. 190: 175n15
21. 43–45: 52
23.183–201: 52

**Hyperides** (*Hyp.*):
3: 68n57, 243, 287, 287n121
2: 283
6.9–10: 252
15: 283
4. 35: 119

**Isaeus** (*Isae.*):
5. 39: 272
8. 35: 268
9. 42–43: 268

**Isocrates** (*Isoc.*):
7. 32: 280
8. 20–21: 6
14. 48: 272
17. 9: 19
11–12: 287

**Leonidas**:
6.205.204 (Greek Anthology): 172

**Lucian**:
Demosthenis Encomium (*Dem. Enc.*):
15: 235
On Dreams (*Somn.*):
9: 220

**Lycurgus** (*Lycurg.*):
Against Leocrates(*Leoc.*):
22–23: 138, 219, 252
58: 138, 219, 302

**Lysias** (*Lys.*):
1. 4–10: 275
5. 5: 285
12. 4: 138
18–19: 12, 28, 139, 143
13. 18: 282
23. 2: 160
24. 6: 273, 285
20: 240
30. 22: 191
32. 20: 240
Fr. 38: 26, 68n57

**Menander** (*Men.*):
Epitrepontes (*Epit.*):
378–80: 287n122
Kekryphalos (*Kek.*):
2: 178
Sikyonioi (*Sic.*):
315: 283n107

**Oxyrhynchus papyrus**:
22.23410: 158

**Pausanias** (*Paus.*):
Histories:
1.9.4: 217

**Pherecrates** (Kock):
Savages: 271, 282
Fr. 64: 240n50
Fr. 70: 278

**Philostratos** (*Philostr.*):
Life of Apollonius of Tyana (*VA*):
5.200: 217

**Pindar** (*Pind.*):
Nemean Odes (*Nem.*):
  10.37: 52
Olympian Odes (*Ol.*):
  6.9, 7.1–2: 52

**Plato** (*Pl.*):
Apologia (*Ap.*):
  18b (schol): 163n75
Gorgias (*Grg.*):
  463–65: 214
  490d: 155
  514c: 7
  514e: 74
  515e: 271
  517e: 155, 231n2
  518b: 231n2
Hippias Minor (*Hp. Mi.*):
  368b: 47
Lachesis (*La.*):
  187b: 7, 74
Laws (*Leg.*):
  705c: 192
  846d: 265
  916a: 283
  945c: 195
Menexenus (*Menex.*):
  4g: 135
Meno:
  82a–b: 282
  90c: 166
  91d: 219
Phaedo (*Phd.*):
  87b–c: 154–55
Philebus (*Phlb.*):
  56b: 173
Protagoras (*Prt.*):
  315a: 148
  315e: 177
  324c: 7
  325e: 177
  328a: 219
Republic (*Resp.*):
  369–71: 29n143
  370e: 155
  371e: 12
  374b: 155
  404b–c: 232
  496d–e, 524d–31d, 547b: 12
  601c: 166
  616b–c: 195
Symposium (*Symp.*):
  197b: 10

**Plutarch** (*Plut.*):
Moralia (*Mor.*):
  219c: 140
  776b: 167
  843d: 119
On Socrates' Divine Sign (*De Gen.*):
  10.580d–f: 217
Life of Agesilaus (*Ages.*):
  264–65: 11
Life of Alcibiades (*Alc.*):
  7.5: 134
  23.3: 150
Life of Antony (*Ant.*):
  67.3: 196
Life of Cimon (*Cim.*):
  11.2–3: 190
  13.7: 203
Life of Lycurgus (*Lyc.*):
  7: 191
  9: 177
Life of Lysander (*Lys.*):
  16: 132
Life of Nicias (*Nic.*):
  28.5: 139
  29.1: 259
Life of Pericles (*Per.*):
  1.2: 161
  2.1: 12
  9.2–3: 271
  12.2: 204n7
  12.6–7: 211
  13.4: 224n109
Life of Solon (*Sol.*):
  13.7–8: 203n2
  21: 240n50
  22.1: 6, 7
Life of Sulla (*Sulla*):
  14.7: 193
Life of Themistocles (*Them.*):
  1.4: 203
  2: 191
  22: 203n3
Life of Theseus (*Thes.*):
  25.2–3: 7

**Pseudo-Plutarch** ((*Plut*)):
Life of Isocrates (*Isoc.*):
  1: 12, 183, 273
Life of Lysias (*Lysias*):
  1: 138

**Pollux** (*Poll.*):
  3. 9.30: 226
  **6**. 9: 176
  **7**. 1: 283n107
  78: 155
  **10**. 34: 175
  35: 176, 180

36: 175
61: 178
91: 179

**Sappho**:
Fr. 154 (LL): 52

**Pseudo-Socrates**:
Cynic Epistles (*Soc. Epist.*)
8, 18.2: 167

**Sophocles** (*Soph.*):
Antigone(*Ant.*):
313–14: 10n43
365–66: 10
Fr. 482 (LS): 74

**Strabo**:
7. 6.20: 157
58: 127
9. 1.15: 193
1.23: 121

**Theophrastus** (*Theophr.*):
Characters (*Char.*):
6.9: 231n2
17.6: 283n107
25: 141
30.5: 231n2
History of Plants (*HP*):
4.2.7: 148
5.7.2: 192
5.55.2: 180
5.6.2, 7.3.4: 173
9.3.1–3: 238
On Odours (*De Od.*):
15–6: 241
17: 242
37: 243
38: 241
42: 240
57: 242
On Stones (*De Lapid.*):
68: 155

**Thucydides** (*Thuc.*):
1. 2.2: 17
4: 185
6.3: 149
10.4: 186
13: 7, 150n9, 186
80, 142.6–7: 190
2. 13: 6, 117n9
31.2: 301
40.2: 274
84–86, 89: 190

94: 192
3.17.3: 190
22.3: 140
49.2–4: 192n84
68.3: 175
4. 12: 194
16.1: 259
96.2: 140n111
6. 8.1: 190
22: 231n2
27–28: 175
31.3: 190
43: 135n90
97.7: 117
7. 12: 190, 192
25.6: 5
34: 194
63: 280
87.2: 259
8. 5.5: 132
25: 136
45: 190n72

**Xenophon** (*Xen.*):
Anabasis (*Anab.*):
2. 4: 140
7. 1.27: 6
3.21: 178
Apologia (*Ap.*):
29: 28, 163
Constitution of the Lacedaemonians
(*Lac.*):
7: 11
Cyropaedia (*Cyr.*):
5. 3.39: 231n2, 277n76
8. 2.5: 29, 168
Hellenica (*Hell.*):
1. 1.36: 192
5.7: 132
5.10–11: 190, 192
4. 3.17: 140n111
5. 4.33: 140
6. 2.27: 194
4.13: 141
7. 1.31: 140n111
8. 9–10: 202
Memorabilia (*Mem.*):
2. 3.3: 273
5.2: 283
5.3: 260
7.3–6: 155
7.5: 153
7.6: 150n9, 160, 231n2, 273
7.7: 155
7.11: 157, 252
7.11–12: 25

## 368  Index Locorum

Memorabilia (*Mem.*) (*Cont.*)
  **3**. 5.18: 190
  7.6: 274
  10.9: 126, 137
  **4**. 2.1: 167
Oeconomicus (*Oec.*):
  **2**. 5–6: 23n106
  **4**. 2–3: 12
  **6**. 4: 292
  **7**. 3: 275
  6: 153
  9.5: 282
  14.7: 287
  22: 275
  32, 35–43: 19, 276
Poroi (*Vect.*):
  **2**. 1–6: 6, 279
  **4**. 4–16: 8, 26, 99n105, 110, 120, 257, 283
  23–24: 257, 261
Symposium (*Symp.*):
  2.1: 178
  2.4: 240

**Pseudo-Xenophon** ((*Xen.*)):
Constitution of the Athenians (*Ath. pol.*):
  1.11–12: 6, 19, 280
  19–20: 190
  27. 3: 271

**Zosimus**:
Historia Nova:
  5.20: 185

## ROMAN AUTHORS

**Cicero** (*Cic.*):
De Oratore (*De Or.*):
  1.14.62: 193
De Legibus (*Leg.*):
  2.64–65: 217

**Horace**:
De Arte Poetica (*AP*):
  32–35: 219
Juvenal (*Juv.*):
Satires (*Sat.*):
  3. 168: 76

**Lucretius** (*Lucr.*):
De Rerum Natura:
  **1**. 895–901: 10
  **5**. 1091–95, 1241–49: 10

**Pliny** (*Plin.*):
Natural History(*HN*):
  **7**. 12: 193
  57, 191–98: 10
  198: 172
  **9**. 40: 176
  60–65: 160
  **12**. 18, 42–99: 241
  **13**. 1: 240, 244
  92–93: 178
  **16**. 192: 173
  197: 176
  222, 227: 173
  **19**. 87: 176
  **23**. 108: 176
  **27**. 7: 187
  **29**. 33: 150
  **35**. 128–29: 219
  136: 277

**Valerius Maximus**:
Factorum et Dictorum Memorabilium Libri Novem:
  8.12: 193

**Varro**:
Rustica (*Rust.*):
  1.2.21: 158

**Virgil** (*Verg.*):
Aeneid (*Aen.*):
  **8**. 424–25: 10

**Vitruvius** (*Vit.*):
On Architecture (*De. Arch.*):
  Praef. 12: 207
  1.2.4: 191
  2.1: 10
  7.12: 193
  9.3.4: 222n105

## INSCRIPTIONS

**Agora Inscription**:
  1.7396: 166n85

**Code of Gortyna**:
  1 Cr.IV.72: 153

**Corpus Inscriptionum Latinarum** (Berolini, 1869–1892. George Reimer).
  VI. 9185, 1214: 138n103

**Inscriptiones Graecae** (*IG*)
IG I[2]:

343.90, 372–74: 205
**IG I³**:
  1: 135
  21: 192
  24: 193, 205
  35: 204, 205
  36: 204
  45: 205
  49: 204n7
  52: 204, 205, 207
  64: 204, 205
  78: 178, 204
  79: 204
  84: 205
  127, 154: 191
  257: 164
  343: 177, 178
  343–45, 351: 176
  357: 178
  369: 16n68
  382: 191
  386–87: 209
  395: 204
  421, 422, 430: 283
  435A–F: 204
  436–51, 474–79: 209
  546: 231n2
  554, 616, 905: 160
**IG II²**:
  141, 337: 5
  463: 204, 205
  555: 216, 220
  1556.30–32, 1557.68–71: 231n2
  1561.27, 1570.73, 1578.5: 277
  1604.34, 1604.48, 1606.74, 1609.90: 194
  1609.114: 196
  1611.23, 1611.28: 194
  1611.254, 1611.259, 1611.393,
    W1627.449: 196
  1631.671: 195
  1649–50: 203
  1656.64: 202
  1668: 207
  1672.105: 166, 257n26
  3109: 216
  10995, 11681: 231n2
  11688: 243n61
  12073: 277
**IG II⁴**:
  514: 216
**IG II/III²**:
  3869: 178
  4280.415, 4280.671: 195
  4321, 4403: 178
  7593: 122
  8388: 5
**IG III³**:
  68a1–2: 231n2
**IG XI**:
  199A82–85: 178

**Sylloge Inscriptionum Graecarum**
  (**SIG³**) (Dittenberger, 1883. Hirzelius):
  1177: 277

**REFERENCE WORKS**
**Greek-English Lexicon**. H. G. Liddell,
  R. Scott, 9th edition. 1940.
  Oxford: Clarendon Press.
New Pauly Encyclopaedia of the Ancient
  World. 2003 edition. Boston: E. J.
  Brill.

# GENERAL INDEX

*Usage and spelling follow the* Oxford Classical Dictionary *Third Edition (Oxford University Press, 1996) wherever direct references are found therein.*

Abrasive, 129, 222
accounting, 22, 26, 28, 208–9, 209n34, 222, 261–62
accountability (public), 203–4, 207
Achilles, 52, 186, 272
acrolithic, 224
*adunatoi*, 271
Aegean Sea, 162, 172, 283
Aeschines, 12n49, 26, 167, 242, 252, 269
Aeschylus, 9, 188, 194n91
Africa, 23, 87, 109, 124, 125, 161, 182, 237, 240, 241
Ageladas, 219
Agora,
   archaeology, 13, 15, 79, 81, 94, 125, 166n85, 167, 183
   buildings and monuments, 203, 216, 217, 225, 226
   *gunaikeia* (women's), 275
   items on sale, 81, 99, 103, 105, 163, 166, 169, 181, 183, 197
   meeting place, 2
Agoracritus, 219, 224
agriculture. *See* food
   manufacturing in agricultural societies, 1, 48–51
   nonfood products, 149, 237–38
Alcamenes, 224
Alcibiades, 99, 118, 149, 175, 176, 177, 275n67
Alcmaonid, 217
Alexander, 1n2, 135, 217, 240
Alexandria, 129, 157, 241–42
aliens, 19, 189n70, 209, 215, 279–80, 302, 304, 314
Amorgos, *amorgina*, 150, 154, 154n27
Amphipolis, 140
*amphora*, 74, 77–79, 81, 83, 98, 102–3, 105, 109, 160, 166, 179, 234, 235
anchor, 194, 196–97
Andocides (orator), 12. See also *Index Locorum*
Andocides (potter), 75, 89
*andron*, 226

Antenor, 7, 217
*antidosis*, 118
*antilabe*, 139
anvil, 53, 61, 88, 126, 127, 133
Anytos, 10, 28, 163, 269
*apeleutheroi. See* slaves, freed
*aphanes* (wealth), 23, 268
*aphlaston*, 193, 194
Aphobus, 254, 264
*apodektai*, 204
Apollo, 15, 79
Apollodorus, 215, 256
*apophora*,
   definition, 8, 22, 24, 28, 40, 120n28, 154, 168, 211n47, 248, 253, 270, 284, 288
   instances, 167–69, 198, 238, 242–44, 253–68, 286, 303
appliqué, 181n45, 223
apprentice(ship), 7–8, 86, 89, 90, 106, 125, 127, 170, 208, 214, 219, 243, 261, 309
archaeological evidence, 13–16, 45, 49, 65, 75–83, 84, 94, 96, 105, 125, 129, 131, 148, 151, 154, 156–57, 161, 162, 167, 178, 188n65, 191, 216, 240, 241, 292
Archaic Age, 5, 186, 194, 205
architect, 7, 193, 203, 205, 207–8, 214, 215, 228, 249, 271
   naval architect, 188n65, 195, 200, 201
architecture, 2, 7, 80, 173, 215, 216, 219, 229
   naval architecture, 190
Areopagus, 156, 228
*arga* assets, 262, 265–67
Argos, 216, 219, 220, 224
Aristarchus, 25, 155, 252, 269, 287
Aristophanes, 10–11, 13, 17, 30, 45, 82, 106, 126, 142, 147, 166, 181, 183, 202, 219, 242, 253, 263, 265, 273, 277, 282, 285, 292, 299, 313n18. See also *Index Locorum*
Aristotle, 12, 17, 24, 187, 259, 273, 285, 292. See also *Index Locorum*
Arkwright, 159

371

## General Index

armor, 10, 11, 45, 52, 56, 67, 116, 125, 127, 128, 134–38, 139, 142–43, 145–46, 167, 168, 219, 225, 249, 273, 278, 280, 302. *See also* breastplate; bronze technology; cuirass; greave; shield
armorer, 15, 138
armrest, 175–76
aromatics, 240, 245
Arretium, 109–10
arrow (arrowhead), 127, 135, 145
Arsenal, 193, 207
Artemision, 197
artisan, 2, 7, 11, 65, 110, 158, 211n46, 212, 213, 287. *See also* craftsman
Asclepius, 203, 206
Asia, 149, 182
assayer, 210
assembly, legislative, 6, 97, 184, 203n3, 204, 208, 271, 274
  production, 25, 29–31, 52, 168, 173, 181, 185, 199–200, 218, 221, 249
*astunomoi*, 226–28
*ateles*, 259–63
Athena, 10, 52, 53, 132, 150, 153, 154, 157, 162, 204, 206, 207, 209, 214, 216, 218, 220, 224, 275
Athenogenes, 25, 243–45, 252, 287
Athens,
  coinage, 6n33, 50, 64, 67, 117, 117n11, 126, 127, 131–34, 145, 210, 249
  economic development, 1–8
  income opportunities, 2–3, 53, 65, 67, 100–102, 105, 116, 120, 122, 128, 130, 154, 170, 183, 203, 210, 215, 230, 237–38, 247, 248, 250, 252, 269, 270–74, 276–81, 285, 287, 294, 295, 299, 301–5, 309
  housing, 225–28
  legal system, 18–19, 27, 49, 153, 250, 257, 271, 274–76, 279, 283, 286–87
  naval power, 5, 185, 193
  population, 5n28, 282, 285, 300–303
athletics, 52, 142
Attica, 118, 203, 218, 230, 233, 236, 250–52, 272, 279, 300
auction, 82, 103, 283n107
*autarchaia*. *See* self-sufficiency
axe, 127, 145, 173
Ayer, Alfred J., 291

bag, 148, 157, 236
Bacchius, 103
banking, 9, 19, 21, 139, 251n8, 256, 267, 272, 275–76, 287

barbarian, 138, 278, 282, 288
barley, 233–34, 239, 259
barriers to entry, 26, 32, 33, 38–45, 73, 91, 98, 101, 113, 115, 116, 122–23, 126, 143–45, 156–157, 159, 163, 164, 170, 180, 201, 228, 244–246, 270, 272, 274, 278, 281, 294
basket (weaving), 15, 148, 160, 166, 237, 246
batch, 91–92, 96, 110, 124, 151, 160, 235, 237, 241
Bdelycleon, 285
beam, 151, 152n17, 162, 173, 184–85, 191, 193–94, 197, 209, 213, 226, 236
bed, 32, 52, 122, 148, 172, 174–77, 180–81, 254–68, 315
beeswax, 237
bench, 111, 166, 177, 180
bending (wood), 173, 181, 192, 195
beneficiation, 20n87, 119, 121
Berlin Foundry Cup, 126n52, 137
biscuit, 239
Black Sea, 234, 283
blacksmith. *See* smith
blade, 144, 146
block and tackle, 226
bloomery, 125
boat, ship, 15, 77, 122, 150, 216, 253, 280. *See also* trireme
boatbuilding, 5, 11, 35, 44, 64, 156n38, 169, 172, 173n5, 174, 185–200, 213, 214, 215, 220, 229, 238, 249, 315
  components and suppliers, 193–200
  industry structure, 197–200
body rub, 240, 245
boot, 165–66, 313
Bosporus, 252
Boston Consulting Group, The, 30, 33
*boule*. *See* council
bow (and arrow), 135
branding, 34–35, 38–39, 41, 44, 113, 128, 138, 143, 144, 146, 157, 159, 170, 183, 184, 224, 238, 245
Brasidas, 140
breastplate, 126–27, 134–35
broth, 239
brothel, 69, 153, 158, 227, 288
Bryaxis, 219
building program, 7, 202–05, 271, 286
butter, 240
Byzantine period, 94, 164, 185

cake, 231, 239
calipers, 143, 173, 223
Callicrates, 207
Callistratus, 287

*General Index* } 373

Campania, 109
cape, 155, 273
capital. *See* industry, investment in; investment; lending
Capital Asset Pricing Model, 291
Caputi hydria, 85–86, 90, 277n73
carding, 74, 147, 152, 160
carpentry. *See* woodwork
cart, 1, 184
cartage, 184, 214, 228, 229, 234, 237, 249
carter, 209
Carthaginian/Punic, 187, 189n70, 192–93, 195, 222n105, 234. *See also* Phoenician; Punic Wars
casserole, 239
casting, 7, 29, 125, 219, 221, 223
    pit, 15, 125, 218
casual participation, 73, 97, 99, 100, 105, 114, 116, 145, 158, 183, 269, 270–74, 281, 284, 304
cathead, 192, 194, 197
*cella*, 212
Celtic, 218
Cephalus (envoy), 273
Cephalus (father of Lysias), 138, 144, 281
Cephisodotus, 7, 219
ceramics. *See* pottery
Ceramicus, 79, 84, 94, 103, 125, 156, 218
cereal, 39, 231
chair, 174, 176–77, 180–82, 315
Chairedemus, 142
Chaironea, 122
Chalcidice, 79, 197
charcoal, 15, 122–23, 231, 246, 285, 287
    technology, 237–38
chariot, 10, 184
cheese, 231, 234, 238
chef, 231, 246–47, 249
chest, 174, 178–82, 315
children, 153, 155, 157, 166, 197n104, 256, 260, 261, 276, 277, 280, 283, 309
China, 48n8, 87, 111, 159
Chios, 176, 235
chisel, 117, 136, 173, 205, 212, 222, 263
chock, 194, 197
*choinix*, 259–60
*choris oikountes*. *See* slaves
Choristes, 285
chorus, 9, 10, 268, 272
Chremes, 285
Chremyles, 285
chryselephantine, 224
Cicero, 178, 193. See also *Index Locorum*
Cimon, 118, 203
Ciron, 268

citizen,
    attitude to manufacturing, 11–12, 23, 250–53, 270, 272, 290
    craftsman, 2, 5–8, 40, 42, 52, 114, 130, 133, 136, 146, 273–74, 278, 294, 305, 307
    income, 2–3, 53, 65, 67, 100–102, 105, 114, 116, 120, 122, 128, 130, 154, 170, 183, 203, 210, 215, 230, 237–38, 247, 248, 250, 252, 253, 269, 294, 295, 301–5, 309
    investor, 12, 15, 20, 22, 24, 117–20, 122, 154, 168, 248, 250–71, 273, 274–78, 286, 291–92, 300–12
    landowner, 4n19, 5, 100, 237, 248n1, 250–52, 270, 273, 274–75, 300–12
    population, 5n28, 300–02
Cittus, 103
civic activities/duties. *See* duty, civic
clay, clay beds, 4, 14, 15, 25, 79–80, 87–91, 93–94, 97–99, 104, 106–7, 109, 111, 129, 151, 206n19, 215, 221, 223, 226, 237, 316n22
Cleisthenes, 204, 217
Cleon, 8, 10, 11, 28, 163, 253, 269, 271, 273
Cleonymus, 140
Cleophon, 269, 271, 273
Cleophrades, 103
cleruchy, 5
cloak, 148, 151, 155, 166n84, 273
clothing, 45, 53, 63, 69, 138, 147–62, 170, 183, 214, 249, 260, 274, 276, 286, 305, 308, 309, 312–13. *See also* textiles
cobbler. *See* shoemaking
coinage, 50, 58, 59, 64, 116, 131–34, 210
    *Athenian units* (Athenian currency), 297
    industry structure, 126, 131–34, 145, 249
    symbolism, 50
    technology, 133
column, 110, 184, 191, 205, 207, 209, 212, 212n55, 216
comb, 147
comic poets, 9, 276
commerce, 1, 8–13, 17–21, 23, 27–28, 33, 65, 81, 124, 239, 250–51, 253, 259, 278–80, 284, 287–95
commercial vessels, 199
commission (board), 205, 207
commission (order), 51, 67, 75, 76, 99, 102, 104, 137, 156, 200, 208, 216–17, 220, 224
Comon, 287
competition, 9, 21, 33–46, 50, 57–61, 65, 72, 100, 108, 116, 124, 156, 164, 201, 220, 225, 228, 229, 234, 242, 257, 282, 284

competitive advantage. *See also* branding; cost advantage; reliability advantage; reputation advantage
  instances, 61, 72, 101, 112, 114–15, 123, 127, 138, 142–45, 161, 164, 183, 228–29, 256, 294
  theory, 33–46
Conon, 202, 217
consolidation (industry), 32, 72, 120, 138, 145–46, 159, 170, 184, 230, 237, 245–46, 274
construction. *See* housing; public buildings
consumable, 262
consumer, 34, 38, 43, 112, 231, 238, 245, 248
consumption, 2, 4, 5, 14, 16, 51, 53, 62, 64, 69, 109, 136, 158, 229–30, 233–35, 240, 259–60, 276, 282, 294, 300, 302, 304, 305n13. See *also* demand
  estimation methodology, 311–17
contract, 19, 27, 49, 102, 105, 108, 120, 195, 197, 200–205, 208, 211, 212, 227–29, 252, 284
contractor, 12, 133, 185, 190, 195–96, 199, 200, 208, 211, 214, 215, 228, 280
cooking, 11, 31, 36, 75, 76, 82, 88, 122, 144, 179, 231, 239
cooperative, 3, 56, 61, 115, 236–37, 247
copper, 113, 124–26, 129, 131, 144, 215, 262–63
cord, 139, 141–42, 192
Corinth, 7, 75, 78–79, 81, 82, 89, 131, 150, 151, 186, 194, 207, 215n62, 234
Coronea, 140
cosmetics, 66, 68, 230, 238–42
  industry structure, 242–49
  technology, 242, 244
cost advantage, 35–38, 72, 115, 127, 137, 142, 163, 169
cotton, 149
couch, 5, 174–82, 213, 226, 254–67, 314–15
council (*boule*), 118, 204
craft, 1–16, 23, 24, 27, 29, 32, 42–44, 52–61, 62–65, 97, 114, 116, 122, 130, 153, 159, 164, 166, 167, 170, 204, 210–14, 228–29, 246, 249–50, 270–74, 277, 278, 280, 282, 284–88, 294, 309
craftsman, 5, 6, 10–16, 21, 40, 42, 45, 46, 52, 57, 65–70, 73, 84, 87, 99–100, 102, 104, 108, 109, 111, 114–15, 116, 123, 126, 128–31, 133–34, 136, 142–43, 144–46, 163, 166, 167, 170, 175, 179, 182–83, 200–201, 202–3, 207–14, 214–25, 228–29, 248, 250, 256–57,
268–69, 270–74, 277, 280, 281, 294, 299, 301–11
apprenticeship, 7–8
  definition, 3n8, 42–44
  income. (*see* citizen; income)
Crates, 167
creative artist, 213–15, 219
credit, 22, 24–27, 264, 272
Crete, 173, 178
crushing, 121, 160, 231, 234n24, 235–36
Ctesicles, 301n6, 302
cuirass. *See* breastplate
cupboard, 148, 179
cupellation, 122–24
currency. *See* coinage
curtain, 134, 148, 195
cutwater, 192, 194, 197
Cyclades, 216
Cydathon, 164
Cynics, 167
Cyrus, 150

dagger, 144
Dark Age, 49, 51, 61, 64, 125, 216
debt, 19, 26, 61, 242–43, 252, 263, 268, 283. *See also* interest rate
deck, 187–89, 193, 196, 198
decoration, 5, 7, 43, 45, 52, 74–78, 80, 82, 84, 86–91, 97, 98, 99, 102–7, 112–14, 116, 130, 134, 139, 141, 146, 148, 165, 166, 174–82, 184, 186, 193, 208–14, 217, 237, 240, 249, 285, 312n15, 316
dedication, 14, 77, 103, 154, 161, 166, 216, 277, 281, 304, 308, 313
default, 27, 253
Delos, 108, 207, 211, 220, 257
Delphi, 211, 220
demand, 3, 6, 7, 12, 16, 17, 35–43, 45–46, 47, 50, 53, 56, 58–61, 66, 70, 96, 99–101, 106–8, 110, 112–13, 116, 123, 127, 130, 136, 138, 142, 144, 146, 154, 158, 169, 174, 182, 200, 201, 210, 215, 217, 220, 233, 234, 238, 240, 244, 248, 249, 251, 257, 263, 283, 290–92, 295, 300, 304, 309, 311–17
*demarch*, 204
deme, 189, 204, 209, 251, 269, 279–80
Demeas, 155, 272
Demeter, 215n62
Demetrius (sculptor), 207, 219
Demetrius (statesman), 217
demographics, 155, 276, 294, 302–11. *See also* Athens, population
Demos, 169, 274, 285
*demos*, 203

Demosion Sema, 79
Demosthenes (orator), 2, 12, 17, 19, 28, 85, 119, 122, 126, 144–45, 149, 181–83, 235, 243, 254–56, 269, 283, 286–87, 291–92, 302, 314–15
Demosthenes senior (father of the above), 8, 26, 254, 268–69
depreciation, 123, 139n105, 255, 261–66
die, 131, 133–34, 145
diet, 230–32, 260
differentiation (product), 34, 35–37, 41–44, 67–71, 82, 99–106, 114–15, 128, 130, 134–36, 145, 151, 156–58, 163, 170, 173–74, 179–81, 183–85, 201, 225, 228–29, 234, 239, 245, 246–47, 249, 269–70, 273–74, 276–78, 281–82, 294, 305, 309
*dikai emporikai*, 19, 279
*dike apostasiou*, 280, 280n91
Dicaeopolis, 285
*diobolon*, 271
Dionysus (cobbler), 166
Dionysus (helmet maker), 276–277
Dionysus of Syracuse, 187
Dioscurides, 242
Diotimus, 122, 142
dispensing, 244–47, 249
distaff, 151
distribution,
  products, 36, 40 68, 61, 81, 112, 231, 282
  public funds, 119, 189, 204
  wealth, 1, 4, 27
diversification, 63, 83, 118, 250, 253
dockyards, 185, 191, 195, 198
Doric, 149, 216
Douris of Samos, 102, 218, 281
drama, 18, 142, 156, 184, 201, 249. *See also* theater
dress, 147–50, 156. *See also* clothing
drill, 128–29, 172–73, 205, 212, 222
drink, 226, 230, 235
duty, civic, 97, 209, 256, 257, 270, 271–72, 272, 281, 286, 294, 303, 305, 308
dyeing, 4, 15, 43, 69, 152, 156–61, 165, 170, 201, 211, 214–15, 228, 249
  technology, 160–61

economic,
  growth, 3–6, 17, 47–49, 108, 112n48, 236, 284, 299
  rationality, 17–21, 45, 50, 69, 100, 250n3, 256–58, 264–66, 269, 290–94
economies of scale, 25, 31–42, 66, 110, 114–15, 120, 122–23, 127, 130, 137, 142, 234, 237, 241, 272, 274

efficiency, 11, 19–20, 22, 26, 28, 39, 60, 70, 110, 113, 125n45, 129, 144, 155, 192n80, 229, 235–36, 316
efficient size, 31–33, 42, 73, 86, 92–93, 111, 182, 184, 246
Egypt, 11, 48n8, 49, 109, 135, 149, 150n9, 151, 152, 158, 160n157, 175, 176, 178, 205, 216n63, 217, 221, 225, 243, 261n39
*eisphora*, 301
*ekklesia*. *See* assembly
Eleusis, 156n43, 203, 209, 211, 213, 257, 277, 282
elite, 23–24, 102, 109, 118, 139, 211, 251, 307
embeddedness paradigm, 16–22, 290–93
embossing, 211–15, 216
employment, 29, 31–33, 36–38, 42, 44, 45, 50, 55, 57, 62, 64, 66, 67–68, 79, 80, 83–84, 93, 95, 100, 104, 107, 109, 110, 112, 116, 120, 122, 126, 130, 134, 139, 144, 147, 153–54, 158–59, 181–83, 185, 190, 199, 200, 203, 206, 209–13, 214–15, 219–20, 223–25, 229, 242–43, 247–48, 251, 269, 271–74, 280, 283–84, 285–86, 314n19
*emporoi*, 253
*energa* assets, 254, 266–67
*ephebes*, 135
*epibatai*, 188–89, 197n104
epic poets, 9–10, 51–62, 217
Epicrates, 25, 119, 243–44, 249, 280
Epidaurus, 11, 211, 220
epigraphy, 13–15, 73, 74, 98, 154n25, 166, 172, 203–5, 211, 277, 283, 304, 312
*epimeletai*, 191, 205
*epinetron*, 160
equilibrium, 13, 34, 38, 142, 258, 269
equity, 253, 255
*eranos* loan, 276
Erechtheum, 126, 187, 206–13, 224, 277
*ergasterion*. *See* workshop
Ergoteles, 103, 108
Ergotimus, 102–3, 108
estate, 49, 51–60, 62, 65, 68–70, 109, 114, 152, 162, 163, 178, 236, 246, 251, 254, 268, 279
Etruria, 102, 109
Eubulus, 193
Euphrainus, 287
Euphranor, 219
Euphron, 287
Euphronius, 75, 102, 218
Europe, 8, 23, 110–11, 120, 125
Eurymedon, 188
exchange, 50–51, 53–59, 61–66, 69, 77, 110, 123, 154, 275, 279, 292

experience curve, 30–31
exports. *See* trade

factory, 3n8, 28, 30–32, 112n148, 113, 126, 139, 142–43, 144, 158, 182, 254–69, 281, 303, 315
famine, 4, 20n87, 52
farming, 4, 6, 9, 10, 28, 48–53, 61–65, 79, 110, 121, 162, 166, 207, 230–39, 246, 251, 270–72, 274, 284, 299, 301, 304. *See also* agriculture
festivals, 2, 5, 63, 67, 153, 156, 157, 231, 238, 257, 270, 271, 299
fiber, 149, 151–52, 155, 159–60, 237
fig, 233–34, 239n43
figurines, 49, 67, 106
filigree, 129
finance, 1n2, 12, 24–25, 28, 39, 117n9, 190, 203–6, 210, 247, 253, 265, 275, 280. *See also* capital; investment; lending
fine garments, 7, 69, 148–50, 154–57, 170, 249
finishing, 150–52, 159–61
Finley, Sir Moses I., 3n10, 11n46, 13, 16–24, 29n143, 50, 56, 153, 158, 251, 255, 260, 264, 284, 289–93
firing, 15, 25, 74, 79–80, 87–98, 110–11, 237, 316n21
firm size,
  by product. (*see* industry structure *by specific products*)
  theory, 22–44
fishing, 173, 231–34, 238, 240, 278
fish paste, 232
fishing boat, 200
fixed assets, 25, 40–41, 99
fixed workshops, 60–61
flax, 149, 154, 231, 237
fleece, 148, 160
flock (glazing), 113
flower, 231, 233, 237, 246, 278
flute, 12, 166, 183–84, 273
fluting, 207, 212n55, 213
foil, 216
food, 20, 30, 34, 39, 49, 51, 53, 54n34, 58, 62, 64, 77, 178–79, 226, 230–39, 249, 260, 270, 277–78, 286, 303
  partly processed products, 231
    industry structure, 233–38
  prepared products, 230–31, 238–39, 275
    industry structure, 239
  preservation, 233–34
  unprocessed products, 231–32
    industry structure, 233
footstool, 176, 180, 182

footwear. *See* shoe
foreigner. *See* aliens; metics
foreman, 1, 8, 24, 40, 93, 120, 123, 144, 154, 169n93, 181, 199, 200, 203, 205, 208, 215, 223, 224n109, 228, 250, 253–55, 256–57, 260, 262–64, 266, 275–76, 278, 281–82, 284, 286, 287
forging, 124–26, 220
formulation, 239–46, 249
foundry, 25, 218. *See also* kiln
Foundry Painter, 218–19
fountain, 226
fowl, 232
frame, 175, 180, 181, 183, 184, 192n80, 220, 226
frame saw, 173
France, 9, 110, 111, 114, 153, 282
freed slaves. *See* slaves, freed
freelance, 104, 196, 228
fruit, 231–33, 239n43
fuel, 106, 110, 124, 172, 230, 231, 233, 237–38, 260
fulling, 69, 147, 152, 159–62, 170–71, 249
funerary monuments, 74–75, 79, 106, 212, 217, 224. *See also* tombstone
fur, 196
furnace. *See* foundry; kiln
furnishings, 148, 155, 181, 182
furniture, 4, 15, 25–26, 43, 62, 116, 144, 172–85, 200–01, 210, 225, 249, 254–69, 311–17

gall, 144, 162, 262–63
game, 232
garland, 231, 237, 246, 277
*garopoles*, 234
Gaul, 109
Germany, 82
glass, 48, 91, 108, 129–30, 174, 215, 216
glaze, 77, 89–90, 95, 98–99, 103, 109–13, 151, 218n77, 221
glue, 141, 173, 223
gold, 5, 29, 52, 90, 123–31, 178, 215, 216, 222
goldsmith, 15, 44, 53, 126, 130–31, 211–13
graffiti, 75, 80–82, 110
grain, 5n28, 16, 62, 77, 148, 231, 233–35, 246, 260, 287
  primary processing, 234–35, 237, 246, 249
  supply, 4–6, 16n68, 17, 49, 173, 252
granulation, 129
grape, 62, 234–35, 237, 246, 249
Graufesenque, 110
gravestone. *See* tombstone
greave, 52, 127, 134, 136, 138
grooming, 4, 272, 305
guard (armor), 134, 136

Gylon, 254
*gynaikon(tis)*, 275

haggis, 231
halyard, 193–97
hammer, 1, 53, 117, 121, 124–27, 129, 131, 133, 134, 141, 143, 144, 173, 181, 212, 221, 222, 241, 263
handle, 87–89, 124, 144, 173
hangings, 148, 157, 162
harbor, 191
 tax, 5, 5n28, 6, 12
heat control, 87, 90–91, 112, 122, 124–25, 126n49, 133
Helen of Troy, 240
Hellenistic, 78, 130, 132n71, 135, 146, 159, 175, 179, 218, 220, 236, 240–41
helmet, 126, 127, 134–36, 166
helmet maker, 276
Helot, 282
Hephaestus, 10, 85, 125, 224
 temple of, 206, 209
herbs, 15, 231–35, 238, 240–41, 244
Herculaneum, 110
herding, 48, 51–52, 231, 272
herm, herm carver, 175, 182, 216, 217
Hesiod, 9, 13, 47, 51, 61–65, 285. See also *Index Locorum*
hide, 15, 48, 52, 139, 162–64, 240
Hippolytus, 253
Hipponicus, 119–20, 257
historian, 2, 11–13, 15, 21, 23, 29, 32, 50, 96, 147, 157, 185, 188n65, 253, 275, 284, 289–94, 299, 302, 317
historic cost, 258
*hodopoioi*, 228
hollow casting, 221
Homer, 9, 10, 13, 47, 51–61, 66, 125, 127, 139, 148, 152, 163, 172, 174, 175n15, 178, 186, 188, 191–94, 196, 232, 259, 285. See also *Index Locorum*
honey, 231, 233–35, 238, 239n43, 241, 277
hoplite, 134–36, 139–41, 213
*hoplon*, 139. *See also* shield
hopper, 235
horticulturalist, 233
Hotelling's Law, 14n57, 169
House of Many Colors, 156
House of the Tholos, 14n56, 79, 82
House of the Vettii, 241
household. *See* oikos
 objects. (see *by specific products*)
housekeeping, 153, 309
housing, 3, 4, 225–28, 301
hull, 185, 190–93, 195–201, 249, 315, 317

Hume, David, 17
hunter-gatherer, 233
Hymettus, 205
Hyperbolus, 106, 269, 273
hypothecation, 253

Ilyssus, 164
imports. *See* trade
incense, 106, 240–42
income. *See* Athens, income opportunities; citizen, income; wage
India, 5n25, 23, 48n8, 87, 131, 152, 159, 164, 237, 241
Industrial Revolution, 3, 24, 32, 108, 112–15, 152, 154, 159, 238, 265, 275, 293, 295
industry, 1, 7, 9, 12, 14, 16, 21, 23, 25, 29, 30, 32–46, 101, 116, 201, 210, 247, 248–49, 269–70, 272, 274–75, 278, 281–82, 286–87, 290–95. See also *by specific products*
 definition, 3n8, 43–44
 formation, 48–72
 investment in, 15, 22, 25, 40, 122, 163, 248, 250, 253–54, 259, 304, 308–12, 317
ingredient, 68, 161, 231–32, 239–46
inhalation, 240
inheritance, 8–10, 12, 17, 28, 85, 108, 119, 144, 163, 181, 213, 251, 252, 253–56
inlay, 174, 180, 181, 183, 211, 213, 215
inspector, 210
inscriptions. *See* epigraphy
intention, 50, 53, 291–92
interest rate, 16n68, 26, 252–53
inventory, 36, 41, 55, 57, 66, 68–69, 100, 145, 182, 195, 201, 238, 244, 245, 263, 265–66, 269, 301
investment. See *by specific products*
 capital requirements, 24–26, 39–41, 80, 272, 276, 303
 returns, 243, 250–68
Ionia, 81, 149, 150
iron, 29, 49, 77n12, 87–91, 116n2, 117, 123, 125–26, 144, 173, 180, 182, 196, 205, 215, 220, 222, 262–63
Iron Age, 110, 129, 139, 162, 172
Isaeus, 269, 272
Ischomachus, 276
Isocrates, 12, 183, 253, 269, 272, 273, 280
Italy, 109–10, 138, 158, 173n5, 225, 241–42
ivory, 144, 167, 174, 178, 180–82, 211, 213, 215–17, 220n92, 224, 262–63

Japan, 87, 111
javelin, 127, 135
jewel. *See* gem

joinery, 173, 179–85
journeyman, 212, 215
judge, 10, 13, 27, 271
jury, 28, 163, 279

*kalathos*, 160
Kamid-el-Loz, 129
Kant, Immanuel, 291
*kapeleia, kapeleides*, 235, 277n77
keel, 192, 194
Keynes, John M., 17, 26n124
kitchen, 45, 76–77, 127, 178–79, 226
kiln, 29, 67, 73, 74, 78–87, 90–99, 102, 104, 106, 109–13, 114, 124, 316–17. *See also* foundry
  supports, 94, 110
*kline*, 175, 180–81
knife, 122, 125, 144, 166, 210, 219, 225, 254–69
*koite*, 179–80
*kolakretai*, 204
*kosmesis*, 223
*kothon (kothizein)*, 235
*kothornos*, 165n79, 166

labor, 3, 4, 7, 16, 18, 24, 25, 39–41, 45, 50–58, 62–66, 68–69, 80, 86, 87, 92–98, 103–4, 107, 113, 120, 123, 128, 136n94, 141, 142–44, 154–56, 158–59, 162, 168, 170, 190, 198–99, 202–3, 210–12, 220, 221, 223, 225–28, 236, 242–43, 249, 251, 261–63, 272–73, 278–79, 283–85, 288, 294, 300, 307, 309–16. *See also* productivity
  division of, 22, 29–32, 138, 142, 152n17, 168, 215
labor market, 24, 39, 40, 62, 64, 98–99, 104, 143, 250, 255
ladder, 194, 197, 226
lamp, 6, 78, 83, 106, 115, 249, 273, 274
  lampstand, 127, 179, 180
Lampis, 19, 287
Lampon, 204
Lampsacus, 24
land, 4, 5, 20, 48n5, 49–51, 53, 54, 58, 62, 64, 100, 119, 182, 237, 248n1, 250–52, 258, 263–65, 270–71, 272, 274–75, 279–80, 293, 300–12
landowner. *See* citizen, landowner
lathe, 24, 141–43, 172n2, 173, 181, 262
Laurium, 6, 15, 117–22, 132, 189, 195, 261
lead, 8, 15, 113, 121–24, 240
  dog lead, 166, 166n84, 169
Leagros *hydria*, 82–85

lease, 9, 14, 26, 109, 117, 135, 207, 250, 251–52, 260, 263, 287. *See also* mining, lease
leather, 54n33, 68–69, 134, 139, 141, 142, 148, 161n61, 162–70, 193, 195–97, 201, 249, 313
leatherworker, 6, 52, 164–70, 197, 274
leisure, 11, 63–64, 232, 270–72, 300
Lemnos, 224
lending, 23, 27, 209, 248n1, 253, 280
  as an investment, 24–26, 158, 250–52, 280, 301
  for production, 25, 157, 255
  maritime loan, 19, 27, 242, 250, 252–53, 259, 280
  security, 25, 252–53, 275, 279
  terms, 253, 264, 267
Leocrates, 138, 219, 223, 269, 302
Lesbos, 192n84, 235
Levant, 124, 152, 193
lid, 74, 82, 93, 178, 180
limestone, 4, 205, 215, 222
linen, 148–49, 155, 160n57, 195–96
Littleton, Edward, 261
liturgy, liturgiast, 19, 25, 138, 189–90, 203, 251, 268, 300–01
livestock, 48n5, 232
living standards, 3–5, 9, 49, 55, 57, 63–67, 155, 225, 260, 299
loom, 1, 151–52, 154, 156, 159, 184, 201, 214, 262, 315
  weight, 15, 147, 151, 156, 226
lost-wax method, 15, 136
luxury, 49, 52, 66, 69, 112, 129, 130, 148, 152, 157, 158, 174–82, 201, 210, 225, 232, 249, 254, 263, 272, 314–15, 317
Lycon, 285
Lycurgus (statesman, orator), 119, 191, 193, 219. *See also Index Locorum*
Lydia, 64, 150
lyre, 183–84, 273
lyric poets, 9, 52, 61, 172, 179n37
Lysias, 12, 28, 32, 138–44, 269, 285, 311. *See also Index Locorum*
Lysippus, 218–19, 224

machinery, 22, 24, 29–32, 141, 162, 170, 184, 198, 201, 237, 249, 261, 282, 313
maintenance, 18, 40, 56, 97, 119, 135, 142, 156, 168, 189–90, 198, 199–200, 203, 205, 211n47, 212, 225, 227–28, 229, 259–62, 268, 284, 286, 288
*machairon*. *See* knife
make-or-buy decision, 36, 47, 51–61, 70–71
mallet, 222

Mantias, 26, 252
manufacturing, 1–18, 21, 22–23, 25, 31–33, 36, 39–46, 51, 52, 248–88, 299–317. See also *by specific products*, industry structures; technology; Athens, income opportunities
  earliest evidence, 47–51
manumission, 262, 284–88
Marathon, 197
marble, 4, 177, 179, 202, 205, 212, 214–18, 220n92, 221–24, 229
margin, 26, 36, 58, 99, 106, 124, 135, 142, 163–64, 170, 239, 250, 270
  marginal competitor, 34, 40, 200, 291n5
  marginal cost, 154, 156
maritime loan. *See* lending
market (demand/exchange), 3n8, 6, 16n68, 20, 21, 24, 35, 36, 44, 50, 55–58, 66, 69–70, 76, 78, 79, 81, 89, 96, 98–100, 102–6, 108, 110–14, 115, 120, 123, 125n48, 127, 130, 143, 146, 149, 156, 158, 159, 164, 167–71, 181–82, 183, 211, 212–13, 217, 220, 227, 238n41, 239, 241, 243–45, 251, 256–58, 273, 281, 285, 291, 293
  (place), 8, 30, 50, 74, 99, 147, 166–67, 231–34, 275. *See also* Agora
  share, 18, 29, 32, 33, 36, 42, 44, 142–43, 174, 182, 315
  *See also* labor market
Marshall, Alfred, 17, 292
mason, 54n33, 208, 212, 214, 225, 228
mass production, 3, 29, 89, 109, 131, 138, 223
Massachusetts, 159, 164
mast, 193–97
mattress, 148, 174–75, 181
meat, 51, 231–34, 238
medicine, 230, 239–42, 246–47
*medimnos*, 260
Mende, 235, 252
merchant, 6, 44, 159, 234, 274, 283n108, 304
  ships, captains, 191–92, 199–200, 253
Mesopotamia, 59
metallurgy, 10, 152
metalwork, 2, 4, 52, 66–68, 86, 116–38, 145, 197, 202, 213, 218, 249, 252, 274, 277, 280, 305, 308
  applications, 115
  technology, 120–23, 124–26
metics, 19, 97, 100, 142, 149, 154n25, 197n104, 203, 206, 209–12, 228–29, 248, 251, 253, 259, 276, 301–11
  population, 301–2
  rights, 19, 278–81
  role in manufacturing, 248, 249, 279–81

*metoikon*, 279, 281
microeconomics, 16, 34, 38, 45, 47, 69
Midas, 243, 287
Middle Ages, 111–12, 158–59
middle class, 58–61, 67–68, 135, 300
Miletus, Milesian, 150, 175–76
military procurement, 135
  service, 271–74, 279, 283
miller, 231, 235
Milyas, 254, 263
mining, 1n2, 4, 10, 21, 26–27, 35, 41, 43, 45, 67, 116–20, 121–24, 204, 213, 252, 260, 276n71, 284–85, 305–7
  industry structure, 119
  lease, 15, 118–20, 123, 250–52, 276n71
  services, 120. *See also* ore processing industry structure
  technology, 117–18
  wealthy miners, 118–19, 252
Minos, 185, 240
*misthos*, 271
Mnason, 285
mobile craftsman, 9, 56, 64
money. *See* coinage, Athenian units
monopoly, 17, 109, 142, 146, 202
monument, 212, 214, 224, 230
  monumental sculpture, 45, 213
Moriades, 264, 269
mortise and tenon, 173, 192
Moschion, 287
mold, molding, 15, 89, 94, 109–11, 113, 129–30, 133, 136–37, 146, 211–12, 221, 223–24, 226
*murepsos*, 243
murex, 160–62
*muropoloi*, 240, 245–47
musical instruments, 12, 183–84, 201
Mycenae, 48, 84, 128, 152
Myron, 7, 219
Mysteries, the, 251

nail, 30, 173, 181, 192, 262–63
Naples, 109
*naukleroi*, 253
naval architecture, 188n65, 190–91, 195, 200–01, 249
  capability, 5, 7, 189,
  lists, 185, 187, 194–96
  supplies (*see* boatbuilding)
Neanderthal, 48, 239
Near East. *See* Asia
Nearchus, 102–3, 108
neolithic, 75, 172, 235
*neoroi*, 191
Nestor, 49, 53, 186, 240

## 380 } General Index

Niceratus, 257
niche business, 42–43, 101, 105–6, 115, 170, 245, 249
Nicias, 8, 31, 118, 120, 126, 139, 253, 257, 260–61, 279

oar, 166, 185–86, 187–89, 193–95
   -port cover, 166, 196–97
Odysseus, 51–52, 172, 177, 186, 192
*officinae*, 241
*oiketai*, 265
*oikos*, 19, 43, 46, 47, 50, 52, 54n33, 66, 68, 69, 116, 276, 285, 292, 294, 301, 303–305, 307, 309
oil, 1, 74, 162, 176, 222, 240–41, 262.
   *See also* olive oil
ointment, 74, 240
oligarchy, 64
oligopoly, 41–43
olive oil, 4, 6, 54, 105, 109, 231, 234–40, 246, 316
   press, 235–37, 240
Olympia, 67, 116n2, 220
Olympias, 188n65
Olynthus, 156–57, 175, 292
*opson*, 232
orators, 9, 11–12, 23, 120, 131, 138, 183, 268–69, 292
ore, 10, 20n87, 28, 35, 41, 52, 53, 55–57, 66–67, 116–19, 120–25, 143, 145, 230, 249, 252
   acquisition, 53, 56–57, 67
   cupellation, 122–24
   processing industry structure, 25–26, 121–25, 143–45
   washing, 119, 121
   *See also* smelting *and* smelting, technology
organization, 36, 143, 158
ornament, 49, 67, 90–96, 116, 126, 127, 128–31, 136–37, 145, 217, 222, 228, 249, 280, 317
outsourcing, 51, 58, 65, 70, 121, 133, 159, 161–62, 170
oversupply, 53–54
oxen, 207, 232

Paestum, 242
painting, 7, 31, 131, 134, 141, 147, 186, 190, 196–97, 201, 208, 211, 214–15, 219, 222, 224, 228–30, 249. *See also* vase painter; vase painting
palace system, 48–49, 51, 128–30, 152, 240
Panathenaic festival, 74, 102–3, 157

panoply, 134–37
Pantainetus, 25–26, 122, 252
Paphlagonian, 163
*paradeigmata*, 205
Parthenon, 176–78, 191, 205–7, 209, 220, 222
participation in industry,
   by population segments; *see* citizen population; metics, population; slaves, freed; slaves, population; women
   estimation methodology, 301–17
Pasion, 139, 142–44, 255n21, 267, 276, 281, 287, 303, 311
paste, 129. *See also* fish paste
pastoralist, 233
Pausanias, 7, 13, 216, 218, 259. See also *Index Locorum*
pay. *See* wage
peasant, 49, 52–53, 61–66, 152, 285
Peiraeus, 15, 184, 188n65, 191, 225, 280
Peloponnesian War, 6, 117, 132, 142, 185, 189–90, 197, 206, 209, 217
*pentecontor/pentereis*, 187, 192
Penteli (Mt. Pentelicon), 205, 216, 221
*peplos*, 148, 154, 157, 214
perfume, 15, 25, 26, 35, 39, 41, 55, 66, 74, 94, 130, 148, 230, 235, 239–47, 249, 252, 287
   industry structure, 68, 242
   technology, 240
Pericles, 84, 100, 117n9, 138, 144, 204, 271, 274, 300
Persia, 7, 117, 240, 241
pestle, 235
Pheidias, 7, 207, 219–20, 224
Pheidias Alcamenes, 224
Pheidippus, 119
Phereclus, 52
Philemonides, 120, 257
Philip of Macedon, 256
Philistine, 162
Philocles, 207
Philocrates, 269
Philon, 193, 207
philosopher, 9, 11–12, 17, 240, 292, 293
Phoenician, 5, 89, 105, 160, 186–88, 195
Phormion, 19, 144, 287
Phrygian, 10, 283
*phyle*, 204
pick, 117, 205, 222
pickling, 233
pillow, 148, 174–75
*pilos*, 134
pin factory, 30–32
Pistias, 126, 137n100, 138, 143

pitch, 136, 190, 192, 195, 238
pitchfork, 127
pit-prop, 195
plane, 141, 173, 263
plank, 192, 195, 197
Plataeans, 140
Plato, 2, 7, 12, 24, 259, 263, 265, 273, 292. See also *Index Locorum*
plunder, 271
Pluto, 285
pole, 183, 184, 194, 197, 237
*polemarch*, 279
Polemarchus, 138–44
Polyclitus, 218–19, 224
Pompeii, 110n142, 162, 241
*porpax*, 139
porridge, 233, 277
portfolio, 33, 248, 251
potter, pottery, 1, 2, 7, 8, 14, 15, 25, 43, 49, 52, 73–115, 124–128, 145, 146, 150, 157, 173, 183, 225, 229, 249, 269, 273, 274, 277, 280, 286, 288, 305, 308, 309, 316
  archaeological evidence, 14, 73–83, 125
  coarse (utility) ware, 73, 75, 77, 89, 99, 101, 105, 108, 109, 111, 316–17
  containers, 44, 49, 74, 75, 77, 81, 98, 99, 109, 115, 229, 235, 240–41, 244, 249, 316–17
  fine ware, 6, 102–5
  industry structure, 83–115, 126, 145, 170, 173, 292, 304
  technology, 29, 87, 108
  trade, 6, 75–77, 81, 102, 105
Praxiteles, 7, 215, 219, 224
precious metals, 4, 49, 126, 129, 180–81, 218. See also gold; silver
pressing, 111, 121, 129–30, 152, 161, 173, 222, 235, 240–41. See also olive oil press
price(s), 4, 12, 20, 32, 34, 40, 44–45, 49, 57–61, 63, 68–72, 91, 107, 124, 127, 137–38, 142, 156, 164, 178–84, 191, 198, 224, 227, 229, 234n24, 237, 262, 274, 291, 294, 314n19, 317
  armor, 13–38, 135, 142
  clothing, 148
  fish, 232
  furniture, 179, 182–83
  labor, 18, 24–25, 29, 40, 97–99, 103, 107, 120, 122–23, 128, 135, 142–43, 147, 154–58, 159, 168, 198–99, 211n47, 213, 220, 229, 242–44, 259–61, 266, 283, 294. See also labor market
  metal objects, 128
  perfume, 240–45
  pottery, 81–82, 98–114

premium, 34–35, 38, 44, 57, 184, 213, 224
setting, 16n68, 45, 76, 143, 151
shoes, 166, 168–71
priestess, 275
primary process. See food
*proboulemata*, 204
production, 1–3, 11, 13–15, 19, 21, 22, 25, 29, 31–34, 37, 40–45, 48–49, 51, 55, 60–63, 65–66, 69, 255, 263, 266, 272–76, 282, 285, 290, 293, 302–3, 311. See also manufacturing; *by specific products*
productivity, 29n143, 30–32, 41, 50, 65, 107, 113, 114, 118, 119, 134, 154, 157, 163, 168, 169, 199, 286, 314, 316n21
profit, profitability, 8, 9, 12, 13, 16–23, 26–28, 33–41, 42–45, 64, 69, 73–74, 81, 106, 113, 119, 122, 132n71, 135, 142, 143, 155–58, 163–66, 170–71, 182–83, 228–29, 237, 243, 245, 253–55, 260–62, 266, 269–70, 284, 287, 289–94, 300. See also investment, returns; margin; yield
project management, 195, 201, 204–5, 207–8, 211, 228–29, 249, 271
property, 19, 27, 248n1, 252–53, 280, 287, 301, 303. See also land
Propylaea, 116n2, 209, 224
*prostates*, 279
prostitution, 11, 153, 157, 256, 260, 272, 286n116, 305, 309. See also brothel
*proxenos*, 279
public buildings, 174, 201, 202–14, 225, 228–29,
  funds, 6n33, 157, 190, 203–4, 209, 211, 261, 271, 301
  records, 203, 205, 209. See also accountability; epigraphy
pulse, 231
Punic Wars, 109, 187
Pylades, 267
Pylos, 49, 156
pyrometer, 113

ram, 185–86, 189, 191, 194, 196–98
rasp, 222
raw materials, 4, 6, 14, 25, 31, 39–40, 41n159, 44, 55, 57, 58, 63n45, 65, 113, 123, 127, 130–31, 135, 142, 145–46, 150, 158–59, 162, 182, 183, 198–99, 217–18, 243, 246, 247, 252, 260–63, 265–67, 269, 285, 312n17
ready-to-eat. See food, prepared products
real estate, 251, 279. See also land

382 { General Index

reinvestment, 64, 143, 256–57, 261–62
reliability advantage, 44, 45, 105, 114, 144, 169, 184, 200, 229
relief, 89–90, 97, 166, 172, 179, 181, 186, 187, 212, 215–17, 222
repair, 67, 128, 145, 190, 198–200, 205, 212, 249
reputation advantage, 38, 44–45, 104, 106, 107, 111, 113, 130–31, 137–38, 143–45, 167, 174, 182–83, 188n65, 197, 215, 219, 224–25, 234, 273
research and development, 36, 237, 245
reselling, 1n2, 2, 7, 11, 13, 77, 99, 105, 107, 145, 149, 169, 171, 231, 238–39, 245–47, 282, 299
retailing. *See* reselling
return on capital. *See* investment, returns
ribbon, 148, 277
ridge beam, 184–85
risk, 20–21, 22, 26, 27, 33, 48–49, 52, 62–63, 69–70, 73, 90, 95, 101, 104, 105–7, 129, 137, 143, 146, 156, 183, 208, 225, 238, 244, 250–59, 260, 262, 266, 286–87, 291
  and return, 20, 28, 250–59, 262, 266, 291
  management, 9, 96
Rome, manufacturing, 109–10, 138, 146, 158–59, 161–62, 164, 203n2, 216, 219, 225, 236, 241
  technology, 10, 80, 109, 120, 121, 125, 151, 152, 173n8, 181n45
roof, 213, 225–26
rope, 15, 123, 156n38, 157, 192–97, 201, 249
rotary action, 235–36
rug, 148, 157, 174–75

sack, 148, 166
sail, 54, 156n38, 157, 185, 189n67, 193–97, 214
sailyard, 194–95
Salamis, 117, 135, 185, 188, 197
salt, 150n9, 160, 233–34, 235, 241, 277
salted fish, 231–32, 234, 238, 240
sanctuary, 203, 206–7
sandal, 52, 165–66, 168, 313–14
sausage, 6, 169, 231–32, 274
saw, 15, 173, 178, 181, 183, 195, 263
science, 17, 18n78, 23, 33, 245
scouring, 147, 150–51, 152, 159–60, 170, 249
screw, 120, 173
  -press, 236
sculptors, 7, 172, 215, 216–19, 224
sculpture, 1, 13, 15, 54n33, 67, 125–26, 138, 165, 201–2, 208, 211–14, 214–29, 249
  bronze technology, 220–21
  industry structure, 223–25

marble technology, 221–22, 224–25
Scythia, 161
Scythian archers, 210, 282
seasonality, 45, 62, 67, 79, 86, 97, 99, 105, 106, 116, 211, 251, 294, 304
second hand goods, 6, 82, 98, 102–5, 109, 148, 183, 266, 316
secondary process. *See* food, partly processed products
segmentation, 3, 8, 42–46, 67–70, 75, 101, 105–6, 108, 114, 116, 125, 128, 145–46, 157, 170–71, 174, 183–84, 200–01, 213, 238–39, 239–47, 248–50, 262, 273–78, 290, 294, 299–300, 302–3, 311, 314, 317
self-sufficiency, 3, 9, 16n68, 48, 51–53, 56, 59–60, 61–62, 68, 154–56, 167
semiprecious stone, 129
serf, 49, 285
service business, 1n2, 4, 11, 12, 37, 39, 111, 120, 184, 230–31, 238–39, 247, 268, 272, 280, 284, 287, 303, 305, 309
sesame, 239n43, 241, 277
sewage, 210
shaping, 29, 84, 87, 88–89, 92, 93, 97, 100, 102, 104, 113, 129–30, 136, 141, 144, 149, 168, 173, 176–81, 212, 220n92, 222
Shareholder Value Analysis, 258
shed (boatshed), 15, 187, 191–93, 196, 198
sheet, 15, 129, 136, 139, 141, 148, 181, 221, 224
shield, 24, 28, 31–32, 45, 52, 116, 122, 134–36, 138–44, 145, 146, 163, 174, 182, 210, 225, 249, 256, 303
  industry structure, 142–44
  technology, 141–42
ship, shipbuilding. *See* boat
shipping, 81, 99, 101, 105, 107, 109, 124, 130, 184, 205, 230, 247, 312, 317. *See also* pottery containers
shipyard. *See* dockyards
shoe, 49, 165–66
shoemaking, 7, 29, 44, 68, 158, 162, 163–64, 165–71
  industry structure, 167–71
  technology, 168–69, 170
shroud, 193–94, 196
Sicily, 138, 178, 231, 234
sideboard, 179
Sidon, 5–6, 160, 186, 220
Silanion, 218
silk, 148, 149, 154
silver, 4–6, 20n87, 29, 90, 116–20, 120–24, 125, 126, 128–31, 133, 145, 178, 215, 216, 249, 251, 257, 266–67, 284. *See also* coinage; mining

silversmith, 15, 77n12, 130
technology, 121–24
Simon the Shoemaker, 166–67, 169
Siris, 136
*sitos*, 233n15, 271
skill, 10, 12, 15, 17, 18, 25, 30–31, 37, 39, 42, 52–56, 62, 65–70, 90–91, 94, 99–104, 116, 121–22, 125, 130–31, 133, 136, 141, 143, 145, 155, 167, 169–70, 175, 179, 181, 183–85, 187, 191, 195–97, 200, 202, 208–14, 216, 220–25, 228–29, 230, 238, 242–45, 249, 250, 257–58, 273, 276–78, 281, 285, 287, 303, 307–8
slaves/slavery, 1–4, 7–8, 10–12, 14–15, 18–19, 22, 23–26, 27, 28–29, 31–32, 40–41, 42, 45, 47, 51–54, 56–57, 60, 62, 64, 67–70, 73, 96–101, 106, 107–9, 117, 118–20, 121–23, 126–27, 130, 131, 133–34, 135–46, 148, 150, 152, 154–55, 156–58, 161, 163, 167–70, 181, 183, 185, 190, 195, 198–202, 206–7, 208–15, 219–20, 223, 225, 226–28, 229, 238, 239, 242–47, 248–53, 254–70, 271–73, 275–76, 276–78, 279–80, 281–88, 290, 292–94, 301–17
*choris oikountes*, 19, 251, 287, 314
family, 97, 260, 302
freed, 11, 24, 100, 139, 161n66, 212, 248–49, 250, 254, 259, 275–76, 278, 280–81, 282, 286, 287, 302–14
maintenance costs, 40, 97–98, 119, 135, 142, 198, 259–60
manufacturing, 1–3, 8, 12–15, 19, 25–26, 28, 31–32, 40, 42, 47, 52, 67–70, 107–9, 118, 120, 126–27, 130, 131, 133–34, 136–37, 138–44, 144–46, 152, 154–55, 156–58, 161, 167–70, 181, 183, 202, 203, 210, 211, 214, 221, 227, 229, 230, 233, 242–47, 248–50, 253, 258, 268, 275–76, 276–78, 281–87, 290, 293, 295, 302–10, 312, 313, 317
manumission, 154n25, 262, 286–87
population, 4, 118, 302
prices/capital costs, 25, 40, 97–98, 99, 122, 127, 142–44, 219, 242–44, 255, 257–58, 265–66, 268, 283, 301
public, 126, 133–34, 206, 210, 228, 257, 271
replacement/depreciation, 97–98, 260–62, 263, 266, 268
source, 282–83
slipper, 148, 166, 168, 313
smelting, 10, 52, 117–18, 120–22, 124–27, 136, 144–45, 249
technology, 120–22, 124–25

Smith, Adam, 28–32
smith, smithy, 1, 10, 15, 29–31, 57, 62, 67, 116, 121, 124–28, 173, 211–14, 219, 228, 273. *See also* goldsmith; silversmith
snack, 239. *See also* prepared food
soap, 231, 238, 246
Socrates, 6, 137, 155, 166–67, 213, 240, 273, 274
solder, 129, 221
Solon, 4, 7, 27, 217, 240, 283n104
Sophocles, 9, 74, 186, 259, 273
Sophroniscus, 213
Sosias, 120, 257, 261
Spain, 109, 234
Sparta, 1, 7, 11, 132, 135, 140, 191, 235, 282
spear, 10, 48, 126, 127, 134–35, 140n111, 145, 166
specialization, 7–10, 29–31, 48n7, 53–59, 62, 64, 65–72, 73, 79, 81, 83, 86, 93–96, 100, 105–6, 110, 114, 116, 121, 125–28, 129, 136, 138, 145, 149, 150, 154–55, 157, 161, 163–64, 166, 168, 170, 182, 183–84, 185, 195–96, 200–202, 208, 210, 213, 214–15, 222–23, 226–27, 236–37, 238, 244–45, 270, 280–81
Sphacteria, 135
spice, 4, 238, 244
spindle, 151, 152
whorl, 15, 147, 152
spinning, 69, 147, 150–59, 160, 170, 260, 278, 308–9, 312–13
technology, 151–52, 159
stacking (kiln), 94–98, 110, 316–17
stamp, 75, 80–82, 110, 151
statues. *See* sculpture
statuettes. *See* ornament
status, 2, 20, 27, 46, 50, 53, 62, 110, 135, 195, 200, 202, 209–15, 244n62, 250, 253, 269, 271–72, 275–77, 279–80, 289–90, 292, 299, 300–02, 307, 309, 312, 314. *See also* citizen; metics; slaves; women
stew, 231, 238, 239, 249
Stoa, 206
stock. *See* inventory
stone, 1, 4, 10, 15, 24, 25, 48, 80, 121, 129, 131, 177, 180, 184, 191, 201, 205–6, 208, 212–15, 215–17, 219–24, 227, 235–36, 263
stonemason (*see* mason)
stool, 176, 177, 180–81
storage, 15, 20n87, 49, 53, 57, 61–64, 67, 74, 77, 109, 121, 135, 179, 187, 193, 218, 234, 238, 241, 247, 263, 269, 276

## General Index

Strabo, 13, 129, 218. See also *Index Locorum*
*strategos*, 189
strategy, business, 3, 33–37, 101, 211, 245
    investment, 118, 250–53, 257, 270
Stration, 285
Stratocles, 268
Strepsiades, 285
subsistence, 4, 24, 43, 44, 47, 49, 51, 53, 62–64, 100, 114, 183, 226, 248, 260, 269, 274, 281, 299, 301
supervisor. *See* foreman
supply and demand, 12, 16–17, 39, 44–46, 47, 58–61, 64, 66–71, 100–101, 108, 116, 171, 174, 249, 289–91, 295
surplus, 11, 48–49, 53–55, 64, 115, 155, 204n7, 209, 271, 299, 301, 303. *See also* profit
sword, 126–27, 134, 144–45, 249, 254
symbol, 50, 131, 132, 196
*syngraphe*, 205
Syracuse, 135, 138, 187, 192, 280

table, 5, 121, 166, 173–82, 213, 315
*talasiourgos*, 154, 277
*tamiai*, 205
tannin, 162
tanning, 11, 24, 43, 52, 68–69, 161n61, 162–64, 170–71, 210, 249, 313
    industry structure, 163–64, 170–71
    technology, 162–63
    wealthy tannery owners, 28, 163, 269, 273
tapestry, 148, 151, 157, 170, 249
*tarichopoleia*, 234
tavern, 239
taxation, 4–6, 19, 26, 64, 117–18, 204, 253, 259, 265, 268, 271, 281, 283, 301. *See also* harbor tax; metoikon; xenika
technology, 9, 10, 12–14, 23–25, 29, 32, 36, 38–41, 52, 73, 80, 87, 108–9, 111–15, 117–19, 120–28, 135, 141–42, 143, 146, 151–52, 159, 160–61, 162–63, 170, 173, 215, 222, 224, 234, 237–38, 242–44, 274, 290, 293–94
*teichopoioi*, 205, 207
Telemarchus of Acharnai, 203
temple, 15, 49, 53, 67, 79, 116n2, 130, 149, 164, 174, 184, 193, 203–15, 217, 224, 257, 277, 282, 299
tetradrachm, 6n33, 132
textiles, 14, 52, 66, 147–59, 169–71, 185, 195–97, 214, 249, 275, 277.
    *See also* clothing
  gender roles, 152–55

    industry structure, 152–59, 169–70
    technology (*see* spinning technology; weaving technology)
thalamian, 187
Thasos, 215, 235
theater, 121, 177, 270–71, 299. *See also* drama
    equipment, 184, 262
Themistocles, 117–18, 189, 191, 197n104, 198, 203
Theodorus of Samos, 172, 218
Theophrastus, 24, 242, 285. See also *Index Locorum*
Theopompus, 251, 254
*thetes, thetia*, 53, 62, 272
Thirty Tyrants, the, 139, 143, 201, 251
thong, 136, 163–69, 173, 175, 179–83, 196, 313
Thrace, 193, 257, 283
thranite, 187
throne, 174–76, 180
Thucydides, 11, 158, 259, 273. See also *Index Locorum*
tile, 15, 78, 83, 95, 99, 105–6, 112, 114, 226
Timarchus (citizen investor), 122, 154–55, 167–69, 256–57, 260, 268, 269, 287, 302
Timarchus (sculptor), 219
timber, 4, 15, 61, 118, 151, 172–73, 179–81, 184–85, 186, 190, 192–93, 198, 200, 213, 226
Timochares, 219, 252
tin, 124–25
Tleson, 102–3, 108
tombstone, 14, 163, 216–17. *See also* funerary monuments
tongs, 53, 96, 127
tool, 15, 25, 48–49, 53, 56, 116–17, 119, 124, 126–27, 129, 143–45, 147, 172–73, 198, 212, 217, 221–22, 249, 262–63, 274
torch, 188n65, 235
trade, 1, 4–6, 14, 17, 21, 48–49, 50n21, 56, 64, 69, 76–77, 81, 100, 102, 105, 108–14, 130, 131–32, 137n99, 149–50, 156–57, 159, 160, 172–73, 184, 187, 191–95, 198, 202, 232, 234–35, 241, 245–46, 249, 250, 253, 259, 265, 272, 279–80, 283, 287, 289–90
    finance, 19, 27–28, 242, 250, 253, 280
tradesman. *See* craft; craftsman
tragedy, 9, 270. *See also* drama; theater
transport, 15, 36, 43, 77, 78, 105, 109, 113, 121, 123–24, 128, 172, 184, 192, 201, 205, 207, 222, 233–34, 244, 247, 249, 299, 315. *See also* shipping
*trapetum* press, 236

treasure,
  private, 51
  public, 117, 204
tribe, 204
tribute, 6–7, 132, 150n9, 190, 204, 253, 259
*tricotylos*, 235
trident, 127, 145
trierarch, 23, 119, 189–90, 196, 219, 268
*triereis.* See trireme
*trieropoios.* See boatbuilder
trireme, 11, 15, 189–201, 313n18
  components, 193–201, 315–16
  configuration, 187, 188n65, 192
  construction (*see* boatbuilding)
  maintenance, 190, 192, 198, 200
  responsibility, 189–91
  1987 recreation, 188n65
Trygaeus, 285
tunic, 135, 148, 155, 312–13
turning, 6, 24, 141, 143, 172n2, 173, 175–76, 181, 210, 274
tyrant, 118, 131n67, 138, 203. *See also* Thirty Tyrants

urban, urbanization, 3–4, 47, 49, 64–66, 68, 112
  topography, 14
utensil, 62, 67, 76, 99, 127, 144, 201, 249, 274
utilization, underutilization, 34–36, 47, 54–61, 65–71, 106–7, 127, 137, 143, 223, 236, 276, 293
utility ware. *See* pottery, coarse (utility) ware

value, 18, 21, 25, 26, 32, 35–36, 41, 45, 65–66, 70–72, 89, 99, 103–4, 121, 131, 139n105, 155, 158, 181, 201, 213, 238, 240–44, 246, 250, 254–58, 263, 266, 268, 276, 283, 289–94, 299. *See also* competitive advantage
vase painter, 104, 109, 157, 219, 277, 316
vase painting, 7, 29, 45, 52, 75, 82–86, 105, 136–37, 147, 154, 166, 170, 172, 174–75, 186, 189, 218, 219, 277
vegetable, 160–62, 231, 233–34, 238, 239, 277
Vicus Actionum Ferrarium, 138
vinegar, 231, 234–35, 239
Vix *krater*, 218
wage, 4, 24, 63, 112n48, 119, 135, 148, 190, 198n106, 213, 232, 284. *See also* price, labor
wagon. *See* cart
washery, 121
water, 14, 24, 74, 87–88, 113, 120, 121, 124, 126, 141, 159–60, 162–63, 187–94, 226, 233–34, 235, 240, 275

wealth, 1–6, 11, 12n49, 19, 23, 27–28, 51, 57–60, 62, 65, 81, 100, 102, 118, 119, 130, 134–35, 150, 163, 204, 219, 224, 227, 240–41, 248, 251–53, 257, 266, 268, 269, 273, 282, 284, 286, 287, 299–301, 305, 315
weaving, 15, 69, 148, 151–55, 166, 170, 275, 277n77, 308–9, 313
  technology, 152
wedge, 205, 222, 241
Wedgwood, Sir Josiah, 112–13
weft, 151
well, 14–15, 105, 121–23, 226
wet-nurse, 278
wheat. *See* grain
whetstone, 263
whorl. *See* spindle whorl
widow, 19, 148, 154, 156, 275–76, 301, 303, 308, 314
wig, 216
window, 226
wine, 4, 6, 15, 35, 54, 74, 77, 81, 99, 105, 109, 166, 169, 179, 231, 234n23, 235, 238–40, 242, 246, 316
women, 2, 5, 14, 19, 21, 51, 69, 74, 128–29, 148, 151–55, 158, 159, 162, 166–68, 170, 176, 197n104, 226, 233, 237, 240, 250, 274–78, 301, 302, 304, 308, 309, 313
wood. *See* fuel; timber
woodworking, 48, 141–42, 172–201, 209, 213, 220n92, 274, 305, 313–14, 316–17
  industry structure, 181, 200–201
  supplier to construction, 249
  supplier to shipbuilding, 195, 197–200
  technology and tools, 172–73, 176–77
wool, 15, 74, 147–60, 231, 242, 246n64
work, workforce, 22, 25, 73, 92–94, 100, 106, 130, 133, 143, 169, 198–200, 203, 209–15, 220–24, 242. *See also* labor
working capital, 26, 131, 143, 245, 263, 266, 269, 292. *See also* inventory
working year, 257, 314
workshop, 3, 8, 10, 12, 14–15, 19, 22, 24–25, 26, 28–30, 40, 44, 60–61, 62, 64, 66–67, 69, 73, 75–86, 92–108, 110, 116, 122, 124–28, 131, 135, 138–39, 141–46, 156–58, 162, 167, 169–70, 181–84, 195–201, 210–14, 217, 224, 228–29, 238–39, 242, 245, 249, 250, 253, 254, 256, 261–63, 265, 269, 273, 274, 276–78, 284–87, 289, 294, 301, 303, 308–9, 312, 314, 316n21
wreath, 231, 237
*xenika*, 279

Xenocrates, 218–19
Xenon, 287
Xenophon, 12, 17, 167, 261, 263, 292. See also *Index Locorum*
*xenos. See* aliens; barbarian; metics
yarn, 151–52

yield, 20, 28, 121, 238, 241, 254–58, 265–66. *See also* investment, returns; margin; profit

Zenothemis, 19, 287
zygians, 187